MAGIC AND THE MILLENNIUM

MAGIC AND THE MILLENNIUM

A SOCIOLOGICAL STUDY OF RELIGIOUS
MOVEMENTS OF PROTEST AMONG
TRIBAL AND THIRD-WORLD PEOPLES

Bryan R. Wilson

HARPER & ROW, PUBLISHERS

NEW YORK, EVANSTON, SAN FRANCISCO, LONDON

1817

FIRST U.S. EDITION

STANDARD BOOK NUMBER: 06-014671-0

LIBRARY OF CONGRESS CATALOG CARD NUMBER: 72-9762

Contents

v

For Jess

Acknowledgements

To put institutions before individuals runs very much counter to the principles which for years have informed my practice in social relations, but in writing this book my obligations to four institutions are such that, even though institutional generosity was always mediated by individuals, it is the institutions themselves to which I owe the first (and last) word.

The Harkness Foundation elected me in 1957 to a Commonwealth Fund Fellowship, which allowed me to spend the next academic year reading, thinking, and travelling in the United States, and it was at that time that my interests turned to the subject treated in this book. In 1966, I was elected a Fellow of the American Council of Learned Societies and returned to the United States to spend a year, much of which was devoted to learning about the religious movements that have arisen at various times among the North American Indians. To those two foundations this book owes a great deal: the awards they made to me were of the greatest importance to my development as a sociologist, and perhaps more important was what their trust meant to me. I hope that those who administer these benefactions will feel that in the publication of this study their trust was in some small measure justified.

To hold both of these fellowships at the University of California at Berkeley was, of course, of my own choosing. The excellence of the university's facilities, and the stimulation that I derived from the sociologists there during my first visit made it clear that this was where I should spend the second spell of research time in America, rather than at any other centre of learning. On my second visit, the Survey Research Center at Berkeley offered me research facilities that exceeded my needs, and provided me with generous secretarial assistance which was of the greatest value, both directly to my research and also in allowing me to conduct the correspondence of academic business quickly and efficiently. It was a luxury to which, coming from the University of Oxford, which had never provided me with secretarial help for any purpose, I was quite unaccustomed, and the value of which I soon learned to appreciate.

The individuals to whom I should like to express gratitude are mainly those who were at the University of California during the period of my two visits. Charles Glock was instrumental in arranging my second visit; his help in this respect and his unfailing interest in my work have been of continuing importance. He was also a member of a small group of distinguished scholars to whose fortnightly meetings I was privileged to be invited during my stay in Berkeley in 1966–7. Those evenings of sustained, critical, and learned discussion were a most important formative experience, not least the occasion on which the group met to discuss some draft chapters of this work, which had been circulated to each member. That evening led me to amend and re-organize my thoughts in various respects, for which I should like to thank the members of the 'Scholars' Group'—David Apter, Charles Glock, Ernst Haas, Eugene Hammel, Martin Malia, Neil Smelser, and Ivan Vallier—some of whom may recognize that some of their sug-gestions have influenced the final moulding of this study. Eugene Hammel invited me to participate in the seminar that he was conduct-ing with graduate students in anthropology on topics similar to those treated here, and I was glad to have the opportunity to listen and talk with others about millennialism and related subjects.

Friends who, over the years, have asked what I was doing must from time to time have thought that when I referred loosely to 'my millennial book' I alluded not to the subject-matter but to the unconscionable time it was taking me to finish it. Some of them have listened to me discuss the ideas, perspective, and the method of treatment, and have made helpful suggestions: in particular Asa Briggs and Allan Eister have both, at different times, asked penetrating questions which made me think a little harder. Donald MacRae, with a persisting kindness to which I was introduced years ago when he supervised my first uncertain efforts in sociological research, read and commented on an early draft of a concentrated exposition of part of the subject-matter. At a late stage two other friends influenced this study: Philip Rieff made sug-gestions which were most important in the final shaping of the book; and, in the final stage of writing and revision, Terence Bull devoted hours of his spare time to reading carefully through the typescript, saving me from many of the errors, inconsistencies, and infelicities of which I was guilty, and it is to him that I owe the bibliography.

Some of my graduate students have listened to me talk about millennial movements and out of genuine concern for scholarship, and with the care and courtesy that I have always been lucky enough to find in my students, they have not forborn to raise the really awkward questions and to identify just those ambiguities that marked places where one had failed to deal with all the issues. Colleagues whom I do not know well have sometimes been more than kind. Dr Harold W.

Turner took time and trouble to correct a number of details about the Church of the Lord, about which he knows so much, and on matters touched on in Chapter 14, Professor Walter J. Hollenweger, from his extensive knowledge of fringe Christian groups, suggested sources that have brought me more up to date. Various scholars at the University of Edinburgh where I was invited to deliver the Gunning Lectures in 1971, and at the University of Dundee where I delivered a series of Public Lectures in 1972, gave me the benefit of their reactions to some of my ideas on millennial movements and for their comments and criticisms I was, and remain, most grateful.

   Of the four institutions I referred to above, I have so far mentioned only three. The last of them I can scarcely think of as an institution at all—such is the personal friendliness of its atmosphere—and its contribution is least specifically restricted to the writing of this particular book. But there should be occasions on which to acknowledge the diffuse goodwill, the wide-ranging support, and the sustained atmosphere of concern for scholarship and for scholars which are so important to academic activity. During the last decade of work on 'my millennial book' I have enjoyed the benefit of living and working in the unusually amicable fellowship of All Souls College. What I owe to All Souls is not confined to this present study, but, since this work has been in hand ever since I came to All Souls, this seems the appropriate place to express appreciation for all that the College—Warden, Fellows, and Staff—have contributed to my life and work.

Bryan R. Wilson

All Souls College, Oxford
1973

Introduction

NEW religious movements arising among less-developed peoples follow-ing cultural contact with westerners have today come to command increasing attention in several different social sciences—among anthropologists understandably, but also among political scientists, sociologists, and historians. Even some comparative religionists and theologians have been tempted to abandon writing new commentaries on often over-worked texts from the past for the excitement of more contemporary, if less literary, products of religious sentiment. The specific focus of interest in new religious movements differs for each of these disciplines. For the sociologist they are of more than merely phenomenological interest. They are significant not only in themselves, as examples of religious innovation, but also for what they reveal about spontaneously expressed social needs, about styles and levels of social consciousness, and about the consequences of social disruption and the patterns of response to it. Each new movement may be regarded as a pattern of sustained social action stimulated by new supernaturalist interpretations of contemporary processes of social change.

The ethnographer, the religious phenomenologist, and the student of comparative symbolics have discovered mines of new material in the minutiae of the artefacts and action patterns of participants in the new movements. The exhaustion of traditional materials, the over-supply of scholars working in these fields, and perhaps new doubts about the significance of the past, have no doubt all been responsible in some measure for the new-found interest in the new religions of less-developed peoples. The focus of the sociologist's concern is different: the minute details are not ends in themselves. Their full value is realized only if they contribute to the understanding of wider social processes, which embrace, but which also transcend, specifically religious phenomena.

In the pages that follow, therefore, much descriptive detail has been consciously sacrificed—but not, one hopes, to a point where information of sociological significance is lost, or the history or orientation of a movement becomes obscure.

Most of the scholarly monographs, reports, and articles on which this study relies are the works of anthropologists, and their interpretations of their data are much closer to my interests than those of some other disciplines. None the less, as a sociologist, I ought perhaps to proffer some excuse for entering the field. That excuse rests on the conviction that something might be gained from a more explicitly comparative analysis than anthropologists have usually been ready to pursue. One has heard, and I hope sufficiently heeded, their cautions on this matter, and one has gone ahead. Deliberately I have looked for continuities between sectarianism in western countries and the new sectarianism of the third world, without, I hope, being insensitive to the many discontinuities—which, indeed, are themselves an important issue of the theoretical discussion.

The few comparative studies of the new religions among less-developed peoples have not employed the type of general conceptual framework which provides the structure for this study.[1] The conceptual apparatus that I have used is not derived from the *most* general theoretical perspectives that sociology has to offer—the abstract, reified concepts of structural-functional analysis. That approach has sometimes led to increasingly elaborate, internally coherent, and well-articulated representation of systemic order. Not only does any such postulation appear to be of little immediate value as a heuristic device for the explanations of new religions of protest, but it is a form of theorizing that appears to preclude the necessity for further social research rather than to stimulate new enquiry. Definitive formulations are not part of

---

[1] Two of the most impressive comparative studies, Peter Worsley, *The Trumpet Shall Sound* (MacGibbon and Kee, London 1957; Rev. Edn 1968) and Katesa Schlosser, *Eingeborenen-kirchen in Süd- und Südwest-Afrika* (Walter G. Mühlau, Kiel 1958) confine themselves to movements arising in one particular cultural tradition. This is also true of David Barrett, *Schism and Renewal in Africa* (Oxford University Press, Nairobi 1968), whose interesting attempt at causal analysis confines itself to new religions that have split off from existing missions. Maria Isaura Pereira de Queiroz, *O Messianismo no Brasil e no Mundo* (University of São Paulo, São Paulo 1965) covers a wider geographic canvas but confines herself to (rather loosely defined) 'messianic' movements: this is an important study. The ambitious work by Vittorio Lanternari, *Movimenti religiosi di libertà e di salvezza dei populi oppressi* (Feltrinelli, Milan 1960), English edition, *The Religions of the Oppressed* (MacGibbon and Kee, London 1963) is essentially descriptive (and by no means always accurate). It lacks a coherent analytical procedure, and even the order of presentation of material seems to me to be likely to mislead the reader. The short study of Kenelm O. L. Burridge, *New Heaven, New Earth: A Study of Millenarian Activities* (Blackwell, Oxford 1969) is perhaps the most exciting attempt at synthesis: the emphasis is, however, very much more on a general explanation of behaviour than on comparison of religious responses in different cultural contexts.

my prospectus of sociological theory.[2] Conceptualization is indispensable to the sociological enterprise, of course, but no one conceptual framework is indispensable. The end sought is not the subsumption and encapsulation of all reality in a set of (therefore necessarily tautological) formulae, but the interpretation of reality by principles of greater generality than are to be derived from a particular case, and by the conscious application of comparative method. Results are always interim results, are always *only one way* of perceiving phenomena, one way of organizing data. Enquiry remains open-ended.

Nor have I found it possible to use what I believe to be the most interesting sociological theory of collective behaviour, that of Neil Smelser.[3] Smelser's conceptual framework, which is basically structural-functionalist, provides a method of looking at many widely divergent forms of collective behaviour and identifying them by reference to the point at which those involved have experienced dislocation in terms of the values, norms, facilities, etc., of the social system. Smelser's concerns are wider than mine: he seeks to distinguish types of collective behaviour that include the religious as one mode of action among many. He defines religious movements as value-oriented movements, and this one readily accepts. But my own concern has been more with the specific interpretation of evil in particular movements, and the course of action prescribed to deal with it.

All structural-functional theories—Smelser's included—necessarily see new religions of protest as evidence of 'strain' in the social system. That strain is experienced by deviant religionists, and is the condition for which they seek remedy, is implicit (where it is not indeed explicit) in most, if not all, explanations of new religious movements. Anomie, relative deprivation, frustration-aggression, compensation, are the sociological concepts most commonly employed in such explanations. Religionists themselves, in very different terms and with persuasive, evocative, and emotive language, also point to contemporary evils and the need for salvation from them. Salvation may be demanded rather specifically from immediate discomforts—from illness, bereavement,

---

[2] It is perhaps instructive to recall the stricture of Max Weber on theorizing of this kind: 'Laws are important and valuable in the exact natural sciences, in the measure that those sciences are *universally valid*. For the knowledge of historical phenomena in their concreteness, the most general laws, because they are most devoid of content are also the least valuable. The more comprehensive the validity—or scope—of a term, the more it leads us away from the richness of reality since in order to include the common elements of the largest possible number of phenomena, it must necessarily be as abstract as possible and hence *devoid* of content. In the cultural sciences, the knowledge of the universal or general is never valuable in itself.'—Max Weber, *The Methodology of the Social Sciences*, trans. E. A. Shils and H. A. Finch (Free Press, Glencoe, Illinois 1949) p. 80.

[3] Neil J. Smelser, *Theory of Collective Behaviour* (Routledge and Kegan Paul, London 1962).

trauma, or ill-defined psychic pain—or it may be demanded from much more general conditions, and be offered as reassurance about life after death, the restoration of social order, or the acquisition of a wholly new and superior way of life. In the movements discussed in this study, strain is certainly not at issue. Such indeed is the incidence of strain, that the usefulness of a concept of social system in application to the social conditions in which many of these movements arise must be seriously in doubt. The very word 'movement' often implies something with far more coherence, more order, and more organization than the actual manifestation of collective behaviour in reality possesses. I have been concerned with the specific mode of response of movements that are readily defined as religious, rather than with the location of strain within a social system. It is the nature of the salvation men seek that has been my primary focus of interest, and the general cultural conditions in which specific soteriological conceptions are attractive and successfully capture the minds of men.

II

The most explicit central concepts of this study are drawn from the sociology of religion rather than from any body of general sociological theory. In spite of significant differences, new religious movements among less-developed peoples have much in common with the sects that have arisen in Christendom since the Reformation. With due respect to these similarities and differences, I have tried to examine third-world movements within the context of wide, evolutionary social processes by employing analytical procedures that have previously been applied to sects. The general applicability of concepts developed in the sociology of sectarianism is discussed in Chapter 1, and the theoretical framework is there set out. The relationship of this perspective to an evolutionary context is developed in Chapter 2, where the specific types of movement found among under-developed peoples are compared with those that have arisen in Europe and the United States. Brief reference to the sects in western history provides a foil for the discussion of deviant religious responses in relation to levels of cultural and social development. The most characteristic types of movement in tribal and de-tribalized societies are then compared, together with one or two instances of movements that appear to contradict the generalizations about religious deviance in less-developed societies that initial comparative study has suggested.

What follows in subsequent chapters is not a catalogue of new religious movements. No attempt has been made to describe, or even to mention, every movement about which reports are available. Yet the sample offered in these pages is large, and intended to be sufficiently extensive to indicate three different general connections: first, to provide examples of the types of movement that arise at various stages of cultural contact; second, to indicate what types of movement arise at the many different points in the balance of subordination and domination of indigenous and invading peoples; and third, to indicate the correspondence of varying levels of cultural development and consciousness and specific modes of religious response to a disrupted and evil world.

Just as this work is not exhaustive, so it follows neither a geographic nor a chronological order in grouping the accounts of various movements. The order that I have followed has been dictated by essentially sociological considerations. In the many new religious movements of less-developed peoples what may be seen is a pattern of response appropriate to particular constellations of circumstances. Mere geography and mere chronology are inadequate charts to the sea of human experience, human inventiveness, and human behaviour. I have tried to be sensitive to the specific cultural peculiarities of various regions: thus, although I have looked for significant differences among cargo cults, dealing with one as an essentially thaumaturgical movement in Chapter 3, and another as a rational mutation of millennialism, in Chapter 14, most of them I have treated together (Chapter 10), in deference to the distinctive Melanesian cultural inheritance which they share. The general arrangement of this book has, then, been informed by sociological rather than geographic or chronological determinants. Thus it is, to give an instance, that North American Indian, Zulu, Tanganyikan, and Maori movements are treated together, in Chapter 8, as cases of millennialism in association with military enterprise.

The argument implied in the ordering of these data, however, is that thaumaturgical (or more simply if not quite synonymously, magical) preoccupations are the fundamental orientation of new religious movements among simpler peoples—just as they were of their indigenous religion. This orientation shows itself to be fundamental in two ways. Movements arising among indigenous peoples soon after cultural contact with white men are, understandably, fundamentally magical. Even where some vaguely apprehended millennium is expected (in the arrival of a cargo, for example) it is the magical implication of this, rather than the idea of social transformation, which is evident in the movements that arise at, or very soon after, the very first impact of cultural contact. Secondly, even in movements that are much more explicitly revolutionist, there persists among many individuals a much more personal conception of salvation: the demand for immediate assuagement of ills may, for a time, be mobilized into support for ideals of salvation that are expressed in terms of changing the social order, but such demands always precede the vision of a transformed society, and they often persist when such a vision has come, been widely canvassed, and then faded. This cycle is evident in some branches of the congeries of movements associated in Kimbanguism (Chapter 11). It is altogether understandable that personal ills and needs are capable of persisting after some transformative vision of the millennium has momentarily generalized and 'universalized' the prospects of salvation. Men go on experiencing evil when the promised millennium has not come into being, and their personal concerns are always capable of transcending a collective social vision. This is perhaps truest for the most helpless members of society—for the least intellectual and those with least energy. Contemporary millennialism is the millennialism of an age when the young are a rapidly growing proportion of total population, and when the young, particularly those gathered into institutions of learning, have attained a position of much greater relative influence than they have previously enjoyed.

Millennialism may operate as a type of catalyst in the thinking of less-developed peoples. However briefly and however misguidedly, millennialism represents a type of social consciousness which transcends the personal and the local, the bodily ailment and the neighbouring witch. It presents—even if only by the elimination of all witches (although usually the conception of the future is more widely transformative than that)—a vision of a different social order.[4] That this catalytic agency does not always produce new levels of rationality, must be explained in

[4] Mary Douglas, 'Techniques of Sorcery Control in Central Africa', in John Middleton and E. H. Winter, *Witchcraft and Sorcery in East Africa* (Praeger, New York 1963) pp. 123–41, considers that witch-finding cults among the Lele sometimes carry the idea of the elimination of all witches to whose activities death (except from old age) is always attributed, and thus of an age free from tensions, of general 'peace and prosperity' (pp. 138–9). Lucy P. Mair, 'Independent Religious Movements in Three Continents', *Comparative Studies in Society and History* 1, 2 (1959) pp. 113–36, emphasizes that millennial movements 'usually combine healing and sometimes also the detection of sorcerers and witches with the preparation for the millennium' (p. 135). Whilst accepting this point I cannot entirely agree with the advice she offers in her extremely perceptive brief review of the field covered in this book, namely, 'Millenary cults . . ., are sometimes treated as if they belonged to a class by themselves. I do not believe that a sharp distinction should be drawn between them and movements which attest religious autonomy without promising the immediate coming of the millennium, or between them and the cults which limit their activities to healing and the detection of witches.' (p. 113). Whilst a combination of such diverse ends is certainly not uncommon in new religious movements, it is usually possible to distinguish dominant from subsidiary themes. The interplay between thaumaturgical and revolutionist responses is an important issue in the analysis attempted in the following pages.

relation to the diversity of prevailing circumstances, and in particular the relation of subordinate millennial dreamers to dominant colonial settlers (among whom one must number the white Americans and New Zealanders). In its own terms, millennialism is almost always doomed to utter failure: almost, if not quite. The association of millennialism with military activity (Chapter 8) was often little more than the attempt of particular magicians to universalize their magic and to enlarge their claims in the face of a new scale of the social needs that it had always been their social role to supply. The association was always disastrous of course. Nativistic millennialism (Chapter 9) has, in the face of the westernization of the third world, done no more than momentarily re-assure men with promises of the return of the world they have lost. Where such reassurance has been sustained, in suitably withdrawn circumstances, as in the case of Smohalla, millennialism has itself faded as a dream, in effect to be virtually replaced by an introverted response, such as is found in the latter-day expressions of indigenous religious creativity among subordinated peoples (Chapters 12 and 13).

The catalytic impulse of millennialism has not, however wholly failed even in these cases. The vision of a transformed social order has at least lifted the consciousness of men to some measure of awareness about the conditions for the maintenance of a separate and different way of life, and however fashionable it may be to condemn the withdrawal from involvement with a wider world that typifies an introversionist movement, for many people such movements have created a secure context for living, a type of this-worldly salvation.

It is perhaps in the rational transformations of millennial dreams that the catalytic function may more convincingly be said to result in failure less than total. When the dream of a transformed social order, a millennium that will come into being 'by magic', gradually undergoes mutation to become a new world to be planned, to be discussed by rational procedures, and to be worked for—as in the Paliau movement (Chapter 14)—one sees the secularization of the revolutionist world-view. A new way of thinking, a new dawn of social consciousness occurs, and whatever the ultimate inabilities of men to create the millennial order may be, they are, none the less, stimulated to create something: by taking thought they do, in the very long run, add cubits to their stature, security and longevity to their lives.

It is not of course contended that thaumaturgical perspectives dis-appear, although they too undergo a process of mutation. The broaden-ing of local boundaries, the individual's transcendence of his own local community, the increased reliance on pragmatic procedures and empirical knowledge, make miracles less likely, the search for them less devout. Magical explanations give place to better-tested hypotheses, and claims to supernatural intervention in everyday life become more circumscribed. Thaumaturgical movements themselves embrace more rational procedures, and more systematic patterns of organization, as in some Aladura churches in West Africa (Chapter 6). Sometimes they come to accept the insights of science to augment their own sometimes inadequate thaumaturgical performances, as in the increased endorsement and provision of educational and medical facilities by groups such as the Kardecists of Brazil (Chapter 4).

The processes of mutation of response of primary religious orientations are, of course, themselves an aspect of the secularization, the rationalization, and the westernization of the third world. It is not contended, however, that either thaumaturgy or millennialism are doomed totally to disappear as soteriological prospects. Both persist, if in muted, circumscribed, and spasmodic incidence, at the periphery of the modern world, and in attenuated forms within major religious traditions. If they have lost credibility for most men, they have not lost their fascination. Indeed, as the social order imposes increasingly rational procedures, technological methods, and impersonal organization on men, involving them in networks of restrictive role-relationships, so the fascination of radical and dramatic solutions—of salvation of a wholly other kind—appears to grow. This book has nothing to address to that phenomenon directly, but it has been written in the hope that the study of these diverse and exotic schemes of salvation may none the less be not without significance for the understanding of contemporary man and society.

1

Sociological Analysis and the Search for Salvation

THE sociology of religion has suffered for a long time in captivity to its own concepts. That captivity occurred partly because of the difficulty of establishing adequate generalizations about complex and highly diversified phenomena, and partly because of the derivation of concepts from the Christian tradition of the west and its theological formulations. In the wider perspective of history, Christianity and sociology are, of course, related phenomena in the cultural inheritance of the western world. Whatever the differences in their perspectives—western assumptions about human personality; freedom of will; the norms of human interaction; the character of voluntary association; the emotional and intellectual implications of commitment, and its exclusiveness; the concept of rationality, and its realization in the patterns of religious organization—all inhere in a greater or lesser degree in both the Christian tradition and in sociology. Inevitably—the attempted objectivity of the discipline notwithstanding—concepts in the sociology of religion have been heavily stained by these assumptions. Difficulties arise when concepts evolved in relation to religion in Europe and America are applied in other cultural contexts, and it is evident that comparative religionists and, in lesser measure, anthropologists have faced similar difficulties.[1]

This accounts, in large part, for the lack of uniform terminology in reference to even everyday phenomena in the field. Each analyst, dissatisfied with existing terms, feels not only the need, but almost the obligation, to coin a new terminology for his concepts and categories. This circumstance in sociology may be regretted, but perhaps it can be regretted overmuch, and particularly by those who liken sociology to the natural sciences. Despite the inconvenience, the situation may be one not without advantages, and it may be a situation endemic in the social sciences. The humanistic content, the diversity, variability, subtlety, elusiveness, and complexity of human interaction are kept in

[1] See, on the philosophical problems involved here, the essays in particular of Peter Winch, Alasdair MacIntyre, and Steven Lukes in Bryan R. Wilson (Ed.), *Rationality* (Blackwell, Oxford and Harper, New York 1970).

9

mind by the range of our diverse terminologies. The analogy with languages is apparent: a world with numerous tongues is one in which universal communication is hindered. What is preserved is the affective quality of language—the immediacy, intimacy, subtle parochiality (and the parochial is an important source of satisfaction in that the lives of most people are lived, necessarily, at parish levels) of moods, sentiments, and thoughts. But local experience, because it is local and because localities have distinctive qualities, is unique and perhaps incommunicable in other tongues and in other places. Consequently, comparison becomes difficult. The standard terms in which it can be undertaken are always likely to be inexact. Sociologists are perhaps committed to believing that there are a number of important qualitative similarities among widely spread local and individual phenomena which justify both their categories and their generalizations. But in the multiplication of terms, there is a recognition, even if it is only implicit and involuntary, of the diversity of data. Were sociologists to impose a completely standard terminology on those diverse data, they would not of course—except perhaps very slightly and slowly—influence the actual diversity of phenomena in the real world, but they would reduce their discipline, if not to dogma, at least to sterile insensitivity.

New concepts may sensitize us to facets of data to which, were standardized terms accepted, we should remain blind: the chaos of concepts may reflect constantly changing phenomena which lack the universality that we so easily credit to them. It is appropriate that there should be many ways of approaching phenomena which are themselves inconstant and mercurial, of which we cannot hope, any more by computers than by concepts, to obtain any permanent or abiding pictures that capture their complete complexity. We need not even assume that our analytical procedures or conceptual frameworks bring us progressively nearer to any final picture—the fixed goal is hypothetical, and progress towards it has no yardstick. The contributions to the subject are contributions to our contemporary understanding rather than steps to any *final* statement about the nature of social phenomena.

There are, then, no definitive typologies, no correct terms. The typology employed here is offered only in the hope that types of this kind may illumine some relations in a diverse body of phenomena in new ways: that it has its own limitations and blind-spots one cannot doubt.

Nowhere has the proliferation of terminology and typologies been more apparent than in the discussion of religious organizations, the very diversity of which has made classification difficult. The sociologist seeking to generalize has, following theologians and comparative religionists before him, sometimes transferred the types evolved in one context to another where they have had only dubious applicability, since the elements commonly associated in one culture might not be normally associated in another. Would anyone today seriously wish to employ Durkheim's definition of 'a church' in the type of primitive society that he was then examining?[2] It is evident that this concept is culture-bound to Christian society. The sect, however, in many more of its characteristics, is a phenomenon that transcends Christendom, and it is a term which has been more widely and more appropriately employed, in common usage as well as in sociology, for separate minority religious movements within the context of various dominant religious traditions. The concept is less culture-bound than that of the church; paradoxically one might say that the sect is a phenomenon of greater universality than the church!

Of 'sect' and 'church'

The sociological concept of 'the sect' was evolved by Ernst Troeltsch specifically in reference to Christian data. He first gave the concept precision, using it in direct contradistinction to the concept of 'the church', in continuity, of course, with earlier theological practice. The concepts were elaborated as a dichotomous pair: the conservative church and the perfectionist sect.[3] His procedure served an important

[2] Émile Durkheim, *Elementary Forms of the Religious Life* (The Free Press, Glencoe, Illinois 1957).

[3] Ernst Troeltsch, *The Social Teaching of the Christian Churches*, trans., O. Wyon (Macmillan, New York 1931).

As Troeltsch typified them, the sect was egalitarian, radical, appealing to the outcast: the church was hierarchic, traditionalist, appealing to the dominant classes, for whom it operated as an agency of social control. The sect worked from below against the state: the church from above for, and with, the state. The sect had a subjective fellowship, the church distributed objective grace. The church mobilized differential commitment—monks and priests and laity, of whom the first two were more totally committed; it enjoyed a division of religious labour in the activities of ritual, sacraments, and prayer, as well as government: the sect demanded total commitment from all. Whereas the church had specialists to maintain, for instance, ascetic practices, the sect was totalitarian—all were expected to be equally ascetic. Whereas the church became in itself an object of reverence—as well as an objective reference —for the individual, and existed as an entity external to him, the sect had no such sanctity or external identity, but was the shared experience of the inner community. The church stressed a relation of the individual to the institution, the sect emphasized the fellowship of love. The church was integrated with the world, the sect in tension against the world: the church conferred ascriptive status, its members were in-born; the sect conferred status only by achievement—by voluntary adherence and the proof of merit. Troeltsch saw sect and church as polar opposites; the sect was an almost uninstitutionalized (and sometimes virtually anomic) movement; the church was a highly institutionalized and even an over-institutionalized organization. For Troeltsch the types were 'a logical result of the Gospel . . .' in which the strains of conservatism and revolutionism were to be discerned.

explicatory purpose, but the constant reference back to Troeltschean typifications of church and sect has sometimes obscured the realities which 'ideal type constructs' are meant to clarify. Abstract typifications, instead of stimulating empirical enquiry and analytical rigour, have sometimes been substituted for them. Even though numerous refinements of the Troeltschean types have been developed, these have all too often overlooked important empirical data that should have called into question the gross categories of 'church' and 'sect'.[4] It is especially necessary to be aware of the limitations of the Troeltschean categories when examining new religious movements that have arisen outside the traditional milieu of Christianity. In particular, it is important to divest ourselves of theological conceptions of religious protest: 'the sect', if we continue so to call such movements, is no longer to be understood by direct contrast with 'the church'.[5]

While the sect may be regarded as a self-distinguishing protest movement, its protest in the contemporary world is not (and formerly may not always have been) normally levelled specifically against the church. It may be against the state, against the secular institutions of society, or in opposition to or separation from particular institutions or groups within the society. The change of social circumstances, in which, even in Christian contexts, state and church are no longer so closely identified, has made evident that sects are not necessarily protesting specifically against church organization. The point is as relevant in the analysis of religious movements in less-developed societies as it is for contemporary, western, sectarianism. The conceptualization of the sect is liberated from a restricting assumption that placed the sociological category 'sect' in bondage to specifically Christian theological preoccupations.

[4] It is unnecessary here to trace the development of ideal-type analysis of church and sect. H. Richard Niebuhr, in *Social Sources of Denominationalism* (Holt, New York 1929), made explicit the dynamic character of sectarianism, and sought to show that in one generation the sect became a denomination. This misleading conclusion arose from a failure to distinguish among sects in respect of important characteristics affecting sect development: see B. R. Wilson, 'An Analysis of Sect Development', *American Sociological Review*, 24, 1 (February 1959), pp. 3–15. For earlier developments of the typification of religious groups, see Howard Becker, *Systematic Sociology on the Basis of the Beziehungslehre and Gebildelehre of Leopold von Wiese* (Wiley, New York 1932), who distinguished 'cults' from 'sects' by criteria criticized above. J. Milton Yinger, in *Religion in the Struggle for Power* (Duke University Press, Durham, N.C. 1946) and *Religion, Society and the Individual* (Macmillan, New York 1957), distinguished, together with refinements of the church-type, 'established' from incipient sects. E. T. Clark, *The Small Sects in America*, Rev. Edn (Abingdon Press, New York and Nashville 1947), mixed theological and other criteria in his categories in his extensive catalogue of sects. For an important development in the differentiation of different types of sect, see Peter L. Berger, 'The Sociological Study of Sectarianism', *Social Research*, 21 (Winter 1954), pp. 467–85.

[5] This point is argued by Allan W. Eister, 'Towards a Radical Critique of Church-Sect Typologizing', *Journal for the Scientific Study of Religion* VI, 1 (Spring 1967), pp. 85–90

Two of those preoccupations have considerably influenced sociologists of religious movements: organization and doctrine. Sociology has grown up in societies the dominant ideologies of which have been Christian, and even though the sociological tradition has been very largely positivist and its aspirations those of the ethical neutralism of science—and hence, in large measure, specifically non-Christian—there is no doubt that the new social science received a significant inheritance from the old religious ethic, and the humanistic disciplines that it had nourished. The more obvious value-commitments could be disavowed, but the intellectual assumptions, style, and logic were a fundamental groundwork harder to abandon, or even to recognize as potentially prejudicial. The specific preoccupations of the Christian church with formal organization, role-differentiation, the unambiguous delineation of power, prerogative, privilege, and hierarchic status, were precursors of the consciously-developed structures of organization in western society in the industrial era. It is not surprising that the elaborated post-Troeltschcan classifications of religious bodies focused very considerably on the degree of institutionalization discernible in an ascending order from cults (regarded by some as ephemeral and charismatic); sects; advanced sects; denominations; and churches. But the conscious creation of formal and systematic organizations is in large measure a phenomenon that is culturally specific to western society. (And even if the western dominance of other parts of the world leads increasingly to the adoption of rational organization in other cultures, that dominance has *not yet* eliminated, nor even significantly modified, other styles of group association and activity in all non-western societies.) Because this factor is culturally limited, classification of religious movements by the extent to which they are institutionalized is a clearly inadequate procedure for movements that have arisen outside the boundaries of established Christianity.

It is true, of course, that the earliest Christian sects had initially only limited prospects of creating a formal structure—it had taken the Church itself a long time to do so. It is also clear that one of the most powerful of sectarian impulses in Christianity has been the rejection of such systematic patterns of organization. Sects have often sought to 'de-structure' existing religious practice, to replace formal ritual with spontaneous manifestations of devotion. But even as early as the Reformation some of those joining new religious movements recognized, almost from the beginning, the need for some stable pattern of procedure in their religious, and perhaps also in their social, concerns. To protect their members and to maintain their ideals, some sort of organization was necessary: in some considerable degree they inherited the distinctively Christian preoccupation with a coherent and internally consistent system of beliefs. The early models of organization which they adopted, however, were often minimal. Either from lack of knowledge of alternatives, or from commitment to what was taken to be a 'natural' pattern of social organization, the model that was frequently adopted for sect organization was that of the local community. Even among such communal types of sect, varying degrees of formality were possible, of course. But groups which, once formed, settled to a way of life in which voluntarism was not much emphasized could, by isolating themselves, effectively imitate the local communities of peasant society without need for much, if any, formal constitutional arrangement.[6]

Whilst spontaneity, informality, and the sense of community have remained important features of some persisting sects, and have continued to be, at least until well into the twentieth century, powerful impulses in stimulating new ones, some sects have evolved more elaborate and more formal patterns of organization. The impress of the increasingly rational systems of procedure and organization that have developed in the extra-religious areas of western society has imposed upon sects the need to adopt more systematic and more formal arrangements and structures.[7] Since the established churches were ideologically committed to a traditional ecclesiology that they were obliged to regard as timelessly valid and viable and divinely warranted, a sect could regard its acceptance of more rational forms of organization as a continuing affirmation of its divergence from churchly forms. More rational forms of organization occurred even in sects committed to styles of worship and activity in which emotional and expressive features remained prominent. The Primitive Methodists and the

[6] Such a group is exemplified in the Amish Mennonites, who have remained insulated from the wider society by a different language, a divergent culture, and vicinal segregation. In comparison with the Hutterians and with the early fifteen-century Taborites, their social organization is less formal and more imitatively communal. John A. Hostetler, in *Amish Society* (Johns Hopkins Press, Baltimore 1963) treats them more as a community than as a sect, while still according primacy to their religious orientation to the world. The Hutterians have a more formal but essentially communal, indeed communitarian, organization. See Victor Peters, *All Things Common: the Hutterian Way of Life* (University of Minnesota Press, Minneapolis 1965), and John W. Bennett, *Hutterian Brethren* (Stanford University Press, Stanford 1967). Non-communal sects such as Quakers necessarily relied much more on voluntary commitment without the support of a separated community of believers and, indeed, in the face of a largely hostile public among whom Quaker believers continued to live. Even so, Quaker suspicion of formal organization is evident in the minimal character of the arrangements they have traditionally endorsed for their continuance as a worshipping collectivity.

[7] There are many examples of this process. For one, see B. R. Wilson, *Sects and Society* (Heinemann, London and University of California Press, Berkeley 1961), pp. 277–80.

Salvation Army provide, in their different ways, good nineteenth-century examples. It is not our specific concern to pursue the matter here, but it is clear that the rejection by Protestantism, and in particular by sectarian groups in the Protestant tradition, of the sacerdotal, sacramental, and ritual-magical aspects of Catholicism, facilitated this steadily strengthening disposition to embrace more rational patterns of organization. (Clearly, certain types of sect more consciously imitated the formal organizational patterns of other institutions, particularly of education, of medicine, and even, in part, of business corporations and mail-order companies: usually in these cases there were doctrinal departures from the dominant Christian tradition which were congruous with, and which legitimated, their secularized procedures and organization.[8])

Despite the increasing proximity of the organization of some religious movements to more general patterns and structures of association in western societies, it is clear that no organizational style is to be regarded as a defining criterion of minority religious movements. Although a broad distinction sometimes exists between highly institutionalized churches, and the loose, spontaneous, and volatile arrangements of sects, the Troeltschean dichotomy of church and sect leads to facile assumptions that are frequently not justified.[9]

The distinction of religious movements purely in terms of doctrine clearly suffers from similar defects. The identification of sectarianism with heresy (and the further identification of heresy, may it be said, with moral deficiency or wilful and perverse espousal of evil, which has been very readily assumed by Christian theologians) clearly limits any

---

[8] The typical cases are the movements that are designated in this book as *manipulationist*, and they have been most conspicuous in the United States. For some discussion of their organizational styles see B. R. Wilson, *Religious Sects* (Weidenfeld and Nicolson, World University Library, London, and McGraw-Hill, New York 1971), pp. 141–66.

[9] Dichotomization is a common tendency among sociologists who construct ideal-types of particular widespread phenomena. Thus even those who go beyond the church–sect dichotomy and who seek to distinguish types of sect tend to content themselves too readily with dichotomies. Martin E. Marty, 'Sects and Cults', *Annals of the American Academy of Political and Social Science* 332 (November 1960), pp. 125–34, approaches a sociological distinction in dividing minority movements into the negatively oriented and the positively oriented. But this division is both too gross and too evaluative to facilitate further analysis. David A. Martin, 'The Denomination', *British Journal of Sociology* XIII (March 1962), pp. 1–14; *idem, Pacifism* (Routledge, London 1965) divides sects, perhaps following intimations in Troeltsch, as being 'either communist or anarchist, revolutionist or quietist, nudist or uniformed, ascetic or licentious, completely sacramental or non-sacramental, worshipping in a wild communal rant or, like the Seekers, in utter silence'. Colourful as this complex set of dichotomous choices is, it is not true. The analysis mistakes some sects for all sects, and it does not help us to understand sects if we prejudge them as necessarily extremist in one direction or the other. Werner Stark, *The Sociology of Religion*, Vol. II *Sectarian Religion* (Routledge, London 1967) follows exactly the same misleading procedure.

objective depiction of innovatory or protesting religious movements.[10] Worse, it directs attention away from the social, economic, and cultural circumstances by which sociologists would seek to explain these social phenomena and their development. Perhaps the most important defect of the characterization of sects by doctrinal divergence from orthodoxy is that, like characterization in terms of organization, it puts too much emphasis on specifically Christian preoccupations. The Christian church for centuries devoted its intellectual energies to the establishment of an elaborate and internally consistent body of doctrine, making it the vital test of purity and faith, and eliminating all contrary, competitive, and deviant statements of faith, and all groups that espoused such divergent ideas. Such a preoccupation with logically consistent, hierarchically and rationally co-ordinated statements of the pseudo-historical, philosophical, and metaphysical, and the derivation of a body of moral prescriptions from them, is a distinctive feature of the Christian religion. A taxonomy based on assumptions about religion defined in these terms must signally fail to do justice to religious phenomena in other cultures where doctrinal preoccupations of this type have not been typical.

An alternative approach to new religious movements

We may, therefore, entirely with profit abandon both the traditional theological basis for sect classification in terms of doctrine, and the sociological attempts to distinguish new religious movements by the degree of institutionalization that they have achieved. Whilst this last type of categorization may be of interest in tracing the dynamics of certain sectarian movements over time in certain circumstances of western society, it cannot be shown to have universal validity or to be suitable for universal application. From specific 'stages' of organizational development, and doctrinal niceties (designated, usually, by the names of the first Christian to espouse them) we may pass to the more socio-logical concern with the relation of doctrine, organization, form of

---

[10] Such theological judgements are to be found very widely, of course, even in the work of so urbane and charitable a theologian as Ronald Knox, in *Enthusiasm* (Oxford University Press, Oxford 1950). Some writers who regard their perspective as sociological betray the same normative theological perspective which very much diminishes, where it does not altogether destroy, the sociological value of their work. See, for example, W. Stark, *The Sociology of Religion* Vols. I–IV, op. cit. This criticism of this work is developed in my review article, B. R. Wilson, 'Establishment Sectarianism and Partisanship', *The Sociological Review* 15, 2 (July 1967), pp. 213–20, and ibid., 16, 1 (March 1968), pp. 120–3; 18, 3 (November 1970), pp. 426–8.

association, social orientation, and action—all of which may change in some measure independently of each other. Sects, after all, are phenomena that are not confined to Christendom, even though, in the way in which we are accustomed to think about them, there are certain characteristics that are specifically or predominantly inherited from the Christian tradition. If the wider aims of sociological analysis are to be met it is essential that our categories should be freed from the presuppositions of one particular cultural tradition or of one historical period.

Clearly the type of comparative cross-cultural study that is here proposed is not without difficulties. Minority religious movements in other cultures have developed against an orthodoxy radically different in structure and operation from that of the church in Christendom. The typically Christian concerns of conversion, exclusiveness of religious allegiance, the institution of and insistence upon one unified dogmatic system of doctrine, are not features of all religious traditions. Movements in other cultures frequently lack the organizational durability of most Christian sects. There are, in some cultures, fewer models of organizational structure for new movements to adopt: people are much less literate; there is less knowledge of constitutions and rational co-ordination; and there is often less emotional stability and much less of a time-perspective to make such forms workable. The absence of exclusivity of religious commitment, of those assumptions of the impossibility of simultaneously espousing two (or more) contradictory beliefs, inevitably make movements in many cultures—and especially in those less-developed societies that are the subject-matter of this book —significantly different from the stereotypical Christian sect. To avoid too easy a total identification of Christian sects and the movements here under review we shall refer to them simply as new religious movements. The basis of our earlier categorization of sects, because it is fixed on neither doctrine nor organization, remains applicable, however. These movements are regarded in terms of their dominant social orientation, their response to the world.

If sociology is not itself to be a culture-bound discipline like theology, it must have fundamental categories of this type, which recognize the similarity of social processes in diverse contexts, and provide a common stock of analytical apparatus capable of extensive application. The common social processes that lie behind the specific context of different cultures is the theoretical bedrock on which such concepts rest. The tools may need modification in the light of application, but should ultimately reach a point of very wide applicability, and be something more than a collection of categories which are ethnocentric or christocentric. Obviously, if this is to come about the derogatory implications of terms such as 'sect', as it is sometimes used by the theologians, must be avoided.

That any such apparatus must miss some of the local quality and richness of phenomena is evident. To formulate new categories and to coin a new terminology, and perhaps especially one that aims at generality and width of applicability, is to jeopardize the possibility of grasping the distinctive and peculiar feeling-tone of the diverse phenomena that have been subsumed into these general types, by virtue of their similarities of structure, function, and process. It is at this point that what the sociologist hopes to gain must be reluctantly paid for in the coin of the historian and the anthropologist. The minutiae which are locally significant, and which the historians and anthropologists have carefully noted, are surrendered for grosser resemblances of those dominant configurations that show inter-cultural comparability. In the analysis that follows, the particularities must often be ignored, but it is hoped that to ignore them is not to do them violence or to derogate their value. The constructor of categories must always remind himself that the data are richer than his types—as the data-collector should also remind himself, that the world is richer than his data.

'Responses to the world'

The typological constructs to be employed in this essay are an elaboration of an earlier taxonomy modified and freed from specific Christian connotations to make it applicable to a wider, more diversified range of phenomena.[11] This book attempts to use these theoretical models to explain new religious movements that have developed outside the main body of western Christendom. This is no more than an obvious, small and tentative step in the application of these models to religious movements which have arisen in simpler societies which are at, or even beyond, the fringe of the influence of orthodox Christianity.[12]

[11] This approach has developed slowly and not without some changes of mind in the writer's earlier work. In its early form it is closer to specifically Christian examples of sectarianism: see B. R. Wilson, 'An Analysis of Sect Development', op. cit. For a reformulation of greater applicability see B. R. Wilson, *Religious Sects*, op. cit. For a discussion of the nature of ideal types of sectarianism see B. R. Wilson, 'A Typology of Sects' in *Types, Dimensions et Mesure de la Religiosité*, Actes de la Xe Conférence Internationale de Sociologie Religieuse (Rome 1969), pp. 29–56.

[12] The early versions of the type-constructs outlined here have been applied to sects in one non-western society by Robert I. Rotberg, in *The Rise of Nationalism in Central Africa* (Harvard University Press, Cambridge, Mass. 1965). In respect of Japanese sects they have received valuable criticism from Earl R. Babbie, in 'The Third Civilization: an Examination of

The principal criterion of classification is in terms of a movement's *response to the world*, which should facilitate both the comparative and dynamic dimensions of study. *Response to the world* suggests items that lie beyond the self-conception of the sect, important as that is. The sectarian movement always manifests some degree of tension with the world, and it is the type of tension and the ways in which it is contained or maintained that are of particular importance. In earlier attempts to construct models of sectarianism, I used the term *mission*: *response to the world* is a concept with evident similarities to the idea of mission, but it emphasizes rather more directly the soteriological elements of theodicy. Men seek salvation in a world in which they feel the need for supernatural help. Sectarians necessarily seek that salvation in some other way than by the acceptance of the secular culture and the institutional facilities that it provides for men to attain social and cultural goals. Clearly, by definition, they also reject the orthodox or dominant religious tradition in respects important enough for them to separate from it, at least in worship, and usually also in other ways.

The shift from *mission* to *response to the world* as a basis for typifying sects reflects a gradual shift in my own thinking about the problem of distinguishing among religious movements. It illustrates different stages of acquaintance with data and changed appreciation of the nature of collectivities. The earlier classification of sects was a classification based on empirical observation, arising from years of work with sectarian groups and a first-hand acquaintance with their distinctive styles and orientations. It led me to challenge the generalizations of H. R. Niebuhr and to hypothesize divergent courses of sect development predicated on a knowledge of the cluster of empirical factors that were actually to be found in a number of particular cases. Subsequently it seemed useful to consider (and obviously this could be successfully undertaken only *after* extensive exposure to empirical cases) just what range of orientations was possible for deviant religious movements, always allowing that any one of these cases might or might not be found in the empirical world.

Sokagakkai', *Review of Religious Research* 7 (Winter 1966), and by Russell W. Galloway Jr, 'The New Religions of Japan: A Comparative Study of Sects' (unpub. ms. 1967). More marginally it has also been used by M. D. Gilsenan, 'The Decline of Sufi Orders in Modern Egypt', *Muslim World* LVII (1967), pp. 11–18. Since the first chapter of this book was originally written I have attempted very briefly to make use of the revised model put forward here in application to new religions in contemporary Japan. See B. R. Wilson, *Religious Sects*, op. cit., pp. 218–25.

The reader acquainted with the type-constructs of sectarianism employed in that work will not need to do more than briefly re-acquaint himself with them as they are presented in the following pages of this chapter.

The shift, then, was from taxonomy *somewhat* in the style of ideal types to a much more thorough attempt to ideal-typification. Once an exhaustive set of deviant religious responses to the world has been specified, the incidence of each ideal response in relation to specific empirical variables can be investigated. By using this heuristic device to measure variations from the ideal-typical and to relate them to specific empirical factors, propositions of high explanatory value might be produced. This is clearly a more significant exercise in sociology than is simple classification of sects. It realizes the potential of the earlier set of types, which sought to specify the clustering of empirical factors found in various cases and to explain their significance for sect development. The new typology allows full weight to be given to those movements which do not really approximate to one type or another, and it facilitates recognition of changes in orientation.

The terms by which particular response is designated escape entirely from the theological echoes of the earlier classification and their christocentric culture-bound character. Even more important, what is designated as *response to the world* is not necessarily located in the context of a stable, on-going, self-consciously organized movement. We may discuss responses to the world without necessarily supposing that they occur only in well-established sects which manifest all the cultural connotations of Christendom in respect of exclusivity, internal coherence, and formal organization. *Response to the world*, much more evidently than *mission*, may be manifested in many relatively unfocused, un-purposive activities, and *not only* in activities, but also in life-style, association, and ideology.[13]

Obviously response is affected by teachings and doctrine (where something answering to that designation exists), but it is recognizable in groups in which formal teaching is inchoate or incoherent. Even in movements in which doctrine persists unchanged (or changes only slowly and slightly), change in response to the world may occur independently of doctrine. Ideology, as formally expressed in sect teachings, can become ossified and insensitive to social realities that are expressed by other media and at other levels within a movement. While by no means ignoring the importance of conscious ideologies, this specific item by which ideal types of sect may be distinguished is not confined to ideological concerns. Response to the world may change without specific doctrinal changes, perhaps in relation to changed social circumstances experienced by sect members such as social

---

[13] Insufficient attention to ideology in my earlier discussions of sects is a specific point of criticism in Gary Schwartz, *Sect Ideologies and Social Status* (Chicago University Press, Chicago 1970).

mobility, recruitment of the second generation, changed reactions of the wider society, the process of institutionalization, or other internal or external factors.

Response is perhaps a more completely sensitizing concept than is *mission* in suggesting the probable action-patterns of particular social groups. People of a particular age-group, social class, educational achievement, or ethnic type, or in a particular ecological context, or in a given social situation, are more likely to approximate to particular patterns of response than others. Again, once a movement has come into being the response to the world it has evolved may have stronger appeal in the recruitment of one sex rather than the other; flourish more, persist longer, or spread more readily in particular rural, urban, or suburban contexts; or find more congenial conditions at particular stages of social and cultural development than at others. These probabilities may be hypothesized from preliminary acquaintance with empirical cases, but they may even be tentatively formulated on the strength of logical extrapolation from the type-constructs, the logic of social situations, and the range of *Lebenschancen* prevailing within them. The superiority of ideal typifications over a mere taxonomy lies in their capacity to suggest such hypothetical formulations, and by alerting us to expectable developments, they call attention to divergent cases in which empirical analysis is required to produce explanation.

There appear to be eight basic *supernaturalist* responses to the dilemma which men face in asking how they might be saved. The dominant position is that of acceptance of the world, the facilities it offers, and the goals and values that a given culture enjoins upon men. This orthodox response (whether secular or religious) concerns us only as a base-line. Concern with transcendence over evil and the search for salvation and consequent rejection of prevailing cultural values, goals, and norms, and whatever facilities are culturally provided for man's salvation, defines religious deviance. The seven possible responses of those rejecting cultural arrangements may be simply stated, but it is first necessary to recognize the variability of content of the idea of salvation.

Men apprehend evil in many different ways, and thus look for relief from it in different forms of supernatural action. The various responses to the world embrace different conceptions of the source of evil and the ways in which it will be overcome. Evil may be seen as the work of supernatural agents inhabiting another sphere—the Devil, spirits, ghosts—or as the work of men with supernatural powers—witches and sgrcerers. It may be recognized simply as it occurs, as illness, barrenness, poverty. It may be ascribed to the inherently evil nature of men,

or to their failure in serving God, or in failing to organize their affairs
in accordance with his will. All evil occurrences may be seen as
manifestations of one indivisible agency, or each may be regarded as
discrete and specific. The events or episodes or circumstances depicted
as evil in one society may be regarded neutrally in another. The
incidence of cognitive dissonance, failure of expectations, discrepancies
between ideal and reality, may be subject to wide cultural variability
according to the specific legitimations available in particular societies
and the empirical content of what Peter Berger calls their plausibility
structures.[14] But everywhere there is a problem of evil, and everywhere
men are disposed to seek salvation from it. The scale of soteriological
promise is clearly related to the scale on which evil is depicted, from the
local incidence of illness to the destiny of all mankind. It is thus evident
that salvation may range from limited demand for *ad hoc* instant therapy
to a programme for the reorganization of the world. The seven responses
which reject cultural goals and the soteriological theories and facilities
that exist may be typified as follows:

(1) The world is corrupt because men are corrupt: if men can be
changed then the world will be changed. Salvation is seen not as
available through objective agencies but only by a profoundly
felt, supernaturally wrought transformation of the self. The
objective world will not change but the acquisition of a new
subjective orientation to it will itself be salvation.

Clearly this subjective conversion will be possible only on the
promise of a change in external reality at some future time, or the
prospect of the individual's transfer to another sphere. This is
the ideological or doctrinal aspect of the matter, but the essential
sociological fact is that what men must do to be saved is to undergo emotional transformation—a conversion experience. This is
the proof of having transcended the evil of the world. Since it is
a permanent and timelessly valid transcendence, some future
condition of salvation is often posited in which objective circumstances come to correspond to the subjective sense of salvation,
but the believer also knows, from the subjective change, that he
is saved *now*. Thus he can face the evil of the world, the processes
of change that threaten men with decay and death, because he is
assured of an unchanging condition *and feels this*. This response
is the *conversionist* response to the world. It is not concerned

[14] See P. L. Berger, *The Sacred Canopy* (Doubleday, New York 1967), esp. pp. 45–7.

simply with recruitment to a movement, but with the acquisition of a change of heart.[15]

(2) A second response to evil is to declare that only the destruction of the world, of the natural, but more specifically of the social, order, will suffice to save men. This process of destruction must be supernaturally wrought, for men lack the power if not to destroy the world then certainly to re-create it. Believers may themselves feel called upon to participate in the process of overturning the world, but they know that they do no more than put a shoulder to an already turning wheel and give an earnest of faith: the outworking of the prophesied cataclysm and subsequent restoration is essentially the doing of supernatural agencies. Men have no hope except from a new dispensation, and the creation of such a new order is the intention of god or the gods.[16] In this case men may not claim to be saved now but do claim that they will *very soon* be saved: salvation is imminent. No subjective re-orientation will affect the state of the world: its objective condition must be recognized. It will be changed only by divine action. This response is the *revolutionist* response.

(3) The third response, labelled *introversionist*, is to see the world as irredeemably evil and salvation to be attained only by the fullest possible withdrawal from it. The self may be purified by renouncing the world and leaving it. This response might be an

---

[15] The term 'to convert' is, of course, often used as a synonym for 'to recruit', but the two are in fact quite separate concepts, and although evangelical sects often seek to recruit members by converting sinners they usually subscribe to a theology that admits that at least in theory the sinner may be convicted of his sin and converted without being drawn into any particular movement. The significance of the designation 'conversionist' is not that it indicates a recruitment-oriented movement (after all, Jehovah's Witnesses whom we do not label conversionist, is the movement which recruits most effectively), but that it specifies a response in which a change of heart is the central feature. Movements that approach the ideal-type of conversionist sect frequently 'over-subscribe' to this designation, in fact, adding to the emotionally powerful experience of conversion other events which repeat or intensify its effect, such as belief in instantaneous sanctification as a 'second blessing' in some Holiness sects, and in the baptism of the Holy Ghost and the exercise of gifts of the Spirit in Pentecostal groups.

[16] Just who is to benefit from the establishment of this new order is not always clear. In most movements in the Christian tradition, only true believers are expected to enjoy this new dispensation, or at least to enjoy it in the fullest measure. But even among these movements some participation is allowed to those who even at a late date join the movement and acknowledge the truth. In millennial movements in less-developed countries the matter may be less well defined. The movements are often ephemeral and their expectations are for very early transformation of the world. Often all natives are vaguely expected to participate in the coming benefits, which are ascribed to the effort of ancestor spirits. Millennial movements that predict one objective event often arise in the name of existing social groups— the tribe or 'the natives'—without discrimination between those who 'join' the movement or who participate in required rituals and those who do not.

individual response, of course, but as the response of a social movement it leads to the establishment of a separated community preoccupied with its own holiness and its means of insulation from the wider society. Even if the ideology posits only its future realization, in practice, salvation is sociologically a *present* endeavour. The community itself becomes the source and seat of all salvation. Explicitly this prospect of salvation is only for those who belong.

(4) The *manipulationist* response is narrower than those already considered. Whereas revolutionists seek a transformed world, introversionists a purified community, and conversionists a transformed self, the manipulationist response is to seek only a transformed set of relationships—a transformed method of coping with evil. Whereas the foregoing orientations reject the goals of the culture as well as the institutionalized means of attaining them and the existing facilities by which men might be saved, the manipulationist rejects only the means and the facilities. Salvation is possible in the world and evil might be overcome if men learn the right means, improved techniques, to deal with their problems. No less than other responses this orientation is concerned to provide timeless happiness for man: salvation is no less a present, immediate, and permanent possibility. Whatever the ideologies of manipulationist movements may be, this response is very much related to everyday well-being, and this well-being may be vouchsafed by learning universal principles concerning man and the world which will explain evil away. This conception of salvation is neither other-worldly nor transcendental. It is the scarce goods of this world—health, wealth, longevity, happiness, success, and high status—which constitute the saved condition. Illness, incapacity, pain, poverty, and death are the things from which one seeks to be saved. Salvation depends on learning religious precepts which allow men to alter their relation to the world, to see the world differently, to eliminate baleful influences which are essentially mental incapacities. Whilst it is the subjective orientation which must be changed, the objective world will be brought into harmony with this new perception and manipulated by it.

(5) Differing from the manipulationist response primarily by its still narrower and essentially particularistic conception of salvation is the *thaumaturgical* response. The individual's concern is relief from present and specific ills by special dispensations. The demand for supernatural help is personal and local: its operation is

magical.[17] Salvation is immediate but has no general application beyond the given case and others like it. There is little likelihood of generalizing this response or producing elaborate ideological formulations for it: where doctrine is developed it is often of little importance in the attainment of salvation. Healing, assuagement of grief, restoration after loss, reassurance, the foresight and avoidance of calamity, and the guarantee of external (or at least continuing) life after death are the elements of the salvation which is sought. The evils feared are all highly specific, and it is from their particular incidence (not from their universal operation) that salvation is sought. Miracles and oracles, rather than the comprehension of new principles about life, are the instruments of salvation in this case.

(6) The *reformist* response to the world recognizes evil but assumes that it may be dealt with according to supernaturally-given insights about the ways in which social organization should be amended. Amendment of the world is here the essential orientation, and the specific alterations to be made are revealed to men whose hearts and minds are open to supernatural influence. Clearly this response is close to reformist attitudes of secular men who seek only rational justification for their advocacy. It differs only in the belief that divine inspiration operates to indicate the focus of reformist effort. This perspective has considerable convergence with some secular positions, but it is clearly maintained that although man will save himself he will not do so without the prompting of supernatural agencies. It is evident that this orientation is less likely to lead to total conviction concerning salvation than are other responses: there is a gradualist assumption involved and a much larger element of accommodation to the wider society.

(7) The final response is to reconstruct the world according to some divinely given principles, to establish a new social organization in which evil will be eliminated. This response differs from the demand that the world be overturned (revolutionist), in insisting that men re-make it, even if they do this work strictly at divine

---

[17] The demand for salvation by thaumaturgy is found not only in deviant religious movements, of course. It is the demand for magical solutions of problems and it is thus an ancient orientation and one which, despite their rationalizing thrust, is found as at least a mythical element in the great founded religions. The founders and their associates are typically credited with oracular and miraculous powers. In Christianity disciples for several generations were credited with such thaumaturgical ability, and in the theory of sainthood it may be said to live still in the Catholic Church. In Islam the same power has, unofficially but widely, been credited to persist as a hereditary property.

behest. It is much more radical than the reformist response in insisting on complete replacement of social organization. It is more active and constructive than the introversionist response of simply withdrawing from the world. That is a *utopian* response.[18]

Responses and movements

These responses are complex orientations to the wider society, its culture, values, and cultural goals, the experience of evil and the means of escaping it and attaining salvation—which together we have referred to simply as 'the world'. The focus of response may be external reality and subjective apprehension of it. Inevitably many slightly varying emphases are possible for deviant religious movements in actual fact, and the seven types of responses might not appear in any high degree of purity in the real world. The beliefs of religious movements are often volatile, inconsistent, many-sided, and internally contradictory. Since they are the beliefs of a collectivity this diversity is altogether expectable.

[18] It should be clear that although utopian movements are always concerned with colony-building, not all religious movements that build colonies manifest a utopian response to the world. Whereas utopians regard the colony as the way of salvation, other movements—typically introversionist movements—may in certain circumstances find colony-building highly expedient. Such groups as the Amana Society, the Rappites, the Shakers, and some Mennonites have been communitarian in practice, although communitarianism was not part of their pristine vision. The separated community is less a way of withdrawing from the world—the location for salvation—than in itself the agency of salvation; less the response to the world than a vehicle facilitating the response. It was an appropriate way to come to terms with an alien society within which such a group might be dispersed and be steadily assimilated piecemeal. For migrant groups adjusting to new social conditions—for Tyrolese Hutterians in Moravia, Transylvania, Russia, and North America no less than for Württemburg Rappites—communitarian life refabricated the benefit and security of the kinship relations that they had surrendered in migrating. Brethren in Christ became a substitute for blood kinsfolk until, by practice of endogamy, fictive and biological kinship had again converged. Communitarianism, often assisted by distinctiveness of language, became a device by which to insulate their own, more holy, way of life. Since land was cheap, or there for the clearing, vicinal segregation became an almost ready-made defence for the sect.

Communitarianism often became invested with great significance by a movement, and its role in creating a specific type of mutation within introversionist movements cannot be ignored. It imposed new functions on the sect, and stimulated the development of new internal divisions of labour, new processes of social control to support the original ideological totalitarianism of the movement. As the original inspiration became less emphatic in groups such as the Shakers and the Amana Society, which had claimed special inspiration at their origins, so communitarianism may well have become an end in itself, regarded as the criterion of a good life, rather than simply as an expedient means towards its realization. The ideological demand to withdraw from the world became confused with the specific means of withdrawing in particular social contexts (although many such sects continued to permit the existence of associated members who lived in the wider society). Communitarianism became itself the object of defence-mechanisms and rationalizations, and doctrinal or inspirational legitimation was then retrospectively discovered for what had originally been merely expedient. Clearly this development differs from a utopian response to the world.

Since in many cultures the formal rules of western logic are not evident even in the highest formulations of idea-systems, they must not be expected in a matter of such emotional significance as the way to attain salvation. Since movements persist over time, changes in composition, opposition, general circumstance, and shifting orientations are a necessary aspect of their existence. None the less these ideal-types of response appear useful as hypothetical points of orientation for movements that reject established cultural resolutions of the problem of theodicy.[19] They may be briefly summarized as prescriptions for changing the relation of men to 'the world'. The objectivists focus on the world, saying:

God will overturn it (revolutionists);
God calls us to abandon it (introversionists);
God calls us to amend it (reformists);
God calls us to reconstruct it (utopians).

The subjectivists say:
God will change us (conversionists).

The relationists, if we may call them that, say:
God calls us to change perception (manipulationists).
God will grant particular dispensations and work specific miracles (thaumaturgists).

In this formulation, manipulationists appear nearer to a subjectivist position, although they have a more specific, more intellectual, less total,

[19] There is a numerically unimportant but widely known group of religious movements which deviate from orthodoxy in practice but not in orientation, and which in consequence do not fit into any of these patterns of response. It is tempting, following Merton's use of the term and because the word has a substantive descriptive justification, to call such groups *ritualist*: see Robert K. Merton, *Social Theory and Social Structure* (Free Press, Glencoe, Illinois 1957), pp. 149–53. The categories of sect that I first developed were similar to, but were not derived from, Merton's categories of anomic behaviour. See also Karen Horney, *Neurotic Personality of Our Time* (Norton, New York 1937). These groups are separate from but maintain a response identical with conformists. Unlike those in Merton's *ritualist* category, these groups have not in fact abandoned the goal of salvation, but like them they have become very much obsessed with the conformist and orthodox means—religious rituals. These imitators of orthodox practice accept all but limited elements of orthodox ecclesiology, in that they seek to break the claim to monopoly of performance of established priests. They seek ordination as priests and consecration as bishops and since in Catholic, Orthodox, and other branches of Christianity there are a number of *episcopi vaganti*, who are duly and validly consecrated but who have broken with their churches, numerous lines of apostolic succession have arisen. Such imitators have small followings but grand titles, vestments, and claims to ecclesiastical jurisdiction, and are found in several 'denominations' in England, and America, where a group of this kind, the African Orthodox Church, exists among negroes. Such imitators also exist in other religious traditions besides Christianity. There is not, however, a real deviation in response to the world in these instances but only a separation arising from a dispute over power and privilege in religious practice. See on this subject Peter F. Anson, *Bishops at Large* (Faber, London 1964), and A. C. Terry-Thomas, *The African Orthodox Church*, 1956 (no publisher or place of publication given).

and less emotional conception of the subjective change which is needed, and thaumaturgists are nearer to objectivists, although they demand change only in specific self-affecting events. The manipulationists do expect a change in objective reality in accord with changed perception, of course, and may present their position as objectivist by declaring that the special knowledge that they claim to possess is objective truth: they work on the shadow-line of man's epistemological dilemma. Compared with this the thaumaturgical demand is a simple, immediate demand for *ad hoc* changes.

As set forth here these basic orientations may be classified in another way. Three positions, the revolutionist, thaumaturgical, and conversionist, place far greater emphasis on the autonomous operation of the supernatural than do the others. God—the convenient symbol for supernatural power, however that power is conceived and designated in particular cultures—is seen as the active agency. Men need do little but realize this and believe it. (In the other cases it is men who have to act in the world, minimally in the introversionist case, since here they are called upon to leave the world. In the manipulationist case, which is in some respects a polar opposite, men are told to remain active in the world but to alter their thinking about it.) There is reason to suppose that the degree of dependence on the supernatural itself reflects significant differences in cultural development: only in more advanced societies are responses of diminished dependence on the supernatural likely to be manifested in religious movements. In some respects, then, this is an oblique measure of a degree of secularization—a greater circumscription of the autonomy of the supernatural. This, of course, is merely a very general association: even in the most advanced societies there are movements of all kinds. Even in societies in which cultural attainments are most impressive in the arts, science, and philosophy of the highest sophistication, there are those who continue to voice belief in the autonomous activity of God in the world.

The simple paradigm of response presented above ignores the complexities of actual social situations. In a religious tradition such as that of Christianity even those who emphasize extreme dependence on God in practice qualify this dependence by strong demands on the behaviour of men who want to be saved. The conversionist case is particularly instructive since this response was embraced by powerful movements in Protestantism in the nineteenth century. The cardinal expectation of evangelical movements was that God would work on the hearts of men to convert them. They would be 'born again' through what was often called a 'heart experience'. In such movements, however, there was usually also a demand that the converted should enlist to aid God convict sinners of their need for repentance and to prepare them to receive a conversion experience. Men were thus active in helping God to change men, although no conversionist would accept that any agency could effect this change but God himself. We need not become involved in the theological issues of this position: the extent to which it is God who awakens faith in men; the relation between information and opportunity to be saved; the desire for it, faith in and attainment of it. Such issues are complex. The terms employed often lack precision and participate in the strategic ambiguities of all religious discourse. The concepts seek simultaneously to fulfil two ultimately irreconcilable functions—intellectual and cognitive precision and emotional awakening. They seek to describe and explain whilst at the same time summoning responses. It suffices to acknowledge that in the actual case of conversionist responses in nineteenth-century Protestantism an elaborate structure of injunction to act was constructed on the basis of ultimate dependence on the supposed action of the supernatural: 'we love Him' (and help Him in respect of our fellow men) 'because He *first* loved us'.

We can avoid contingent theological considerations since we seek to distinguish essentially sociological relationships and, for immediate purposes, to lay bare the exhaustive range of primary responses. How men conceive the supernatural to solve the basic problems of meaning and experience for which their society and culture offer no acceptable solution is our task in defining these responses. We are not, as must by now be evident, concerned about the specific cultural content of ideas of the supernatural itself—whether it is God, spirits, ancestors, or forces —but with the posited relationship of man, the world, and the supernatural. It is men's response to their human situation by application to the divine which is crucial. Our problem is conceived sociologically, not theologically: as the sociology of religion, not as comparative religion or symbolics. Thus, the groups which espouse particular responses and the circumstance of their emergence and persistence concern us, but the intricacies of their theological argumentation do not.

The orientations of deviant religious movements are empirically often much more complex than the logic of the typology employed to analyse them. It is already clear from what has been said that processes of mutation of response occur in long-persisting movements. Religious groups are sometimes volatile, and if not volatile sometimes so complex that divergent means of salvation are espoused. Mutation, volatility, and internal complexity are all ways in which pure types of response are adulterated in the real world. Christian sects usually manifest mutation and internal complexity, and, especially in a group dominated by a charismatic founder or leader, volatility also occurs. Of mutation more will be said in the following chapter, but internal complexity as a more obvious and general condition must be briefly mentioned now.

The orthodox teachings of Christianity offer diverse and not always easily reconciled prospects of salvation to men, of which the chief are the post-mortem glory for the soul and the eventual resurrection of the body. More important, there are divergent emphases on the means by which salvation will be attained, for example by faith, by the administration of grace through the church, by good works, or by God's inscrutable choice. These diverse means have been the subject of heresies and of subtle theological rationalization, since divergent elements are to be found in the central tradition and must be reconciled. Subsiduarily there is a persistence of demand for that limited and proximate form of salvation in this world—healing. This, too, must be accommodated. Many sects that have arisen among those nurtured in orthodox Christianity retain these diverse soteriological elements, but usually emphasize one very much more than the others (even though emphasis may change over time—the process of mutation already alluded to). Thus in movements such as the Exclusive Brethren, the Mormons, or in the various Pentecostal sects, belief in the literal second advent of Christ and an ensuing millennium is an indisputable tenet. But in none of them is it given dominant emphasis. Salvation by faith is likewise a general inheritance, but among these movements it characterizes Pentecostal groups very much more fully than the others. Exclusive Brethren do not disavow this aspect of Protestant faith, but salvation for them is in the withdrawn community: they do not elaborate the conversionist potential of the doctrine of salvation by faith. Within the diverse doctrinal inheritance of many such sects certain emphases, orientations, action-patterns, and styles of comportment become discernible once the investigator penetrates behind formal ideology. The deviant religious movements in Christendom, despite their many-sided traditions, generally approximate at any given time more to one or other of the types of response we have set out. Movements in the tribal or less-developed societies that are the subject of this study appear to do so no less. We shall then readily characterize these movements by the dominant orientations that they exhibit as a convenient shorthand for the term 'approximate to' this or that response. All cases are likely to be somewhat mixed: some, such as Mormonism, are extremely complex. But our purpose is to consider the cultural circumstances in which approximations to each pure type of response arise, and beyond this the social conditions and internal imperatives which lead a movement to shift in its orientation from an emphasis on one form of salvationary quest to another.

2

The Cultural Contexts of Religious Deviance

Western 'sects' and 'third-world movements'

ALL minority religious movements manifest, with whatever degree of ambivalence, a general response to the world, and suggest the means by which men save themselves from evil. In passing, we have already noted that there are certain profound differences between the sects of the western world and many of the religious movements that arise in other cultures in which similar responses are manifested. Where the term 'sects' is employed in this discourse, its use is not technical but is in general continuity with popular usage, even though that usage is sometimes extremely loose, covering at different times various phenomena, from such tightly-organized movements as Jehovah's Witnesses and the inchoate expression of religious unrest represented by Congolese Ngunzism. All too often, however, the use of the word 'sects' for movements in other cultures suggests all the characteristics of the sects in western Christendom. But in fact, in such cases most of these particular characteristics are absent. The extension of the term to the many and varied phenomena of religious protest suggests that the common element which *is* recognized, is the response of protest against the way in which things are in the world, and the demand for salvation from it.

In the west, a sect is generally a movement with a distinctive organizational structure: its boundaries are usually evident both to its own members and to outsiders. It shares the exclusivism of Christianity at large—the assumption that religious belief should be so articulated and defined that there can be no doubt about the doctrines to which an individual is committed, the authorities that he obeys, the rituals in which he participates, and the body to which he belongs, *to the exclusion of all others*. Plural allegiance is inconceivable in the Christian sect of western countries. Where dual allegiance occurs, 'sect' is not the term we employ. Thus Moral Re-Armament and British-Israelism are movements which, whilst maintaining distinct ideological positions with their own procedures, proselytizing agencies, and financial organizations, none the less have members who retain other affiliations.

31

Since the beliefs of these two movements are essentially additional to, not contradictory of, those of orthodox Protestant churches to which their members often also belong, dual membership readily occurs.[1] We call neither of them a 'sect', any more than we do religious orders or ancillary organizations.

This principle of exclusivism is more emphatic in the Judeo-Christian tradition. But it has not been fully impressed even in all the areas nominally Christian. And in less-developed societies, and particularly in tribal societies, or societies only partially de-tribalized, the logic which excludes simultaneous acceptance of contradictory propositions, and the propriety which excludes simultaneous allegiance to competing organizations, are often unknown.

Since the sixteenth century, some western sects have managed to persist by the evolution of stable patterns of organization. Exceptionally, some of the earlier movements were able to reinforce initial voluntarism by community organization, to insulate themselves from the outside world by language, ethnic differences or, as in the case of the Waldensians, by a high degree of geographic concentration and isolation. The pattern evolved by the groups that arose later was more typical. Voluntary entry was maintained, and instead of imitating 'natural' communities, more conscious structures of organization as voluntary associations were adopted. Many of these sects have sought, none the less, to keep their formal organizational arrangements to a minimum. Most sects have a vigorous life that far transcends that of a mere interest-group, and one which approximates—usually without the vicinal or economic basis of communitarian sects—the life of a self-selected and intermittently operative community. The individual's affective life and leisure are lived within the sect, even if his economic activities are undertaken in instrumental roles in the wider society. Such sects clearly vary considerably in point of formal organization, from loose associations of local communities such as Christadelphians and Plymouth Brethren, who as far as possible reject conscious forms of organization, to a centrally directed system of local branch meetings, such as is maintained by Jehovah's Witnesses. Even within a centrally administered movement, however, there may be a powerful evocation of community. The whole Jehovah's Witness fraternity, despite its size and international character, maintains through a system of conventions and meetings, and in a powerful ideology, a strongly fostered self-conception of the movement as a community. Other centrally organized

---

[1] On the British Israel case see John Wilson, 'British Israelism: the Ideological Restraints on Sect Organization' in B. R. Wilson (Ed.), *Patterns of Sectarianism* (Heinemann, London 1967), pp. 345–76.

movements, such as Christian Science, abandon such 'blown-up' models of local *Gemeinschaft* entirely, and base their organizational form on quite different conceptions.[2] But whatever variations there are among these groups, all these western sects have, none the less, some pattern of stable procedures, not only for worship and association, but also for decision-making and the maintenance of group-identity. This is as true for the minimally organized as for those with the most elaborate and consciously constituted arrangements.[3] In this stability they all differ from a large number of minority religious movements among less-developed peoples which very frequently rely on the direction of a charismatic leader. However erratic such leaders may be, charisma solves the organizational problem. Trust in the leader rather than reliance on set procedures is the basis of continuity in these cases.

Separatist movements which are commonly called 'sects' are to be seen in relation to the cultural context. In African countries movements that have separated from mission churches protest more against the religious dominance of white men than against a specific religious ideology. These movements are 'sects' by virtue of having broken away from missions in the assertion of racial or tribal or national independence. They stand in uncertain relation to the dominant values of the communities within which they exist—in protest more against existing religious organizations than, necessarily, against secular culture or political organization. Thus, there is the paradox of protest movements that seek to be more 'orthodox' than the already established European mission churches, of which the African Greek Orthodox Church of Reuben Spartas in Uganda is an example. For Spartas, who was, even after ordination as a priest, a political activist during part of his career, the search was to establish a more authentic style of Christianity than was available in the Anglican (CMS) and Roman missions. With the eventual recognition of his movement by the Greek Orthodox Patriarch of Alexandria, he achieved that goal.[4] Even one such case unsettles the established sociological expectations of the styles that a sect might adopt. Its long-term relationship to the values that will eventually emerge as dominant in Ugandan society remain uncertain

[2] The very names of these groups indicate a divergence in self-conception. Christadelphians, Jehovah's Witnesses, and Plymouth Brethren reject any abstract title which suggests a corporate entity separate from the collectivity of individual participants. The plural form of nomenclature suggests a profound element in sectarian protest. In contrast, Christian Scientists readily accept 'Christian Science' (or 'the Christian Science Church'), an appropriately abstract designation for their movement. They lack any pronounced communal sense of themselves which this abstract nomenclature could offend.

[3] On the variability of sect organization, see B. R. Wilson, *Patterns of Sectarianism*, op. cit., Introduction.

[4] On this see F. B. Welbourn, *East African Rebels* (SCM Press, London 1961), pp. 77–110.

as that society itself undergoes a transformation more profound and accelerated than anything that western nations—from the experience of which our existing theory of sects arises—have ever known. The range of cultural borrowing is wider, the incongruities are unresolved, and social movements may carry implications, fulfil functions, and become the crystallization of aspirations in combinations unknown in western experience. Such movements may persist as foci of protest or they may collectively become expressions of a new pattern of pluralism.

Minority protest movements in less-developed societies usually manifest less stability, less routinization, and less persistence of procedures than sects in the west. The responses of protest displayed by these movements—loosely and popularly referred to as sects—are thus not necessarily associated with any particular organizational patterns. They may not enjoy so explicit a social context of tolerance as western sects, and the phenomenon of voluntary allegiance may have quite different implications. Such movements may be persecuted or suppressed if they come to the knowledge of the religious, civil, or military authorities, or if they appear to be socially disruptive. They may, reflecting the generally lower degree of discipline of the emotions in less-developed societies, engage in more ecstatic practices and expect more immediate consequences. The involvement of those who practise may not even be predicated as a permanent commitment: it may be no more than the shared enthusiasm of a wider social group. The individual's voluntary dissociation from his kin-group as an expression of permanent, total, and transcendent loyalty to a new intellectual position or even to a new set of emotionally stirring practices, may be simply inconceivable. Choices of this kind are not available in such societies. Fundamental allegiance to family or to a wider group may render involvement in a 'sect' haphazard or ephemeral.

All these cultural variations, however, leave untouched our typification of responses. As long as it is these to which reference is made, and organizational and other factors are recognized as by no means invariably associated with responses, we may continue to use the word 'sects' loosely and in general as pseudonymous with 'minority religious movements'. We are not using a term that stands in emphatic contradistinction to the more culturally bound category of 'church', nor are we positing specific organizational characteristics. Hence, acknowledging the range of cultures in which 'sects' are commonly recognized, we can proceed to discuss these movements, under that name, without entering into further debate about the whole range of elements which might normally be considered to enter into the elaboration of a Christian ideal-type sect.

Mutations and sectarian response

A typology of minority religious movements should emphasize, rather than obscure, the fact that all such movements undergo mutation processes, and that this is so not merely in the best documented case of the sect becoming a denomination. All organizations are likely to experience the attenuation of their original value-commitments, and this is particularly true of protest movements. It is in terms of response to the world that this can be most clearly seen in the case of sects—since organization, formal offices, and official doctrines are all much more resistant to change. It is the more-developed articulation of these aspects of sect organization that both facilitates the persistence of sects in the western world, and sustains them in a recognizably consistent pattern of beliefs and procedures. Western sects show gradual changes of response, but those in less-developed societies display much greater volatility precisely because they lack, or possess in so much less a degree, the organizational structure and doctrinal formality of western sects. The features of religious systems emphasized in less-developed societies —symbolic representation, emotional expression (which includes far more than merely verbal formulations), receipts of inspiration, assurance, or solace—are all less subject to the demands of rationality and consistency than are the ideological and organizational aspects. Ideological movements claim to present the truth to their adherents. and in the sophisticated cultural context of the western world they seek to avoid contradictions and inconsistencies in their teachings, and between their teachings and their practices and organizational structure, Consistency over time becomes an aspect of this commitment for all movements which profess to have discovered the truth, and to have a monopoly of it. While in less-developed countries such claims are less frequently asserted as matters of intellectual conviction, in some cases intense allegiance to the movement is a functional substitute for intense belief in an exclusive body of doctrine: belief in a particular leader (whether as a semi-charismatic evangelist, a headman, or as a tribal or racial representative), or a set of rites, or a prophecy, may indicate very similar intensity of commitment.[5]

---

[5] Of many possible illustrations of these points, the following may be mentioned: William Wadé Harris represents the semi-charismatic evangelist in the movement which he called into being in the Ivory Coast before the First World War, and a part of which was much later affiliated to the Methodists. See W. J. Platt, *An African Prophet* (SCM Press, London 1934); Katesa Schlosser, *Propheten in Afrika* (Albert Limbach Verlag, Braunschweig 1949).

Whatever may be the demands for constancy of ideological orientation, the ethos and self-image of a religious movement, which are formed in the context of its dialogue with the world, undergo change. Such mutation is most emphatically illustrated in the revolutionist sect, which, while remaining essentially sectarian, and not becoming denominationalized, may gradually amend its response. Intense revolutionism is difficult to maintain. The expectation that the world is to overturn by supernatural action is necessarily subject to repeated postponement. Of several possible mutations of revolutionist religion, two appear as the most typical.[6]

In the one case, the sect may become so much concerned with the idea of active revolution that it actually mounts rebellion: in such a circumstance it becomes difficult to maintain the original religious position in anything like its first form. Examples of such development are provided by Sudanese Mahdi-ism;[7] in the Marching Rule Movement of the Solomon Islands;[8] and in the T'ai-p'ing Rebellion;[9] and perhaps also in the case of the Fifth Monarchy Men of seventeenth-

---

pp. 240–64; B. Holas, 'Bref Aperçu sur les principaux cultes syncrétiques de la Basse Côte d'Ivoire', *Africa* XXIV (1954), pp. 55–60. The formation of the Tembu Church was an assertion of tribal integrity; Nehemiah Tile, a former Wesleyan, made the Tembu High Chief, Ngangelizwe, its presiding bishop. Robert H. W. Shepherd, 'The Separatist Churches of South Africa', *International Review of Missions* XXVI (1937), pp. 453–63; O. F. Raum, 'Von Stammespropheten zu Sektenführern', in Ernst Benz (Ed.), *Messianische Kirchen, Sekten und Bewegungen im heutigen Afrika* (E. J. Brill, Leiden 1965). The breakaway of several of the more prominent indigenous leaders from the Rheinischen Missionsgesellschaft in South West Africa in 1946, and the affiliation with the African Methodist Episcopal Church (and the whole history of that church itself) illustrates the extent to which schism can represent racial protest: see K. Schlosser, *Eingeborenenkirchen in Süd- und Südwest-Afrika* (Walter G. Mühlau, Kiel 1958), pp. 71 ff. The strength of feelings concerning the imminence of strange events could be evidenced from many studies: it is particularly well brought out in the study of Melanesian cargo movements by Kenelm O. L. Burridge, in *Mambu: A Melanesian Millennium* (Methuen, London 1960).

[6] On this problem, see below pp. 272 ff.

[7] P. M. Holt, *A Modern History of the Sudan* (Weidenfeld and Nicolson, London 1961), contrasts the Mahdi's reputation among modern Sudanese, as *Abu'l-Istiqlal*, the Father of Independence, a nationalist leader who united the tribes under Islamic ideology, drove out alien rulers, and founded a nation-state, or as a mujaddid, renewer of the Muslim faith, with Muhammed Ahmad's self-interpretation. He claimed to be the Imam, the Successor of the Apostle of God, the Expected Mahdi, whose advent foreshadowed the end of the age. For the transformation of the Mahdi movement into a theocracy, and thence into secular despotism riven by internal rivalries, see P. M. Holt, *The Mahdist State in the Sudan* 2nd Edn (Clarendon Press, Oxford 1970), and Robert O. Collins, *The Southern Sudan 1883–1898: A Struggle for Control* (Yale University Press, New Haven, Conn. 1962).

[8] It may be doubted whether this movement can be counted as a religious sectarian movement in the strict sense. For an account of the interplay of political aims and cargo-cult elements, see pp. 328, 347 and the literature there cited.

[9] This is the interpretation of the development of the rebellion offered by Anthony F. C. Wallace, 'Revitalization Movements', *American Anthropologist* 58 (April 1956), pp. 264–81.

century England.[10] The militaristic mutation leads to radical transformation of the sect whether the rebellion is successful or not. With success the movement develops into a political administration and must make some adjustment of its attitude to millennialist promises. With failure, it is suppressed by the state authorities, and may continue its existence only as an underground party, again more political than religious.[11]

The alternative mutation is likely to be less dramatic and less perceptible. Nothing is done: the millennium is simply awaited. The expectation of a cataclysmic event is difficult to sustain over long periods, and it is possible that it is sustained most readily by the recruitment of new converts, fervent for what is, to them, a new vision, rather than by the recruitment of the second and subsequent generations of existing adherents, who have lived too long with the expectation. But if the sect is well insulated from the wider society and has good possibilities of maintaining internal recruitment, then it is likely that its response to the world, in spite of continuing minimal allegiance to established doctrine, exegesis, and organization, will gradually shift. The persisting revolutionist sect appears, given these circumstances, to become more devotional, more indrawn, and thus to approximate more to the position of the introversionist sect. Such would appear to have been the mutation that occurred early among the Quakers, and which is occurring, in some measure, among the Christadelphians.

Such mutations do not always occur unnoticed within the sect, and do not always go unchallenged: indeed, such processes are themselves progenitors of schism within revolutionist sects, in much the same way that denominational processes have been recognized as progenitors of schisms in conversionist sects. Further mutation, from revolutionism to introversionism and thence to social reformism, may also occur, as it appears to have occurred among the Quakers, not merely as individual Quakers have developed an interest in good causes, but as the concerted

[10] The Fifth Monarchy Men were less a sect than a party among Cromwell's Puritan supporters, and those among them of greatest social consequence—Major General John Harrison, for example—were probably innocent of direct rebellious intentions. The leaders, and particularly the pamphleteers among the Fifth Monarchy Men, were, as Solt points out, neither *fighting* saints ready for revolution nor *suffering* saints prepared to wait for the fifth monarchy by progressive revelation of the Holy Spirit. Leo F. Solt, 'The Fifth Monarchy Men: Politics and the Millennium', *Church History* XXX, 3 (September 1961), pp. 314–24. Once the rising of Thomas Venner had failed in the early months of Charles II's reign, the Fifth Monarchy party disappeared from view. For a detailed account see P. G. Rogers, *The Fifth Monarchy Men* (Oxford University Press, London 1966).

[11] This appears to be the case with the Lazzarettists from the account provided by E. J. Hobsbawm, *Primitive Rebels* (Manchester University Press, Manchester 1959), pp. 65–73, although Hobsbawm, unlike one of his sources, tends to argue that the movement was not completely religious even at its beginnings.

action of the whole movement. All this has come about without any attempt—and this is the significant thing about the reformist position—to use this type of good works to induce recruitment, and without the sect surrendering its sense of its own distinct identity. The reformist work becomes the *raison d'être* of the sect, central to its mission and its self-conception—a changed response to the world.[12] In simpler societies where organization is less developed and intellectual commitment less articulated, these mutations may, as we shall see, be less readily manifested within one clearly sustained and continuing movement, but nevertheless may be evident in changes occurring as one movement rapidly replaces another.

The cultural conditions of sectarian response: conversionists

The mutation of sect response to the world is to be understood in terms of internal factors (such as disappointment of advental hope or the recruitment of the second generation) and the consequences of imperative external action. But our immediate concern is more with the prevailing external conditions in which different types of sect can develop. It appears that social conditions in which reformist and utopian sects arise are very limited, and that manipulationist and introversionist sects, whilst arising in different types of society, do so only at certain stages of social and intellectual development.

Conversionist sects appear to arise most readily in circumstances in which a high degree of individuation occurs. Such a condition may occur through the atomization of social groups in a process of profound social upheaval in which more stable social structures are impaired or destroyed, communities are disrupted, and individuals are forcibly detached from their kinsfolk in enforced or induced migration by conquerors or invaders. Thus, many individuals may find need of spiritual and social accommodation in an alien social context. Likeness of circumstance—as with slaves, displaced people, foreigners—may be sufficient to overcome differences of cultural background and ethnicity in the welding of new religiously-based communities. Such may have been the conditions of the early spread of Christianity. This, then, is a socially enforced process of individuation of social circumstance: it may

---

[12] Just how far this orientation towards social reform can go is illustrated not only by the range of good works undertaken by Quakers, such as prison reform, war-time ambulance service, rehabilitation of refugees, etc., but also in the type of less activist reformatory zeal expressed in *Towards a Quaker View of Sex* (Friends Home Service Committee, London 1963), in which even their traditionally rather austere moral standards are surrendered.

not go deep into human consciousness, but it is a situation in which the individual is separated from his home culture and must make some new accommodation for himself. The obvious accommodation is to reunite himself with a group—a group which cannot be a natural grouping, but must be one which capitalizes the commonality of circumstance of detached individuals and which draws them into a new synthetic community of love.

Alternatively, we can also see a phenomenon of individuation taking place as a long-term consequence of a process of cultural development, in which a steadily more extensive division of labour and increasing geographic and social mobility have promoted the breakdown of ascriptive status systems. Disruption of traditional community structures has led to less collective involvement in the socialization of children, as families have been shorn of wider kin-groupings, and children have come to depend on smaller groups of adults for their formative experiences. The diversity of the culture, the multiplication of the agencies of its transmission (by the reduction of size of kin-groups) and the smallness of the groups in which children are reared contribute not only to differences in the socialization process but also to the growing sense of uniqueness and individual identity of men. This process of heightened individuation was, in the eighteenth century, considerably reinforced by the social disruption of the industrial revolution.

In this situation men had been both dramatically detached from stable social contexts, and had acquired the independence of mind and the degree of emotional control to respond to a new and orderly system of psychic security and intellectual explanation. The system which Methodism introduced went further, as a secondary socialization process, in the extension of this system of order and in the diffusion of its influence beyond its own boundaries, into wide ranges of public and social life. The period was conducive not only to this new conversionist response, of course: millennial movements were by no means uncommon, and the political unrest arising from the French Revolution and the subsequent Napoleonic Wars stimulated millennial speculation even among the orthodox. Yet the most marked feature of the period is the emergence of conversionist religion and the increasing competition of conversionist groups. The general quietism into which the Congregationalists and even the Baptists had passed in the late seventeenth and early eighteenth centuries was challenged and transformed once Methodism developed. Having challenged Calvinist élitism by Arminian Free Will teachings, Methodism was at once much less restrained than earlier nonconformity. Its emphasis on free will in conversion amounted to an implicit democratic tenet of equality of opportunity for salvation (although Methodism rejected democracy in this world, and even in its own chapels and band-meetings).

The American frontier and the transformation of an 'awakening' (implicitly of the somnolent faithful who were Calvinists and thus an élite) into 'revival' (implicitly of the society at large, by the conversion, on the basis of Arminian free will or of a radically modified Calvinism, of those who had never before rightly belonged) contributed further conditions propitious for movements that made conversion their primary concern. The development of a laissez-faire economy and the abandonment by entrepreneurs of concern for their workers except in their strictly economic activities, further strengthened the ideal of a free choice of religious affiliation, and the free opportunity to establish new religious systems, beliefs, and practices as an extension of the free will by which men might choose Christ. The sects which arose in the wake of Methodism—many of the Holiness groups, the Salvation Army, and later the Pentecostalists—drew a great deal from Wesley's teachings, but even more significant than this doctrinal inheritance was the somewhat competitive orientation towards the conversion of the world.

Christianity had, of course, from its beginnings emphasized the need for a change of heart, but once established this voluntaristic element had become routinized and ritualized. Whether its early recruitment typically followed a pattern anything like that of the highly stylized conversions of the nineteenth century is an open question, but certainly this period saw an intensification of the idea of free choice, personal commitment, and an almost contractual balance of worship now for present reassurance of post-mortem advantage. In large part the conversionist movements relied on mass situations, and on promoting a sense of unmediated relationship between the saviour and those they would convict of sin. Free choice, which had always operated in Christianity, albeit often in a restricted way, now become the paradigm for individual religious commitment: the conversionist sects made their primary goal the eliciting of such commitment.

Conversionist sects appear to have had another significant characteristic in the period of their greatest pullulation, which in some respects provides a degree of functional correspondence with a nativistic movement in less-developed societies. Such sects have frequently emphasized their continuity with the native values of rural society. Their typical fundamentalism and emphasis on literal moral precepts were associated with their re-creation of a folk community in their chapels and meeting halls, the development of a close-knit *Gemeinschaft*, an abode of love in which fraternity, free and easy expression, spontaneity, and informality were emphasized. Intellectualism, ritual, and aesthetic religion were all set at a discount in the primary concern with the 'heart-condition' of the sinner and the affectivity of the fellowship. Conversionist sects have frequently needed the services of a pastor to weld together their membership, and this he has done best by entering into the folk culture of his group, and providing it with biblical legitimation. In the city such sects have frequently been 'accommodative' for displaced rural people, and even in the countryside they have tended to be repositories of the idealized folk values of rural life in revulsion against the impersonality, sophistication, and anonymity of the city.

The cultural conditions of sectarian response: manipulationists

Movements manifesting a manipulationist orientation are also dependent on social circumstances in which men have become highly individuated. These movements are not familial or communal in composition. It seems unlikely that such movements could arise in traditional societies, or indeed in societies which lack at least some degree of social mobility. They appear to arise in achievement-oriented societies, where physical, economic, and social well-being are open to at least some measure of competitive action, and where the means of competitive achievement are already diversified, as by scholarship, business acumen, professional expertise, and success in administration (as well as, in some cases, by political skills). In such an impersonal social context other means to gain wealth, power, and status may also exist— gangsterism, fraud, charlatanism, nepotism, and intrigue, as well as the use of esoteric knowledge. In social circumstances of this kind the individual's sense of identity may appear to depend on success in the competitive struggle for status. The manipulationist sect offers both objective achievement and psychic reassurance in a world in which the direct reassurances of participation in community life have been weakened. Some of the cults of the later Roman Empire might have fulfilled these functions, even if they began in different social contexts, and even if they played a different role in the accommodation of diverse groups to a complex social structure. The metropolitan context, with its mixture of peoples and cults and its attendant social confusion, anonymity, and opportunities for social mobility, provided a propitious climate. A movement which at the time of its origin is concerned with traditional thaumaturgy, or the maintenance of ritual obligations, or which promoted supererogatory spiritual exercises in the search for essentially other-worldly benefits may, if transposed to another context, take on the characteristics of a special cult which, when adjusted to the needs and tensions of the new environment, acquires the style of a manipulationist movement. The middle-eastern mystery cults in Rome, and the Indian meditation cults in contemporary America are examples of such accommodation to a more cosmopolitan, secular, and sophisticated clientele.

A manipulationist sect can develop only when metaphysical thinking has been developed within the religio-philosophical traditions of the society. Such sects tend to thrive among the semi-sophisticated who are aware of, and who imitate in some measure, the genuine reasoning of the philosophers and the scientists. Their organization often owes as much to the development of other social institutions as it does to the prevailing pattern of religious organization. Thus such sects may have classes, instruction, lectures, exercises, lessons, courses, colleges, and diplomas, as well as—and even sometimes in place of—services, rituals, worship, prayer, and retreats. Their authorities may be teachers and lecturers rather than priests, or mystics rather than ministers. The *guru* is sometimes the model, though he is a *guru* entrenched in a set system of doctrine and a firm structure of organization. He may act as therapist as well as teacher, and his teachings may be the basis of his therapeutic system. Manipulationist movements generally emphasize mental hygiene, and sometimes also a physical regimen of some kind, even if only a system of abstinences, such as vegetarianism in Theosophy, and abstinence from tobacco, alcohol, and drugs in Christian Science. They have typically been concerned with systems of self-control from which beneficial consequences—physical, economic, and social, as well as spiritual—are believed to follow. (The newer movements of this kind have tended to concern themselves more with mental health as a primary orientation, tacitly leaving bodily health to the increasingly effective medical practice of secular society, and even older movements such as Christian Science have, despite the difficulty of departing from set dogmas, become less anti-medical than once they were.)

Manipulationist sects are universalist, and this, too, is a cultural variable occurring only at relatively advanced stages of cultural development. These are the sects of the more articulate, which offer short cuts to prestige and power, and appeal to those groups whose ambitions in these directions rely largely on verbal manifestations of power. The special means which they offer to these ends are metaphysical theories and verbal reassurances. (The taboos that they enjoin function more to reduce reliance on material things and to manifest 'power' by self-control—overcoming the 'tobacco habit' for example—than as moral norms that facilitate social relations. They have similarities, apart from their universality, to the taboos by which individual shamans in some North American Indian tribes maintain their shamanistic power.) Worldly well-being becomes the pragmatic sanction for sect teaching. As widespread phenomena, sects of this type have been particularly evident in the nineteenth and twentieth centuries in the cities of advanced industrial societies, where those concerned with bodily health appear to exercise a particular attraction for middle-aged and older women, and those dominantly concerned with mental health and the expansion of consciousness for a wider— often younger—section of the population.

The cultural conditions of sectarian response: introversionists

For rather different reasons the introversionist response also occurs only in limited types of social circumstance. Withdrawal is a possible reaction for individuals or groups only when social institutions have achieved a certain degree of autonomy one of another, and when religious expression and practice have ceased to be a necessarily public performance for all members of the wider society. Withdrawal implies rejection of society and of the prevailing religion (as distinct from withdrawal as an intensified expression of it, as in the case of monasticism). It can occur only when social diversity obtains. Ideological diversity reflects this social diversity in which religious value-consensus can no longer be too thoroughly enforced.[13] The idea of religion as a private commitment (whether familial or individual) in which there is at least recognized freedom of choice, not only in intensity of devotion and religious practice but also in the patterns of religious expression, must have been established before introversionist tendencies can occur. Such a development is possible only in a society in which the family itself has acquired privacy and separation from wider kinship and neighbourhood groups, or in which sectarian groups are free to establish themselves as communities that insulate themselves from the people at large. Monastic withdrawal was undertaken under the auspices of the dominant social ideology into a way of life that was separate from the world, but which could also be interpreted as undertaken on

[13] Thus the Rappites in Württemberg in the 1790s were called upon to account for themselves by state and church authorities for worshipping independently, but they were not very seriously persecuted. See Karl J. R. Arndt, *Georg Rapp's Harmony Society 1785–1847* (University of Pennsylvania Press, Philadelphia 1965), pp. 20–9.

the world's behalf: introversionist withdrawal is from the wickedness of the world, not for its good.

In the case of the introversionist sect, withdrawal is a more radical 'contracting out', not necessarily out of all social relationships but essentially out of the dominant moral and religious consensus. It can thus occur only in a society in some measure secularized. One would expect to find it only where social diversification has occurred and where some degree of disintegration of divergent social roles has taken place. For the introversionists themselves, a degree of social participation in secular activities may continue, but if participation in secular life creates difficulties for religious practice, or threatens the maintenance of group identity, then the sect may—in suitable social conditions—isolate itself and develop communitarianism.

But introversionist sects have not always been able, or inclined, to become communitarian: withdrawal is basically into an inner religious association, not necessarily into the vicinal segregation of the separated community. Privacy is not necessarily regarded as jeopardized or tainted by those activities in the world which are held to be 'necessary'. Thus some pietist groups and the Exclusive Brethren demand that their members keep their private lives unspotted from the world, while admitting the need for them to undertake business in the world. They may, of course, restrict their members in various directions by prohibiting certain ways of making a livelihood, particularly those that imply allegiance to a social organization other than to the sect itself. Service in the agencies of national defence or even of social control are sometimes forbidden or at least disapproved of. Quakers would not be found in the armed services, perhaps not even in a police force, and neither would Christadelphians, who would, equally, not permit one who became a lawyer to remain in their fellowship (although Christadelphians never completed the process of transformation into an introversionist sect). Recreation, entertainment, and sport would also represent areas of employment too much tainted by the pleasures and lusts of the world for an introversionist movement. The Exclusive Brethren and Christian Apostolic Church go further and prohibit their members any employment that involves membership in a worldly association such as a trade union or professional association.[14]

Separation from the world is in some ways a more acute problem in the urban, industrialized world with its high degree of role-interaction, than in the agricultural context; yet it should be noted that intro-

[14] On the Exclusive Brethren, see B. R. Wilson, 'The Exclusive Brethren' in B. R. Wilson, *Patterns of Sectarianism*, op. cit. On the Christian Apostolic Church, see H. H. Gerth, 'A Mid-western Sectarian Community', *Social Research* XI, 3 (September 1944), pp. 354–62.

versionist movements cannot arise in feudal or semi-feudal societies, and in the context of peasant society usually only for those who are themselves not initially peasants, or who, as farmers, have attained some degree of independence of higher social strata. Thus, for example, the Rappites appear to have been as often tradespeople or village artisans as farmers. It has often been easier for introversionists to adopt a basically agricultural economy as a way of establishing their separation, whether as a communitarian sect, such as the Rappites and Hutterians, or more simply as a farming community, more or less settled together, like the Amish and other Mennonite groups.[15] Agricultural pursuits permit a high degree of social and economic independence of the wider society; perhaps more important, they also permit direct expression for folk virtues and simple moral precepts in an uncomplicated pattern of work activities. The impersonality of urban society does, of course, allow a high degree of privacy, but at the cost of intensive role-interaction, interdependence, and situations in which simple moral truths are difficult to sustain and to apply. Introversionist sects such as the Exclusive Brethren have evolved a *modus vivendi* for urban society. In their worldly associations they withhold all affectivity and personal involvement, which they confine to relationships within the religiously-defined community, which the outsider is not readily given opportunity to join. Whereas conversionist and revolutionist sectarianism demands public expression in testifying to 'the truth', the introversionists deny the value of such activity, and do not look for the augmentation of their numbers that often comes from it.

Introversionism became a possible sectarian response in many parts of western Europe in the seventeenth and eighteenth centuries, but it appears that the social climate has now become less conducive for this particular religious orientation. Compulsory education; health and sanitation regulations; increased economic control of individual activity by the state and by trade unions; extensive taxation; the imposition of military service or of state-approved means of securing exemption from it; the development of mass communications; the extensive division of labour; the development of large-scale agencies of employment—all of these make effective insulation increasingly difficult to achieve.

This change in general social conditions appears to have made the

[15] On the Rappites, see K. J. R. Arndt, op. cit. For a recent account of the Hutterians in Canada, see V. Peters, op. cit. On the Amish, see J. A. Hostetler, op. cit. On the Mennonite communities there is an extensive literature, but see, for a sociological account of their adaptation to new living conditions, Joseph Winfield Fretz, *Pilgrims in Paraguay* (The Herald Press, Scottsdale, Pennsylvania 1953).

emergence of new introversionist movements less likely; to have made it less likely that existing sects undergoing some transformation of response would espouse an introversionist position; and to have made new difficulties for sects of this type already in being. Thus most of the sects that manifest an introversionist response appear to be sects that have been in existence for several generations. Modern sectarianism has few, if any, clear examples of pristine introversionism to offer, except where such sects arise as schisms from existing introversionist movements, as in the case of some groups of former Exclusive Brethren that have been 'withdrawn from' by the main body. The transformation of response among Christadelphians from revolutionism has been partly in an introversionist direction, but this response is apparently being overtaken by another—the disposition to reformist activities in the world, as some Christadelphians have become involved in refugee rehabilitation and the 'Freedom from Hunger' campaign.[16] What took perhaps a century and a half among the Quakers—the passage from revolutionism through a long period of introversion, into, by way of evangelicalism and the reaction to it, a philanthropic disposition—appears to have occurred much more rapidly among Christadelphians.[17]

Despite the growth of freedom and choice, modern society has in many ways become compelling and conformist, and an introversionist response is not now easily evolved or sustained. The growth of formal organization, mass provision, and technological dependence make it difficult for men to contract out of obligations defined within the principal economic, political, legal, educational, and even recreational, domains of modern life. Mass society is necessarily conformist within a given framework of permitted pluralism—but radical withdrawal is far less easily arranged than in the past. Social approval of reformist sectarianism and disapproval of introversionism—exemplified in the very different public response in England to the Quakers on the one hand and the Exclusive Brethren on the other—indicates new criteria of tolerance in society. As developed industrial societies have come to rely increasingly on consciously-organized regulative agencies, on technical and often mechanical regulation, communal nonconformity has been more difficult to assert and less readily accommodated.

---

[16] The beginnings of this new response among Christadelphians are evident in the publication of *The Endeavour Magazine*, which began in 1961, and in the group of (mainly English) Christadelphians who are associated with it. Whilst claiming to be doctrinally orthodox this group has emphasized attitudes to social welfare and responsibility to the wider society that stand in marked contrast with traditional Christadelphian responses.

[17] The development of Quaker philanthropy, and of changing attitudes to public affairs and politics in Britain in the nineteenth century, is documented in Elizabeth Isichei, *Victorian Quakers* (Oxford University Press, London 1970).

Ideological tolerance may have grown but technical tolerance has diminished. When the regulative agencies of society were less mechanized in their operation there was a wider range for humane discretion than is easily inbuilt into the bureaucratic machines of the modern state. Thus, although nominally *religious* tolerance *per se* appears to have grown, paradoxically, the freedom to subscribe to the 'religion of your choice' is available on the implicit assumption that that choice has no particular social significance. It is a private preference for a largely private ideology, which should not entail any *social* nonconformity. The enlarged religious tolerance is, perhaps, merely indifference to variations that have no social consequences for society at the public level. This tolerance does not readily extend to groups whose social disengagement threatens the smooth operation of the technical and bureaucratic procedures of the state and of economic and social organization. Thus there is increased difficulty for the introversionist sect, whose members necessarily seek to dissociate themselves from a variety of public activities.

Established introversionist sects have also experienced a renewal of tension with the wider society. Problems of land-holding, registration of births, and especially of education, brought the Sons of Freedom section of the Doukhobors of British Columbia into direct conflict with the provincial government, even though it was on the promise that in that country they should enjoy such freedoms that the Doukhobors (and Mennonites and Hutterians) migrated to Canada.[18] The disappearance of the conditions which favoured the small enterprise may be important in this respect, since introversionist sectarians appear to have frequently been independent small-scale entrepreneurs. The individual's increasingly multiform dependence on the institutional and bureaucratic agencies of society makes his total withdrawal more and more difficult. The local community which once supplied such a large part of man's needs, including, in a totally affective context, his instrumental needs, is no longer able to meet even a small part of man's wants in advanced industrial society. The failure of the local com-

---

[18] For an account of the Doukhobors and their issues of conflict with the authorities, see Harry B. Hawthorn (Ed.), *The Doukhobors of British Columbia* (University of British Columbia Press, Vancouver 1955), and for a probably definitive history, George Woodcock and Ivan Avakumovic, *The Doukhobors* (Faber, London 1968). Communitarian groups have commonly experienced the growing intolerance of the state and of their fellow citizens, especially as the state has grown more efficient, and as the communities have prospered. The Doukhobors in late nineteenth-century Russia, the Mennonites after the Russian Revolution, and the Hutterians in both the United States and Canada, have had similar experiences of growing state oppression and increased hostility from formerly welcoming neighbours. On the Mennonites, see J. W. Fretz, op. cit.; Fritz Kliewer, 'Die Mennoniten in Brasilien', *Stadenjahrbuch* 5 (São Paulo 1957), pp. 233-46.

munity to meet his instrumental needs—now met elsewhere by consciously-organized commercial and political agencies—also weakens even its affective functions.

In the early stages of the breakdown of the self-sufficient community, introversionist sects may well have gained some impetus from their capacity to sustain community functions in a new community structure based on the voluntary fellowship of love, replacing kinship and neighbourhood ties. But as the conditions disappeared that made viable the model on which they were constructed, eventually they too were less easily established and sustained. The extension of men's experience into a wider range of accessible social and cultural activities has also made the way of life of the withdrawn sect not only less attractive but also less conceivable. The organic solidarity that Durkheim described as the character of complex advanced society with its extensive division of labour might not lead to an increased allegiance to that wider society, but it makes complete independence of it harder both to achieve and to contemplate. The alienated minority who reject the values of contemporary society tend to do so in negative terms, and not typically because they accept a more coherent and compelling system of values, as do introversionist sects.

Sects in the mission territories

Turning from the world which has been completely christianized to the less-developed societies, it can be seen at once that some types of sect are most unlikely to be in evidence there—the manipulationist, reformist, and utopian types. In the early stages of culture contact and social disorganization *indigenous* and *spontaneous* conversionist and introversionist sects are equally unlikely. But under certain conditions, when there has been sustained inter-ethnic contact subsequent to conquest and colonization, the revolutionist response, which is frequently found among primitive peoples, often associated with dreams of nativistic restoration, gradually gives way to something closer to the introversionist syndrome of response. We turn to a more extended discussion of cases of this kind in Chapter 12.

The manifestation of a secondary response as a consequence of mutation is paralleled by the appearance, in certain conditions, of movements that display marked conversionist orientations, sometimes in a complex matrix of alternating and equivocal responses to the world. These movements have usually acquired their conversionist traits from

Christian, and sometimes from distinctly sectarian, missions from which they have broken away, or by which they have been deeply influenced. They have often acquired something of the fundamentalist evangelical tradition of radical Protestantism. Where the conversionist response becomes really dominant over the adventist ideas and thaumaturgical practices with which—in western sects, as well as those in less-developed societies—it is often associated, such movements may develop, as have some western sects, into a more specifically denominational mould. A good example of this type of movement is that led by Nicholas B. H. Bhengu in East London and Durban, South Africa. Bhengu practises faith-healing, but sees it as a mere means to an end— that of recognizing God. He claims no organic healings and he is not opposed to the use of scientific medicine. In this he differs from the thaumaturgical sects of South Africa. On the other hand, he is not opposed to *Apartheid*, and he rejects the idea of a black Christ, saying that the colour of Christ's skin does not matter. In this he clearly rejects ideas which have often been central to revolutionist sects in Africa, and elsewhere. He is prepared to serve as a revivalist for other movements, and claims to have done so for the Lutherans and South African General Mission, as well as for the Assemblies of God (and other western-inspired Pentecostal groups) by whom he was originally ordained in 1937.[19]

It will be evident from the foregoing that at any given time a movement may manifest more than one response to the world, even though an examination of its history will usually enable the analyst to say unequivocally which particular response was dominant at particular stages of a movement's development. Obviously there are sometimes exceptions. Since exclusiveness of commitment is not much emphasized and there is usually very little stability of organization in movements in less-developed societies, consistency of ideological orientations also tends to be low. Emotional reaction rather than new intellectual interpretations characterize these movements, and thus their response to the world reflects the range of volatility of emotional dispositions rather than intellectual consistency. Some exceptions, however, occur in a form that cannot be so readily accounted for by these foregoing considerations. The two most frequent types of movement in less-developed societies are the thaumaturgical and revolutionist. The exceptional movements do not respond in either of these ways, nor

[19] This account is based on K. Schlosser, *Eingeborenenkirchen . . .*, op. cit., pp. 12–58. Similar cases appear to be found among the African churches which James B. Webster, in *The African Churches among the Yoruba 1888–1922* (Clarendon Press, Oxford 1964), carefully distinguishes from the syncretistic Aladura-Apostolics, the doctrines and practices of which, he informs us, do not differ from those of the missions from which they separated.

conform to the patterns of mutation or of inheritance which account for the introversionist and conversionist movements that we have noticed above.

Two exceptional cases

Neither of these two cases presents itself clearly as a case of an autochthonous religious movement. Some external influence is evident in each case. None the less, it is not easy to suggest what prompted them, nor the specific conditions against which their leaders and members have reacted.

(i) The so-called *Sect of the Second Adam*, sometimes called the Agu people, at Nkwakabio, near Anum in Ghana, appears to have been established in 1911, and in 1934 was under the leadership of Filipo Tse, and consisted of about forty people. The members wore no clothes, practised celibacy and vegetarianism, and refused to accept money for work, but took vegetables instead. Property was owned in common. Filipo regarded himself as divinely inspired, enjoying the same spirit as had Adam in the garden of Eden. Through him, God was believed to have re-established paradise. Filipo prophesied war between the British and Germans on the one hand and the French on the other, and the return of Napoleon, on the strength of Revelation 13. Thus, although there were some nativistic ideas—the abandonment of clothing and the rejection of money—there were also distinct millennialist elements echoing ideas concerning the advent which had been current in Europe in the nineteenth century. (The Basel Mission had been active in the neighbourhood for seventy years.) There is also a marked introversionist element in withdrawal into their own compound, and the secrecy of their own chapel, to which visitors were not admitted.[20] It would appear that there is little that can be said to be genuinely autochthonous in this case: all the practices have been embraced by Christian sects of one sort or another at different times, and with the exception of nudity, some of them have done so in very much this type of combination. At the same time, neither the lines of influence nor the appeal of the group are particularly evident.

(ii) The *Community of the Holy Apostles* at Aiyetoro, Nigeria, appears as a case of a semi-introversionist group which has not undergone the mutation process typical of most such groups in less-developed soci-

[20] This account relies on G. Stoevesandt, 'The Sect of the Second Adam on the Gold Coast', *Africa* VIII (1934), pp. 479–82.

eties.[21] The Community was founded on 12 January 1947, when a group of fishermen settled on a beach some 104 miles east of Lagos, having become dissatisfied with their way of life, and having decided to adopt simple Christian principles as their rule for communal living. They had broken away from the earliest form of the Nigerian independent church, the *Cherubim and Seraphim*, after trouble had occurred between the church and some of the local population, and after some rioting. Not all of those who had broken with the Church had in the end come to this place, subsequently named Aiyetoro—which means *Everything is at Peace*. Those who did, followed E. O. Peter, a leader who had a vision of the need to live together. They adopted a simple khaki uniform and began the work of building a settlement, constructing their own huts and digging a canal. The site of the community, which is surrounded by ocean, creeks, and swamps, is unconnected by road to other parts of the country. Only the beach provides a continuous land communication with other places; apart from this the community had relied on the boats which they built for themselves.[22]

From May 1948, the Apostles decided to hold all property in common, and, under divine guidance, organized their community through a number of committees. Initially their programme was one of austerity, until gradually they produced the equipment to improve their yields of fish, and to augment their way of life. Within ten years they were reported to have a higher standard of living than any other community in Nigeria, and at that time they numbered about 3,000 people. They had created their town on stilts, including sections of roadways of wooden planks (all their timber had to be brought by boat); they had dug some seven miles of canal, which took three dry seasons of labour in which every man and woman in the community participated. They had invented their own type of nets and had had their sample copied and manufactured in England. Thatched roofs had been replaced by corrugated aluminium; there were twenty-two canoes for fishing, with a total of over two hundred men as crew; and they were building their own boats in their own shipyard. A synchronized three-generator three-phase full voltage power station had been purchased for £20,000,

---

[21] See Chapter 12.

[22] Two brief and largely pictorial accounts of Aiyetoro have appeared in the magazine issued by the Crown Agents for Nigeria. Anon., 'A Visit to the Apostles and the Town of Aiyetoro', *Nigeria* 36 (1951), pp. 387–442; and Anon., 'Aiyetoro', *Nigeria Magazine* 55 (1957), pp. 356–86. (The magazine has borne different titles at different dates.) A further account is in E. M. McClelland, 'The Experiment in Communal Living at Aiyetoro', *Comparative Studies in Society and History* IX, 1 (October 1966), pp. 14–28. The most extensive analysis of Aiyetoro is Stanley R. Barrett, *God's Kingdom on Stilts: A Comparative Study of Rapid Economic Development*. Unpub. Ph.D. thesis, University of Sussex, 1971, which pays special attention to the process of innovation. Unfortunately this study was not available before my own book went to press.

for which they had paid 'cash down'. They are reputed to have 're-invented' the narrow loom, before they later learned about broad looms, which they then purchased. The community included its own weavers, as well as dyers, soapmakers, tinsmiths, carpenters, and other craftsmen. Altogether Aiyetoro is virtually an economics textbook case of Robinson Crusoe-style production—austerity; work; surplus; saving; division of labour; capital production; increased consumption. Although we do not know just what expectations of economic growth its members originally had, it appears, from its religious commitment, to be virtually a test case of the salience of the Protestant ethic in the process of economic growth. God had instructed the leader, E. O. Peter, that his followers should 'be severe with [themselves] so that no indulgency of the body shall take away the energy that should be kept for God's work',[23] and 'God's work' appears in practice to have been ordinary economic activity.

The community structure and religious beliefs of the Apostles are somewhat unclear. Their original leader, who was known as 'Father', was elected by the community to be their *Oba*, and his inspiration was said to come from God. He acquired the style and traditional circumstances of a Yoruba king, although he also worked alongside other members in the shipyard. They abolished bride-price, and although they did not encourage polygyny, neither did they prohibit it. The men and women lived in two separate parts of the town, and men visited their wives at night, or women, usually chaperoned by a child, visited their husbands. Children were regarded as age-classes, and, once they had been put down from their mothers' backs, they were brought up very much by the community. Catering, clothes-making, and laundering were centralized, and the dressmakers, laundresses, and cooks were specialists, so that once mothers had finished nursing they returned to their work in the community. Although workers looked after their own tools and equipment, these were supplied by the community, and the produce reverted to the community. By 1957, the severe uniforms had been abandoned, and workers were permitted to choose their own cloth from the communal store, for the clothes which would be made for them by their own specialist craftsmen and women. All goods were bought from the communal purse and anyone might propose how money should be spent.

Committees regulated all the activities of the community and the sale of its surplus products after all the needs of the Apostles themselves were met. They regarded themselves as essentially religious committees, whose decisions were taken under Christian rules and

[23] E. M. McClelland, op. cit.

divine guidance. There were early morning religious services before work, with the drums and hand-clapping that are typical of Nigerian religion. The beliefs of the Apostles were biblical, but the particular emphases have not been reported. Work was reported to be central to the life of the community; laziness was condemned, although the only sanction was said to be the disapproval of the group itself. Running about and loud shouting were frowned upon, and early reports said that this was also true for smoking and drinking. Silence was valued; manual workers sang at their work, but gossiping was held to be a sin. The community had a positive attitude towards education, although the dominant emphasis was on the learning of crafts. Early reports that book-learning was regarded as divorcing children from village interests do not appear to have prevented the whole community from learning to read Yoruba, in adult schools, where later all were also learning to read English. The teachers were members of the community who had been trained outside. By the mid 1960s boys were sent to high schools outside, but the community planned to construct its own, in addition to a teachers' training college and a hospital. By 1957, few had left Aiyetoro, and the community had had a number of recruits from outside, although at a later date recruitment had ceased and the 'intentions of the world outside were held to be evil'.[24]

Whether this movement should be regarded as utopian or introversionist is not easy to decide. It is not utopian in the sense that its establishment of a colony was not undertaken to provide a prototype for new patterns of social organization. Indeed, it appears to have been a distinctly subsequent and expedient decision after the settling of the community at its new location. In this sense, it seems to parallel the decision to embrace communitarianism of various introversionist groups in America, such as the *Amana Society*, and those among the Dunker following of Peter Becker who left with Conrad Beissel to found the *Ephrata Community*. Its religious teachings appear to have increasingly insisted on this separation from the world, but their exact status as an intellectual and emotional response, remains unclear. Aiyetoro appears to be an introversionist group, although on the reports available, it remains uncertain whether it came into being *primarily* at the behest of religious impulses.

Thaumaturgical responses

The vast majority of religious minority movements arising in less-developed societies manifest one or other of the two responses to the

[24] Ibid.

world which we have designated thaumaturgical and revolutionist. Even with only rudimentary organization, some of them continue over long periods of time. Where the organizational pattern of 'the church' is known some take this as the obvious religious form for their own movement, particularly those which begin in schism from missions. Yet others appear as a congeries of inchoate rumours, rites, assemblies, and pilgrimages. Variation in organizational type, and in its persistence, need not conceal the basic similarities in response to the world of the movements in less-developed and those of more-advanced societies. Thaumaturgical practice is usually part of the tradition of primitive religion itself, and when a society develops to a point of complexity in which diversity of religious expression can occur, thaumaturgical movements are likely to arise. They frequently prescribe ritual practices similar to those prevailing within the traditional religion and their preoccupations are often of the same kind. Thus, it is as new social movements, rather than as a *distinctive* type of response, that this category merits attention. It is entirely expectable that such new movements should initially offer similar satisfactions, address them-selves to similar needs, and often employ similar techniques, to those already prevalent in the society. Despite these continuities, they are recognized as *new* movements. Their appearance is related to one or both of two sets of circumstances: the recognition of the inadequacy of traditional procedures, which is particularly evident following the impact of a superior culture; and reactions to prohibitions on tradi-tional practices imposed by the new authorities. The relationship of these new thaumaturgical responses to revolutionist responses will be examined below.

Thus, to take a case almost at random, the *Tigari* (or Tigare) cult, one of a number of movements which has developed in West Africa in the course of the last seventy years, and which flourished in Ghana especially in and after the Second World War, sought, like its pre-decessors, to re-institutionalize belief in magic.[25] The ideas about causality which were implicit in its operations, and the taboos which it enjoined on its votaries, were not unlike those associated with indigenous tribal religious belief. Whether Tigari was a deity or an impersonal supernatural agency was disputed by Christensen's Fanti informants—the Tigari priests usually declaring Tigari to be a deity, an *obosom*

---

[25] Tigari is discussed by H. W. Debrunner, in *Witchcraft in Ghana* (Presbyterian Book Depot, Kumasi 1959); K. A. Busia, *Report on a Social Survey of Sekondi-Takoradi* (Crown Agents for the Colonies, London 1950), pp. 80–1. For a detailed account on which this paragraph chiefly relies, see J. B. Christensen, 'The Tigari Cult of West Africa', *Papers of the Michigan Academy of Science, Arts and Letters* XXXIX, Part IV (1954), pp. 389–98.

(pl. *abosom*), the type of god usually associated with natural phenomena such as lakes, rivers, groves, or stones, and the adherents regarding it more as an *edur*, a medicine or charm of an animatistic type. Tigari exponents among the Fanti used drums and percussion instruments of a type native to the Sudan, whence Christensen states that the cult came (although other writers sometimes attribute its origins to northern Ghana).[26] But its three-day ceremonies every six weeks, its animal sacrifices, and the mores it enjoins—prohibitions on evil-speaking, stealing, defrauding, committing adultery, gossiping, lying, practising magic, killing, or challenging the religious power embraced in the cult —are continuities of more traditional cultural practices of the Akan tribes, of which the Fanti are one. The apprenticeship system by which the individual may become a Tigari priest, although of shorter duration than in traditional religion, follows a very similar pattern. The type of sanction for non-payment of fines prescribed by the cult for male-factions—fear of the vengeance of god—is essentially similar in its operation to that found, for example, at the shrine of Akonedi at Larteh, which is, if not traditional, a much older-established, Ghanaian cult. Other features are common to many African movements. Healing, and the relief of barrenness in women are two characteristic traditional demands for religiously provided benefit; others are the demand for protection on journeys, success in courtship, and, betraying more markedly western influence, requests for employment and success at school. Although there are some Christian elements, and there are taboos on pork, and on the wearing of sandals in the shrine, which appear to manifest Muslim influence, the cult appears primarily to offer a more efficacious fulfilment of functions already well-established within Akan religion. Thus requests to Tigari 'are of the same type as the favours asked of the ancestors and the native deities, except that because of culture change, more requests are now directed toward economic improvement'.[27]

One of the most important factors in the success of Tigari was its claim to efficacy in affording protection against witchcraft, the fear of which is, today, widespread in Ghana and other African countries. The extent to which belief in witchcraft, the search for protection from it, and the function of religious movements in identifying witches and forcing them to confess, have been traditional concerns in West Africa,

---

[26] H. W. Debrunner, op. cit., states that Tigari was discovered by a priest at Ypala, near Wa in northern Ghana, where he has visited the modest parent shrine.

[27] J. B. Christensen, op. cit., p. 392.

has been disputed.[28] Christensen considers that the fear among the
Fanti has grown in association with the uncertainties of kinship relations
in a society experiencing new pressures towards individualism; dissatisfaction with the avunculate (among the matrilineal Fanti);
tensions concerning the non-achievement of new aspirations newly
introduced with the impact of European culture; and perhaps also by
the decline in the number and activity of native priests of the traditional
abosom. Whether witch-finding is a traditional activity or one relatively

[28] Thus Barbara E. Ward, 'Some Observations of Religious Cults in Ashanti', *Africa*
XXVI (1956), pp. 47–60, considers that witches were not a traditional preoccupation of the
Ashanti—the old gods did not provide protection from witchcraft. She attributes the ubiquity
of such shrines in the 1940s to the disruption of traditional social structure by increased
contact with Europeans, and with rapid social change as manifested in the expansion of
cocoa-farming, mining, and the introduction of English law, for example, the problems
arising from which were beyond the competence of the old cults. She considers accusations
of witchcraft as symptoms of kinship tensions, which have increased because evasion of kin
responsibilities was less common in the older order. Taking issue with this thesis, Jack
Goody, in 'Anomie in Ashanti', *Africa* XXVII (1957), pp. 356–62, holds that the increase
of witch-finding cults is not evidence for the increase of witchcraft, which may have been
dealt with in other ways in the past. Even so, he holds that shrines similar to those established
by contemporary cults existed in the past, even if transiently. The mobility of West African
shrines occurs, he maintains, because gods fail, and new cults are accepted on pragmatic
grounds. M. J. Field, in *Search for Security* (Faber, London 1960) investigated twenty-nine
shrines and found that three were ancient, and that all the rest had been founded after 1914,
most of them being of less than ten years' standing. It is not known how many shrines have
arisen and failed without leaving evidence of their existence. Field, op. cit., pp. 29 and 87,
relates new shrines to the growth of the cocoa industry and to the anxieties arising from
circumstances of social change. Elsewhere she refers to the probable increase in witchcraft
as 'no doubt part of the new sense of insecurity in supernatural affairs which we have already
seen favouring the growth of privately owned medicines and fetishes. In Tema where we
have the old *Kple* gods in undiminished vigour, witchcraft is practically unknown.'—M. J.
Field, *Religion and Medicine of the Gã People* (Oxford University Press, London 1937), p. 135 n.
David Brokensha, *Social Change at Larteh, Ghana* (Clarendon Press, Oxford 1966), p. 188,
rejects any single explanation for the continued vitality of shrines. From mission records
H. W. Debrunner, *Witchcraft in Ghana*, op. cit., p. 106, found the activity of a witch-doctor
reported in 1855, when he believes that anti-witchcraft shrines first began, after government
interference with native customs. He tends to accept a stress theory of culture contact,
similar to that of Ward. Discussing prophetism rather than shrines, C. G. Baëta, *Prophetism
in Ghana* (SCM Press, London 1962), p. 6, suggests that 'the rise of ever new cults to meet the
prevailing spiritual and emotional needs of the people is a well-established feature of African
life, some periods throwing up more prolific outcrops than others'. He considers the emphasis
on the anxieties of acculturation have been overdrawn, '. . . prophetism appears to me to be
a perennial phenomenon of African life . . .'. This view is shared by J. B. Christensen, 'The
Adaptive Functions of Fanti Priesthood' in William R. Bascom and Melville J. Herskovits
(Eds.), *Continuity and Change in African Cultures* (University of Chicago Press, Chicago 1959),
pp. 257–78, who writes, pp. 277–8, 'The introduction of new gods, shrines and medicine
has been a continuing process among the Fanti, and it in turn is accompanied by the rejection
or abandonment of other gods and shrines. . . . However there can be little doubt that the
new cults have increased at a rate that requires them to be considered as something more
than "replacements" for defunct deities.' Although there was no mass neurosis among the
Fanti, when social structure and the economic and political systems have been greatly
modified 'a situation is created where uncertainties are likely to exist because the new norms
are in conflict with the old. What is posited here is that increased anxiety has resulted from
accelerated cultural change. The new cults and their priesthood have provided a new
combination of beliefs and rituals to assuage these uncertainties.'

recently evolved in response to new social and cultural uncertainties, Tigari, at least in Ghana, sustained a preoccupation found in at least nine earlier movements of a similar type.[29] The reports we have of Tigari itself emphasizes its preoccupation with witch-finding and protection from witches. Whether this was activity at a new level of intensity or not, it persisted in a succession of cults each with its own practices, priests, and shrines.

Thaumaturgical sects, in addition to manifesting these continuities of cultural tradition, evolve new preoccupations of their own, and often also owe something to the thaumaturgical tradition of Christianity itself. The Christianity presented to peoples in less-developed countries has often been heavily biblical, with simple and direct emphasis on the miracles recorded in the Scriptures. These are easily identified with the religious preoccupations of paganism. Some of the numerous so-called Zionist sects of South Africa illustrate the syncretism of pagan and Christian practice. These sects acquired their name because of the inspiration that they drew from Alexander Dowie's *Christian Catholic Apostolic Church in Zion*, at Chicago, whose African mission spawned a number of imitators.[30] Sundkler describes these movements as a third people between heathens and Christians, since the important elements in their religious practice are derived from both tribal and mission traditions, often with special emphasis on elements drawn from the

[29] See H. W. Debrunner, op. cit.

[30] The African movements which Dowie's missionary in Johannesburg influenced show remarkable convergence in style with Dowie's own church in Chicago. That church (then known simply as the Christian Catholic Church in Zion—a title to which it returned after Dowie had been deposed from its leadership in 1906 by Wilbur Glenn Voliva and others) had been founded in Chicago only in 1896. By 1901 Dowie had purchased 6,500 acres of land 42 miles north of Chicago on Lake Michigan, and his followers began to settle there. The acquisition of a piece of land has had special significance to native churches in South Africa, both because of land scarcity and because new churches sometimes function almost as surrogate tribes. Dowie's central concern was with healing; he held an almost dualistic belief concerning demons and possession of the body by the Devil, which could readily be absorbed in Africa. He preached taboos on drink, smoking, swearing, medicine, gambling, dancing, secret lodges, and the consumption of pork. With the exception of dancing these closely resemble taboos among African Zionists. He founded the Zionist Restoration Host whose members took an oath of allegiance to him in which they held all 'family ties and obligations, and all relations to all human governments . . . subordinate to this vow'. He created a church with many offices, the incumbents of which dressed in splendid robes: both features characterize African Zionist sects. He claimed successively to be the Messenger of the Covenant, Elijah, and the First Apostle, styles which are often assumed (or surpassed) by African sect leaders. His theology was rudimentary, and this, too, may have made easier the communication of his ideas to Africans. Obviously, Africans accepted those features in Dowie's organization that suited local circumstance and crystallized their own tendencies of religious response, but Dowie's movement provided them with a seminal model. For details of Dowie's Chicago church see the contemporary account by Rolvix Harlan, *John Alexander Dowie and the Christian Catholic Apostolic Church in Zion*, a Dissertation submitted to the Faculty of the Graduate Divinity School, University of Chicago, 1906; and also Walter J. Hollenweger, *Enthusiastisches Christentum* (Zwingli Verlag, Zürich 1969), pp. 124–30.

Old Testament.[31] Their leaders are prophets who claim divine inspiration, and who sometimes claim more than this. They frequently
resemble the diviners and witch-finders of tribal society, and the very
successful ones among them sometimes come to take on the status
characteristics and to acquire the prerogatives of tribal chiefs.[32] The
movements themselves are preoccupied with healings obtained by faith,
sometimes with glossalalia, ecstatic dancing, invocation of—and perhaps possession by—the Spirit, all of which stand in direct continuity
with tribal traditions. They engage in purification rites, and in baptism,
which is itself sometimes regarded as an important purification rite,[33]
and this is also linked to the old Zulu use of pools and streams for
ritual practices. The baptismal pool is often supposed to be full of
snakes and monsters which the baptizer must overcome. The angel of
the pool is the christianized heir of the old water-spirit of Zulu religion.[34]
Dreams and visions are often of particular importance, dictating confessions, procuring healings, issuing warnings, or requiring interpretations. Illness is attributed to evil spirits, and the movement functions
as the agency that promises its votaries the retention of, or the acquisition of, good health. Resurrections from death are sometimes claimed
as the pinnacle of the healing power of the leader or of the Holy Spirit.
In some cases the Holy Spirit is fused with the older conception of
ancestral spirits.

These South African sects obviously reflect local social circumstances
in being vehemently anti-white, with strong nativistic elements. But
whilst they disdain many European religious, moral, and medical
practices on the one hand, they also combat, albeit with methods not
entirely dissociated from the tribal past, pagan diviners, and medicine
men. They claim a monopoly of therapeutic power, and employ the
style of western evangelical faith-healing in their own operation, condemning what they regard as evil, magical practice, and protecting
their own following from witchcraft. These two aspects of *many* of the
so-called 'Zionist' sects, their hatred of whites, and their many-sided
inheritance from the tribal traditions of South Africa, should not obscure
the facts that they are on the one hand not millennialist in their
orientation, do not maintain a revolutionist response, and that they do

[31] This account of 'Zionist' sects is derived principally from Bengt G. M. Sundkler, *Bantu
Prophets in South Africa* (Lutterworth Press, London 1948).

[32] This is very clearly so for the Nazareth Baptist Church, which many of its followers see
as a tribe, and its leader, Johannes Galilee Shembe, who is often referred to as chief, and who
receives from followers and outsiders respect similar to that accorded to old Zulu chiefs,
according to K. Schlosser, *Eingeborenenkirchen . . .*, op. cit., pp. 264–6.

[33] Ibid., p. 273.

[34] B. G. M. Sundkler, op. cit., pp. 200 ff.

manifest many similarities of a thaumaturgical kind with movements in other cultural contexts which enjoy differing particular traditions.[35]

The central preoccupations of these movements are echoed in sects found in quite different cultural contexts. Thus if we examine the movements known collectively under the name of *Pocomania* in Jamaica, we find a list of practices, rites, taboos, and issues of concern which very largely reproduces those of many of the 'Zionist' churches of South Africa.[36] Pocomania sects focus on essentially emotionally gratifying exercises: singing; the invocation of saints, prophets, and angels; the experience of visions and the reception of messages from the dead; the safeguarding of members from witchcraft, from *obeah*, the form of black magic believed in, in the West Indies; and the procuring of healing for the sick. Rival sects are accused of witchcraft and are anathematized. The leaders usually give interpretations of dreams, and they also are reputed to be able to distinguish genuine from simulated Spirit-possession occurring at meetings—usually accompanied by groaning, screams, and rolling. There is an elaborate pattern of taboos, including prohibition of pork, of indecent language, of social dancing, and of sexual intercourse within several days of important religious festivities— a collection quite similar to those found in sects in South Africa. Services are dominated by singing and short speeches, and may last for several hours. As in Africa, water often plays a significant part in ceremonies, together with a wide array of ritual objects. Baptism and purification ceremonies are emphasized and animals are sometimes sacrificed. Apart from healing, cures for sterility are very much sought, and—an interesting variation, reflecting the chronic instability of the West Indian kinship system—sometimes prescriptions for abortion.

[35] It will be evident that the groups under discussion here are not all of those categorized by Sundkler as 'Zionist' in the somewhat unfortunate terminology that he introduced: B. G. M. Sundkler, op. cit. That terminology introduced confusion for the public at large and obscured both important, and in my view salient, differences among sects within each category, and certain convergences and similarities between sects in different cultures. In the ensuing discussion I shall abandon the category of 'Zionist' sects, unless referring directly to Sundkler's work, and shall use the term 'Ethiopian' (Sundkler's contrasting type) only in inverted commas. I agree with Shepperson's comments on this problem when he says that Sundkler and Schlosser popularized 'three terms which have often brought confusion rather than clarity into the discussion and analysis of African forms of Christianity: Ethiopian, Zionist and prophet movement'. To him the Ethiopian movement 'includes churches and other independent African religious groups which could be called both "Ethiopian" and "Zionist" '. He continues, 'Ideally the historian would like to see the words such as "Ethiopian" . . . or "Zionist" used within their specific historical contexts, and new terms for the various general categories into which they fall'. George Shepperson, 'Church and Sect in Central Africa', *Rhodes-Livingstone Journal: Human Problems in Central Africa* 33 (June 1963), pp. 82–94. Just such an endeavour is made in this volume.

[36] This account is based on George E. Simpson, 'Jamaican Revivalist Cults', *Social and Economic Studies* 5, 4 (1956), pp. 321–442.

The significance of direct cultural continuities between African and West Indian ex-slave communities has been widely explored, and some specific elements in West Indian religion do derive from African society. But in general this is less evident in Jamaica than in other West Indian islands, and what is perhaps more striking is the similarity in the range of preoccupations and the measures of adjustment they have inspired in two very different social contexts: an only partly de-tribalized society (and it is often on the reserves that 'Zionist' sects flourish most) on the one hand, and a non-tribal, under-developed society which has suffered centuries of social disruption from slavery and economic exploitation, on the other. Both societies have been characterized by unstable patterns of social and familial relationships (Jamaica more extensively and for far longer than South Africa); racial antagonisms; the strong sense of persistent exploitation; populations that are largely illiterate and that lack, and often seek, authoritative interpretations of their social circumstances and expectations. Both communities (including the tribal peoples in South Africa) have experienced chronic social disorganization. Whilst South African peoples have suffered military defeat and the destruction of tribes, Jamaica has lacked the coherent tradition, the community organization, and the in-group authority structure that prescribe life-orientations, that support the stability of commitment, and that provide emotional reassurance and intellectual conviction. Thaumaturgical response in minority religious movements shows remarkable similarities in the two societies, despite the differences in social conditions, and the differing extent to which traditional patterns of action may be re-summoned. The demand for reassurance, participation, and salvation in a wider and more meaningful universe bear close resemblance, when shorn of particular cultural elements— the degree of ease of emotional release, the expectation of ecstasy, and credulity concerning visions, messages and divine interventions—with those manifested by spiritualistic cults in western societies, and even among some migrant groups in the orient.[37] The preoccupation is still with personal, or at most familial, spiritual gain, whether physical or strictly psychic. To be recognized by God, or by the spirits, to have communication that transcends everyday experience in both manner and content, to be able to claim healing and deliverance, and often continuity with the ancestors, are the compensations that are sought.

[37] The extent of the similarity of such preoccupations among orientals is evident from Alan J. A. Elliott, *Chinese Spirit-Medium Cults in Singapore* (London School of Economics and Political Science, Monographs in Social Anthropology, No. 14 [New Series], 1955).

Revolutionist responses

Religious movements that manifest a revolutionist response are a common type in less-developed societies, and especially in non-literate cultures, although they have a long history in western societies where such sects still flourish. For the moment, we may confine ourselves to examples from the two societies which have provided our cases of thaumaturgical sects, South Africa and Jamaica.

In Africa, at least some of those sects which have been labelled—or which have labelled themselves—'Ethiopian'[38] manifest this response, even though a distinction may be made between those movements that rely on essentially religious and supernatural agencies to achieve their *revolutionist* vision, and those which, even in limited degree, manifest a more political *revolutionary* disposition. Other sects that evidence this disposition have been termed 'messianist', although this name, given the diversity in the messianic conceptions of movements, seems a partial and perhaps misleading designation.

Typical of revolutionist sects, and one which brought its response to active conflict with the authorities, was the movement of *Israelites* led by Enoch Mgijima (1858–1928) at Bulhoek, near Queenstown, which emerged as an independent movement in the years after the First World War.[39] Mgijima had originally been a Wesleyan Methodist who, after receiving visions—the first of them in 1907—joined the *Church of God and Saints of Christ*, an American negro movement which had, through its bishop, Msikinya, undertaken evangelism in South Africa. Mgijima succeeded Msikinya as bishop in 1914, but fell into difficulties with the movement's American authorities because of his continued pronouncement of his own visions. Mgijima's following came increasingly to adopt a hostile position in relation to the South African government. By 1917, his followers were reputed to be carrying weapons, and Mgijima had

[38] The term is derived from the emphasis given to a verse in the book of Psalms, 68:31, 'Ethiopia shall soon stretch out her hands unto God'. It has been used for separatist movements that emphasize African leadership and independence of white missions since the first separatist 'Ethiopian' movement arose in South Africa in the 1880s. A number of movements in South Africa and in other parts of Africa have adopted the name, and it has been applied to some which do not themselves employ it, e.g. by G. Shepperson, 'Ethiopianism and African Nationalism', *Phylon* XIV, 1 (1953), pp. 9–18; K. Schlosser, *Propheten in Afrika*, op. cit.; and Thomas Hodgkin, *Nationalism in Colonial Africa* (Muller, London 1956). See also, Lloyd Allen Cook, 'Revolt in Africa', *Journal of Negro History* XVIII, 4 (October 1933), pp. 396–413; Diedrich Westermann, *Africa and Christianity* (Oxford University Press, Oxford 1937); Edward Roux, *Time Longer Than Rope* (Gollancz, London 1945); and, a perhaps less reliable book, Daniel Thwaite, *The Seething African Pot* (Constable, London 1936).

[39] A detailed account, from published and unpublished primary and secondary sources, on which this and the two subsequent paragraphs heavily depend, is provided by K. Schlosser, *Eingeborenenkirchen . . .*, op. cit., pp. 125–80.

visions of the future when whites would be annihilated by natives. He had become virtually independent of the Church of God and Saints of Christ by 1918, directing the affairs of his followers from the village of Ntabelenga, near Bulhoek, where he was the headman.

In 1920, Mgijima took the style of prophet, and at passover his followers congregated at Ntabelenga. The concentration of Israelites at his village and the construction of many unlicensed new dwellings aroused the hostility of other natives, and in 1921 caused the authorities to seek the dispersal of the sect. Mgijima first temporized on the issue, and then defied the local authorities, parleying with the police and persuading them to withdraw their encamped members, and subsequently refusing to permit a medical officer to enter the Israelite compound to deal with an outbreak of typhus. The government finally offered free railway travel and food to the Israelites if they would depart for their own homes, but Mgijima's followers, having stood their ground for some time, and having succeeded in 'forcing' the police to withdraw, were convinced that they were fulfilling God's will, and that earthly powers could not interfere with them: if the authorities attacked them, Jehovah would protect them and give them victory, turning the bullets of the soldiers to water. The Israelites believed that they alone were true to God, and that Enoch Mgijima had the seven keys to heaven, which comprised: belonging to the sect; avoiding wine; using bread and water at the evening meal; footwashing; receiving new members into the church with a prayer and a kiss; the apostolic prayer; and the ten commandments. They kept Saturday as their Sabbath, baptized by total immersion, prayed with raised hands and upturned faces, and wore special badges of Israelitish identity. They were the chosen people, Ntabelenga was holy ground, and they must prevail. Enoch Mgijima stood between man and God as God's prophet, who knew how Jehovah would preserve his people in the face of persecution.

The eventual outcome of the long months of resistance to the authorities, of drilling and preparing for military conflict, was the battle at Bulhoek in May 1921, after Mgijima had again defied the order to disperse his followers. The military had offered to protect persons and property as long as no resistance occurred, but to Mgijima's followers this was a war of the God of Israel who would protect them. Over 180 men were killed, more than 120 wounded and 112 arrested. Mgijima was imprisoned, but was released in 1923, when he again collected his following, which again came into connection with the American-organized Church of God and Saints of Christ. In the mid 1950s the Israelites still existed, acknowledging Mgijima (and sometimes Msikinya) as their founders. They wore small photographs of them on their clothes, and regarded Ntabelenga as their principal tabernacle. Whether they still adhered to the millennial prophecies of their prophet is unclear.

Obviously Christian adventism, though in this instance with very little emphasis on Jesus, influenced the Israelites of Bulhoek, as it has influenced many other revolutionist movements. The Israelites were preoccupied with some aspects of the Old Testament, and for them the Jews provided the obvious model of a people who, despite current persecutions, were in fact the chosen people of God. Despite their original title, which included the appellation 'Saints of Christ', existing accounts of the movement say very little of Christian theology in its daily life or divine aspiration. As in many such sects the dominant concern is the emotionally stirring issue, and this is the new order to come, and not the subscription to a set of coherent doctrines. For them the Old Testament, or the New, is simply an allegorical foretelling of their own struggle, a typological foreshadowing of the circumstances in which they find themselves, with such persons and places from the Scriptures as fit, taken as archetypes for the locations and *dramatis personæ* of the situation in which they live.[40] This sect, then, was hardly messianic in the usual sense of the term, although the imminence of a new dispensation, to be supernaturally established, induced a climactic manifestation of faith in the early pre-Bulhoek phase of their existence. They are, however, if not messianic, certainly *revolutionist*, as is evident from their early faith in resort to arms in the holy cause. The Israelites were one revolutionist movement of many which have existed among the various South African independent sects, the estimated number of which was, in the late 1950s, not less than 2,000. Conditions in South Africa have proved conducive to revolutionist as well as to thaumaturgical movements: elsewhere in Africa, and particularly in West Africa, this has not always been so.

The visions that Enoch Mgijima claimed to have literally experienced are little different in their purport from those dreams of a changed social order which have inspired the congeries of volatile and fissiparous Jamaican movements known collectively as the *Ras Tafarians*. The movement, which in 1953 had at least a dozen groups within it,[41] has had numerous leaders and a variety of organizations, some religious, others more political, and some which have been explicitly revolu-

---

[40] This point is brought out clearly by Ernst Dammann, 'Das Christusverstandnis in nachchristlichen Kirchen und Sekten Afrikas', in E. Benz (Ed.), *Messianische Kirchen . . .*, op. cit., p. 9.

[41] George E. Simpson, 'Political Cultism in West Kingston, Jamaica', *Social and Economic Studies* 4, 2 (1955), pp. 133–49.

tionary.[42] This ideological position included racist assertions of the superiority of the negro, and hatred of the white man. Together with the black nationalist movement in Jamaica, the Ras Tafarians regard Marcus Garvey (1887-1940) as their prophet. Garvey spent his life seeking to promote the independence of the black people by ambitious schemes for shipping lines (the Ghanaian *Black Star* line takes its name from the original line founded by Garvey, though there is no actual continuity, of course), colonization in Liberia, and appeals to the League of Nations to found a state in Africa for negroes.[43] He had ideas of a black religion and a black god (one of his fellow West Indian associates in the United States, George Alexander McGuire of the African Orthodox Church, preached the blackness of God). He admired white racists as his own counter parts, and preferred the Ku Klux Klan to American negroes like W. E. B. DuBois. He proclaimed himself to be the first fascist, and his campaigns were likened to those of Theodor Hertzl's (Jewish) Zionism. In Jamaica, to which he returned after the failure of his various schemes in the United States, he is regarded as a great native son, and in the 1960s, a quarter of a century after his death in London, he was reburied there.[44] Ras Tafarians believed that he prophesied that his people would return to Africa in the 1960s. He was reputed to have said, 'Look to Africa when a black king shall be crowned, for deliverance is near'. Thus when Haile Selassie was crowned in 1930—an event which was given wide press coverage in Jamaica—many took this to be the king of whom Garvey had spoken. They took the name Ras Tafari, the Emperor's name before his coronation.[45]

Ancillary teachings quickly grew up: they came to regard themselves as re-incarnated Israelites, descendants of the lost tribes, under alien dominance similar to that of Babylon. They emphasized particular parts of Scripture, particularly chapters 3, 9, 34, 43, 44, and 47 of Isaiah, Proverbs 8, and Jeremiah 2, 8, 50, and 51. They let their hair and beards grow and preached peace and love among blacks, and hatred of whites. They regarded themselves as Ethiopians, with Haile

---

[42] See the report produced for the Jamaican Government by Michael G. Smith, Roy Augier, and Rex Nettleford, *The Ras Tafari Movement in Kingston, Jamaica* (University College of the West Indies, Institute of Social and Economic Research, Mona, Jamaica, 1960), on which I have drawn for this section. See also the paper by the same authors, 'The Ras Tafari Movement in Kingston, Jamaica', *Caribbean Quarterly* 13, 3 (September 1967).

[43] On Marcus Garvey, see Edmund D. Cronon, *Black Moses: The Story of Marcus Garvey and the Universal Negro Improvement Association* (University of Wisconsin Press, Madison 1955).

[44] Sheila Kitzinger, 'Protest and Mysticism: The Rastafari Cult of Jamaica', *Journal for the Scientific Study of Religion* VIII, 2 (Fall 1969), pp. 240–62.

[45] Katrin Norris, *Jamaica: The Search for an Identity* (Oxford University Press, London 1962), p. 44.

Selassie as the living God, who would soon arrange for them to go back to Ethiopia—to heaven. Events stimulated their enthusiasm. The Italian–Abyssinian war of 1935 was easily interpreted as a war between blacks and whites and as further evidence of oppression, and the later return of the Emperor in 1941 was seen as the fulfilment of prophecies in the Book of Revelation.

Throughout the 1930s the various preachers, some apparently independently of each other, proclaimed Haile Selassie, King of Kings, to be the messiah promised by Garvey. Some Garvey-ites, whose interests had been largely political, associated themselves with the various Ras Tafari groups. The most effective of these in that period was the Ethiopian Coptic Faith, led by Leonard P. Howell, who appears to have been the earliest Ras Tafari preacher. After a period in prison for sedition, Howell collected his followers on an abandoned estate, Pinnacle, where ganja (marijuana) was grown and where an extreme and fanatical development of Ras Tafari teaching occurred. The estate was raided by police in 1941 and 1954, by which time Howell, who had come to claim his own divinity, had lost credit in the movement.[46]

An extremist wing of the movement had arisen in the late 'thirties, the Niyamen, who swore an oath *Niyabingi*, 'Death to the white oppressors and their black allies'. The name is derived from a newspaper article published in the *Jamaica Times* on 7 December 1935, which may have been produced by the Italian Fascist propaganda office to discredit the Emperor of Ethiopia. The article purported to describe the Nya-Binghi order of Ethiopia and the Congo, which was supposedly planning to end white dominion in Africa by resort to arms: Haile Selassie was represented as the head of this anti-white secret society.[47]

[46] M. G. Smith, *et. al.*, op. cit., pp. 9–12.

[47] Ibid., p. 11. The authors appear to be unaware, as do other writers on the Ras Tafarians, that such a cult did exist in Ruanda. Its priests, *bagirwa*, prophesied the return of Nyabingi, a woman who may have been a Hamitic queen, as the deliverer of their followers from the Belgians and the English in Uganda, according to Marcel Pauwels, 'Le Culte de Nyabingi', *Anthropos* 46 (1951), pp. 337–57. M. J. Bessell, 'Nyabingi', *Uganda Journal* VI, 2 (October 1938), pp. 73–86, traces the name to N.W. Tanganyika as the title of a murdered queen who had reigned over Karagwe, and around whose memory a cult evolved. Travellers brought the cult to Ruanda in the early nineteenth century, and it recrudesced when various prophetesses claimed the spirit of Nyabingi in subsequent decades. The cult was used in the early twentieth century by Muhumusa, the widowed mother of an unsuccessful claimant to a kingdom, as a way of arousing the enserfed Bahutu against the dominant Batussi. She sought, in 1911, to liberate Ndorwa from the Europeans when the Anglo-German-Belgian boundary commission was at work in the territory. Although Muhumusa was captured, Nyabingi priests encouraged indiscriminate marauding against German, British, and Belgian posts until 1919, and again in 1928. The cult offered protection for tribute, and special prayers and rites to be saved from Europeans. Would-be priests were faced with easier initiation, less discipline, and less complicated secret language than in the

The self-declared Niyamen at Pinnacle adopted the practice of plaiting their hair and twisting it into spikey points, presumably in imitation of African warriors, and became known as 'dreadlocks'. In the 1950s, and particularly after the break-up of Howell's estate, the 'dreadlocks' appeared among the Ras Tafarians of Kingston.

There is great diversity of style among Ras Tafarians. The Niyamen use ganja; their ranks have been infiltrated by criminals; and they live —perhaps from necessity—on or near the rubbish dumps of Kingston, without water, light, or sewage disposal. Other, puritanical, groups renounce ganja, tobacco, and alcohol and are said to 'go tidy' and have a reputation for kindness.[48] But all groups have two central ideas in common. They all accept Ras Tafari as the living God: and they all believe that black men can achieve salvation only by repatriation to Africa. Beyond this their doctrines and practices differ. Some regard black men as the true Israelites, and Britain as Babylon. Many support their beliefs from the Bible but assert that whereas white men worship a dead god, their god lives. They generally reject European ways, and some even refuse food prepared by anyone outside the faith; they reject second-hand clothes; refuse blood transfusions (and any penetration of the skin by, for example, a hypodermic needle). Some urge the rejection of all wealth and property—anything which can tie man to Jamaica. Some live for periods in camps where they have no traffic with women, and where they cook for themselves. There is an assertion of masculine dominance, which runs counter to the general pattern of relations between the sexes among the Jamaican poor, where women tend to be a more stable element. They often regard ganja as their medicine, and they reject birth control as a white devil to destroy the black people. Many refuse to acknowledge death or have anything to do with it, and some believe that it comes only to Ras Tafarians who have sinned, or who have been poisoned by white medicine or food.

Ras Tafarian services are fervent, and their sermons emphasize economic oppression. They have a strong sense of persecution. 'The movement is rooted in employment', and Ras Tafarians differ 'from the rest of the population in that a much larger proportion of them are unemployed; not because Ras Tafarians are difficult to employ, but

---

traditional Kubandwa religion, according to J. E. T. Philipps, 'The Nabingi: An Anti-European Secret Society in Africa, in British Ruanda, Ndorwa, and the Congo (Kivu)', *Congo: Revue générale de la Colonie belge* I, 1 (January 1928), pp. 310–21. Although for a long time a vigorous anti-European movement, the cult was not, of course, associated with Haile Selassie, as the newspaper report suggested. See also, May Mandelbaum Edel, *The Chiga of Western Uganda* (Oxford University Press, New York 1957), esp. pp. 148–57, and William R. Louis, *Ruanda-Urundi 1884–1919* (Clarendon Press, Oxford 1963), pp. 153–6.
[48] S. Kitzinger, op. cit., p. 35.

because it is the unemployed who are most easily attracted to the movement'.[49] There are good workmen among them and some craft work is undertaken, some fishing, and some have set up communal workshops, but the movement has also been penetrated by criminals, who have perhaps fostered among them the cult of violence and hostility to law and order. All Ras Tafarians look forward to a time when white men will be obliged to serve them. For the present they have sought to maintain economic independence, regarding those who work for whites as 'slaves'. Many live in extreme poverty in the shanty town of Kingston with huts made from cardboard, corrugated iron, and other rubbish from the adjacent town rubbish dump. They have had bad relations with the authorities, police, and public, particularly since extremist groups—attracted by Ras Tafarians' rejection of law and order—have infiltrated into their midst. Insulting behaviour, especially to white tourists, and the addiction to ganja have led to frequent clashes with the police and public, who, however, have sometimes too readily identified innocent Ras Tafarians with those who have been active in disorders.

Despite their display of tough-mindedness, their deliberately disorderly behaviour in the face of persecution, and their frank condemnation of religion and politics, the Ras Tafarians are clearly a highly suggestible group not dissimilar from other revolutionist sects in less-advanced countries. Their simplicity of faith in the living God; the pictures of him; their singing of the Ethiopian national anthem; and their own hymns—'I wanna go home to my yard in Ethiopia . . .';[50] their banners, sashes, flags—all point to uncontrolled emotional orientations. In 1958, one of their leaders, Prince Edward C. Edwards, summoned an all-island convention to a twenty-one-day celebration. About 3,000 adherents attended. Some, under the impression that the convention would be followed by immediate embarkation for Ethiopia, sold up all they had.[51] In the following year the Rev. Claudius R. B. Henry returned from the United States to found the *African Reformed Church*, and promised to lead his followers back to Africa by the end of 1959.[52] He sold some 15,000 tickets at one shilling each together with

[49] M. G. Smith, *et al.*, op. cit., pp. 25–6.

[50] K. Norris, op. cit., p. 96.

[51] Except by some *a priori* argument of a false consciousness, it is difficult in view of this typical millennialist response to follow the thesis propounded by Orlando Patterson, in 'Ras Tafari: The Cult of Outcasts', *New Society* No. 111 (12 November 1964), pp. 15–17, that the last thing which the cultist wants 'in the depth of his being . . . is for the ship to come'.

[52] K. Norris, op. cit., pp. 49–50. M. G. Smith, *et al.*, op. cit., and a report in the *Sunday Telegraph* of 21 April 1963 (a later time of Ras Tafarian troubles).

travel instructions, and again many Ras Tafarians sold all their possessions.[53]

In April 1960, the police made a series of raids on Henry's headquarters, and discovered a number of home-made bombs, dynamite, and small arms: the raids 'also disclosed letters between Mr Henry and Dr Castro, the Cuban Prime Minister'.[54] Henry and twenty-four others were arrested, and Henry, accused of plotting to overthrow the government, was charged with treason and subsequently sentenced to ten years' imprisonment. American negroes appear to have been prominent in disturbances which occurred in June 1960, when Henry's son, Ronald, apparently tried to lead an insurrection.[55] The younger Henry and three others were held responsible for the murder of three other Ras Tafarians: two British soldiers were killed in the disturbances. Henry and his three associates were condemned to death. One consequence of these disturbances was the commissioning of the report on the Ras Tafari movement by Michael G. Smith and his colleagues at the University College, which was prepared and presented to the government within a month.[56] Political revolutionaries infiltrated into the Ras Tafari movement easily because of the diversity of the groups and organizations which had arisen to espouse the cause. The diverse levels of sophistication prevailing in Jamaica facilitated easy association within one movement of those who held simple-minded literal expectations of the advent of Ras Tafari and the almost magical transportation to Africa, and those who were prepared to exploit such naïveté either for personal economic gain or for active revolutionary ends. Ras

[53] This episode caused the Ethiopian World Federation to dissociate itself from Henry at its 20th Annual International Convention, for bringing its name into disrepute. The Federation had been established in New York in 1937 by Dr Malaku E. Bayen, with the authority of Haile Selassie (at that time seeking the support of negroes in America following the Italian invasion of Ethiopia). Although retaining its headquarters in New York, the Federation had its largest following among Jamaican Ras Tafarians.

[54] As reported in The Times, 12 April 1960.

[55] K. Norris, op. cit., pp. 50–1; G. E. Simpson, 'The Ras Tafari Movement in Jamaica in its Millennial Aspect' in Sylvia L. Thrupp (Ed.), Millennial Dreams in Action (Mouton, The Hague 1962), pp. 160–65.

[56] The authors recommended repatriation for those who wanted to go to Africa (although recognizing the difficulties in making such arrangements). Subsequently, an unofficial mission, including three Ras Tafarians, was permitted to go to Ethiopia, Liberia, Sierra Leone, Ghana, and Nigeria, to explore this possibility. In Ethiopia the mission was received by the Emperor. Little seems to have been accomplished, despite the Emperor's obvious pleasure at the devotion of his Jamaican 'subjects'. Haile Selassie was reported to be deeply moved by the reception he received from the Ras Tafarians on his official visit to Jamaica in 1965, when he received these sectarians at a garden party and distributed medals. In the meantime the Jamaican government's problems with the Ras Tafarians had continued: eight people were reported to be killed in the Rosehall area, near Montego Bay, in 1963. The government decided at that time to attempt to prohibit the cultivation and use of ganja: The Times, 19 April 1963.

Tafarians have at times stressed their peaceability, particularly since the times of these troubles; they have denied race-hatred but emphasized race-consciousness. None the less, in the terms in which we have defined it Ras Tafarianism is a revolution*ist* movement, even when not exploited by potential political revolutionaries. Despite the missions to Ethiopia, and their choice of a living, and involuntary, messiah, they have a distinctly supernatural conception of their utopia and the means of getting there.

These introductory examples have provided us with an indication of the basic similarities of response to be found in the spontaneous religious movements of pre-industrial societies, even though there are vast differences in historical circumstances, in social, economic, and political structures, and in inherited religious traditions. There are, obviously, also differences in the specific cultural elements that are embraced in new religious movements, but these must not obscure the syndrome of response in which specific cultural symptoms are organized. To emphasize factors of this kind is not to dismiss as unimportant the intrinsic details of ritual, doctrine, or ethical practices; these are all, obviously, legitimate and important subjects of study, and without such studies comparative analysis could not be attempted. Our necessarily slight regard for the minutiae of religious worship, teaching, and practice in this context, is justified only by the broad comparative exercise in which we are engaged—the attempt to delineate patterns that have wide application. The difficulty of showing specific relationships (e.g. between leader and followers; between antecedent circumstances of particular adherents and their decision to join a movement; between one set of ritual observances in a new sect and those of the inherited traditional religious practices of the culture) makes all such comparisons both hazardous and tentative. We may, with this point always in mind, now turn to examine the range of, first, thaumaturgical, and then, revolutionist, movements in tribal and other pre-industrial societies, and subsequently proceed to a discussion of the conditions of their emergence, their style of development, and their distinctive characteristics.

3

Miracles and the Control of Magic

THAUMATURGY is the primal stuff of primitive religion. Curing ceremonies, protective devices, and miracle-making are found very widely, if in differing combinations, in almost all preliterate societies. The 'received religion', whether it is actually of great antiquity or whether it represents a steady accretion of practices and beliefs acquired by culture contact, is largely concerned with the magical amendment of nature. Thaumaturgical elements persist in all the great religious traditions. In the countries of Theravada Buddhism, thaumaturgical practice, despite its essentially alien character, is closely integrated with authorized religious acts, to a point where there is a virtual division of religious labour between priests and astrologers and herbalists.[1] In Mahayana Buddhism the penetration has gone much further, of course. In Christianity, religious functionaries claimed monopoly of all thaumaturgical practice that orthodox theology permitted them to embrace, suppressing, when conditions permitted it, all other would-be practitioners. The exorcism of ghosts, the blessing of ships, and the claims to miraculous healing at Lourdes and Fatima continue as evidence of persisting thaumaturgical demand. Even in Judaism, where, in association with the adventitious discontinuance of full priestly rites, thaumaturgical elements have atrophied into ritual recollections, they continue as received myth.

The thaumaturgical response is a refusal to accept the testimony of the senses and natural causation as definitive. It is the belief in, and demand for, supernatural communications and manifestations of power that have immediate personal significance. If, in the orthodox religious traditions of the western world, these elements appear as a survival, and perhaps especially so to the religiously sophisticated, they none the less persist as an undercurrent among the laity. They exist as superstitions, sometimes as superstitious explanations of religious practices within orthodox churches themselves. And they exist in a number of

---

[1] See, for example, Michael M. Ames, 'Magical Animism and Buddhism: A Structural Analysis of the Sinhalese Religious System', *Journal of Asian Studies* XXIII (June 1964), pp. 21–52; Winston L. King, *A Thousand Lives Away: Buddhism in Contemporary Burma* (Cassirer, Oxford 1964), pp. 50–2; and Richard F. Gombrich, *Precepts and Practice* (Clarendon Press, Oxford 1971), esp. pp. 146–50, 208–9.

religious movements. Such belief in thaumaturgy has greatly declined in the nineteenth and twentieth centuries, as empirico-rational explanation has expanded, and has declined perhaps even more sharply than specifically religious belief and practice have declined.[2] But there are still today movements in which thaumaturgy is the dominant concern, and even in manipulationist and conversionist movements thaumaturgical elements are sometimes present, particularly in faith-healing. But in these movements a rather different significance is attached to healing activity. Whatever may be its actual role in attracting recruits —recognized when Christian Scientists claim, 'Christian Science recruits from the cemeteries', or when Pentecostalists aver in their revival and healing campaigns, that in Pentecostal churches Christ is still working his miracles—both these types of sect reject the idea that healing is either their principal concern or, in the ultimate scheme of things, a particularly important activity for them. In each case it is an activity which is merely a small indicator of what faith can do.

In some ways the manipulationist sects in advanced societies are the developed equivalent of the thaumaturgical religion of simpler societies; in conformity with their cultural context they have made appropriate adjustments, and offer their knowledge as objective, de-mythologized, and universalistic in its implications, and acceptable in terms of scientific principles. Manipulationist sects have not, however, superseded thaumaturgical sects in advanced societies. Thaumaturgy persists particularly in spiritualist movements, in which 'miracles' (usually as transformations and materializations) are still believed, and in which healing is also often practised. Their orientation is particularistic and their theological interpretations are often either exiguous or eclectic, and as might be expected from the particularism of their ministrations, usually unsystematic. The specific clientele of manipulationist and thaumaturgical movements is socially easily distinguishable from that of the others, and might normally be expected to correlate inversely with socio-economic status and education.

The thaumaturgical response is essentially a special claim for personal dispensation from the normal operation of natural causation by the invocation of particular spirit aids. It is a less total response to the world,

---

[2] Occasionally, public opinion polls reveal that there is in Britain a more extensive readership of newspaper astrology columns, or a more widely spread belief in witches than there are regular readers of the Bible or attenders at church services. See, for example, the NOP Survey on Religion, January 1971. The value of such evidence is not easily assessed, since astrology, witchcraft, and magic may make an easy, transient, and frivolous appeal which is scarcely comparable with abiding religious commitment. The spasmodic recrudescence of these interests does indicate a certain convergence in the essentially individualistic, personal, and particularistic character of thaumaturgy and the process of 'privatization' of religion in contemporary society, however.

especially in advanced societies, than is manifested by other types of deviant religious movements. Only where the activity of spirits is widely believed in, as in simpler societies, do such *movements* tend to dominate the individual's life activities, and then, usually, only where conditions make it possible for a man to contract out of the normal life of society. Thus in countries such as Brazil or South Africa these movements show greater organizational cohesion than in tribal societies, where however, they may arise as transient cults or passing enthusiasms. Even in more advanced societies, these movements often exert only transitory appeal and spasmodic involvement as needs arise, rather than evoking stable lifetime commitment. In simpler societies such movements are by no means always organized to demand total commitment from adherents; they persist as optional healing facilities, loosely associated with special practitioners, shrines, or rituals. Thus on a strict interpretation, these distinctive and often competitive clusters of religious practice are usually not sects as sociologists employ that term, although they may be so called in loose, popular usage. They do sometimes adopt sectarian styles of organization, and do so specifically where they arise out of, or in imitation of, other movements—most typically, in less-developed societies, from missions.

In the preceding chapter we discussed three somewhat different thaumaturgical movements in Ghana, Jamaica, and South Africa: the very different stages of cultural development at which these movements emerge and persist is already evident. The durability of such movements and their specific preoccupations are equally subject to cultural variation. Thaumaturgical movements seek to cope with evils that exist in the social system or the prevailing environment, supernatural, natural, or social. These evils are personal and particular, and the afflicted individual needs protection, therapy, or propitiation. When a movement arises to cater for individual needs (however widely diffused among individuals those needs may be) a wide range of organizational style is open to it. It is less bound organizationally than a revolutionist movement, the enemies of which are enemies of the community, whether that community is the tribe, the ethnic group, the race, or the self-selected sect, and for which the enemy is, usually, socially rather than individually identifiable—as the church or the government, as conquerors, colonists, or missionaries. The ills recognized in a revolutionist movement are ills which affect men commonly and collectively as part of their social situation, rather than individually and haphazardly as do the ills with which thaumaturgical practice is concerned. The response is collective belief (and may ultimately give rise to collective action); the arena of response is the total social situation; and the expected consequence of belief, prayer, and of the soon-expected supernatural action, is to affect the whole social system, the whole prevailing dispensation. In contrast the thaumaturgical demand is frequently for a personal service, a personal and immediate release (rather than an ultimate salvation) provided by a leader who usually practises—sometimes in a social context—for individuals one at a time. When he performs for a whole society, as he may in rain-making or in witch-finding, he does so to restore, by influencing nature or discovering and purifying or eliminating individual malefactors, the normal balance of a disturbed social system, not to re-distribute the wealth, authority, and status distributed within it. Thaumaturgical anxieties may be specific to the cultural context, or will, in any case, be expressed in terms of that context, but their intensity and the combinations in which they occur may vary from individual to individual, and from religious practitioner to practitioner.

Thaumaturgical movements in Papua

The succession of movements in the north and north-east divisions of Papua, which began in 1911 and which had become firmly rooted among the Orokaiva by 1928,[3] illustrate a thaumaturgical response readily espoused by a people only slightly removed from their primitive circumstances. In 1911, Maine, a native of Tufi, declared himself to have been killed by a snake and to have been subsequently restored to life, having learned the facts of existence from the snake, *Baigona*. He promulgated this vision as a new set of practices and prohibitions relating to reptiles. Snakes and lizards were in native belief reincarnations of spirits, and the new teachings developed this cultural idea in demanding that henceforth all snakes be treated affectionately. The leader appointed his agent in each village. The Baigona man, who was both curer of diseases and sorcerer, was said to terrorize his village by threatening to withhold cures. He ceased to work, devoting himself entirely to sorcery and healing. The Baigonas claimed to make or prevent rain.[4] The district had been disrupted by the bad relations of natives and whites arising from conditions of labour in the near-by gold mines, and although the movement expressed some anti-white

[3] The following section relies heavily on F. E. Williams, *Orokaiva Magic* (Oxford University Press, London 1928).

[4] E. W. P. Chinnery and A. C. Haddon, 'Five New Religious Cults in British New Guinea', *Hibbert Journal* XV (1917), pp. 448–63.

sentiment its principal emphasis was on personal problems rather than millennial aspirations.[5]

It was followed by other cults, the *Kava-Keva* and *Kekesi* movements. Both were animistic but both showed elements of white influence. Buninia, the founder of Kava-Keva, which arose near the mouth of the river Mambare, claimed to have been struck down by the spirit of taro, the principal crop and staple food of the natives: this was a similar explanation of the way in which new knowledge is acquired to that current in the Baigona cult. Meetings were held at which people were visited by the spirit of taro and shaking fits were experienced, and special new agricultural knowledge was obtained when under the spirit's influence. The teachings of the cult urged that food be handled with care, gardens be weeded, waste avoided. The Kekesi version of the movement was only slightly different. Its founder represented himself as an agent of the spirit Kekesi, a friend of Jesus Kerisu (Christ) and of the government. He prescribed songs in his own honour and exhorted obedience to tribal law and to the government, at the risk of loss of food supplies. He also ordered regular marching to work in the gardens, and gave words of command in imitation of the English. The rites involved shaking, and taro was again an important element in the songs.

Apparently the interest in the Kava-Keva cult waned, but was resumed when a girl had a trance experience which caused a new interest in Buninia and his taro-spirit. The movement now became known as the *Taro* cult, although the spirits involved had undergone some transmogrification from being spirits of taro to being the spirits of the ancestor, in keeping with traditional preoccupations.[6] Thus an ancestor cult was associated with a fertility cult, since the rituals of songs, dances, and violent shaking of the limbs (*jipari*) were meant to ensure an abundant taro crop. The cult, which diversified into many different local traditions, recapitulated ideas about the concern of the ancestors with the crops. In Manau, in the Kekesi version of the movement, Christian elements were stronger, even though Bia, the leader, had been one of the leaders of the Baigona cult. Taro 'priests' were all dreamers in their own right, although each dreamed very much what his initiator had 'taught' him to dream,[7] even if they often claimed that the inspiration had come to them directly. The Taro men were in fact often the old medicine men of the society, who used traditional

[5] Peter Worsley, *The Trumpet Shall Sound: A Study of 'Cargo' Cults in Melanesia* (MacGibbon and Kee, London 1957), pp. 54 ff.
[6] E. W. P. Chinnery and A. C. Haddon, op. cit.; P. Worsley, op. cit., pp. 59–60; F. E. Williams, op. cit., p. 9.
[7] F. E. Williams, op. cit., p. 36.

'medicines' both in curing and to 'feed the crops'. (This phenomenon, of traditional religious specialists joining new cult movements and retaining their religious leadership, is by no means uncommon in thaumaturgical movements.) Taro followers held aloof from Christian missions, indicating that the cult was an alternative at least to the introduced religion, the orientation of which had, perhaps, much less meaning for Orakaiva.[8] At the same time, though the Taro men did not oppose traditional ceremonies, the cult tended to displace traditional ceremonial which had, perhaps, become less significant to the natives with the disappearance of native warfare, and changing food-growing techniques.[9]

The preoccupation with food and the material well-being of the community is part of the cultural complex evident throughout Melanesia, and one which heavily influences newly-emerging religious movements there, whether their response be, as in the foregoing cases, thaumaturgical, or revolutionist. Cultural preoccupations of a different type are evident in other parts of the world, organized in movements sharing this basic response. The more pronounced concern of African movements, both at the level of early cultural contact, and even among peoples who have experienced prolonged and intense association with western culture, has been protection from witchcraft rather than the insurance of material abundance. Preoccupation with healing we may take as a universal concern of thaumaturgical movements.

The incidence of witchcraft

Belief in witchcraft and/or sorcery is extremely widespread among simpler peoples, although exceptions among very primitive groups have been claimed.[10] It is necessary to refer to both witchcraft and

[8] P. Worsley, op. cit., p. 70.
[9] F. E. Williams, op. cit., pp. 97–8.
[10] For example by Colin M. Turnbull, 'Tribalism and Social Evolution in Africa', in James Charlesworth (Ed.), *Africa in Motion, Annals of the American Academy of Political and Social Science* 354 (July 1964), pp. 22–32, who maintains that 'in those areas where people are hardly even grouped in recognizable tribes but, rather, live in small independent bands, at this extreme level of "primitive" organization, there is almost total lack of magic, witchcraft, and sorcery. Here a true religion pertains, a clear, simple, direct belief in a supernatural power who is, let it be noted, benevolent. I am thinking particularly of the Bushmen and the Pygmies. . . . It is only as the complexity of life increases that, in Africa we get a greater incidence of the phenomena of witchcraft and sorcery.' E. E. Evans-Pritchard, 'Witchcraft', *Africa* VIII, 4 (October 1935), pp. 417–22, says 'There are few, if any, African societies, which do not believe in witchcraft of one type or another. . . . In many communities . . . witchcraft is a function of a wide range of social behaviour, while in others it has little

sorcery, since usage among anthropologists is unstandardized. Witch-craft is regarded, by British Africanists, as a psychic and sometimes an unconscious act, while sorcery is always effected deliberately, by the use of 'medicines', rites, or spells which operate magically.[11] This distinction is not always employed by American Africanists, who sometimes prefer to speak of good and evil magic.[12] Writers on other areas, for example on Melanesia, sometimes use the word 'sorcery' for all evil magic, while common English usage tends to embrace the Africanists' conception of sorcery within what is generally understood as the wider generic category of witchcraft. In Africa, the belief in witches is a belief that certain people have an inherited capacity for causing evil to others, whether they are conscious of it or not. The body of the individual is supposed to contain a witchcraft substance, and evidence of witch power might be discovered by ordeal or divination, or, after death, by autopsy. Special diviners and witch-doctors, whose functions are some-times associated, and sometimes separate, exist in many African societies.[13] Evil emanates from the witch, whose soul may go forth

---

ideological importance.' With different emphasis, Evans-Pritchard confirmed this view almost thirty years later in the Foreword to John Middleton and E. H. Winter (Eds.), *Witchcraft and Sorcery in East Africa* (Praeger, New York 1963), p. vii: '. . . most, perhaps all African peoples have witchcraft or sorcery beliefs—or both—in some degree'. The editors of this volume have a similar interpretation, saying of witches and sorcerers: 'in Africa their occurrence is almost universal'—ibid., p. 1.

[11] This distinction was first established, on the basis of Azande concepts, by E. E. Evans-Pritchard, *Witchcraft, Oracles and Magic Among the Azande* (Clarendon Press, Oxford 1937), pp. 9–11, 21–32, 387, and has been widely accepted. Other writers have emphasized the involuntary or unconscious element in witchcraft, for example, M. J. Field, *Religion and Medicine of the Gã People* (Oxford University Press, London 1937), p. 137; Hans-Jürgen Greschat, ' "Witchcraft" und kirchlicher Separatismus in Zentral-Afrika' in E. Benz, op. cit., pp. 89–104; G. Hulstaert, 'La Sorcellerie chez les Mongo' in Meyer Fortes and G. Dieterlen (Eds.), *African Systems of Thought* (Third International African Seminar, Salisbury, December 1960) (Oxford University Press, London 1965), pp. 165–70. See also Lucy P. Mair, 'Witch-craft in the Study of Religion', *Cahiers d'Études Africaines* 15, Vol. IV, 3 (1964), pp. 335–48. J. D. Krige, 'The Social Function of Witchcraft', *Theoria* (Pietermaritzburg) 1 (1947), pp. 8–21, says in making this distinction among the Lobedu of the north-east Transvaal 'Sorcery is neither wonderful nor above matter-of-fact physical laws: but witchcraft involves supercausation, is mysterious and transcends the operation of natural cause and effect'. C. M. N. White, in 'Elements in Luvale Beliefs and Rituals', *Rhodes-Livingstone Papers* No. 32 (Manchester University Press, Manchester 1961), says of sorcery 'there is nothing super-natural about it except the possibility that magical manipulation of matter is involved . . .'.

[12] For example by J. B. Christensen, 'The Adaptive Functions of Fanti Priesthood', op. cit., who prefers to write of 'evil magic'.

[13] For example, among the Azande of the Southern Sudan, see E. E. Evans-Pritchard, op. cit., p. 11; among the Nandi, see G. W. B. Huntingford, 'Nandi Witchcraft', in J. Middleton and E. H. Winter, op. cit., pp. 175–86; among the Gisu of Uganda, see Jean La Fontaine, 'Witchcraft in Bugisu', ibid., pp. 187–220; among the Gusii of South-west Kenya, see Robert A. LeVine, 'Witchcraft and Sorcery in a Gusii Community', ibid., pp. 221–55; Witch-finding by ordeal has been common among various peoples.

for evil ends—often flying, but in some societies, it is said, walking—while he or she sleeps. The witch causes death, among some peoples by a slow wasting disease, elsewhere more dramatically. The sorcerer, in this usage, becomes the practitioner of black magic, usually using his art against people in his own community. Sometimes the sorcerer is a specialist who is commissioned to act for others; sometimes merely a specialist who prepares 'medicines' for others to use. In other cases evil magic is used by those who are possessed by a familiar spirit, which demands that the individual kills for it, in return for which he or she acquires the spirit's power for his own concerns: he, then, often kills his own kinsfolk. Theories and practice vary between peoples, but both witches and sorcerers are regarded as the enemies of men, and collectively we may refer to them, in accordance with the practice of some modern authorities and to avoid the confusions of these two variously used terms, as wizards.[14]

Against wizards there are usually protective agencies. Counter-magic is obviously the usual form of protection, but sometimes traditional deities act as protectors from wizardry and its baleful influences. Protection may be privately sought and administered, or may be a public exercise, and traditionally might be the function of a village headman. The exposure of wizards, sometimes as one operation and sometimes as the combined activity of two types of specialist, was usually in the hands of diviners, who employed various methods of divination, and witch-finders, who might 'smell out' witches or administer ordeals. [15] Thus there is often a demand for magical practice for protection from wizardry, and also a demand for the effective discovery of wizards, which again may admit of further diversity of magical arts, particularly since even within these divisions some specialists, in some societies, restrict their talents to particular types of wizardry-detection. Witch-finding in its various forms is clearly a long-established activity among African peoples, although it is one which has undoubtedly shown a capacity for the incorporation of new ideas

[14] Max G. Marwick, 'Some Problems in the Sociology of Sorcery and Witchcraft', in M. Fortes and G. Dieterlen, op. cit., pp. 171–91.
[15] The range of practice is so diverse that detail cannot be considered here. In addition to the works cited in footnote 11, above, a detailed analysis of methods of divining is provided in V. W. Turner, 'Ndembu Divination: Its Symbolism and Techniques', *Rhodes-Livingstone Papers* No. 31 (Manchester University Press, Manchester 1961), p. 21, who writes 'From the Ndembu point of view, the diviner is a man who redresses breaches in social structures, enunciates the moral law and detects those who secretly and malevolently transgress it, and who prescribes remedial action both on the social-structural and cultural levels in the form of redressive ritual.' For an interesting division of functions between diviners and witch-finders, see Barrie Reynolds, *Magic, Divination and Witchcraft among the Barotse of Northern Rhodesia* (Chatto and Windus, London 1963), especially pp. 48–127.

as these have arisen.[16] It may be expected that in periods when fear of wizardry is mounting, such innovations—offering more effective means of detecting or destroying wizards—will be all the more readily accepted. It is in this context that those new thaumaturgical movements which offer protection from and exposure of wizards, but which are distinguishable from the traditional clusters of religious belief and practice, have their importance for this discussion.

There is considerable evidence that Africans themselves believe that there has been a growth in the activity of wizards in recent decades. Although we shall concern ourselves principally with East and Central Africa in the ensuing discussion, evidence of such increase under conditions of acculturation comes from other societies both in Africa and beyond.[17] The uncertainties and insecurities of rapidly changing social and cultural conditions appear to be directly related to increased fears of the activity of wizards, and indeed, to the demand for extra-empirical help in attaining new goals, new securities, and new stability.[18]

[16] Within traditional protective and divining practices, the use of protective needles and the supposed 'radio' test in divining are examples: B. Reynolds, op. cit. The prevalence of new cults disseminating ideas alien to particular cultures are other examples.

[17] The best known is perhaps the North American case of the Navaho: Clyde Kluckhohn, *Navaho Witchcraft*, Papers of the Peabody Museum of American Archaeology and Ethnology, Harvard University XXII, Cambridge, Mass.: The Museum, 1944. See also the discussion above, Chapter 2, footnote 28.

[18] This contention seems to me to be a thoroughly plausible hypothesis, particularly taken in conjunction with the effect of the destruction of traditional anti-witchcraft agencies (see p. 81). Confining opinion to Central and South Africa, however, we find the following comments: Audrey I. Richards, 'A Modern Movement of Witchfinders', *Africa* VIII, 4 (October 1935), pp. 448–61, '. . . economic and social changes have so shattered tribal institutions and moral codes that the result of white contact is in many cases an actual increase in the dread of witchcraft and therefore in whole incidence of magic throughout the group' (p. 458). Employing a psychological theory of witchcraft-accusations as a response to repressed anxiety or repressed aggression (in part a consequence of the prevention of inter-tribal warfare), M. G. Marwick, in 'African Witchcraft and Anxiety Load', *Theoria* (Pieter-maritzburg) 2 (1948), pp. 115–29, has argued that anxiety has increased in African societies and that consequently—expressing a view which he believes is shared by most fieldworkers—'African witchcraft beliefs, far from having decreased with the advent of Western culture have actually increased. It is, of course, the intensity of witchcraft beliefs rather than their incidence that has increased. Incidence has probably kept at a steady 100 per cent; but the average African's preoccupation with witchcraft beliefs, and, on a more observable level, with defensive magic, has undoubtedly increased.' —pp. 125–6. (Marwick would, today, if I read him aright, substitute the word 'sorcery' for 'witchcraft' in the foregoing.) Marwick has subsequently re-iterated this point: M. G. Marwick, 'The Continuance of Witchcraft Beliefs' in Prudence Smith (Ed.), *Africa in Transition* (Max Reinhardt, London 1958), p. 106. J. Middleton and E. H. Winter, op. cit., p. 20, report: 'It is commonly held by people in a large number of African societies that the practice of secret maleficent acts is on the increase'.

C. M. N. White, op. cit., p. 65, writing of the Luvale, believes that witchcraft charges are less common today, and believes that even if social change has brought new insecurities, it has—for example by the introduction of health services, which have been very eagerly accepted by the Luvale—reduced others. L. H. Gann, *A History of Northern Rhodesia* (Chatto and Windus, London 1964), p. 232, writing of the murders which involved a Barotse prime minister and other notables in witchcraft charges in 1929, asserts that 'no historical evidence

The factors producing new tensions are numerous: disruption of traditional kinship relations; diminution in chiefly authority; difficulties of maintaining traditional patterns of reciprocity when changes occur in economic activity, and through new, government-provided social welfare; the breakdown of the agencies which formerly elicited social conformity and maintained social control. Disparities of opportunity between migrants and villagers reflect the significance of the conflict of values and give rise to new jealousies.[19] There have always been occasions of differential success, and typically religion has legitimated status discrepancies. But when new avenues of mobility are opened for some, traditional ascriptive status systems are disrupted. New envies grow and new tensions arise. Africans themselves often relate the use of magic to envy. Then, in the absence of any sociological analysis of conditions, and the impossibility of making such analysis meaningful to those undergoing such changes, the 'best' explanations available are those in terms of the operation of wizardry by the successful against those who suffer illness, death, or failure.

Economic and technological developments in African societies are circumstances in which belief in wizardry—and perhaps the attempts to use wizardry—appears to grow. Another feature of this situation is the interference of European missions and governments with native social control of disruptive tendencies in their own society. The typical colonial-government prohibitions on the old style of wizardry detection, particularly of poison-ordeals, have destroyed mechanisms which at least held witchcraft and sorcery in check. The so-called 'witch-finders' were regarded as charlatans, and prohibited. Often it was not the wizard but the diviner, whose activity was essentially purgative and socially therapeutic, who fell under the censure of government witch-

---

has been brought forward that ritual murders increased in numbers under white rule, as compared with the pre-colonial period, when some chiefs as individuals suffered from a much greater sense of personal insecurity during lengthy periods of civil strife . . .'. Gann, however, is hoist by his own petard, since if no historical evidence has been brought forward concerning the numbers of ritual murders, it is even more certain that none can ever be brought forward about the greatness of the 'sense of personal insecurity'. Such inter-personal psychological comparisons are even more emphatically mere matters of conjecture. The type of evidence we do have relates to (i) the impressions of natives themselves, which, if fallible, must be taken into account; (ii) the persistence, in spite of governmental prohibition, of the activities of diviners and witch-finders, and the appeal of new anti-witchcraft movements; and (iii) the remarkable proliferation of witchcraft accusations from time to time, as in 1956 in Barotseland, when ninety-four cases of witchcraft arose and an epidemic of accusations occurred.

[19] M. G. Marwick, in *Sorcery in its Social Setting: A Study of the Northern Rhodesian Ceŵa* (Manchester University Press, Manchester 1965), cites cases of migrants who, returning to their native village, preferred to arrive at night in order to avoid arousing antagonisms and envy of their wealth 'and so perhaps avoid the attention of sorcerers' (pp. 248–54).

craft legislation. 'It is an ironical feature of the cases prosecuted under the Witchcraft Ordinance that diviners are the people commonly charged with naming a witch although they are generally merely the mouthpiece of corporate hostility towards the suspected witch.'[20]

Sometimes it is Christianity which has, even more ironically, provided the circumstances in which this native belief in the supernatural has acquired renewed vigour. This has occurred with traditional practices of spirit possession in some societies,[21] as well as with wizardry, which more directly concerns us. Christian evangelization has sometimes eliminated the agencies within a society which protect men from wizardry without effectively supplying anything in their place. Thus among the West African Fang of the Gabon, the old ancestor cult, *Bieri*, regulated the aggressive and egoistic activity of a competitive and assertive people, in accordance with ancestral demands for harmony. The missions brought the ancestor cult into desuetude. They also attacked the old anti-witchcraft societies, the activities of which were public ceremonies. The wizardry against which these societies were directed, however, was necessarily secret, and, being beyond the effective reach of the Christians, persisted uninterrupted and undetected. Indeed, once Christian action had rendered the counter-

[20] C. M. N. White, op. cit., p. 65. For an account of the varying governmental ordinances relating to witchcraft in British Africa, see G. S. J. Orde-Browne, 'Witchcraft and British Colonial Law', *Africa* VIII, 4 (October 1935), pp. 481–7. No uniformity existed between codes. The ordinance for Northern Rhodesia of 1914 proposed three years' imprisonment for anyone who indicated that another was a witch or a wizard, and seven years, a £100 fine and twenty-four lashes for anyone who was proved to be by habit or profession a witch-doctor or witch-finder. Conducting ordeals, and even presence at ordeals, were punishable offences. Definitions were often inadequate, but Uganda law also punished witch-finders and witch-doctors, although these were not mentioned specifically in the provisions for Tanganyika: in Nigeria ordeals were the main concern of the law. The Northern Rhodesia ordinance, as amended in 1952, still concerned itself primarily, in the first clauses, after definitions, with 'whoever names or indicates or accuses or threatens to accuse any person as being a wizard or witch . . .' that is, with witch-finders and diviners rather than with witches. Europeans regarded witchcraft as a wicked illusion, belief in which was perpetrated by the witch-finders. This was a serious misconception of the dynamics of African social structure, in the operation of which the witch-finder and diviner had positively functional roles. Frank Melland and Cullen Young, in *African Dilemma* (United Society for Christian Literature, London 1937), had pointed out that colonial witchcraft ordinances accused the detective as if he were the criminal.

[21] Thus John Beattie, 'Group Aspects of the Nyoro Spirit Mediumship Cult', *Rhodes-Livingstone Journal*: Human Problems in British Central Africa, XXX (December 1961), pp. 11–38, says that 'despite rigorous repression by both Government and missions, spirit possession is still widespread in Bunyoro, but its practice is now nocturnal, furtive and highly secret. . . . Nyoro say that there is more spirit possession than there ever was before. . . . But despite the breakdown of the old group cult, men and women today have just as much need, perhaps more, for spiritual consolation and support, a need which, for the majority, the mission cannot as yet be said fully to meet. . . . It is often said, and I believe that it is true in Bunyoro, that at least a temporary consequence of the breakdown of traditional values is an increase of insecurity and anxiety, with consequent increase in recourse to occult consultations.'

agencies ineffective, wizardry flourished with increased vigour. A vacuum was created, and the *evus*, the spirit which possesses a *nnem* or sorcerer, flowed into it. Whereas in 1908 it was reported that only a minority of the Fang had been prepared by their parents for the possession of the *evus*, informants today 'maintain that over half the Fang are so prepared'.[22]

What had occurred among the Fang in West Africa had long ago been recognized as a general condition by a missionary and a magistrate with knowledge of Central Africa, who wrote,

> the very causes which are breaking down or altering out of all recognition the old religions are actually encouraging the persistence of this malign belief [in wizardry] . . . shorn of ancestral spirit-help it [wizardry] becomes more and more potent, for natives throughout Africa did believe that their ancestors could afford protection from this curse, and our imported religion, which in its modern and westernized form denies the existence of the cure, obviously cannot help against it.[23]

Despite the advance of the introduction of scientific and medical practice into Africa, and the widespread acceptance of European ideas about how disease originates, Africans have not abandoned a teleological style of thought in which they seek not only to understand *how* disease occurs in the body, but *why* it occurs in this particular person rather than in that one, why an accident happens to one man and not to another.[24] Belief in wizardry provides such an explanation, and since Africans do not need to encounter the basic premises of scientific thinking, their witchcraft ideas are not directly challenged, but rather science itself becomes assimilated to the prevailing explanatory system, as a particularly powerful magical agency.[25]

[22] James W. Fernandez, 'Christian Acculturation and Fang Witchcraft', *Cahiers d'Études Africaines* Vol. II, 2 (1961), pp. 244–70.

[23] Frank Melland and Cullen Young, op. cit., p. 153.

[24] This function is brought out by Max Gluckman, *Custom and Conflict in Africa* (Oxford University Press, London 1955); J. Middleton and E. H. Winter, op. cit., pp. 19–20. For a particular instance of adaptation of sorcery to a modern application, see Norman A. Scotch, 'Magic, Sorcery and Football among the Urban Zulu: A case of reinterpretation under acculturation', *Journal of Conflict Resolution* V, 1 (March 1961), pp. 70–4.

[25] M. G. Marwick, 'Continuance of Witchcraft Beliefs', op. cit. Robin Horton, 'African Traditional Thought and Western Science', *Africa* XXXVII, 1 and 2 (January and April 1967), pp. 50–71, 155–87, argues for strong similarities between African thought and scientific thought. He sees the principal difference as resting in the 'personal idiom' in which African thought is expressed. I believe that the personal idiom indicates much more important differences, however. It indicates how subjective African thought must be, and how much less abstract it must be. Without abstract conceptualization the distinction of factual and evaluative elements is impossible. Cognitive and emotional orientations remain inextricable, and this is precisely the circumstance in which witchcraft beliefs can flourish—calamity through natural causes must be laid to someone's charge. This is emotionally demanded, and cognition is re-structured to fit these emotional demands.

The increasingly rapid introduction of new techniques, ideas, and values, and the alteration of traditional social, political, and economic organization are widely assumed to produce new tensions. On a commonly accepted hypothesis mounting tensions lead to increased belief in witchcraft. But Europeans have prohibited the traditional means of detecting witches. In consequence, Africans have been ready to accept new agencies to relieve anxiety. The Christian missions, however, have characteristically refused to accept the task of uncovering witchcraft and protecting men from it. Christians had long since rejected their medieval inheritance, their devices for dealing with witchcraft as exemplified in *Malleus Maleficorum*. They no longer understood the fears which had persisted into the late seventeenth century in some places. Most missionaries showed themselves incapable of understanding the Christian past or the African present. They rejected the widespread belief in witches as mere native superstition, and they declined the role of protectors. The extent to which new anxieties have been caused by the Christian refusal even to countenance the idea of witchcraft is inestimable. Its significance in promoting separatist religious movements has often been ignored in favour of more political explanations of religious separatism.[26]

Fear of wizardry probably increased when the authorities prohibited ordeals, and itinerant witch-finders arose. Some of them made money from their practice.[27] They, and those who employed them, were in breach of the law in most British East and Central African territories, and thus their activities brought them into conflict with the authorities, and disposed them to be, or become, anti-white. Movements devoted specifically, and at times almost exclusively, to witch-finding emerged. Later, perhaps in response to government prohibition of witch-finding, some movements emphasized rather the purification of witches (which in certain circumstances was not considered illegal) and protection from witches. The recrudescence of movements specifically concerned with witchcraft in one form or another indicates the persistence of the thaumaturgical demand.

---

[26] Such in particular has been the tradition among writers especially about South Africa. The importance of a search for adequate protection from evil as a stimulus to the creation of separatist movements is briefly discussed by Jean Comhaire, 'Sociétés Secrètes et Mouvements Prophétiques au Congo Belge', *Africa* XXV (January 1955), pp. 54–68; J. W. C. Douglas 'African Separatist Churches', *International Review of Missions* XXV, (1956), pp. 257–66; Hans-Jürgen Greschat, op. cit., pp. 92–104.

[27] See, for example, T. O. Beidelman, 'Witchcraft in Ukaguru', in J. Middleton and E. H. Winter, op. cit., pp. 57–98.

Thaumaturgy and revolutionism in Central Africa

At the time of the First World War other religious influences were conspicuous in Africa, especially in Central Africa. Millennialist ideas had been disseminated, perhaps beginning with the adventist preaching of Joseph Booth in Nyasaland at the turn of the century. In this period they gave rise to the *Watchtower* or *Kitawala* movement. *The Watchtower* is the best known periodical of Jehovah's Witnesses, who had sent emissaries to South Africa and for whom Booth had been, for a time, an agent. Its millennial teachings had found a ready reception, and many had taken them up who were never, or did not long remain, responsible to the Brooklyn headquarters of the Jehovah's Witnesses proper.[28] At this point, our concern is not with this imported and readily accepted revolutionist response, but rather with the fact that even such a response, in Central Africa, quickly became associated with, and at times subordinate to, the thaumaturgical demands of the population. Watchtower teaching, remote as it is in its pure form from any kind of thaumaturgy, became, in Central Africa, yet another vehicle for those preoccupations which were more persistent and more immediate than the promised millennium. This becomes readily apparent in the *Mwana Lesa* movement.

In 1925 Tomo Nyirenda (some accounts say Ngengwa), who appears to have been a Henga from Nyasaland (other accounts say he was a Luangwa of Northern Rhodesia), went to Broken Hill seeking work. He had been converted to Watchtower beliefs by one Gabriel Phiri. The Watchtower movement (as Jehovah's Witnesses were then called), relied on converts to preach the message. Africans responded eagerly, but quickly departed from official doctrine and practice. African independent Watchtower or Kitawala movements emerged. Recurrent adventist and millennial rumours and expectations of the resurrection of the dead circulated over various parts of the Rhodesias, Nyasaland and the Congo. Nyirenda soon began asserting that black liberators would come at the second advent, that whites would be expelled, that

[28] According to L. H. Gann, op. cit., p. 234, 'the official American organization, the Watch Tower Bible and Tract Society . . . until 1935 was not permitted to maintain an accredited representative in the country'. Robert I. Rotberg, in *The Rise of Nationalism in Central Africa* (Harvard University Press, Cambridge, Mass., 1965), says that six deported Kitawala adherents from Southern Rhodesia had preached the doctrine in the Mkushi, Serenje, Abercorn, Fife, and Chinsali districts in 1918, and in the last two districts gained thousands of followers. They preached the usual millennial message of the Witnesses, but with ecstatic accompaniments quite unknown among orthodox Jehovah's Witnesses. Arrests and imprisonments failed to subdue the movement in 1919 (pp. 136–9). J. R. Hooker, 'Witnesses and Watchtower in the Rhodesias and Nyasaland', *Journal of African History* VI, 1 (1965), pp. 91–106.

their property would be made available to natives, and that taxation would cease.[29] At some stage in his short preaching career among the Lala he picked up the idea, which also had currency in Southern Rhodesia among those converted by Jehovah's Witnesses, or by the African imitators of the movement, that dipping—the practice of baptism by immersion on which the Witnesses place great emphasis—was an ordeal for the detection of witches. The Lala Chief, Shaiwila, urged him to use his power to help destroy witchcraft, and he began to preach that the advent could occur only when the land was pure. Baptism now became an order, and those who would not dip were regarded as *afiti*, witches.[30] Clearly, none of the other promises of millennial bliss or the ending of taxes, nor even of the efficacy of baptism in conferring eternal life, could be given proof of fulfilment, but dipping as a witch-finding ordeal was both in accord with expectations about witches and had the merit of being a self-fulfilling prophecy. It became the touchstone of success. Nyirenda was now known as Mwana Lesa, 'the Son of God', in Lala and Lamba areas. Sixteen of Shaiwila's people were killed as witches, and several more in the Ndola sub-district. Nyirenda then crossed into Katanga, where he indicted 176 other victims. Pursued by the Belgian authorities, he returned to Serenje where, despite the efforts of the natives to protect him, he and Shaiwila were captured and subsequently hanged. Thus, despite the currency of revolutionist response that had been stimulated by the excitements of the war, in which natives had often helped in the legal killing of other white men (German colonial forces), and the dissemination of Watchtower ideas and rumours, none the less the preoccupation with a thaumaturgical concern became dominant. This is a pattern found in other instances.

Anti-witchcraft movements

The *Mcape* or *Bamucapi* movement, which had its point of origin in Nyasaland, was observed in 1934 by Richards some 500 miles away among the Bemba of Northern Rhodesia.[31] A cripple, Maluwa, supplied

[29] J. R. Hooker, op. cit. Similar ideas had been current earlier in the preaching of another Kitawalan, Hanoc Sindano: R. I. Rotberg, op. cit., pp. 136, 138.

[30] Hans-Jürgen Greschat, op. cit., p. 96. The account in R. I. Rotberg, op. cit., pp. 142–6, includes some differences of detail. The early account of Carl von Hoffman, *Jungle Gods* (Henry Holt, New York 1929), pp. 42–68, which includes the author's own photographs of the *Mwana Lesa*, differs on many points, including the point in his career at which he began to practice dipping as a method of witch-finding, attributed by von Hoffman to his stay in the Congo.

[31] A. I. Richards, 'A Modern Movement of Witchfinders', op. cit., p. 448.

a red substance which his salesman sold as both a detective and curative medicine. Those who consumed it would either be protected from, or cured of, witchcraft. Those who sought to practise witchcraft after treatment, it was maintained, would die. The myth which grew up around the substance imputed to it a wide range of thaumaturgical powers which passed beyond specific concern with wizardry: it conferred immunity to poison and drove away all evils. There were, however, elements of Christian-type preaching associated with the cult's diffusion, although without specific Christian mythology. The washing away of sins was a predominant theme of the preaching; a parousia was promised of a saviour who would come when the land was entirely cleansed of witches. The high God, Lesa, who used to be called on to provide protection from witches, had raised up a prophet, Kamwende, who, however, as the price of the revelation he had received, had had to pay with an eye, an arm, and a leg which remained dead. The movement fell foul of the law which forbade witch-finding ordeals, and because money was charged for the treatment.

In the late 1940s a new movement, *Bwanali-Mpulumutsi*, also beginning in Nyasaland, spread in the same part of Rhodesia. Bwanali was a Ngoni herbalist who began to experience a great increase of cures, because, it was asserted, God was helping him. Wizards began to go to him to confess. The steady increase in his fame led many to make journeys which were sometimes of three weeks' duration, on foot, to see him, or to see his disciple Mpulumutsi in the Tete district of Mozambique, to be cured of, or protected from, wizardry. The two leaders did not accuse people of wizardry, thereby avoiding the direct breach of the law which had occurred in the Mcape movement. Those who went for treatment became incapable of suffering harm from wizardry thereafter, and would die if they attempted to practise it themselves. Thus the movement acted as a selective wizard-killer of the really evil. Old evil medicines were to be destroyed, and a set of moral prohibitions accompanied the treatment, which indicated the extent of intrusive Christian principles: after treatment men were no longer to steal, lose their tempers, swear, to damage others' property, or seek vengeance. There was a sharing of sins by confession, and there were Bible readings. Thus whereas Mcape appeared more as a commercial venture, this movement, which avoided administering an ordeal, appeared somewhat more like a religious revival.[32] The pattern of increasing assimilation of Christian elements is noteworthy, but as Greschat has pointed out, none of these movements succeeded in

[32] M. G. Marwick, 'Another Modern Anti-Witchcraft Movement in East Central Africa', *Africa* XX, 2 (1950), pp. 100–12, on which this and the foregoing paragraph rely.

establishing a stable pattern of religious practice or of institutionalizing itself. They were ephemeral responses to meet the need for sudden miraculous action to reduce tensions in societies in which the old mechanisms of adjustment were inadequate to cope with new patterns of social relationships. Competition for achieved status, anxiety and security about personal well-being, and envy of others had been rationalized as intense concern about wizardry, probably leading to an increase in accusations, which contributed further to general social maladjustment.

The need for new institutions to keep in control some of the new tensions, and to replace those prohibited by European colonial authorities, has been analysed for the Lele of the Belgian Congo.[33] Within this tribe no less than seven named anti-sorcery movements had occurred in the period from 1910 to 1952. All had apparently been introduced from neighbouring tribes, and all had promised to eliminate sorcery. The sorcerer typically perverted his own duties and obligations in order to acquire the knowledge with which to harm his enemies. The cost of obtaining such knowledge was thought to be the magical killing of his own clansmen—an assumption itself indicative of the tension between clansmen, particularly between the old men, who were those usually accused of sorcery, and the young accusers. Before it was abolished by the Belgian authorities in 1924, accusers and accused could seek vindication in the poison ordeal. If the accused vomited and did not die, then his accusers had to pay him compensation: if he died, there was an end of the matter, and a new alignment of social forces could occur. Without the ordeal, an old man against whom accusations multiplied might find himself socially ostracized, and so social tension would persist without the opportunity of purgative action and without a new basis for social re-integration. The abolition of the poison ordeal, however, may not alone have led to the emergence of cult movements, since one is reported before the ordeal was prohibited, and there were probably others. Clearly, Lele society was also facing other strains from culture contact.

The cult movement *Kabenga-Benga*, which the Lele obtained from the Kasai in 1952, may have been more than a thaumaturgical deviation (by definition a movement espoused by only a minority). But it was a thaumaturgical deviation in the sense that, like its predecessors, it commanded enthusiasm for only a short time, and then passed into desuetude. Anti-sorcery movements have their own methods of compelling everyone in a community where they gain even a little support,

[33] Mary Douglas, 'Techniques of Sorcery Control in Central Africa' in J. Middleton and E. H. Winter, op. cit., pp. 123–41.

to accept them, on pain of otherwise being branded a sorcerer. The Lele had sent two men to Kasai to obtain the cult and, according to their usual practice, they paid to receive its rites, myths, songs, and secrets. Returning, the emissaries would hope to profit from their investment, by charging those whom they inducted into the methods of treating sorcerers. In this particular cult social relations of any sort between the purified and those uninitiated were forbidden. By ostracizing the impure, the cult gained added force in proselytizing. Old diviners gave up their magical equipment—horns, rubbing oracles, and whistles—and took up positions as officials of Kabenga-Benga; thus the rites of the new cult superseded all previous rites. The officials of the cult promised that communities which adopted it would henceforth live free from sorcery. In effect, since all deaths and all illnesses, except for those in great old age or childbirth, were attributed to sorcery, such a promise implied that there would be a 'new era of peace and prosperity'. Such is Douglas's interpretation.[34] Thus the new cult is a type of group resolution not to believe in or practise sorcery again, perhaps in the hope that if all abided by this resolve, a life without social tension might be lived. Analogically, it is a 'currency reform' of social relations and emotional life. The endeavour is made, perhaps, among a people for whom tensions have become unmanageable, among whom tensions are no longer circumstances adding zest to the business of daily living, as they can be when controlled and regulated by specific social mechanisms. But since discrepancies between the expectations and the realities of life without sorcery are noticed, the problem of explanation remains: either purification rituals must be repeated, or their efficacy is doubted; the cult wanes and sorcery beliefs persist till a new purgative movement comes along.[35]

Movements of this kind promise relief from genuine circumstances of social unease, and the promise is made in thaumaturgical terms. A new medicine will be employed which will purge the society of its witches, and the purging may indeed provide relief. Something, and something powerful, has been done. Like so many other social phenomena, the medicine is credited with power, and therefore it has power: faith in the operation makes the operation successful. The result may be no more than a displacement of anxiety on to scapegoats; the scapegoats are likely to be a pre-selected class that occupies a focal position in the accumulation of tensions, and will usually be a group whose activity

[34] Ibid., pp. 138–9.
[35] M. Douglas, ibid, p. 141, notes that in 1959, when Belgian administration was collapsing, but before independence was declared, the poison ordeal had been resumed in parts of the Congo, causing many deaths.

(or inactivity) arouses envy and resentment. The victims are frequently old, and sometimes they are exclusively men or exclusively women— people who have lived beyond their period of usefulness to the community, and who are now either a burden or a hindrance. They may be economic charges on the community; or they may monopolize property or control, which, were they dead, would be redistributed to younger people.

It is in this context that Bohannan has written of anti-witchcraft movements among the Tiv of Nigeria as 'extra-processual events'— events that are unlegitimated in the theoretical functioning of the society, but which appear to be periodically necessary to its smooth operation.[36] Among the Tiv there was, before British rule, relatively little accumulation of power in the hands of any one set of persons: the effect of British rule was to create a system of authority in which some men became power-holders. The Tiv regard success or power as necessarily due to supernatural force, which in some men is simply an endowment, but which may be strengthened by evil magic, in particular by eating human flesh and practising sorcery. The *mbatsav* are an organization of witches who bewitch people who will then kill for them. The bewitched kill their kinsfolk and the corpses are eaten by the *mbatsav*. The word applies both to men with power and to a group of witches: *tsav* may thus be genuine power or may be power re-inforced by witchcraft. The Tiv consequently distrust men with power, and the system of authority introduced by the British was followed by periodic anti-witchcraft movements (although similar movements appear to have also occurred before British rule was imposed). The movements appear to be aimed at the power structure: the men with authority, and particularly those who have abused their positions, are the people who are generally indicted as witches, as men with *ijebu*—counterfeit power. In 1939, when the *Nyambua* cult, the fifth of these recorded movements, occurred, social and economic life came to a standstill, since effective leadership had been brought to an end. Guards protected bodies of the dead until they had decomposed, after which they were burned, to prevent their consumption by the *mbatsav*: when the guards discovered witches they were pursued and invited to a Nyambua chapel to be cleansed, or had their heads shaved. The shrines became important meeting centres, and appear, in the distribution of statuses, to have shown some signs of re-institutionalizing the power structure of the society, this time within the anti-witchcraft movement itself. But, as in so many other similar cases, in later years the Tiv were reluctant to talk

[36] Paul Bohannan, 'Extra-Processual Events in Tiv Political Institutions', *American Anthropologist* 60, 1 (February 1958), pp. 1–12, on which this paragraph relies.

of the Nyambua cult: they said that it was folly and was now forgotten.

In effect the anti-witchcraft movements among the Tiv had the function of a re-distributing power, or, at least, of a de-institutionalizing power. In one case, the *Ijôv* cult of 1912, one of the spirits, Wainyoru, appears to have promised that if *mbatsav* gave up the human flesh they were hoarding, then the world would be handed over to the Tiv as a chosen people. But in general the aim of the movements has been more restricted—the removal of particular office-holders, rather than a promised re-structuring of society.

The association of thaumaturgical demands with hopes for some type of new dispensation have appeared in several of these anti-sorcery movements, but this association is to be expected, given the welter of Christian ideologies circulating in Central Africa, the social circumstances that have prevailed, and the co-existence of other movements with a more distinct millennialist response. The expectations of a movement may usually be characterized in terms of the dominant preoccupation, and these movements, whatever subsidiary ideas of a golden age may exist, were clearly primarily oriented to assuagement of social ills by supernatural therapeutic agency. In some clearly millennialist movements we shall encounter subsidiary concern with healing practice. Like other responses to the world, these two may supersede each other within the context of a movement, or—more typically in less-developed societies—within a congeries of movements. But unlike certain other cases of mutation of response, the succession of a revolutionist response by a thaumaturgical response does not represent the normal logic of development. In advanced societies it is probably rare: in less-developed societies there may be special circumstances to account for the decline of a millennial movement and the emergence among the same people of a thaumaturgical movement.[37] An example from Central Africa is the *Munkukusa* (or *Mukunguna*) movement in the Belgian Congo.

The Congo, of course, at the time that this movement arose, in 1951, had been the scene of a recrudescent congeries of movements following in the wake of Kimbanguism, and the misinterpretation by many

[37] L. P. Mair, op. cit., p. 348, notes that millenarian leaders often promise the elimination of witchcraft as one of the features of the golden age to come. When such movements become what she calls 'total reactions', the theme of resistance to the colonial regime becomes central, and the fight against witches is temporarily forgotten. 'But since it is not really possible to achieve the golden age, the fight against witches is liable at any time to be renewed.' The concept of totality of reaction fits closely with the analysis in terms of response, that is offered here; the thaumaturgical response is less total than the millennialist response. Mair appears to see the anti-witchcraft orientation as a residual concern for many movements when other external circumstances are less pressing, and this appears to accord with our failure to discover a logic in the sequence of changed response from millennialist to thaumaturgical.

Congolese of the functions and intentions of the Salvation Army, which had at first been seen as an agency attacking witchcraft and undertaking curing. It seems more than likely that the Munkukusa movement caught up in its following some of those who had previously participated in the millennialist movements of the preceding three decades, although without detailed investigations we can do no more than regard this as probable.[38]

The movement swept over the Congo (Belgian and French) with great speed. It began with a man whose wife left him after their child had died and she had accused him of eating it through *kindoki*, sorcery—a typical sorcery allegation. To win her back he decided to confess to *kindoki*, but also to assert that his wife had participated, so that her kinsfolk would turn her out. He and she would then go through a *kukusa* rite and be reconciled by promising never again to eat human flesh (*kukusa* meaning 'to cleanse', an old usage connected with swearing oaths). The particular rite now instituted was to rub their mouths in different excrements and earth from graves. The rite spread with the idea that all who wished to be 'free of carrying on *kindoki* had to *kukusa*'.[39] Other thaumaturgical ideas became associated with it: that it would eliminate all disease; that blacks would now live long like whites, and suffer only illnesses sent from God (since whites abjured sorcery and evil spirits, and did not suffer from disease attributed to sorcery and the operation of spirits—thus it followed that Europeans had undergone such a rite and had declined to reveal it to natives). The rite was also held to prevent animals sent by the *bandoki*, sorcerers, from eating crops.

There may have been an anti-white element in these ideas as first propounded, but when the movement was opposed by the authorities this aspect became more pronounced, even though the movement apparently remained essentially concerned with its thaumaturgical practice. Its agents were not like the old *nganga zaminkisi*, the smellers-out of sorcerers, nor were they paid. There was no organization and no attempt to establish community life among the purified, although the rites, initially intended as an all-time purification, were repeated periodically. The rituals tended to become longer, sometimes including a fertility rite, and whole villages or clans came to be assembled for the ceremonial, which had continuities with the old ancestor cult. Later it seemed that Munkukusa was regarded as a deity. Christian symbols, in particular the cross and the Bible, were used, and oaths such as, 'If I

---

[38] This account rests entirely upon the detailed study of Congolese religious movements by Efraim Andersson, *Messianic Popular Movements in the Lower Congo*, Studia Ethnographica Upsaliensia XIV (Almquist and Wiksells, Uppsala 1958), pp. 201–13. On Kimbanguism generally, see Chapter 11.

[39] Ibid., p. 202.

have eaten any human being I shall die', or 'We cast away our sorcery' were sworn. As in the Kabenga-Benga cult among the Lele, which was flourishing at about the same time, and may have been influenced by the same ideas, those who opposed Munkukusa were accused of being sorcerers, and gradually the purified withdrew from association with others, as dangerous people. Thus was the enforcement of this type of public hygiene extended.

The organization of thaumaturgical movements

It is evident that in the later cults there is an increasing tendency for forms of activity to be incorporated that are similar to those of religious ceremonies and practice, yet typically—and this appears to be true even of advanced society—the thaumaturgical movement, focusing so intensely on the state of individual grace and wholesomeness, finds organization, direction, and permanence difficult to achieve.[40] The cults rely on dissemination through agents, and even where the ultimate medical 'power' is ascribed to some individual healer or herbalist, it is difficult for him to use the myth of his thaumaturgical prowess as a means of acquiring religious or political power, though in the earlier movement he sometimes gained economically. Thaumaturgical movements, even if their purifying practices spread long distances, appear to be essentially local and particularistic in their operation, reflecting their ideological orientation in the pattern of their organization. Men are not mobilized for social action by such cults, except in extending their own security by enforcing purification on others, or by 'selling' their secrets and initiating new officiants.

Some distinction arises here, however, between these Central and East African witch-finding movements and the pattern we have already observed in West Africa.[41] Thaumaturgical movements in West Africa are frequently organized by the proliferation of shrines. While these movements are no less particularistic and while little centralization of

[40] For the difficulties which spiritualist movements in Britain have encountered in seeking to establish a permanent organization see Geoffrey K. Nelson, *Spiritualism and Society* (Routledge, London 1969), and the critical review of this work, *The Times Literary Supplement* (26 June 1969), p. 707. Even in advanced society thaumaturgical movements manifest practitioner–client relationships rather than community services. Demand is spasmodic and personal and the medium's charisma is equally intermittent. At best mediums may establish a 'professional organization': they are much less likely to create stable and enduring church structures with congregations as diffusely committed as in churches or as totally involved as in sectarian groups.

[41] See pp. 54 ff.

organization has occurred, none the less this arrangement has sustained movements of greater permanence than those which we have examined in Nyasaland, the Rhodesias, and the Congo, which appear to have had a life-cycle of only a year or two. Thus, though the Tigari cult in Ghana had lost much ground by the mid 1960s, at that time it was still extant, two decades after its period of great popularity, and a longer time after its period of early dissemination. One might suppose that these differences are related to the differences of tribal organization and traditional religion between these societies; for examination of that hypothesis we must, however, await a comparative anthropological analysis. At levels of more advanced cultural development, Central and East Africa have not been without thaumaturgical movements of greater durability. Although they have not so effectively discovered the organizational pattern of European denominationalism, as have the West Africans in cases we shall consider below, nor blended it into a surrogate tribal structure as effectively as have some of the thaumaturges of South African sectarianism, none the less two examples are available from Rhodesia of relatively enduring religious associations dominated by thaumaturgical attempts to control wizardry and secure healings.

The *Twelve Society* was founded in 1944 by a trader in the Mongu District of Barotseland, and in 1957, after an epidemic of witchcraft accusations had occurred in this area, was found to be still thriving by the administrative officers who then began systematic investigation of wizardry and anti-wizardry in the area.[42] Rice Kamanga, the founder of the Twelve Society, had become mentally ill in 1944 and had run away into the bush. Subsequently he reappeared and claimed to have been visited by a spirit, which had cured him of his ailment, *bindele*. He claimed to have received a commission from the spirit to treat this affliction and to found a church from the first twelve patients he cured. The illness, *bindele*, was one of the modern Lunda-Luvale *mahamba*—an ailment caused by the possession of spirits other than those of one's own ancestors, and 'may be considered to reflect a tension between the society of the victim and that of the group represented by the spirit'. In this case *bindele* is the Luvale word for European, and sufferers are thus believed to be ill because they are possessed by the spirit of a European. When a man was cured of a traditional *mahamba* ailment, caused by possession by an ancestor spirit, he might choose to be initiated by the curer into the methods of curing, and so set up in practice himself.

Kamanga was clearly following an accepted pattern of local therapeutic socialization in transmitting the methods of his own practice to

[42] This account is drawn from B. Reynolds, op. cit., pp. 133 ff.

those he cured, but in organizing them into a 'church' he was following a model introduced by Europeans. Kamanga, who came to call himself Chana (known as Chana I) diagnosed his clients' complaints by a process of ringing bells, until the patient, if suffering from *bindele*, began trembling and shouting. Other rituals followed within the church, and thereafter the patient went to his home village under the care of a subordinate doctor to be treated for a period often lasting several months. The emphasis in treatment was on cleanliness; the patient had to live apart in a small circular windbreak with clean blankets and daily or more frequent baths. He underwent spiritual cleansing by surrendering all witchcraft charms. Once cured the patient was taken back to Chana's compound for his cure to be checked. On the following Saturday he was taken into the church for a ceremonial in which the cure was further proved. At the church service Chana preached, exhorting people to cleanliness, the care of children, and wholesome diet, and later in the day, after the patient had paid his fees and brought an animal, the congregation would hold a feast with drumming and singing. The patient was then installed as a doctor in his own right and a *pazo*, a small courtyard with a hut, would be built for him in his own village where he could receive patients and bring them to Chana for diagnosis.

This thaumaturgical movement symbolizes, even in its choice of ailment, *bindele*, the tensions experienced by those living in a society in which diverse value-systems are given simultaneous and conflicting expression, in the acceptance and rejection of the 'European spirit'. The cult itself manifests similar syncretism. Chana had been at a school run by the Seventh Day Adventists from 1928 to 1934, and the extent of his borrowing from them is obvious, not only in the cross, the apostles, and the restriction of the use of the church to Saturday, which Reynolds mentions, but also in the emphasis on hygiene, which has become a major characteristic of the movement in its missionary work. His concern with witchcraft and his method of recruiting new practitioners are indigenous. But the authority that he has managed to retain over their activities, by controlling diagnoses and checking cures himself, reflects the hierarchic character of European organization and is in contrast with the autonomy of traditional diviners and healers. It appears, however, that the organization has remained local, and from the report available it is not clear that there were any other actual congregations than the one over which Chana himself presided. Such centralization is typical for a movement with a charismatic or semi-charismatic leader who claims direct supernatural experience and revelation. But dependence on the principal thaumaturge was obviously also a limitation on the movement's growth. The abilities and facilities necessary for a more elaborate structure, however, were probably not yet available in Barotseland: beyond a certain point of growth, it is difficult to exercise effective control without established bureaucratic techniques. Precisely because of the particularistic dependence on the thaumaturge, the usual pattern of growth of thaumaturgical movements is the proliferation of agents, or of schism and the emergence of healers and mediums who act in their own right. Only where an organizational model of another type of movement can be imitated should we expect thaumaturgical responses to take on those structural characteristics which we associate with sects in advanced society. Such imitation, combining strong central direction with branch churches over a wide area, first occurred in this region in the *Lumpa Church*.

The Lumpa Church: the mission as organizational model

In the ten years from its beginnings to its dramatic conflict with the newly independent Zambian government, in 1964, the Lumpa Church had grown phenomenally and had become one of the most vigorous churches in Northern Rhodesia. Alice Mulenga Lenshina Lubusha, a simple woman of the village of Kasomo in the Chinsali district in the country of the Chief Nkula, in the north-eastern area of Northern Rhodesia, claimed, in September 1954, to have had a vision.[43] She had died, had been to heaven, and had been given a book of hymns by God. Making a claim common among such prophets[44] that she was not yet ready to enter heaven, she said God had sent her back to earth to preach 'the good news'. She was instructed by God to relate her experience at the Lubwa Protestant United mission a few miles away. The missionary, the Rev. F. MacPherson, received her kindly, baptized her, giving her the name Alice, and put her under instruction. She knew some of her hymns at that time, and could sing them at once. Mac-Pherson accorded her no special status, and for a time she appears to have remained content in this situation.[45] Her revelation became widely

[43] The specific account of the visions vary. In this account of the visions I have followed R. I. Rotberg, 'The Lenshina Movement of Northern Rhodesia', *Rhodes-Livingstone Journal*: Human Problems in British Central Africa, XXIX (June 1961), pp. 63–78.

[44] The frequency of the claim to precisely this type of experience among prophets is arresting: it is found, for example, in very similar form in the case of John Slocum, founder of the Shaker Church among the North American Indians of Puget Sound. See pp. 353 ff.

[45] For a different account of the visions and the events which immediately followed, see John V. Taylor and Dorothea A. Lehmann, *Christians of the Copperbelt* (SCM Press, London 1961), pp. 248 ff.

known and large numbers came to the Lubwa Church for services. She testified against adultery, hatred, cursing, stealing, and telling lies, and in particular she told people to 'Bring your magic horns and charms, then you will be saved in God's judgment'.[46]

Some months after her initial revelation she distributed seeds for people to mix with their own seeds to get a blessing on their crops, and she began to give advice to those who sought it of her. Her fame spread over a wide area, and people came on pilgrimages to see her from places as far away as Abercorn on Lake Tanganyika, the Copperbelt, and Nyasaland. For about two years no distinctive or separatist movement emerged, despite her fame and the continually growing body of pilgrims who came to her village throughout 1955 and 1956. She was not labelled a heretic and did nothing to magnify her own claims to leadership. It is conceivable that the very acclaim of her growing following may have been partly responsible for creating Lenshina-ism as a separate movement, although the developing hostility of the missions, and especially of the Roman Catholic White Fathers' Mission at Ilondola, a few miles away, was also important. The pilgrims built their own wattle-and-daub churches when they returned to their homes, 'in which they held services "with a good deal of enthusiasm", in many places three times a week, singing the simple evangelical phrases which Lenshina had taught them, set to indigenous tunes, and listening to the self-appointed priests, many of whom were ex-mission catechists and teachers who asked Lenshina's permission to pass on her message'.[47]

Rotberg suggests that it was after MacPherson's departure that Lenshina began to advise those who came to see her. 'Her tirades against the evils of witchcraft and sorcery began in this period. She also baptized adherents for the first time, including many who were otherwise members of the Lubwa Church.'[48] At this time some of the native evangelists and teachers of the Church of Scotland Mission (presumably of the Lubwa Mission of the United Church of Central Africa in Rhodesia) were expelled, and these displaced preachers, used to the exercise of leadership, were eager to take up new roles of a similar kind. We can only suppose that the growing movement round Lenshina was vulnerable to the intrusion of this displaced priestly class, who had every reason to seek a share in its success, to espouse a purely African

---

[46] From the report of the African missionary of the congregation 'in which the prophetess entered the catechumenate and was being prepared for church membership', quoted by J. V. Taylor and D. A. Lehmann, ibid., p. 250.

[47] Ibid.

[48] R. I. Rotberg, op. cit., p. 69.

movement, and to promote its separation from the mission. The precise force of the differing factors at work are impossible to estimate. The departure of MacPherson from the Lubwa Mission may have been a factor in her growing estrangement from it, since others were less sympathetically disposed towards her. Or Lenshina may have become increasingly 'managed' by her husband, Petros Chintankwa, and others who aspired to leadership roles in what was now a thriving movement. Once Lenshina began to baptize—a function which priests have usually regarded as their own prerogative—and especially since she baptized some who had previously been baptized in the missions, the separatist course of her church became inevitable.

The movement now became the Lumpa Church. Within the years from 1955 to 1961, the Lubwa Mission and the large Roman Catholic station at Ilondola had been seriously affected; their 12,000 members or catechumens had vanished and 'less than 600 spiritually strong Christians are all that remain'.[49] The Lumpa Church had an estimated following of more than 85 per cent in the leader's home district, and large numbers of Bemba, Nyanga, and Tumbuka-speaking peoples in surrounding areas, and all this in the face of growing opposition from the missions, and the hostility of the Senior Chief Nkula, who saw the Lenshina movement as a rival claimant to authority in his own precincts. The Lenshina-ists came into active conflict, first with the missions and then with the authorities who attempted to evict illegal immigrants from Kasomo. But the arrest of Petros and sixty-four other leaders in 1956 appears only to have accelerated the growth of a separate organization, which formulated its own ordinances and presented them to the District Commissioner at Chinsali.

The rules of the Lumpa Church (*Lumpa* is a term meaning 'highest', 'excelling', or 'above') are an intensification of the moral ideals of the Church of Scotland, whose influence had been paramount in the area. The laws state that the church is 'to worship God and his son Jesus Christ'; disavow unruly behaviour; affirm the brotherhood of black and white men; prohibit backbiting, insult, lies, pride, boasting, hatred, anger, harsh(ness), false-witness, selfish(ness), rudeness, cunning, and stealing; and enjoin sincerity, kindness, trustworthiness, love, patience, and truthfulness. Christians must 'keep away from . . . coveting, witchcraft, stealing, adultery, sorcery, witches, drunkenness, bad songs and all primitive dances'. Good manners are enjoined; divorce, polygamy, beer and primitive dances at weddings, smoking and snuff-taking in church, and beer-drinking before going to church, are all prohibited.

[49] Ibid., p. 64; J. V. Taylor and D. A. Lehmann, op. cit., p. 261; 'It has been estimated that about half of Lenshina's followers came from the Roman Catholic mission churches . . .''

A special clause permits widows to re-marry if they wish, but declares that they shall not be forced to do so. Attendance at church whenever 'the congregation takes place' is demanded. The final summary returns to the theme of witchcraft, 'Who does not obey these laws is the one that God also does not like the Almighty God says do not practice witches, keep my love. Anyone who practice witchcraft, he will at the end also suffer and be punished' [sic].[50]

The Lumpa Church, understandably for a movement arising in the remoter parts of a territory in which Christian mission activity itself was considerably less than a hundred years old at the time of its emergence, developed no systematic theology as an independent movement. It accepted a simple evangelical faith, and its services were largely devoted to the singing of the distinctive songs which Lenshina had taught, set to old Bemba tunes which resembled the repetitive choruses sung in evangelical assemblies in the western world and which are a common form of church singing in many parts of Africa. Many of the songs expressed very simple hopes for redemption, and exhortations against sin.[51] The prayers and sermons at the services emphasized the same themes. Lenshina received the sick and those seeking her advice at her own village, 'Zion' as it was called, and when visiting the towns, but she appeared to administer no special healing grace, nor to make promises or predictions for the afflicted. None the less there was always a great press of people to take their troubles to her, and because she had returned from the dead she was believed to have healing power.

Rotberg says that by 1961 the priests had formed a carefully regulated hierarchy, and that new priests were admitted only by Lenshina; they were apparently not paid, and some, at least, earned their livings in other ways, for example in the mines of the Copperbelt.[52] Taylor and Lehmann saw no evidence of financial exploitation in their investigation of the Church, although Rotberg believed that Lenshina's husband, Petros, and other leaders may have made considerable financial gains.[53] Lenshina herself remained a simple woman, although she employed servants and had a car, in the usual style of African religious leaders whose material well-being—in the most thorough thaumaturgical spirit —is often demanded by their followers as an evidence of their spiritual prowess.

With the exception of the Catholic missionaries, who had perhaps

[50] The complete text is given in J. V. Taylor and D. A. Lehmann, op. cit., pp. 253-4.
[51] Ibid, pp. 255-9.
[52] R. I. Rotberg, op. cit., p. 74; J. V. Taylor and D. A. Lehmann, op. cit., pp. 263 ff.
[53] R. I. Rotberg, op. cit., p. 69; J. V. Taylor and D. A. Lehmann, op. cit., p. 255, reject the idea that she was 'used by ruthless and politically ambitious men'.

reason to be hostile towards a very successful female rival who swept away within a couple of years their proselytizing work of decades, most commentators appear to accept the sincerity of Lenshina as a religious leader. The precise story of her visions is perhaps now beyond recall, since Lenshina's own accounts appear to have differed (a matter not usually of much importance to prophets). She was held in great awe by her followers, but she herself told interviewers that she had nothing new to teach, only opposition to greed and selfishness, and that in her church people found the power to resist temptations. Her status was in many respects similar to that of a woman chief, rather than that of a semi-divine person, but her injunctions were impressively obeyed by her adherents.

The thaumaturgical character of the Lumpa Church is evident in the importance attached to Lenshina's healing ability; in the emphasis on baptism (by sprinkling) at her hands alone; in the stories of a never-diminishing supply of holy water with which she performed baptism; and most of all in the movement's potency against witches. Lenshina gathered from her converts all their implements both for making magic and for protection from magic, and accumulated these in a large hut at her village, Kasomo—to illustrate their impotence against God's power. Adversaries have likened her healing practice to the traditional cult of *ngulu* possession, a name used for secondary deities who dwell in waterfalls, large trees, or pythons, and for a person possessed by such a deity. 'The *ngulu* prophesy and heal, that is they have the power to find under whose authority is the spirit who troubles the sick person. When this is established, the sick person is initiated, and on joining the society of the *ngulu*—"It is a kind of church", one of our informants said—his sickness will stop.'[54] Lenshina's name, Mulenga, is that of one of the best known *ngulu*, and may evoke 'the idea of a supernatural being, whose concern is with healing'.[55]

The importance of the Lumpa Church as an anti-witchcraft movement is readily evident. The fight against witchcraft was the subject of some of Lenshina's earliest discourses, and it features prominently in the laws of the church. 'Since 1955 Lenshina's energies have been devoted primarily to the eradication of witchcraft.'[56] Her movement almost amounts to a holy war against witches. It will be recalled that this area of Northern Rhodesia had previously known anti-witchcraft movements. It was among the Bemba that Richards saw the vigorous operation of the Bamucapi in 1934, and the Bemba were especially

[54] J. V. Taylor and D. A. Lehmann, ibid., p. 267.
[55] Ibid.
[56] R. I. Rotberg, op. cit., p. 70.

suggestible about the efficacy of their anti-witchcraft medicines. It seems unlikely that the same areas which accepted Lenshina in the late 1950s were not also influenced by the Bwanali-Mpulumutsi movement in 1947–8. At an early date in the emergence of Lenshina's following the District Commissioner at Chinsali interviewed Lenshina about her vision to discover to what extent she was acting as a witch-finder—a role strictly forbidden by government ordinance. But Lenshina was not accusing individuals of witchcraft: like members of the Bwanali-Mpulumutsi movement, she allowed those with wizardry objects to bring them to her and be cleansed. 'A District officer wrote in 1955: "The extent of her following—60,000 pilgrims to her village in one year —is an indication of how unsatisfying the modern missionary approach to witchcraft is for the majority of Africans. Lenshina does not say that witchcraft is nonsense, but that she has been given the power to neutralize it." '[57]

Unlike earlier movements the Lumpa Church had, perhaps almost by fortuitous circumstance, come to evolve a relatively stable church structure, and to embrace a persisting preoccupation of African religion within it. It accepted the Protestant mission pattern and the body of mission teaching, and adapted it to African demands. The movement was not anti-white in origin, and Lenshina always rejected the suggestion that it was, even though some of her followers were suspicious of whites (perhaps understandably after their condemnation by the Catholic missions). Europeans believed that the movement was probably under the control of men with strong anti-white sentiments. Robert Kaunda, the brother of Kenneth Kaunda, first prime minister of Zambia, was active in the movement. According to one report, a song beginning 'The white men are your enemies' was also popular among Lenshina's followers.[58] The rules of the movement, however, emphatically rejected racial discrimination, and declared, '. . . white and black men and women shall be Brotherhood and love each other'.[59] The question which puzzled some observers, when in 1964 armed conflict arose between the Lumpa Church and the government forces, was, 'What has been the reason for turning a reformist sect into a

[57] Cited by J. V. Taylor and D. A. Lehmann, op. cit., p. 266. The significance of the control of magic in the establishment of the church is also recognized by the Government Commissioners who enquired into the church after its dissolution in 1964. They wrote 'It was undoubtedly Alice Lenshina's reputed ability to release people from witchcraft on which the strength of the Lenshina movement was to be based'.—*Report of the Commission of Inquiry into the former Lumpa Church* (Government Printer, Lusaka 1965).

[58] Christine Heward, 'The Rise of Alice Lenshina', *New Society* 98 (13 August 1964), pp. 6–8.

[59] This quotation is from the version of the rules of the church given by Canon M. A. C. Warren, in a letter to the *Guardian*, cited in *East Africa and Rhodesia*, 20 August 1964, 40, p. 940.

fanatical one ?'[60] The millennium was little stressed, perhaps surprisingly little, in a region long infiltrated by Jehovah's Witnesses and the local Watchtower variant of their ideas. But the continuities in healing practice are evident, and, in a society in which the traditional protectors of the social order from evil, the witch-finders and diviners, were prohibited by government ordinance from operating, the Lumpa Church legitimated in Christian terms the thaumaturgical response to persisting need.

*   *   *

The examination of thaumaturgical movements in the country that is now Zambia and in immediately adjacent areas reveals a steady evolution of organizational structure in such movements, as western models of religious institutions have been increasingly imitated, and traditional preoccupations have been regulated by these new organizational patterns. The thaumaturgical response, as we have noted, does not readily lend itself, even in the context of western society, to stable sect organization of the type found in conversionist, revolutionist, and introversionist movements. The frequent particularism of thaumaturgical concerns, and the usual dependence of such movements on the

[60] Canon M. A. C. Warren, ibid. The specific causes of this conflict, in which 587 people died in three weeks of fighting, do not directly concern us. The trouble appears to have arisen from resistance to being canvassed by the United National Independence Party. The party, which formed the first Zambian government, regarded Lumpa members not only as indifferent to politics, but 'anti-politics', according to Mainza Chona, Minister of Justice in Northern Rhodesia. Ibid, p. 941.

An 'Official Description of the Lumpa Church' printed in *East Africa and Rhodesia*, 20 August 1964, 40, pp. 941-2 and 950, suggests that in fact the Church lost members to UNIP in the period 1960-2, and that 'No Lumpa Church members registered as voters in the general election in October 1962, following Lenshina's decree that members should have nothing to do with politics'. Lenshina-ists feared government action against them when it became evident that UNIP would win the election, and their desertion of their villages and establishment of separate settlements (twenty-two illegal settlements were established in the Chinsali district, six in Kasama district, three in Isoka district, and six in Lundazi district, with a total of over 6,700 adults) appears to have led directly to government action. A relatively minor incident led to the fighting. In the early conflicts between members of UNIP and the members of the Lumpa Church, the Lumpa had suffered 14 persons murdered, 121 houses, 28 churches, and 28 grain bins destroyed by fire. UNIP had suffered 7 persons murdered, 2 houses and 2 grain bins destroyed by fire.—*Report of the Commission of Inquiry*, op. cit. Although the party was almost certainly mainly responsible for beginning the trouble with the Church, it was the Church which was banned: the party, of course, was the Government party.

Central African political parties have shown themselves persistently intolerant of religious sects where members wish not to vote. The UNIP in Zambia attacked Jehovah's Witnesses in Luapula Province in early 1969, burning down their Kingdom Halls: *East African Standard* 6 February 1969. Later that same year hundreds of Jehovah's Witnesses were forced to flee into the bush when UNIP members set fire to their homes: *Daily Nation* (Nairobi) 26 June 1969. In October 1972, Malawi's Congress Party members caused more than 8,000 Jehovah's Witnesses to flee from that country to Mozambique and over 10,000 to Zambia: *Daily Telegraph* 19 and 23 October 1972.

special competence of the thaumaturge, make it difficult to establish persisting organizational structures. The search for therapy, relief from spirit possession, or the overcoming of witchcraft are primarily individual concerns. Momentarily, witches are seen as a social problem, but only because there is a distributive incidence of witchçraft: the anti-witchcraft movement is a vehicle for men to make common cause to meet a widely-spread but individually-felt evil. The movement is an ephemeral fashion in problem-solving, and lacks the shared basis of action to become an enduring organization. Since evil is seen as a consequence of spasmodic and random individual action rather than as a consequence of permanent deficiencies in social structure, what is needed to destroy evil is not a programme, a policy, or a prophecy of transformation, but only repeated performances, *ad hoc* and *ad hominem*. Strictly, such performances do not require more than limited local organization, although thaumaturgy may be co-ordinated within organized movements with complex bureaucratic structures.[61] But in simple societies such organizational models are frequently not available, and there is a manifest dissonance between the emotional orientations of thaumaturgy and the rationalism of bureaucratic structures. It is, then, all the more remarkable that West African movements of an essentially thaumaturgical type should have developed relatively stable organization. They have done so, of course, in direct imitation of missions, which, because of their rejection of belief in wizardry and their surrender of healing practice to medicine, do not provide expression for thaumaturgical response or for any other type of sectarian response to the world.

---

[61] Thaumaturgical movements modelled on tribal systems are discussed in Chapter 5.

4

Thaumaturgical Persistence in Non-Tribal Societies

THAUMATURGICAL preoccupations are not easily embraced within stable, consciously-organized associations which serve local congregations. The commitment of the clientele is particularistic, and the independent entrepreneurship of practitioners difficult to contain within such stable systems. But thaumaturgy has become organized into such associations in some instances. It is an apparent paradox that this should not have occurred so conspicuously in advanced countries, but in Africa. That thaumaturgical movements are so unstable in advanced western nations, illustrates again the dissonance between thaumaturgical response on the one hand, and the dominant cultural, intellectual, and emotional sophistication of these industrial societies, on the other. Africans have welded the many individual thaumaturgical demands into synthetic and persisting communities similar to other sects, and this is a unique syncretistic achievement.

Thaumaturgy is diffuse and institutionalized in tribal society. If anxiety causes greater recourse to sources of supernatural aid, and there is evidence to suggest that this is so, then, when tribal structures are disintegrating, thaumaturgical practice is likely to be stimulated. Growth may occur haphazardly in the multiplication of many different and unassociated local practices. It also occurs in the spread of very specific thaumaturgical techniques of curing, protection from witches, and miracle-working instituted through a movement. Traditional community organization, however, is now a less viable context for thaumaturgy, but among peoples being detribalized new models of religious organization do already exist. These are the missions, which have been everywhere imported. But the missions—a few small sects apart[1]—have traditionally made little accommodation for local

---

[1] The influence of western sectarian missions not only in accommodating, but often also in reinforcing, thaumaturgical demands in African communities has never been specifically studied. (There are studies, as earlier chapters have shown, of their influence on revolutionist millennial movements.) Many sects, the basic orientation of which is conversionist, none the less emphasize healing. Some of these groups have considerably strengthened African thaumaturgy and have unwittingly given it new forms of expression. See, for excellent

thaumaturgical demand. These two cultural deficiencies, the unsatisfied growing demand for the supernatural assuagement of anxiety, and the breakdown of traditional community organization, have readily become associated with another: the absence of leadership roles in colonial (and post-colonial) African societies. In the colonial period new religious movements provided one of the few opportunities for social mobility and for the exercise of leadership. Given the failure of the missions to accommodate the principal religious preoccupations of the indigenous population, and their rigorous attitudes towards various aspects of African culture, of which polygyny is perhaps the most important, an incentive to satisfy various social needs was created.[2] New religious organizations could meet all these demands simultaneously. The European mission, with its rational authority structure and co-ordinated hierarchy, becomes a model for indigenous movements. Without the model of the mission, various West African movements and the Lumpa Church in Rhodesia would hardly have been possible. Nor perhaps would even some of the movements that arose in South Africa, even though these were developed on more specifically tribal lines.

The thaumaturgical movements in advanced societies tend to serve unadjusted and marginal individuals, and particularly those who are marginal by virtue of sudden affliction and inability to benefit from, or even to accept, culturally prescribed remedies. (The marginal ethnic and migrant groups of advanced societies do not normally respond thaumaturgically to their situation, which is more completely *socially* conditioned. Their more typical responses are more total than those of thaumaturgy, and tend to involve more *implicit* collective, and sometimes even communal, bases of organization—found most typically in conversionist movements.[3]) Those who are marginal by virtue of affliction to which they have not adjusted are those with ailments, bereavements, and spirit preoccupations, or who seek reassurance about

---

illustrations of this process, J. D. Y. Peel, *Aladura* (Oxford University Press, London 1969), in which the significant role of the (British) Apostolic Church—a pentecostal body which practised divine healing—on two Nigerian independent churches is brought out. Some aspects of similar developments are mentioned in J. M. Assimeng, *A Sociological Analysis of the Impact and Consequences of some Christian Sects in Selected African Countries*, Unpub. D.Phil thesis, University of Oxford, 1968. The Christian Apostolic Church in Zion of Alexander Dowie had an extensive and widely diffuse influence in South Africa.

[2] For evidence of the extent of this particular incentive for Africans to establish separatist churches, see David B. Barrett, *Schism and Renewal in Africa* (Oxford University Press, Nairobi 1968).

[3] See, on the religion of immigrant ethnic minorities, M. J. C. Calley, *God's People: West Indian Pentecostal Sects in England* (Oxford University Press, London 1965); R. Poblete and T. O'Dea, 'Anomie and the "Quest for Community": the Formation of Sects among Puerto Ricans of New York', *American Catholic Sociological Review* XXI, 1 (1960), pp. 18–36.

their prospects. Such a collection of individuals does not correspond to particular communities or social strata, but they are drawn together in meetings which offer specific forms of thaumaturgical solace. Quite apart from this explicit thaumaturgical practice, there is, among the general populace of advanced societies, a fainter but more widely diffused demand for mild thaumaturgical practice, which is not organized in a distinctive thaumaturgical movement. The great religions are multi-functional and, despite their preoccupation with the suppression of magic,[4] thaumaturgy is part of their tradition, and has sometimes been an important part of their practice. Dramatic thaumaturgy, even in the mock re-enactment of mythical miracles, persists in liturgy or festivals in the practice (if not in the teachings) of all these religions. There is a widespread and sustained demand for religious solace, and for mental and spiritual healing, if not for physical healing, in contemporary Christendom.[5] Wonder-working, and even simulated wonder-working, fulfilling recreational as well as religious functions, has been a commonplace outside, as well as within, religious traditions. Even today clairvoyance and fortune-telling, although less seriously regarded, still evoke interest. Stories of witches and magicians—perhaps even serious discourses on witchcrfta movements!—have their appeal. Imaginings of invisibility and of the ability to transport oneself instantly by thought to far-away places, of power to transcend normal causation in space, time, and matter, are the stuff of day-dreams as well as of television serials. The use of the words 'magic', 'witchcraft', and 'fantastic' in songs, advertisements, and everyday speech, and the persistence of astrology columns in mass-circulation newspapers, even if they are 'only for fun', indicate the sustained power of thaumaturgical ideas.

Even the sophisticated populations of more advanced countries are liable to accept new movements which promise new, normally unattainable, powers of mastery, mind-control, cosmic consciousness, radiance, or inner calm. These are usually manipulationist movements, of course, but among less-educated and less emotionally controlled sections of the population thaumaturgical cults sometimes persist.

---

[4] The suppression of magic in the great religious traditions is given particular attention by Max Weber, in *The Sociology of Religion* (Methuen, London 1965), translated from *Wirtschaft und Gesellschaft* (Mohr, Tübingen 1925) by Ephraim Fischoff. On England in the sixteenth and seventeenth centuries, see Keith Thomas, *Religion and the Decline of Magic* (Weidenfeld and Nicolson, London 1971).

[5] For a careful documentation of the persistent demand in the United States for comfort and pastoral care (which is in itself a mild and attentuated demand for the thaumaturgical aspects of religion), see Charles Y. Glock, Benjamin B. Ringer, and Earl R. Babbie, *To Comfort and to Challenge* (University of California Press, Berkeley and Los Angeles 1967).

Their continuance as religious affiliations for some may coincide with interest in them as recreational activities for others. Popular spiritualism, ouiji boards, up-turned glasses, and other 'home-made' devices have their periods of spasmodic fashion; the seance, the encounter with the occult, and the sight of spirit-possession are excitements to people who do not give complete credence to such things as 'genuine' religious phenomena.[6] Our interest in thaumaturgical practice is as a religious response to the world for people who feel the need for immediate and personal reassurance that benevolent, supernatural agencies are active on their behalf. In America and Europe religious thaumaturgy is manifested most in relation to bereavement. This development has occurred at a time when the efficacy of religious rites and the truth of Christian teachings concerning death have become subject to increasing and pervasive scepticism, and when attitudes towards death are unsupported by intellectual convictions and stable social norms.[7]

In less-developed societies, where medical practice has been intimately involved with religious ritual, and where modern medical services are scarce, thaumaturgy has been concerned with healing as well as with death. In societies where empirico-rational assumptions about the material world are less comprehended, insights, reassurances, and magical practices of older cultural traditions persist. They are sustained in special cult developments, as substitute religions, which continue as an expression of widespread but tolerated doubt and ignorance about the way in which the social system functions. Where the certainties of everyday life are threatened by the inefficiency and corruption of the social system; where coercive political agencies operate in unpredictable, spasmodic, or uncomprehended ways; where a modern state apparatus has been imposed on a population with limited literacy and sophistication; and where there is an amorphous admixture of traditions, religions, values, and life-styles—we can expect the thaumaturge to have a thriving practice. He is the agent who offers particularistic reassurance in a situation where no general reassurances are credible.

[6] The incidence of possession among peoples of diverse religious traditions, including the Judeo-Christian religion, both in its biblical traditions and in the lives of the saints of the Catholic Church, is documented in T. E. Oesterreich, *Possession: Demoniacal and Other* (University Books, New York 1966), translated from the German by D. Ibberson.

[7] For a discussion of the significance of *rites de passage* in an otherwise largely secular context, see B. R. Wilson, *Religion in Secular Society* (Watts [New Thinkers' Library], London 1966), especially pp. 2–18. Although not specifically concerned with the difficulty of contemporary Christianity in handling the problem of death and bereavement, a discussion of the decline of mourning rites, and of the embarrassment felt in contemporary society concerning death, will be found in Geoffrey Gorer, *Death, Grief and Mourning* (Cresset Press, London 1965).

Thaumaturgy in a Catholic context

Circumstances such as those described above are to be found in many parts of the world, but perhaps there is no society with so rich a profusion of thaumaturgical cults as Brazil, with its part-acculturated indigenous population, and the uneradicated traditions of its immigrants. In some measure similar considerations apply to the Caribbean countries, but these cults are exceptionally profuse in Brazil. Strong elements of African religion persisted among the slave populations, and thaumaturgical practices survived more easily in the new environment than did those rituals and practices which had meaning only within the social structure of tribal life. Tribal deities and deities associated with fixed locations necessarily lost significance or acquired new functions among detribalized slaves. The integrative functions of religion for tribal groups were now no longer relevant, but the therapeutic and psychic functions of traditional religion, the practice of the thaumaturge in putting individuals into contact with ancient and traditional sources of power and reassurance, acquired new appeal. In a limited way, and without the firm social structural foundations of religion in the African context, these practices developed, not as manifestations and exacerbations of anomie as some have supposed, but to provide both personal and group satisfactions.[8]

Neither in Brazil, nor in those parts of the Caribbean where Catholic colonists were dominant, was there an intensive effort to eradicate these magical practices. Protestantism in the southern states of the United States did attain that end, partly as a consequence of the dominance of the white colonists and the segregation of Africans, and partly because of the rigour of Protestantism itself.[9] Protestantism eliminated the persisting magical elements in Christianity and its sacramental and sacerdotal aspects. In its more rigorous forms it denied men any possibility of manipulating supernatural agencies. The practice of any-

---

[8] The social functions of the Afro-Brazilian cults are emphasized by Roger Bastide, *Le Candomblé de Bahia (Rite Nagô)* (Mouton, Paris 1958), who writes (p. 215), 'Certains Blancs ont voulu voir dans le candomblé une orgie; c'est bien plutôt une *éthique*. L'élévation sociale ne se réalise pas par une rupture de la solidarité; elle en est, au contraire, le base la plus solide.'

[9] Protestantism in the British West Indies worked in the same direction in the elimination of magic. The African inheritance in Jamaica is much more attentuated than that which persists in Brazil or Haiti, although it is continued in *Cumina* ceremonies: it is regarded by some writers as evident in Pocomania (see p. 59), and certainly in Obeah magic. Except in the last case African elements are vague and perhaps simulated in a structure overlaid by Christian procedures and practices. For a brief discussion, see Joseph G. Moore, 'Religious Syncretism in Jamaica', *Practical Anthropology* 12: 2 (March–April 1965), pp. 63–70.

thing suggestive of sympathetic magic, such as occurs in a Roman mass or in the theory of transubstantiation, was rejected. Catholicism was less able to eliminate aboriginal magical practice, and tended rather to absorb indigenous practices and re-interpret them. In Brazil, Catholicism co-existed with both aboriginal and imported thaumaturgical traditions, and they acquired from it elements that were built into their syncretistic configuration. Protestantism emphasizes the appeal to scripture, tolerance, and liberty of conscience in interpretation, but it insists upon exclusivity of commitment, and rejects irrational acceptance of the mutually contradictory. It rejects diversity within the fellowship, but often requires free association and congregational democracy.

Thus Protestantism creates circumstances propitious for the growth of sects. Catholicism, by contrast, accommodates local, indigenous peculiarities by permitting divergences within the church, but is intolerant towards groups which remain outside, and particularly to those which do so by appeal to alternative Christian standards. Whereas Protestantism relies on the self-control of the laity, Catholicism relies on hierarchic control of the priests: once priestly authority is recognized, the actual commitments of the laity may, in some circumstances, be not too closely questioned. In the face of Protestant rigour, and partly as an expression of that rigour, sects arise. Catholicism suppresses sects but permits cults, which though not formally sanctioned, are often not too closely examined, as long as their members remain within the church. In the heavily Catholic countries, such cults are regularized and formalized into part of the church life, but where, as in Brazil, the church has never had sufficient numbers of priests to control the religious life of the population, many cultists are only nominal Catholics, and the cults stand alongside the church. The church lost the support of the secular power when the Brazilian republic was created in 1889. Church and state were separated in the following year, and thereafter the allegiance of cultists to Catholicism might well be no more than a matter of form. Occasionally, nominal allegiance to the Church became a protection for cultists, but they were not usually orthodox believers: their religious satisfactions were principally from thaumaturgical practice.[10]

The thaumaturgical movements in Brazil usually operate in highly

[10] Thomas Lynn Smith, *Brazil: People and Institutions*, Rev. Edn (Louisiana State University Press, Baton Rouge 1963), p. 511, writes, 'Most of the differentiation along religious lines has occurred within or been incorporated into the general framework of this universal body [the Roman Catholic Church]. Even the members of the African cults that survive in Bahia, Rio de Janeiro, Pernambuco and other states are nearly always nominal Catholics.' And 'where religious syncretism has involved the blending of cultural elements derived from aboriginal Indian sources with Christianity, the process also has gone on within the broad framework of the Catholic faith'.

localized centres. They may be readily grouped in certain broad species, each species including many individual local places of assembly, with independent operators. There is no central hierarchy and no denominational structure. They do not conform to the organizational pattern of church, sect, or denomination. The Protestant mission, which in Africa supplied the model for thaumaturgical practice, has been a marginal phenomenon in Brazil, and one which came upon the scene long after thaumaturgical cults had become widespread. Thaumaturgy is usually practised in a context over which the thaumaturge has complete control. Those he serves are less likely to be a settled congregation than a clientele: he needs a centre rather than a constituted association. The organizational focus is not 'the group' so much as 'the shrine', the *terreiro*. Shrines may be numerous, but they are more often replications one of another (even if with variations) than elements in an organized system. The power of the thaumaturge is local, immediate, and particularized, and in Brazil there appears to be less association between shrines than in Africa.

Possession cults in Brazil

The Afro-Brazilian cult movements are dramatic manifestations of the continuance of thaumaturgical demand among less-privileged populations in Brazilian cities.[11] They are highly localized in different urban contexts, where the slaves, who were freed in 1888, largely remained. The slaves in the north and north-east were predominantly from West Africa, and included Yoruba, Nagô, Oyo, Ibeju, and Egba from what is now Nigeria; Ewe and Fon of the Gêge group from what is now Dahomey; and Fanti, Ashanti, and other tribes from present-day Ghana. Elements of Gêge-Nagô culture seem to have survived best, and this term is now commonly applied to the African culture of the north-east, and in particular to that of Bahia (mainly Yoruba) and Maranhão (mainly Dahomean).[12] Bantu culture was dominant and is still evident further south in the cult movements of Rio de Janeiro and

[11] The most thorough discussion, on which this section relies, is R. Bastide, *Les religions africaines au Brésil* (Presses universitaires de France, Paris 1960). Healing success is achieved, according to Ribeiro, by the projective mechanisms that the operational techniques of the cults elicit. He administered a Rorschach test to a cult adherent, and this was interpreted by cultists as itself a new divinatory technique. Each subject gave interpretations based on personal preoccupations. René Ribeiro, 'Problemática Pessoal e Interpretação divinatória nos cultos afro-brasileiros do Recife', *Revista do Museu Paulista* X (1956/8), pp. 225–42.

[12] Arthur Ramos, 'The Negro in Brazil' in Thomas Lynn Smith and Alexander Marchant (Eds), *Brazil: Portrait of Half a Continent* (Dryden Press, New York 1951), pp. 125–46.

Niterói, in which Angolan influences are still predominant. The Afro-Brazilian thaumaturgical cults that flourish in thousands in the cities of Brazil are thus regionally distinguished according to the distribution of negro cultures. In some places they have also been fused with thaumaturgical practice and traditions of spirit possession from indigeneous Indian culture. The Gêge-Nagô cult of Bahia is known as *candomblé*; in Recife the cults are *xangôs*, after the name of the deity (Shango), who is also prominent in those Caribbean islands in which African religion persists; in part of the north-east the cults are known as *catimbós*; in Rio de Janeiro and Niterói they are *macumbas*; in Port Alegré the corresponding phenomenon is called *batuque*; and in Maranhão it is *Tambor-de-Mina*. All of these cults have much in common, and in particular the centrality of spirit-possession.[13]

A common feature of these cults is the multiplicity of deities who attend at one shrine, each of whom possesses his own particular *filhas de santo*, novice priestesses. The deities are common to the shrines within a given cultural tradition and many of them can be directly traced to African origins.[14] In the course of time, local cults have been affected, however vaguely, by the Catholic church, and these deities have, in consequence, acquired corresponding Christian designations, as members of the Trinity, the Virgin Mother, saints, or angels, in an elaborate syncretism of nomenclature and symbolism. Some authorities believe that this identification of the spirits of the shrine with entities from the Catholic pantheon was a deliberate attempt by the negroes to avoid police persecution at certain periods.[15]

The typical *candomblé* in Bahia is a small shrine, a cluster of buildings in which the various gods, the priest (*babalorixá* or *candomblezeiro*) or priestess (*ialorixá*), and the *filhas de santo* all have rooms. Most important, there is also a space in which dancing and spirit possession take place. There is usually a special place for drums and a Catholic-type altar, and a prominent central post which some authorities have described as a cosmic phallic symbol.[16] Each *candomblé* is autonomous under its *babalorixá* or *ialorixá*, usually called *pai-de-santo* (holy father) or *mãe-de-santo* (holy mother). This leader magically prepares the fetiches, and commands a retinue of the *filhas de santo*, sacrifice-priests, altar-boys, and

[13] This nomenclature is derived from R. Bastide, op. cit.; T. L. Smith, op. cit.; and Anatol H. Rosenfeld, 'Macumba', *Stadenjahrbuch* III (1955), pp. 125–40.

[14] For a detailed discussion of the diffusion of African elements, see R. Bastide, *Le Candomblé de Bahia*, op. cit.

[15] Kalvero Oberg, 'Afro-Brazilian Religious Cults', *Sociología* (São Paulo) XXI, 2 (May 1959), pp. 134–41. 'Later to protect themselves from police persecution the Negroes identified their deities with Christian saints and put their images in their temples', p. 134.

[16] A. H. Rosenfeld, op. cit.

assistants. The *filhas de santo* (called *ebomin* when they have spent seven years of dedicated service) are the vehicles for spirit-possession.

The deities, *orixás* (*orishas* elsewhere in africanized Latin America) have their own distinctive traits. In Bahia, the high god Oluran is no more than a presiding deity: the others are active deities, who represent both cosmic forces and ancestor cultural heroes, who are vaguely believed to be resident in Africa. One of the principal deities is Obatalá (also called Orixala or Oxala), who is often identified with Jesus or with the Holy Ghost, but who is also regarded as a bisexual deity representing the reproductive forces, who receives sacrifices of goats and pigeons and whose special day of celebration is Friday. Xangô, the thunder god, is popular, and in some areas in Brazil and in the Caribbean the whole cult is named after him. Yemanjá (or Janaína) is regarded as goddess of the sea, and is the object of a separate cult outside the *candomblés*. At one time she was a maternal figure but today she has been transformed into a Brazilian beauty: she has been identified with Our Lady of Rosario and with Nossa Senhora de Piedade. Identifications vary, but a god who is widely believed in is Exú, who is dually regarded as the spirit of evil or the Devil, but also, if correctly approached, as a messenger or servant of men. He alone is depicted by an idol: the rest are represented through their fetiches. He must be placated before *candomblé* activities begin, and he is given a preliminary sacrifice to induce him not to interfere with the proceedings that follow, since this would endanger the daughters of saintliness during their possession.[17]

The thaumaturgical performance of the *candomblé* is an elaborate ritual. The *filhas-de-santo* invoke the deities until each is possessed by her god. The *filhas* are recruited in response to a call or vision which draws them into the service of the god, and they then occupy their leisure hours at the shrine. They use their own money to provide offerings for the deity to which they are dedicated. The deities are each offered three songs by their votaries, in the presence of the large numbers who crowd in to see the gods appear in the persons of *filhas*, and who seek blessings from them. One by one the *filhas* are possessed, the phenomenon of *queda ho santo* (falling into the saint): they then withdraw and reappear dressed as the god, behaving in whatever way the god desires. They may counsel those who seek advice, receive obeisances, resolve quarrels, and always they dance out the history and story of the god. The observers come for solace, comfort, healing, and the experience of that sense of awe which is central to primitive religion.

Macumba in Rio shares many essentials with *candomblé* in Bahia,

---

[17] For fuller details see R. Bastide, *Les religions africaines au Brésil*, op. cit., and for a short account, A. H. Rosenfeld, op. cit.

although its rituals are less intense, and the *macumbas* lack the developed cults of fetich gods, although they have elaborate funeral and totemic ceremonies, and magical medicine.[18] The high priest, *umbanda*, is a typical thaumaturge, who has, however, a less elaborate liturgical style of his own, and who has often adopted the style of the Gêge-Nagô culture from further north. Importance is attached to the role of the *defumador*, who purifies the shrine or *terreiro* with a censer. Spirit-possession normally occurs in the priest, but the spirit is less a protector than a familiar, usually an old negro, such as Pai Joaquim or Vehlo Lourenqo. He gives advice, and undertakes healing. Identification of deities occurs, as in the *candomblés*—the Senhor do Bomfin (Jesus) with Oxalá, St George with Oxossi, and São Jeronomo with Xangô.

Both cults represent thoroughly characteristic thaumaturgical responses to the world. This is most pronounced for the *filhas*, of course, who are devotees whose status is that of a third order. They are usually lower-class working negro women, laundresses, seamstresses, maids, who at night become living gods, ecstatically possessed, dispensing solace, advice, comfort, and admonition. They participate in a religion which, for them and for the congregation, is more than mere symbolic representation. In the ecstasy of the dance the self is abandoned, and the sufferings of the world are transcended in the very being of the god or in his presence and intimate contact. 'The living thus hold communion with the gods, and ancestral spirits. This is not a remote symbolic spiritual communion as in Catholicism nor a largely accidental contact with the dead as in spiritualism. The celestial world is not remote and superior. The gods mix with the living, they can be touched, talked to. . . .'[19]

The diversity of African cults in Brazil, and the mutations and variants of practice and belief, make difficult the systematic categorization of the many movements involved. Categorization itself belongs to an ordered world where distinctions are made clear, where principles of exclusivity and rejection of intellectual contradiction are established, and where boundaries are firmly drawn and well maintained. This is not the condition of the innumerable local autonomous cults of Brazilian cities. The various traditions have influenced each other and perhaps re-infected each other and, as we shall shortly see, have merged with other thaumaturgical currents in the stream of Brazilian culture. Before turning to that particular syncretism, however, one case of Brazilian spirit-possession which illustrates how thaumaturgical religion is almost

[18] T. L. Smith, *Brazil: People and Institutions*, op. cit., p. 541.
[19] K. Oberg, op. cit., p. 140. A. H. Rosenfeld, op. cit., writes of the meaning of possession: 'es ist nicht nur Zelebrierung des Göttergeschehens, sondern ist zugleich dieses selbst. Das Symbol und das Symbolisierte sind Eins' (p. 137).

explicitly adapted to fulfil recreational functions is worth mentioning.

Among the *butuques* in Belém, the port city of the Amazon, where some forty Afro-Brazilian *terreiros* cater to the local population, one variant of the *candomblé* style has been influenced by Amer-Indian culture. Drums and dancing occur as in the *candomblés*, but the less-elevated spirits, *encantados*, who possess their devotees in these *terreiros* are described as *senhores* (nobles) or *caboclos* (yokels).[20] The *caboclos* are essentially fun-loving deities, *brincalones*, jokers, who, though occupying lesser roles in the ritual, and never having festivals organized in their honour, none the less provide these cults with a distinctive character. While the *senhores* are identified with Catholic saints, the *caboclos* are semi-illegitimates in the pantheon whose status allows them to behave less responsibly. The procedure is similar to that of the Bahian *candomblé*, but the devotees are possessed by a *senhor* and a *caboclo* in succession, although in theory the latter is not supposed to appear before midnight. In practice, possession by the condescending *senhor* quickly gives place to a *caboclo* possession which may last hours or days. The *caboclo* sometimes cures, but frequently jokes, goes wild, smokes, drinks, strips naked —all while the medium is, of course, unconscious of the acts which the god is performing in her person. The mixture of ritualism and hedonism does not stem from Indian shamanism, where curing is always serious and deities are often malicious: it may derive from the child-like deities of African tradition, associated with the developed demand for the entertainment of the fiesta, which characterizes Brazil.

Syncretic spiritualism: Umbanda

An unusual syncretism which has occurred in Brazil has been the fusion of African traditions of spirit-possession, particularly as represented in *macumba*, with a rudimentary type of spiritualism derived in the later nineteenth century from the modern style of spiritualism then developing in America and Europe.[21] This movement, again more a congeries of autonomous local shrines, takes its name from the *macumba* priests (or mediums) of *Umbanda*, and had acquired an independent character by about 1930, but gained a mass following only after the Second World War.[22] Unlike the spiritualists of the western tradition, the Umbandists do not seek communication with the spirits of the recently dead. They seek instead the spirits of individuals long dead, whose lives earned for

[20] This paragraph relies entirely on Seth Leacock, 'Fun-Loving Deities in an Afro-Brazilian Cult', *Anthropological Quarterly* 37: 3 (July 1964), pp. 94–109.
[21] See p. 117.
[22] R. Bastide, op. cit.

them a blessed condition in the hereafter. The cult *terreiro* is organized similarly to the more African *macumba terreiro*, and liturgical practice is similar, with the possession of the medium by Petros Vehlos or some other named spirit. The deities who are invoked are classifiable into seven different lineages, each with its own nominally traditional character. Thus the *linha de Oxalá* (Jesus) are all Christian saints; those of the *linha de Oxosse* (St Sebastian—a saint of particular importance as the awaited cultural hero who will return heading the holy armies, in Portuguese-Brazilian messianic tradition) have exclusively Indian-Brazilian names; the *linha africana*, though headed by St Cyprian, has deities with African names.[23] The officers of the *terreiro* include the *pai-de-santo* or *mãe-de-santo*, *filhas* as mediums, with *cambones* (assistants) and a *defumador*, but also, and this appears to be distinctive, there is usually a president who judges community officers and other secular officers, who are distinguished from those on the spiritual side.

Umbanda is also distinguished from other Afro-Brazilian cults by its rejection of animal sacrifices. Nor is the *despachos* of *macumba*, the ritual in which offerings are made (for example to placate Exú and to induce him to go away), performed, although there is a similar ritual which is regarded as *obrigações*, thank-offerings. Umbandists regard themselves as free from the more primitive elements of other cults of the Afro-Brazilian tradition.[24] They distinguish themselves from other spiritualists by their rejection of communication with any but those who, through saintly lives, have attained the wisdom to act as guides to the living, and these are seen rather as deities than as mere spirits. They also distinguish their own ritual sharply from the practice known as *quimbanda*, which is a form of black magic and sorcery. During spirit-possession glossalalia occurs, graphic symbols are employed, burning ordeals are sometimes undertaken, and the drumming, singing, dancing, and consultation with the gods found in the other cults that draw on the African tradition. The leader of the session retains a certain control in Umbanda *terreiros*, and although practice varies from shrine to shrine, the leader is usually master of the spirits.[25]

[23] According to Richard W. Brackman, 'Der Umbanda-Kult in Brasilien', *Stadenjahruch* 7/8 (1959–60), pp. 157–73, and Candido Procópio Ferreira de Camargo, *Kardecismo e Umbanda: Uma interpretação sociológica* (Livraria Pioneira Editôra, São Paulo 1961), pp. 36–8.

[24] R. Bastide, op. cit., p. 432.

[25] Ibid., p. 438. The extent to which Umbanda practice derives directly from Africa as a Bantu tradition need not detain us. Bastide has suggested this in his extensive treatment of the subject. Ferreira de Camargo, op. cit., p. 34, says of this theory: 'E possível. Não cremos, entretanto, que tenha havido na cidade de São Paulo uma *continuidade* cultural de tradição africana que chegasse até nossos dias, como sucede na Bahia. A Umbanda paulista é importada dos outros Estados e seu poder de expansão se encontra na functionalidade de seu sistema e não na fôrça de inercia de uma tradição cultural. Alem do mais, a Umbanda não constitui um fenômeno racialmente africanista em São Paulo.'

In the typical tradition of thaumaturgical practice, the Umbandists are locally autonomous, and display many variations of liturgical, doctrinal, and organizational detail. But just as they have sought to distinguish themselves from cruder elements in the African tradition, they have also sought to adopt more sophisticated organizational forms. The patterns of organization introduced by the spiritualists of the western world have provided an imitable pattern, even though Umbandists feign to despise the spirits evoked in *Kardecism*, the more westernized and intellectual form of spiritualism. Their *terreiros* are, today, organized into a number of unions, of which the chief is the *Confederação Espírita Umbandista*,[26] which attempt to represent the cultists and to protect them from police interference. At local level the Umbandists are a group of thaumaturges and clients, although some have tried to make their audiences into something more like a congregation. The gods are said to be wrathful when followers fail to participate in ritual activities, or to make suitable offerings to them.[27] (Such propitiations are extensively offered to the spirits, on highways, at crossroads, and at shrines throughout Brazil.[28]) This attempt to draw the clientele into a more stable pattern of involvement may represent an attempt to establish a more regular structure of religious organization. The Umbandists also appear to be developing an incipient theology and ecclesiology in keeping with their role as an urban religion.

Because Umbandists are only a loosely organized aggregation of cult centres, their numbers in Brazil are difficult to estimate. Typically they are officially registered as Catholics, and some writers regard the phenomenon as a typical paganization of Catholicism.[29] As many as eight million believers have been claimed, but it is not easy to distinguish Umbanda *terreiros* from *macumba* and other Afro-Brazilian cults, if indeed a real distinction exists. Reports suggest that such groups (and it is unclear what is included and what not) have grown from forty to four hundred in Bahia in fifty years; in Recife they grew from forty-eight to over a hundred in the period from 1947 to 1951; in São Paulo, whereas *terreiros* were scarcely known in 1925, there were 269 in 1945, and in Port Alegré they have grown from thirteen in 1937 to 211 in 1952.[30]

[26] C. P. Ferreira de Camargo, op. cit., p. 51, gives the name as Federação Espírita de Umbanda, with 260 *terreiros*.

[27] Emilio Willems, 'Religious Mass Movements and Social Change in Brazil' in Eric N. Baklanoff (Ed.), *New Perspectives of Brazil* (Vanderbilt University Press, Nashville, Tennessee 1966), pp. 205–32.

[28] For an account, see T. L. Smith, *Brazil: People and Institutions*, op. cit., especially pp. 543–9.

[29] Boaventura Kloppenburg, OFM, 'Der Brasilianische Spiritismus als Religiöse Gefahr', *Social Compass* V, 5–6 (1959), pp. 237–55.

[30] R. W. Brackman, op. cit., pp. 157–73.

Urban magic and rural Protestantism?

The growth of thaumaturgical movements in Brazil may, of course, be deceptive. It is likely that belief, and spasmodic if not sustained involvement, in thaumaturgical exercises has long characterized the bulk of the population of American-Indian and African descent. Since Catholicism did not eradicate magical ideas and activities, these have persisted in many places—not as distinctive cult movements, but as part of the general religious tradition.[31] Now in the urban centres the cult movements begin to take on new functions. They become conspicuous if only because their votaries are self-selected and go voluntarily to the *terreiros*. This pattern of thaumaturgy is not a traditional activity of total local communities, as thaumaturgy may have been in more rural settings. It begins to appear as a distinguishable and voluntary response, in isolation from the dominant religious tradition, and ill-adapted as it is as an orientation, it comes to be articulated in its own organizational structures. Thus, it may well be, not that there is a new commitment to thaumaturgy, so much as that this commitment has become more separated and more visible. In a period of urbanization and also of increasing religious differentiation in other directions, the development is entirely to be expected.[32]

[31] R. Bastide, 'Religion and the Church in Brazil' in T. L. Smith and A. Marchant, op. cit., pp. 334–55, writes 'Brazilian rural Catholicism is turned more toward the worship of the saints and the Virgin, than of God, and these saints vary according to the regions as well as according to families' (p. 346). Even in the cities there is, 'and especially in their lowest strata, a popular Catholicism, characterized by miraculous revelation and cures, and . . . the extraordinary and supernatural' (p. 348).

[32] This differentiation has occurred as Protestantism, and especially Pentecostalism, has grown in Brazil, partly in response to missionary activity, but largely as indigenous movements. See W. R. Read, *New Patterns of Church Growth in Brazil* (Eerdmans, Grand Rapids, 1965); E. Willems, op. cit., and E. Willems, *Followers of the New Faith* (Vanderbilt University Press, Nashville 1968). Tiago Cloin, 'Aspects socio-religieuses et sociographiques du Brésil', *Social Compass* V, 5–6 (1959), pp. 200–37, writes 'Actuellement, le Brésil est parmi tous les pays latino-americains l'État où le protestantisme gagne le plus de terrain' (p. 228), and this he attributes to the larger proportion of Protestant ministers to Protestants than of priests to Catholics: 'Tandis qu'en 1953, les 51,948,000 catholiques (soit 93 per cent de le population) avaient à leur disposition 8,712 prêtres (ce qui signifie un prêtre pour 5,393 catholiques) les 2 millions de protestants (3.4 per cent de la population) n'avaient en 1954 pas moins de 4,600 à leur disposition (1 pasteur pour 434 protestants).' A rather different picture is given by Isadoro Alonso, *La Iglesia en America Latina: Estructuras ecclesiásticas* (Feres, Freiburg, Switzerland, and Bogotá, Colombia 1964), working with later figures. He shows that there was one Roman Catholic priest (secular or religious) for approximately every 6,400 people in Brazil, and one for every 2,900 in Chile. Alonso seeks to show that in the areas of Chile and Mexico where there are the highest proportions of Protestants, there are also higher ratios of people per Roman Catholic priest. Of Brazil he writes, 'En Brasil, si se comparan las cifras al nivel de las extensas unidades civiles o Estados, no sólo no aparece la relación entre mayor numero de habitantes por sacerdote y mayor proporción de protestantes, sino que, en general,

The paradox of religious development in Brazil and other South American countries is that while the new incursions of Protestantism, and particularly of Pentecostalism, have had greatest impact in rural areas, where the control of the Catholic church is least effective, the Afro-Brazilian cults have, together with Kardecism, grown steadily in the cities where they originated.[33] Umbandist cults have multiplied. Not only has there been growth and the search for new organizational patterns, but even though very diverse practices persist, there has also been a development of doctrinal and ethical formulations. This may, as some authorities assert, be an accommodation of possession phenomena to the increasingly sophisticated urban context.[34] Mediumistic religion appears to be coming to terms with the problem of welding its votaries into more stable congregational organizations, and, in the new emphasis on ethical prescriptions, to be encouraging adherence to new and more intense personal norms, appropriate to urban life. The effectiveness of this development could no doubt be overstated, since even among the more sophisticated Kardecists, the mass of adherents are still interested more in physical and spiritual healing than in the maintenance of a rigorous ethical code.[35] Thaumaturgical demands do not cease as a movement adjusts to a changing environment, and develops, in some cases, more stable organizational forms. There may, however, be a more subtle shift of response involved in the attempt of some Umbandists to establish principles of doctrine. This may be the first sign of a re-interpretation of thaumaturgical practice into something that approximates an incipient form of manipulationist response. Among the Umbandists the process is so nascent that its development is

aparece en sentido opuesto. Efectivamente, en los Estados del Sur, donde se relativamente más abundante el clero, es donde se dan los mayores porcentajes de protestantes. Una causa historica, explica el hecho; la importancia de la inmigración protestante recibida por esta región en décadas pasadas' (p. 139). It is evident, however, that this relationship is scarcely operative between different countries, since Chile, which has a larger number of priests in relation to its population than Brazil, also has a larger percentage of Protestants (many of them Pentecostalists). See on Chilean Pentecostalism, C. A. Lalive d'Epinay, *Haven of the Masses* (Lutterworth Press, London 1970).

[33] C. P. Ferreira de Camargo, op. cit., p. 88. The following paragraph relies considerably on his analysis.

[34] Ferreira de Camargo, op. cit., p. 49, emphasizes that the doctrine of evolution, and the increased emphasis on personal ethics, serve as an instrument of adaptation of the African traditional religious practice to the style of rational urban life.

[35] Of the regular participants in Umbanda, Ferreira de Camargo, op. cit., p. 72, says 'Possuem um conhecimento precário de doutrina e estão afastados de intimidade do ritual'. Of the ordinary adherents of Kardecism, he says, 'Esta categoria constitui-se de indivíduos que vão buscar no Espiritismo sòmente confôrto espiritual ou alívio para seus problemas físicos e morais' (p. 74). Of all the mediumistic religions, he writes, 'Dificilmente poderíamos superestimar a importancia da esperça de cura no preceso de conversão ao "contiuum" mediúnico' (p. 94).

by no means clear. The existence of a flourishing rural Pentecostalism may even yet provide a different—more conversionist—model, particularly since Pentecostalism itself in some measure caters for thaumaturgical concerns. This is, of course, speculation: as yet, Kardecism is perhaps a clearer model for the Umbandists. It is itself an example of a thaumaturgical response, even if of a more sophisticated kind, that is undergoing some modification in the direction of manipulationism. But the eventual convergence of conversionist movements on the cities seems, given the policy that such movements pursue, almost predictable. Their central direction, whatever the appearances of local ecstasy and emotionalism, gives such movements a facility for operating in urban contexts. If Brazilian cities increasingly draw people from the countryside, Pentecostalism is likely to come with them, as fundamentalist and holiness religion has done in other countries, notably in the United States. The differences of the total social context might affect the extent to which such sects could facilitate urban adjustment, not least in respect of the dominant Protestantism of North America and the official Catholicism of Latin America. Rapid secularization of the total urban context might, of course, make such fundamentalist Protestantism itself incongruous, in which case the more rational and secularized style and the more limited collectivism of manipulationist responses might prove a more viable and congruous development.

Intellectual spiritualism

Brazil has inherited more than African and American traditions of thaumaturgy. It has been the world's most willing recipient of the thaumaturgical traditions evolved in nineteenth-century America and Europe. This tradition had its impact in Brazil in the 1870s, in particular in the writings of Léon Hyppolyte Dénizart Revaill (1804–69), whose works on spirit doctrine, published under the name of Alan Kardec,[36] rapidly gained a popularity there which they never enjoyed in his native France. Subsequently his teachings about mediumship and the temporary incarnation of the spirit of a dead person in a medium, were given a Brazilian interpretation by Francisco Candido Xavier, who claimed, perhaps not without justice, that Brazil was the world's centre for spiritualist Christian revival.[37]

[36] Kardec's best known works were *Le livre des esprits contenant les principes de la doctrine spirite* (1857) and *Le spiritisme à sa plus simple expression* (1864). His works, and those of his followers, C. Flammarion and L. Dennis, were translated and circulated in Brazil. B. Kloppenburg, op. cit.; C. P. Ferreira de Camargo, op. cit.

[37] E. Willems, 'Religious Mass Movements . . .', op. cit.

Kardecism, as a western religious system, lacks the animistic and poly-theistic elements of Umbanda. But its operation, accompanied with less ecstasy and more mysticism, appears to fulfil similar functions for its adherents. The mediums receive the spirits of light in their being, and through them advice, counsel, and solace are distributed. They acquire spiritual power, represented as fluids, which may be transmitted through them to the heads, arms, or shoulders of supplicants, and this has beneficial and therapeutic effects. The process of communication is held to be as beneficial for the dead as for the living, helping men to achieve perfection both in their earthly and spiritual lives. Men are believed to exist in a number of habitable worlds, through which spiritual progress is possible, dependent not on grace but on merit. Like Buddhism, Kardecism emphasizes charity as the principal virtue, and it accepts reincarnation theory. None the less belief in God is enjoined, albeit as a remote being who governs the world, and who has given men spirit-guides, chief among whom was Christ.[38] An articulated body of doctrine that can be set out as a set of interrelated propositions reflects the intellectual sophistication of the western world, although Kardecism in its official expression seeks to emphasize moral regenera-tion as well as its Christian inheritance of doctrine. It includes a theory that illness is caused by the 'fluidic' actions of disembodied spirits, or by Karmic tribulation.

Kardecism has been organized into associations since a *federação* was established in 1884, but it had ramified into twenty-one different associations by 1951.[39] The movement, unlike spiritualism in Europe or the United States, has concentrated on providing institutional welfare in hospitals, clinics, asylums, shelters, and schools on a scale which, given the estimated size of the movement, is more impressive than anything achieved by either the Roman Catholic church or the growing Protestant denominations in Brazil.[40] This is an entirely

[38] The principal doctrines of Kardecism are: (1) the possibility and ease of communication with spirits; (2) reincarnation; (3) no cause exists without an effect, so that no one can escape the consequences of his acts; (4) the plurality of inhabited worlds, each of which represents a stage of spiritual progress; (5) no distinction of natural and supernatural, or of science and religion: there is no grace, and individual progress depends exclusively on personal merit accumulated in earlier incarnations; (6) the principal virtue is charity as exercised towards the dead, the disembodied, and the living; (7) God is an immense distance from men; (8) there are important spirit-guides who help men; (9) Jesus Christ was the greatest incarnated being. These doctrines are set out in the two works on which this para-graph relies: C. P. Ferreira de Camargo, op. cit., p. 7 ff; and C. P. Ferreira de Camargo and J. Labbans, 'Aspects socio-culturels du spiritisme au Brésil', *Social Compass* VII, 5–6 (1960), pp. 407–30.
[39] E. Willems, op. cit.; B. Kloppenburg, op. cit.
[40] E. Willems, op. cit., p. 219.

unusual development for thaumaturgical movements, and may be the focus that provides a degree of organizational coherence in Kardecism, which spiritualists elsewhere have often lacked.

The absence of clear distinctions between spiritualists of different kinds (particularly between Kardecists and Umbandists), and the fact that many meet privately, and are officially classed as Catholics, make it difficult to estimate numbers. Some 680,000 spiritualists were officially recorded in Brazil in 1960.[41] But in the late 1950s there were some 7,000 spiritualist centres (of all kinds) in Rio alone, and one Catholic estimate for the archdiocese of Curitiba (capital of Paraná state) suggested that 40 per cent of the population was sympathetic to spiritualism.[42] In 1958, the spiritualists (who might include some Umbandists, although perhaps most were Kardecists) had almost as many welfare establishments in Brazil as the Roman Catholic church. They claimed to have provided hospital treatment for some 6,992 persons (compared with the Roman Catholic figure of 38,781, and the Protestant figure of 1,038), and they had provided assistance of some sort for 374,000 (compared to 503,000 persons assisted by the Catholics and 34,000 by the Protestants).[43] Camargo discovered in his study of São Paulo that over 5 per cent of pharmacists and 7 per cent of dentists were prepared to describe themselves as spiritualists, and similar proportions were prepared to describe themselves as 'sympathetic' to spiritualism. Very few—in each case less than 1 per cent—were prepared to be described as 'Umbandists'.[44]

The appeal of thaumaturgical religion in Brazil appears in part to stem from the persistence in the population of only partially assimilated elements, who have become prominent in the urban lower strata. Wonder-working is an important compensation for these groups, particularly when whites of higher social strata become votaries at the *candomblés* or *terreiros*. Then the negroes become the embodiment of the gods, before whom white men must humble themselves.[45] This explanation does not, however, hold for Kardesicm, the appeal of which was to other social groups. The prevalence of a rather unrefined thaumaturgy may, however, have stimulated enthusiasm for Kardecism, which grew

---

[41] Loc. cit.

[42] B. Kloppenburg, op. cit., p. 238, who writes, 'Der Spiritismus befindet sich in einer Blüteperiode, sein Fortschritt ist offenbar und gerade zu beängstigend. Von Jahr zu Jahr nimmt er zu, dehnt sich aus bis in die entlegensten Ortschaften des Binnenlandes, durchdringt alle sozialen Schichten, erfasst auch die Reichen und Intellectuellen und hat gegenwärtig in Militär seine besten Propagandisten und Beschirmer gefunden.'

[43] C. P. Ferreira de Camargo, *Kardecismo e Umbanda*, op. cit., pp. 127 ff.

[44] Loc. cit.,

[45] R. Bastide, 'Les religions africaines au Brésil', op. cit., pp. 467-8.

rapidly in a way unparalleled elsewhere.[46] Spiritualism, often of a less intellectual type, had spread widely in western countries in the latter half of the nineteenth century. Its appeal has subsequently declined, especially among the middle classes. In Brazil, it emerged at a time when church and state were separating. Theoretically non-Catholic religion now had better opportunities to spread than ever before, but in fact there was little religious diversity. Kardecism may thus have appeared as a symbol of religious liberation. It possessed, too, the attraction of a semi-intellectual body of teachings.

Just as some Umbandists have increasingly approximated the Kardecists in their organization and practice, eliminating the more primitive animistic elements, so the Kardecists have also been undergoing change.[47] They emphasize, or at least their more heavily-committed votaries emphasize, the spiritual, cosmological, and ethical aspects of their teaching. The directors and mediums stress the importance of leading morally exemplary lives, and they give evidence of their convictions in the extensive social work that they undertake.[48] Kardecism, although functioning very largely to perform cures for the mass of its following, begins to take on some aspects of a manipulationist movement. Such movements also emphasize therapy, as do the Kardecists. But today the Kardecists reveal rather less readily the extent to which followers—often gathering in private homes—engage in the more traditional spiritualistic activities of levitation and materialization.[49] It is perhaps too early to write of a clear process of the mutation of response, but the developmental continuity between thaumaturgical and manipulationist responses appears to be evident.

[46] According to B. Kloppenburg, op. cit., there are about three hundred spiritualist groups known in Argentina, with between 70,000 and 100,000 followers: the largest grouping is the Escola Científica Brasilia, founded in 1917.

[47] C. P. Ferreira de Camargo, op. cit., p. 14, considers that there is a continuum among spiritualists, even from the subjective point of view. 'De maior importância, entretanto, é a consciencia popular de continuidade, senão da identidade religiosa, entre a Umbanda e o Kardecismo. Effectivamente a anologia da experência religiosa e das interpretações que giram em tôrno do fenômeno mediúnico, reduzem, aos olhos do fiel, o "terreiro" de Umbanda e a "mesa" Kardecista ao "continuum" de uma vivencia espiritual unificada.' On the increasing similarity to Kardecism of the Umbandists, he mentions the increasing prohibition on alcohol; the exclusion of smoking; the simplification of the cult; and the exclusion of the altar of Exú—among other things (p. 49).

[48] Ibid, p. 73.

[49] Ibid. As we have already seen, the ordinary adherents still come to look for healing. Ferreira de Camargo considers that cures are responsible for perhaps 60 per cent of those who practice in São Paulo. 'Cremos que, a despeito de restrições doutrinárias de alguns Kardecistas, no que tange ao alcance, à conveniência e às possibilidades da actividade terapêutica, ela constitui o caminho principal de que o "continuum" mediúnico se utiliza para interessar possiveis adeptos' (p. 95).

Pentecostalism reinterpreted

In Brazil and elsewhere in Latin America the appeal of Pentecostalism, which in America and Europe we should regard as a conversionist movement, may have much less to do with the specific elements which have been significant in its spread in Protestant societies, and more to do with those thaumaturgical aspects which are part of its inheritance.[50] Thus we find that in missionary activity—and it is a factor we shall meet repeatedly—the ostensible configuration of doctrine, organization, and practice that is offered, is not accepted as a whole: certain elements are more readily embraced than others. In cultures with strong indigenous religious traditions it is entirely expectable that the appeal of any missionary denomination which includes thaumaturgical elements should be precisely these, rather than other features of its teachings, activities, or organization.

One example of this process, taken from Latin America, may suffice. The Toba Indians of the northern Argentinian Chaco, in the Saenz Pena, represent an indigenous and unassimilated group of some 10,000–15,000 people. In the early twentieth century, their way of life came under severe pressure, and was undermined as the *criollos* (non-Indians) settled increasingly among them. The Toba response was a mixture of hostility, escape, and uneasy symbiosis. Intoxication increased among them; destitute Tobas went begging in the towns, and they engaged in occasional depredations against their *criollo* neighbours. Government armed intervention had to be used against them in 1916 and 1924.[51] From their association with urban Argentinians, the Tobas acquired some knowledge of Pentecostalism, and from 1935 Pentecostalists were active among them, leading to extensive conversion of the Tobas once their *caciques*, headmen, had adopted the new religion. Pentecostal preaching was directed to the elimination of the dissolute behaviour that had become common among the Toba in the period of intensified culture-contact and conflict—stealing, fighting, drinking, and failure to work. But Protestant morality was not the aspect of

[50] Eugene A. Nida, 'The Indigenous Churches in Latin America', *Practical Anthropology* 8:3 (May–June 1961), pp. 97–110, considers that in Chile the Pentecostalists are perhaps four times as numerous as all other Protestant denominations, and equal to all others in Mexico. There are variations of doctrine and practice, but he comments, significantly for the point made above, that divine healing, speaking in tongues, filling with the Spirit, deep emotional fervour, dancing, shouting and crying, and spontaneous, vocal congregational prayer, are the usual characteristics.

[51] This paragraph relies principally on William D. and Marie F. Reyburn, 'Toba Caciqueship and the Gospel', *International Review of Missions* ILV (1956), pp. 194–203.

Pentecostalism that specifically appealed to the Tobas. The Old Mennonites, among whom these ethical prescriptions are sustained with greater rigour, had also been active among the Toba, but they had failed to make converts. The elements in Pentecostalism that made it acceptable were its emphasis on divine healing, which could be regarded as corresponding in some ways to Toba shamanistic practice; its encouragement of singing, which the Toba had traditionally associated with healing; and its expectation of the direct operation in the assembly of the Holy Spirit, which corresponded to the spirit-activity already known to the Toba.[52]

Given these affinities, the 'Christianization' of the Toba occurred with only a rather minimum selective missionary influence. After some time the orthodox Pentecostalists found sustained association impossible, because the Toba too vigorously re-interpreted the thaumaturgical elements of their faith, and too much ignored many of its other elements. In recent years, 'Pentecostal ministers and churches have consistently refused a more than casual involvement with what they considered a highly pagan expression of the Christian faith'.[53] Traditionally the Toba ascribed illness either to the action of bad spirits or to the action of sorcerers (who were also shamans or healers). The sorcerer was believed to shoot evil substances into the bodies of his victims, or to steal their souls, or occupy their bodies with his own evil soul. Curing was undertaken by three different types of shaman, *pi'oxonaq*, a doctor who had learned to heal; *natannaxanaq*, who had been endued with power; and the most potent, *napinshaxaic*, who had spirit-power with which he could

[52] E. A. Nida, op. cit., writes, 'In their period of disillusionment, however, a Pentecostal message had a tremendous appeal, for whereas before only certain persons could be medicine men, and enjoy ecstatic experiences of fellowship with ancestral spirits, as Pentecostals all people could be possessed by the Spirit of God and could enjoy the thrill of this new religious ecstasy. Moreover the message of God's redeeming grace was explained as a way in which God "shared" his Son with men, and his Son "shares" his Spirit. This theme of sharing struck a responsive chord, for willingness to share is a basic feature in Toba life.' (For a comparable analysis of the compensatory functions of Protestantism, with its distribution of new prestige, see Benson Saler, 'Religious Conversion and Self-Aggrandisement: A Guatemalan Case', *Practical Anthropology* 12:3 (May–June 1965), pp. 107–14.)

[53] Jacob A. Loewen, Albert Buckwalter, and James Kratz, 'Shamanism, Illness and Power in Toba Church Life', *Practical Anthropology* 12:6 (November–December 1965), pp. 250–80. The Toba had not been sympathetic to Mennonite missioning, but when the Pentecostalists refused to accept Toba practice as Christian, the Mennonites re-evaluated their own missionary endeavour and decided to stay to help the new movement to acquire the necessary registration it required for government recognition, which was granted to twenty-four churches as the Iglesia Evangélica Unida. The Mennonites remained as friends and advisers, and have provided a measure of coherence especially for I.E.U. conferences, although Toba Christianity is very remote from Mennonite practice. Here is an example, not dissimilar from Quaker activity at the origins of the Handsome Lake Gai'wiio᷄ religion among the Iroquois at the end of the eighteenth century, of a tolerance and patience of endeavour that has perhaps seen few equals among the major missioning bodies of the Christian Church.

heal or harm. Shamans were engaged in a struggle for power, and even in curing for their clients were also pitting themselves against other shamans. Toba reactions to white medicine are very much affected by this complex of belief. In Pentecostalism, however, a general and more readily available spiritual power was offered, with which the Toba could free themselves from the exploitation and negligence of their shamans, of whom many complained.

Pentecostalism appealed because 'physical healing is obviously a very central concern for the Toba. . . . Many Toba Christians date their conversion as following an experience of healing.'[54] Illness, which was shameful, was viewed as an absence of power, while death has sometimes caused relatives such shame that they have stayed away from church for some time after a death has occurred. In a Toba church service an individual seeking healing is brought forward and surrounded by a group who pray aloud and seek to transmit their power to him, to drive out the alien element in his body which is causing sickness. In the fashion of a traditional college of shamans, they may touch and rub the patient, and at times they also undertake a sucking cure. For the shaman, abandonment of shamanistic power is clearly difficult, and thus there are continuities of traditional belief and procedures in church practice. Dancing, singing, incantations, spirit possession, loss of power, transmission of spirit power, the experience of trance, and the acquisition in trance, while the soul is away from the body, of new songs, are all features of the Toba *Iglesia Evangélica Unida*. The Bible is carried, often as an object of spirit power, since many are illiterate. The loud spontaneous prayer, offered by everyone individually and simultaneously, does not interrupt, any more than need the sermon, the dancing which prevails in church services.

Syncretism and thaumaturgical demand

The origins of the various elements entering into the syncretistic movements of Latin America and the Caribbean, and their documentation, is not our concern. It is sufficient, perhaps, for us to note that very similar, essentially thaumaturgical movements, are widespread throughout the region, whether it be a combination of African ideas and practices with indigenous beliefs, as in the cities of Brazil, or the acceptance of organizational patterns from the conversionist sects of Christen-

[54] Ibid, p. 268.

dom, as among the Toba. In some areas, the syncretic elements are even more diverse. Thus, in Trinidad we find fifteen or more Yoruba deities worshipped, including Shango (Xangô of Brazil), the thunder god who is here equated with St John. Obalufon, who is identified with the Eternal Father, and Eshu (Exú). Dancing, animal sacrifices, revelations, possession, and the intervention of the gods in human affairs, occur here as elsewhere, but there has also been assimilation with the local Christian sect of Shouters (*Spiritual Baptists*), and there appears to be much more extensive use of the Bible than in the Brazilian cases (where Protestant influences have, of course, been largely absent). There are also more ascetic rules, particularly demands for sexual restraint, and fasting before ceremonies, and prohibition of gambling, stealing, homosexuality, and the consumption of pork.[55] This asceticism is derived from Protestantism, and, typical of Protestant tradition, it is an obligation not only of the functionaries, as among the Catholic-influenced *candomblés*, but also of the laity.

Entirely similar ascetic orientations are found in the even more highly syncretistic movement led by Norman Paul in Grenada.[56] The influences which operate here are derived from Paul's earlier association with the Seventh Day Adventists. He claims to be less worldly than the Shouting Baptists, although he believes in spirit-powers and visions, and has a thoroughly thaumaturgical practice.[57] In Martinique, south-Indian elements are prominent among the immigrants who came from India, although they now speak no Tamil, maintain no caste structure, have no contact with that continent, and are nominally Roman Catholics. Entirely similar identifications of Maldevidan with Christ and of other deities with Catholic saints are found, and the practice of the faith is seasonal, and does not attempt to displace other forms of worship. The ceremonies and animal sacrifices are largely sponsored by private individuals, and there is an elaborate practice of healing,

---

[55] George E. Simpson, 'The Shango Cult in Nigeria and in Trinidad', *American Anthropologist* 64:6 (December 1962), pp. 1204–19; G. E. Simpson, 'The Acculturative Process in Trinidadian Shango', *Anthropological Quarterly* 37:1 (January 1964), pp. 16–27. Similarities between negro cults in Brazil, Cuba, and the *vodun* cults in Haiti are discussed in Melville J. Herskovits, 'African Gods and Catholic Saints in New World Negro Belief', *American Anthropologist* 39:4 (1937), pp. 635–43.

[56] An account, together with a long tape-recorded description of his movement by Norman Paul himself, is given in M. G. Smith, *Dark Puritan* (Department of Extra-Mural Studies, University of West Indies, Kingston, Jamaica, 1963).

[57] Paul himself says, 'Since I came back to Grenada, all the time people are coming to me for help, those people who believe in the old people, the dead people, when the dead are troubling them; sometimes people come because somebody have put obeah on them; sometimes they come because loupgarou [witches] troubling them; sometimes they sick; sometimes it is an evil spirit that is with them.' Ibid., p. 127. One could scarcely seek a more comprehensive description of a thaumaturge's clientele.

and consultation with the possessed priest, who, in characteristic Asiatic fashion, practises self-immolation while possessed.[58]

The significance of syncretism for this analysis is not the tracing of lines of cultural diffusion, but rather the recognition that in the persistence of the deities, beliefs, and practices of thaumaturgical religion, there is more than a mere continuance of cultural forms. There is also the sustained and unrelenting demand, or very slowly relenting (and then relenting in degree rather than in kind) for thaumaturgical benefits, for reassurance, personal gratification, protection, health, and relief from mental anguish in daily life. As long as these functions appear to be fulfilled by the gods and the rites, and as long as men experience social circumstances that produce the demand for them, the gods and the rites are unlikely to be relinquished. They will, rather, be subject to an intensification of demand when circumstances render men more insecure: emigration, new life activities, uncertain status-orders and authority structures, can be expected to increase the sense of insecurity. Old 'cosmic', tribal, or territorial gods who were to be placated for society's sake may then acquire functions of personal protection, or lose their place to gods who offer greater reassurance. New gods, from other traditions, may be readily accorded a place, if they appear to be powerful and appropriate agents of benevolence.

But not all thaumaturgical traditions are syncretistic in the sense in which the *candomblés*, Umbanda, and Caribbean cults are. In some cases, the organization of older religious systems has been re-structured, both to suit new social circumstances, and to meet enhanced thaumaturgical demand, but where migrants have retained a segregated social system and are still emotionally attached to the homeland, syncretism has not occurred. Old gods acquire new status, and a new social organization of religion, detached from kinship and territorial principles, may occur (and may be reflected in loose hierarchies and vaguer cosmic associations among the deities themselves, who now function in a much more particularistic way, at special shrines for self-selected individual votaries). Such is the development of the spirit-medium cults among the Chinese of Singapore.

Dislocated religion and thaumaturgy

The Chinese immigrants to Singapore have added relatively little to

[58] The account rests on Michael M. Horowitz and Morton Klass, 'The Martiniquan East Indian Cult of Maldevidan', *Social and Economic Studies* (Jamaica), 10:1 (March 1961), pp. 93–100. Similar cults are found in Guadaloupe. Horowitz found some seven temples in Martinique, each of which might contain about twenty images of deities: M. M. Horowitz, 'The Worship of South Indian Deities in Martinique', *Ethnology* II, 3 (July 1963), pp. 339–46.

the religious ideas which they brought from mainland China, although spirit-medium religion has flourished. The growth of these cults reflects the difficult life circumstances of the immigrants, and the tolerance of new forms of religious organization in Singapore. Following the principal authority, we may call these spirit-medium practices *Shenism*, from the name of the gods who are principally invoked in the search for blessings, and it represents 'the most typical, although rather extreme, manifestation of the major religious orientation of the overseas Chinese'.[59] Spirit-mediumship certainly occurred among the Chinese population of the provinces from which most of the immigrants came, and Shenist practices were undertaken in the home, the fields, and in temples associated with territorial units.[60] In Singapore spirit-medium practice has become more strongly associated with temple worship. The dominant religious traditions had also become suffused with thaumaturgical practice, just as Mahayana Buddhism had been infected in Tibet.[61] Taoism had lost much of its connection with the philosophy of Lâo-Tsze, and had become associated with alchemy, divination, and sorcery; its practitioners devoted their time and occult knowledge to the invocation of forces to counterbalance evil powers.[62] The ancestor cult, too, in addition to providing implicit support for the rank order of seniority, and the supremacy of filial duty in this world, satisfied demands for a flow of blessings to their faithful, living progeny: 'the ancestors maintained an essentially benevolent interest in the doings of their descendants. They were not agents of moral control.'[63]

The Chinese immigrants to Singapore came in as cheap labour in the second half of the nineteenth century. The ancestor cult continued among them but since they were detached from their traditional patrilineal lineages, it did so in a somewhat attenuated form, and in accommodation to the rather different kinship structure that developed there, when, eventually, a larger proportion of women came from China to join the men who had constituted the vast majority of the early migrants. The changes in social structure; the lost significance of the agricultural religious cults; the attenuated ancestor cult, the corruption

[59] Alan J. A. Elliott, *Chinese Spirit-Medium Cults in Singapore* (London School of Economics, Monographs in Social Anthropology No. 14, London 1955), p. 5. The following paragraphs rely principally on this work.

[60] Majorie Topley, 'The Emergence and Social Function of Chinese Religious Associations in Singapore', *Comparative Studies in Society and History* III, 3 (April 1961), pp. 289–314; pp. 290–1.

[61] See, for example, Robert B. Eckvall, *Religious Observances in Tibet: Patterns and Functions* (University of Chicago Press, Chicago 1964).

[62] A. J. A. Elliott, op. cit., p. 25.

[63] Maurice Freedman, 'Religion and Society in South Eastern China', *Man* LVII (April 1957), article No. 62, pp. 56–7. See also C. K. Yang, *Religion in Chinese Society* (University of California Press, Berkeley and Los Angeles 1961).

of both Taoism and Buddhism, and the tolerance of the British government, all facilitated the emergence of autonomous thaumaturgical cults
in Singapore. Chinese religion, had, in Confucianism, the traditions of
a state cult. In Buddhism and Taoism there was a more intellectual
strain. But at the level of folk religion it was a 'system of belief which
postulated a set of guiding forces behind the universe and human
conduct'. Among these forces were included 'beings who are capable
of influencing worldly affairs'. The disappearance, in Singapore, of the
more elevated aspects of traditional religion, and of the social structure
appropriate to the operation of the ancestor cult, left the opportunity
for the development in puissant form of thaumaturgical practice.
'Religious endeavour has been almost entirely devoted to the attainment
of material success, through the manipulation of one's luck.' 'This has
led to emphasis upon methods of placating spiritual influences, and,
more significantly, of divination which had . . . provided a rich field
for the enterprise of professional practitioners who claim to be versed
in the old Chinese ways.'[64]

For the Chinese the religious world is peopled by powerful, anthropo-
morphically conceived gods and spirits who possess miraculous powers,
who are capable of dispelling misfortune when propitiated, and who
are susceptible to the blandishments of their votaries, when properly
approached through specialist intermediaries. The *Shen* are ghosts,
spirits, or souls who enjoy this positive spiritual influence, and the name
is also used for the mediums whose bodies the spirits possess. Wide
ranges of thaumaturgy are practised, from the reading of horoscopes,
divination, and fortune-telling, to the self-immolating practices during
the state of possession by the *Shen* of the *dang-ki*, or medium. The *dang-ki*
may be possessed by only one *Shen* or by several. Whilst possessed he
must, in a manner often found in thaumaturgical practice, be protected
and revered by all his assistants and by the temple clientele who come
to watch the trance, the feats of self-mortification, and to obtain cures,
advice about their difficulties, and protection. 'The immediate reason
for most consultations is physical illness, but more often than not this
is allied with other kinds of worry. Men most frequently complain that
"their luck is bad" while women often have family worries. . . .'[65] The
dang-ki may prescribe drugs, to be taken in connection with prescribed
actions, and often with the use of charm-papers smeared with blood
from the tongue of the medium (which is often pierced while he is in a
trance state). Images are consecrated, charms are sold, shirts are

[64] A. J. A. Elliott, op. cit., pp. 21–2.
[65] Ibid., p. 90.

stamped with the temple stamp to bring luck to the wearer. There is a diverse and ingenious range of practices by which the clientele can seek benefit.

Special rituals take place to protect children from illness or to obtain cures for children who are ill. The danger in which a child stands may be worked out by horoscope, and a propitious day will then be chosen for the rite to be performed for him. The highly complex rituals that are performed, though much less elaborate and taking much less time than the rites performed in Foochow, might typically include exhortation to the deity (the Mistress of the Golden Flower, in the case reported) to cure the child, and the propitiation of the devil who is causing the illness. The child is stroked with the scapegoat effigy of a child, so that the illness may be transferred to this figure; he is stroked with special charm-paper called 'The Reliever of a Hundred Catastrophes', and money and coins are burned. If the devil is 'satisfied' by this performance, and by being told that it is getting everything it wants, the real child will then be relieved of its illness. Other rites include those to 'pray away the little man' who represents the burglar, thief, pickpocket, rumour-monger, or, more rarely, the practitioner of black magic. The little man may be chained with a paper chain and beaten with a paper hand, and wrapped together with charm-papers and set alight at the altar. Altars devoted to spirit beings, such as the White Tiger, Gold Cock, or Heavenly Dog, all of whom are considered to be very bad, may be found in the temple usually under that of the major god, and women are likely to pray to them when any ill-luck occurs in their families. Other rites are concerned with attempts to change fate, or to relieve barrenness.[66]

At the fringe of the spirit-medium cults with practices of this kind, there are some that specialize in automatic writing. For many practices there is no particular specialized cult, though there is one type of cult with a female *dang-ki*, 'who specializes in raising the souls of the dead for the purpose of communication with surviving relatives'.[67] Communication with the dead is not, however, so much concerned with the solution of the problems of the living, as to learn about the welfare of the recent dead. The seances are private.[68] Other associations that specialize in religious ritual have also their strong thaumaturgical orientations: thus the *Tao-yüan* religion appears to bear resemblances

[66] This paragraph relies on the detailed account of M. Topley, 'Some Occasional Rites performed by the Singapore Cantonese', *Journal of the Malayan Branch of the Royal Asiatic Society* XXIV, 3 (October 1951), pp. 120–44.

[67] A. J. A. Elliott, op. cit., p. 67.

[68] M. Freedman and M. Topley, 'Religious and Social Realignment among the Chinese in Singapore', *Journal of Asian Studies* XXI, 1 (November 1961), pp. 3–33.

to Brazilian Kardecism in its preoccupations, and perhaps in the social status of its votaries.

> The syncretistic religion of Tao-yüan with its 'outer works' philanthropic association for non-members, the Red Swastika Society, . . . stresses internationalism as well as promotion of 'things Chinese'. It includes Christ and Mohammed among its objects of veneration. . . . The Tao-yüan holds regular meetings at the headquarters of the Red Swastika association, and members of the latter, who are mostly middle-class Chinese of diverse origins and dialects may attend. The meetings generally consists [sic] of a seance, a planchette producing automatic messages about policy.[69]

Thaumaturgy and organization

Thaumaturgical movements generally lack the capacity to establish large-scale organizations. They depend so closely on the powers of the particular thaumaturge that operations have an inherent tendency to be localized. The particularism of the response itself almost implies the particularism of its organizational pattern. Yet there are ways in which thaumaturgical practice can be organized at a wider level. There are various possibilities. The thaumaturge may train acolytes who then eventually establish themselves as the operators of shrines. This is a pattern in Ghana with the shrine of Akonedi, and in the diffusion of the Tigari cult. Obviously, this is scarcely a pattern of organization so much as the diffusion of a set of practices through ecologically dispersed local agents. Usually there is no effective hierarchy of control, even when there is a recognized central shrine with a functionary of higher status. But even the originator or teacher in such a diffused set of rituals is also a local operator, and normally he has neither facilities nor opportunities to supervise the activities of other practitioners. The strong tendency to localism often eventuates in rivalries and competition between practitioners, and this can occur though they belong to the same ideological tradition, and practise essentially similar rites and feats. The particularism of their operation, their need to claim superior powers in order to sustain patronage and to satisfy their clientele, readily generate competition of this kind, with mutual disparagement, accusations of extortion and exploitation (typical, for example, in Singapore) or allegations that rivals practise black magic.

The grouping of practitioners in leagues or associations is also a possibility for thaumaturgical religion, and this is the pattern that has

[69] M. Topley, 'The Emergence . . . of Chinese Religious Associations . . .', op. cit., p. 310.

evolved in Brazil. The fragility of such associations is evident from the ease with which they are formed, undergo fissure, and dissolve for want of support. Centralization of control is difficult to achieve in thaumaturgical practice. It is in this respect that manipulationist movements show marked distinctions of organizational potential from thaumaturgical movements. They control ideology and evolve distinct, objective categories of heresy and malpractice, and they regulate procedures of training, socialization, and initiation. In universalizing their principles and practice, manipulationist movements establish agencies of control. The effect of rationalization, which is evident in the development of doctrine, is also effective at the level of organization. The movements among both Kardecists and Umbandists in Brazil manifest a nascent attempt to adopt the organizational structure that has been effective for some manipulationist cults (although this organizational pattern is by no means universal among them, and the organizational dimension is not part of the primary criterion by which we have distinguished responses to the world).

The organization of thaumaturgical practitioners into leagues is a possibility which is open most typically where thaumaturgy is practised in an urban context, in a society in which other social institutions are conspicuously organized on rational bureaucratic lines, and in which rational-legal types of authority structure, role-specificity, and rational decision-making procedures are available models.[70] In traditional societies, where thaumaturgy is still the dominant form of indigenous practice, such models are rarely available. But the thaumaturgical response may none the less acquire new forms if it is to reassert itself in the face of religious proselytizing of imported religious systems (in the African case, in the face of Christianity and Islam). Thaumaturgy continues at a local level, but the general social circumstances may provide prospects for organization which were not formally available to religious enterprises. Some of these are traditional patterns of organization, in which the religious movement adopts the style, and some of the functions, of the tribe. This can perhaps occur only where the process of de-tribalization has reached the level of undermining tribal structure without eliminating the strong desire for tribal identity or some surrogate form of identity. The alternative is to adopt the modes of organization imported by the proselytizing faiths.

[70] This is the case among spiritualistic mediums in Britain who have an organization similar in style and spirit, as far as charismatic claims permit, to a professional organization. It is the functionaries who organize, however. Their clientele is, despite rudimentary church and congregational arrangements, too volatile to conform to stable sectarian or denominational patterns.

The thaumaturgical response, as we have noted, is a recurrent, and as yet inextinguishable, characteristic of religion. It outcrops in all the great religious traditions, and—more vigorously and with far fuller expectation of effectiveness—in the movements which espouse a different deviant response to the world. It stands in tension, often, with the revolutionist response; but it is much more readily accommodated in conversionist movements. The conversionist model, exported from more advanced societies, has perhaps provided the best organizational base for the thaumaturgical response; it provides, in the emotional freedom on which conversionism relies, a context suitable for wonder-working and the distribution of special, particularized benisons. Local discretion is often sufficient to allow considerable latitude in the interpretation of basic teachings, and doctrine is never a supreme concern of conversionist movements. The emphasis on a heart-experience can readily accommodate the direct operation of the deity in offering miracles, even if these contravene the specific expectations which a conversionist movement—at its most doctrinally pure—would acknowledge as legitimate. The amalgamation of conversionist orientations and the demand for wonders, healings, and reassurance, is perhaps the most effective pattern of regulation for thaumaturgy. The thaumaturgical response itself is broadened once it is associated with conversionism. Typically there is compromise, for instance in the way in which a miracle is conceived: it becomes less of an objective event and more of a subjective evaluation. The extreme claims and expectations are modified. The personal special pleading for dispensation from normal causative processes is diminished, and often reassociated with the pleading of a group, with lowered expectation of 'signs following'. The fellowship begins to provide the context of the miracles, becomes *in itself* the miracle, the evidence of the deity's operations. As this occurs the thaumaturgical response is given a stability, which in its pristine form it normally lacks; it acquires wider application; it becomes a more total orientation of the individual to the world, and so, steadily, a re-orientation. This mutation of response is most evident in the modern world in the acquisition of conversionist organization by a clientele which is still largely preoccupied with the operation of the thaumaturgical, and is nowhere more apparent than in West African Christianity.

5

Thaumaturgical Responses and Social Organization

DISCUSSION of thaumaturgy must involve us, to an extent greater than is necessary in the case of other responses to the world, in consideration of the range of possibilities available for the organization of thaumaturgical movements. The reason for this lies in the aboriginal and indigenous character of thaumaturgy, which had no distinctive organizational form, but which was, in the hypothetical static state of an underdeveloped preliterate people, an integrated part of the total social system. Only when the social system had been disrupted were traditional thaumaturgical orientations likely to be challenged, the need for ritual practice denied, and natural and social forces explained in non-religious terms. Thaumaturgical beliefs persist among individuals, of course, even after the decay of the social order in which they had once occupied a more fully integrated place. The old associations such as cult societies may also continue, but as the society is affected by external influences—colonial governments, missions, new types of economic relationship—so the thaumaturge may increasingly act only for clients and less for the community as a whole. His status changes and he ceases to have an important public role even where he continues as a ceremonial functionary. Communal rites—rain-making or witch-finding or crop-blessing—have only perfunctory continuance or fall into complete desuetude. The thaumaturge becomes dependent on a voluntary clientele by whom the performance of this role is still demanded, from whom he can exact fees and by whom he is accorded status.

In such societies, however, the terms of voluntaristic allegiance, and the cultural pluralism which it implies, are little understood. Only the missions provide an introduction to a range of ideological choice and its consequences. They become possible models for the thaumaturge. But other bases of allegiance have existed in the traditional society, and these, too, may provide an appropriate model. Since the demand for thaumaturgical practice may in itself be enhanced by the disruption of traditional social organization, it may be entirely appropriate for the thaumaturge to attempt, on his own part, to adopt a tribal type of

132

organization for his own practice. How consciously this is an attempt to revitalize a tribal system is not always clear. It may be no more than an obvious pattern of organization, perhaps not always consciously chosen by a man whose claims to status are, if uncertain, now also unbridled— for in the disruption of fixed places in the traditional structure, there is the possibility not only of loss of social standing, but also the prospect of suddenly and dramatically increasing it. If chiefly authority has fallen low because alien authority has usurped its functions; if tribal associations have lost their vitality; and if traditional communities have lost their economic, social, and political integration, religious authority may still make traditional claims. Without traditional hindrances, religious authority may now indeed be the only effective authority available within the indigenous society.

The thaumaturge as messiah

In societies in which economic and political activities have been differentiated from religion the role of the religious leader has undergone devaluation. In such societies—and increasingly in all societies— religion is of less consequence for the working of the social system than are these specialized instrumental spheres of activity. Thus diversity of religion becomes tolerable, and claims to religious leadership constitute much less of a threat than in less-developed societies. Where indigenous political leaders have been replaced by new, externally-imposed leaders, the religious practitioner may persist as a tolerated indigenous claimant to power. Because the power he claims is power over the supernatural he appears to constitute no threat to secular authorities. Yet the source by which he legitimates his claim presents itself as ultimate and transcendent. If a population concedes that claim to any considerable degree the religious leader may indeed pose a threat to those whose claim to power is secular, instrumental, and pragmatic. The thaumaturge is normally only a local worker of wonders, but there are circumstances in which he may re-evoke the sentiments appropriate to a community and a social system that has been destroyed and which exists only as a memory. In resuscitating it in recollection and in simulating its organization in the movement he creates, he works a very special type of miracle—bringing back into being a social system by persuading men that they can re-create it by an act of faith. In the vacuum which exists when a society is in decay, he may fictively reconstitute the system and so work miracles which were never possible in a more stable social context. The thaumaturge becomes the charismatic leader who not only performs miracles, but is himself also the miracle. By winning allegiance, the thaumaturge can become the messiah, buoyed up on the confidence of his followers. The hope, reassurance, renewal which he claims as an intrinsic quality of his thaumaturgical skill, are realized by the confidence he generates and the practical steps which he takes to win and keep his following. In such circumstances of de-tribalization the thaumaturge becomes the messiah, the chief, the now-and-coming king.

The living god, the man who claims to be a messiah, must of necessity be a thaumaturge. He may not practise much and he may rely largely on legendary feats, but usually he will be obliged to appear and to manifest power. The self-styled messiah can rarely claim political power, and rarely does he challenge it. Rational economic ability is alien to the whole style he must adopt, and represents the procedures of the world, with which he contrasts his own abilities. He may, of course, offer economic benefits to his adherents, but these are benefits which he does not claim to provide on the strength of his organizing ability, his capital, or his manipulation of the economic system: rather they are claimed as direct fruits of his supernatural power. Thus such messiahs can be expected in social conditions where men are either excluded from normal political and rational economic relationships, or where it is possible to contract out of them. In underdeveloped societies, the non-political messianic thaumaturge is found most usually among populations that have no access to political and economic power: *he* is a living embodiment of a claim to transcendental power that far surpasses the power that is denied *them* in secular affairs. His role is symbolic and expressive, rather than directly instrumental, even though in certain contexts, and especially in relation to psychic and physical well-being, pragmatic proofs of power are also demanded, and even though economic and political consequences may occasionally ensue from his activities. The power he claims explicitly challenges only rival claimants to supernatural ability, who are necessarily held to be evil deceivers. Casting out demons and countering such evils, healing the sick, and purging or curing wizards, are his speciality.

Messiahs must be capable of wonder-working, even if this is not what is primarily stressed in their mission. For the living claimant to messiahship this is the touchstone of legitimacy. Since he cannot, without coming into direct conflict with the civil authorities, claim political or military power; since he must eschew the sphere of rational economic activity, since he claims a unique quality, and thus does not teach others to emulate him but rather only to serve him and rely on him, he has few styles of action in vindication of his claims other than wonder-working. He cannot justify himself by an overt claim to change the social order—the claim frequently made on behalf of a future messiah. His vindication is in alleviating present ills. He does not challenge the existing system in direct political terms, as, implicitly, does a future messiah. Thus existing messiahs are not revolutionist. The response to the world which they canvass cannot be as direct as that of even the typical revolutionist sect, for whom the overturning of the world will be a possibility only when the messiah arrives or decides. A living messiah cannot make claims that are postponed in this way. There is no leeway of latency. His world-transforming potential cannot be stressed. It must be muted. In consequence it is his therapeutic and thaumaturgical powers that are extolled.

It is thus evident that in designating new religious movements as 'prophetism' or 'messianism' important differences in their character are concealed.[1] The messianic claim excludes, in the case of a living messiah, certain possibilities of action. Such movements cannot persist as revolutionist movements without inspiring political action against them (as occurred in the case of Enoch Mgijima and his Israelites[2]) unless they can insulate themselves completely, and thus disavow millennial ambitions relevant to the wider society. A promised messiah opens the way for quite different expectations of action. Thus, the designation of a movement as 'messianic' indicates nothing of a movement's central preoccupations. Some movements that are led by men who make, or have made for them, messianic claims, are better regarded as thaumaturgical movements. But where a *future* messiah is expected, the likelihood of a revolutionist response to the world is considerable.

Millennialism, as such, need not be messianic in the usual sense: some millennial movements have expected the restoration of the ancestors, rather than the coming of the new messiah. Equally, mes-

[1] In the revised edition of his book *Bantu Prophets in South Africa* (Oxford University Press, London 1961), B. G. M. Sundkler adds to his existing classification of the independent sects in South Africa a new type, 'messianic' (p. 302). His earlier typology, of 'Ethiopian' and 'Zionist' sects, employed as its criteria the original sources of sect teachings. As we have seen, this led to the inclusion of sects with completely different response to the world under one label. The *ad hoc* addition of a new type to this classification, defined by a criterion which is not of the same logical order as the others, and which may readily overlap with them (particularly in the 'Zionist' case) makes confusion worse confounded. It must include, for example, groups as divergent in their response to the world as the revolutionist Israelites of Enoch Mgijima, and the thaumaturgically oriented Nazarites of Shembe. Religious movements may, of course, be categorized by reference to their organizational (and leadership) characteristics. But organization appears to vary independently of orientation to the world, which is a better indicator of the functions that sects fulfil for their membership, the sections of the population from which they recruit, and their consequences for the wider society. Organizational style may, of course, make its own independent contribution to the development of a movement in association with its orientation to the world. To this problem we return on pp. 156 ff.

[2] On Enoch Mgijima, see pp. 61–3.

sianism need not be millennialist. A living messiah is not, in the normal
sense, offering the establishment of a millennium, though he may be
offering an extensive range of blessings to those who acknowledge his
claims. Salvation may be from present bodily ills, rather than in a
future state of bliss. Such messiahs are sometimes in a position, and this
is true of the two whose movements are examined below, to create, for
certain occasions or for particular periods in the individual's life-cycle,
circumstances that do, in a limited sense, amount to the re-making of
social experience for their adherents. By using the wealth and man-
power that their adherents make available and which they, as messiahs,
can mobilize to build retreats or communities, or for economic re-
distribution, they perform the miracles demanded of them, and this
they do without political action or revolutionist orientations. They
create something approaching heavenly enclaves—'abodes of love'. The
limits of economic resources that a messiah commands restricts the size
and permanence of such establishments. But were they larger, longer-
lasting, and more conspicuous socially, they would represent a challenge
to the political order of the wider society. In practice, in the societies
with which we are concerned, they constitute small permanent settlements with a shrine or church of pilgrimage and a surrounding area
that may become a camping ground for periodic ceremonial gatherings.
They are not settled millennial societies with routinized and institutionalized social systems but places of occasional assemblies for ecstatic
and festive events. They are a foretaste of heaven, if such is promised;
an occasional refuge; they are not politically-conscious attempts to
create permanent communities of *all* followers under messianic rule.
(There may be a local headquarters, where a special élite live according
to special regulations.) The 'heavenliness' of such communities is
related to the breakdown of stable community organization in the
wider society—and in the cases with which we are concerned, to the
partial dissolution of the tribal structure. These communities provide
circumstances for the continuance or renewal of tribal beliefs and
tribal activities.

The messianic thaumaturge among the Zulus

Circumstances propitious for the emergence of thaumaturgical messiahs
prevail most conspicuously in South Africa. Such a messiah brings into
being a new community as a surrogate of the tribe, and so reassures and
protects his following both by his supernatural powers, and by his
social achievement. His messianic claims acquire reality in the locally

best-known terms in which honour might be conferred—the assimilation of the messianic style to that of the paramount chief. The chief who is powerful beyond all that conquerors can do re-creates the tribe. In the face of general social disruption, he controls a territory, a feasting ground, establishes a festive season, and inaugurates socially integrative rites which re-emphasize aspects of the tribal past. Together these things constitute the miracles that sustain the system. In practice, the new messianic figure might frequently seek confirmation of status by close association with the old chiefly houses whose power and status he may rival. It is a common pattern for men claiming status in new terms to seek marriage alliances with older aristocracies. The claimants to new status in South Africa, however, are not capitalist farmers or captains of industry, brewers, or trade unionists who, in turn, acquired aristocratic connections in Britain, but sect-leaders and thaumaturges. Thus Johannes Galilee Shembe, the leader of the *Nazareth Baptist Church*, pays homage to the Zulu Paramount chief, to whose predecessor his sister was married.[3] Chiefs commonly visit the temples of separatist sects, and different sect leaders have claimed visions of dead kings who have come to them with advice. Many prominent Zulu chiefs attend the principal festivals of Shembe's movement.

Shembe's sect provides the best example for this particular adaptation of indigenous social organization to the practice of thaumaturgy. The leader is able, in such a surrogate tribe, to retain the particularism of his practice: his functions are rarely delegated, and then only within his presence. A messiah may take disciples who become agents under his control, but this is not an effective decentralization of authority, so much as an enhancement of the messianic status of the thaumaturge himself. The principle of the 'living god' makes it difficult to establish branch organization and rational delegation of authority, but where organization is based on the tribe the personal authority and communication on which the thaumaturge depends are easily maintained.[4]

Johannes Galilee Shembe was the son of Isaiah Shembe, the founder

[3] The relation of the leaders of new sects to chiefs is brought out in B. G. Sundkler, 'Chief and Prophet in Zululand and Swaziland', in M. Fortes and G. Dieterlen, op. cit., pp. 276–90. Sundkler distinguishes between the power of sect leaders among the Zulu, where chiefly power has considerably broken down, and where the new messianic leaders have moved forward to occupy roles similar to those of chiefs, and those among the Swazi, where kingship remains important. The 'Zionist' leader, Stephen Nkonyane, after a period of tension between the sects and the tribe, has, by recognizing tribal festivals, established amity with the royal house, and come to occupy a position of influence, though other sect leaders are also entertained by the Swazi royal family.

[4] B. G. M. Sundkler, in *Bantu Prophets in South Africa*, 1st Edn (Lutterworth Press, London 1948), p. 117, comments on the distinction between the more politically-conscious, separatist 'Ethiopian' churches, and the 'Zionist' churches. In the former the church leader's influence is mediated by a nucleus of adherents, whereas in the latter it is merely transmitted through them—and may also be transmitted personally.

of the Nazareth Baptist Church which flourishes among the Zulu in
the Durban area of South Africa. Isaiah Shembe had been a preacher
in the *African Native Baptist Church*, from which he separated to found
his own Nazareth Baptist Church (NBC) in 1911. One issue on which
he differed from the parent body was that the Sabbath should be the
seventh day.[5] Isaiah Shembe had visions, left his wife, and devoted
himself to this new religious work. He rejected all comforts, led an
ascetic life, and was worshipped by his followers as a living god. Before
his death, he named his son, J. G. Shembe, as his successor as leader
of the movement. The son has inherited something of the father's
messianic claim and some of his followers refer to him as God. But the
father appears to have been a more vigorous, more fully charismatic,
figure than the son, who is an educated man—he holds a B.A. from
the University of South Africa—and who appears to be less comfortable
in the messianic role.[6]

The NBC is typical of the 'Zionist' movements which we have already
discussed.[7] It is one of the largest and most successful, and one of the
most avowedly messianic. Its membership has been variously estimated
as between 10,000 and 80,000.[8] As in all similar movements, women
appear to be more numerous among the following than men. The
identification of the Church with the tribe is sometimes explicit, and
Shembe himself may be referred to as 'the chief'. Members bow as long
as Shembe is in sight, and even outsiders, including a brother-in-law
who is an Anglican, do likewise. He receives gifts, and employs a
herald, *imbongi*, who orates his praises, after the same fashion as a
chief. Like a chief, he too is first judge of his people. The organization
of the movement appears to be based on old Zulu social structure, with
the leader in the role of the deified cultural hero, a role which Zulus
have in the past attributed to their kings.[9]

[5] Katesa Schlosser, *Eingeborenenkirchen in Süd- und Süd-west Afrika*, op. cit., p. 229. This
section relies very largely on this work. B. G. M. Sundkler, op. cit., refers to Shembe's church
as 'Nazarites'.

[6] K. Schlosser, op. cit., p. 225.

[7] See pp. 57 ff.

[8] B. G. M. Sundkler, op. cit., p. 135, reported 50,000 in 1948; Schlosser, op. cit., p. 251,
said that Shembe himself claimed only 10,000 in 1958.

[9] K. Schlosser, op. cit., pp. 264, 243. She writes, further, 'Zum Problem der Entstehung
neuer Sozialgebilde demonstriert die Nazareth Baptist Church anschaulich, wie aus den
alten Stammesbindungen herausgelöste Menschen sich zunächst zu einer religiösen Gemeinschaft zusammenschliessen können, aus der sekundär ein neuer "Stamm" entstehen kann
. . .' (p. 291). This particular social function of religious movements has gained widespread
recognition: the statements of 'the Eiselen Commission on Bantu Education, that the
Christian Churches became new forms of tribalism, attests to this general tendency of the
church to become a new form of organization, usurping the functions previously performed
by traditional institutions'. Absolom Vilakazi, *Zulu Transformations: A Study of the Dynamics
of Social Change* (University of Natal Press, Pietermaritzburg, 1962), p. 94.

White mission churches have often tried to treat all black men as equal, making no distinctions for native orders of rank: the radical Christian tradition of treating all men as equally miserable sinners, which was necessarily set aside in dealing with the princes of European society, could be given full expression among conquered peoples, whose status systems and sense of social honour could be disregarded. One of the functions of the new separatist movements was to reassert native dignity, by establishing or re-creating status distinctions within native society. Not only are chiefs welcomed and honoured in the church, but the new thaumaturge assimilates his own life-style and claims to that of the great chiefs, who were traditionally also men whose claims to status rested on their magical prowess.[10] A function of separatist movements is often to provide a new status system: the status conferred on the leader becomes the basis for re-allocations of status to the followers. A system of honours, and even of offices, comes into being. Thus in the NBC there is a small council of elders (set up by Isaiah Shembe to advise his son); a committee on discipline and liturgy; ministers (some of whom have Bible school training); evangelists; preachers; and (male and female) leaders of age-groups. Status is a necessary part of the largesse distributed by such chiefly messiahs. Uniforms, rich ceremonial, semi-traditional costumes for dancing, and graduate age-classes are all further evidences of the significance of status and status-symbols in the organization of the movement.

Vital to the maintenance of the surrogate tribal character of such a movement is the existence of a territory. The NBC, like other movements in which thaumaturgy is associated with messianism, owns an area of land. This is both of tribal significance—an ancestral territory—and also an important assertion of prestige, of special appeal since the Land Acts have made purchase of land difficult for natives. The sense of belonging to a kraal remains important for many South African natives: the church group in the town becomes an important location as a community centre, while the estate in the country, such as Shembe's village at Ekuphakameni, becomes an ancestral home and a place of refuge.

Besonders die detribalisierten Menschen der Städte dürfen es sein, die von der Führung ihres Verbandes erwarten, dass sie ihnen eine neue Heimat mit allen ihren seelischen Werten der Geborgenheit biete. Da sie aber zugleich sehr stark die Tendenz haben, Bargeld zu verdienen, und dieses Ziel am ehesten in städtischen Arbeitszentrum zu realisieren ist, stellen viele von ihren an eine neue Heimat möglicherweise weniger Anspruch,

---

[10] B. G. M. Sundkler, op. cit., pp. 101–4. K. Schlosser, 'Profanen Ursachen des Anschlusses an Separatistenkirchen in Süd- und Süd-west Afrika' in E. Benz, op. cit., pp. 25–45.

sie möchte ihnen als dauernder Wohnort dienen als vielmehr, sie möchte ihren Zufluchtstätte in Krankheit und Not gewähren und auch eine Stätte der Erbauung sein.[11]

There Shembe maintains his hostelries for unmarried girls, who are thus protected from the moral dangers of the towns. There are shops owned by the messiah. His church seats 4,000 people. There the movement's following can gather, especially for the July festival, which lasts a month, and there they can behave as a tribal grouping, and engage in ceremonials evocative of tribal reunion.

A movement such as this is clearly more than merely a thaumaturgical cult; but thaumaturgy is central to it. This is evident in the visions that are typically claimed by the leaders: Isaiah Shembe claimed visions at the inception of the church, and frequently thereafter; his son has claimed to receive new hymns from his father in spiritual auditions and so have others in the movement. The benefits that the thaumaturge-messiah figure distributes are, however, more than status and reassurance of tribal identity. He is also a healer, and all medicine is to be avoided other than the water which Shembe has blessed, either directly, or by his having used it to wash in. Witchcraft is taken to be the cause of all fatal illnesses, and possession is an evil to be cured. Prayer, the laying on of hands, and especially the touch of Shembe himself, are principal curative procedures. Healing, indeed, is considered by the principal authority on the movement to be its primary appeal: the yearning for new community organization to replace the tribe is secondary.[12] Healing is not attained in highly emotional states, and although Shembe takes many patients himself, and often spends ten or fifteen minutes with his hands on them, he behaves impersonally.[13] But even a picture of Shembe is often regarded as sufficient to procure a healing.[14]

The sect is not, and cannot be, the re-created Zulu tribe. It adopts the available model of group association less as a conscious choice than as an evocative focus of allegiance. The community in which men were previously protected, in a sense 'saved', was the tribe: thus it is this, or something modelled on it, which the movement seeks to re-create. The symbols, ceremonies, styles, and sentiments of the Zulu people are re-enacted, but the necessarily peaceful purposes of the Nazarites prevents

[11] K. Schlosser, *Eingeborenenkirchen* . . ., op cit., pp. 303–4; see also B. G. M. Sundkler, op. cit., p. 33.
[12] K. Schlosser, op. cit., pp. 252–3. The essentially thaumaturgical character of the 'Zionist' groups is well brought out by W. J. Knoob, 'Ethnologische Aspekte der religiösen Bewegungen in Südlichen Afrika', in Wilhelm E. Mühlmann, *Chiliasmus und Nativismus* (Reimer, Berlin 1961), pp. 87–110.
[13] K. Schlosser, op. cit., p. 225.
[14] B. G. M. Sundkler, op. cit., p. 285.

complete replication of Zulu social organization. It is an extended allusion to the tribe rather than a direct imitation of it; it maintains at least some parts of the Zulu culture, in however confined a context. The essence of the movement is religious, and its religious character is deeply thaumaturgical. The messianic leader himself is no more than a primary manifestation of the miraculous. Cultural continuities are evident, and in most of the thaumaturgical movements—and they number many hundreds in South Africa—there is, at least among the Zulu and the Xhosa-speaking tribes (Xhosa, Thembu, Mpondo, and Mfengu) special regard for ancestors. Ancestral spirits are credited with helping faithful men, and prophets sometimes instruct followers to perform ancestor ceremonies (though this preoccupation is, also, sometimes associated with the Holy Ghost).[15]

The thaumaturge-messiah and the surrogate tribe

A similar movement to that of Shembe, at least in respect of its assimilation of the messianic and thaumaturgical elements, is that of Edward Lekganyene, the *Zion Christian Church* of North Transvaal. A significant difference, however, is that whereas Shembe's church is distinctly Zulu, and recaptures the spirit of that tribe in its rituals and reunions, the Zion Christian Church unites people of different tribes within its membership. Although most of Lekganyene's followers appear to be northern Sutho, there are some Venda; the movement has made progress in Bechuanaland, and there are some followers in Johannesburg, Pretoria, and Germiston. Lekganyene's sermons are translated into Zulu, Ndebele, and Afrikaans. He himself is of the Pedi tribe. Thus, in this case, there is less of a surrogate organization of an actual historical tribe than an adaptation of tribal styles and structure for partially de-tribalized peoples of various tribes of origin.

Edward's father, Ignatius Lekganyene, founded the Zion Christian Church perhaps in 1924 (although earlier dates are also claimed). It split in two after his death, when his two surviving sons both sought leadership. Like the church or churches from which Ignatius Lekganyene seceded, the Zion Christian Church traces its inspiration in large measure to the activity of Alexander Dowie's agent in South Africa, and like Dowie's Church in Illinois, this movement, too, has

[15] This syncretism with ancestor cults is brought out by B. A. Pauw, 'African Christians and their Ancestors' in Victor E. W. Hayward (Ed.), *African Independent Church Movements* (Edinburgh House Press [International Missionary Council Research Pamphlets, No. 11], London 1962), pp. 33–46. See also A. Vilakazi, op. cit., pp. 87 ff.

built its own Zion—Zion City Moria, some twenty-five miles from Pietersburg, where Edward Lekganyene is reported as living.[16] The city itself has perhaps three hundred residents, although the adherents of the movement probably number some tens of thousands (more than 27,000 were claimed in 1942 when Ignatius unsuccessfully sought government recognition of the Church).[17] Zion City Moria serves as the territory of a surrogate tribe, as the home of the chief, and the reunion ground for the sect's festivities.

The thaumaturgical character of the movement is intimately bound up with the messianic claims of Edward Lekganyene, who is today, as his father was before his death in the late 1940s, regarded as God. He transmits power to objects, which then themselves carry it. Thus he transforms paper into healing material, and the smoke from burning such blessed paper is a curative or a prophylactic. He heals by transforming water into medicine; by touching the afflicted; and perhaps by unspecified processes by which he also protects his faithful followers from unemployment. Illness is caused by witchcraft, and the movement neutralizes the power of witches: its prophets destroy the effects of magic, sometimes by blessed pieces of khaki materials which are sold. Purification ceremonies occur before baptism, and speaking in tongues occurs in the religious services. Strains of a more revolutionist orientation, are, however, also found in this movement. Like most native movements, the Zion Christian Church is anti-white, and there is also a prediction, perhaps stemming from the adventism of Dowie-ism, of a future time when Christ will descend to Zion City, which God has chosen as his holy place. But since Edward is regarded by his followers as God, this doctrine is perhaps only partially asserted, even though Zion City is expected to be the paradise of the future, and in some respects is seen as a present paradise.

The Zion Christian Church has an elaborate status hierarchy. There were some fifty-five ministers in 1955, but the Church also has overseers (above ministers) and, below them, headmen, deacons, class-leaders, local preachers, and lay-preachers. In Zion City Moria special ranks exist, including the bodyguard of the leader, trumpeters, policemen, and watchmen. Special insignia, stars of David, are distributed to followers as a protective device. The Church organizes elaborate and spectacular festivities in which dancing, noisy processions, and free spontaneous prayer are conspicuous features. As in other native

[16] This section relies heavily on K. Schlosser, op. cit., pp. 181–218.
[17] The figure of 80,000 adherents of Lekganyene is given by Jacqueline Eberhardt, 'Messianisme en Afrique du Sud', *Archives de Sociologie des Religions* 4 (July–December 1957), pp. 31–56.

movements in South Africa, there is in this movement—again many of these elements are probably derived directly from Dowie's Church— a mixture of Old Testament practices in association with both New Testament ideas, and elements drawn from the indigenous culture, such as sacrifice, polygamy, and the need to counteract witchcraft (though clearly there is also Old Testament sanction for all of these things).

Thaumaturgy and the social context

The pictures of both the Nazareth Baptist Church and the Zion Christian Church which come to us are heavily coloured with the depiction of the leaders, father and son in each case, and their personalities and activities. Sundkler has attempted to depict movements in terms of their types of leadership; he believed the chiefly style to be associated with what he calls 'Ethiopian' churches, those separatist churches which break away from missions largely to assert independence, and the prophetic style of leader to be characteristic of the 'Zionist' churches.[18] To the degree to which these two types converge with revolutionist and thaumaturgical orientations, the plausibility of this association seems warranted. But prevailing social circumstances also influence leadership styles, and we cannot expect any automatic association. In these two well-documented cases, where attention has been concentrated on the leaders, it is apparent that, although neither sect is 'Ethiopian' in Sundkler's usage, the present leaders, whom Sundkler regards as 'messiahs', behave rather more like chiefs than like prophets in many respects. Thaumaturgy is their real concern and they are credited with miraculous powers, but the patterns of deference that the sects have evolved, and the status-orders of their social structure, have been borrowed in large part from the traditional political and social organization of tribal society. J. G. Shembe, indeed, appears to be at most a reluctant prophet, under some strain in the prophetic role. In contrast to Edward Lekganyene, who has had only three years of schooling, J. G. Shembe is a well-educated man.[19] It may, indeed, be

[18] B. G. M. Sundkler, op. cit., chapter V.

[19] K. Schlosser, op. cit., p. 225. In her earlier studies, Schlosser paid even greater attention to prophets than in this book, where considerable attention is paid to history, rites, composition of membership, and other features. See K. Schlosser, *Propheten in Afrika* (Albert Limbach, Braunschweig 1949), and *idem*, 'Die Prophetismus in Niederen Kulturen', *Zeitschrift für Ethnologie* 75–76 (1950–1), pp. 60–72, where her judgment is, 'Die Ursachen für das Auftreten von Propheten sind—abgesehen von rein persönlichen Ehrgeiz—überwiegend wirtschaftlicher und politischer Natur ausschliesslich religiös nur in den selteristen Fällen.' The contrast in the education of these two second-generation messiahs is pointed out by J. Eberhardt, op. cit.

that prophetism is scarcely transmissible from father to son, but the fact that these sects follow such an inheritance system is itself further evidence of the influence of tribal models. Thaumaturgy, after all, differs from other religious responses to the world, in that it was once an orthodoxy. It may thus readily reassimilate itself to political institutions. It becomes heterodoxical only as it differs in technique from orthodoxy, or as thaumaturgy as such ceases to be a culturally dominant response, and as new religious orientations become established that accept the secular world *as it is*.

The relationship of leadership-type and sect-type, which Sundkler sought to establish for South Africa, has been challenged in the case of the Phuduhutswana chiefdom on the Taung reserve of the north Cape Province on the Transvaal border, where some nineteen separatist churches of various types flourish, in addition to eleven denominations and sects introduced by Europeans.[20] It does not appear that the chiefdom has lost influence to the degree evident among the Zulu, and although secular leadership opportunities have declined, all headmen today come from the royal lineage, and fewer opportunities for non-hereditary leadership are available than in the past.[21] These separatist sects do generally show strong tendencies to tribal exclusiveness, but they do not appear to operate as surrogate tribes. The ritual and belief of the sects, many of which are preoccupied with typical thaumaturgical concerns, 'do not resemble traditional ritual and belief so much in respect of external form, but in respect of their magical character'.[22]

Nor is tribalism, or its subsequent transmutation as African nationalism, given much support by these sects, which are not nativistic in inclination, and which stand apart from traditional tribal practices and concerns.[23] The model of the tribe, the reconstruction of communities

[20] B. A. Pauw, *Religion in a Tswana Chiefdom* (Oxford University Press, London 1960), p. 46.

[21] B. A. Pauw, op. cit., p. 77, writes, 'Church leadership also makes up for a lack of opportunity for non-hereditary leadership which always used to exist even in traditional society . . .'.

[22] Ibid., p. 146. Traditional thaumaturgy has been replaced by the thaumaturgy of the new movements, which represents a distinct difference in techniques but a close similarity of ends.

[23] We have already noted, in other cases, that some sects become virtually tribal churches (see p. 137 and footnote 3). In this area, the Maidi were involved in one of the earliest tribal secessions. Because they objected to any implication that they were subject to the Phuduhutswana (Tlhaping), they withdrew, with their chief, from the LMS at Manche to found the Native Independent Congregational Church, which they still tend to regard as their tribal church. B. A. Pauw, 'Patterns of Christianization among the Tswana and Xhosa-speaking Peoples' in M. Fortes and G. Dieterlen, op. cit., pp. 240–57. Of the Tswana tribes of the Bechuanaland Protectorate, I. Schapera, in 'Christianity and the Tswana', *Journal of the Royal Anthropological Institute of Gt. Britain and Ireland* 88, Pt. I (January–June 1958), pp. 1–9, writes that many who became Christians did so only as a matter of fashion because chiefs were converted. Schapera is sceptical of the significance of the claims that Christianity affected tribes very much.

on a territory, which was evident in the case of both the Nazareth
Baptist Church and the Zion Christian Church, appear to be lacking in
the context of life on the Taung reserve. There is no similar vacuum of
tribal order to fill, and the sects, whether they are separatist and similar
in style to the mission churches from which they broke away, or
primarily thaumaturgical, do not adopt this organizational pattern.
(It is not only thaumaturgical sects that are likely to respond to the de-
tribalized situation, of course. The generally conversionist movement of
Nicholas B. H. Bhengu, in the east coast towns of East London and
Durban, has its community structure, and the distinctly revolutionist
sect of Enoch Mgijima at Ntabelenga built its community organization.[24]) It is thus evident that thaumaturgy shows an adaptability to
organize according to available circumstances. It may be engrafted into
a decaying tribal structure; it may be organized as a synthetic, surrogate tribe; it may persist as a dispersed set of rites and practices for a
following which is less than fully committed to a thaumaturgical view
of the world; it may acquire the style and durability of a western-style
fundamentalist mission.

Although our examples of the affiliation of thaumaturgy to the
rational denominational style of organization are drawn primarily from
West Africa, they do arise elsewhere, as is evident from the study made
among the Tlhaping of the Taung reserve of north Cape Province.
The separatist churches among this group of tribes include schisms
from mission churches found elsewhere in South Africa. They also
include groups that are thaumaturgical in orientation, even though
they have adopted the organizational forms of the missioning sects that
have influenced their religious practice. None of the churches found in
the Phuduhutswana chiefdom originated there, and there are relatively
few cultural continuities from traditional religious practice embraced
within the new sects. Rather, those new churches that are more
markedly thaumaturgical[25] replace most traditional elements with new

[24] On Nicholas Bhengu, see p. 49. An account is to be found in K. Schlosser, op. cit. For a
discussion of the influence of Bhengu's revivalism on the un-schooled 'Red' Xhosa, see Philip
Mayer, *Townsmen or Tribesmen: Conservatism and the Process of Urbanization in a South African City*
(Oxford University Press, Cape Town 1961), pp. 192–205. For an interesting discussion of
the various forms of native adjustment to white rule, in which the author contrasts Enoch
Mgijima, Nicholas Bhengu and James Limba (of the Ibandla Lika Krestu movement), see
O. F. Raum, 'Von Stammespropheten zu Sektenführern', in E. Benz, op. cit., pp. 49–70.
[25] B. A. Pauw, *Religion in a Tswana Chiefdom*, op. cit., Pauw employs an unusual distinction
among separatist churches (p. 44), distinguishing those that split from missions without
much (if any) doctrinal divergence; those that are keepers of the seventh day as the Sabbath;
and those that he calls 'Pentecostal', but which differ from the second type principally in the
matter of seventh-day observance. For our purposes the distinction of these last two types has
no particular significance: both appear to employ conversionist types of organization for
largely thaumaturgical concerns.

types of magic. But the magical power of baptism by immersion (which among the Tlhaping is not a traditional rite), the emphasis on holy water, the idea of a staff endowed with holy power, and the list of ritual avoidances, are all elements in the pattern of widespread thaumaturgical practice. The church's own methods of healing displace traditional methods, and herbalists and witch-doctors are both rejected. Sorcery is an accepted cause of illness, to be countered, however, by essentially new techniques of prophylaxis rather than by traditional practices. Simultaneous but individual vocal prayer is common, with 'a rigmarole of cliches and of sounds which in ordinary conversation have no meaning, but which are interpreted as speaking in tongues'.[26] Revelations from the Spirit are frequent in some of these churches, and 'the revelations received are mostly concerned with the treatment or prevention of illness; they are about the causes of illness (including sorcery), about what clothes or figures should be worn, whether to use holy water, whether to use ashes, and so on'.[27] The Phuduhutswana chiefdom is said to be 'in an advanced state of transition from paganism to Christianity',[28] but it is also clear that that part of Christianity which has been taken up is the thaumaturgical practice to be found in the scriptures.

If the Tswana chiefdom is in an advanced state of transition from paganism to Christianity, this is certainly no less true of many societies of West Africa, and particularly of those coastal tribes, some of whom have been exposed to European influences for centuries, and to systematic Christian influences from the early nineteenth century.[29] Since the firm establishment of missions, and particularly since the latter half of the last century, the European Protestant model of religious

[26] Ibid., p. 191.
[27] Ibid., p. 202.
[28] Ibid., p. 237.
[29] The first organized mission in what is now Ghana was that of the Society for the Propagation of the Gospel in 1752, one of whose pupils, Philip Quaque, became the first non-European Anglican to be ordained. He ministered in the area for fifty years from 1766: Robert T. Parsons, *The Churches and Ghana Society, 1918–1955* (E. J. Brill, Leiden 1963). The Basel Mission arrived at the Danish settlement at Christiansborg (later Accra) in 1827, and moved, after the severe loss of several missionaries by disease, to Akrapong in the Akwapim mountains in 1835. Thomas Birch Freeman, the Wesleyan, had been at Kumasi, Abomey, and Abeokata in 1839, and was followed by George Chapman as a permanent missionary. The Bremen Mission was established east of the River Volta in 1847. Conflicts between pagans and Christians among the Fanti occurred in 1849. A training institute was established at Fourah Bay, Sierra Leone, by the Anglicans in the 1840s, and at the same time the Roman Catholics sought priests in France for service in Liberia. C. P. Groves, *The Planting of Christianity in Africa*, Vol. II (Lutterworth Press, London 1954), pp. 218–19, 224–5. Roman Catholic influence through the Portuguese was, of course, very much older, and had already, at much earlier dates, given rise to some dramatic syncretistic cults much further south: see Erika Sulzmann, 'Die Bewegung der Antonier im alten Reiche Kongo' in W. E. Mühlmann, op. cit., pp. 81–7.

organization has been increasingly available. The missionary impact of many decades is complicated by the diversity of missionary bodies—a diversity which has markedly increased in the twentieth century, and particularly from the 1920s, with the steady increase in the number of European and American sectarian movements that have entered the mission field. Whatever success Christian missions may have had in actually converting Africans, it would be surprising, given the resilience of thaumaturgical orientations that we have already noted in other contexts, had not the central concerns of traditional religion—albeit usually in other forms—persisted both within the newly-imported religious organizations, and in movements arising in imitation of them. Once sectarian proselytizing missions had been established, the indigenous thaumaturgical preoccupation acquired reinforcement, for even in conversionist sects thaumaturgical elements often persist—in glossalalia, faith-healing, and prophesying. In the African context, such elements had a special appeal, and in some cases they had a direct continuity with traditional preoccupations and practice. The autonomy of the sects, and their defiance of what must initially have appeared as more or less 'official' religion, was a further stimulus to native separatism and particularly to those who broke away in order to enjoy a fuller opportunity for thaumaturgical practice.

Our purpose here is largely to illustrate the way in which thaumaturgical preoccupations have been the real focus of concern in movements that have adopted the characteristically conversionist type of organizational structure. But we need also to remember that one religious response may be found in widely differing cultural conditions and levels of development. Perhaps this is most true of the thaumaturgical orientation, which is a fundamental religious position. West Africa presents us with many cultures at differing stages of development, and many societies that are culturally relatively autonomous of the states into which, by the accident of colonial policies, they are politically amalgamated. In those societies that have experienced less association with European cultures and where, despite modifications induced by cultural contact, indigenous traditions have persisted, we might expect to find new movements that are not very far removed in their forms of expression and standards of practice from primitive religions. In the cities and especially in areas near to the coast, there is a much heavier cultural overlay of western forms, especially of organization, and perhaps also of practice and belief. The number and diversity of such movements is undoubtedly greater than the reports that are available concerning them, but brief reference to some of them will indicate the range of cultural variability found in even one religious response.

Transient and persisting movements

We are already acquainted with thaumaturgical movements of an ephemeral character which arise in, or are brought into, a particular region to fulfil a cleansing and purifying mission, and which then move on or wither. Such witch-finding cults have occurred in West Africa, as in Central and East Africa. Such a cult is reported of the Dagomba at Savelugu in the northern Gold Coast (now Ghana) in 1955.[30] Medicine was drunk at a shrine some distance away, either as a way of protecting oneself from wizardry, or of gaining the power to see wizards. At first outsiders were brought in as wizard-finders, but subsequently young women acquired this power and accused other women, who were (usually more senior) neighbours or co-wives. A similar outburst of wizard-finding is reported in 1950 among the southern Yoruba, and was introduced among them by travellers from Dahomey. This movement, the *Atinga* cult, was a somewhat modified version of the Tigari cult of Ghana,[31] but whereas in Ghana the cult acquired semi-permanent shrines of its own, and appears to have operated through one priest at each shrine, among the southern Yoruba it was brought by a migratory band of practitioners, drummers, and dancers. Its incidence was of short duration, and interest waned when the heavy farming season began.[32] In this instance a cult which became somewhat

[30] David Tait, 'A Sorcery Hunt in Dagomba', *Africa* XXXIII, 2 (April 1963), pp. 136–46. From the account, the wizards appear to have been sorcerers in the technical sense: they used medicines and they consciously destroyed their victims. The accused sorcerers were typically old women, and the victims were young men. The wizard-hunt was a hunt of older and senior women by younger ones, and all the accused were married to, or lived in, the homes of prominent men. Tait presents the Dagomba as a people fearing the coming of independence to Ghana because of the dominance of the south, and the outbreak as occurring in a year when Ramadan had fallen at a difficult time of year for fasting, thus increasing tensions.

[31] On Tigari, see pp. 54–7.

[32] P. Morton-Williams, 'The Atinga Cult among the South-Western Yoruba: A Sociological analysis of a Witch-finding Movement', *Bulletin de l'Institut français d'Afrique noire*, T XVIII, ser. B. Nr. 3–4 (1956), pp. 315–34. The Atinga cult was invited to particular townships, and the Alatinga band would make accusations after a performance of dancing, drumming, and the killing of domestic animals (from the blood of which, with kola nuts, the special anti-witchcraft medicine was made). Those taking the medicine would be immune to witchcraft, provided that they also maintained four taboos: (1) not to steal, nor to take paw-paw or pepper from another's farm; (2) not to commit adultery, or, if committing it, to confess it to one's spouse; (3) not to murder; (4) not to think evil against anyone. Atinga would kill anyone who practised witchcraft after taking the medicine. Those not immediately confessing to witchcraft when accused were obliged to sacrifice a chicken, which, in dying, indicated by its final posture the guilt or innocence of the accused. Morton-Williams suggests that Yoruba witchcraft fears and accusations arise particularly from the anxiety of older women who can no longer fulfil their child-bearing functions, and from the ambivalent sentiments in men. He relates these phenomena to the character of Yoruba social structure, in which a woman lives in her husband's compound, where she is insecure unless she has adult sons to protect her. Traditionally the Yoruba in their ancestral cults had danced to placate witches—to overcome them by goodwill—but the cults were themselves falling into decay at this time.

institutionalized in Ghana, failed to acquire even incipient institutionalization among the Yoruba, perhaps because those Yoruba who became practitioners of the cult were less feared, we are told, than the Dahomeans who introduced it. The tensions prevailing within the society—in this case, hostility especially towards older women who, in the absence of sons to take care of them, became resented, as economic burdens on other relatives—did not disappear with the short-lived cult. Although the demand for thaumaturgical and therapeutic practice appears to persist at high levels in less-developed societies (and, perhaps, in some respects and with appropriate cultural modifications, in all societies), none the less, because of its essentially local and particularistic character, it is not easily institutionalized except in the context of the traditional social structure.

It is evident that the specific objects of attack in witch-finding movements vary with the social structure of the society concerned, and perhaps with the points in the system at which the cult finds expression. In many instances, older fetiches are attacked by the new cults, as we have seen in the Central African movements, in the Nyambua, and some of the earlier cults among the Tiv. This was also the case in the Atinga cult among the south-western Yoruba, although in the parent Tigari cult in Ghana, whilst the surrender of medicines was demanded, other fetiches were superseded rather than actively destroyed.[33] The cults appear as initiators of sudden social change, accelerating the normal process of social dynamics; effecting redistributions of power (among men of the Tiv) or of prestige (among women of the Dagomba); working off resentments against older women, and perhaps making evident their dependence (among the Yoruba). Where respect for elders is the norm, as it is in most primitive societies, the anti-witchcraft movement becomes an occasion when resentment against elders can be legitimately expressed. In the process of wider social change, it may become the vehicle by which younger and more progressive men assert themselves. It provides them with a religious justification for their claims to prestige and power, and it offers a protective function from the envy of others while they establish themselves.

Functions of this type may be accomplished by a transient and recrudescent anti-witchcraft movement, but thaumaturgical demands, for healing, reassurance, and protection, are persistent and endemic in human society. New thaumaturgical movements do not readily become fully institutionalized within traditional social structure; but where some such structure can be 're-made', as with the Zulu, a process

---

[33] On the Tiv, see pp. 88–9. The account rests on P. Bohannan, op. cit.

resembling traditional institutionalization may occur. The secret society may provide an alternative model. Where the new thaumaturgical preoccupation can assimilate itself to older patterns of religious practice, it may, rather like a secret society, acquire a certain stability and persistence as an integrated part of the social system. In such cases it is assimilated to, or becomes a facet of, traditional religious preoccupations.

Such a re-working of the ancestral cult with many syncretistic features is found in the *Bwiti* cult, which has flourished, even if in somewhat changing form, for several decades among the Fang of Gabon, and among the Bakale, Bateke, Bangala, Aduma, and other tribes in the Gabon, Cameroons, and Spanish Guinea.[34] The cult divides into a number of sub-cults, but appears to be generally characterized as a re-working of traditional religious practice, and as a strengthening of already known medicines by new rites, the accretion of Christian ideas, and in particular by the important place accorded to an indigenous hallucinogen, the *iboga* shrub.[35]

Bwiti co-exists with other religious movements, although it is active in proselytizing and inducting initiates into its secret rites. The secrets of Bwiti are held to be incommunicable, but they are experienced in the initiation. They are closely associated with the intense experiences induced by *iboga*, which include highly stereotyped visions, to which specific symbolic meaning is accorded. The visions establish communication with the dead, and are an encounter with God and Jesus. This special secret knowledge is of particular importance in creating a sense of group identity among initiates and in facilitating sect cohesion.[36] Cult practices include: sacrifice of fowls (which may perhaps be a modification from earlier human sacrifice); all-night dancing and drumming in the forest and at the little chapels of the cult; re-enactments of the crucifixion, when the initiate undergoes a type of 'hazing' by carrying a cross in procession and, in imitation of the sufferings of Christ, is made to suffer at the hands of other members.[37]

The elaborate imagery, creation mythology, the use of fire, of a

[34] This account relies principally on Georges Balandier, *Sociologie actuelle de l'Afrique noire* (Presses universitaires, Paris 1955), pp. 218–30; and on Antonio de Veciana Vilaldach, *La Secta del Bwiti en la Guinea Española* (Consejo Superior de Investigaciónes Científicas [Instituto de Estudias Africanos], Madrid 1958).

[35] The botanical and pharmacological character of *iboga* (Tabernanche Iboga) and the alcoloids which can be extracted from it, are given briefly in A. de V. Vilaldach, op. cit., pp. 29 ff.

[36] G. Balandier, op. cit., p. 229.

[37] James W. Fernandez, 'The Idea and Symbol of the Saviour in a Gabon Syncretistic Cult', *International Review of Missions* LIII (July 1964), pp. 281–89, provides details additional to the above-cited sources.

central pillar, and of a traditional harp-like instrument of special importance in ceremonies, illustrate the richness of the cult, but do not directly concern us. Bwiti is a multifunctional secret society related to established fertility cults, purification from witches, ancestor cults, and the transfer after death of the *banji* (devotee) to the land of the dead, with which, through ritual and the influence of *iboga*, he is already acquainted. It reinforces a sense of the potency of the tribe, or, perhaps more characteristically, of the supra-tribal indigenous culture. It has an elaborate hierarchic order, and the *okambos*, masters of ceremonies, are often young and mission-educated.[38] As a movement it has acquired considerable influence in native affairs, and is at the centre of all native activities among the Fang. In the 1930s and 1940s the cult network was used by Gabonese politicians, in particular by Léon Mba, who later became President of Gabon after independence.[39] But although Bwiti has been a response to the frustrations of European domination, particularly among the Fang, and has encouraged anti-European sentiment and activity, 'the search for messianic satisfactions and apocalyptic promise . . . have never been dominant'.[40]

The Bwiti cult, it will be noted, had become well integrated with indigenous society; it did not depend on any one leader, and its rituals and procedures had become elaborated on existing models and perhaps on older established secret societies. This undoubtedly contributed to its persistence over so long a period, in which it has been more markedly successful than many of the movements that have imitated Christian models, or the typical anti-witchcraft movements and purification cults. It has become thoroughly institutionalized, which is by no means the achievement of all religious impulses that seek a synthesis of new ideas with elements of traditional culture. It appears to be less easily achieved where a charismatic prophet prevails except when, as in the South African cases reviewed above, he adopts tribal organizational styles for his movement. The *Déima* cult of the Ivory Coast offers an example of a movement of greater duration than the typical anti-witchcraft enthusiasms, but without the capacity either to assimilate to the traditional pattern of social organization, or to acquire the new organizational strength of the imitative movements to which we shall shortly turn.

[38] A. de V. Vilaldach, op. cit., pp. 55 ff.

[39] J. W. Fernandez, 'Politics and Prophecy: African Religious Movements', *Practical Anthropology* 12, 2 (March–April 1965), pp. 71–5; and Virginia Thompson and Richard Adloff, *The Emerging States of French Equatorial Africa* (Stanford University Press, Stanford, California, 1960), p. 314.

[40] J. W. Fernandez, 'The Idea and Symbol . . .', op. cit.

Thaumaturgy as an innovative and as a restorative agency

Déima is a neologistic term invented by Marie Lalou, the founder of a purification cult among the Bété and Dida of the lower Ivory Coast. In some respects the movement has similarities with the usual anti-witchcraft movement, and it is in this sense that it might be described as relying on traditional ideas.[41] Marie Lalou had had some experience of the Protestants when young, and after the death of her three children and her husband she appears to have experienced visions, in particular of a strangely shaped snake, which became the object of a personal cult.[42] She learned how to prepare water which the snake would enter and purify, thus conferring upon it healing powers. She herself became a seer, who could detect sorcerers on sight, and these powers were sufficient to make her the object of pilgrimages from various tribes. The extent to which she owed inspiration to Christianity is disputable, but it seems that, whatever may have been her attitude towards William Wadé Harris, the Liberian prophet, who had so extensively affected the Ivory Coast before the First World War, and in whose wake her movement arose in the 1920s and 1930s, she drew people out of the missions and suggested that the missions did not practise religion according to the will of God.[43]

[41] B. Holas, Le Séparatisme religieux en Afrique noire (Presses universitaires, Paris 1965), emphasizes the cultural continuities in Déima, pp. 304 ff. He had written at an earlier date, 'Le culte, fondé par une femme godié, Marie Dahanon, surnommée Lalou, reste, par opposition au harrisme, fortement redevable aux croyances autochtones'—B. Holas, 'Bref Aperçu sur les principaux cultes syncrétiques de la Basse Côte d'Ivoire' Africa XXIV, 1954, pp. 55–60.

[42] The significance of the death of children, of still-births, and miscarriage in the immediately anterior experiences of prophetesses remains to be analysed. One is reminded of the history of Mother Ann Lee, foundress of the Shakers in Lancashire, whose teachings also emphasized sexual continence (in her case for her followers as well as herself); of some of the suggestions made in regard to the inspiration of Mrs Hutchinson in the 1630s in Boston (on which see Emrys Battis Saints and Sectaries [University of North Carolina Press, Chapel Hill, N.C., 1962]); the asceticism imposed on her Christian Science schismatics by Mrs Stetson in the American Church Triumphant; and the hints of sexual abstinence as a higher path in the teachings of Mary Baker Eddy, after the double widowhood of her brief first and third marriages, her second apparently unhappy marriage that ended in divorce, and her inability to bring up her own son (for brief accounts, see B. R. Wilson, Sects and Society, op. cit). There are other cases: their detailed analysis might be rewarding. Marie Lalou opposed the compulsory re-marriage of widows, and this idea, a significant assertion of feminism, was also enunciated by Alice Lenshina in the Lumpa Church in Zambia.

[43] B. Holas, Le Séparatisme religieux . . ., op. cit., p. 314, writes, 'In truth, and despite appearances, the dogma of Lalou is little dependent on that which was preached by Harris, even though his name is often posted at the front of their sanctuaries . . .' (my translation). Denise Paulme, in 'Une religion syncrétique en Côte d'Ivoire: le culte déima', Cahiers d'Études Africaines 9, vol. II (1962), 1er Cahier, pp. 5–90, says that Marie Lalou regarded Harris as an enunciator of true faith. It is evident that certain preoccupations of the two movements were similar, but Harris appears to have stood rather closer to western tradition than did Marie Lalou, and to have introduced fewer specifically traditional elements of myth or ritual. On William Wadé Harris, see p. 174, footnote 4.

The central concerns of the Déima cult were relatively simple: they were the restoration or preservation of health; protection from wizards; and the abandonment of traditional fetichism. The elements are combined in a clearly syncretistic complex of beliefs and practices. Thus Marie Lalou imposed upon herself a rigorously ascetic regimen, sleeping on the ground, using a stone for a pillow, avoiding meat, fish, and spices, rejecting the idea of taking another husband or of having any sexual relations. These ideas are not part of the indigenous religious tradition. They are indeed very typically the ways in which religious leaders who arise outside the established traditions seek to impress their authority. But the use of water as a protective, purifying, and life-giving force is widely diffused in Africa, and occurs in many new cults. There appears to have been an element of ancestor worship in Déima, and there was the typical preoccupation with sorcery. Regular weekly services were held, in which songs, preaching, and the use of a bell were prominent, but of perhaps greater significance were the occasional services when men came to be relieved of sickness. The sick person had to confess his faults publicly to a Déima priest, and had to abandon all evil thinking about others. He then paid five francs (a fixed fee), drank holy water, and was anointed with a specially prepared and consecrated ash, which together represented life-giving water and purifying fire. Protecting oneself from evil was the first preoccupation of the faithful. To this end old cult objects were destroyed and the weapons furnished by Marie Lalou, and in particular the sanctified water, were usually kept at hand.[44] Something of the asceticism of the prophetess has entered the cult, however, and a puritanical and impassive attitude to the world, even in the face of death, is evident in the strictness and regulation of the emotions at funerals.

The cult has its creation myths in various versions, and has stories of Jesus and another son of God, Abidise, who was reputedly king of the black race. Stories from the Old Testament were evolved to explain the dominance of white peoples over black. Marie Lalou said that as the white men had their religion, so black men should have theirs. This was an incipient anti-white element, which was more pronounced in the reverence that the movement gave to Félix Houphouët-Boigny, who, after independence, was deified as the man who had driven the French from the country. Marie Lalou died in 1951, and thereafter the movement was disrupted by schism, and in many areas has fallen into disregard. Various successors arose, including two other women prophets, Princess Geniss and Ble Nahi (who took the name Jesus Onoi, or Jesus

---

[44] B. Holas, op. cit., p. 321.

Woman).[45] In the areas in which it had first arisen, and in the village of Marie Lalou herself, the cult has dwindled to small proportions, and followers have returned to the missions, even though aspirants to the Déima priesthood, to which there is ready access, still make pilgimages to her tomb, and obtain their basic equipment from the village.

In one significant respect Déima represents an interesting variation from some of the earlier anti-witchcraft movements that have arisen in many African countries—it is, of course, a more elaborate religious system than movements that confine themselves simply to the elimination of wizardry. Whereas previously a man's illness was regarded as clear evidence of the evil magic of others, Déima represented an attempt to relocate culpability. The sick individual was himself blamed for attempting to work evil magic on others, and it was he who needed the purification of the holy water and ashes. Marie Lalou had a ghost army of 'gendarmes' which attacked with illness those who were attempting to practise sorcery, and only confession would induce her spirit soldiers to cease the attack.[46] In many ways this might be taken as a significant step in the process of the internalization of values, and the creation of a more ascetic and objectified morality.

The function that has impressed some investigators, more, however, is one which bears some resemblance to that mentioned above in relation to anti-witchcraft movements, namely, the catalytic function of facilitating generational change, innovation, and the provision of an agency of protection for those whose wealth, modernity, or power represented a challenge to a traditional status system. Déima is a protection from institutionalized envy. Köbben reports that one man had said, '. . . people are jealous of me because I am young and give orders here. It is just as well that Deima is here—in earlier times I would have been dead by now'.[47] Witchcraft, he considers, helped in time past to reinforce the power of the gerontocracy: anti-witchcraft movements permitted the threatened newer groups to retort. Although Köbben does not take his analysis so far, it is conceivable that the reallocation of culpability to the sick man himself might have gone further to reduce envy by fear of its consequences, and might have been a particularly potent weapon against more senior, older, and perhaps therefore more sickness-prone individuals.

---

[45] D. Paulme, op. cit., traces the subsequent history of some of these successors and the schisms that occurred.

[46] This characteristic is brought out by A. J. F. Köbben, 'Prophetic Movements as an Expression of Social Protest', *International Archives of Ethnography* XLIX, Pt. 1 (1960), pp. 117–64, on the basis of his own research, and is discussed by B. Holas, op. cit., pp. 321 ff.

[47] A. J. F. Köbben, op. cit., p. 141.

Not all new thaumaturgical movements necessarily fulfil functions of this kind, however. Some are distinctly supportive of existing social structures, and are essentially conservative of patterns of social relations, even where they incorporate new elements of myth or ritual or moral prescription. The weakness of an analysis of the functions of religion for the whole society, is the failure of this approach to recognize that in societies in which the balance of social strata is changing, and in which social relationships are acquiring new forms (and this has been a common condition in preliterate societies in the last hundred years) divergent religious orientations, or even, at times, competing religious movements, are likely to arise to accommodate those experiencing this process. Changes in social experience or social position may cause men to demand a new *Weltanschauung*, a new response to the world, and in societies where religious modes of thought predominate, this will probably lead to reinterpretations of man's conception of what God will (or should) do in the world. New movements may arise to give expression to these new orientations, or—and this is by no means unusual—the same movements, in some of their facets, may accommodate the divergent interests of different groups.

An example of a new thaumaturgical movement serving essentially conservative interests, although doing so through a new synthesis of elements drawn from indigenous and external cultures, is the *Massa* movement of the northern Ivory Coast. Massa is at once a more primitive movement than Déima, occurring in a less-developed area, and occurring later in time. But it has important features in common with similar cults, such as Tigari, which found followings in the more sophisticiated coastal towns of Ghana. In the period of the early 1950s, Massa spread widely through the northern Ivory Coast and the southern French Sudan. It arose in 1946, in Wolo, a village in the canton of Dielizangasso, Cercle de San, halfway between Bamako and Wagadugu, when a man, Mpéni Dembélé, had a vision of God who gave him a new fetich and a cult for its worship. The fetich was to replace all previous fetiches, which were to be destroyed. It promised the fertility both of the fields and of women, and the restoration of old customs and practices, in every regard except that the new fetich was now to be the object of worship. Mpéni Dembélé had previously preached the traditional cult, the *nia*, and was thus well versed in traditional agricultural practices and their attendant ritual. The new cult regulated agricultural days of work, which were old traditions of the area (for example, that on Friday no old person or chief of a family should work). Practice of the cult ensured that thanks were given to the Fertilizer of the Crops. Disobedience to it would bring rain. The cult spread rapidly among the Senufo, Bambara, Marka, Bobo, Gouin, Dian, Pougoul, Wile, Dagara, and other peoples.[48]

The cult strongly emphasized obedience to superiors, and it was established an an essentially community cult, not as a private practice like Tigari. A village deciding to adopt Massa would send delegates to Wolo to learn the necessary rituals. Temples were built, and elaborate sacrifices marked the inauguration of the new shrine in which the fetich was to be kept. The fetich was a visible object of somewhat indescribable character—a mound of horns, iron rings, and encrusted blood from sacrifices.[49] It presided over special feasts, which were associated with the agricultural season. Water was of special importance in this cult, as in most of the new religious movements of the Ivory Coast. It was kept in a large pot in the temple, and there might also be two baths of water, known as the Spring of Massa, which were used for bathing, and the water from which was afterwards drunk.

Massa was available to individual supplicants through his priests, to whom both sacrificial animals and money had to be provided. Massa's acceptance of a sacrificial hen with the determination by its death-posture of guilt or innocence was identical with that found in Tigari and Atinga. Its principal function, we are told, was the abolition of wizardry,[50] although Massa was invoked in all kinds of trouble. Ideally, Massa replaced older fetich cults, but it appears that in fact it often existed side by side with them, or adapted the masks and rituals of other religious practices to its own worship. It was not an abandonment of fetich belief, but a reformation of it, from 'polyfetischismus zum Monofetischismus'.[51] Old sorcerers and seers became the priests of the movement, and respect for traditional bearers of status was reinforced. Traditional society had acquired new consolidation.[52] At the same time, the cult put a new premium on righteous behaviour by forbidding evil works.

Functions and organization

Massa thus appears as an essentially restorative movement, focusing on thaumaturgical practice, and re-interpreting past ideology and ritual

---

[48] This account relies principally on B. Holas, op. cit., pp. 343–63.

[49] This is the description provided by Hans Himmelheber, 'Massa-fetisch der Rechtschaffenheit', *Tribus* (Zeitschrift für Ethnologie und ihre Nachbarwissenschaften) Stuttgart, 4/5 (1954/5), pp. 56–62.

[50] Ibid.

[51] Ibid.

[52] B. Holas, op. cit., p. 361.

in support of existing status-groups. We have already seen that, fundamental as thaumaturgy appears to be as a religious orientation, its practice may be adapted to the needs of new social strata, as in the Déima movement, or may, as among the Tiv, prevent the enhancement of status differentiation. Clearly the functions of such a movement must vary with a variety of cultural and social structural factors, and this in itself may make us hesitant about the acceptance of any dogmatic theories concerning the social significance of particular religious responses.

Thaumaturgy is obviously closely concerned with the troubles of individual men, and with their struggle for status one with another. Whatever *groups* thaumaturgical activities serve, a cult always claims to seek the regulation of evil. In practice it provides mechanisms to reduce the tensions and jealousies of some, whilst also claiming more general social functions in the eradication of sickness and death and the distribution of reassurance. It is concerned with the affairs that are close to people, with their adjustment in the social relationships of normal everyday life, and so with the perennial tensions that individuals experience. But such tensions may be structurally induced in the social system: they need not be—even if sometimes they may be— tensions distributed purely as probabilities of age (sickness) and sex (infertility) or as more random phenomena. Thus witch-finding movements may be directed at—and by—certain sorts of individuals with particular locations in the system, whilst at the same time being generally available for application to a wider range of problems, and this is especially true of the more persistent movements.

The very persistence and recrudescence of such tensions, however, is perhaps one factor that prevents movements attaining stability. Unless there is a large public to whom these cults can offer services when and as their various needs arise, permitting such votaries to come and go, it may be difficult for them to persist. The more total a community's acceptance of a new movement, the more likely is it that the cult will be seen to have failed, for its promise of remedy for all types of tensions and strains cannot in the nature of the case be fulfilled for all men, all of the time. A temporary movement may be sufficient to facilitate the adjustment of status claims as new social strata emerge, giving them 'cover' while they consolidate their new positions—whether these are generationally determined, or are readjustments between innovators and those with traditional claims to status. It may provide for brief social regeneration or revitalization, but in the nature of its own practice it is unlikely to succeed in the long run. The result is that such movements, when they rely on the charismatic leader, or when they are espoused by villages (as were the cults among the Lele, or the Massa cult), lack a sufficiently independent organizational structure to withstand the disenchantment of votaries. Only where a thaumaturgical movement has an organizational pattern that is, over the long term, independent of local community organization, and that is independent even of its *particular* following at any one point in time, is it likely to endure.

This, as we have seen, may be achieved in a variety of ways. The new movement may emphasize tribal identification, and so provide itself with a social basis—but this is possible, clearly, only in certain circumstances. The disruption of tribal life in South Africa, together with the 'freezing' of these partially disrupted units, and the prevention of any reformulation of native power structure on other lines, as an effect of government policy, make the tribe the viable unit of assimilation and identity for sects like that of Shembe among the Zulu, and that of Stephen Nkonyana among the Swazi.[53]

In the West African cases messianism and Christian influences have been less strong; the context of the dominant culture is less oppressively evident, and tribalism, although affected, has not been frozen in a position of half-decay. Here the new movements readily extend across tribal lines, although many do so as essentially migratory phenomena, taken into, and absorbed within, local community organization. There is no implication of permanent or significant allegiance to founders or originators, who are merely the sellers of secrets and the legitimators of ritual. The capacity of these cults to unify men supra-tribally is not very pronounced in these cases, and this is certainly far from being an articulate conception of their *raison d'être*, or even a latent function.

At local level, the new cults may, as we have seen, have varying effects on the status claims of different groups. Thus although they do not establish an orientation for more permanent alternative allegiance than that of existing tribal and communal authority, they may affect local *distribution* of power and status. They do not present a frontal assault on the *structure* of power or status. But where they persist, and where they impose new moral practices, taboos, and rites, they may promote a steady erosion of the existing legitimation of traditional authority. But these movements do not show, even in the case of Tigari or Déima, the durability of movements which have adopted the tribal base or have imitated the mission model.

[53] B. G. M. Sundkler discusses the relationships of various 'Zionist' churches with the Swazi kings in various places: op. cit., Rev. Edn, pp. 315 ff; *idem*, 'Chief and Prophet in Zululand and Swaziland', in M. Fortes and G. Dieterlen, op. cit., pp. 276–90; *idem*, 'The Concept of Christianity in the African Independent Churches', *Africa* 20, 4 (1961), pp. 203–13.

In the context of more advanced societies, thaumaturgical practice is faced with similar problems in retaining a clientele, as individual votaries join and leave. The *terreiros* of the Brazilian *candomblés* have a clientele that may not manifest more than occasional commitment. The spiritualist churches of western Europe similarly appear to cater for people who, at particular times, need reassurance about continuance in the after-life, but who probably only rarely remain in a spiritualist movement all their lives.

The organization of the Christian missions has, of course, precisely the pattern which allows (though it tries not to encourage) the periodic commitment of its clientele. It provides a structure that is independent of its lay support; it establishes offices, and necessarily (especially in its early stages) mans those offices with individuals who are not rooted in the local community; it creates a pattern of authority that is quite unlike that of the society in which it operates. In all these ways— essentially by introducing the rudiments of rational organization—the mission creates a permanent, independent, self-sufficient, externally-supported organization.

Although they can never be so wholly independent of their local lay supporters, since they do not have external sources of financial support, some African thaumaturgical movements have adopted the structure of the mission churches. In some respects, as they have themselves embarked on missionary activity in other countries, they have more nearly approximated to missionary styles, but in their normal operation they must be content with a more limited similarity. It follows that this type of organization does not depend on the power of a particular visionary, who establishes himself at a central shrine and who dispenses a physical substance (holy water) or special secrets to those who would acquire the cult. There is more emphasis on the stability of worship and commitment, although the physical elements do not entirely disappear. The pilgrimage, which is a more primitive and essentially thaumaturgical conception of the action necessary to get benefit, becomes less important, and persists as a work of supererogation. The new movement is not offered for adoption to whole villages; rather it takes its votaries out from the midst of other men and into its own places of devotion as frequently as it can. It creates a new—and nascently alternative— allegiance. It represents a new pluralism, and arises where new patterns of general social organization are evolving. Consequently, the God-man nexus that it presents is more individualistic. But from these individuals the movement might create (albeit without the circumstances to ensure it of that degree of success enjoyed by the denominations and sects of western society in their early stages) new community structure. It is to such thaumaturgical movements that our attention must now turn.

Thaumaturgy and rational organization

The large and enduring movements known as 'spiritual churches' or 'independent churches' in West Africa are essentially thaumaturgical movements, their westernized, bureaucratic organization notwithstanding. The search for salvation, even where a relatively christianized conception of salvation is well-entrenched, is predominantly a search for miracles of healing through the agency of the Spirit.

> . . . *every* Church in Africa is concerned with Christian healing. . . . 'This is not a church, it is a hospital' . . . proclaimed one prophet to his Zionist congregation, according to Dr. Sundkler . . . direct healing of physical illness . . . without the use of any medicine . . . is proclaimed as of the essence of the Gospel and is perhaps the most universal characteristic of the Aladura or Zionist type of Independent Christian Church.[54]

But unless it is also remembered that healing is more than merely a restoration of physical and mental well-being, the significance of this preoccupation cannot be completely understood. Healing includes fertility; it is also purification, protection from wizardry, and is associated with the abandonment of magical practices, although the ends that are sought by Christian means, and particularly by the inspiration of the Spirit, are very similar to some of those for which traditional magic was practised. Possession, the search for visions, the interpretation of dreams, were the agencies by which various blessings were sought.[55]

It would be impossible to examine the origin of all of these West African *aladura* (which means, *owner of prayer*) churches. Most of them began among prayer groups or visionaries who had previously been affiliated to Protestant missions, but who had found these churches lacking in the very things which Africans sought in religion. They came to regard these missions as 'not spiritual' and, sometimes after existing as prayer groups and unions within these churches, they separated from them.[56] The influence of various, more fundamentalist, European and American sects is often also evident.

Various estimates of the number of adherents of these churches have been made; thus in Western Nigeria they have been said to have

---

[54] Robert C. Mitchell, 'Christian Healing' in V. E. W. Hayward, op. cit., p. 47.
[55] This wider preoccupation of the spiritual churches is made apparent in E. G. Parrinder, 'The Religious Situation in West Africa', *African Affairs* 59 (January 1960), pp. 38–42.
[56] E. G. Parrinder, *Religion in an African City* (Oxford University Press, London 1953), pp. 115 ff.

80,000 members, and to represent about a quarter of the active Christians in Ibadan.[57] These are merely estimates however. The spiritualist churches appear to have a following of marginal members around a central nucleus of more permanently committed adherents. Not only is volatility in evidence, but it is also clear that dual membership and 'ensampling' are common practices. But several of these movements are well established and can accommodate in a more stable context the often casual and volatile clientele who seek thaumaturgical solutions to their problems. The movements have grown, and have often established many branch churches, not only in their own regions, but even in other countries, and they have a pattern of organization which, at least formally, imitates, and usually elaborates, that of western ecclesiastical organizations. That they are also susceptible to schism, and to internal disputation that sometimes stops short of actual division, does not reduce the importance of the expansion and organization that they have achieved.

The independent churches that had earlier separated from the various missions were largely prompted by disagreements about the extent of African authority; they retained the teachings of the missions from which they had come, and they adapted, rather than amended, the structure of church organization. Most important, they became African-run churches. Those who broke away to form the spiritual churches, in contrast, did so, in the main, much less precipitately. They had different religious preoccupations from those of the low-church Anglican Church Missionary Society and the Methodists, and they were more intense about them. The prayer group that eventually grew into the *Christ Apostolic Church* among the Yoruba in Nigeria began soon after the great influenza epidemic of 1918, when a small group in an Anglican church at Ijebu Ode began to experience visions and to seek healing. The influence of the Faith Tabernacle, a small American sect in Philadelphia, with whom David Odubanjo, one of the group's leaders, was in communication, caused them to differ from the Anglicans concerning infant baptism; they formed an independent church in 1922, and, although there was no formal link, they became known by

[57] R. C. Mitchell, op. cit., makes this estimate. Jean L. Comhaire, 'Religious Trends in African and Afro-American Urban Societies', *Anthropological Quarterly* XXVI (1953), pp. 95–108, estimates that in 1950 8.5 per cent of the population of Lagos belonged to African churches; but this category appears to include separatist movements that are orthodox in doctrine as well as the spiritual churches. In 1965 the Christ Apostolic Church had over 100,000 members and was the third largest church in Western Nigeria, and the Seraphim and Cherubim had about 50,000, according to John D. Y. Peel, 'A Sociological Study of Two Independent Churches among the Yoruba', Unpub. Ph.D. Thesis, University of London, 1965. Dr Peel's study appeared as a book, *Aladura* (Oxford University Press, London 1969) in substantially unamended form: my page references are to the thesis.

this name thereafter. For a time these churches were a group of 'small independent congregations of sectarian cast whose members were renowned for their fanatical belief in the efficacy of prayer alone for healing'.[58]

After a period in which they discontinued their belief in visions, perhaps through the influence of Pastor Clark of the Faith Tabernacle, they adopted it again, noting the great success of their rival body the *Society of the Seraphim* (later *Cherubim and Seraphim*), which they attributed to that Society's acceptance of visions and dreams as appropriate forms of divine revelation. The emergence of a new young visionary, Joseph Babalola, who soon joined the group, and whose success as a preacher was essentially similar to that of an American or British evangelical revivalist, restored beyond doubt the legitimacy of visions—at least as an appropriate power for the leadership—since he attributed his very considerable power as an evangelist entirely to his ability to receive visions.

At this period a number of visionaries were arising in Yorubaland, and Babalola's practice was not new, but he appears to have been the most successful of these revivalists, particularly among his own people, the Ekiti, and among the Ijesha, Akoko, and Yagba groups of the Yoruba. He acquired a remarkable reputation for healing, and the revival in north-eastern Yorubaland continued for a period of many months. His ministrations led to an almost embarrassing flow of people into the under-staffed Methodist and CMS missions, and the missionaries were initially disposed in his favour. When the *Nigerian Faith Tabernacle* began to establish its own churches, however, the missionaries objected to Babalola's activities, and found more reason to cavil at his distribution of holy water (which was not a Faith Tabernacle practice) and at his curative practice (which was, of course, associated with the purification of witches).

Babalola's power as a revivalist was enhanced by the impunity with which he burned fetiches and charms, in defiance of the power of the gods to whom they were sacred.[59] As in so many of the new thaumaturgical movements, and this appears to be true even in cases where, as in Massa, there is no special infusion of Christian ideals, a process of de-mystification occurred: old cult objects were de-sacralized, and traditional artistic endeavour and traditional religious practice were equally condemned. Such movements have a new, rational,

[58] R. C. Mitchell, 'The Babalola Revival: A Non-Arrested Prophet Movement', mimeographed, p. 4. (To be published in J. Middleton and V. W. Turner (Eds.), *Modern African Religious Movements*.) This paragraph and the two that follow rely entirely on this source.
[59] Ibid., p. 23.

puritanical spirit. They seek to simplify the faith. They employ more commonplace objects, the production of which involves less investment of time and skill: thus, water replaces masks and fetiches.

Despite the powerful thrust of such movements against traditional religion, neither their innovations nor their accommodation of persisting cultural demands has usually reconciled the missionaries to them. Even if at first they seem like spontaneous revivals of an acceptable kind, sooner or later the missions discover the persistence of indigenous preoccupations and practices which they cannot accept. The principal authority considers that there is no doubt that Babalola was seen as a 'witch-cleanser', even though this was only a subsidiary aspect of his role, and perhaps the use of water was itself a continuity of the former practice of compelling witches to drink sasswood as a poison ordeal. It was eventually on accusations of administering an ordeal that the colonial authorities imprisoned Babalola for six months, although 'the most striking thing about the exercise of control was the restraint of the colonial authorities'.[60]

In the early 1930s the leaders of the Faith Tabernacle entered into association with the pentecostalist Apostolic Church, and in due course Babalola also joined this movement, whose British missionaries had greater success than the Nigerians themselves had had in getting approval for the building of independent churches and schools. The Apostolic Church delegates from Britain co-operated with the original Faith Tabernacle leaders in discouraging the use of holy water. The movement had 170 churches, thirty schools and religious classes, two missionaries, and sixty native workers in 1939, shortly before the Nigerians broke away from the Apostolic Church to found their own Christ Apostolic Church.[61]

The spiritual churches are ubiquitous in the more developed areas of present-day West Africa. Seventeen independent African churches were counted in Ibadan in 1955, and more than forty (varieties) were reported in 1963. These churches might include some that were separatist rather than spiritual, but in 1965–6, over 150 aladura congregations, strictly defined, were reported.[62] One further example from Nigeria will make evident the significance of thaumaturgical response in this particular organizational mode.

[60] Ibid., p. 31a.
[61] Ibid., p. 43.
[62] The 1963 estimates are given by H. W. Turner, 'African Prophet Movements', *Hibbert Journal* 61, 242 (April 1963), pp. 112–16. R. C. Mitchell, 'Sickness and Healing in the Separatist Churches', University of Ibadan, Institute of African Studies, Special Seminar on 'The Traditional Background to Medical Practice in Nigeria', April 20–23, 1966, reported some 150 aladura congregations in Ibadan in 1965–6. In 1968 D. B. Barrett, in *Schism and Renewal in Africa*, op. cit., reported 6,000 independent movements in sub-Saharan Africa.

The cluster of movements known as the Cherubim and Seraphim began with a number of independent visionaries who were led to found prayer groups. The contrast with the distinctly messianic claims made by some visionaries in South Africa is striking, and so, too, is the association (which did not always last) of people among whom several leaders claimed very powerful visions. Moses Orimolade Tunolase, of Ikarre in Ondo province, is reputed to have had visions by which he was cured of a lame condition from which he suffered.[63] At a later time, a girl, Abiodum Akinsowon, had visions, and subsequently, when sick, demanded that Orimolade be sent for to pray for her. Followers were to stay in their churches, according to the early pronouncements of Orimolade. The members of the Seraphim Society tended, however, to regard themselves as something of an élite. Engendering the typical hostility that arises against 'holy groups' that recruit *within* existing church fellowships, they were opposed by other church members because they likened themselves to seraphim in heaven. By 1935 the movement had broken away.[64] Orimolade took the title Baba Aladura (father of the owners of prayer) and open-air evangelism was practised. Abiodum styled herself Captain. The movement was affected by the pentecostalism being disseminated in Nigeria by the Apostolic Church missionaries from Britain, and perhaps by other pentecostalist bodies, but the central idea of gaining spiritual power was certainly indigenous. In its early activities it directed itself to the burning of fetiches, and to condemnation of the *babelawos*, the traditional priests.[65]

The original society did not long remain unified: a split occurred between Orimolade and the more educated praying band. In 1929, Abiodum Akinsowon had broken away to form her own movement. Despite recent attempts at reunion, the tendency has been for the movement to become increasingly fragmented.[66] And yet its fragmentation has not affected growth, and may indeed have been a concomitant of it, since we are told, 'In contrast to the African churches, which tended to lose their impetus after a generation of growth and activity,

[63] The name is given in an unsigned article, 'Cherubim and Seraphim', *Nigeria* 53 (1957), pp. 119–34; it is given as Moses Tunolashe of Ikare by E. G. Parrinder, op. cit., p. 119. J. D. Y. Peel, op. cit., refers to this man as Orimolade, and refers to his brother (who divided this branch of the movement after Orimolade's death) as Tunolase (p. 186). Peel's account is much the most extensive and thoroughly documented, and these paragraphs rest largely upon it.

[64] Ibid., p. 188.

[65] Ibid., pp. 130 ff.

[66] In 1957 there were ten different sects in Lagos alone: — 'Cherubim and Seraphim', *Nigeria*, op. cit. J. D. Y. Peel lists some thirteen groups of Cherubim and Seraphim. He considers problems of succession to leadership to be one of the important occasions for schism, but there are also sporadic factions on more personal grounds (p. 482).

the Aladuras are expanding more quickly today than ever before. . . .'[67]

The difficulty for movements that emphasize thaumaturgical elements is to institutionalize the oracular and miraculous in such a way that they acquire legitimation without losing immediacy and spontaneity. The various Yoruba churches have had an abundance of prophets and visionaries among their leaders, and if the divisions which have occurred have followed largely from differences among them, none the less, they have come about without marked hostility.[68] The secessions occur not for ideological reasons, but rather through claims to undiluted spiritual power. Techniques rather than doctrines are important.[69] The movements that become independent of each other are thus not mutually anathematized in doctrinal terms, since power can be dispensed in relatively small units. When one recalls the essential localism of most thaumaturgical practice and the inherent particularism of its ministry, the considerable fragmentation of these new spiritual churches is less impressive than the extent to which, by their imitation of other organizations (and relatively few of their leaders have been fully socialized to bureaucratic roles, it must be remembered) they have established widely-spread and relatively coherent structures. They had set centrifugal organizational patterns into counter-motion against the essentially centripetal and fissiparous tendencies of thaumaturgical practice.

All members of these congregations seek personal blessings—health, longevity, fertility, protection from witches, success in the world.[70] Spiritual power is the faculty by which these things will be attained, and it is the diffusion of power throughout congregations that appears to be the principal factor in the creation of these relatively permanent thaumaturgical movements. Power is available *in the churches*, and since such power is itself partly an artefact of the presence of a believing and supportive group, one sees the dependence of the believer on the context in which power arises. Individual thaumaturges may arise in such movements. Unless they can be absorbed into the institutionalized leadership, they set into motion the characteristic thaumaturgical

[67] Ibid., p. 400.

[68] Ibid., p. 502. As Peel comments, in a church in which the aim is dispension of power, unity is superfluous and hostility pointless. This is the characteristic circumstance of thaumaturgy, as long as thaumaturges are not competing for power in one location or in respect of similar objects.

[69] Ibid., pp. 496–7.

[70] J. D. Y. Peel, op. cit., p. 521, regards the Yoruba as having a distinctly this-worldly concern with religion, which is seen largely instrumentally. In the aladura churches, ends such as these are sought with religious means, just as previously they used medicine, herbs, magic, doctors, and prayers. Emphasis on this-worldly benefits was apparent in the majority of responses from Christ Apostolic Church members and Cherubim and Seraphim members to Peel's inquiries.

sequence—new miracle-workers require new contexts which they can manage and in which they can monopolize power. It is the diffusion of charisma, a type of spiritual democratization, which appears to be essential for the success of these spiritual churches. 'Any one of the congregation may become endowed with the power to work miracles by prayer: may learn to see visions and prophesy.'[71]

As in other spiritual churches, the central belief of the Cherubim and Seraphim is that all prayer is answered, and prayer offered in the proper way obtains quick answers. Prayers are themselves like recipes. The types of requests which are made include not only the traditional ones for fertility and physical healing, but also modern demands such as help against unemployment. This perhaps accounts for the high proportion of migrants who are to be found in the church. In both the Christ Apostolic Church and in the Cherubim and Seraphim, the proportion of the indigenous members in a city like Ibadan is reputed to be very small (although they are also a minority in the Anglican churches).[72] The early members of the Cherubim and Seraphim were largely clerks, and the movement spread as clerks were transferred. It provided an avenue of mobility, and a strong assertion of a new and modern orientation, particularly in its activity of breaking fetiches and jujus.[73] More recently artisans and clerks appeared to be the principal classes in membership of the movement. Because so many of these churches have attracted immigrants, they have had a clientele which in itself has facilitated the spread of the movement, as migrant workers have returned to their villages. Clearly, as a class this group has special needs for strong affiliations, living, as immigrants do, in conditions of insecurity and anomie. To a section of a traditionally religious society that was preoccupied with the search for new status (itself evident from their migrancy) the aid of prayer in the attainment of these goals was attractive. Traditional religion had to be amended to accommodate these new demands. New demands required new techniques. New techniques were available in the syncretism of old practices and mission teachings. Thus the 'spiritual churches' offered 'prayer-power' for the widely diffused new goals—an accommodation of the 'boundless aspirations' diffused throughout these societies—the evidence of a

[71] — 'Cherubim and Seraphim', *Nigeria*, op. cit.

[72] J. D. Y. Peel, op. cit., p. 345, gives figures as low as 25 per cent indigenes of his Ibadan sample of Christ Apostolic Church members; and only one man in forty-five in a group of Cherubim and Seraphim members.

[73] Ibid., p. 147. Mitchell reports of the early Faith Tabernacle in the period of the Babalola Revival that 'Babalola had "most of the clerical staff of the Government and the Native Authorities and many of the police"' (reporting the Secretary, Southern Provinces to the Resident, Oyo): R. C. Mitchell, 'The Babalola Revival . . .', op. cit., p. 38.

chronic condition of anomie. A growing class provided the basis for recruitment for the thaumaturgical movements in new countries like Nigeria, where the pains of transition and the immense social relocation which occurred has perhaps created an especially large body of people for whom traditional religion could no longer function, and for whom the provision of the orthodox ex-mission churches was in many ways inadequate.

6

Thaumaturgy Denominationalized

MANY of the thaumaturgical groups that we have examined rely on the charismatic gifts of a single thaumaturge, who by adopting particular pre-existing patterns of organization, particularly that of the tribe (in societies where tribes are large), may command a considerable movement. Such a pattern of organization is legitimated by the past. So, too, is thaumaturgical practice. Thus organization and practice represent cultural continuities and are mutually reinforcing. Such a new movement depends on traditional devices for the (sometimes considerable) degree of stability which it attains: on patterns of deference: hereditary succession; the gathering of followers at the holy place; and participation in occasions of reunion. Nor do these features immediately disappear even when thaumaturgical practice is embraced in a different pattern of organization. In some contexts tribal structure may represent too much of an identification with a now discredited past to be acceptable as the organizational model for new religious movements. Thaumaturgical demand itself persists even when the ends sought are innovative ends, learned in a new non-tribal social context. In such circumstances the actual style of thaumaturgy is likely to be ostensibly and conspicuously distinguished from traditional thaumaturgical practice, and from traditional forms of social organization.

All of this implies some immediate loss in stability. Outside traditional contexts, thaumaturgy attracts a volatile clientele, and its practice is likely to be local, transient, and haphazard—unless there are stable procedures and structures which new movements can imitate. Within new organizational forms, however, the difficulty which arises is that of socializing a clientele to the idea that flashes of miraculous power may be associated with, may even depend on, persistent commitment to a regular pattern of worship and a formal system of belief. It is in this socializing process that we may see the beginnings of an ethical orientation among thaumaturgical movements (most noticeable in urban contexts, for example among the Kardecists and even among the Umbandists of Brazil). As long as thaumaturgy was located in tribal organization, and undertaken for collective tribal ends, the volatility of individual clients was unimportant: communal solidarity ensured adequate religious solidarity. But in a pluralistic context, thaumaturgical practice for a permanent clientele may bring into being a long-continuing religious association gathered around one or more thaumaturgical specialists. Such a movement rests on assumptions quite alien to tribal society. It depends on voluntary adherence. Its solidarity is primarily and specifically religious. The movement becomes a cause which is independently worthy of support; some recognition and regular provision must be made for the sustenance and support of leaders. Above all, awareness grows of the need for conscious persistence of commitment. These are the attributes of institutionalized social movements which operate in a diversified social system. They are necessary attributes of the religious movement *per se*, if it is to persist.

Yet, as we have seen, thaumaturgical practice as such, being highly particularistic, offers little leverage in these respects. The thaumaturgical demand is a demand for service, and it often appears as an almost reciprocal commercial relationship. These characteristics make difficult the maintenance of stable commitment. Once tribal structure has broken down, sooner or later tribal identity, the traditional, corporate locus of social solidarity, may be discredited or regarded as inappropriate, as in the urban areas of West Africa.[1] In those circumstances religious expression and religious needs—and traditionally these are largely thaumaturgical—must either acquire new forms of organization which both accommodate the particularism of thaumaturgical pursuits and provide new foci of identity in stable and enduring structures, or revert to local entrepreneurial thaumaturgy. Both phenomena are found. Our concern now is with the enduring movements.

Leaving aside the cases in which surrogate-tribal organization has been adopted, thaumaturgy is a mode of religious orientation that normally requires a certain ecological distribution. Particularism limits the number of clients a given thaumaturge can accept; his fame, except in those cases where government prohibition of traditional practices has left a thaumaturgical vacuum (as in the Central African witch-finding movements, and in the case of the Babalola revival) is not likely to transcend local level. For every Babalola, Kimbangu, or Mwana Lesa, there are many local men promulgating new patterns of thaumaturgical practice. The local man competes with others, but the locality (or the tribal group) provides his clients. The whole logic of the parochial

---

[1] The extent to which tribal organization remained a model, even after very considerable influence of western denominations, is evident in the case of the Musama Disco Christo Church in Ghana, which adopted 'circuits' in imitation of the Methodists, but maintained them very much according to the pattern of the old military formations of settlement among Akan tribes, according to C. G. Baëta, *Prophetism in Ghana* (SCM Press, London 1962), p. 61.

organization of Christendom—the even distribution of religious functionaries among a population—arises from the similar need, to provide full opportunities for salvation to all (even if, in this case, the distribution has long been centrally organized). Although thaumaturgy was tribally based, none the less, a similar distribution of shamans or diviners might, no doubt, also be found in many societies. Curers, healers, and savers of souls are functionaries whose services are, at a given level of social development (and perhaps excluding only modern secularized societies), likely to be more or less equally demanded among men. They have arisen locally to meet needs that are found universally. On what principle, then, can thaumaturgical practice, always widely distributed and particularistic, be drawn together in an organization that itself transcends the purely local level?

The obvious pattern, and the one that is adopted in West African independent churches, is to retain the localism of the thaumaturgical operation, but to diffuse and democratize its practice, whilst establishing a hierarchy of control, which in itself partly rests on distinctions of graduated thaumaturgical power. This is both an institutionalization and in some measure a rationalization of thaumaturgy, and its long-run consequences may well be the increasing subjection of the thaumaturgical to purely organizational goals. (Just such a process appears to have occurred to the considerable, but not dominant, thaumaturgical preoccupations in American and European conversionist sects, particularly the Pentecostal sects.)

In adopting the denominational model of the Protestant missions, the thaumaturgical movements have transformed the Protestant demand for 'every man his own priest' into 'every man his own thaumaturge'. The problem of reliance on the one indispensable possessor of charismatic power is overcome by the dissemination of charismatic gifts in a congregation. It is the congregation, however, that must be firmly settled as the place in which the principal manifestation of charisma occurs: the individual's charisma must be validated in a charismatic community, in which the gifts are manifested in some sense for the corporate benefit. If wonders are worked elsewhere it is to the congregation that they must be told, and within it that gratitude must be expressed. The provision of facilities for widespread charismatic manifestations involves the need to impress on individuals their dependence on the rest of the congregation and, in some measure, on the hierarchy, in whom charismatic quality is differentially distributed and personified. Reliance on physical objects—such as holy water—persists, but its potency is now impersonally acquired from the specific operations of a minister, who brandishes a symbol of office in a hierarchic structure. The clientele relies on the superior powers of the organization's officers both for validation of their personal charisma and for the regulation of the dispersed and free-flowing power discharged in the meetings, rather than regarding them as its specific source.

The test for such movements is the extent to which they can anchor charismatic manifestations in a firmly established context of regulation and socialization. The thaumaturgical clientele is normally volatile, and these movements do not inherit the relative stability of even the surrogate tribal structure. They are obliged to forge new relationships, particularly in contexts where movements embrace people of different tribal origins, and where tribalism is in itself associated with a backward-looking perspective. The people it recruits are not those seeking their past tribal identity (though they may seek new identity in the religious community). They seek new personal power for the attainment of new goals in a changing social context. Such particularistic and personal goals are not in themselves easily accommodated to stable involvement in the life of a movement, and it may well be that the new movements have a more volatile clientele than the thaumaturgical movements which imitate tribal organization. But just as schools are necessarily full of uneducated people and hospitals of sick people, such volatility is a characteristic quality of socializing agencies, of agencies that mobilize commitment, inculcate norms, summon allegiance, and create mutual obligations among people who are neither a natural nor a social group, and whose orientations are not, at this point, primarily corporate. The benefits of new community allegiances appear to be secondary (a fact evident in the slow development of exclusivity of commitment, and the persistence of dual allegiances, as well as in spasmodic attendance). The process by which thaumaturgical demands are institutionalized implies, therefore, a process of socialization with consequences that may have far greater significance for the wider society than the mere establishment of well-organized religious movements. To this we shall return later. For the moment, we need only recognize that it is the diffusion of charisma, and the democratization of participation in the manifestation of supernatural power—albeit still defined within a basically hierarchic structure—that are necessary for thaumaturgical demand to be institutionalized as a viable religious orientation. That in the process the very character of thaumaturgical preoccupations may change for some participants, is in itself only a further indication of the dynamic relationship between religious *Weltanschauungen*.

Thaumaturgical response and rational organization

We have so far reviewed various accommodations of thaumaturgy: the half-mystical adoption of tribal structure, associated with a tribal location in South Africa; the partial delegation of preliminary diagnosis to assistants in the Bindele movement; the identification of thaumaturgy with a particular shrine, or a particular medium, in the *candomblés* of urban Brazil; the diffusion of a cult by the purchase of secrets in the Déima and Tigari movements; the establishment of a holy village and the maintenance of a church in the near-denominational pattern of the Lumpa Church. All these, however, have failed to establish a persisting, centrally directed and fully institutionalized movement. Even the Cherubim and Seraphim society, for all its considerable success, has manifested by its fragmentation the characteristic strains of thaumaturgical practice. Organizational stability and rational procedures stand in sharp contrast with thaumaturgical pursuits, which congregational participation does not alone resolve. As long as thaumaturgical power is personalized, whim may transcend order. But if fixed locations and an ordered hierarchy with an undisputed principal thaumaturge can be established, then the volatility of the wonder-seeking clientele might be withstood and accommodated.

The framework of rational organization is not easily established in societies with low standards of literacy, limited traditions of voluntaristic action, and very little internalized sense of disinterested goodwill. The models of relationship and reciprocity are those of tribe, community, and kin. The only prospect of establishing relationships within newly created groups is by evoking kinship ideals fictively—a pattern typical of the early European sects. The organization that is wholly legal-rational relies on inter-related, disinterested role-performances, the willingness of the individual to accept segmentary participation in systems of relationships which offer him far less than total security or involvement, and in which only a portion of his personality dispositions are mobilized. Such organizations—civil service, industrial concerns, even large stores—are difficult to organize in less-developed countries, precisely because tribal-type particularism, affectivity, and diffuseness of roles persists in new contexts, even if the tribal ascriptive basis of status systems is more readily displaced. Religion in its very nature does not readily adopt legal-rational organizational form. It maintains the particularism, affectivity, and diffuseness of primitive institutional complexes, and it does this even in advanced societies. Yet in advanced societies elements of rational planning steadily affected the organizational character of religion, particularly in the evangelical denominations as, over three centuries or more, they promoted large-scale missionary activity. The paradox occurs that religious groups, which are so often almost surrogate kinship systems, and which use language of fictive kinship, steadily adopt rational organizational form, and socialize their clientele to disinterested role-performance in the wider society. The Protestant ethic required just such a process of socialization. The sect or the congregation was modelled as an affective and particularistic surrogate family, and like the family, on the basis of affection it socialized its members for non-affective, universalistic participation in the wider society.

In under-developed countries, the new denominationalism of thaumaturgy may perform a function similar to that of the early Protestant sects of Europe, albeit as yet in limited degree. The volatility of the clientele, the difficulty with which exclusiveness of commitment is established, and the persisting strength of real kinship groups, militate against its complete success. We have already noted that many of the early votaries of these new movements were migrants, and often clerks—the very group most in need of surrogate family participation, confirmation of achieved status, *and* socialization for segmentary role performance. Doctrinally, thaumaturgical groups do not manifestly function to meet these needs: they offer, rather, power. But power is a highly generalized commodity, capable of manifold application, both for man's abiding concerns and gratifications, and for the attainment of new goals, even if these are expressed as rewards rather than as competences. Their efficacy in socialization may be less than that of early Protestantism, since they rely more heavily on leaders; they cater for a clientele with a more limited background, and whose general socialization and experience in societal institutions is generally at a lower level. Yet, in the adoption by some of these movements in West Africa of a denominational model directly borrowed from the Christian missions, there is a more direct influence of rational-legal organization than new religious movements in Europe acquired for some long time. The African local congregation is linked to a wider denominational structure. Even though the mass of the clientele may be only vaguely aware of this wider organization, a cadre of local leaders is made increasingly aware of it, and socialized by it. In western denominations this form of organization could grow only steadily and often only surreptitiously, since doctrinal emphasis sometimes elevated the *Gemeinschaft* as the agency through which God operated, as for example, among the Baptists and Congregationalists.[2] But in Africa it has been accepted at a relatively early stage in movements the orientation of which is dominantly, if not wholly, thaumaturgical, and thus a particularistic and non-rational response to the world.

The origins of institutionalized thaumaturgy

The process by which thaumaturgical movements in West Africa came to accept denominational organization is already evident from the history of the Christ Apostolic Church and Cherubim and Seraphim society in Nigeria. The gradual emergence of prayer groups within missions which paid little heed to native demands for more emotional styles of worship, the acceptance of the ideas and support of sectarian mission bodies such as the Faith Tabernacle of Philadelphia and the pentecostalist Apostolic Church, and the eventual appearance around a cadre of leaders of separated movements with their own form of worship, were the steps in this process. Not all the groups arose in this way.[3] Thus the less successfully denominationalized *Church of the Twelve Apostles* in western Ghana, with its succession of illiterate or near-illiterate leaders, was one of the numerous descendants of the activity of William Wadé Harris, whose evangelizing efforts just before the outbreak of the First World War brought into being many groups in the Ivory Coast and the then Gold Coast.[4] The Church of the Twelve

[2] For a discussion of this process among a Baptist denomination in America, see Paul M. Harrison, *Power and Authority in the Free Church Tradition* (Princeton University Press, Princeton 1959).

[3] For a brief account of the history of these churches see Chapter 5. R. C. Mitchell, 'Sickness and Healing in the Separatist Churches', op. cit., distinguishes between 'Spiritual' churches, which emphasize the Holy Spirit in their worship (among which he would include Cherubim and Seraphim, and the Church of the Lord) and the 'Apostolic', which place greater reliance on the Bible as the source of inspiration. He also distinguishes younger, freer, and less-disciplined churches in each category. In terms of the responses we are employing, it may be that the 'Spiritual' churches have retained a much fuller thaumaturgical orientation, whereas the 'Apostolics' (and this appears to be evident from Mitchell's own work on their history) approximate to the conversionist response, which is found in the fundamentalist evangelical Protestant sects of western Christendom.

[4] William Wadé Harris was a Grebo, a Liberian who was taught by the American Methodist missionary Jesse Lawry. According to W. J. Platt, *An African Prophet* (SCM Press, London 1934), Harris said in 1926 that he had not had visions before his missionary campaigns of 1913–14 but had felt the inspiration of the Spirit. Harris had extensive knowledge of the Bible, and he preached the destruction of fetiches, the forsaking of theft and adultery, and reliance on the Bible. His success in the Ivory Coast was such that although he was deported in 1915 by the French authorities, who feared that the movement might challenge their authority, Platt discovered many *Harristes* (as B. Holas, op. cit., calls his followers) still with their Bibles, which they were unable to read, and still waiting for Harris to return to lead them. The French governor, M. Angoulvan, found no particular fault in Harris, but his encouragement of the maintenance of Sunday as a day of rest interfered with

Apostles had only indirect opportunity to imitate mission models, although in the 1930s it made contact with the missionaries of the Apostolic Church, until a dispute concerning the use of the rattle, which the native leaders regarded as particularly effective in the dispersion of evil spirits, caused some members of this movement to dissociate themselves from these British sectarians. It is typical of such movements in that,

> no importance whatsoever is attached in this Church to doctrine. . . . Emphasis is laid, to the total exclusion of all other matters, upon the activity of the Holy Spirit, in enabling certain men and women to predict future events, warn of impending misfortunes, detect evil-doing, and, above all, to cure illnesses. Asked to put in a nut-shell what their Church stood for, Mr. Nathan (one of the leaders, who had himself been baptized by Harris) had no hesitation at all in exclaiming: 'We are here to heal'.[5]

Another movement left in the wake of Harris's meteoric itinerary through these territories became known as the cult of *Boto Adaï*, a leader who claimed to be the successor of Harris. This movement, thoroughly dependent on the austere personality of Papa Adaï himself, was even less denominationalized than the Church of the Twelve Apostles, which maintained some ninety-eight 'sub-stations' in two of its four divisions (the other two divisions appeared, in the late 1950s, to be in a state of near-schism).[6] Adaï claimed visions in which he got a commission 'pour sauver tous ceux que souffrent sur la terre'.[7] As in so many other of the so-called 'spiritual churches' of West Africa, holy water was regarded as the principal curative agency. Adaï had assistants, but was himself very much the absolute leader of his 5,000 adherents. The main focus of his thaumaturgical attack were the devils which caused illness, failure of the plantations, and barrenness in women. The confessions, made in public, as in so many similar movements, were principally about recourse to sorcery. But the movement remained uninstitutionalized, and depended too heavily on its founder to bear promise of a secure future after his death.[8]

---

the work of road-building (Platt, op. cit., p. 61). Despite French destruction of many of the churches which the *Harristes* had built, the movement persisted and spawned others such as Déima and the cult of Boto Adaï, in addition to providing a nucleus of some 23,000 people for the Methodist Church which Platt introduced from Dahomey in the mid 1920s. According to K. Schlosser, *Propheten in Afrika*, op. cit., p. 250, Harris was not concerned with faith-healing, but given the association of protection from witchcraft and curative practice, his attack on wizardry may have amounted to something similar to therapeutic practice.

[5] C. G. Baëta, op. cit., p. 15. This account relies entirely on Baëta.

[6] Ibid., p. 11.

[7] B. Holas, *Le Séparatisme religieux* . . ., op cit., p. 78. Holas provides an extensive account of this movement, including its use of consecrated water, its public confession, cult ceremonies, and liturgical texts.

[8] Ibid., p. 195.

Perhaps the most successful adaptations of thaumaturgy on a denominational pattern have occurred in the *Church of the Lord*, which is often also known simply by the word which is often used as a generic term for churches of this kind, *Aladura*.[9] Since 1930 this Church has grown rapidly in Sierra Leone, Liberia, and Ghana as well as in Nigeria, the country in which it originated.

The origins of the wider *aladura* movement lay in the activities of the Faith Tabernacle of Philadelphia. The official literature of the Church of the Lord has now little to say of this connection. The Church was founded by Josaiah Olunowo Ositelu in the Lisa chieftaincy house at Ogere, Ijebu Remo, in the Western Region of Nigeria, in 1930. Today, the official literature of the Church attributes a variety of early wonder working to Ositelu,[10] who was a pupil in CMS schools at Ogere and Porogun, Ijebu-Ode, and who subsequently trained to be a catechist. Ositelu had visions and engaged in fasts and abstinences which in 1926 caused his suspension as a catechist by the African Anglican missionaries. In 1929 he held open-air meetings, preaching against Islam and against idols and shrines; he prophesied famines, flood, world war, and locusts, and proclaimed the kingdom of God to be at hand.[11] In 1930 he was associated with the Faith Tabernacle, and with those Africans who subsequently became prominent in the Christ Apostolic Church and the Cherubim and Seraphim society. He was more millennialist than Babalola or the Cherubim and Seraphim preachers, and in at least one pamphlet he prophesied destruction for 1931, the resurrection of the dead, and the uprooting of false and deceptive government.[12]

Perhaps for expedient reasons the government did not find his writings seditious, even though in one pamphlet he condemned those who collected taxes, and predicted that all Europeans would die in a smallpox epidemic which would soon occur.[13] In 1930 he participated in the revival in Ibadan and Abeokuta led by Daniel Orekoya, who was

[9] E. G. Parrinder, *Religion in an African City*, op. cit., p. 123, translates the Yoruba title of the churches of this movement in Ibadan, *Ijo enia Oluwa*, as 'The Church of the Lord's People' (a title not used by the Church itself), and provides a short note about them. C. G. Baëta, op. cit., pp. 119–27, uses the title 'The Church of the Lord (Aladura)' which is the style employed by the Church. The bulk of the following sections rely on my own participant-observation in the churches of this movement in Accra, Ghana.

[10] Thus according to the official life by M. Sam Wobo, *A Brief Resumé of the Life-Course of Dr. J. O. Ositelu, Psy.D.* (The Church of the Lord, Ogere Headquarters, Shagamu 1955), a diviner told Ositelu's parents, soon after his birth, that he would become 'the Head of his people'. At the age of eleven he was once punished for disobedience to his father, and 'on the third day (thereafter) his father slipped off the palm tree and suffered bodily injury from which he did not recover untill [*sic*] after two years'.

[11] Ibid., p. 9.

[12] J. D. Y. Peel, op. cit., p. 170. See also, H. W. Turner, *African Independent Church* (Clarendon Press, Oxford, 2 vols. 1967) vol. 1, pp. 28–9.

[13] Ibid., p. 171; R. C. Mitchell, 'The Babalola Revival . . .', op. cit., p. 39.

closely associated with the most impressive of the prophets of the whole amorphous revivalist movement, Joseph Babalola. Ositelu was already, at this time, employing the special holy names, or seal words, which have persisted in the Church of the Lord. To these names, and to his reputed 'leanings towards polygyny', the African leaders of the Faith Tabernacle took exception. By the end of 1930 Ositelu had broken with the Faith Tabernacle. Twenty-three candidates had been baptized into the Church before the end of that year. At a meeting in January 1931 Eshinshinade (J. B. Shadare's adopted name), Akinyele, Odubanjo, and Babatope criticized the use of the names as unnecessary and unbiblical, and reaffirmed their opposition to polygyny.[14]

The first pastor of the Church of the Lord was ordained in 1931, and the first hymn-book was published in the following year. Considering the religious ferment among the Yoruba at this time, the early growth of the Church was not dramatic. Ositelu appears to have lacked the dramatic charismatic qualities so apparent in the evangelistic activities of Babalola. The organizational structure of the Church of the Lord was equally slow to evolve, and its pattern of devotions also steadily underwent change. Only in 1937 was the important Tabbieorrah ceremony first held, at Ogere, and only in that year was the important lay status of cross-bearer established for faithful members of long standing. The creation of this status was a recognition of differential charisma among the laity, which rested on institutional, not on personal criteria. The Church thus began to distribute charismatic power, or at least began to legitimate men's claims to some of the more elevated forms of charisma. In 1945 the Church added an apostle to its growing hierarchy, as a lieutenant to the Most Reverend Prophet Doctor J. O. Ositelu, Psy.D., Primate and Founder (the doctorate of the Founder was conferred upon him by the Spiritualists' National Union of Nigeria, in 1948).[15] In 1947 the first bishop and the first reverend mother were elevated. Some twenty churches are mentioned by Wobo as being founded in the first thirty years of the movement, while other reports suggest that in Nigeria alone there were over seventy in 1962. The growth in other African countries, and particularly in Ghana, has been much more impressive. The first Apostle of the Church, Emmanuel Owoade Adeleke Adejobi, received a vision instructing him to

[14] M. Sam Wobo, op. cit., p. 10, declares the Church of the Lord to have been founded on 27 July 1930 in the Lisa Chieftaincy house at Ogere, with ten people. According to Wobo, on 28 December the first baptisms took place at Abeokuta, conducted by Pastor I. B. Akinyele (later to become Olubadan of Ibadan). The meeting at which Akinyele and other Faith Tabernacle leaders criticized Ositelu is described in R. C. Mitchell, op. cit., pp. 25–6.

[15] Michael Banton, 'An Independent African Church in Sierra Leone', *Hibbert Journal* LV (October 1956), pp. 57–63.

go to Freetown to begin the movement there in 1947.[16] Adejobi gained a reputation for prophecy, and by 1952 a large church had been built in the city.[17] The movement had early difficulties in Sierra Leone, but within two years a quarterly magazine had been started, the training of ministers was undertaken (although most defected sooner or later), and thirteen subsidiary organizations, some of 'uncertain existence', were established.[18]

Disagreements appear to have arisen in the development of the Church in Ghana between Apostle Adejobi, who was missioning from Sierra Leone, and whose work in Ghana centred on Kumasi and Takoradi–Sekondi, and the churches established in Accra by Samuel Omolaja Oduwole, who had become the second Apostle of the Church in 1949, and who had been in charge of missionary activities in Liberia from 1947. The Church made rapid progress in Ghana from 1953, but there were differences between the two branches of the movement there in style of worship and dress, and these were not even resolved by a visit from the Primate himself, who appointed Adejobi as Administrator General, and Oduwole as Administrator, with autonomy in Liberia, for all the churches outside Nigeria.[19] Even in 1964, however, individuals in the Accra churches considered that the operation of the Spirit was less vigorous in Kumasi than in Accra, even though congregations were larger there. There appeared to be fifty-nine churches in Ghana in 1959, and in 1964 members spoke loosely of 'over a hundred'. In Sierra Leone, 'at the end of 1960 there were seven centres manned by a full-time leader' but it was less successful in the hinterland, where this mission of an African independent church 'met with an experience similar to that of most Western missions in the previous century and a half'.[20] However, the Church had extensive contacts of a more informal character, and harvest festival services in 1959 were listed for fifty-five places with a date and the name of a preacher.[21]

Worship in the Church of the Lord (Aladura)

Services in the Church of the Lord are characterized by a mixture of spontaneity and routinized procedure.[22] The local hierarchy maintains

[16] Harold W. Turner, 'The Church of the Lord: The Expansion of a Nigerian Independent Church in Sierra Leone and Ghana', *Journal of African History* 3 (1962), pp. 91–110.
[17] M. Banton, op. cit.   [18] H. W. Turner, op. cit.
[19] Ibid.   [20] Ibid.   [21] Ibid.
[22] This description appeared to be general at least for Accra, Ghana. Movements of this kind, however, frequently evolve variations in accord with local cultural practices, and, as one

a framework of order, within which, however, the fullest opportunities for free expression prevail. The occasion for the operation of the Spirit is the principal feature of services. Members are, in the main, clad in white prayer gowns; they remove their shoes, and many wash their feet outside the church; they there await the minister and the congregational officers who, after consecrating themselves for the service in a nearby 'Mercy Ground', arrive in procession, ringing a bell and singing a hymn. The church, which may be a corrugated iron structure, has a sanctuary of a few feet square, a place of special power, curtained from waist-height to the floor, and entered only by the minister. Hymns and prayers begin the service, with an official calling out the words of each line of the hymn before the congregation sing it. The prayers are largely of supplication.[23] A sequence of choruses ('shouts') often follows, similar in style to those employed by Pentecostalists in Britain, but rather shorter and lending themselves to much greater rhythmical

---

of the more prominent missionary churches among independent African movements, the Church of the Lord has had to contend with this problem. Some variations of interpretation appear to me to be evident in the church literature which I have seen. For a detailed description of The Church of the Lord, which does not, however, purport to be a sociological analysis, see H. W. Turner, *African Independent Church*, op. cit.

[23] The Litany of the Church includes very strong condemnation of witchcraft. A printed version is available and includes the following responses:

Priest:	From all attacks of wizards and witches,
Congregation:	Good Lord deliver us
P.	From pestilence and sudden death,
C.	Good Lord deliver us
P.	In the days of confusion by the flies
C.	Good Lord deliver us

. . . .

Priest:	Over sooth-sayers and those who curse us,
Congregation:	Good Lord give us Victory
P.	Over those who harm us and feign sympathy with us
C.	Good Lord give us Victory
P.	Over all those who wish us bad everywhere
C.	Good Lord give us Victory
P.	Over all bad and wicked juju men
C.	Good lord give us Victory
P.	Over tale-bearers and gossips
C.	Good lord give us Victory
P.	Over magicians and necromancers
C.	Good lord give us Victory
P.	Over quack doctors and herbalists
C.	Good lord give us Victory

H. W. Turner, 'The Litany of an Independent West African Church', *Sierra Leone Bulletin of Religion* (December 1959) 1, 2, pp. 48–55, notes that the Aladura litany does not make intercession for 'our enemies, persecutors and slanderers', and that it 'reverts to the level of the ancient litanies in their preoccupation with deliverance from dangers'. Another part of the litany employs the repeated response of the congregation, 'We use our mouths as brooms before thee' (and the members push their lips through the dirt). Turner believes that this particular idea may have stemmed from a form of deference before a Yoruba king.

development. The repetition of the words and the intensification of the tempo, with drums, timbrels, and other musical instruments (except in Lent), quickly leads to swaying and dancing, led by the two bands of officials—the (male) 'Army of Jesus' and the 'Ladies' Praying Union' (both of which are uniformed with short capes). Each individual dances by himself. Rapid gyrations are performed by some members with arms flailing. Eventually a dancer may fall, to be caught by the officers, and made to bow before the altar in prayer. If they are unruly, they are taken out into the Mercy Ground to thrash about in the sand, which is regarded as an especially beneficial exercise.

Bible-lessons and prayers are followed by the announcement of visions received by the congregation during prayer, and interpretations of these visions by a warden. Typical interpretations promise blessings to the church and benefits to individuals—a child for a woman who has not yet borne children, promotions in their jobs for men, and perhaps a new car to someone in the congregation. Perhaps more important than these congregational interpretations are the revelations which are received by the wardens and the members of the Army of Jesus, who move around the congregation at a fixed time, approaching in turn most of those present, to give immediate and personal spiritual advice that they have received directly from the Spirit for the individual concerned. (Sometimes the more advanced members of the congregation, the cross-bearers, carrying the wooden crosses that they have received for sustained and faithful membership, join this activity.) The recipient falls to his knees, and the typical message, which always begins with the formula, 'The Lord has revealed unto me . . .' warns him of dangers, and advises him how to avoid them.[24] Many write

[24] A typical revelation, among several noted, was given as: 'The Lord has revealed unto me, that you must pray, pray, pray. Use Psalm 67 and Psalm 32, and pray fervently to the Lord, because there will be a great trouble for you unless you do this. There is a letter coming from a long way, and it will have good news, the Lord has revealed unto me. There will also be sickness in your family, but the Lord has said unto me, you must read Psalm 25 three times every evening, with a lighted candle at your bed. Use holy water, plenty of holy water, get holy water, sprinkle it around your room, and the Lord will protect you. You must be careful: read Psalm 108 every morning before going out, to guard against misfortune. Pray, pray unto the Lord.' On another occasion, an important item in the message was that there was to be a terrible accident whilst driving, within seven days: the form of protection was to make a sign of the cross over the steering wheel of the car every time one was about to drive. Usually, however, the specifics against danger and illness were confined to the Psalms. This follows Ositelu's own advice, in which the powers of various psalms are described. Thus of Psalm 7 he wrote, 'If enemies arise against thee, recite this Psalm standing facing East in mid-night with the Holy Name—Ell Ellijjoni. You are to [be] nacked [sic]. And the enemy will be Defeated at will.' Of Psalm 19: 'I. To take delivery of new baby, kneel with your left knee, recite 7 times in water with the Holy Name, Jehovah He, give the woman to drink of the water and bath with the rest. She will deliver in peace. II. For power of remembrance— Read on a glass of wine or honey with same Holy Name JEHOVAH HE 7ce for drinking and you will always remember your lessons.' Psalm 20: 'For victory over litigation, read

down the messages, and particularly the specifics to be used to counter the dangers that beset them. Whilst this goes on other members of the congregation hum, listen in to the revelations being received by those about them, read Bibles, tracts, or carry on *sotto voce* conversations with their neighbours. This activity is the least corporate aspect of the procedures of the Church, and yet there can be little doubt that to many it is the principal manifestation of the true spirituality of the Church. Despite the difference of its cultural style, it appears entirely similar to the functions of the possessed priestesses in the Brazilian *candomblés*, or the *dang-kai* of the spiritualist temples of Singapore.

Other forms of revelation are also known. An individual may be possessed by the Spirit and give a message to the whole congregation. Such a message is not preceded with the formula, 'The Lord has revealed until me . . .'; rather the Spirit speaks, through the possessed individual, 'I say unto you . . .'. The message may contain a number of readily accepted sentiments, but may also include specific directions for fasting or other congregational activity, and exhortations against magic (implying that some members of the congregation have 'medicines' or protective devices in use).

Individuals also reveal their blessings from revelation when thanksgiving to the Lord is called for. There is some pressure on people to give thanks, and those who do so must give an additional sum in a special collection when they prostrate themselves before the altar. The group of those giving thanks (men and women do so separately) are also called on to perform spiritual exercises, which consist of jumping seven times, touching one's head to the ground seven times, saying 'Hosannah' seven times, saying 'Allelujah' seven times, and laughing out loud seven times.[25] Further opportunity for individual attention is provided in the prolonged valedictory proceedings, which, after further

---

seven times over water with Holy Name JEHOVAH. Wash with the water and you will gain the favour of the Judge.' Other Psalms are to escape the danger of imprisonment, against witches, to win the favour of a noble person, in order to dream about a particular thing, to prevent thieves, to disgrace one's enemies, if they 'spoil you to your master whereby your master hates you . . .', to gain a post, as well as for a variety of named ailments. Source: Dr J. O. Ositelu, Psy.D., *The Book of Prayer with uses and powers of Psalms and Precious Treasures Hidden Therein* (The Church of the Lord, Ogere Headquarters, Shagamu n.d.).

From the account available, the practice in the Musama Disco Christo Church (Army of the Cross of Christ Church) is not dissimilar. A local prophet describes the spiritual condition of those who go forward for healing, and the precautions necessary for their safety, and perhaps he might say something of their future. This appears to be a type of institutionalization of prophecy restricted to more limited occasions than in the Church of the Lord, but otherwise the operation seems essentially similar. The account is given in C. G. Baëta, op. cit., p. 58, who, however, describes it as a custom 'peculiar to this Church'.

[25] M. Banton, op. cit., reports similar proceedings from Freetown, Sierra Leone, though with some differences of detail from those in Accra.

prayers and hymns, involve a procession into the Mercy Ground. At this time any individual may ask for special congregational prayers to be said on his behalf. The sick, travellers, and sometimes others, may be prayed for: the individual is surrounded by all the office-holders of the congregation (who may number between a dozen and twenty) and the cross-bearers, all of whom proceed to pray individually, spontaneously, and simultaneously in loud and emotional tones.

An important activity is the blessing of holy water, which is undertaken by the minister, who invokes the Holy Ghost to bestow power on the water collected into various bottles and jars beside the sanctuary. The minister communicates this power to each receptacle with the metal wand of office that symbolizes his status. The water plays little part in corporate proceedings, except that it is in this prayer that visions are seen. The water is distributed as a therapeutic agent to those who want it. The Church is thus the distribution point for this powerful commodity, which, however, is used privately. Unlike prayer, which is both an individual and corporate activity, the holy water has a rather subsidiary role in the Church of the Lord. The special seal words are believed to be of great potency, and they are periodically pronounced, often with great vigour, by the minister, and more rarely by other congregational officers. The words themselves are said to have no meaning, but they evoke well-established responses from the congregation, usually the cry 'Holy', or 'Jesus'.[26]

The organization of the movement

The freedom and spontaneity of the typical service of the Church of the Lord (there were different types of services on Sunday morning and evening and on week-nights, and a special Watch-night service on Wednesdays) conceals a firm framework of order. The deployment of a large group of congregational officers who know their stations and duties may be concealed by the apparent abandon with which activities proceed, by the freedom with which particular parts of the service

[26] The use of holy names is related by R. C. Mitchell, 'Sickness and Healing in the Separatist Churches', op. cit., p. 10, to the Christo-pagan magical traditional found in such works as *The Sixth and Seventh Books of Moses*. Books of this kind have had a wide circulation in parts of Africa and in the West Indies, and appear to have had special influence on thaumaturgical movements. They are briefly discussed by B. Holas, *Le Séparatisme religieux . . .*, op. cit., p. 220 ff., and by H. W. Turner, 'Pagan Features in West African Independent Churches', *Practical Anthropology* 12, 4 (July–August 1965), pp. 145–51. Their influence in the Caribbean is made evident in the sect of Norman Paul in Grenada, and is no doubt also widespread. See M. G. Smith, *Dark Puritan*, op. cit., p. 6. A number of American and British firms advertise books of this kind, charms and other religious objects in the popular press of less-developed countries.

(especially individual testimonies during the period of Thanksgiving) continue for a very long time, and by the usually joyous, sometimes casual, and sometimes diverted, expressions of congregants and officials. The pattern of service is laid down for the Church in Ghana in a well-written constitution which is far more lucid than most of the literature of the Church, and which reveals considerable legal expertise on the part of its (anonymous) author.[27] This document sets out the times, proceedings, and offices in the local congregation, districts, regions in the Ghana See of the Church. It reflects the increasing significance of the rapidly expanding Ghanaian branch of the movement in the late 1950s and early 1960s, and the wish of many Ghanaians in the Church to enjoy some degree of independence, although allegiance to Dr Ositelu and the Ogere headquarters was firmly stated.[28]

The extent to which the Church of the Lord, especially in Ghana, has adopted western-style denominational provisions, illustrates the accommodation of thaumaturgical orientations to a rational-legal organization structure. Thus the government of the Church is through three houses of clergy and laity, a Conference, Minor Conference, and Standing Committee. The hierarchy of the Church is given as: Primate and Founder; Apostle; Bishop; Archdeacon (or Archdeaconess); Deacon (or Deaconess); Senior Prophet (or Senior Prophetess); Prophet (or Prophetess); Evangelist (or Lady Evangelist); Acting Prophet (or Acting Prophetess); Captain (or Lady Captain); Teacher; Follower (Minister in Training); Leader; Cross-Bearer. In addition, an Apostle, who is the effective head of the Church in Ghana, may appoint a Chancellor and a Registrar, the latter to concern himself with property and documents. There are also a Secretary-General, a Treasurer-General, and their assistants, and secretaries and treasurers at regional, district, and branch levels. At the local level there is a church council, and each church council nominates elders for a four-year period. Each church has a General Warden and his deputy, a corps of officials in the Army of Jesus under its own Captain, and a Ladies' Praying Union under its Leader. Each church must be under the charge of a full-time minister.[29] An elaborate range of local societies is listed, relatively few of which appear to operate in any given congregation, however.

[27] *The Constitution of the Church of the Lord (Aladura) Ghana (Comprising Definitions, Laws and Regulations)*, mimeographed. No author or date.

[28] H. W. Turner, 'The Church of the Lord: The Expansion of a Nigerian Independent Church . . .', op. cit., refers to pressure by the Ghanaian churches in 1959 for a resident spiritual head of the church in Ghana, and adds, 'Apparently some support was secured from a Cabinet minister of the Government'. The preoccupation with firmly establishing the Ghana Church was evident during my participation in church meetings in 1964.

[29] *The Constitution . . .*, op. cit.

In many ways the constitution of the Church in Ghana manifests a literalism and an inclusiveness of regulation that perhaps equals that of denominations of western Christendom. It provides elaborate procedure for discipline of both members and clergy, regulations for services, for fasting, burial, marriage, divorce, and intestacy, among other things. Particular attention is given to schismatic tendencies, and the danger of the diffusion of charisma is recognized in the specific mention of Cross-Bearers (the highest order of laity):

> Members of the Organization, especially Cross Bearers who have been imbued with the divine spirit and power to prophesy, to give divine messages, to be seers of visions, to heal and to interpret dreams, are forbidden from establishing a private praying place or a place of worship or a Branch Church under the aegis of this organization without the approval and consent of the Apostle and the Standing Committee. New Branch Churches may only be created on recommendation of the District Church Council and the Regional Board concerned, by the Apostle with the consent of the Standing Committee.[30]

The senior members of the laity, in whom the Church recognizes charismatic gifts, are clearly seen as a potential threat to church order. With the ministry itself, emphasis is put upon their call, to which the minister's life is to bear testimony; their capacity for expression; and their education.[31] Two years' training at a hostel attached to the Ghana See were stipulated for the ministry, where the curriculum was to include Old and New Testament Theology; Expository; Dogmatic Theology; Pastoral Theology; Moral Theology; Ethics; Church History—but in fact no such hostel existed. In the 1960s the Apostle went to a British bible institute of strong evangelical persuasion for a course of instruction.

The development of rational-legal forms in the administration of the Church extends to matters beyond those dealt with in the Constitution, wide-ranging as that document is. In 1948, a Church committee on which the Primate and the two Apostles sat pronounced in detail on the robes to be worn by members and ministers of the Church, although considerable latitude was allowed to senior officials to 'wear a robe of any colour or design he likes except those the Primate forbids'. (Interestingly this latitude was expressed as a matter of personal preference, not

---

[30] Ibid., p. 44.

[31] Ibid., p. 6. 'Although Candidates with the highest possible education are needed for the Ministry of the Church, it is not only the present stage reached, which the examination seeks to find out, but the possibility there is of advancing further in mental development . . . only Candidates with sufficient educational background, that is, holders of the Middle School Leaving Certificate or its equivalent shall be accepted for training for the Ministry.' Those not satisfying these conditions were acceptable for training only as catechists; all catechists were required to be able to read and write the vernacular.

of Spirit guidance.) For the lower orders there were more precise details.[32] The Church has also issued a matrimonial guide, which seeks, in particular, to induce ministers to regularize their marital relationships and to contract marriage through the Church. Choice of spouse is to be justified by divine findings, and for ministers divorce, except for the adultery of a wife, is forbidden.[33] The document is silent on polygamy. Some members maintained that the Primate had more than one wife, that the practice was therefore not forbidden, and might, indeed, be divinely warranted.

The teachings of the Church of the Lord

In common with many other independent movements in West Africa, the central preoccupations of the Church of the Lord are oracles and miracles. The liturgical details of these movements differ, as does the degree of sophistication in organization and regularization of procedures, and the inherited cultural forms they employ, but there are also striking similarities which need not be ennumerated. The precise points of syncretism are obviously likely to differ increasingly as movements undergo internal evolution. The Christian inheritance of this Church was transmitted initially and primarily through the CMS, with subsequent influences from the Faith Tabernacle. Wherever its early adventism came from, it is now no longer emphasized or of particular importance. The order in which the teachings of the Church are stated reveals its central preoccupations, and their accommodation to Christian scriptures. The first three of twenty-seven 'fundamental beliefs' are on visions, dreams, and divine revelation; consecrated waters of healing; divine healing and present-day miracles: the fourth is on prayer and fasting.[34] Then follow items usually given greater prominence in western fundamentalist churches: the divine inspiration of the Bible; the Trinity; human depravity; redemption through Christ; confession of sins, repentance and restitution; justification. Entire sanctification is stated to be 'through sprinkling of Holy Water for Cleansing'. The typically pentecostalist elements of the baptism of the

[32] J. O. Oshitelu (et al.), Order of the Official Robes for the Ministers and Members of the Church of the Lord (Aladura) (no place of publication [Ogere?], n.d. [1948?])
[33] Apostle E. O. Adeleke Adejobi, Holy Matrimonial Guide (no place of publication, n.d.). Similar close attention to matrimonial matters is reported from the Musama Disco Christo Church of southern Ghana. Spiritual consultation is advocated, a form of marriage counselling, and meetings for the married are also held in that church. C. G. Baëta, op. cit. p. 59.
[34] — The Fundamental Beliefs of the Church of the Lord (Aladura) Throughout the Whole World. Founded in Nigeria, 1930 (no place of publication, n.d.).

Holy Spirit, and the gifts and fruits of the Spirit, warrant two of the twenty-seven statements. Resurrection Day is included as the nineteenth item, and the second coming of Christ as the twentieth, with the judgements following—all preceded, however, by a statement of belief in civil government. A later publication, seeking to justify the Church's beliefs and practices in scriptural terms, leaves adventist ideas altogether unmentioned, but provides elaborate scriptural support for a wide range of practices, including singing, dancing, clapping, lively entertainments in worship; the use of Holy Water; the institution of Cross-Bearers and the conferment of rods of office on ministers; fasting; food taboos; the prohibition from the house of worship of women during menstruation; rolling on the ground; making spiritual enquiries for guidance; disallowing corpses in the house of worship.[35] The preoccupation is characteristically thaumaturgical: the adventist and millennialist concerns have largely disappeared, in the literature as in the emphasis in worship.

Some attention is given to ethical prescriptions with the usual Christian exhortations to humility, steadfastness, truth, faith, obedience, and love. The Constitution, which emphasizes salvation by faith, also emphasizes avoidance of drunkenness; going to law; railing; buying and selling uncustomed goods; usury; 'uncharitable or unprofitable conversation, particularly speaking evil of Magistrates, Ministers, or for that matter the Government'; wearing costly apparel; engaging in diversions that cannot be used in the name of the Lord Jesus; singing songs and reading books that do not tend to the knowledge of the love of God; and self-indulgence. They are exhorted to do good, 'especially to them that are of the household of the faith, or groaning to be so. . .'.[36]

Any purely formal analysis of the teachings of a church like Aladura is likely considerably to overstate the importance of ideological and ethical aspects in the life of the movement. At a service relatively little weight is attached to doctrine. Although there is a sermon, it is usually

[35] Apostle E. O. Adeleke Adejobi, *The Bible Speaks on the Church of the Lord*, with a foreword by J. A. Adenuga, B. A. Dunlem [*sic*] Dip. Theology, London, 2nd Edn (Free Town, Sierra Leone, January 1950).

[36] *The Constitution* . . ., op. cit., p. 5. H. W. Turner, 'The Catechism of an Independent West African Church', *The Sierra Leone Bulletin of Religion* II, 2 (December 1960), pp. 45–57, has commented on the extent of doctrinal material included in the Church's catechism, which is greater than that of the Anglican, though he also acknowledges the discrepancy between its catechistical 'mildly Africanized evangelical Baptist position' and the actual life of the Church. The Catechism includes strong ethical precepts—'To order myself lowly and reverently to all my betters. . . . To keep my hands from picking and stealing, and my tongue from evil-speaking, lying and slandering. . . .' J. O. Ositelu, *Catechism of the Church of the Lord (Aladura) throughout the World and the Holy Litany* (Ogere 1948), p. 8.

a simple moral tale, often involving considerable display of dramatics by both the minister and the translator (into, or out of, the vernacular —with considerable freedom for the linguist to embellish the story in his own way). The sermon, however, despite the considerable Protestant inheritance of the Church (and it regards itself as distinctly in Protestant tradition, despite the use of incense, candles, sanctuary, etc.) is no more than an interlude in the ritualism and inspirational and ecstatic practices of the service. Power and the means of unleashing it are traditional preoccupations, evident in the use of seal words, holy water, and in the importance of the name of Jesus (the congregation always bows when the name occurs, for example, in a hymn).

This primitive concern is nowhere more manifest than in the attitude towards the small wooden crosses which are distributed to faithful members. The order of Cross-Bearers was established by the Founder in 1937 at Mount Tabbieorrar, at the command of the Lord.[37] A special service is held each year at the national ceremonies which commemorate this event, and crosses are conferred on those who are recommended by the local church after four years of faithful member-ship. That service, which begins with the hymn 'Take up thy Cross the Saviour said', includes prayers of sanctification, anointment, cross-giving, the distribution of victory leaves, and the hymn, 'In the Cross'. The cross is not only a symbol of power and a testimony of power achieved, it is a source of intrinsic power. It is to be held always when praying, in services, during spiritual visits, when preaching, when telling visions or conveying revelatory messages. Certain taboos are associated with it: it must not be touched by unanointed ones, nor by 'women behind the tent'; it must not be allowed to drop carelessly, 'for the falling of the Cross means (i) you have committed a sin, or (ii) a Death, or (iii) a loss, or (iv) a bad fortune or occurrence'.[38] The cross is an agency through which God will speak to the individual in dreams and visions, and, in particular, dreams about the cross have special significance. 'The position of a Cross-bearer in the Church of the Lord is higher than that of a communicant in other Churches, even very higher.'[39] The Cross-Bearers are looked upon as anointed to preach, heal the sick, raise the dead, work miracles, and even to run a church

[37] The Mount Tabbieorrah Anniversary is the principal festival of the Church calendar, and is held in the various provinces independently on 22 August. The feast is preceded by thirty days of fasting (abstention from salt, oil, fats, sugar, milk, fish, and pepper), and is regarded as an occasion of penance. E. O. Adeleki Adejobi, *Mount Taborrar's Anniversary* (The Royal Press, Tka, probably 1962). (There are several variant spellings of Tabbieorrah.)

[38] Rules concerning the crosses are given in Apostle Samuel Omolaja Oduwole, *'Ell Tieggah Vicottieorrius', The Holy Cross (in the Church of the Lord)* (no place or date of publication, but probably 1962), pp. 11 ff.

[39] Ibid., p. 3.

if the minister is not available. A variety of obligations are also associated with the office.

The cross thus acquires a power which is almost magical, much as does water in this and other West African movements.[40] The seashore, where some congregations go to bathe and hold spiritual exercises in the nude at periodic intervals (a practice which seems to vary with the nearness of the individual church to the sea), and the Mercy Ground attached to each church, are similarly regarded as places endowed with special power. Holy Communion, though practised, is less frequent, and is a less popular vehicle for the transmission of supernatural power. Certainly, older pagan forms of acquiring power are abandoned, but, as in Christianity proper, there are distinct continuities at the ritual level (rather than at the ideological) with the magical practice of pre-Christian days.[41]

Inspiration and institutionalism

Inspirationalism always creates problems of institutionalization. Where prophets abound, order is difficult to attain. This was a problem in the Pentecostalist churches in Britain and the United States in the early years of the twentieth century. The difficulty of establishing authority without bridling the Spirit was only slowly resolved in these highly emotional sects. In many, a degree of informality and a lightly-sustained pattern of casual order persisted for a long time. In others, centralized control developed, as the means of organizing local services in an orderly fashion were gradually evolved. Some of them, and the (British) Apostolic Church which influenced the early independent spiritual churches in Nigeria was one, established a pattern of authority based on the directions of Paul concerning the offices and gifts of the Spirit, and thus claimed pentecostal structure as well as pentecostal doctrine and liturgy. In institutionalizing officers such as Senior Prophets, Prophets, and Assistant Prophets, the Church of the Lord has attempted a similar method of containing inspirational challenge to stable church order. But it has harkened back to the Old Testament rather than to the New Testament designations of Paul. The attempt

[40] We have noted this in the Déima movement and the Massa movement, among others. It is equally pronounced in Musama Disco Christo Church, which maintains a special House of the Holy Well, from which alone holy water is available, and which is under the charge of the head of the movement. C. G. Baëta, op. cit., p. 48.

[41] A discussion of the syncretism of West African independent churches, from a Christian point of view, is provided by H. W. Turner, 'Pagan Features in West African Independent Churches', op. cit.

at centralization, even though in the case of Ghana it appears to be nationally defined, is greater than that of most Pentecostal sects: so, too, is the extent to which charismatic superiority is credited to the Founder. The nomenclature reveals a considerable syncretism of various traditions, with the Anglican predominant. With its many status positions, the church offers opportunities for service, and thus institutionalizes the dispositions of all prominent personalities. The opportunity to prophesy is widely diffused, and while personal references are avoided in the messages given to a whole congregation, there is still opportunity for everyone to receive individual messages. Conventions grew up in western Pentecostalism concerning what messages might be congregationally received, and the early tendency for very explicit directions and personal references to occur was gradually eliminated by agreement among pastors and by the socialization of congregations. Some such process has obviously occurred in the Church of the Lord. Perhaps the wide dispersal of offices especially facilitates the reduction of jealousies about spiritual power.

Particular conventions have arisen that reflect the movement's thaumaturgical preoccupations concerning the recognition of witches. Those who have the power to receive messages, and they are numerous in a congregation, also acquire the capacity to discern spirits (as the Scriptures put it) and thus to recognize witches (a traditional function of thaumaturgy). Accusations of witchcraft are, of course, punishable in most countries, and so congregational officers who recognize a witch do not announce the fact. Obviously, such accusations would have disruptive consequences in a congregation. But witches *are* seen, and those who receive revelations attempt to convey to witches the fact that they have been recognized, without making a direct statement to this effect. Some members claimed that as they moved about in their daily lives they recognized witches, and from what these congregational officers said, they regarded witches as particularly prevalent and dangerous phenomena against which the Church had given them the blessings of protection. In the recognition of witches, as in the regulation of other charismatic power, a process of socialization and institutionalization has occurred. This is the cost of stability. The urgency, intensity of personal involvement and emotionalism that characterize thaumaturgical demand persistently challenge the routine of order and decorum, as when the local minister, concerned for punctuality, urges in vain the loquacious givers of thanks, 'Short, short, short'.

Despite the formality of its constitution and the elaboration of its hierarchy, the services of the Church of the Lord were conspicuous for the freedom which prevailed within their fixed order. At local level, the times and order prescribed in official documents were not taken seriously. The authority of the minister, whilst not challenged, could be exercised only lightly. The norms of the movement had not been internalized in a way characteristic of a western religious movement. The very acceptance of free expression over a wide range of emotional responses—joy, anguish, sorrow, fear, enthusiasm—precluded the appearance of that degree of decorum characteristic of European Protestant styles of worship. Although the movement requires that followers wear white robes at services, there were always men dressed in white shirts and trousers and some in coloured shirts and flannels, and this despite the regularly intoned threat of the warden that such improperly dressed people would in future have to sit outside the hall. There were always people who did not even give the appearance of following the proceedings of the service, particularly in its less dramatic parts. There were occasional outbursts of quarrelling between partici- pants during the service (for which they might be sent to the Mercy Ground to do penance).

Limitations on rational bureaucratic procedures were evident in a number of circumstances. Tithes and dues were necessarily collected in the services, since the movement lacked an organization which could obtain these by post or house-call, and services would be held up for a considerable time while collections were taken, and tins (for tithes) collected. A characteristically non-rational pattern of collecting dona- tions prevailed: groups, often designated by the common day of their birth, would be induced to compete in giving donations. When the total sums were announced each group would be given an opportunity to improve its status by adding more to its total. The prize for the winning group was to choose a set of choruses to be sung. Nor was attendance particularly high or constant among the five hundred nominal members. Characteristically, many members maintained dual memberships: they attended Aladura services but were sometimes prepared to regard themselves primarily as 'Roman Catholics' or 'Presbyterians', who came to the Church of the Lord for 'more spiritual' exercises, or when they had troubles for which the orthodox Christian churches made no provision.

The thaumaturgical orientation and the accompanying manifesta- tions of power were the attractions for these casuals and pluralists. Despite these various manifestations of limited socialization to the Christian style of religious practice, Aladura members were not primarily drawn from the lower strata of Accra society. No detailed list of occupations was available, but there were among the more strongly committed members, a postmaster, a policeman, a teleprinter operator, the headmistress of an infant's school, two law students at the University, an air hostess, a tailor, several clerks, and drivers. Most of the men were in greater or lesser degree literate in English, although some of the women spoke only Twi or Gã, and may not have been able to read even the vernacular. Despite the absence of specifically European conceptions of decorum, a sense of orderliness prevailed. This was no sectarian expression of the disprivileged strata of Accra society, and this was confirmed by the fact that prophetic emphasis was, when not concerned directly with overcoming illness, barrenness, danger, and evil, often placed on the status preoccupations typical of people who have already attained some degree of status.

At local level, and as its literature reveals, the Church of the Lord is essentially a thaumaturgical movement. But it has been heavily informed by evangelical mission Christianity, with which many of its leaders have been associated, and as a mission church itself, it has acquired the formal apparatus of the typical conversionist movement. It lacks the social context in which to regularize its activities as a sect or as a denomination, in the western sense of those terms: but its efforts to impress ethical commitment, to enjoin its members to hold themselves apart from non-Christian people and from the places they frequent, and to regulate the charisma it so readily and so widely distributes, indicate its endeavours in this direction.

There are, however, other models available, besides those of the missions, from which a movement like the Church of the Lord might acquire its legal-rational style. Many members have been associated with the army, others are engaged in the police force or the civil service, or in concerns which are run on western lines. Only a full analysis of the background of the strategically deployed personnel of the movement would show the extent to which learning in these agencies has been employed in the service of the Church. There is a marked difference between the early pronouncements of the Founder, which are brief and in poor English, and which display almost magical dispositions, and the lengthy, formal, well-written, and legally acute Constitution of the Ghanaian branch of the movement. That document, too, and perhaps others emerging from the rapidly growing Ghanaian See, displays concerns of a type characteristic of a society in which there is keen awareness of the new foci of authority in a (then) some-what dictatorial nation-state. The pressure of the Ghanaian See to obtain national autonomy and the emphasis on respect for government, and perhaps the very need for an elaborate and detailed constitution, making these matters very plain, reflected the conditions then prevailing.

Conclusion

Our concern with thaumaturgical movements has not been to provide a catalogue of all such movements that are known, but rather to make apparent the frequency of new thaumaturgical manifestations among less-developed peoples. In a world in which magical forces are believed to be ubiquitous, new events and new manifestations of power are likely to be interpreted in magical terms and to give rise to new patterns of thaumaturgical practice. The power of strangers, and particularly of Europeans, is impressive, and in the desire to share such power, their spiritual and 'magical' styles are likely to be imitated for whatever ends power is culturally employed. We have seen that even in movements that are essentially restorative in orientation, important elements have, none the less, been acquired from cultural contact with Christianity or Islam—the procedures by which the strangers acquire their greater spiritual and physical power. We have paid special attention, not so much to the actual rites and formulae that have been imitated, as to the organizational forms into which traditional ideas have been transplanted. Clearly, as Tylor long ago noticed, there are self-evident continuities in preoccupation in religious practice from the magical consumption of tabooed foods among very simple peoples to the solemn rites of the Catholic Church, but the persistence of magical elements in higher religions has not been the burden of our enquiry. We have not been concerned with the way in which the more elevated forms of widely spread rites have influenced native practice. Western religion has developed most conspicuously by the adaptation of rational forms of organization, even though these have necessarily constituted a secularizing process. The diffusion of more rational patterns of organization among those whose interests are primarily thaumaturgical is a phenomenon to which very much less attention had previously been given.

New thaumaturgical movements represent a deviant religious response—a sectarian religious response—largely because of the *newness* of their ritual procedures and organizational forms. They become a protest against traditional religious practice—itself highly thaumaturgical—because they pit new measures, and (often) new conceptions of social nexus, against the old. As a 'protest' such new movements are muted comments on the inadequacy of previous procedures rather than an articulate condemnation. Their practice, however, is often enough to make evident at least a temporary rejection of older procedures, and of those who control them. When new organizational forms are adopted, the vigour of the protest becomes more apparent and sometimes more articulate. Such movements cannot but be innovative in some respects, even if their innovation is undertaken in the name of restoration, or in defence of tradition (as in the Massa movement). They rely on new men, who have a new perception of the social situation (or on old ones who make dramatic adjustment to new situations) and who re-work old elements into new systems. Often, as in the case of the spiritual churches of West Africa, the new men have acquired a wide range of western knowledge, and even if their thought-forms are not wholly rationalized in the western sense, and even if they maintain religious and even magical conceptions of causality, they do so on the model of agencies which, for all their rational organization, are themselves the custodians of the remnants of such patterns of non-rational thought in western society—the churches.

To say this is to make no value-judgement about the worthiness of the spiritual churches (or of any other new religious movement). They may themselves be socializing agencies in the development of more rational habits of thought. Rational ways of thinking may best be learned through involvement in the procedures of rationally organized institutions, and in the underdeveloped countries, in contrast to the more developed, even élites may acquire their rational perceptions of the world from involvement in rational structures, rather than by a more individuated psychological and philosophical process.[42] (The same is perhaps true for the masses in contemporary western society.[43]) The disciplining of the emotions in the maintenance of rational structures is itself an important exercise in the diffusion of rational thinking, even when those structures are first embraced in order to provide a stable context in which the emotions may be unleashed. But the very agencies which facilitate that emotional expression also regulate it. Organizational goals will evolve in the spiritual churches, and commitment to these goals is likely to be a process of commitment to rational order, to means rather than to the ends of emotional liberation.

That rational organization should be adopted for non-rational activities is merely a paradox in a process of cultural socialization. The pattern is not new. Methodism in its early stages fulfilled similar social

[42] The persistence of magical patterns of thought occurs even among élite strata: the belief in 'money-doubling' among Cabinet ministers in Ghana was revealed in some of the political intrigues during the government of Kwame Nkrumah. On 'money-doubling' see Gustav Jahoda, 'Money Doubling in the Gold Coast', British Journal of Delinquency VIII, 4 (April 1958), pp. 266–76.

[43] For brief discussion of this see B. R. Wilson, Religion in Secular Society (Watts, London 1966), pp. xvi–xvii.

functions; the Holiness movements, the Salvation Army, and Pentecostalism, did so at a later time. In the case of Pentecostalism, its
attractiveness to immigrants (to Italians in Brazil and to Italians,
Mexicans, and Puerto Ricans in the United States—all of whom had an
inheritance of Catholicism from their old cultures[44]) is perhaps indicative of its 'power' as an agency of acculturation in mobilizing thaumaturgical demand, and in steadily transforming it. What is lost in this
process of rationalization is not our concern here. That something is
felt to be lost is perhaps in itself evident from the long persistence of
thaumaturgical orientations, and the emotional intensity that accompanies them. That intensity is steadily reduced in the new forms of
thaumaturgical movement.[45] The free expression of grief and joy in the
spiritual churches is part of their appeal. Eventually the elements of
asceticism and austerity (evident in many of the prophets themselves,
for example in Papa Adaï, Marie Lalou, Isaiah Shembe, as well as in
the prescriptions promulgated in many such movements) are likely, on
all the evidences of religious evolution, to grow in importance, and the
emotionality to decline. The spontaneity and joy of the spiritual
churches is a feature not very evident in the churches of advanced
countries, but neither is the free expression of mental anguish which
these churches facilitate. Among a more sophisticated population,
thaumaturgical demands become more instrumental, more mechanical,
and more a matter of manipulating forces, or manipulating oneself, as
more practical and more rational orientations predominate. The
manipulationist movements of western society are the inheritors, albeit
in more sophisticated and universalistic style, of the thaumaturgical
demands of men. Those demands have never been entirely silenced in

[44] See on the Puerto Rican Pentecostalists, Renate Poblete and Thomas O'Dea, 'Anomie
and the "Quest for Community": The Formation of Sects among the Puerto Ricans of New
York', *American Catholic Sociological Review* XXI, 1 (Spring 1960), pp. 18–36; Anne Parsons,
'The Pentecostal Immigrants', *Journal for the Scientific Study of Religion* 4, 2 (1965), pp. 183–97;
Scott Cook, 'The Prophets: A Revivalists Folk Religious Movement in Puerto Rico',
Caribbean Studies 4, 4 (January 1965), pp. 20–35. Cook estimates that more than 10 per cent
of the Puerto Rican population, once wholly Catholic, were enrolled in Protestant (largely
Pentecostal) groups in 1964. On Protestantism among Mexicans in the United States, see
Margaret L. Sumner, 'Mexican-American Minority Churches, U.S.A.', *Practical Anthropology*
10, 3 (May–June 1963), pp. 115–21.
[45] This is implicit in the very regulation that they impose, in their emphasis on discipline,
hierarchy, and the institutionalization of levels of thaumaturgical power. Increasing regulation of emotion has been a feature of western Pentecostalism. It has also occurred in a variety
of movements in less-developed societies which have manifested other responses besides the
strictly thaumaturgical. Thus among North American Indian movements, most conspicuously in the injunctions of Wovoka, regulation of grief in mourning has been conspicuous. The Bwiti of the Gabon manifest the same discipline, and similar injunctions to
control grief are found in Te Kooti's Ringatu Church.

the most orthodox churches, and it might be maintained that they stand at the very heart of religion, even though in contemporary orthodoxy they are demands not for wonder-working, but for mental therapy, comfort, pastoral care, and reassurance.[46]

[46] This is very fully brought out in the study of contemporary Episcopalians by Charles Y. Glock, Benjamin B. Ringer, and Earl R. Babbie, *To Comfort and to Challenge* (University of California Press, Berkeley and Los Angeles 1967).

7

The Social Sources of Millennialism: three ambiguous cases

REVOLUTIONIST religious movements are readily recognizable i the Christian tradition. They are those groups which emphasize the second advent of Christ, and believe that that occasion will be associated with divine intervention in the affairs of men by the over-turning of the social, and perhaps also the physical order. They are not, of course, revolution*ary* movements, since they do not necessarily expect themselves to implement God's will. In less-developed societies this point of distinction cannot always be drawn so readily, for a number of reasons. In the first place, the relations of indigenous peoples with European invaders are often warlike in the early phase of contact, and for such peoples war is an activity for which religious rites are usually necessary. Secondly, Europeans observe the behaviour of primitive peoples long before they learn to understand the motivations and thought processes associated with that behaviour: they have often been inclined to interpret religious activity as political activity, since this is more immediately meaningful to them. Third, colonial action in response to such political interpretations of religious activities has sometimes had the effect of a self-fulfilling prophecy. Religious practices or meetings have been prohibited and leaders persecuted as political rebels, and have thereby been induced to become rebels, their religious ideas undergoing appropriate modification to become ideological justifications for revolutionary activity.

In their nature, revolutionist movements face inherent difficulties in attaining stable and persisting commitment. The hope or expectation that God will act to transform the world most easily mobilizes support when the hope is newly canvassed, and the expectation is of action suddenly and soon. In western countries such movements have acquired stability and institutionalization, even though their initial revolutionist orientation has sometimes receded as a consequence. In less-developed societies such stability has only rarely been achieved. Most of the reported cases are of prophecies about divine intervention in human affairs that have brought into being short-lived movements, most of which have quickly disappeared or been repressed. Often they have gone without trace although sometimes they have recrudesced.

There has been a high incidence of such movements. They are reported from most parts of the world (although there appear to have been no clear cases of revolutionist religious movements in India among Hindus and few among tribal peoples[1]). Among tribal societies, such movements have occurred in most regions, with the possible exception of Australia during the earlier stages of cultural contact. Just what they owe to Judeo-Christian-Muslim conceptions of the coming messiah and to Christian conceptions of the millennium is debatable. The movements of which there are reports have almost always arisen among men with some knowledge of Christian or Muslim ideas. This influence is often apparent even when it is dominated by indigenous conceptions.

Our reports come from missionaries, frontiersmen, government agents or colonial officials, or (western) anthropologists. We can learn very little of movements that might have arisen before regions were affected by western ideas, and before western observers were there to record them. If movements arise from spontaneous prophecies, indigenous and recurrently remembered native myths and beliefs, then they might be found in a variety of circumstances. If social disruption alone were sufficient to give rise to the revolutionist response, then myriads of movements would have arisen in the course of history. If they spring from particularly dramatic contact of much more-advanced with much less-advanced peoples, we might expect them to occur among tribal groups living at the periphery of all the great civilizations.

There seems to be no *a priori* reason why a people in distress, particularly from human oppression, should not seek relief from the ancestors— from those stronger men, in whose time suffering is supposed to have been unknown. The intensity of demand, among highly suggestible peoples who often have faith in dreams and visions, *might* give rise to strong convictions of soon and sudden salvation by the action of the ancestors. But we simply do not have firm empirical evidence of such movements.[2] Obviously the specific and associated conceptions of the

---

[1] The many cases of religious reform movements and actual rebellions in India chronicled by Stephen Fuchs, in *Rebellious Prophets: A Study of Messianic Movements in Indian Religions* (Asia Publishing House, London 1965), appear to me to include no clear instances of a revolutionist response or unambiguous millennialism.

[2] Great importance is attached to such indigenous myths by Maria Isaura Pereira de Queiroz, in *O Messianismo—no Brasil e no Mundo* (University of São Paulo, São Paulo 1965), pp. 10–11, and also to indigenous ideas of a returning messiah as the basis for active new religious movements, pp. 14–15. Undoubtedly such myths may give movements their character, but—for obvious reasons—we lack well-documented and indisputable cases of millennial movements that can be shown to be entirely free of the Judeo-Christian-Islamic millennial ideas. The myth of world destruction is not uncommon among simpler peoples. F. Rudolf Lehmann, in 'Weltuntergang und Welterneuerung in Glauben schriftlöser Völker', *Zeitschrift für Ethnologie* Vol. 71, Heft 1–3 (1939), pp. 103–15, lists a number of cases

messiah and the millennium, with a belief in the overturning of the world, constitute a Judeo-Christian-Muslim cultural complex, and this association of items is likely to be found only where one or other of these cultural influences has prevailed. But revolutionist responses may occur in many ideological and mythological forms. Some of these elements may be found without the others. Three possible cases of spontaneous movements with some type of revolutionist connotation may be briefly examined, as indications that such movements *might* arise more or less autochthonously, without the impress of the cultural ideas transmitted by the three middle-eastern religions.

Many simpler peoples have regarded the first white men to visit them as supernatural beings,[3] sometimes, it has been suggested, because they had pre-existing myths about return of the gods (or the ancestors).[4] For a time, the superior power of the strangers has been sufficient to sustain this belief. These ideas adumbrate a faintly revolutionist orientation—a belief in the transformation of the world. If these ideas are indeed part of the indigenous, autochthonous religious tradition, they resemble similar conceptions within Judaism, Christen-

---

of such myths, some springing from actually remembered floods and volcanic eruptions. The Bukawa believed eclipse to portend the death of all men. The Paiute believed that they must frighten the monster that, at times of eclipse, was swallowing the sun. The Incas had stories of a permanent eclipse, and Aztec ritual constituted a priestly protection of the world from destruction. There was a Choctaw tale that the world would be burned by fire, but would be made new when the ghosts returned. Lehmann rejects, with Radcliffe-Brown, E. H. Man's report of a similar idea of world-renewal among the Andaman Islanders, partly on the ground that the language of this people lacked a future tense. George Shepperson, 'Nyasaland and the Millennium' in S. L. Thrupp, op. cit., pp. 144–59, finds nothing particularly Christian about the millennial ideas current in Nyasaland, and thinks it unlikely that the Arabs had introduced Islamic theology. He recounts that 'the last Malawi hero, chief Kankhomba who, when overwhelmed by the Yao, retreated to Soche Hill . . . it is believed, is still waiting there in a cave to come again when his people most need him' (p. 148). But Shepperson is far from wanting to press the case for an autochthonous tribal millennialism.

[3] There are numerous reports of simpler peoples entertaining this type of conception of the first Europeans to arrive among them. The Samoans called the British *papalangi*, the cloud-piercers, or heaven-sent ones, according to J. D. Freeman, 'The Joe Gimlet or Siovili Cult: An Episode in the Religious History of Early Samoa', pp. 185–220 in J. D. Freeman and W. E. Geddes (Eds), *Anthropology in the South Seas* (Thomas Avery, New Plymouth, N.Z. 1959). It was the general belief of Australian aborigines that whites were the returned spirits of the dead of their own people, according to Helmut Petri, 'Das Weltende im Glauben australischer Eingeborener', pp. 349–62, in A. E. Jensen (Ed.), *Mythe, Mensche und Umwelt* (Bamburg 1950), p. 362. (This volume is also Vol. IV of the journal *Paideuma: Mitteilungen zur Kulturkunde*.)

[4] The Maoris of New Zealand had legends of a fairer race of semi-divine character, and this dictated their reaction to Cook on his landing: I. L. G. Sutherland, *The Maori Situation* (Tombs, Wellington, N.Z. 1935), p. 14. James Mooney in *The Ghost Dance and the Sioux Outbreak of 1890*, Fourteenth Annual Report of the Bureau of Ethnology to the Secretary of the Smithsonian Institution, Washington, D.C. (Government Printing Office 1896), whilst allowing that missionaries might have sometimes inspired such stories, says, 'The faith of the return of a white deliverer from the East opened the gate to the Spaniards at their first coming, alike in Haiti, Mexico, Yucatan and Peru' (p. 658).

dom, and Islam, and they may not be more socially disruptive than they are within those traditions. In three cases, however, such ideas appear to be more than merely fossilized elements in a wider mythological context. In two of the cases the supportive mythology is *possibly* indigenous, and may not have been diffused from Christian or Muslim sources, but this is only a possibility. In these two cases, the myth, however and whenever it was acquired, appears to have become a relatively stable element of the cultural inheritance, but one capable of precipitating religious response when external circumstances or prophetic idiosyncrasy have brought the myth to the forefront of attention. In the third case, the mythological elements are almost certainly the result of recent diffusion: the analytical importance of this case is, however, of a rather different order.

Three special cases: the Koreri movements

The *Manseren* cult, or *Koreri* movement, of the island of Biak-Numfor, one of the Schouten Islands, situated in the Geelvink Bay, on the coast of north-western New Guinea (now Irian), is a recrudescent revolutionist movement which rests on an established local myth of unknown provenance. The islands were infertile, and the society was itself labile and insecure. By Indonesian conquest the islands became acquainted with iron, bronze, cotton, and porcelain, but because of difficulties of communication none the less maintained considerable cultural localism.[5] Ascribed status was important: one class, the Manseren, were masters who stood above newcomers and slaves. But, as elsewhere in Melanesia, the outstanding individual, whether as warrior or successful trader, could always acquire status. 'Long before the advent of modern colonial power, the acquisition of new commodities obtained in the trade with East Indonesia brought enhanced prestige, and such commodities were absorbed in the traditional rituals of marriage and trade.'[6] The islands came under the dominance of the Sultan of Tidore, and from some time after the sixteenth century the Biaks became pirates in his service and in their own right.[7] Thus from

[5] The foregoing description is from Justin M. van der Kroef, 'Patterns of Cultural Change in Three Primitive Societies', *Social Research* 24, 4 (Winter 1957), pp. 427–56.

[6] Ibid., p. 430.

[7] According to Ernst Wilhelm Müller, 'Die Koreri-Bewegung auf den Schouten-Inseln (West Neuguinea)' in W. E. Mühlmann, op. cit., pp. 141–64, European contact began in 1572 with the Spaniards, followed in 1616 by the Dutch. Missions were active in New Guinea from 1855, but not until 1905 in Geelvink Bay. The colonial agents of the Dutch made visits to the islands from 1898, and were established on Biak from 1913 to 1940.

early times 'the west' was associated with an abundance of prestigious commodities, and the subsequent impact of Europeans enhanced this conception.

The complex myth of Manseren may be briefly recounted. The full myth provides a story of the creation of clans, and of one Jawi Nusjado, who inherited all the hero titles and who visited the underworld where his desire to stay was refused. He returned to live in sadness, neglected his gardens, failed to wash, and became known as Manamakeri, 'he who itches'.[8] He proposed ways to make the world as perfect as the paradise he had seen: in particular he prohibited spilling blood and killing swine, but he was mistreated, and left Biak for the island of Moek Wundi. There he made wine, but he discovered that someone stole his wine, and he set himself to catch the thief. The thief was the Morning Star, Kumiseri, whom he caught. In return for releasing him, Manamakeri obtained from him magic fruit which, when thrown at the breasts of a maiden, would make her pregnant, and a staff with which whatever he drew would become real when he stamped his foot.

After acquiring, by these magic means, a wife and a child (who magically recognized his own father) Manamakeri was deserted by all the people. He then transformed himself into a young man, now to be known as Manseren Mangundi, 'The Lord'. The child whom he had magically fathered recognized his transformed father at once. In the baptism of fire by which he became young again, some versions recount that he first became white, but that he disliked the colour and returned to the fire to become brown. At first he had European clothes, but then returned to the old costume of Biak. He sought to preach the Koreri truth again, but eventually, saddened by the failure of the people to live up to his requirements, he departed for the west. The earliest accounts of the myth did not specifically claim that he would come back again, but from 1860 the versions suggest that he would return.

[8] This very concentrated account of the myth relies principally on E. W. Müller, op. cit., and on P. Worsley, op. cit., pp. 126–30, in each of whose works fuller (but somewhat different) versions may be found. The most complete version is F. C. Kamma, *De Messiaanse Koreribewegingen in het Biaks-Noemfoorse cultuurgebied* (J. N. Voorhoeve, The Hague 1954). Names vary in versions of the myth from different localities and according to the orthographic practices of the reporter's own language. A particularly attractive account of the myth as a song employs the name Manarmaker, with Manapureri as a nickname for Manseren Mangundi before his transformation. The first part of this song from Korido is put into the mouth of Manarmaker himself, and tells his story in brief but graphic terms, with considerable emphasis on such incidentals as the places he visited in the course of the tale, so that the consequential elements, which appear to be significant as ideology—the theft by the morning star, his capture by Manarmaker, the magic fruit, begetting of the child, etc., receive rather less attention. The second part is the complaint of the natives about the disappearance of Manseren, and ends with their call to him that the morning star still steals. F. W. Hartweg, 'Das Lied von Manseren Mangundi (Biak Sprache)', *Zeitschrift für Eingeborenen-Sprachen* XXIII, 1 (October 1932), pp. 46–58.

Some subsequent versions assert that he went to Holland, Europe, Soep Kalinga, or Japan specifically, and declare that he was in fact white, and would make all the Biaks white.

The myth has been the excuse for a number of prophets, *konors*, to arise in the Schouten Islands, most of whom have claimed to be the son of Manseren Mangundi, and who claim revelation of the Lord's coming from a vision or a dream. The *konors* have arisen periodically since the earliest recorded case in 1854, and have usually demanded that preparations be made for Manseren Mangundi. Larger houses are needed since the ancestors will return: foodstuffs must be destroyed, gardens laid waste, and pigs killed, since Manseren will bring all that is necessary. Dancing, drunkenness, and nightly vigils continue through the nights of expectation. More than thirty such movements of varying intensity have been recorded.[9] The *konors* sometimes contented themselves with extravagant claims, but sometimes they led their followers against the Dutch. The headman of Mokmer in 1884 proclaimed the coming of Manseren, and led his men against a Dutch ship, killing the captain. The *konor* was defeated, offered tribute, but subsequently became a chief by appointment of the authorities, which the natives saw as a remarkable victory,[10] and which in itself is an interesting case of the transfer from traditional to charismatic, and thence to nascent bureaucratic authority.

Over the years the periodic outbreaks of prophetic activity prompted accretions to the myth. Many of the *konors* showed marked magical and therapeutic tendencies. Some were previously medicine men, who claimed powers to heal and to transform objects[11] (elements evident in the original myth). But growing tendencies to xenophobia, to the incorporation of Christian elements, and to the inclusion of ideas of a cargo of European goods coming with the returning Manseren (who was often now identified with Jesus) are also manifest in the twenty-first recorded *konor* movement in 1897.[12] These and further developments are associated with the growing impress of colonial administration on this Melanesian society; the imposition of taxes and public works; the suppression of head-hunting and piracy; the introduction of elements of a money economy; and the arrival of various groups of immigrants,

[9] J. M. van der Kroef, op. cit.
[10] E. W. Müller, op. cit. Worsley's account, op. cit., pp. 131–2, suggests that these episodes were events that occurred in relation to two different *konors*.
[11] J. M. van der Kroef, op. cit., makes this apparent.
[12] E. W. Müller, op. cit., suggests that Christian elements become conspicuous in the 1894 outburst, and that Jesus was expected with a ship full of trade goods in 1897. P. Worsley, op. cit., p. 135, gives a later date for the incorporation of Christian elements—'after 1908', which is the date also given by J. V. de Bruyn, 'The Manseren Cult of Biak', *South Pacific* 5, 1 (March 1951), pp. 1–11.

including Chinese, Indonesians, and the Dutch.[13] The earliest conflicts between the Dutch and the natives of the area were not couched in terms of the Manseren myth, but were protests against forced labour and other grievances, in 1906, 1921, and 1926.[14] Xenophobic feeling was, however, manifest in the Manseren disturbances in 1911, and refusal to pay taxes and engage in forced labour was urged by the self-styled *konor*.[15] Despite more secular troubles, the Manseren myth did not lapse. It persisted in folk tale and as a song. In 1931 a movement led by one Wasjari began among Biak immigrants of the so-called Radja-Ampat Islands. He exacted tribute to save men at the forthcoming sinking of the world that he prophesied. Natives were to cease cultivating and to stop paying taxes. The movement spread to the gulf, and Tanda, another prophet, emerged promising the arrival of a great ship carrying Manseren.[16] Other *konors* arose in the area in the late 1930s, although not on the island of Biak itself. One promised a ship with four funnels, and the arrival of a 'factory' (which natives now understood to be the place in which highly valued trade-goods were somehow created). Despite the Christianization of Biak and the other islands, there was widespread local messianism in some parts, and expectations of war between Holland and Japan followed.[17]

The most important manifestation of the recrudescent Koreri movement, perhaps stimulated by the effects of the outbreak of world war, and certainly by its local consequences, began in 1939. Angganita Menufar, a woman of about 35 years of age from the island of Insumbabi, had, after the death of her husband and three children, and after catching beriberi, retired to live on the small island of Aiburanbondi.[18] There she was supposedly visited by Manamakeri, who commissioned her to preach Koreri. She was miraculously healed of her complaint, and this experience resembled that of Manseren himself. She began to have visions and auditions, and became celebrated, particularly after returning to her own island. The myth as she presented it involved a syncretistic conflation of Manseren and Jesus, but she preached vigorously against the missionaries, whom she said had torn out a page from the Bible before giving it to the natives,[19] thus depriving them of the full efficacy of the faith by which Europeans had achieved so much

---

[13] J. M. van der Kroef, op. cit.

[14] P. Worsley, op. cit., p. 135.

[15] Ibid., p. 134.

[16] F. C. Kamma, 'Messianic Movements in Western New Guinea', *International Review of Missions* XLI (1952), pp. 148–60.

[17] Ibid.

[18] E. W. Müller, op. cit. P. Worsley, op. cit., p. 138, describes Angganita as 'an old leper woman'. Müller suggests her date of birth as about 1905.

[19] This idea was of course common in Melanesian cargo cults.

wealth. Angganita took the title of Maiden of Judea. She organized an advent ceremony with songs of her own composition, instituted initiation rites, and at her meetings there was speaking with tongues. Originally Angganita had preached, as the Manseren had preached, against the spilling of blood. She had also commanded the protection of all animals that changed their skins, prohibited eating pork, bathing in salt-water, and a variety of other things.[20] When meetings under local village leaders were held in 1941, the government arrested Angganita (for a second time), and she was imprisoned in May 1942. With the coming of the war the movement acquired strong anti-Dutch sentiments. Manseren's arrival was expected: dancing was inaugurated in anticipation of this event, gardens were harvested, and pigs slaughtered.

Leadership passed from Angganita to Stephanus Simiopiaref, a convicted murderer, after the arrival of the Japanese in June 1942. The new teaching was that Holland was being defeated because Manseren had left Holland, where he had gone for cargo before the war. A further period of excitement with visions followed.[21] Strong nationalistic sentiments now developed in the movement: a Papuan flag was adopted; Angganita was proclaimed as Princess of New Guinea; and Stephanus Simiopiaref put forward a new programme. Whilst belief in Koreri, the appropriation by the leaders of mystical titles, and the claims to special revelations and visions all continued, new aims were now emphasized. Dutch New Guinea was to be federated, and an army which he called the A B army was to be created to join America, Britain, Holland, and China.[22] Initially the Japanese had been accepted, but later the movement had become hostile, although it had also fragmented into numerous local groups, and the extent of their co-operation with the Japanese appears to have varied. Stephanus himself was impressed by an Allied bombing raid on Manokwari, a small town on the coast, in which many Japanese but no Papuans were killed, and this he took to indicate that the Papuans had a special destiny.[23]

The grandiose ideals of a united Papua stood in sharp contrast with the many local variations of the cult belief that actually came into being. Stephanus led his group, assured of their magical invulnerability against enemy bullets, against the Japanese who attacked by sea. According to

[20] E. W. Müller, op. cit., gives an account of these teachings.
[21] J. V. de Bruyn, op. cit.; P. Worsley, op. cit., pp. 139 ff.
[22] The visions and titles are listed by P. Worsley, op. cit., p. 140. The plan of Stephanus Simiopiaref is given in E. W. Müller, op. cit., following F. C. Kamma, De Messiaanse Koreri-bewegingen . . ., op. cit.
[23] Hugo Pos, 'The Revolt of "Manseren" ', American Anthropologist 52 (1950), pp. 561–4, recounts this episode, but without very much historical background. It is also related in F. C. Kamma, 'Messianic Movements . . .', op. cit.

Müller, Stephanus wanted to negotiate with the Japanese for the release of Angganita, for the recognition of the Papuan flag, removal of the Indonesians, freedom for New Guinea according to its old customs, and economic advance for Papuans. Other natives attacked the Japanese ship, however, and many were killed. Stephanus was taken to Manokwari and was probably killed there.[24] At Mokmer, the Japanese machine-gunned crowds of supporters who had settled on an airstrip with Jan Simiopiaref (brother of Stephanus), killing about five hundred.[25] Another group under Korinus Boseren on Biak had sticks which they believed Manseren would change into rifles; they, too, believed in their invulnerability in battle.[26] Unrest continued, but the Japanese defeated the Papuan dissidents, who, according to Kamma, represented a diverse range of positions, both in regard to Koreri beliefs and in the extent of their willingness to be involved in active resistance to the Japanese. The activists appear to have been nationalists and opportunists seeking spoils. Manseren became identified with the daily bombing raids against the Japanese, and finally with the coming of American ships, and cargoes, and the establishment of an army camp on the island of Meok Wundi, many believed that Koreri had at last arrived.[27]

The judgement of commentators on the Manseren movements is extremely varied. Kamma sees the cults as a product of culture contact, 'contra-acculturative' movements which attempt to stress the value of aboriginal ways of life. The original myth made evident the tensions between everyday reality and the longed-for situation.[28] In contrast, van der Kroef considers that the movement of 1938–44 'is to be interpreted as an attempt to channel the host of complex acultural influence in an increasingly unsettling environment by resort to ancient and hallowed cultural mechanisms'. He rejects the designation of the movement as 'contra-acculturative', and considers it to be a revitalization movement, 'an attempt to guide acculturation in understandable terms'.[29] It was ethnocentric, but used accepted mechanisms of autochthonous tradition to explain alien elements and to assimilate them.[30] Worsley has emphasized the shift from more magical towards more secular political action, and summarizes the course of the movement as one beginning with the use of 'indigenous

[24] E. W. Müller, op. cit., who is more detailed concerning this point than other sources.
[25] P. Worsley, op. cit., p. 142; F. C. Kamma, op. cit.
[26] F. C. Kamma, op. cit.
[27] P. Worsley, op. cit., p. 144; E. W. Müller, op. cit.
[28] F. C. Kamma, op. cit.
[29] J. M. van der Kroef, op. cit., p. 437.
[30] Ibid., pp. 437–8.

myth as a passive and non-violent millenarian reaction to Administration and mission control. It ended by the creation of well-organized
and disciplined bodies which used armed force in the effort to drive
the foreigners from Papua'.[31] But Müller stresses the hostility to foreigners found in early reports, distinguishes the attitudes towards the
Japanese from those shown towards the Americans, who were the
bringers of new material abundance. At the same time he rejects the
designation of the movement as a mere cargo-cult, and as a nativistic
or revitalistic movement.[32] For de Bruyn the movement was less a
religion than a self-conscious Papuan nationalist movement.[33]

As with other movements which, without central direction, recrudesce
and mobilize diverse groups, the Manseren movement was a many-
sided expression of discontent with the prevailing social order. Following centuries of cultural contact, vassalage and, latterly, increasing
colonial regulation, and suffering from the recent dramatic consequences
of war, the social order was necessarily fragile and subject to the
accretion of new interpretative elements, and the attrition of others.
Prophets, organizers, ideologues, and exploiters leave their impress on
particular groups, deflecting them from specific concerns, and en-
hancing the significance of others, as they provide answers to the
question of 'What shall we do to be saved?' In the broad sense, in the
context of a persisting myth of this kind, the answer is always in
revolutionist terms. Salvation is related to objective events soon to take
place. Despite the nationalistic elements in the movement, there was
also the expectation of return to a paradisial past, and of the restoration
of the customs associated with Manseren. The inherent contradictions
between sudden new wealth and restored old customs, between Papuan
nationalism and localism, are the inevitabilities of both revolutionist
and thaumaturgical responses.

The Manseren legends obviously ante-date European settlement on
the islands of Geelvink Bay. Culture contact with the Islam-influenced
islands of Indonesia may have caused some similar ideas to be disseminated, but in the main the myth appears to be indigenous. Certainly
it is a myth widely diffused in this area, and similar cultural heroes
occur in various tribal mythologies. When the people have paid for the
error of their ways the cultural heroes will return, and help them to
master the strangers, who in recent times have become masters of the

---

[31] P. Worsley, op. cit., p. 145.

[32] E. W. Müller, op. cit., writes, 'Vor allem kann von einem "Kult der Güter" keine Rede
sein. . . . Mit den Termini "nativistisch" oder "revivalistisch" sind diese Bewegungen nicht
ausreichend zu characterisieren' (p. 162). And, on p. 163, 'Teilweise will man europaisieren,
teilweise die alten Formen wieder herstellen.'

[33] J. V. de Bruyn, op. cit.

land.[34] The idea of the hidden father (which is evident in the details of the Manseren myth)[35] and of the recognition of the father by the child, has been found even among unchristianized tribes (although Christian ideas have been disseminated among them) and has fed the millennial expectations which some authors regard as autochthonous.[36]

We are left with some suggestion that the mythological basis of the revolutionist response is indigenous in the religion of at least some groups in north-western New Guinea. How such myths originally arose remains a matter of conjecture, although the circumstances of long cultural contact, and of subservience to more powerful and more advanced peoples may, as with the Jews, have been the seed-bed for such ideas to grow. The island of Biak was in some respects a class-stratified society of lords, strangers, and slaves, with the dominance of tribute-exacting outsiders. Tribal structure no longer existed as it did on the mainland. Millennial myths might easily take root in such a place, and once established they are available for subsequent generations. As seems evident from the history of *konor* movements of the Schouten Islands, they may provide a nucleus for the accretion of new ideas and interpretations of circumstances, and even, as in the war years, provide a stimulant for violent action.

Three special cases: the Tupi-Guaraní movements

The celebrated myths of the Tupi-Guaraní and other Guaraní tribes of South America provide a clear example of revolutionist religious orientation in a more emphatically tribal context than does the considerably de-tribalized society of the Schouten Islands. Our fragmentary knowledge of these now decimated peoples is of their various migrations from the sixteenth century onwards, and of their mythology (our knowledge of which has been very much more recently acquired). The Guaraní tribes of conquistador times have largely disappeared although they once occupied large areas. In the sixteenth century,

[34] Thus the Waropen, who were (then) a pagan tribe living on the east coast of Geelvink Bay, had legends of mythical miracle-working ancestors, cultural heroes who had established the social order, before its destruction by a flood, and whose return was expected. G. J. Held, *The Papuans of Waropen* (Martinus Nijhoff, The Hague 1957), pp. 317–20.

[35] See p. 200. These elements of the myth, and other mythical conceptions of the hidden father, are found among the Waropen. See G. J. Held, op. cit., pp. 303 ff.

[36] This appears to be Held's opinion (op. cit., p. 320). J. V. de Bruyn, op. cit., considers that the legend may be centuries old, and appears to consider some elements of the legend as possibly autochthonous. He notes similar myths among other New Guinea tribes, particularly the Miganis.

the Tupi-Guaraní were found on the Brazilian shore from the Amazon to Cananéa in the south of the state of São Paulo.[37] Yet they appeared to have been not long in possession of the coast. Since they were superior as warriors to most other groups it is inferred that they had not been driven there. They had only a modest knowledge of boats, and relied on agriculture and hunting rather than on fishing for their livelihood. The principal authority considers that their migration was not forced, but was impelled by deeply held religious reasons.[38] Linguistic and archaeological data and the persistent tendency noted since the beginning of European settlement for these tribes to migrate is offered as supplementary evidence. In 1539, a Tupinamba group of 12,000 was reported to have left eastern Brazil, under a medicine man, Viarazu (or Curaraci), to seek 'the land of deathlessness'. He was assisted by two Portuguese. In 1549 three hundred arrived in eastern Peru, who may have been of the same group.[39] If this did constitute one migration, it was only the most spectacular of the numerous migrations by various groups that followed in subsequent centuries.

Messianic outbursts were apparently frequent among the Tupinamba and Guaraní tribes. The Guaraní first allied themselves to the Spaniards who had explored the Paraguay in the 1520s and 1530s, but later rebelled, 'often led by native messiahs, the most famous of whom was Oberá, who promised the Indians supernatural support and convinced them that the happiness of native times would be restored after the final expulsion of the White men'.[40] Oberá, who had been baptized as a Christian, claimed to be God's son, conceived and born of a virgin. He carried a cross as his emblem, and combined the prestige of the traditional shaman with a claim to monopolize all that was really true in the teachings of the missionaries. He was extremely eloquent and was

[37] Alfred Métraux, 'The Tupinamba' in Julian H. Steward (Ed.), *Handbook of South American Indians*, Vol. III (Smithsonian Institution, Bureau of American Ethnography Bulletin, Washington, D.C., 1948), pp. 95–133.

[38] Curt Nimuendajú Unkel, 'Die Sagen von Erschaffung und Vernichtung der Welt als Grundlagen der Religion der Apapocúva-Guaraní', *Zeitschrift für Ethnologie* 46, 1 (1914), pp. 284–403. Considering the various circumstances, Nimuendajú Unkel declares, p. 364, 'Solche Betrachtungen haben mir die Vermutung nahe gelegt, die Haupttriebfeder für die Wanderungen der Tupi-Guaraní sei nicht ihre kriegerische Expansionskraft, sondern ein anderes, wahrscheinlich religiöses Motiv gewesen. . . .'

[39] Well-documented accounts of this, and other, early migrations are provided by A. Métraux, 'Migrations Historiques des Tupi-Guaraní', *Journal de la Société des Américanistes* (N.S. XIX, Paris 1927), pp. 1–45. For discussion see Wolfgang H. Lindig, 'Wanderungen der Tupi-Guaraní und Eschatologie der Apapocúva-Guaraní' in W. E. Mühlmann, op. cit., pp. 19–40.

[40] A. Métraux, 'The Guaraní' in J. H. Steward, op. cit., pp. 69–94 (p. 78). This paragraph relies on Métraux.

idolized by the Indians, to whom he was a 'man-god'.[41] The Spaniards led a campaign against him in 1579. The use of medicine-men in war is not easily distinguished from the occasional upsurge of religious responses that lead to violent action: were these early uprisings merely part of a conventional pattern of religious validation of arms, or were they essentially prompted by distinctly new religious responses? Certainly the Guaraní of the upper Paraná River and the Uruguay River basin, many of whom came under the strong Jesuit influence in the region in the seventeenth and early eighteenth century, were frequently involved in warfare, particularly with the Marmelucos of São Paulo, and subsequently with the Spanish and Portuguese.

Similar elements of messianic prophetism occurred among both the Tupinamba and Guaraní tribes. From the beginning of the conquest, the Guaraní tribes were stirred periodically by announcements of the end of Spanish rule, and by the prospect of a new golden age in a 'land without evil'.[42] Similarly among the Tupinamba, prophets exhorted departure 'for the "land of immortality", where the cultural hero had retired after his earthly adventure'. After Portuguese colonization, prophets promised a golden age

in which digging sticks would till the soil by themselves, and arrows would kill the game without the intervention of hunters. The Indians were

---

[41] A. Métraux, 'Les hommes-dieux chez les Chiriguano et dans l'Amérique du Sud', *Revista del Instituto de Etnología de la Universidad nacional de Tucumán* II, 1 (1931), pp. 61–91. Métraux likens Oberá to the man-god of the African or Polynesian chief (p. 77), and writes 'La doctrine de ce puissant magicien est un bon exemple de l'étrange adaptation que les Indiens guaraní ont fait subir à la religion catholique, et du mélange qui s'est produit entre les anciennes traditions et les nouvelles croyances imposées par le vainqueur' (p. 76). The range of response among the Chiriguanos was perhaps typical of other Guaraní groups, although, for obvious reasons, our best documentation is of those messiahs whose activities led to warfare against the Spaniards and Portuguese. Some were no doubt essentially restorative, seeking only to escape the conquerors. Others were accommodative, but perhaps equally anxious to avoid any interference with their way of life from the invaders: of one such among the Chiriguanos we have an interesting, but very incomplete, report. The report is in instructions from Don Francisco de Toledo, Viceroy of Peru in 1573, to his investigator, García Mosquera, and a report from Mosquera to the Viceroy (both of which are marked by a very genuine humanitarianism and tolerance). The messiah, Santiago or San Diego, had appeared near Saipurú, in present-day Bolivia. He was credited with healings and miracles, causing crops to grow magically, and of being able to fly. He claimed to have been sent by Jesus to urge the Indians to be good. If they were not good—and he enjoined them not to kill or eat flesh, or touch women other than their own—a great man from far away would make war on them and destroy them. He distributed wooden crosses to the *caciques* and others, but they had only vague knowledge of him. The Viceroy was prepared to believe in the genuineness of this young man whom 'the Father . . . has seen fit to send', but wanted fuller information. The Indians, according to Mosquera's report, had had no contact with Christians, although on his own evidence there was one baptized person—a negress—among them. They professed peace as long as they did not have to have Spaniards living in their towns and were not compelled to be stable boys, to draw water, or do other women's work. The reports are given in full in Jack Autrey Dabbs, 'A Messiah among the Chiriguanos', *Southwestern Journal of Anthropology* 9, 1 (Spring 1953), pp. 45–58.

[42] A. Métraux, 'The Guaraní', op. cit., pp. 93–4.

assured of immortality and eternal youth. . . . The followers . . . gave up their normal activities, dedicated themselves to constant dancing, and even started mass migrations to reach the mythical land of the culture hero. . . . Several of the late Tupinamba migrations were caused by the urge to enter the promised land as soon as possible. . . .[43]

Leaders were often deified, and appear to have 'represented a new type of wonder worker, who had been influenced both by the early traditions of their tribes and by Christian ideas, preached to the Indians by the Catholic missionaries'.[44] Successive migrations of the Tupinamba in the region of Maranhão are recorded in the later sixteenth and early seventeenth centuries. In 1605, a shaman of Portuguese birth, but who was thoroughly assimilated to the Indian way of life, promised miraculous sustenance to those who would follow him, and some ten to twelve thousand natives went with him on a futile march to the Sierra da Ibiapaba.[45] Each new shaman or messiah interpreted a set of myths already in existence, but it is evident from the emergence of a leader who was not an Indian, and from the assistance given to Viarazu by the two Portuguese, that the myths were, even at an early date, likely to have received the imprint of European, and therefore Christian, ideas. This was quite explicit in the teachings of Oberá, and of the messiahs who arose from the sixteenth to the nineteenth century among the Chiriguano, a detached branch of the Guaraní tribes in Bolivia.[46]

There have been many new outcroppings of religiously inspired action among the Tupi-Guaraní, whether as rebellion or migration. These are responses to new situations in terms of a pre-existing mythology, represented by leaders who have often claimed charismatic authority. We do not know how extensively such leaders, who were shamans rather than community chiefs, exerted effective authority. At times they commanded thousands of followers, at others they led relatively small, particular bands. Nor do we know the exact character of the pre-Christian myths: the myths that are now known include many Christian elements.[47] But the idea of paradise appears to be a central element in the myths of the Guaraní and other South American tribes. Nimuendajú Unkel, who first suggested that pre-colonial migrations were inspired by essentially religious motivations, has emphasized the extent to which the Guaraní have maintained their early religious

[43] A. Métraux, 'The Tupinamba', op. cit., p. 131.
[44] Loc. cit.
[45] A. Métraux, 'Migrations historiques . . .', op. cit., pp. 10–11.
[46] For an account of messianic prophets among the Chiriguanos, and for an account of Solares, who led a movement at Tandil, Argentina, in 1872, see A. Métraux, 'Les hommes-dieux . . .', op. cit., pp. 81 ff.
[47] A Métraux, 'The Tupinamba', op. cit., p. 94.

ideas—ideas not readily revealed to neo-Brazilians and especially not to priests, before whom the Indians have feigned Christianity.[48]

Nimuendajú Unkel recounts the myths of the Apapocúva-Guaraní, which he learned in the early twentieth century, and which prompted their migrations in the nineteenth, and uses them to interpret the past migrations of the Tupinamba and other Tupi-Guaraní peoples. All these peoples understood the world to be replete with spirits who were mainly malevolent, and ghosts who were somewhat more impersonal. Among the Tupinamba, shamans, rain-makers, diviners, and healers were the intermediaries with the supernatural world; they interpreted the will of the spirits in mediumistic fashion; and they were accorded prestige and tribute.[49] The Apapocúva believed that although demons and spirits might seek to prevent it, at death one of a man's two souls would go to the 'land-without-evil'. The other, animal, soul was exterminated. The souls determined temperament, and dreams were the experience of souls. Communication with the dead was important, and each adult learned a chant from a dead relative: shamans owned many such chants with which to protect the community from accidents. Shamans were also prophets, miracle-workers, and the unmaskers of sorcerers.[50] Within this rich religious context, in which secular singing and dances were unknown, the myths of creation and of the 'land-without-evil' were of the greatest importance.[51] Recent medicine-men have justified myth and their sense of its eventual fulfilment as the primary causes for the migrations that they have inaugurated.[52]

Omitting many details, the creation myths of these tribes recount that Ñanderuvuçú, with his helper, Ñanderú Mbaecuaá, was creator of the earth, which rests on two struts. He took an earth woman as his wife, and after she had been deflowered by Ñanderú Mbaecuaá she bore him twins. When the woman told Ñanderuvuçú that these were not his children, he withdrew from the earth, leaving a tiger to bar the path to his dwelling. One son, Ñanderyqueý, then sought to communicate with his father through a dance, and when he succeeded he was given responsibility for the earth. A variety of supernatural figures were involved in the rich mythology, which was told without consecutiveness. In some versions, a bat threatened to eat the sun, but the

[48] C. Nimuendajú Unkel, op. cit., p. 284, finds it remarkable that the remnants of the Guaraní, 'ihren Bekehren zum Hohn, and der umringenden Zivilisation zum Trotz, die alte Religion in solch verhaltnismässiger Reinheit bis heute bewahrt haben'. See also p. 300, concerning the adoption of a superficial Christianity.
[49] A. Métraux, 'The Tupinamba', op. cit.
[50] A. Métraux, 'The Guaraní', op. cit.
[51] C. Nimuendajú Unkel, op. cit., pp. 335 ff.
[52] Ibid., p. 332. The account of the mythology rests on this source.

medicine men were able to persuade the creator to hold back its assault. The tiger also threatened men, but the principal threat to mankind was that one day Ñanderyqueý would pull out one of the struts supporting the world to the east, causing fire to begin in the west. Destruction would flow from west to east. Sometimes a period of darkness, preceding the coming of the blue tiger, was also predicted.

The Apapocúva described the earth as being old, and the tribe as decreasing, and expressed their wish to see the dead. Not only was the tribe tired, but so was the whole of nature. The earth cried out to the creator that it was weary and awaited its end, according to the medicine-men, who in their dreams visited Ñanderuvuçú. The Guaraní expected no future. Their one hope was flight from the impending disaster. Thus they had no messianic hopes, only the hope of discovering in the east, the 'land-without-evil', thought to be over the seas in the middle of the earth.

In modern versions of these myths, white men were sometimes blamed for the evil in the world: the Guaraní themselves, because of their manifold sins, might reach the promised paradise only after death. But paradise, where their ancestors persist in the old way of life, is only for Guaraní.[53] Originally only the privileged dead—great shamans and warriors—were thought to go to the 'land-without-evil', and then only after many ordeals. 'Later when life on earth became unbearable even the most humble sufferers on earth came to believe that they also might be admitted to the Land of Promise, provided that they showed enough courage.'[54] Among groups of Mbüá, the myth, fortified by the prophecies of medicine-men, caused migrations as recently as the 1940s. But among them, and especially those who had been least influenced by Christianity, the idea of world destruction was not conspicuous. Nor did this group, which had had little contact with white men, and which still maintained a tribal structure, identify the 'land-without-evil' with the idea of 'not working', as was the case among groups more closely associated with neo-Brazilians. To them the land was across the seas, perhaps in Portugal—whatever they understand by the name. The myth was still well known among the Kaiová, who in the early 1950s lived in reservations in the southern Mato Grosso and near the borders of Paraguay, and who were also reputed to have once migrated to the coast. When threatened—for instance when Indian lands were granted to settlers—they have acted out the requirements of their shamans by

[53] Egon Schaden, 'Der Paradiesmythos in Leben der Guaraní-Indianer', *Stadenjahrbuch* III (São Paulo 1955), pp. 151–62, on whom this paragraph relies.
[54] A. Métraux, 'Messiahs of South America', *The Interamerican Quarterly* III, 2 (April 1941), pp. 53–60 (p. 54). (This article has more recently appeared as 'Les Messies de l'Amérique du Sud', *Archives de Sociologie des Religions* 4 [July–December 1957], pp. 108–12.)

dancing fervently in the way associated with the attempt to bring the myth into reality.

The typical pattern of recorded migrations was for a group to reach the coast and to attempt by dancing to make themselves light, to be lifted up and carried to the 'land-without-evil'. Failure after days of dancing was frequently attributed to European food and clothing that had made them heavy, so that neither fasting nor dancing were sufficient to raise them up. After some time they might then withdraw inland again. Nimuendajú Unkel reported encountering small groups who, although speaking no Portuguese and only a word or two of Spanish, had in the early years of the century trekked from Paraguay to São Paulo, wanting to cross the sea to the east.[55] This mythological complex, whatever its origins, has exercised a compelling influence on many of the Tupi-Guaraní for a very long time.

Not all commentators are as convinced as Nimuendajú Unkel that the myths are wholly of Indian origin. He rejects the idea that the Jesuits transmitted the notion of the destruction of the earth to the Indians, since they failed to transmit so much else of Christianity. The fire, flood, animal demons, the medicine dance, and the journey to heaven he regards as all originally Indian.[56] Yet the myths as now recounted have acquired Christian elements. Nimuendajú Unkel believes that Indians had ideas of racial decline before European contact, and that their pessimism is associated with the idea of world-weariness rather than with any conception of sin, although the idea of sin is now found among Guaraní groups settled on or near the coast.[57] The shift from the present search for the 'land-without-evil' and the expectation that it could be reached only after death are no doubt an accommodation to Christian ideas.

It seems possible that the ideas found among the Tupi-Guaraní (and they are found very widely spread among South American Indians[58])

[55] C. Nimuendajú Unkel, op. cit., p. 361.

[56] Ibid., p. 382; W. H. Lindig, op. cit., pp. 35–6, believes that some of the migrations may have been the result of culture contact, and believes that the influence of the Jesuits was probably greater than Nimuendajú Unkel allowed. Nimuendajú Unkel was a participant in one of the migrations of the Apapocúva, by whom he was 'adopted' (and from whence the name Nimuendajú comes). In Lindig's opinion, his close association with the Indians m. have affected his objectivity.

[57] C. Nimuendajú Unkel, op. cit., p. 380; E. Schaden, op. cit., writing of the Ñandevá who live on the coast.

[58] René Ribeiro, 'Brazilian Messianic Movements' in S. L. Thrupp, op. cit., pp. 55–69. The idea of impending cataclysm, associated with offence given to the Creator, as a repetition of the cataclysms of ancient times, are the driving ideas of cult movements among the Tukuna, who live on the banks of Solimões River in Brazil, and on the Camatía and along the lower Jandiatuba. The cataclysm will destroy the *civilizados*, but prophets, usually adolescents, reveal ways in which the Indians may be saved. C. Nimuendajú Unkel, *The Tukuna* (University of California Publications in American Archaeology and Ethnology, 45, Berkeley and Los Angeles 1952), pp. 137–8.

embrace elements of millennialism uninspired by the Judeo-Christian inheritance. Prophetism is certainly an indigenous phenomenon. That the form and central ideas of the myth are found so widely spread suggests that they are of older provenance than the post-Columbian era. One authority, however, appears to distinguish between supernatural messianism and the recurrent messianic claims of shaman-prophets: the movements

> did not center round the personality of the Messiah or Saviour. In fact these revivalistic movements among the South American Indians were mainly fomented by certain individuals who succeeded in convincing others that they had been entrusted with a supernatural mission. . . . All of them preached a holy war against the whites, and they encouraged their followers by a promise of immunity from the deadly weapons of the Europeans.[59]

Whatever earlier movements may have been, the post-Columbian movements appear to have had many of the traits of direct revolutionist responses to a situation of subordination. Métraux, who uses the terms 'messiah' and 'mysticism' rather loosely, adds, 'More messiahs appeared in Paraguay than in any other part of South America. The influence of the Jesuits is perhaps responsible for this blossoming of native mysticism.'[60] Of the migrations the evidence is less clear, and we do not know what social conditions might have stimulated them. In more recent times, the disruption caused by cultural contact and the exploitation of Tupi-Guaraní groups by conquistadors, Jesuits, Paulinist Marmelucos, and warfare with other tribes, particularly the Mbaja and Caingang Indians, in addition to epidemics, may have been adequate causes to bring the myth of salvation, and its achievement by migration, into prominence.

In its very nature the revolutionist response defies institutionalization. While the mythological elements may become an established part of the ideological stock of particular peoples, myths only periodically become a focus for compelling action. They have become such when a new prophet has arisen, claiming special knowledge of the imminence of the fulfilment of the mythological prophecies. A new movement arises from the prophet's appropriation of the myth, and usually by his own claims to a part in its final enactment. The migration, the fasting, the dancing, begin. When the migrants have reached the sea and wearied of the dance, the active stage of the movement ends. Only the myth persists— to be re-activated by another prophet at another time.

[59] A. Métraux, 'Messiahs of South America', op. cit., p. 56. This generalization is unwarranted, however. See above, footnote 41, p. 208.
[60] Loc. cit.

The distinctive character of the Koreri movements and the movements among the Tupi-Guaraní lies less in their content—every culture contributes a unique stock of specific mythological and magical items to the movements that arise within it—than in the probability that their mythological stimulus ante-dates Christian cultural contact. In both cases, the myths appear to have been inherited from some earlier social context. Although in each case they acquired elements of Christian teaching and assimilated western ideas, none the less the continuity of the ideological element cannot be ignored. Later movements reacted against new features of the assimilated cultural system—missions, taxes, or work for the white men. The substance of the promised paradise correspondingly changed: the introduction of cargoes of western type in place of Indonesian commodities, in the later Koreri movements; and the escape from sin, as well as from destruction among later Guaraní migrations.

The extent of this distinctiveness should not be overstated, however. Other movements have risen in response to mythological complexes that stem more particularly from local apprehension of Christian ideas, or from a fusion of Christian and aboriginal elements. Sometimes they have become the stimulus for a series of outbursts. Whether one should regard these as several movements or as one recrudescent movement is not easily determined, particularly in the absence of detailed information about the continuity of commitment of leaders, core personnel, or mass following. Myths may change somewhat whilst basic elements continue to reveal their debt to native interpretations of western culture-contact and of particularly attractive elements in Christianity. Kimbanguism and the Jonfrum movement were both such recrudescent movements, in which, because of the continuity of significant elements and the persistence of the names invoked, a series of outbursts have been regarded as phases or renewals of one movement.[61] Where organizational elements are identifiable, however, distinctions of leadership and control are often taken as appropriate criteria by which to designate movements, even where common ideological elements are found in different organizations. The distinction of the Brooklyn-controlled Jehovah's Witnesses in Central Africa from the Watchtower followers of Elliott Kamwana and from Mwana Lesa are cases in point.[62]

A revolutionist tradition that ante-dates western cultural contact may, of course, be associated with earlier cultural contact between

[61] On Kimbanguism, see pp. 368–73. On the Jonfrum movements, see pp. 322–6.
[62] On Mwana Lesa, see pp. 83–4. On Jehovah's Witnesses and the Watchtower (Kitawala) in Central Africa, see pp. 83, 253–4.

peoples, or, more specifically, as in the case of the Koreri movements, may be associated with an earlier period of conquest, oppression, and subservience to foreign lords. Yet need such ideas arise in response only to cultural contact, disruption, or oppression? The millennial myth has no self-evident appeal to contented people, but the range of popular discontents may arise from causes other than conquest or social disruption due to the intrusion of alien peoples and their ways of life. The range of possible antecedent conditions may go beyond conquest to include such phenomena as 'culture shock' or anomie. These are possibilities, but conquest is, empirically, the most evident circumstance in the background of the revolutionist movements arising after the impact of western culture has been experienced.

The significance of these two cases is that they suggest very strongly, although they do not firmly establish, that revolutionist responses (and we are concerned, be it remembered, not with active revolution, but essentially with a religious orientation) may arise from traditions other than the Judeo-Christian. The myth the Jews created or learned about in Babylon may not be an original ideology that has proliferated and re-emerged wherever the Judeo-Christian-Muslim inheritance has been transplanted, but merely one particular (undoubtedly influential) instance of a response that has arisen among other peoples undergoing subjection, or experiencing the trauma of contact with an alien culture that is overwhelming (whether militarily, technologically, or intellectually). The revolutionist ideology becomes institutionalized, even though it is sufficient to stimulate a movement only from time to time, in propitious circumstances, and when some prophet arises who sets himself into special relation with the deities, and who justifies his specific prophecies in terms of the fund of received myth.

Neither the Koreri mythology nor the myth stimulating Tupi-Guaraní migrations maintained itself unadulterated over the long periods for which records of movements are available. Each assimilated new elements in interpretation of changed circumstances of the natives themselves, and their relation to the strangers who had imposed themselves and their alien culture. Neither set of movements, occurring over the course of decades or centuries, may be easily described as specifically a 'nativistic' response, a restoration of the imagined past, particularly in the restoration of ancestors, although this idea existed at times within each tradition. Each is a demand, not so much for a return to a particular past, nor for the revitalization of a particular way of life, as for a completely new environment, a new beginning. Just what is sought has no well-articulated definition: it is a total transformation of the present situation, but with only the vaguest conceptions of the new social structure. So indeed it must be, among peoples whose conceptualization of social order is necessarily predicated on what has been legitimated by inheritance, and who have acquired neither the capacity for distanciation from the social order, nor even an objectified perception of it.

Three special cases: New Guinea highland peoples

The third example illustrates similar points in a somewhat different way. In this case the pattern of millennialist response appears to have been acquired by a process of cultural diffusion from other tribes. What this case illustrates is that conquest and domination as such are not prerequisites for the emergence of a religious response that seeks to bring about a transformation of the environment. Cultural shock and anticipation induced by rumour appear to be sufficient to induce demands for cultural transformation. If such slight impact can bring about a profound religious re-orientation, then, at least within the Melanesian context, a probable consequence of any more persistent cultural contact may be a more articulated form of revolutionism.[63] This case reveals the cultural continuity of basic religious orientations, which are necessarily associated with thaumaturgy. In being intensified, rendered urgent, and given a societal connotation the demand for thaumaturgy may take on what amounts to intense desire for total cultural transformation. Where magic has been used to enhance personal prestige, by the acquisition of material possessions, the collective demand for such prestige through such possessions takes on a much more culturally transformative significance. The votaries of the cargo cult may initially expect simply cargo without the social transformations that are often also voiced by prophets—the reversal of roles of natives and intruders; the elimination of white men; the enjoyment of abundance and the end of work; and perhaps, withal, the transformation of the material environment and normal experience of it, by the elimination of problems, diseases, and suffering. But, although a

[63] The issue adumbrated here is taken up again later, see pp. 309 ff. It is not suggested that revolutionist religious responses *always* arise from cultural contact of much more advanced with much less advanced peoples: revolutionism has arisen rarely and insignificantly in India, Australia, and West Africa. Nor, and the case of Tupi-Guaraní illustrates this, does the revolutionist response arise only as a consequence of cultural contact. It need not, therefore, be asserted that such responses arise *only* from the cultural diffusion among subject peoples of the (usually Christian or Muslim) mythological inheritance of revolutionist orientations of conquerors or settlers.

conscious overturn of the social system and the natural environment may not be consciously demanded or expected by the cargo-cultists in rudimentary cultures such as that which we shall now consider, this is, none the less, the implication of their efforts to dance into being the new dispensation.

Among the peoples of the Eastern Highlands of New Guinea, the coming of the first white men was necessarily explained in religious terms. The white men were assimilated to the spirits, who were as much part of the world as were humans. This was the obvious explanation for these newly appearing beings. They manifested power and they had valuable goods, rumours of which had preceded them from one native group to another. From the work of Berndt, we know that when these peoples learned about white men they experienced an emphatic reaction of fear, curiosity, and tension concerning the rumours that had circulated.[64] Shivering and visions occurred, and promises of wealth were experienced in dreams. The spirits of ancestors gave instructions about necessary rituals and purification in order to obtain the wealth which was now coming. The spirits were believed to play dual roles, and there was uncertainty about their behaviour. In consequence, a mixture of hostility and desire to curry favour was manifested. The instruction of the spirits was to build houses in preparation for the goods that were coming. Pigs were to be sacrificed. A ghost wind which caused men to shiver was widely felt as a manifestation of the 'power' that was abroad.

At this stage there had been no disruption of older traditional patterns of life, only the intrusion of white men and the first intimations of the different values that they represented, most especially in the material artefacts of their way of life. But the first reaction was one of fear and hysteria: the desire for the material possessions was a secondary motive. Those receiving spirit communications acted on them, although this was not a normal feature of their way of life, but a matter of personal *mana*. When the expected goods did not arrive after spirit instructions had been obeyed, those who had acted as the mouthpieces of the spirit were ashamed, and anger and disillusionment were widespread.

Berndt sees these movements as primarily adjustative towards the comprehension of new situations: these patterns of response to the scarcely comprehensible might be repeated several times over the years. Yet, he considers that 'there is no reason to suppose that they [cargo

[64] This and the subsequent paragraph rely on Ronald M. Berndt, 'Reaction to Contact in the Eastern Highlands of New Guinea', *Oceania* XXIV (March and June 1954) pp. 190–288, 255–74.

movements] would not or could not occur if there was no alien contact whatever'.[65] Certainly the elements in the phenomena in this and other areas of New Guinea were remarkably similar, even in movements that occurred after much longer contact with Europeans and much more disruption of native life. But Berndt is convinced that in the Highlands of New Guinea the 'cargo movement did not arise from an acute crisis of social and cultural change'.[66] Although external stimuli induced them, the manifestations were expressed in the indigenous context, without any untoward consequences for indigenous religion and without, in this instance, the emergence of particular mediums, or the evolution of a separate mythology. In those cases willingness to transform the culture in order to obtain the cargo goods was evident— natives obeyed Europeans in the matter of building roads; they got their hair cut and changed their physical appearance; they behaved like Europeans in order to acquire their 'power' over goods. There was, in a secondary stage of contact, the imitation of European military tactics, and symbolic rifles which would be transformed into real rifles were used against the Europeans who by some means had refused to deliver the goods which natives so keenly expected. Berndt is convinced that even at these more-developed stages such movements may be seen as autochthonous cults that express the natives' desire to be free from alien control, even though these movements often recoil, and themselves disturb native traditions.

Conclusion

Are we to accept these relatively spontaneous responses to very slight culture contact as evidence of autochthonous revolutionism? In this last case no developed millennial ideology was involved: the movement might be regarded as a basically thaumaturgical response of the total community. The people seek spiritual power and its manifestations, and have initially no conception of the transformation of their culture as a concomitant process. That their responses do, in some measure, begin a transformation of their culture is the justification for describing these movements as 'adjustative' or 'adaptative'. That result may, however, be neither an intended nor a necessary consequence: new

[65] Ibid.
[66] R. M. Berndt, 'A Cargo Movement in the Eastern Central Highlands of New Guinea', Oceania XXIII (September and December 1952), pp. 40–65, 137–58 (p. 144).

movements may be as unintentionally disruptive as adaptative. The incipient cargo movement, such as Berndt describes, may be regarded less as a revolutionist movement than as a communal thaumaturgical movement. Subsequently, when the movements begin to acquire conceptions of overturning the existing social dispensation, of reversing the roles of natives and white men, or of some cataclysm that will radically affect the existing balance of 'power', and that will, either by native action or by supernatural action, sweep the white men away—then we have a more convincing case of a revolutionist movement.

At this early stage, however, there is little more than a hysterical demand for a new and more powerful magic, for thaumaturgy on a societal scale. This demand, which occurs in other cases besides this one, is a response not simply to cultural contact as such, but to the confrontation of men from a simpler, and, in ways that they themselves begin to recognize, a less adequate culture with the manifestations of a physically and technically superior one. It is the response to the intrusion of men whose culture—and their culture is perceived as their 'magic'—is enormously powerful, and self-evidently superior. The expectation of acquiring some of this power or its fruits is the first magical demand. It is only with failure, with growing subjection, and the increasingly evident weakness of all that has previously appeared powerful, that a more extreme response arises. It is then that transformative ideologies occur that incorporate dreams of a changed order of things, whether that changed order be a restoration of the past, an acquisition of the alien culture, or a mixture of the two.

The responses of New Guinea highlanders to the first experience of culture contact embrace some elements that become prominent at later stages of contact in typical revolutionist movements found throughout Melanesia—in particular, the shaking, the expectation of cargo, the building of stores for its reception, and the emergence of mediums who receive the promises of the spirits. But there is, at this stage, no conscious millennial expectation, none but the vaguest conception of a transformed world, and then only in regard to material goods, with no conception of changes in role structure, in relationships with aliens, or in the practices of everyday life. This particular case, then, makes manifest that a genuinely transformative conception, even with dramatic cultural contact, is not an immediate response, but one that evolves only relatively slowly, and even then perhaps only in certain circumstances.

Thus, it cannot be said that such responses are implicit in the situation of culture contact (since there are areas where, as we have remarked, revolutionist responses have not occurred, even though other religious manifestations have been in evidence).[67] They often appear to arise in situations where rudimentary Christian (or sometimes Muslim) teaching, with its elements of adventism, has been diffused through the missions. Yet, in regard to the Koreri movements and the migrations of the Tupi-Guaraní it cannot be asserted with absolute certainty that millennialist ideas are necessarily acquired from Christian sources. What can be said, *en passant*, is that Christian sources have undoubtedly frequently stimulated such developments, and have provided a ready-made ideology of transformation for peoples seeking just some such explanation of how things come to be as they are, and just some such hopes for their radical amendment. And Christian explanations have been all the more attractive, of course, because they have been offered as the real source of the white man's power, the mystery of his success. Since religion, in its thaumaturgical aspects, is precisely the agency to which less-developed peoples typically ascribe their own prowess, Christianity, as the white man's medicine, was readily accorded that role, and since many missionaries were convinced that it was the truth of the power of God which was responsible for the white man's success, the communication of its teachings was undoubtedly facilitated.[68]

[67] Australia is an area in which the aborigines have not manifested direct revolutionist responses. Religious reaction to conquest has taken somewhat different forms. The demand for white goods occurs, but not in the context of a millennialist cargo cult. The principal characteristics of a movement such as that among the Arnhem Islanders is the syncretism of aboriginal and Christian ideas. In this case the tribesmen were willing to make public an erstwhile essentially private cult, as a 'gift' to white men (particularly perhaps to the anthropologists whose interests in the cult objects may have impressed the aborigines with their preciousness and power in a reference group wider than their own tribe). They hoped that in response the white Australians would make available their precious material possessions. See, on this particular movement, R. M. Berndt, *An Adjustment Movement in Arnhem Land, Northern Territory of Australia* (Mouton, Paris and The Hague 1962). More general myths (as distinct from movements) of the end of the world are known among some Australian tribes, for example the Ungarinyin, Worora, and Unambel in the Prince Regent River district, who believe that, were they to leave the ritual objects of their cultural heroes unserviced, the springs would dry up and animals, plants, and men would fail to increase. They believed that this was already happening in the late 1930s, but less as a consequence of white contact than of the infiltration of new forms of black magic from tribes further south, according to H. Petri, op. cit.

[68] Missionaries with this belief were looking at Christianity in terms of its more direct significance than sociologists, who might ascribe, particularly to the Protestant ethic, a similar role to religious values in the development of the modern west. On the significance of Christianity for revolutionist responses, see pp. 338 ff. For the influences of Christianity in providing organizational form and some degree of incidental and qualified support for thaumaturgical orientations in less developed societies, see pp. 159 ff., 169 ff.

8

Religious Responses and Military Enterprise

It has been a usual procedure to include among the 'religions of the oppressed' or among 'nativistic movements', the religious activities occurring among native peoples at war with colonial powers and European settlers.[1] This example is followed here, but there are differences between the cultural circumstances of peoples still at liberty, who, however much their warfare may be inspired by new prophetic visions, interpret their action very much as a war for their way of life against intruders; and the responses arising among natives who have already been subjected to the relatively effective government of the intruders. There is usually a role for the shaman or the magician in warfare: the war-dance and war-paint are themselves heavily endowed with magic as a mystical underwriting of military enterprise. But new magical claims, more powerful than those made in the past, become necessary if military activity against enemies with superior weapons is to be effectively encouraged.

Warfare as such is a response which is frequently predicated by the whole structure of inter-tribal relationships from the past. In itself it needs no new ideological justification. It is the odds against which it is mounted (or the scale on which it is launched) that calls for new supernatural support. The role of the ideology may, however, be secondary. Warfare may be viewed as either a relatively rational response to external threat, or as the extension of a biological response to intrusions into the territory of the in-group. Neither completely rational action nor completely instinctive action would require ideologies, of course.[2] Little human action, much less social-group action,

[1] Thus, in his great pioneer work on North American Indian religious movements, Mooney prefaced his account of the Ghost Dance of 1890 with a long account of earlier prophets; James Mooney, *The Ghost Dance and the Sioux Outbreak of 1890*, Fourteenth Annual Report of the Bureau of Ethnology to the Secretary of the Smithsonian Institution, Washington, Part II (Government Printing Office, Washington 1896). Lanternari, who indiscriminately labels very diverse movements as 'messianic', includes them: Vittorio Lanternari, *The Religions of the Oppressed: A Study of Modern Messianic Cults*, translated from the Italian by Lisa Sergio (Alfred Knopf, New York 1963). They are also included by Wilhelm E. Mühlmann, *Chiliasmus und Nativismus*, op. cit.

[2] The point was long ago made by Vilfredo Pareto in *The Mind and Society*, translated from the Italian by A. Livingston and A. Bongiorno (Cape, London 1935), 4 vols., Pareto used the term 'derivations' in the sense in which the word 'ideologies' is used here.

conforms to either of these polar cases, and even ordinary routine tribal warfare awakens the need for sustaining magical acts. In the warfare of tribal groups against more advanced invaders, the demand for supernatural support is enhanced since prospects of success appear manifestly slimmer. The solidarity of the warriors is complemented by exceptional claims to supernatural power. But in these cases, warfare is still the primary focus, and supernatural stimulus subsidiary. The magician or prophet does not claim so much that his power, in and of itself, is to be sufficient to overcome the enemy. The action of the warrior is still essential, indeed primary. It is warfare rather than millennialism. The prophet is still subsidiary to the warrior chief even if the prophetic role is indispensable, otherwise we should see a different pattern of action— migrations; dancing-in the millennium; expectations of the ancestors; hysteria; the abandonment of cultivation and possessions. These are manifestations of a more fundamental millennialist response, which relies on the action of ancestors or spirits to dispel the invaders and restore the land, rather than on the relatively rational procedure of taking up arms against the intruders.

Whether cases that fall close to the arbitrary line which is drawn between political and religious responses should be regarded strictly as millennial movements is open to doubt. In the movements with which we are concerned men express their wishes about the world, and their action towards the world in relation to supernatural power (whether or not they believe that they have access to that power, can manipulate it, or predict its courses). When, in warlike action, the supernatural element is enhanced, as, for example, occurs when the traditional role of the religious man is itself changed from magician to prophet, we may regard these cases as at last partial transformative responses. The achievement of transformation relies considerably on what men do for themselves, but their attempt to do something is prompted by belief in the efficacy of the supernatural forces that have now been mobilized on their behalf.

Cases of this type occur at stages of cultural contact prior to the complete annexation and control of native territories and peoples. In subsequent stages, natives cannot promote warfare in quite the same way; if they then mount action they do so usually with stronger expectations of supernatural intervention in their affairs. Only much later, when a sizeable educated and politically-conscious native élite has emerged, does this supernatural element recede again in importance. Thus the cases with which this section is concerned are of two types. The first occurs when a people experiencing defeat, but not as yet defeated, turns at this juncture to millennialist theories to support their warfare and to prophesy their victory. The prophets in these movements are unlikely to have been the principal instruments in inducing the militant response, even if their visions are important in re-activating it. The second are cases of rebellions of subject peoples in which there is reason to suppose that the leadership is not expectant of supernatural action, but whose following may be stimulated by religious hopes or fears.

In the first set of cases the prophet may act as a catalyst. Through his unifying perception he may be instrumental in effecting a re-grouping of native peoples, in providing a focal point of unity for previously, and otherwise, hostile tribes. His prophecy transcends the particularistic in-group loyalties of tribes that have hitherto had no occasion to make common cause. Their unity in accepting the new prophecies indicates both the commonality of their situation, and some awareness of that commonality. It does not, however, indicate an abandonment of traditional authority and leadership. The prophet does not replace the chief: rather he justifies his authority. His claims are not directed to the displacement of leaders, although in cultures where social groups are small and leadership sometimes insecurely established, as among some North American Indian tribes, bands under new leaders who accept the prophetic message may split away from existing chiefs. This is not the acceptance of a new style of prophetic chieftainship, but a process of fission under new chiefs who, if new men, stand in an old tradition. Only when the traditional authority-structure as such has become evidently inadequate are prophets likely to make effective bids for direct, political leadership. It is when the tribal system falls into decay that a prophet may emerge who claims authority of the same type as a tribal chief. We have seen this process in some decaying tribes in South Africa, the further decay of which has, however, been arrested by the policies of the South African government.[3] (In this instance, government control also circumscribes the possibility of a very manifest expression of a revolutionist response, although this did occur in the case of Enoch Mgijima.[4])

The millennialist augmentation of war may, indirectly, come to constitute a threat to established patterns of authority, but this is an unexpected development. The prophet enrols himself in the service of a past dispensation, and his visions are of the restoration of previously existing conditions and customs. The promotion of action to reduce or eliminate external threats inevitably has consequences for the structure of tribal groups, and for the relationships between them: the very

[3] See pp. 136 ff.
[4] See pp. 61–3.

measures taken to preserve the past become measures that, in one way or another, are likely to ensure that such a restoration can never come about. The prophet is a self-styled agent of social change, but the prophet who wins great acclaim is an agent of more radical change than he ever conceives, and in directions of which he is unaware. It requires supernatural sanction, of the type that the prophet embodies, to draw together otherwise dissociated or mutually hostile groups for common action. Shared acceptance of prophetic visions provides a basis for new alliances among independent groups, since it constitutes a super-empirical reference point that does not threaten local authority, but which rather, indeed, validates it. But the courses that the prophet advocates are mainly courses of failure, and his intervention is likely to weaken existing secular leadership in the long run, even though it promotes it, and often extends it, at the outset. As long as tribal authority is still vigorous, the role of prophecy must be to support it. It is only where such authority has been severely weakened that subsequent prophets, and usually prophets who accept a more total supernaturalist position, are likely to emerge as surrogate chiefs.

The prophets of the American Indian frontier: the Delaware Prophet

The number of tribes and their wide dispersion over an extensive landmass makes any summary statement of the characteristics of the religious ideas of North American Indians subject to inexactitudes. None the less, certain broad generalizations appear to be true. Indigenous religion was essentially thaumaturgical. 'Few groups had any consistent theology. Their interest was in action which would secure health and prosperity and protect them from danger. Explanations of the spirit world in the average man might be fragmentary and even contradictory. . . .'[5] Since primary groups were mainly rather small, the spirits, although they were concerned with breaches of taboo and ceremonial, had no social control functions and relatively little connection with ethics. It was usually regarded as necessary to conciliate spirits, although some groups saw the spirits of the dead as guardians, and others, most typically in the west, believed that they might steal the souls of the living. Little evidence of belief in a high god is found, and concepts such as that of 'the Great Spirit' are said to 'turn out to have

[5] Ruth M. Underhill, 'Religion Among the American Indians', *Annals of the American Academy of Political and Social Science* 311 (May 1957), pp. 127–36 (p. 127).

been very limited concepts either of a distant creator who later ceased to function, or merely of a spirit higher than the others'.[6] The vision quest, in which each young man sought a mystical experience intended to provide him with guidance, protection, and power, was particularly pronounced among the hunting tribes of the plains. In many tribes the shaman was the arch-visionary, who derived special power from contact with the supernatural. His chief function, however, was curing, and he might also employ techniques for control of the weather, success in war, and divining, although the line between priest and shaman was sometimes made apparent.

The occasion for shamans to be prophets probably did not occur in pre-Columbian times, and the evidence concerning belief in messianic cultural heroes is fragmentary and subject to differences of interpretation.[7] It is by no means inconceivable that the prophetic style among the North American Indians was acquired by imitation from the white man, as an additional shamanistic art.[8] The indigenous vision quest, which was a private matter, might have provided the basis for such prophetism, and the public style of prophetic activity might have been learned from the missionaries. The tales of the missionaries, and the emphasis that they gave to the word of biblical

[6] Ibid., p. 130.

[7] R. M. Underhill, op. cit., does not include prophetism or messianism as aboriginal features. Thomas R. Henry, in *Wilderness Messiah: The Story of Hiawatha and the Iroquois*; (William Sloan Associates, New York 1955), suggests that the Iroquois had a complicated mythology, a god, Teharonhiawagon, and two messiahs, the semi-legendary Degandawida and his disciple Hiawatha, although these two were often 'fused'. He also claims for them 'a legend of a flood, and . . . prophecies of a saviour to come', but adds that these were 'possibly inherited from unknown early white visitors with a Christian tradition' (p. 25). This seems particularly likely, since the history of the messiah was also like that of Jesus (p. 31). To Hiawatha was credited the creation of the *Pax Iroquoia*, and the confederacy of the five nations: Mohawks, Cayugas, Onondagas, Oneidas, and Senecas. Wolfgang H. Lindig and Alfons M. Dauer, 'Prophetismus und Geistertanz Bewegungen bei Nordamerikanischen Eingeborenen', pp. 41–74 in W. E. Mühlmann, op. cit., regard concepts of paradise, world end, and a messiah as widely spread elements in American Indian religion. They see the associated ideas of paradise and life after death as a common response to contact with a higher culture, and as part of a search for the old culture before contact occurred and disrupted it. They concede that messianism as such might arise only from the influence of Christian conceptions. From their discussion, it is evident that they refer to Indian religious conceptions after cultural contact. William Christie MacLeod, in *The American Indian Frontier* (Knopf, New York 1928), pp. 513–14, suggests that supernatural interpretations of misfortune had occurred among Indian tribes in the seventeenth century, but that only in the 1760s did there appear a real prophet, the Delaware Prophet. (Unless MacLeod is deliberately excluding the Indian frontier with the Spaniards in the south and south-west, as he may be, he overlooks the Pueblo prophet, Popé, a Tewa medicine man, whose teaching led to an outbreak against the Spaniards in 1680: Alexander F. Chamberlain, 'New Religions Among the North American Indians . . .', *Journal of Religious Psychology* 6, 1 [January 1913], pp. 1–49.)

[8] Many prophets were shamans or medicine-men: e.g. Popé among the Pueblo Indians; Wovoka, the Paiute originator of the Ghost Dance of 1890; Da'takan, the Kiowa; Nakai' dokli'ni, the Apache. Tenskwatawa appears to have practised medicine before he became a prophet.

prophets, to the advent, and to the resurrection might have provided the content. But all this is conjectural. Missionaries had been active in the seventeenth century, if with small success, and in the mid-eighteenth century, David Brainerd, a Presbyterian, had affected some Indians with mass hysteria, had established camp-meetings, and made mass conversions among the Delawares. The communities of the Herrnhuter Brethren had also arisen in this period.[9] Missionaries, then, may have been the models of the new style of religious declamation, and since white men were conspicuously successful in many ways (even if their way of life was much less envied by North American Indians than in the nineteenth century, it was to be envied by Polynesians, and even more emphatically in the twentieth by Melanesians) these new styles of commanding power were no doubt impressive.

Indians near the east-coast settlements had had prolonged contact with whites by the 1760s. Some tribes had been pushed from their lands; the Shawnees and Delawares had suffered enforced expulsion from Pennsylvania in 1759.[10] Relations with Europeans became increasingly disturbed both by this process, by some assimilation to white ways, and by the struggles occurring in this period between the English and the French. The French sought to assure the Indians that they did not intend to dispossess them of their lands, and, unlike the English, they settled among them, participating in their amusements. Indian preference for the French, instanced in the 1750s, when some thirty-three tribes declared on the wampum belt that the French were their brothers, is thus understandable.[11]

The message of the prophets who arose among the Delawares in the 1760s was similar to that which they had heard from missionaries—they preached against adultery and drunkenness, and urged supplication to the Master of Life after the manner of their brothers (in this instance, the French).[12] The greatest prophet, Neolin, known as the Delaware Prophet, appeared at Tuscarawas on the Muskingum, in 1762. He claimed to have made a journey, led by a vision of a woman in white, to the spirit land, where he had learned the will of the Master of Life for his people. His message was a combination of diverse elements. He had acquired a prayer stick carved with hieroglyphics,

[9] Anthony F. C. Wallace, 'New Religions Among the Delaware Indians, 1600–1900', *Southwestern Journal of Anthropology* 12, 1 (Spring 1956), pp. 1–22, on which this paragraph in part relies.

[10] Henry R. Schoolcraft, *Information Respecting the History, Conditions and Prospects of the Indian Tribes of the United States* [also called *Archives of Aboriginal Knowledge*], (Lippincott, Philadelphia 1860), 6 vols, Vol. VI, p. 242.

[11] J. Mooney, op. cit., p. 662.

[12] Ibid., pp. 667–8.

with a prayer to be repeated morning and evening. He also had a skin map, which he called the 'Great Book of Writing', from which he used to preach, and for a price he would draw such a map for Indians to remind them of his teachings. It depicted the way in which their forefathers had achieved happiness, and, by representative lines, the prophet now showed how the white men impeded them in their quest.[13] The sins and vices that they had learned from the whites were the source of their present woes. If they would purify themselves from sin, so the Master of Life had revealed to the prophet, he would provide them with everything of which they had need.

That purification was to be undertaken with the use of emetics. They were to forsake the drinking of alcohol; to abstain from carnal knowledge; to keep one wife, and not to chase unmarried girls or the wives of other men; to make fire by rubbing two sticks together, as in the past, and not by the use of flint and steel; to cease using firearms; they were not to 'make medicine', which could only increase the influence of evil, but to pray; and altogether they were to return to their old way of life before it was affected by the white men. If this were done, the Master of Life would give them the power to drive the white men from their country. According to contemporary accounts, the prophet delivered his disquisition with great conviction, weeping most of the time.[14] Indians from other tribes travelled long distances to see and hear the Delaware Prophet.

Christian elements are conspicious in the prophet's teachings, particularly in the idea of a book of learning; the concept of sin; the prohibition of magic; the vision of the lady in white; and the Master of Life himself. But the import of the message was restorative, the use of emetics as a purification technique was probably indigenous, and the ultimate purpose of the teaching was xenophobic. Whether the prophet's vision implied the elimination of the white men by supernatural action or by warfare is not entirely clear, although he predicted that war would occur.[15]

The teachings of the prophet travelled a long way, and reached the tribes around the Great Lakes, who at this time were experiencing dramatic changes in their relations with the white men, as the British soldiery took over from the French. The victory of the British in Canada, in 1760, brought them much further to the west than they had been

[13] Ibid., p. 667; a thorough account from contemporary sources is given in Howard H. Peckham, *Pontaic and the Indian Uprising* (Princeton University Press, Princeton, N.J., 1947), pp. 98–100.

[14] H. H. Peckham, op. cit., p. 99, citing the diary of James Kenney, a Quaker trader in Pittsburgh.

[15] Ibid., p. 100.

before. Major Robert Rogers, with a body of provincial rangers, marched to Fort Detroit in 1761, and Pontiac, a chief of the Ottawas who had been allied to the French, had met him, and for one night he had held up Rogers, declaring that he stood in the path.[16] The Indians became quickly discontented under the British who were, as a matter of policy, less generous with powder and rum than the French had been.[17] Pontiac, who had waited to see the effects of the British victory, sent ambassadors bearing the wampum belt of war and the red tomahawk to most of the Algonquin tribes, and to the Wyandots and Senecas, in 1762.[18] He heard the story of the Delaware Prophet, 'possibly from the master himself' according to Peckham, and he saw its potential power in drawing the Indians together in a way in which they had never been united before.[19]

Pontiac gathered his own Ottawa people, the Potawatomies, and one band of Huron together on 27 April 1763, and delivered a version of the vision and instructions of the Delaware Prophet.[20] The teachings of the prophet became an important stimulus to the call for war. In Pontiac's version of the prophecy, however, a distinction was made between 'the children of your Father', their brothers, the French, and those who came to make trouble, 'those dogs clothed in Red', the British, thus amending the xenophobic import of the original for his own ends. 'It was an ingenious trick, by which he gained divine sanction for his own scheme.'[21] He drew into alliance the Chippewas and perhaps also the Miamies, Piankashaws and Weas.[22] According to Mooney, he brought the tribes of the Algonquins and the Wyandots, Senecas and Winnebagos into confederacy.[23] Over some 500 miles of frontier, twelve frontier posts were attacked, and nine were taken. Although the ruse by which he attempted to take Fort Detroit failed, Pontiac besieged the fort for fifty days until relief came.

Pontiac had difficulty in keeping his allies from quarrelling, and,

[16] H. R. Schoolcraft, op. cit., p. 243; a detailed account of Rogers' march is given in Francis Parkman, *The Conspiracy of Pontiac and the Indian War after the Conquest of Canada* 10th Edn (Little Brown, Boston 1917), Vol. I, pp. 165-6.
[17] H. H. Peckham, op. cit., pp. 92-3.
[18] F. Parkman, op. cit., pp. 186-8.
[19] H. H. Peckham, op. cit., p. 101.
[20] A contemporary account of this address by an anonymous author is found in *Journal ou Dictation d'une Conspiration*. A translation by R. Clyde Ford, 1910, has been recently reprinted in Milo Milton Quaife (Ed), *The Siege of Detroit* (The Lakeside Press, Chicago 1958), pp. 8-17. This author refers to the Delawares as 'Loups' (Wolves), as they were known to the French. The account of the speech in H. H. Peckham, op. cit., pp. 113-16, and in F. Parkman, op. cit., pp. 204 ff. are based on this source.
[21] H. H. Peckham, op. cit., p. 116.
[22] H. R. Schoolcraft, op. cit., p. 243.
[23] J. Mooney, op. cit., p. 668.

powerful leader as he was, he fell foul of some of them from time to time. Leadership was an uncertain thing among North American Indians even within one tribe, and much more so in a new confederacy.[24] Nor could the alliance persist once the hunting season began, and the tribes separated in search of game. Warriors whose livelihood is by hunting cannot maintain sustained warfare. Neither political and military genius, such as Pontiac displayed, nor millennial prophecies are sufficient to create enduring unity among peoples who live in relatively small hunting bands, and who must be mobile and energetic in search of food as the seasons dictate. The religious response of the Delaware Prophet was a valuable, perhaps in some respects a necessary ideological basis for even temporary nascent union of otherwise dispersed peoples, but without the appropriate economic and social organization these millennial promptings, drawn from aboriginal and intruded sources, were insufficient to sustain new forms of social organization. The objective circumstances for Indian ethnocentricism and nationalism had not yet come into being.

Tecumseh and the Shawnee Prophet, Tenskwatawa

Whatever the sources from which North American Indian prophetism sprang, whether it continued an aboriginal inheritance or was a new cultural response partly learned from missionaries, by the end of the eighteenth century prophets were almost endemic among Indian tribes. Our concern here is specifically with prophetic revolutionist responses in association with military action on the part of unconquered peoples who invoke supernatural aid for their warfare against enemies. Consequently we ignore, for the moment, important figures such as Handsome Lake, who, were we proceeding chronologically, would now force themselves upon our attention as links in the chain of prophetic influence and in illustration of the diversity of prophetic styles.[25] Prophets had by this time become significant respondents to situations of crisis, but the type of crisis which now concerns us is one still couched in military terms. We are told, 'almost every great Indian warlike combination had its prophet messenger at the outset, and if all the facts could be known we should probably find the rule

[24] See, for example, the castigation of Pontiac by Kinonchamek, son of Minavavana, the Chippewa chief, and by a Shawnee; H. H. Peckham, op. cit., pp. 185–8; and Alexander Henry's account of trouble between Ottawas and Ojibwas, following his captivity after the massacre at Michillimachinac, recounted in F. Parkman, op. cit., pp. 351–4.
[25] On Handsome Lake, see pp. 387–97.

universal'.[26] The most famous combination is one that never quite came into being as envisaged by its architect, perhaps through the wilfulness of the prophet with whom he was associated.

The Shawnees were not an important tribe, and probably never numbered more than 2,000, but they were allied to the Wyandots, whom they called their 'grandfathers', and to the Delawares, whom they called their 'uncles'.[27] They may have been forced south by the Iroquois, and, in the period before the emergence of the Shawnee Prophet, they had been engaged in intermittent warfare with the settlers, and had decreased in numbers perhaps more rapidly than any other tribe.[28] They had suffered vandalage from the whites who had steadily penetrated their lands on the eastern side of the Ohio River. In the revolutionary wars they sided with the British, were defeated by General Wayne at Greensville in 1795 and forced to renounce their rights to all territory east of a line running in a general way from the mouth of the Cuyahoga, on Lake Erie, to the mouth of the Kentucky, on the Ohio. The Shawnees, Delawares, and Wyandots were now almost completely shorn of their ancient inheritance, and lived in brooding discontent, faced with the superior power of the whites.[29] The situation could only grow worse, since the policy of many of the United States government agents, and particularly of Governor William Henry Harrison, of Ohio, the administrator of the Indiana Territory, was to alienate Indian lands and to occupy them as effectively as possible.[30]

Towards the end of the century, Tecumseh, the fourth child of a Shawnee, Puckeshinwa, rose to prominence both as a warrior and as an orator. His reputation extended beyond the Shawnees, since he had fought with various tribes, and spoken at conferences with the whites. His younger brother, Laulewasikaw, who was one of twins, announced, in 1805, that he was the successor to Penagashega, a Shawnee 'prophet' (medicine-man?) who had recently died, and from thenceforth he took the name Tenskwatawa, 'The Open Door'. Towards the end of that year he had visions in which he saw all drunkards (he had previously been one himself) taken by the devil, and he now pronounced against witchcraft and drunkenness. He asserted the need to uphold a variety

[26] J. Mooney, 'Prophets', in Frederick Webb Hodge, *Handbook of American Indians* Vol. II, p. 309 (Smithsonian Institution, Bureau of Ethnology, Bulletin 30, Washington, 1910).
[27] John M. Oskison, *Tecumseh and His Times* (Putnam, New York 1938), p. 5.
[28] Benjamin Drake, *Life of Tecumseh and of his Brother the Prophet, with a historical Sketch of the Shawanoe Indians* (Rulson, Cincinnati, and Quaker City Publishing House, Philadelphia 1856), p. 21.
[29] J. Mooney, *The Ghost Dance* . . ., op. cit., p. 672.
[30] J. M. Oskison, op. cit., p. 109.

of traditional customs: the young were to cherish the aged; he opposed innovations in dress and habits; he insisted on community of property. He reasserted ideas that had already established currency among the Shawnees, that their way of life had been superior, but when they had become corrupt, the Great Spirit had removed their power and given it to the white men. One day it would be returned. A Shawnee chief at a convention at Fort Wayne in 1803 had declared that the whites had come and taken away their land in return for goods, 'but the very goods they gave . . . were more the property of the Indians than the white peoples, because the knowledge which enabled them to manufacture these goods actually belonged to the Shawanoes: but these things will soon have an end. The Master of Life is about to restore to the Shawanoes both their knowledge and their rights, and he will trample the long knives under his feet.'[31]

Tenskwatawa's creed bore remarkable resemblances to that of Handsome Lake, and in its restorative aspects it repeated injunctions found earlier in the Delaware Prophet, for example against making fire with flint and steel.[32] This may have become an established prejudice among Indians, of course: prophets frequently announce ideas already well-accepted by their following, 'forthtelling' as distinct from 'foretelling'. The Indians were to kill their dogs, to keep the fires burning in their lodges, to give up their medicine bags and to cease beating their women and children. On accepting these things they were to 'shake hands' with the prophet, by drawing through their hands four strings of beads, supposedly the flesh of Tenskwatawa.[33]

[31] B. Drake, op. cit., pp. 21–2.

[32] J. Mooney op. cit., p. 673.

[33] An especially valuable account of the reception of these teachings among the Ojibwas comes from John Tanner, who, having been captured by the Shawnees at the age of nine, in 1789, lived with the Indians until about 1817, when he rejoined white society. His account, first published in 1830, recounts that 'The Indians generally received the doctrine of this man with great humility and fear. Distress and anxiety was visible in every countenance. Many killed their dogs and endeavoured to practice obedience to all the commandments of this new preacher . . .': Edward James (Ed.), *A Narrative of the Captivity and Adventures of John Tanner, during thirty years' Residence among the Indians in the Interior of North America* (Ross and Haines, Minneapolis 1956).

A contemporary account of Tenskwatawa's teachings, written by Thomas Forsyth to General William Clark (St Louis, 23 December 1812), is given in Emma Helen Blair (Ed.), *The Indian Tribes of the Upper Missouri Valley and Region of the Great Lakes* (Arthur H. Clark Co., Cleveland, Ohio 1912), Vol. II, pp. 274–7. Forsyth sets out as many of the prophet's laws as he can remember. They include: (1) Spirituous liquors were to be avoided; (2) No Indian was to take more than one wife in the future; (3) Indians were not to run after women; (4) The husband had the right to punish misdemeanours in his wife, but thereafter was not to bear ill-will; (5) Indian women living with whites were to be brought home, but the children to be left with their fathers; (6) All medicine bags, dances, and songs were to be given up, the bags were to be destroyed in the presence of the whole group, confession was to be made to the Great Spirit for all misdeeds, and forgiveness sought; (7) Indians were not to sell provisions to whites; (8) No Indian was to eat food cooked by whites or provisions raised

The effects of Tenskwatawa's teachings were dramatic. Some witches were burned (a practice against which the whites sought to intercede, despite the worsening relations of Harrison with the Shawnees and their allies).[34] Drunkenness markedly diminished, even among tribes at some distance from the area where the prophet was preaching.[35] Tenskwatawa pleaded with Harrison to stop the sale of whiskey to Indians. When challenged concerning his teachings, he declared that he taught the holy word and the termination of vices.[36] This was certainly the impression gained by the local Shakers, whose numbers had increased following the Kentucky revival of 1800. The Shaker emissaries to Tenskwatawa elicited from him that he believed in Jesus Christ, and they were impressed by the industry and peaceable disposition of the Indians, by their 'brotherly spirit', 'solemn fear of God, hatred of sin . . . peace, love and harmony'. Subsequently, when several of Tenskwatawa's followers attended the Shaker meeting on the Sabbath, they noted the 'order and decorum' of the Indians.[37]

---

by whites, including bread, beef, pork, fowls, etc.; (9) Indians were not to offer skins for sale, but had to ask for exchange; (10) The Indians were to consider the French, English, and Spanish as fathers and friends, but to keep their distance from Americans; (11) They were to give up all dress introduced by the whites and all dogs not of their own breeds, and to return all cats to the whites; (12) They were to try to do without buying merchandise, 'by which means game would become plenty, and then by means of bows and arrows they could hunt and kill game as in former days, and have independence of all white people'; (13) Those refusing these regulations were to be regarded as bad people, and not worthy to live; (14) Prayers were offered for the earth to be fruitful, and a dance was introduced for amusement. Each tribe was to live in one village.

[34] B. Drake, op. cit., pp. 89, 118 ff.

[35] E. James, op. cit. Tanner recounts this of the Ojibwa of Minnesota.

[36] B. Drake, op. cit., p. 108.

[37] John Patterson MacLean, 'Shaker Mission to the Shawnee Indians', *Ohio Archaeological and Historical Quarterly* XI (1902), pp. 215–29 (pp. 225–8). The Shaker emissaries, David Darrow, Benjamin Seth Youngs, and Richard McNemar (the last-mentioned of whom had formerly been a Presbyterian clergyman) had been refused an interview with the Prophet because white men laughed at him. When they denied this, George Blue Jacket, who spoke English, asked the Shakers, ' "Do you believe a person can have true knowledge of the Great Spirit in the heart, without going to school and learning to read?" A.[nswer] "We believe that they can; and that this is the best kind of knowledge" ' (p. 222). When Tenskwatawa talked to them he told them that he had been a [native] doctor and a wicked man and 'about two years ago while attending on sick people at Attawa in a time of general sickness he was struck with a deep and awful sense of his sins—cried mightily to the Good Spirit to show him some way of escape, and in his great distress, fell into a vision . . .'. The vision had revealed the road of happiness, and the fork in the road represented that stage of life in which people were convicted of sin, and those who took the right-hand way quit everything that was wicked and became good. He saw many people taking the left-hand road in three houses 'under different degrees of judgment and misery. He mentioned particularly the punishment of the drunkard. One presented him a cup of liquor resembling melted lead; and if he refused to drink it he would urge him saying: Come, drink—you used to love whiskey. And upon drinking it, his bowels were seized with an exquisite burning. This draught he had often to repeat' (p. 223). (This vision is very similar to that of Handsome Lake.) Governor Harrison recounted, in a letter to the Secretary of War, that at one point he had employed a Shaker

Tenskwatawa's fame spread, and delegations from various tribes came to visit him. His claims to healing ability and his successful prediction of the eclipse of the sun in 1806 established his credibility. Members of various tribes assembled on what were now regarded as government lands, and a process of negotiation ensued in which the whites attempted to persuade the Indians, whom they saw as a threat to the community at Vincennes, Ohio, to disperse. In 1808, the assembly around Tenskwatawa and Tecumseh re-established itself on the Tippecanoe, a tributary of the Wabash, where a strong body of Chippewas, Potawatomies, and Ottawas collected.[38] The group engaged in religious activities and warlike sports. The association of groups from different tribes suggested a new type of union of Indians: addressing the Governor at one of their meetings, Tenskwatawa said, 'The religion which I have established in the last three years, has been attended to by the different tribes of Indians in this part of the world. Those Indians were once different peoples; *they are now but one:* they are all determined to practice what I have communicated to them, that has come immediately from the Great Spirit through me.'[39] Subsequently there appeared to be about four hundred warriors with the prophet, mainly Kickapoo and Winnebago, whilst the Wyandots seemed willing to see all the tribes 'united in one great confederacy'. They were reputed willing 'to join such a union, and labor to arrest the encroachments of the whites upon their lands, and if possible to recover the lands which had been unjustly taken from them'.[40]

The association of the tribes alarmed the settlers, and the Indian intention to prevent further infiltration into their lands led to the raising of militia companies. Harrison believed, or pretended to believe, that the British in Canada were stimulating Tecumseh to cause trouble for the Americans. By 1810, the prophet was reputedly seeking to influence more westerly tribes, though Drake believes that he was now simply an agent of his brother, Tecumseh. In some areas the prophet's

---

as an intermediary with the prophet, since the Shaker leader 'has assured me that he believes the Prophet to be under the same divine inspiration as he himself is (a circumstance by no means improbable) . . .': J. M. Oskison, op. cit., p. 139. The opinion that the Shakers had of the Shawnee Prophet remained unshaken, despite subsequent events. Visited some years later by the Quaker Thomas Dean, the Shakers, who were settled thirty miles from Vincennes, Ohio, 'thought Tecumseh and the Prophet had been very much misrepresented, they and their people appeared to be peaceable people, and that they were in his [the Shaker's] opinion Christian Indians, opposed to war': John Candee Dean (Ed.), 'Journal of Thomas Dean: A Voyage to Indiana in 1817', *Indiana Historical Society Publications* VI, 2 (1918), pp. 273–345 (p. 308).

[38] B. Drake, op. cit., pp. 104 ff.
[39] Ibid., p. 108 (my italics).
[40] Ibid., p. 114.

message was said to promise the return of dead ancestors, and a cataclysm either against all white men or at least against the Americans, which would usher in a new era.[41] Since these ideas already existed in Shawnee mythology,[42] their inclusion in the prophet's message requires no particular explanation. The prophet said that all lands were the property of the Indian, and Tecumseh declared in 1810 that he was building a dam of tribes against the mighty water of the United States purchase of lands.[43] Few chiefs but many young men had joined him, and the idea grew that if chiefs were signing treaties alienating tribal lands (as they had done again in 1809) then the chiefs might have to be killed. Tecumseh himself appeared to be influenced by the fact that the white men had formed a union: the states were known as the 'seventeen fires', and he told Governor Harrison that it was appropriate for the red men to do likewise. He went to the far south, and the prophet's message so stirred the Cherokees that in 1811 they abandoned their bees, orchards, and commodities gained from the whites, and marched for the mountains of Carolina to be saved from the storm of wind and hail that they expected.[44] He visited the Seminole and the Creek Indians in Alabama, and urged on them that they make no further concessions. When he found that the Creeks would not commit themselves, he said that, when he returned to Detroit, he would stamp his foot and cause their houses to fall. This was Tecumseh's famous prophecy of an earthquake and, on the date that they calculated he might have returned, an earthquake did occur, and destroyed the houses in Tuckhabatchee, causing a frenzy among the Creeks.[45] Whether Tecumseh came to urge war is disputed, but he left behind a prophet named Seekabo, as teacher of the 'Dance of the Lakes' which he had introduced; other prophets, who proclaimed themselves followers of Tecumseh, arose among the Creeks, and led them into the disastrous Creek War.[46]

The great confederacy of which Tecumseh dreamed was aborted by the overreaching claims of his own auxiliary, Tenskwatawa. When

[41] J. Mooney, op. cit., p. 675.
[42] See pp. 226-7.
[43] B. Drake, op. cit., p. 129.
[44] J. Mooney, op. cit., pp. 676-7.
[45] B. Drake, op. cit., pp. 104 ff.
[46] See Theron A. Nunez, Jr, 'Creek Nativism and the Creek War of 1813-1814', *Ethnohistory* 5, 1, 2, and 3 (Winter 1958; Spring 1958; Summer 1958), pp. 1-47; 131-75; 292-301. There appear to have been six Creek prophets at this time: one of them, Paddy Walch, who had been brought up by a white man in South Carolina, led the Creeks in the massacre of Fort Mims by promising them invulnerability against the enemy. Despite his victory, heavy casualties caused resentment against him. The general theme of the prophets was to kill the chiefs; destroy white goods, ploughs, and looms; and to sing and dance the dance of the Indians of the northern lakes.

Harrison got the 4th Regiment of Infantry to protect Vincennes, in October–November 1811, Tenskwatawa, in the absence of Tecumseh, so inflamed the warriors gathered at Tippecanoe with promises that they could not be harmed by bullets that they began an action against the troops and suffered heavy losses. The dream of confederacy died. Although Tecumseh, who took the British side in the war of 1812, sometimes had 2,000 Indians under his command, no stable military alliance came into being among the tribes. Tecumseh was killed at the Battle of Thames in 1813, and was subsequently recognized, by his allies and his enemies, as a very noble savage. Tenskwatawa, discredited by the events at Tippecanoe, played no part in the British-American war but led a band of warriors west of the Mississippi, where he lived on a British pension from 1813 until his death in 1834.[47]

The millennialist ideas that Tenskwatawa learned and disseminated were a valuable stimulus to tribal unity and, with the more rational leadership of Tecumseh, to the prospects of a realistic political and military policy. Communication alone was obviously a hindrance among peoples with many different languages, who could come together in the expectation of supernatural action, but who, once that promise failed, had little capacity to sustain a political organization. Nor did the moral effect of Tenskwatawa's teaching last more than two or three years. The effort to reforge a way of life that was both adequate to the demands of the new competition and a manifestation of the Indian spirit of the past, was, given the existing agencies of social control, too difficult. Subsidiary prophets with similar messages arose in some tribes.[48] Indeed it might not be too much to write of an epidemic of prophetism, but the austerity and imperiousness of Tenskwatawa's demands were not often equalled, and, until the time of Wovoka, the prophet of the Ghost Dance, few subsequent prophets were able to gain allegiance among so many different tribes. But

[47] B. Drake, op. cit., p. 222.

[48] Tanner, in E. James, op. cit., writing of his life with the Ojibwas, recounts that soon after the waning of Tenskwatawa's message, another prophet, claiming visitation from the Great Spirit, arose among the Ojibwa, about whom Tanner reveals his own scepticism, ' "What has he come again so soon?", said I, "He comes often of late . . ." ' (p. 169). The prophet, Manito-o-geezhik, was a man of no particular fame, but he had disappeared for about a year, and claimed to have been to the abode of the Great Spirit (p. 179). His message was interpreted as a taboo on fighting the Sioux who raided the Ojibwa camps: various medicines were prohibited, and only tobacco and birch-bark were to be used in curing. Another prophet known to Tanner was Ais-kaw-ba-wis, who predicted that all the earth would be made new, once old things were done away with. He came to dominate the small band of Ojibwas, although Tanner said of him, to other Indians, ' "We now have these divinely taught instructors springing up among ourselves, and fortunately, such men as are worth nothing for any other purpose . . . here we have one too poor, and indolent and spiritless to feed his own family, yet he is made the instrument in the hand of the Great Spirit, as he would have us believe, to renovate the whole earth" ' (p. 186).

hostilities between Indians and Americans, who were steadily seizing
Indian lands, persisted for some seventy further years, and these were
wars—not outbursts into military action of millennialist dreams. War
continued to be supported by native medicine-men and the millennialist
dreams also occurred—only too clearly in the Ghost Dance—but the
direct connection between the two was no longer as close as in the case
of the Delaware Prophet and Tenskwatawa.

Militant prophets in South Africa

A close association of millennialist prophecy and warfare against
intruders occurred in South Africa during the unsettled period of
European conquest in the first half of the nineteenth century. European
misconceptions of the tribal system of the Bantu and, even more, the
misapprehension of the missionaries concerning native religion, were
important factors in the wars between the Xhosa and the British forces
in the Cape in the early nineteenth century. The British wrongly
credited Gaika (Ngqika), the leader of one group of Xhosa, with supreme
chieftainship west of the Kei. The pattern by which the Xhosa tribes
divided was such that he could not in fact have claimed supremacy
over groups that had split off from the main Xhosa tribe before his
grandfather, Rarabe, had done so.[49] Gaika had rebelled against his
uncle and former regent, Ndlambe, who had been a persistent enemy
of the British and who was pushed over the Fish River by British
forces in the Fourth Kaffir War in 1812.[50] A prophet, Makanna, arose
as Ndlambe's adviser, and he persuaded Ndlambe's following, and the
warriors of the Gcaleka, that with his aid the bullets of the English
would turn to water, and the English themselves would be pushed into
the sea. The numbers involved on the two sides were so utterly dis-

[49] A comparable case, in which the European intruders assumed that a local and lesser
chief was more powerful than in fact he was, occurred, in this same period, in Tahiti, where
the missionaries aided Pomare, who was not even from one of the more distinguished families,
to put down his enemies. Although he was a parvenu and a usurper, he established himself
as king of Tahiti. For accounts, see W. E. Mühlmann, *Arioi und Mamaia: Eine ethnologische
religionssoziologische und historische Studie über Polynesische Kultbünde* (Franz Steiner Verlag,
Wiesbaden 1955), pp. 194 ff., and Peter Henry Buck (Te Rangi Hiroa), *Anthropology and
Religion* (Yale University Press, New Haven, Conn., 1939), pp. 64–7. For this case see Sir
George E. Cory, *The Rise of South Africa* (Longmans, London 1910), Vol. I, p. 370.

[50] O. F. Raum, 'Von Stammespropheten zu Sektenführern', pp. 47–70 in E. Benz, op. cit.,
which this account follows. For a more detailed account of Gaika's relations with Ndlambe,
and for Ndlambe's resentment at Gaika's British-inspired claims to chieftainship, see A.
Kropf, *Das Volk der Xosa-Kaffern im östlichen Südafrika* (Berliner evangelischen Missions-
gesellschaft, Berlin 1889), pp. 47–9; and George McCall Theal, *History of South Africa* 4th
Edn. (Allen and Unwin, London 1915), pp. 328–9.

proportionate that, once bullets were neutralized, such a result appeared a certainty. He would release lightning against them, and ensure victory for Ndlambe's warriors.

Makanna had some knowledge of Christianity, and according to some reports had discussed religious problems frequently with van der Lingen, an army chaplain.[51] He taught that he was the emissary of Thlanga, creator of the Xhosa, who would raise ancestor spirits to assist them in battle. The god of black men, Dalidipu, was greater than the white god, Tixo, and Dalidipu's wife was a rain-giver, while his son was Tayhi, the Xhosa name for Christ. Dalidipu sanctioned the Xhosa way of life, including the customs of polygamy and brideprice, which the missionaries said were sins. Makanna taught that black men had no sins except witchcraft, since adultery and fornication were not sins: on the other hand, the white men were, on their own admissions full of sins. Dalidipu would punish Tixo, and the white men would be destroyed. If the Xhosa danced, they could bring back the ancestors, who would come armed and with herds of cattle. The British were allied with Gaika, who was the first object of attack by Ndlambe and Makanna. His defeat led the British into the Fifth Kaffir War of 1818–19, but their first success against Ndlambe's men beyond the Fish River did not prevent further hostilities between Gaika and Ndlambe, and Makanna's army crossed the Fish River singing that they would chase the white men from the earth. On 23 April 1819 ten thousand warrior, led by Ndlambe's son, Dushane, and Makanna attacked Grahamstown, which they failed to take and where they suffered heavy losses. This failure did not, however, bring about Makanna's downfall, and the war continued with the British driving the Xhosa back as far as the Kei River. In August Makanna gave himself up because his people were starving, and, so he declared, to see whether this would restore the country to peace. He was drowned some months later in attempting to escape, after his fellow prisoners on Robben Island had overwhelmed the guard and made a bid for the mainland. That he was dead was not believed by the Xhosa, who for years expected his return to help them.

Other prophets, who were not directly associated with the support of military enterprise, arose among the Xhosa, among them the celebrated Ntsikana, whose message was concerned with the renunciation of traditional practices, and who (despite the contemporary

[51] Edward Roux, *Time Longer than Rope*, 2nd Edn (University of Wisconsin Press, Madison, Wisc., 1964), p. 11. This paragraph leans on Roux and on O. F. Raum, op. cit. The prophet, Makanna, was also known as Makandha and Nexele (which meant 'left-handed', in consequence of which he was known to the Boers as 'Links', and by the English corruption, 'Lynx').

Xhosa regard for him as a type of national saint) was certainly influenced by missionaries, one of whom he encountered at Gaika's court.[52]
Prophetism in association with military activity occurred again in
1850. The Xhosa chiefs had been temporarily subdued, but discontent
was rife among them, centring on the steady loss both of their lands and
of control over the tribes. The Fingu, after their flight from the Zulus,
had been settled among them by the colonial government, and this
was a further invasion of Xhosa sovereignty. Drought added to the
general unrest. A further cause, according to Cory, was the limitation
that the British had imposed on the traditional practice of the chiefs
of accusing wealthy men of witchcraft, and subsequently of 'eating
them'—seizing their cattle.[53] If this were so, it is interesting that the
new prophet, Umlanjeni, first came to the attention of the British
because he preached the abandonment of all witchcraft medicines. But
Umlanjeni—who was a young man—also advocated war, and either he
influenced the Gaika chief, Sandilli, or was used by him. As the war
went against him, Sandilli became discontented with the prophet and
even suggested that he be killed at one point, though for a time the
prophet's influence persisted.[54] His particular prophecies are not easily
discovered, and whatever they were, with the defeat of the Xhosa and
the Hottentots (who, surprisingly, rose at the same time as their
former oppressors), Umlanjeni fell into obscurity before his death in
1853.[55]

The most dramatic influence of prophecy in South Africa occurred in
1857, after a long period of unsettled relations between the Xhosa and
the British, and the Great Trek of the ten thousand Boers, who were
discontented with a British land policy that seemed to them unduly
favourable to native interests. After conquering the Ciskei (the area
between the Fish River and Kei River) and after the Governor had
fixed the Kei as the eastern boundary of the Colony, in 1834, British
policy had changed. Lord Glenelg gave back the Ciskei to the Xhosa,
but twelve years later the Seventh Kaffir War broke out, and the British
again occupied the Ciskei, this time to keep it. A treaty was imposed on
the Xhosa chiefs, which asserted that Xhosa lands were held from the
British crown, and which condemned witchcraft, murder, theft, and
the 'sin' of buying wives. The Eighth Kaffir War followed in 1848.
The Xhosa, repeatedly beaten in war, and driven steadily from their

[52] O. F. Raum, op. cit., p. 53.
[53] Sir G. E. Cory, op. cit., Vol. V, pp. 292–4. This account relies on Cory's rather exiguous references to Umlanjeni.
[54] Ibid., p. 392.
[55] Ibid., pp. 405, 471.

lands, were further plagued by years of drought, and by a cattle disease that spread with great rapidity throughout the colony and beyond in 1854 and 1855.[56] In the unrest that followed it was rumoured that Umlanjeni, the prophet who had been active in the war of 1850, and 'who was credited with having foretold the great sickness among the cattle', had risen from the dead.[57]

The first prophetess was Nongqause, a young girl who was a niece of Umhlakaza, a counsellor to Kreli, the paramount chief of the Xhosa of the Transkei, although Umhlakaza also claimed this gift of prophecy and visions.[58] The messengers whom the girl saw declared that they were spirits of the dead, and they ordered that all cattle should be destroyed, that corn should be eaten, and no more planted. They would then return, in invincible power, to drive the English beyond the seas. The returning ancestors would bring back cattle, and those who believed would also enjoy the possessions of the whites, once they had been defeated. The day of resurrection was initially expected on 15 August 1856, and in anticipation of this, Kreli and many of the other chiefs began to kill their cattle, or to sell them very cheaply. Not all the Xhosa chiefs were convinced at once, and some were not convinced at all, but sooner or later almost all the Gcaleka killed their cattle, and about half of the Gaika did so.[59] The Fingu, however, who were refugees from the Zulu, were not impressed by the prophecies and they bought cheap cattle from the Xhosa believers.

After 15 August passed without the expected arrival of the ancestors, the cattle-killing waned for a time, to be resumed with a renewal of the prophecies, and the expectation that, on 18 February 1857, two suns would appear in the sky; a great darkness would also occur, and a violent gale—with the resurrection of the ancestors and their cattle to follow. In January, another prophetess, Nonkosi, a girl of about ten years of age, the daughter of a witch-doctor, recounted her experience of seeing a man's head appear in the water of a pond, claiming to be the prophet Umlanjeni, risen from the dead. According to Cory, this 'apparition' was Kwitchi, a councellor to the chief Umhala, who had instructed him to convince the child that dead chiefs and their cattle

[56] Sir G. E. Cory, *The Rise of South Africa* (*Cape Times* [for *The Archives of the Union of South Africa*], Cape Town 1940), Vol. VI, p. 24; O. F. Raum, op. cit., p. 56; G. M. Theal, op. cit., Vol. III, p. 198, suggests that the Xhosa attributed the sickness to witchcraft employed by the Europeans.

[57] Sir G. E. Cory, op. cit., p. 25.

[58] Ibid., pp. 27–8. This section relies on Cory. Cory writes very much as an official historian, however, and his particular interpretation of events has not been followed. A different perspective, but one relying heavily on secondary sources, is provided by Edward Roux, op. cit., pp. 36–44.

[59] O. F. Raum, op. cit., pp. 58–9.

were arising, and to spread the news of her visions.[60] Umhala was, according to this report, acting in conspiracy with other chiefs to produce such destitution among the Xhosa that they would be ready to attack the English, take their cattle, and reclaim the land that had been stolen from them. The plot, if plot it was, failed because the Xhosa did not at once respond to the call to kill their cattle, and some did not do so at all.

It is possible that the original prophecies of Nongqause were genuine, however, and that Umhala was merely aiding a course of action which he, and other chiefs, saw as useful to their warlike purposes. To kill some cattle was a traditional practice before engaging in war, so that some men might be released; in this case it constituted something almost amounting to a collective sacrifice. In earlier wars, the English had destroyed flocks and crops after defeating the Xhosa; without these possessions there might be less to fear from engaging in war. But whether the millennialist prophecy was faked, or partly faked, masses of the Xhosa believed it. New barns and kraals were made to receive the corn and cattle from the ancestors, and skin sacks for the milk that was to be so abundant.[61] After 18 February, however, the Xhosa, some of whom had already died from starvation, were in a state of complete desperation. More than 150,000 cattle had been killed. Despite relief measures on the part of the colonial government, thousands perished.[62] Millennialist prophecy broke the power of the Xhosa tribe; its erstwhile warriors went to the colony as supplicants. The labour that the colonists had formerly found so scarce was now plentiful, and European control became more effective than ever.

Religion and rebellion in Central and East Africa

Religion was associated with military action among the Xhosa through prophets with a new message. Some were counsellors of the Xhosa

[60] Sir G. E. Cory, op. cit., pp. 35–7. Neither Nonkosi nor the confession of Kwitchi is referred to by Roux. G. M. Theal, op. cit., Vol. III, p. 201, attributes the later confession to Nonkosi herself: that she 'had been instigated by men in Umhala's confidence to act as she had done'.

[61] J. Du Plessis, *A History of Christian Missions in South Africa* (Longmans, London, 1911), p. 296; G. M. Theal, op. cit., Vol. III, pp. 202–3.

[62] Sir G. E. Cory, op. cit., p. 39, estimates that 41,791 died in the area of British jurisdiction, that is to say, without taking account of those who died in Kreli's country, for which no census had been taken. O. F. Raum, op. cit., p. 59, estimates 20,000–25,000; and J. Du Plessis, op. cit., p. 297, 25,000. Cory, p. 38, gives the figure of 26,104 as the number relieved by government assistance, in the first year following the failure of resurrection on 18 February 1857.

chiefs, but not necessarily witch-doctors: Nongqause certainly was not. In some central African cases, traditional religious authorities played their part, much as Shakespeare depicts the Archbishop providing Henry V with excuses for his wars against the French. In the rebellions in Matabeleland and Mashonaland in 1896 and 1897, the importance of traditional religious specialists in promoting military action has been well demonstrated.[63] They did not so much provoke as legitimate rebellion, and they did so, in part, by their institutionalized prophetic functions. The priests associated with both the newer tribal cult of the royal house of the Ndebele, and the older religion, the *Mwari* or *Mlimo* cult, of the now tributary tribes, were active in fomenting rebellion. Oracles at the shrines of the Mwari cult provided advice for the young nobles, and groups of dancers associated with the cult spread the message. It was promised that the deity would assist with the war; the bullets of the enemy would become as harmless as water. Important mediums in the spirit-medium cult of central and western Mashonaland also gave this promise. Tribesmen were enjoined not to touch things that belonged to white men, since to do so would cause defeat. Thus the functionaries of three religious systems facilitated the organization of the risings, and did so by legitimating tribal culture, and by attempts both to disavow, and to neutralize, the cultural items introduced by the invader.

Protective magic is a common phenomenon in association with military enterprise among tribal peoples. The encounter with invaders and their superior techniques and weapons stimulated the search for new forms of magical protection. Occasional prophets arose offering such devices and their pronouncements were enough to encourage military enterprise: protection was often associated with the return of the heroes of the past. Where protection was offered in the context of existing magico-religious practice, as among the Ndebele and Shona, political leadership had been largely assumed by religious functionaries in the power vacuum which had arisen. In other instances, the provision of protection for combat was a sufficiently important function to give rise to the emergence and establishment of an entirely new religious system: such is the case of the *Yakañ* or *Allah water* cult, in the southern Sudan and northern Uganda.

The Yakañ cult distributed protective water to combatants, but it led to a well-institutionalized, if recrudescent movement. The myth of

---

[63] This paragraph relies on Terence Ranger, 'The Role of Ndebele and Shona religious authorities in the Rebellions of 1896 and 1897', pp. 94–136 in Eric Stokes and Richard Brown (Eds), *The Zambesian Past: Studies in Central African History* (Manchester University Press, Manchester 1966).

water which conferred invulnerability and ensured success in warfare arose in the Mahdi rebellion in the Sudan in the early 1880s, although it may be older than that.[64] The Dinka had used such water for the onslaught in which they wiped out the station at Rumbek in the Bahr-el-Ghazel, killing eight hundred of the soldiers of Emin Pasha. From the Dinka it spread to the Lerya, Lotuko, and Mundu tribes. The Mahdi had defeated a force of the Emin Pasha, but the Mundu then defeated the Madhists, and in association with the Abukaya, Moru, Fajelu, and Nyangbwara, to all of which tribes the Yakañ cult spread,' . . . combined and waged a successful war against the Azande, who were then at the height of their victorious career of conquest'.[65] In about 1890, a Fajelu named Logworo bought some of the water from Magoro, the chief of the Mundu, and passed it on to Rembe, a Kakwa: it then passed to the Lugbara (Lugbwara) of nothern Uganda, a tribe with cultural affiliations with the Kakwa.[66] The Lugbara used the water in fighting Emin Pasha's garrison at Wadelai, on which they inflicted two, and perhaps three, serious defeats.

Among the Lugbara, who in the 1950s numbered some 240,000 people, gathered in forty-five or more independent groups, the cult became institutionalized and associated with the ancestor aspect of Lugbara religion. The owners of the water became prominent men, who carried a small stick made from the *inzu* shrub as a token of priestly office, and who effectively terrorized their fellow tribesmen into participation in the cult, proclaiming that 'survival after death' was 'dependent on joining the society'.[67] The cult acquired political significance, paradoxically from the hands of the invaders, against whom its magic was directed. When the Belgian officials, who occupied the Lugbara area in the period 1900–1908, sought responsible men to act as their local agents, particularly to collect taxes, the traditional rain-makers of the Lugbara decided not to co-operate with them. ' . . . since the Yakañ leaders were believed to be able to cope with European contact by magical means, they were also thought to be able to deal with them personally as representatives of the local people.'[68] Their assumption of formal political duties led to a decline in the cult for some years, until it revived in 1915, and led to the revolt at Udupi in 1919, in which the Yakañ leaders, now also chiefs, acquired renewed popularity with the people.

[64] This account relies principally on J. H. Driberg, 'Yakañ', *Journal of the Royal Anthropological Institute of Gt. Britain and Ireland* LXI (July–December 1931), pp. 413–20.
[65] Ibid., p. 413.
[66] John Middleton, 'The Lugbara', pp. 326–41 in Audrey I. Richards (Ed), *East African Chiefs* (Frederick A. Praeger, New York 1959), p. 326.
[67] J. H. Driberg, op. cit., p. 415.
[68] J. Middleton, op. cit., p. 329.

The central concern of the cult was the distribution of the sacred water, which was initially more significant in times of war, but which came to be regarded as conferring immunity from death by disease, and which would restore the ancestors to life; resurrect dead cattle; confer immunity in flouting government orders and in refusing to pay taxes; create immunity against government rifles, which could, against the protected, fire only water; and, at some future time, 'provide' rifles for the faithful when they were proficient to use them. Those who refused to drink the water were said to become termites after death.[69] The water, purchased from the priests, was mixed with a drug, locally known as *kamiojo*, which lions were said to chew before they went out to hunt, and which operated as a powerful heart stimulant, sometimes inducing mania. Each dispenser of water had his own temple, each with a guard of *askaris*. A large pole from a particular tree, with a piece of the *inzu* shrub affixed to it, was erected in a parade-ground near the temple, and sacrifice and dance occurred there. The dance, which followed the distribution of the water, was apparently based on the military exercise of marking time; the dancers held imitation rifles, with which they went through the motions of aiming, ordering and presenting arms.[70] The military associations of the cult were apparent in its ritual, as in the myth of the water itself, and on each occasion when, after lapsing, the cult has been revived 'the medical aspect is shortly superseded by the revolutionary idea; during the revival of 1920, the latter was the dominant belief in less than two months'.[71]

The cult was diffused by fighting men: when Major Preston took some of Emin Pasha's 'Nubis' into the service of the Uganda government, a certain Corporal Lemin Marjuk became a principal administrator of the cult. It spread to Kampala and Entebbe, and developed most strongly among troops at Busoga, and the 'Nubis' who took part in the Uganda mutiny were members of the cult: thus a protective device which served the troops in government service also served them when they turned against the government. The protection was effective in all military activity. 'While the cult is directed against aliens, and any form of alien domination, it is not essentially anti-European . . . it assisted the Mahdi in Khartoum, and subsequently contrived the massacre of the Mahdists in the south.'[72] It operated against the 'Nubis', Germans, British, and Azande. It was not, therefore, a specifically 'nativistic' cult, nor was it specifically associated with revolution,

[69] J. H. Driberg, op. cit., p. 419.
[70] Ibid., p. 418.
[71] Ibid., p. 420.
[72] Ibid., p. 420.

but was a special instance of the new religious orientations which arise directly in association with warfare.

The central idea of the Yakañ cult, the protective water, is found again in the *Maji-maji* rebellion, which occurred in Tanganyika in 1905–6, many hundreds of miles south of Lugbaraland. It may have been diffused through the recruitment of 'Nubis' into the German forces, but this is speculation.[73] The rebellion occurred in areas almost unpopulated by the Germans, 'inhabited by tribes which had hitherto been looked upon as the most peaceful in the entire protectorate'.[74] The action was remarkable in two respects; because it had been set afoot more than a year before the actual rising, and was particularly inspired by the chiefs and medicine-men of the Wapogoro and Wagindo; and because it was a combined effort of several tribes.[75] A region the size of Prussia, south of the central railway, and east of a line drawn from Kilosa to the northern point of Lake Nyasa, was the area affected by the rising, which took eighteen months to quell. How important the use of protective water was, is not easy to say, although the rebellion takes its name from the Swahili word for water, *maji*. The words 'Maji maji', and 'Hongo hongo', the name for a medicine-man, were battle cries employed by the tribes. The water was reputedly dispensed by a great medicine-man living in the form of a water monster in the Rufiki River, and was a concoction of water, maize, and sorghum seed. It was sprinkled on the body, consumed, and carried into battle in bamboo sticks. It changed bullets into water, as long as those who used it did not look back in battle. 'The medicine was said to be far superior to the arms of the Europeans, and its power was finally extended so as to make women invisible and secure from capture.'[76] When the medicine proved ineffective, the dead were said to be asleep, waiting

[73] Ibid., p. 415; Gerald F. Sayers, *The Handbook of Tanganyika* (Macmillan, London 1930), in his treatment of the Maji-maji rebellion, offers no information of the source from which the ideas came to the Tanganyikan tribes (pp. 72–5).

[74] Fred Hartman, *Occupation and Colonization of German East Africa*, Unpub. M.A. Thesis, University of California, 1934, p. 120.

[75] George Shepperson and Thomas Price, in *An Independent African: John Chilembwe* (Edinburgh University Press, Edinburgh 1958), p. 501, say that the Ngoni were the only notoriously warlike tribe involved, and that this tribe was seriously split by the rebellion: 'the western group refused to respond to the emissaries from the Maji-Maji leaders'. The tribes concerned were the Ngoni, Bunga, Mwera, Sagara, Zaramo, Matumbi, Kitchi, Ikemba, and Bena, with a number of leaders from the Pogoro tribe, according to W. O. Henderson, 'German East Africa 1884–1918', pp. 123–62 in Vincent Harlow and E. M. Chilver (Eds.), *History of East Africa* (Clarendon Press, Oxford 1965), p. 138 n.

[76] G. F. Sayers, op. cit., p. 73. An account of the military actions of the rebellion is given in W. O. Henderson, op. cit. The principal German source, Gustav, Graf von Götzen, *Deutsch Ostafrika im Aufstand* (Reimer, Berlin 1909), firmly rejects any interpretation of the rebellion as a religious movement, and considers it difficult to determine to what extent religious considerations influenced the rebellion's origin or its diffusion.

to rise again. The water cult alone could hardly have inspired rebellion, but undoubtedly it facilitated its promotion. The very word 'rebellion' is, however, itself scarcely appropriate. Among people so recently experiencing the impact of new invaders, the military and magical action may be seen less as rebellion than as a continuation of normal warfare while conquest remains uncompleted.

The Hau Hau movement

The most important issue in the background of the millennialist *Hau Hau* movement among the Maoris of New Zealand in the 1860s was that of land. British missionaries had been active among the Maoris from 1814, when Samuel Marsden first arrived, and although it took ten years before they made their first convert, thereafter the progress of Christianity and of the arts of reading and writing was rapid. When the first settlers sponsored by the New Zealand company arrived in 1840, the year in which the British crown proclaimed sovereignty over the islands, they found that 'half the native population was regularly attending missionary schools and services, and the best of the chiefs were beginning to reorganize native life on lines drawn from the Scriptures'.[77] Christianity was not the only cultural import to find ready acceptance. In 1820, Hongi, a fighting chief, had visited England, and had returned with all his presents turned into muskets.[78] Thenceforth, the pattern of endemic and savage intertribal warfare, in which *utu*, the pursuit of revenge, was an especially cherished virtue, became even more cruel and more devastating. The spread of European diseases added to the decline of the Maori peoples.

In 1840 the first British governor, Captain Hobson, induced many—

[77] Harold Miller, 'Maori and Pakeha, 1814–1865', pp. 75–95 in I. L. G. Sutherland (Ed.), *The Maori People To-day: A General Survey* (Oxford University Press, Oxford 1940), p. 77. Miller instances the young chief who, in a remote Waikato village, in 1841, posted a notice outside the gate, declaring that those who committed adultery, or stole, or worked on the Sabbath, would be put out of the village, ending (and in this a reflection of Maori religion is found) 'because of these things, God's anger has come upon us; let us put them away, that He may be appeased'. Miller also recounts that on Christmas Day 1846, 'while the Europeans were gathering for a race meeting, across the river nearly four thousand natives had gathered to celebrate the Nativity . . . seven hundred received the sacrament. Some had travelled a hundred and fifty miles in order to be present.' The extraordinary fidelity to Christian principles is evident also in the well-known case which occurred during Heke's war. The Maori defenders of Kawiti's stronghold, Ruapekapeka, who had successfully held it against British artillery, withdrew, when Sunday came, into an outwork for a religious service, only to find that the less scrupulous British took advantage of their religiosity to capture the fort. The incident is recounted by Apirana T. Ngata and I. L. G. Sutherland, ibid., pp. 342–3.
[78] Felix M. Keesing, *The Changing Maori*, Memoirs of the Board of Maori Ethnological Research, Vol. 4 (Avery, New Plymouth, N.Z. 1928), p. 41–2.

but not all—Maori tribes to sign the Treaty of Waitangi, which gave
the Crown the pre-emptive right to buy Maori lands. The measure,
probably conceived as partial protection for Maoris, and a control of
settlement, left unaffected the agreements by which settlers had already
bought lands. Initially the Maoris had sold readily, and tribes had
adopted *pakeha* (whites) as a matter of prestige. Subsequently, the
Crown bought from the Maori at 6d an acre, and then re-sold to
settlers at a price twenty times higher. The Maoris felt cheated.[79] But
worse, Maori titles to land were vague, and led to disputes: 'to offer
land for sale was the readiest mode of revenge open to the losing side in
a quarrel. It was in this way that the celebrated block of land at
Waitara came to be offered by Teira to Governor Browne.'[80] Land
leagues arose among the Maoris, attempts to prevent the sale of the
rapidly diminishing land, but effective control remained difficult.

Maori concern about the alienation of land prompted pan-Maori
movements, despite the bad relations between tribes and the at times
tenuous authority of Maori chiefs within their own villages. The chiefs
also wanted to regain authority over their own people, whose behaviour
had been radically affected by the dissolution of traditional social
controls.[81] Disputes about land led to the creation of the Maori King,
by the Waikato tribes, after a meeting of about 2,000 Maoris at
Rangiriri in 1857. Potatau Te Whero Whero was nominated and
chosen as first king. The Maoris affirmed their loyalty to the Queen of
England, their attachment to the Governor, but asserted that they
wished to maintain a separate nationality, and that they wanted a
magistrate, assemblies, government, and laws of their own.[82] They
took the Old Testament as their model in this creation of kingship.
Ancient hatreds were buried, and the tribes involved undertook never
again to go to war with each other.

Not all Maori tribes joined the King movement, which in this period
was more symbolic than effective.[83] Wiremi Kingi held aloof, and
established a land league of his own, although in his quarrel with the

[79] John E. Gorst, *The Maori King: or, Our Quarrel with the Natives of New Zealand* (Macmillan,
London 1864), p. 67.
[80] Ibid., pp. 70–1.
[81] Ibid., pp. 256 ff., 292. Gorst describes how the traditional power of chiefs had declined:
the Maori had become more democratic in decision-making. Young warriors roamed the
countryside, terrorizing both Europeans and other Maoris, and drunkenness had become an
acute problem in some areas.
[82] Ibid., pp. 191–2. Gorst, who was on the spot among the Waikato, says, that they 'were
conscious of a firm determination to maintain a separate nationality and an independent
King'.
[83] Ibid., p. 279. The King had little real power and no revenues with which to pay his local
officers or his military guard. His foreign policy, however, was strong, and despite weakness
in domestic matters, he became 'a rallying point for Maori nationality'.

Governor about a disputed lot of land, the Waitara block at Taranaki, he induced some of the king's supporters (but not the king himself) to assist him in the first Taranaki war of 1860–1. The course of action followed by the Governor was condemned both by the Bishop of New Zealand and the former Chief Justice, Sir William Martin, but the rapacity of the settlers made difficult any admission of error or injustice to Maoris.

Eventually a new governor, Sir George Grey, who had served in New Zealand earlier, recognized the legitimacy of Wiremi Kingi's claim, but failed to announce his intention to relinquish the Waitara block that Wiremi Kingi claimed, and a series of further blunders and misunderstandings led to steadily worsening relations between the Maoris and the colonists, and the Maoris and the government. War broke out again from 1863 to 1865, and innocent tribes and conciliatory groups among the Waikato, such as the Ngatihaua, were attacked for the misdeeds of the more extreme Ngatimaniapoto.[84] Large areas of land were confiscated, and many Maoris feeling, not without reason, that they had been both cheated and unjustly attacked, were now thoroughly discontented.[85] They had become disillusioned even with the Christian religion to which they had so readily taken, especially when troops burned Maori villages, killing women and children, and particularly since their former friend, Bishop Selwyn, had been with the troops at the time.[86]

The land leagues and the King movement were two Maori responses to the encroachment of the *pakeha*; deliberate and conscious attempts to counter external threat, and, in the case of the King movement, an attempt to provide internal regulation. Circumstances of acute distress are propitious for new visions of less rational solutions, and the Maoris, although they had absorbed many of the white man's ways, and his religion, were now ready for more radical ideas. In this circumstance, a prophet, Te Ua Haumene (also known by his mission name of Horopapera Tuwhakararo, which means John Zerubbabel) arose.[87] Te Ua, who belonged to the Taranaki tribe, had learned the magic arts

[84] The whole complicated process is set out in the classic study by Sir John Gorst, who became magistrate among the Waikato during this period, and was himself a centre of conflict between Maori extremists and moderates: ibid., pp. 337–55. The history of the Waitaro Purchase and its consequences is also set out in detail by Keith Sinclair, *The Origins of the Maori Wars* (New Zealand University Press, Wellington 1957), pp. 110–225.

[85] I. L. G. Sutherland, *The Maori Situation* (Tombs, Wellington, N.Z. 1935), p. 30, puts the land confiscated at three million acres.

[86] Apirana T. Ngata and I. L. G. Sutherland, 'Religious Influences' in I. L. G. Sutherland (Ed.), *The Maori People To-day* . . ., op. cit., pp. 344–8.

[87] S. Barton Babbage, *Hauhauism: An Episode in the Maori Wars 1863–6* (A. H. & A. W. Reed, Wellington and Dunedin, N.Z. 1937), pp. 22–3.

of a Maori *tohunga*, or priest, but he had also studied with Wesleyan missionaries.[88] Perhaps of weak intellect, in 1862 he claimed that the Angel Gabriel had spoken to him in a vision. Since Maoris took the Bible literally and were ready not only to adopt its injunctions, but also to apply Old Testament stories to their own circumstances, Te Ua's claims were accepted, although prophecy appears not to have been an indigenous religious activity.[89]

Te Ua was given the credit for causing a British ship, the *Lord Worsley*, to be drawn on to the Taranaki coast and, although his injunction that the ship should not be looted was not heeded, his fame as a prophet began to spread. Stories about him grew. He was said, in a story that recapitulates that of Abraham, to have maimed his son, and prepared to sacrifice him at the Angel Gabriel's behest, and then, at the angel's intercession, to have healed the boy's broken leg.[90] The importance of Te Ua was an an inspiration in the Maori struggle with the *pakeha*. Three coadjutors were quickly appointed for the new faith, Tahutaki, Hepanaia, and Wi Parana, who acquired divine blessing by inhaling the smoke of Te Ua's pipe.[91] If Te Ua was of weak intellect, then effective leadership must quickly have passed into their hands, and the hands of those who became the prophet's emissaries to the tribes. Tahutaki and Hepanaia persuaded their associates to undertake an expedition to Ahuahu, prophesying that some *pakehas* would be delivered into their hands. A small company of troops was discovered, and quickly overcome, and the head of its officer, Captain T. W. J. Lloyd, who was decapitated, became thereafter the object through which Te Ua received the instructions of the Angel Gabriel. This military success established the credibility of the new religion, which was now quickly propagated.

On Gabriel's instructions, Te Ua now ordered that a *niu*, or post, be set up as a flagpole (the first was part of the mast of the *Lord Worsley*) on which flags were rigged. The assembled company marched around it, with raised hands, chanting incantations. The majority of the chants were unintelligible even to the Maoris, but the word 'Hau', which occurred at the end of many lines of the chants, was a word for the vital spark, besides referring literally to the wind, 'Anahera hau',

[88] A. T.Ngata and I. L. G. Sutherland, op. cit., pp. 351–2.

[89] William Greenwood, 'The Upraised Hand, or the Spiritual Significance of the Rise of the Ringatu Faith', *The Journal of the Polynesian Society* 51, 1 (March 1942), pp. i–vi and 1–81, describes Te Ua as 'the first Maori prophet' (p. 4). However, it was accepted in traditional Maori religion that in a trance one might go to the spirit world: Edward Tregear, *The Maori Race* (Willis, Wanganui, N.Z., 1904), p. 414.

[90] W. Greenwood, op. cit., pp. 4–5; S. B. Babbage, op. cit., p. 25.

[91] S. B. Babbage, op. cit., pp. 26 ff. The account here relies principally on this source.

angels of the wind, who descended from the ropes left dangling from the *niu*.[92] A typical chant included English words, particularly words drawn from church services and from military activity, and the chants were intoned while the naked throng of men, women, and children touched the preserved heads of *pakeha* who had been killed, which were then believed to utter words of prophecy. Shivering, frenzy, and catalepsy occurred during the marching, and the marchers sometimes manifested glossalalia. Te Ua called the new faith *Pai-marire*, which means 'good and faithful', and composed a shout to be used at all meetings: 'Hapa! Pai-marire, hau'—'pass over, good and faithful'.[93] The formula was supposed to ward off bullets.

Te Ua declared victory over the *pakeha* to be near at hand. Gabriel would protect them, and the Virgin Mary was constantly with them. Those who failed to follow the King movement and to become Hau Hau believers would be ruined.[94]

> When the last Pakeha had perished in the sea, all the Maoris who had perished since the beginning of the world would leap from their graves with a shout, and stand in the presence of Zerubbabel, the Great Prophet. . . . The deaf would hear, the blind see, the lame walk; every species of disease would disappear; all would become perfect in their bodies as in their spirits. Men would be sent from heaven to teach the Maoris all the arts and sciences now known to Europeans.[95]

The inspiration of the books of Revelation and Isaiah is evident. The Hau Hauists saw themselves as kin with the Jews, and there was some

[92] Ibid., pp. 30–1; Robin W. Winks, 'The Doctrine of Hau-Hauism', *Journal of the Polynesian Society* 62, 3 (September 1953), pp. 199–236.

[93] W. Greenwood, op. cit., p. 6. A chant, given by S. B. Babbage, op. cit., p. 32, reads:

God the Father, Hau; God the Son, Hau Hau;
God the Holy Ghost, Hau, Hau, Hau.
Attention, save us; Attention, instruct us; Attention
Jehovah, avenge us, Hau. Jehovah, stand at ease, Hau.
Fall out, Hau Hau.
Father, Good and Gracious, Hau.
Big rivers, long rivers, big mountains and sea.
Attention, Hau, Hau, Hau.

Despite the incongruity of some of the military language, the meaning appears to be not dissimilar from that of many Christian prayers.

[94] In some measure the King movement and the Hau Hau movement overlapped in composition, but the King movement never adopted the Hau Hau religion, nor were its principal supporters affected by Hau Hauism. Although it spread among the Taranaki, and as far as Poverty Bay on the east coast, 'it made no headway among the Waikato tribes, since the King movement, and what it stood for, occupied the stage there'. A. T. Ngata and I. L. G. Sutherland, op. cit., p. 352. Te Ua had sent Lloyd's head in circuit to rally the tribes, and strongly prophesied the help of the Lord of Hosts to his people.

[95] W. Fox, *The Revolt in New Zealand*, a series of letters addressed to the Rev. George Townshend Fox (Seeley, Jackson & Halliday, London 1865), p. 129, cited by S. B. Babbage, op. cit., p. 36.

idea of their being the lost tribes.[96] They expected Joshua and his legions to descend to help them, once all Maoris were converted. Thus distinct millennial and resurrectionist elements fused with the promise of active military assistance in the Maori struggle against the *pakeha* for the possession of the land. The Maoris said that the missionaries had taught them to turn their eyes to heaven, while the missionaries had turned *their* eyes to the land.

Te Ua's attempt to rally the tribes led to some premature engagements against the whites. Hepanaia led an attack on the Sentry Hill Redoubt in April 1864, and was repulsed with losses. Other Hau Hauists under Matene fought in the following month. Te Ua disowned the two prophets as disobedient and thus explained their failure to gain the promised immunity to bullets which the upraised hand would ensure when the battle was joined at the proper time. He now sent two groups of emissaries on new routes to arouse the tribes.[97] It was on one of these excursions that in March 1865, Kereopa, one of the delegates, whose daughters had been burned to death by the British soldiers when they razed a village, wrought his vengeance on the innocent Reverend Carl Sylvanus Volkner, killing him and subsequently eating his eyes in traditional Maori fashion, and using his blood for communion.[98] The emissaries converted many natives, but a swift campaign, on both the east and west coasts and in the interior, saw the defeat of the Maoris who were enlisted in its cause. Te Ua was captured early in 1866. He renounced his teachings, and he and Patara were freed; Kereopa was hanged, and several hundreds, including the later founder of the Ringatu Church, Te Kooti—and in his case wrongfully—were deported to the Chatham Islands.[99]

Hau Hauism was a short-lived millennial movement. The authorities differ in appraising its significance. Keesing regards Te Ua as 'a harmless dreamer', and describes Hau Hauism as arising as one of 'a series of religious cults spontaneously within the Maori people, through the forms, ritual and government of which groups of natives were seeking, however crudely and even dangerously, to give expression to their spiritual life'.[100] Babbage maintains that 'It is doubtful whether the cult was ever sincerely adopted by the majority of the Maoris as a religion. As Christianity had allied itself with the political forces of the

[96] R. W. Winks, op. cit., p. 231.

[97] S. B. Babbage, op. cit., p. 44.

[98] Ibid., pp. 50–2; W. Greenwood, op. cit., p. 16. The Hau Hauists, who identified with the Jews, set free the captain of the ship on which they captured the Rev. Volkner, because he, Captain Levy, was a Jew.

[99] S. B. Babbage, op. cit., pp. 66 ff.

[100] F. M. Keesing, op. cit., pp. 49–50.

State, Hau Hauism, too, became inseparably interwoven with the political struggle'.[101] The distinction which Babbage draws here seems unnecessarily fine. Men are capable of believing sincerely in ideas that are to their own interest, whether natural or supernatural. Hau Hauism combined Maori interests with an interpretation of Christianity, which made that recently but widely adopted faith peculiarly relevant to Maori aspiration. Ecstasy and the type of hysteria that accompanied Hau Hau rituals were more vibrant forms of Christianity than that which the now distrusted missionaries had disseminated, and the power of Jehovah, transmitted through the ropes dangling from the *niu*, appeared to have very real consequences. Hau Hauism was both a manifestation of national aspirations that were already finding other biblically-legitimated forms of expression in the King movement, and an attempt to mobilize the powerful millennialist message of Christianity itself (and there can be no doubt that the resurrection, the advent, and the millennium were preached by the Christian missionaries).

Hau Hauism was exactly the type of millennialism harnessed in the service of military action that we have already seen among North American movements, differing in appearance in accordance with the far greater extent to which the Maoris had been christianized. Its expression was less manifestly restorative of the native past. It did, however, disseminate a common stock of ideas, some Christian, some traditional, and it induced tribes that had previously used different incantations and songs to learn new ones, which now became common to all Maoris who espoused the Pai-marire religion. In this respect it resembled Tecumseh's teaching of the songs and dances of the Great Lakes to the far-away Creeks and Cherokee. Like the North American Indian movements, Hau Hauism was an agency of diffusion, but in its promise of a future when Maoris were to enjoy the arts and sciences of Europeans it manifested the more typical acceptance of innovation found in the South Seas. Even the resurrection of ancestors—an idea often associated with essentially restorative movements—lacked this specific connotation in Hau Hauism, where the idea appears to have arisen from the Christian concept of resurrection. The Maori were already a relatively acculturated people (when compared with Indian tribes of the late eighteenth and early nineteenth centuries). The military action on which they embarked came late in their acculturation process, and after they had absorbed many elements of the intrusive British culture. Their patterns of tribal life had been seriously affected by Christianity; traditional agencies of social control had declined; and the dissemination, and use in tribal warfare, of western

[101] S. B. Babbage, op. cit., p. 69.

weapons had completely disrupted the power balance of the past. Their belated millennialism was only very equivocally concerned with the Maori past, but necessarily accommodated the new cultural elements that were now a part of the existential situation.

Religion in the service of secular rebellion: (i) Chilembwe

The foregoing cases illustrate military enterprise supported by millennial prophecies—more immediate and spectacular among the North American Indians and Xhosa, somethat less so among the Maoris. These instances are not, then, typical examples of a revolutionist response since such a response is not intrinsically activist—only in certain circumstances does it give rise to actual armed conflict. On the other hand, a revolutionist response is not *necessarily* millennialist. In a colonial era, less-developed peoples experiencing pluralism of authority, values, and norms may not expect spontaneous *supernatural* action to transform their social situation. In such a situation, the revolutionist response may arise from a reassertion of indigenous religious values which are not in themselves revolutionist, but in the interests of which (and all that they symbolize) a transformation of the present dispensation is demanded. Religious nativism may then become associated with secular rebellion. Before we turn to this, reinvigoration of indigenous religion (or to practices that pass for it) epitomized in some of the precursors of the Mau Mau movement in Kenya (and even as a persisting if distinctly subsidiary strain in that movement) we must briefly look at a somewhat different case, namely the Chilembwe rebellion in Nyasaland.

The brief military career of John Chilembwe, in 1915, does not represent a revolutionist *religious* response to the world. It was not action undertaken at the direct prompting of a coherent and explicit millennial vision. It was not the manifest expression of explicit expectations of supernatural intervention in native affairs. However, it did occur in a situation in which many natives had been extensively exposed to millennial ideas; in which several Christian sects had actively disseminated adventist prophecies; and in which recurrent rumours of both supernatural transformative action, and of war, were canvassed. Thus, Chilembwe's activity in 1915, although not in itself the manifestation of a transformative religious movement, occurred in a social context informed by several such movements. It is important to make these distinctions precisely, because Chilembwe was a minister of religion, and had been closely associated, particularly during his early training under Joseph Booth, with the adventist ideas current in various Christian movements.

John Chilembwe, a Yao, was the steward to Joseph Booth, a pacifist, who had given up his business in Australia to become a missionary in Africa, with the strong idea of establishing industrial missions.[102] Booth baptized Chilembwe, and undoubtedly transmitted to him his ideas about a just land settlement in Africa, and his ideal of Africa for the Africans. Booth (unless, in the service of African independence, he acted purely for expedient reasons) was a restless and volatile man, frequently changing his religious beliefs on matters such as the maintenance of Saturday as the sabbath, and adventism. Booth took Chilembwe to the United States, and there Chilembwe became a Baptist minister in an American negro church, and, under the sponsorship of Lewis Garnett Jordan, he was put through school, and studied at Virginia Theological Seminary at Lynchburg, which conferred A.B. and B.D. degrees upon him.[103] Chilembwe separated more or less amicably from Booth, and appears to have had little contact with him after 1898. On his return to Nyasaland he began his own industrial mission. It was after Chilembwe's separation from him that Booth gained the support of the Seventh-Day Adventists for his missionary activity, and he maintained a station at Cholo, some thirty miles from Chilembwe's Providence Industrial Mission at Chiradzulu. Still later, in 1906, Booth met Charles Taze Russell and became for a time an agent for the dissemination of the literature of The Watchtower Bible Society (whose votaries changed their name, years later, in 1931, to Jehovah's Witnesses).

Although the line of influence from Booth to Chilembwe was no longer a strong one, Chilembwe cannot have escaped the growing influence of Christian millennialism arising in Nyasaland. The Scottish Free Church Livingstonia mission 'from 1895 onwards . . . had encouraged the spirit of revivalism among the Lakeside Tonga', and there were expectations of fire coming down (whether in the pentecostal or the adventist sense is not made clear).[104] Booth's adventism was in evidence from 1901, and later his espousal of the more vigorous adventist teachings of the Watchtower movement led to the preaching activity of Elliott Kamwana, a Tongo, who had been educated at Livingstonia Mission, Blantyre, and who had become one of Booth's

[102] This account draws heavily on the detailed study by G. Shepperson and T. Price, *An Independent African: John Chilembwe*, op. cit. On Joseph Booth, see especially, pp. 18–93.
[103] Ibid., p. 116.
[104] George Shepperson, 'Nyasaland and the Millennium', pp. 144–59 in S. L. Thrupp, op. cit., (p. 150).

converts to Seventh-Day Baptist beliefs, and then to Seventh-Day Adventism. For three years Kamwana prophesied the coming end of the world for October 1914 (Russell's own date), but he gradually turned away from orthodox Russellism. His activities caused the authorities to deport him in 1909.[105] He was believed to have baptized some 10,000 Africans into the new faith in this period, and his version of Watchtower teachings reputedly included elements of nativism.[106] Charles Domingo, another pupil of the Livingstonia mission, was a mission worker who became an outspoken critic of the European administration, and who came into contact with both Chilembwe and Booth: his activity was such that the American Seventh-Day Baptist organization withdrew its support from him.[107]

These were all local influences, stemming from essentially Christian sources, but increasingly mixed with new nationalist strivings that Booth had also fostered in considerable measure. Wilder rumours with more nativistic implications also circulated. Chanjiri, a Chikunda prophetess, arose in 1907, foretelling the departure of the Europeans and the abolition of hut-tax.[108] In 1905–6, in German East Africa, the Maji-maji rebellion, in which 12,000 natives had died, had occurred.[109] All of these millennialist disturbances were in the background of Chilembwe's mission work. In addition, he was himself infused with the nationalist sentiments he had learned from Booth, and perhaps also with pan-racial ideas acquired from the American negroes. Marginally, there was also the fact that the Church of Scotland missionaries themselves, as a minority people in their own right, diffused a rather different mission culture, with rather less automatic support of British authority, than was the usual case with English missions.

There were, however, local factors which had perhaps more influence on Chilembwe. He had become acutely aware of the very limited freedom of his people, and had complained about a variety of injustices, ranging from the employment of his compatriots in wars in Ashanti, to the oppressive hut-tax, and his own difficulties in maintaining a church near to the large Bruce estates, which were managed by William J. Livingstone, with whom Chilembwe's relations were always tense. The estate owners burned down the churches of the squatters, and a general sense of suspended hostility prevailed. Even so, we are

[105] G. Shepperson and T. Price, op. cit., p. 153; George Shepperson, 'The Politics of African Separatist Movements in British Central Africa', Africa XXIV (July 1954), pp. 233–46.
[106] G. Shepperson and T. Price, loc. cit. See also R. I. Rotberg, The Rise of Nationalism in Central Africa (Harvard University Press, Cambridge, Mass., 1965), pp. 66–9.
[107] G. Shepperson and T. Price, op. cit., pp. 159, 163, 164.
[108] Ibid., p. 156.
[109] See above, pp. 244–5.

told that, in spite of his growing sense of national consciousness, Chilembwe's orientation was, even in 1911, 'the Booker T. Washington "petit-bourgeois" ideal, not that of the militant revolutionary'.[110] He had several schools, had attempted co-operative schemes, and had provided sewing classes for the women: his efforts were very much towards the creation of independent industrial organization for Africans. Inevitably, such ideals were neither acceptable to, nor understood by, the European planters.

The growing agitation for native representation, and for education, which were being sponsored by Booth and his associates in South Africa, continued in the years just before the First World War. Drought, famine, and the growth of millennial expectations were added to the growing international unrest.[111] But, as Shepperson points out, there was nothing in orthodox Russellism to encourage Africans to prepare for rebellion, even though in the breakaway groups millennialist ideas may have led to too urgent and precipitate an expectation of the end of white rule. In Chilembwe's own following, some probably mixed millennialist hopes with the public protests that Chilembwe made about the repeated burnings of his church by the estate managers and the use of Africans in the war that had now broken out in Europe.[112] But Chilembwe's own plans were essentially for direct rebellion. There was 'nothing of the messiah about him' nor even of the African prophet.[113] His rising was directed against the planters and the European system, and even its leaders saw it as having little chance of success other than as a gesture: it was not mounted to usher in the millennium. Although the rising has been described by the principal authorities as a mixture of religion and politics, its organization was, even though deficient, none the less rationally conceived. In the event it was a brief affair, quickly subdued.

Livingstone was killed and decapitated as one of the first targets, and on the following Sunday his head was displayed to Chilembwe's church congregation. Apart from this, there was little other indication of atavistic practice in the series of actions fought in the rebellion. The women of the Livingstone household were unharmed. There was not even any looting, and the rebels behaved with considerable discipline. Chilembwe had been in touch with the Germans in Tanganyika, and this was another indication of the extent to which, in rebelling, he was

[110] Ibid., pp. 170 and 146.
[111] These circumstances are documented in detail by Shepperson and Price, ibid., pp. 189 ff.
[112] Ibid., pp. 227 and 233–5.
[113] Ibid., p. 263; R. L. Wishlade, *Sectarianism in Southern Nyasaland* (Oxford University Press, London 1965), p. 42, says that no sects in this part of the country are today led by prophets or messiahs.

inspired by practical aims and resorted to expedient measures. That Africans active in the missions were among the principal architects of the movement reflects a consciousness of the possibilities of using the wartime situation to air their grievances rather than any specifically religious inspiration, much less the dominance of millennial ideals. Millennialism was, as we have seen, in the background, and may have fostered a general expectancy of dramatic events leading to a new social order. The wider goals of the movement were obviously vague. The exchange of British for German control (if that were ever envisaged) could hardly have led to the amendment of the conditions which prompted the rising. There were stirrings of nationalism, particularly with the association of members of different tribes, whose members had never previously joined in common action.[114] But this was not a compact of tribal groups so much as an expression of the new importance of voluntary, as against ascriptive, allegiances—a pattern already diffused in the missions themselves, and something basic in the promulgation of Christianity itself.

Religion in the service of secular rebellion: (ii) The Bambata Rising

The Bambata rebellion was so named after its leader, a lesser chief among the Zulus in Natal, who, after several brushes with the colonial authorities, had resisted their attempt to depose him at the time of the first collection of the new poll-tax in South Africa in 1906. The rising was undoubtedly largely a response to the discontent about payment of the new tax (which was designed both as a method of raising revenue and as a way of inducing the natives to take up wage labour, the means by which they could obtain money with which to pay the tax). It may also have been inspired by the desire to achieve a new political arrangement with the colonists, perhaps through the mediation of the British, who were thought to be less disposed to support the colony now

[114] Shepperson and Price, op. cit., should be consulted for details of the course of the rising. They comment extensively on this association of different tribes, pp. 249–52, and compare it with the Maji-maji rebellion. They consider that the profusion of section names has given a misleading impression in that case, however, since all of these tribes belonged to a common cultural tradition (pp. 420–1). The Maji-maji rebellion was, however, a much larger and longer affair than Chilembwe's rising, and embraced more totally most of the tribal groups that were involved, in contrast to the largely mission-based recruitment of Chilembwe's activists. The conscious sense of national identity in Nyasaland was diffused by aliens like Charles Domingo, who followed Swahili linguistic practice in referring to the various tribes as Nyasas: George A. Shepperson, 'External Factors in the Development of African Nationalism with Particular Reference to British Central Africa', Phylon XXII, 3 (Fall 1961), pp. 207–25 (p. 212).

that imperial troops had been withdrawn, after the end of the Boer War.[115] Dinuzulu, the principal leader of the Zulu nation, who probably aspired to restored paramount chieftancy, had experienced much more kindness from the Governor of St Helena during his earlier exile there than he had received at the hands of the colonists, and this may have inspired his faith in the King of England and induced his complicity (which fell short of direct involvement) in the rebellion.

In the background of the rebellion, and among the factors which prompted its first outbreak, was the growing influence of 'Ethiopianism', in the emergence of new independent African churches that had broken away from the missions. Booth's slogan, 'Africa for the Africans', had been widely heard in South Africa, and 'Ethiopian' sermons dwelt on this theme. In the Ethiopian churches, Africans had attained a degree of independence achieved in no other sphere of activity: in the 1890s, for instance, the subjects of Chief Hemuhemu at Trewirgie had fought a successful court action claiming, as Christians, freedom from the control of the chief. It was among these same Christians, members of the African Congregational Church, now independent members of the area of Hemuhemu's son, Chief Mveli, that the first refusal to pay poll-tax occurred, and this touched off the series of action that led to the Bambata rebellion. Ethiopianism supplied a subsidiary ideological stimulus to the rebellion for a considerable number of its active participants, having provided focal points for the communication of protest ever since it first appeared as a religious phenomenon in the preceding decade.[116]

An interim analysis

The cases of Chilembwe in Nyasaland and of the Ethiopian churches in their association with the Bambata rising in South Africa manifest a

[115] These are the conclusions of J. Stuart, *A History of the Zulu Rebellion, 1906* (Macmillan, London 1913), especially pp. 506–7, on which this account principally relies. A short account is also given by E. Roux, op. cit., pp. 87–99. Stuart also mentions as factors in the background of the rebellion the discontents at the growing demands for money payments by the natives, especially for rents (pp. 94–5); the onset of rinderpest in cattle (pp. 92–3); the appearance of the aphis insect, and its threat to the corn harvests (p. 102); and an exceptional, fierce hailstorm which was widely experienced in 1905 (p. 102). Shortly before the rising a curious injunction, strongly anti-white in character, spread among the natives to kill all pigs (animals which Europeans had introduced), all *white* fowls, and to discard all European eating utensils. Those failing to comply would be struck by a thunderbolt (the typical way of referring to an act of a Zulu king). Some natives complied with the order (p. 103).

[116] J. Stuart, op. cit., refers to Ethiopianism as a significant factor (pp. 506, 521). He notes that of 418 Christian natives in Natal jails in July 1907, 214 had been convicted for participation in the rebellion, although this was not the full total of Christian participation (p. 421).

certain parallelism. In both cases religious organizations became the agencies through which overt revolutionary action was co-ordinated. The new African churches were the focal points for both the expression of political discontent and, in these instances, for action towards the elimination of some of its causes. Several important issues arise from this relationship.

(1) Religious agencies had, in many African societies, been associated with political and military decision-making in pre-European times, and, as in the case of the Ndebele and Shona rebellions of 1896 and 1897, and in the Maji-Maji rebellion of 1905–6, religious authorities, in the indigenous religious system, served both to confirm political decisions to make a war, and to promise supernatural assistance in its waging. Thus, at a later stage of development, the association of the independent Christian churches with political and military action was a continuity of earlier patterns of response.

(2) The significance of religious agencies was reinforced when a chief's power was temporarily weakened (as it had been in Matabeleland with the problem of succession in 1896), and, even more manifestly, when chiefly authority as such was weakened, as was increasingly the case in most tribes. In this circumstance, influence passed to other roles, and as mission-trained Africans rose in prestige it passed particularly to these men, many of whom found their first extra-traditional roles in mission service.

(3) The one avenue of mobility open to Africans once the principal political and judicial functions of their societies had been taken over by Europeans, and once military activity had been effectively prohibited, was provided in the service of the missions. This was not simply a matter of restriction of opportunity to Africans, as it is sometimes presented: it was just as fully the imposition of European standards and European styles of socialization on the native population. Since the missions were the providers of education, advance, in the new style of society that was being created, was regarded as a matter both of civilization in mission schools and conversion to the Christian faith.

(4) The independent African churches, whether represented in the Ethiopian movement in South Africa, or in the separatist churches in West Africa, or in the new missions spawned largely by Booth in Central Africa, were manifestations of the desire to control their own affairs by this new African mission-trained élite. The independent churches became (as did the less

westernized thaumaturgical movements) arenas for the struggle for power in a context from which Europeans had been eliminated.

(5) The churches provided a new basis of organization on lines learned from Europeans and employed by Europeans. This authority system challenged tribal structure. The Europeans, although they had increasingly undermined traditional tribal authority, none the less still tried to use it for the enforcement of social control. In a period of discontentment this paradoxical circumstance of European involvement with chiefly authority made tribal structure even less effective, and made chiefly power increasingly difficult to wield. It was a circumstance in which new loci of power could crystallize around the new men in the churches, with their western education.

Here, then, we have a situation which in itself falls outside the paradigm of deviant religious responses that we have established. It has been necessary to examine these cases, however, to make clear the relationship of these patterns of response with religiously associated, but dominantly secular orientations. These movements have grown in the context of religious millennialism, which was a stimulant of expectancy and unrest. It has usually been a necessary conditioning circumstance for movements in cultural conditions of this kind—however sophisticated the leadership—in their recruitment of a clientele. One other case, which appears to combine religious and political elements in yet other proportions, demands at least brief examination.

Mau Mau: a special case

There are two radically divergent interpretations of the *Mau Mau* movement. Those strongly supporting African independence, who condemned European settlement in Africa and who have generally favoured a left-wing interpretation of history, have regarded Mau Mau as a phase in an African form of the class struggle in which races had become classes. According to this view, the stories circulated about Mau Mau, and particularly attribution of its military activity to the inspiration of witch-doctors and traditional oath-administrators, was simply an official attempt to bring into opprobrium a spontaneous movement of an exploited African people seeking independence. Europeans, in fear or cunning, exaggerated the significance of the administration of an oath of allegiance and depicted it as a symbol of bestiality and perversion. The opposite view, which informed both the military action of the authorities and their attempts to rehabilitate detainees, was that the movement, although politically controlled, recruited its rank-and-file following by employing practices which drew on and elaborated pre-European rituals, and by invoking superstitious, if not magical, sanctions to coerce Kikuyu tribesmen to support the campaign. Thus religious techniques and ideas were disseminated to justify political and military action, to enforce discipline and control among the fighters, and to sustain support for them among the population at large.

The relations of the Kikuyu, the largest and most advanced tribe in Kenya, with the British authorities had been marked by a prolonged and complex distrust arising from a number of causes. Most important was the dispute over land. Different conceptions of land-ownership had facilitated the annexation of land as crown land by the British of uninhabited areas which, however, although not occupied, the Kikuyu regarded as inalienably the possession of their people. The population of white settlers in the highlands grew, but so did the Kikuyu population. A squatter system developed, with Kikuyu settling at the fringes of white estates, with an increasingly complex system of relationships. The attempts at settlement of land problems by, for example, the Land Commission of 1929, left the Kikuyu unsatisfied, and the land question came to occupy a psychological significance of importance disproportionate to the relatively small part of Kikuyu land that had actually been expropriated by white settlers. But evictions occurred, in the interest both of European acquisition of land, and of inducing Kikuyu to take up wage labour. A tax system was introduced in the early 1920s which was also designed to induce the natives to take up wage work.[117] A landless proletariat was brought into being.[118] The situation was made worse by deportations of population which the government enforced from time to time, when squatter populations became too numerous in particular areas.

Kikuyu tribal customs included practices which had met the strongest opposition of the missionaries, in particular the strictly circumscribed, but *apparently* promiscuous, pre-marital *ngweko*, fondling, which took place in the bachelor huts; the non-burial of the dead;

---

[117] For a general account, see F. B. Welbourn, *East African Rebels* (SCM Press, London 1961), pp. 117 ff.

[118] This point is given special emphasis by W. E. Mühlmann, 'Die Mau Mau Bewegung in Kenya', *Politische Vierteljahrschrift* 2, 1 (March 1961), pp. 56–87; see p. 66. See also W. E. Mühlmann, *Chiliasmus und Nativismus*, op. cit., pp. 105–40.

the *ngomas*, dances, which appeared highly lascivious; and most especially the practice of female circumcision, cliteridectomy.[119] The missionaries of the Church of Scotland inaugurated a strong campaign for the prohibition of female circumcision in the 1920s, but without at all appreciating the psychological importance of this initiation, without which a woman was ineligible for marriage.[120] Bride-price and polygyny were also the custom among the Kikuyu, and the missionaries were as intolerant of these practices among the Kikuyu as they were among any pre-literate peoples, but it was their opposition to female circumcision which was of most significance in alienating many Kikuyu and in stimulating the growth of independent Kikuyu churches,[121] and, since the churches were intimately associated with the schools, with the establishment of independent schools.[122]

Kikuyu responses to this situation were multiform, and from surprisingly early dates, and particularly as a consequence of the discontents of ex-servicemen after the First World War, political associations were formed for the reassertion of, first, tribal, and later native (eventually called 'African') rights.[123] Subsequently the independent schools movement—schools controlled by Kenyans and not by the missionaries—arose, and did so in association with separatist churches: the Kikuyu Independent Schools Association, which became associated with the African Independent Pentecostal Church, and the Kikuyu

[119] The ignorance of missionaries in regard to Kikuyu customs is brought out by Jomo Kenyatta, *Facing Mount Kenya* (Secker and Warburg, London 1938), pp. 153–4. For the *ngweko* customs, see ibid., pp. 157–60. For a discussion of Kikuyu initiation ceremonial, see W. S. and K. Routledge, *With a Pre-historic People: The Akikuyu of British East Africa* (Arnold, London 1910), pp. 151–67. The Kikuyu also practised male circumcision, but this was not an object of missionary disapproval, for although through long periods of Christian history this form of ritual mutilation was thought of as the mark of the Jew, by the 1920s it had, on (somewhat dubious) medical grounds, become acceptable to Christians in Britain and the U.S.A. (without, of course, having any ritual significance).

[120] J. Kenyatta, op. cit., p. 132, wrote 'No proper Gikuyu would dream of marrying a girl who has not been properly circumcised, and vice versa' and again (p. 133), 'in the tribal psychology of the Gikuyu . . . this operation is still regarded as the very essence of an institution which has enormous educational, social, moral, and religious implications . . .'.

[121] F. B. Welbourn, op. cit., pp. 138 ff.

[122] Ibid., pp. 144 ff.

[123] See Carl G. Rosberg and John Nottingham, *The Myth of 'Mau-Mau': Nationalism in Kenya* (Praeger, New York 1966), p. 112–33, for discussion of the role of the Kikuyu Central Association in mobilizing political support for the continuance of female circumcision. The KCA contested elections in the name of maintaining native customs: Kenyatta was its secretary in the late 1920s.

The attempt to extend the cause, for which the Kikuyu organized, to other tribal groups is evident from the change of name of their political organizations over time. The Kikuyu Central Association of the 1920s emphasized the tribe: the Kenya African Union of the 1940s emphasized both nation and race. But Mau Mau returned to essentially Kikuyu practices in its oathing ceremonies and never succeeded in drawing in other tribes except the Meru and the Embu, who are closely related to the Kikuyu, and in lesser measure the Kamba.

Karing'a Education Association, which became associated with the African Orthodox Church.[124] These were far from being the first native religious responses to cultural contact in Kenya, but they were in general both more concerned with education and more consciously political than most of the earlier movements, many of which had arisen among the Luo and Kisii in western Kenya.[125] One of the most conspicuously nativistic of these cults was *Mumbo*.[126] It recrudesced from time to time.[127]

Among the Kikuyu, prophet movements arose in the late 1920s, particularly, it appears, in response to the missionary prohibition on cliteridectomy. The most spectacular of these movements was the

[124] F. B. Welbourn, op. cit., p. 144.

[125] One of those with some educational and political concern, the *Nomia Luo Mission*, sprang up as early as 1907, when John Owala, formerly a Roman Catholic, emerged as a prophet. He organized his own primary schools and wanted representation on local councils, but the central focus of his movement was to preach circumcision to the Luo, who, unlike the Bantu tribes of Kenya, did not practice it. See, B. A. Ogot, 'British Administration in the Central Nyanza District of Kenya, 1900–60, *Journal of African History*, IV, 2 (1963), pp. 249–73 (pp. 256–7); and L. J. Beecher, 'African Separatist Churches in Kenya', *World Dominion*, XXXI, 1 (January/February, 1953) pp. 5–12.

[126] Mumbo began in what is today called Central Nyanza in 1913, when Onyango Dunde claimed to have been swallowed by a serpent in Lake Victoria, which, on spewing him up again, revealed itself as the God of Africans. Christianity was condemned; long hair and the use of skins for clothes was advocated; and washing was to be abandoned. Europeans were the enemies, and their cultural artefacts were to be avoided. At a future time the Europeans would disappear: then 'there will be no more need to work. I will cause cattle, sheep and goats to come up out of the lake in great numbers to those who believe in me, but all unbelievers, and their families and cattle, will die out'.—Nyangweso (pseud.), 'The Cult of Mumbo in Central and South Kavirondo', *Journal of East Africa and Uganda Natural History Society*, 38/39 (May–August 1930), pp. 13–17.

[127] In spite of arrests, the cult spread to Kisii, and tribesmen were enjoined not to cultivate, and to consume female stock. A faith cure, effected by a piece of grass tied round the neck, was prescribed. Later investigations in 1915 by the Assistant District Commissioner revealed that possession with trembling and glossalalia occurred. The idea of the coming of the Germans [from Tanganyika] had been added, but the injunctions against cultivation and the killing of cattle were now denied. Respect for elders was strongly enjoined. The cult was said to be growing, and forty Mumboists were detained by the authorities: they were, however, cleared of charges of assaulting eight Seventh-Day Adventist mission boys (of whom the Asst. D.C. had a poor opinion)—*Kenyan National Archives*, DC/KS 3/2, 21 July, 1915. The cult made greatest appeal to older people, and skins were worn by them, according to Pastor Isaac Okeyo, a retired Seventh-Day Adventist pastor, in an interview with the author, 22 August, 1972. In 1918, the D.C. and the Provincial Commissioner disagreed about the political significance of Mumboism, although the D.C. reported that the leaders were still preaching that the whites would soon leave, and that Mumbo would provide food for the faithful. Credulous Kisii tribesmen had paid 155 head of cattle and 98 sheep to the leading preachers to ensure their own salvation: *Archives*, op. cit., DC/KS 3/2, 28 November, 1918. *Bhang*-smoking, communal ownership of women, and incest among Mumboists was reported periodically from 1918 onwards, and Mumbo priests exacted fees for performing cures. Among the Luo, the cult added new practices to traditional sun-worship. In the 1930s, a cult-enclosure existed with a 'phallic' altar-pillar. In 1934, the Mumboists disturbed a local sports-meeting: *Archives*, op. cit., 16 April 1920; 17 August 1921; 6 July 1930; 18 April 1934; and Nyangweso op. cit. The cult was apparently still active in the 1950s, since the Kenyan authorities issued an order for its proscription—*East African Standard*, 17 September, 1954.

Watu wa Mungu, People of God, who refused to wear European clothes, repudiated all foreign customs, and rejected foreign articles and utensils.[128] They claimed direct power from 'Mwene-Nyaga', God, ability to communicate with the spirits of the ancestral dead, and the ability to heal the sick. The prophets of the movement roamed about the countryside, and over time they came to have a reputation for acts of terrorism. Their ritual was to pray with hands upraised facing Mount Kenya, to imitate the howls of lions and leopards whilst in prayer, and eventually to experience trembling at the onset of spiritual power. The weapons which they carried, symbolic of their onslaught against evil spirits, may also have been symbolic of their opposition to Europeans.[129] They maintained passive opposition to medical aid, disease prevention, and soil conservation measures.[130] Eventually a sub-cult, *Dina ya Jesu Kristo*, displayed more extreme Kikuyu nationalism, inveighing not simply against the enemies of God, but against the enemies of the Kikuyu people: but both cults had arisen from the protest against the missions and the mission campaigns for legislation against tribal practices.[131] This sect became a semi-violent group, reputedly given to rituals in which human blood was drunk, although direct evidence on this matter is not forthcoming. But the movement appears to have had something of the character of a special society, if not a secret society, of prophets, and although the rejection of European clothing was not sustained by the movement in the 1940s, periodic acts of violence continued.[132]

Throughout the inter-war years the political activity of relatively

[128] J. Kenyatta, op. cit., pp. 273–9. Kenyatta is not very well informed on the influence of other African movements, however, and confuses 'Ethiopianism' with the Watchtower movement. D. H. Rawcliffe, *The Struggle for Kenya* (Gollancz, London 1954), pp. 30–5.

[129] D. H. Rawcliffe, op. cit., p. 31. J. Kenyatta, op. cit., pp. 278–9, rejects the idea that their weapons had any other than spiritual significance.

[130] These orientations were also evident among the *Dina ya Msambwa*, the cult of the Spirits of the Dead, which had arisen under the leadership of Elijah Masinde, a Suk, who had been expelled from the Friends African Mission for polygyny, and who sought to persuade his thousands of followers to return to traditional practices. Maternity centres were to be avoided—it was said that they prevented child-bearing; soil conservation measures were also attacked. Masinde said Europeans must leave Kenya: the natives must have an African king. A subsequent leader, Lucas Pkiech, promised eternal life to those who would fight the Europeans. He claimed to heal miraculously and conducted meetings with ecstatic dancing. He and twenty-eight other Suk tribesmen were killed in a clash with the police. The cult was active throughout the 1940s. In February 1948 Masinde invoked the spirits of the fallen of the Kitosh tribe to rise and drive the British from the land. At Malakasi, eleven Kitosh sectarians were killed in a battle with police. D. H. Rawcliffe, op. cit., pp. 28–9. The sect was active in Uganda, too; L. C. Usher-Wilson in 'Dina Ya Msambwa', *Uganda Journal* 16, 2 (September 1952), pp. 125–9, attributes arson and riots at various places in Uganda to the sectarians, whose leaders promised them special protection from European bullets.

[131] D. H. Rawcliffe, op. cit., pp. 32–5.

[132] J. Kenyatta, op. cit., pp. 277–9, suggests that the prophets, *arathi*, were not interested in political activities. D. H. Rawcliffe, loc. cit., has a very different interpretation.

small numbers of politically conscious Kikuyu persisted, and they were at times able to mobilize considerable bodies of support. The independent school associations, where the standards of education were certainly extremely low, became politically organized centres of Kikuyu nationalist propaganda. In these, in their incipient political associations, and in the independent churches, the Kikuyu were steadily forging a set of institutions which, however modest, were alternatives to those established by the dominant white society and the missions. The defence of native practices had been a rallying ground, but over time, as is evident from the abandonment by the Watu wa Mungu of their original injunction against European clothing, these essentially tribal restorative elements became less significant in the protest movements, and particularly so in the urban areas. But the issue of the land remained. European medical practice led to the growth of population, and this circumstance, and the government attempt to introduce stock reduction of cattle (itself in the long-run interests of the Kikuyu, of course) aggravated the problem. In the post-war years the Kenyans became increasingly dependent on wage labour, while African income from the market economy grew only very slowly. After the Second World War the wave of returned soldiers reinforced discontent, and strike activity and supra-tribal, social, and vocational organizations sprang into being. The independence of India, Pakistan, and Burma—countries whose affairs were of interest, because of the presence of Indians in Kenya and the knowledge of Gandhi's teachings—and the prospects of increased African representation in the government of the Gold Coast, were further stimulants to the small Kenyan intelligentsia, whose grievances over land issues now passed to wider concerns and the vision of independence for Kenya. The Kenya African Union, the virtual successor to the old, proscribed Kikuyu Central Association, emerged, with Kenyatta as its President, in 1947.[133]

The first reports of a Kikuyu secret society, with rumours of oath-administration and the aim of eliminating Europeans, perhaps by murder, were received by the government in 1947.[134] The use of the oath itself was, of course, an inheritance from the Kikuyu past. Oaths, reinforcing moral and religious obligation, had played an extremely important part in tribal life. Writing long before the emergence of Mau Mau, Kenyatta had pointed to their functions in preventing people from giving false evidence, and 'in bringing offenders to justice through guilty conscience and confession. . . . Among the Kikuyu

[133] This paragraph relies heavily on the account given in Carl G. Rosberg and John Nottingham, op. cit., pp. 194–217.
[134] F. D. Corfield, *Historical Survey of the Origins and Growth of Mau Mau* (Her Majesty's Stationery Office [Colonial Office Cmnd. 1030], London 1960), pp. 72 and 267.

there were three important forms of *oaths which were so terribly feared, morally and religiously,* that no one dared to take them unless he was perfectly sure and beyond any doubt that he was innocent or that his claim was genuine.'[135] A secret mass oath-taking had occurred as early as 1939 to enforce discipline among the landless squatters of Olenguruone whom the government had re-settled.[136] It became the instrument by which new solidarity was emphasized, and the oath of the Kikuyu Central Association, originally taken on the Bible, became an oath using older Kikuyu emblems, which involved the use of sacrificial animals.

To what extent oath-taking was consciously promulgated as a means of creating a mass nationalist party is open to dispute.[137] The oaths were administered by religious functionaries, and their essentially religious effect was described by one oath-taker as 'a mixture of fear and elation . . . I felt exalted with new power and strength'. He called it 'spiritual rebirth'.[138] Leaders who conceived their own ends as

[135] J. Kenyatta, op. cit., p. 223 (my italics).
[136] C. G. Rosberg and J. Nottingham, op. cit., p. 245.
[137] C. G. Rosberg and J. Nottingham, op. cit., say that 'a colony-wide nationalist organization was slow to take root and indeed had hardly done so by the outbreak of the emergency' [1952], p. 219. The oath administered in Kikuyu Central Association was used to draw people into such a nationalist movement (p. 248). They see the Kenya African Union (founded 1944) as the main stimulus for conspiratorial and constitutional politics, with a 'parliament' to control and co-ordinate political action (pp. 263–4). The oath they see as a way of overcoming social fragmentation, with prayers to Ngai (Mwene-Nyaga), God of the Kikuyu, and other religious elements (p. 259). The implications, it seems, are that the oath-taking and religious elements were consciously promoted and co-ordinated for political ends. One of those who took two oaths, and was detained for several years throughout the emergency, has a different interpretation, declaring that, 'There was no central direction or control. The oath was not sophisticated or elaborate, and initially was wholly unobjectionable. It started slowly, indeed regretfully, and was an oath of unity and brotherhood in the struggle for our land and our independence. It eventually spread all over the country. . . .' It was a grassroots movement, according to this writer, Josiah Mwangi Kariuki, in '*Mau Mau' Detainee* (Oxford University Press, London 1963), p. 22. F. D. Corfield, op. cit., p. 269, suggests that the Kenya African Union 'had become almost synonymous with Mau Mau'. C. G. Rosberg and N. Nottingham, op. cit,. p. 261, say that many of the KAU members had taken the oath, but J. M. Kariuki, op. cit., p. 19, denies that the movement called 'Mau Mau' was the same organization as either the KAU or the old Kikuyu Central Association. Kenyatta was sentenced for allegedly sponsoring the Mau Mau movement. His involvement is not our concern: certainly he dismissed officials of the Limuru branch of the Kenya African Union who had condemned Mau Mau for not knowing what KAU policy was: subsequently he closed the branch. F. D. Corfield, op. cit., pp. 128–9. He always denied knowledge of Mau Mau, saying that he did not know the words: when asked by the government to condemn the movement, he was always evasive, and his words, it has been suggested, were always ambiguous. He was reputedly a master of *double entendre*, to which the Kikuyu language, of which he had great command, lent itself. F. D. Corfield, op. cit., pp. 103–4, 304; C. G. Rosberg and J. Nottingham, op. cit., p. 269; on Kenyatta's mastery of Kikuyu language, J. M. Kariuki, op. cit., p. 11, says that on Kenyatta's return in 1946, some believed that he would, after so long a period abroad, have forgotten the language, but 'the doubters found that he knew more old Kikuyu phrases than they had ever heard.'
[138] J. M. Kariuki, op. cit., p. 27.

political may have found it necessary to use religious forms and religious sanctions quite consciously to mobilize a sufficient body of more ignorant Kikuyu for a terrorist guerilla campaign. Alternatively, remote political objectives may necessarily and spontaneously have been translated into religious terms that were commonly understood. What is evident, however, is that the Mau Mau movement, as the organization that emerged through the diffusion of oath-taking rituals became known, owed nothing to direct millennialist preaching, in the typical pattern of religious revolutionist and transformative movements. In some of its forms it shows continuities of concern with the earlier prophet movements, but it stood in perhaps closer relationship with more acute and directly political organizations.

Despite the abundant literature, the exact character of the movement that came to be called Mau Mau remains obscure.[139] It was an organization of guerillas and their supporters, who were bound together by oaths undertaken with traditional symbolism, and who appear also to have cemented their unity by other religious and traditional practices, such as age-group greetings and hymn-singing (with words sympathetic to Mau Mau and promises that blood would be shed to set the people free).[140] Kariuki, who was involved, implicitly denies that the movement was more than an independence movement, and presents it as almost a spontaneous uprising of the Kikuyu.[141] Rosberg and Nottingham go further and suggest that the myth of Mau Mau as a movement made it possible for the authorities to ignore the difference between the form and the meaning of the oath. The authorities became preoccupied with the traditional oathing procedure, and obscured the significance of the oath as an organizational weapon in the context of mass mobilization for political action: thus these authors reject the distinction of political and religious elements.[142] Others saw Mau Mau as a movement with a continuity from the past: thus, Fr Trevor Huddleston declared it to be 'wholly evil', and said, 'It has about it all

[139] Kenyatta said that Mau Mau was a new word: 'The Elders do not know it' (F. D. Corfield, op. cit., p. 304). J. M. Kariuki, op. cit., p. 23, says the word was an anagram of *uma uma*, given as a word of warning at an oath ceremony that was broken up by the police. C. G. Rosberg and J. Nottingham, op. cit., p. 333, say it may have been a corruption of the word *muma*, the word used for the most general oath among the Kikuyu (see also J. Kenyatta, op. cit., p. 223, for the description of this oath in its traditional usage).

[140] F. D. Corfield, op. cit., p. 100; C. G. Rosberg and J. Nottingham, op. cit., pp. 259–61.

[141] J. M. Kariuki, op. cit., pp. 22, 33. He maintains that there were only two legitimate oaths, both of which he describes. According to F. D. Corfield, op. cit., p. 167, General Nderitu, a Mau Mau leader, said that there were ultimately seven oaths among the men in the forest (where Kariuki did not serve), and also cannibalism.

[142] C. G. Rosberg and J. Nottingham, op. cit., pp. 320, 333, 353. But they also suggest, p. 301, that, 'As the isolation of the forest groups became more absolute . . . the small groups that were left . . . came increasingly to rely on the use of prophets for predictive purposes. New oaths were employed to maintain morale and discipline.'

the horror of the powers of darkness; of spiritual wickedness in high places', a verdict that emphasizes magic and witchcraft beliefs, and one in which Corfield concurs.[143] Rawcliffe has maintained, 'At first, Mau Mau was not basically a political movement, but a fanatical and atavistic semi-religious cult which aimed at restoring the old order that had preceded the coming of the British.'[144] Gradually, it became a political movement. Leakey, the son of one of the principal missionaries in Kenya and himself a great authority on the Kikuyu, held that Mau Mau was more than a movement seeking the restoration of the land and the elimination of the English, and that it was in fact a religion, which used Old Testament customs in augmentation of traditional Kikuyu practices. As a religion Mau Mau could succeed, whereas the political organizations had had only limited success.[145] Mühlmann sees political and religious elements meeting, and emphasizes the importance of the African initiation and the secret society as a model of organization.[146] Such societies had existed in the past, merging religious functions and terrorist extortion of money for their ends.[147] The compulsory oathing of tribesmen of the Kikuyu and associated tribes,[148] which became a principal preoccupation of the authorities, was a procedure with religious antecedents for the mobilization of tribesmen for political and military goals.

The political scientists, and the Kenyan intelligentsia for whose motivations political scientists are likely to have most regard, see Mau

[143] Cited in F. D. Corfield, op. cit., pp. 162, 284.

[144] D. H. Rawcliffe, op. cit., p. 35.

[145] L. S. B. Leakey, *Defeating Mau Mau* (Methuen, London 1954) pp. 21, 41. In his earlier work, *Mau Mau and the Kikuyu* (Methuen, London 1952), written before the Mau Mau campaign developed into an emergency, Leakey had tended to see Mau Mau as a continuity with the earlier Kikuyu political associations. In the later book, he recognized the religious character of Mau Mau, the strength of the oath in binding tribesmen, and the force of Kikuyu religious symbolism. He then regarded the Kenya African Union as a cover organization, pp. 53 ff.

[146] W. E. Mühlmann, op. cit.; idem, 'Die Mau Mau Bewegung . . .', op. cit., p. 56.

[147] D. H. Rawcliffe, op. cit., p. 30, provides a brief account of two such societies, *Kagitha*, and *Athi*, among the Meru, a tribe closely related to the Kikuyu. The Kagitha society defied tribal custom largely for sexual amusements, employing vengeance against those who interfered. The Athi society, which had originally undertaken functions of supplying meat when game was scarce, also developed into a powerful terrorist association, employing formidable oath ceremonies with fierce sanctions. 'A special class of medicine man was employed to get rid of the effects of [the Athi oath] by ritual cleaning ceremonies', loc. cit. (The employment of medicine-men to undo coercive Mau Mau oaths was later sponsored by the authorites in the campaign against Mau Mau.)

[148] J. M. Kariuki, op. cit., p. 32, says that oath may sometimes have been forced, although he considers that this was less common than the government suggested. Since he affirms that there was no central control, he is not in a strong position to say what variations of procedure may have occurred. F. D. Corfield, op. cit., p. 167, provides some evidence from those who were forced to take the oath, and of the specific details of some of the oath administration of the more extreme rituals.

Mau as a political enterprise, although they may differ in their estima-
tions of the extent to which it was a consciously organized resistance
movement. The missionaries and those under mission influence were
impressed by the religious aspects of the movement, and believe that
its vigour came more from religiously-induced fear of the oath (which
Kenyatta had himself described) than from the conscious ends of the
leaders. The sociologists have tended to see a convergence of political
ends and religious dispositions. That Mau Mau took the form it did,
employing traditional religious means to recruit or coerce a membership, suggests that it achieved its success at least partly on the strength
of traditional religious dispositions that had recurrently outcropped in
Kenya. That it became militant, and closely associated with the
membership of the Kenya African Union, whatever distinction prevailed between the two organizations, suggests that it was 'used',
locally if not centrally (but perhaps also centrally) to pursue the aims
that the Kenya African Union also embraced. The religious force of the
oaths, and they appear to have evolved into elaborate desecrations of
normal taboos (which is often the character of oaths[149]) gave power to
the leaders to mount a campaign of depredation, arson, and murder.
But, unlike some of the other cases that we have considered, this was
direct action without the expectation of supernatural intervention.

Conclusion

We have now seen several different cases of the association of religious
movements and military action. The cases of outright war at the
instigation of or with the auxiliary blessings of a prophet, occur in
circumstances where tribal peoples are still unconquered, and where
there is not yet too great a disparity between the power that they can
mobilize and that of the invader. Among the South African tribes in
the earlier part of the nineteenth century, sheer numbers—even one
people could muster an army of ten thousand or more—were pitted
against small forces of Europeans with modern weapons. Tribes among
North American Indians and among the Maoris were, of course, much
smaller, and leadership over large numbers, and sometimes even within
one tribe, was difficult to assert. Yet only by association was warfare

[149] J. M. Kariuki, op. cit., p. 33, rejects various descriptions of oath ceremonies, for
example those using menstrual blood, since this was sacred to the Kikuyu and abuse of it a
sin. Oaths, however, usually acquire their sanction from the dramatic juxtaposition of the
highly sacred and the profane in a situation regarded as very specially licensed for what
would, in any other context, be a highly profane act.

possible. The role of the prophet varied accordingly. Whereas among the Xhosa tribes the prophets were almost like court counsellors to particular chiefs, the role of the more prominent prophets among the North American Indians, the Delaware Prophet and Tenskwatawa, was to provide a focal point for inter-tribal unity, which could be achieved when a leader of ability and imagination arose to use the supernatural message. Among the Maoris, too, prophetism became a basis of unity (though it was only one basis, and a more consciously political basis was contemporaneously canvassed).

Thus prophetism became a vital element in itself, set over in the scale against the power of the invader. Prophets both claimed supernatural power and in the temporary unification of tribes achieved a manifestation of power. The promised miracle was in some measure attained by the belief in it, and men's willingness to act in accordance with the promise. Prophetism was not, however, the only style of supernatural assistance. In the Maji-maji rebellion several tribes united (even though they *were* tribes of one cultural complex) in acceptance of a more rudimentary form of supernatural aid, a new medicine, which was to turn bullets into water. This is a widespread promise of sorcerers and prophets who seek supernatural aid in the struggle against invaders: it is the attempt to cope with the principal agency of the white man's power, the cardinal manifestation of his superior magic. It is entirely understandable that bullets should present the principal challenge to the religious functionaries of tribal peoples. Where priests lack the power, prophets sometimes claim to possess it. But priests or prophets were seeking the equivalent of the philosopher's stone, and its utility was to be not gold, but protection from the culture of the white man and from the most potent form of his magic. That this promise was typically associated with another—the restoration of the life of the past, by magical and associated military means—is not surprising.

Four principal cases among these religiously-inspired revolutions may be distinguished. (We refer to the cases reviewed in this chapter, in which active military enterprise has been mounted, and not to transformative or revolution*ist* movements in general.)

(1) There are those movements in which supernatural claims are made that a restoration of the tribal order, the old way of living, and the extrusion of invaders, can be achieved by magical means. There may be a rejection of all European goods. Sometimes these ideas may involve marginal millennial promises, but the pre-existing religious system is not deliberately superseded. The agents are traditional religious functionaries, or assimilate

to such roles, as in the risings among the Ndebele and Shona, the Yakañ cult, and the Maji-maji rebellion.

(2) There are movements which arise in association with the super-natural claims of new prophecies and visions, and in which new injunctions are specified. Even though some elements may have been absorbed from Christianity, the new faith is claimed as a religion for the natives. New agents arise who, if they were medicine-men previously, now claim a new revelation and abandon previous practices. Prophecy may not previously have been part of their function. The newness of the message and its strong millennialist element facilitate the drawing together of tribes previously unassociated or hostile. The movements arising around the Delaware Prophet, Tenskwatawa, and Te Ua exemplify this constellation.

(3) There are secular military actions which use religious agencies for organization, recruitment, and dissemination of information and ideology. Restoration of a former way of life is not now the focus, but rather independence in political and social organization, which may be inspired by already attained religious independence in the style of the dominant culture. Religious rights precede social, economic, and political rights, in the history of most colonially dominated peoples, particularly where the anti-authoritarian elements in Protestant Christianity have been disseminated. Millennial ideas may provide a context of expectation, but with emphasis on their application to the political and secular situation rather than their supernaturalist connotations. Tribal distinctions become irrelevant in the mobilization for this type of revolutionary endeavour: the new voluntaristic allegiance of Christianity becomes the model. The leaders are a new élite, the religious agents of the new order, but also typically the best educated and most progressive members of the indigenous society. John Chilembwe and his associates in the Nyasaland rising of 1915, and, albeit less clearly, the 'Ethiopian' leaders who joined the Bambata rebellion, are examples.

(4) There is the case in which religious sanctions from the past become associated—spontaneously or by design—with secular revolutionary activity. There is no promised millennium nor any explicit promise of a return to the religious order of the past, but the use of past procedures, the promise of rectification of wrongs, and new advantages, satisfy both atavistic and progressive demands. The discontented, whether they attribute their suffer-

ings to the disruption of past order or the inadequacies and tardiness of the new order, can both be mobilized. The atavistic element, as it was found in the Mau Mau movement, limited the extent to which rebellion could be diffused beyond one tribe and those sharing its cultural tradition. Leaders were drawn from both sophisticates and illiterates, who had contrasting and segregated roles to perform. The bond uniting them was identity with a tribal nation and the persisting acknowledgement, even among sophisticates, of the latent power of tribal practices: they were not welded by any more abstract ideological orientation.

Some of our cases do not easily fit into these divergent patterns. Movements do not spring fully fledged, coherent in aim and style from specific social contexts. Each movement inherits a specific set of pre-conditions; styles of leadership; specific patterns of myth; styles of socialization and social action; and degrees of cultural forwardness and forbearance. There are particular geographic, economic, and social determinants of contact, which may include the expropriation of land; the enrolment of native labour; the impress of taxes; the inter-ference with tribal customs; the impact of missions; the diffusion of alcohol; the spread of European diseases. All of these factors and others, such as styles of diffusion of cult ideas and the imitation of one movement by another, make anything more than a broad indication of types of association of religious and military responses impossible. None the less, these general patterns are worth distinguishing and relating to the social circumstances in which they appear.

9

Collective Redemption

REVOLUTIONIST religious responses appear to be manifested in three broad stages of culture contact with less-developed people, although these stages do not occur among all peoples.

(1) In the early stage of culture contact, whilst resistance is still feasible, revolutionist religious orientations appear as prophecies in encouragement of military enterprise. A millennium is promised, and in particular that the ancestors will assist in battle and will abundantly replenish the foodstores of men at war (the destruction of existing herds and crops is a frequent test of faith). Superior magic is promised with which the power of the invader will be counteracted and, in particular, with which the effect of his weapons will be neutralized.

(2) When warfare has failed, revolutionist orientations become more totally religious: reliance is now placed entirely on supernatural action. (It may well be that this is itself a distinct stage of religious development, in which practical techniques have been entirely abandoned for wish-fulfilment at super-empirical levels by institutionalized symbolic acts.) Visions of a transformed society, and especially of a restored society, constitute the revolutionist response.

(3) In the third stage, when the permanence of the alien order has become apparent, the relationships of the invader and the conquered begin to settle in some way. The acquisition of the alien culture now becomes a real possibility for the conquered, and according to the relations of the two groups, their relative size, settlement, and power, so religious responses vary.

(a) When conquerors dominate completely, expropriate the land, reduce the indigenes to minority status, segregation, and inferiority, revolutionism disappears: such has been the case in North America and New Zealand.

(b) Where the power and the technical and educational superiority of the invader remains immensely greater than that of the indigenes, but without the developments set out in (a), imitation, by sympathetic magic and in more practical ways occurs, as among peoples in Melanesia. Revolutionism persists, but the preoccupation is less with magical restoration of the past than with magical acquisition of the artefacts of the new culture.

(c) Where social structure has been radically changed, and where social organization is directly administered in accordance with the requirements and preconceptions of the invaders, but where exploitation has been through extractive industries rather than through settlement, radical movements arise, often in association with religion, and sometimes taking distinctly religious forms. The degree of control exercised by the invader over social situations may, as other forms of organization are suppressed, unintentionally encourage religious revolutionism. Revolutionist ideologies may be disseminated with the rest of alien culture, and become effective agencies of change among the less-developed people themselves (in the case of missionaries like Booth in Nyasaland, or through the diffusion of Watchtower ideas in the Rhodesias).

(d) Where settlers persist in uneasy symbiosis with the indigenes who are the majority, but whose power is effectively neutralized, we see muted revolutionism, as in the declining radicalism of the 'Ethiopian' churches of South Africa.

(e) Where settlement has not been prominent, as in West Africa, we see very little revolutionist religion, and what there is, is largely imported.

This paradigm conceals the diversity of individual cases, of course: mutually contradictory aims often persist in the ideology of a movement, and sometimes divergent goals are simultaneously embraced even by the leaders. Stages are creations of the analyst: they do not inhere in the process of social change. There are regressions to earlier patterns of response within any given movement. and there are anticipations of new patterns of action. The new rational men sometimes lapse into magic, and the old magicians sometimes have uncanny perception of the practical steps that must be taken to achieve their ends. Nor are populations homogenous in these respects: as culture contact increases, and as mobility and diversity of experience occurs, so natives become more highly differentiated and individuated in their awareness of the world. The same movement may thus recruit very differently oriented people, traditionalists or progressives, mystics or activists. Since the goals of such movements are not usually articulated intellectually, these disparities of commitment and assumption need not cause disintegration. The very voluntarism that characterizes new movements is itself a new basis of association. It facilitates increasing self-selection (although self-selection alone does not ensure homogeneity of disposition, intellect or social awareness, at least until men can distinguish facts from values and emotions, and can intellectually appraise their goals and the means appropriate for their realization). The mixture of motivations within movements even in western society is often considerable; but where motivations are prompted by vague wishes and dreams that cannot be adequately expressed, the diversity is inevitably greater, if, simultaneously, less consequential. But a movement as such might create new unities, and in this sense might revitalize a culture. Cultural revitalization is most likely when a movement's dominant orientation is restorative. In practice, of course, much of what the movement regards as the past which it is to restore, is a synthesis of traditional elements and more recently acquired items which have become regarded as 'traditional'.

Militant and quiescent prophets

The second stage of contact, in which warfare has failed, gives rise to religious revolutionism of which we have seen the incipient manifestations among the North American Indians, among whom prophetism was a common phenomenon in the nineteenth century. The militaristic millennialism of the earlier prophets only continued near to the frontier where warfare was still a possibility, and is exemplified in Nakai' dokli'ni, an Apache medicine-man who, in his brief career in 1881, promised to raise the dead, and who prophesied that the whites would soon be driven from the land, and in Cheez-tah-Paezh, a Crow medicine-man, who, in 1887, asserted his own invulnerability, and who died leading a demonstration against the government.[1] It occurred dramatically among the Comanches, whose way of life was under severe threat in the 1870s, when the buffalo herds were fast diminishing, when Ishatai ('Coyote Droppings'), a young warrior medicine-man, who had 'proved' his own immunity to bullets and had 'raised the dead', arose in 1873. The Comanches had resisted confinement in the reservation at Fort Sill, which they were to share with Kiowa and Kiowa-Apaches: some bands were still raiding, and the young men were still seeking prestige in war. Ishatai claimed to have communed with the

---

[1] James Mooney, *The Ghost Dance* . . ., op. cit., p. 704, on Nakai' dokli'ni and p. 706 on Cheez-tah-Paezh.

Great Spirit, and he successfully predicted the appearance of a comet, to be followed by a long summer drought.[2] He succeeded in gathering all the Comanches together—a feat which the great chiefs had never been able to do in the past—to perform the *Sun Dance*, in which all but one band, the Swift Stingers, joined. This was a wholly new venture for the Comanches, although they had watched the Kiowa sun dances and those of the Cheyenne for many years.[3] A buffalo herd was captured, and a buffalo was killed, stuffed, and mounted on a pole. Mud-men clowns (imitated from clowns seen among the Pueblos) provided 'a light hearted gesture in an act of desperation—the inauguration of the Sun Dance for the earthly salvation of the Comanche way of life'.[4] A mock battle was fought, and the people danced in bands for five days before the sun dancers themselves danced, drummed, and sang for three further days, doing without food and water for the duration of the dance. Ishatai had promised that he would share his immunity with others, and that they should drive the whites from the land and restore the old way of life. But in the action they mounted against a post at Adobe Wells, soon afterwards, nine Comanches were killed. Ishatai lost his power, and the Comanches, their spirit broken, entered the reservation in 1875.

In contrast with these militaristic millennialists, among tribes which had been subject to white dominance for a longer time, prophets emerged, whose revolutionist response was entirely pacific, and new medicines were canvassed, which were not concerned with war against the white men. Of these prophets, Känakûk, the Kickapoo Prophet, may perhaps only marginally be considered as a revolutionist prophet at all: in many respects his message, against lying, drinking, stealing, quarrelling, and murder, was closer to the introversionism of Handsome Lake than to the pacific but revolutionist teachings of Smohalla and Wovoka.[5] Känakûk arose in the 1820s after the Kickapoo had been compelled to cede half of Illinois, and had received in exchange a small tract in Missouri which belonged to the Osages, their traditional enemies. Känakûk learned from the Great Spirit that the life of his people was short, that the earth would sink, and that it was mere vanity for chiefs to claim the land as theirs (and to cede it away) when land belonged to the Great Spirit. If only they could continue to live

---

[2] This account rests principally on Ernest Wallace and E. Adamson Hoebel, *The Comanches* (University of Oklahoma Press, Norman, Oklahoma, 1952), pp. 314–27.

[3] E. A. Hoebel, 'The Comanche Sun Dance and Messianic Outbreak of 1873', *American Anthropologist* 43, No. 2, Part 1 (1941), pp. 301–3.

[4] E. Wallace and E. A. Hoebel, op. cit., p. 322.

[5] On Handsome Lake, see pp. 387–97; on Smohalla, see pp. 280–3; and on Wovoka, see pp. 293–7.

on their land, and abandon their bad ways, they might then achieve happiness. They had put away their tomahawks, and wanted to restore their totems (increase their population—many of the gentes had become extinct). His speech, addressed to the United States officer at St Louis in 1827, plaintively expressed what might have been said by many Indians, or by a Maori or a Kikuyu: 'My father, when I talked with the Great Spirit, he did not tell me to sell my lands, because I did not know how much was a dollar's worth. . . .'[6] He sold prayer-sticks, much in the way that the Delaware Prophet had done, and he preached against medicine bags and medicine songs. His message offered a faint hope for a transformative experience, although it was also strongly marked by despair.

Känakûk's was a less specifically Christian message than that of the Potawatomi Prophet, sixty years later, whose new faith was spread among his own people and the Kickapoos at a reservation in north-west Kansas. The ritual was, as in most cases, solely a dance, but the ten commandments were enjoined, together with the prohibition of drinking, gambling, and horse-racing. The agent's comment was, 'As some tenets of revealed religion are embraced in its doctrines, I do not consider it a backward step for the Indians who have not heretofore professed belief in any Christian religion, and believe its worst features are summed up in the loss of time it occasions and the fanatical train of thought involved in the constant contemplation of the subject.'[7]

Indian tribes in the west, however, were generally later in experiencing extensive white contact, and certainly in their more extended acquaintance with, and acceptance of, the Christian religion and white civilization.[8] The upsurge of religious responses that affirmed the propriety of a native way of life continued much later than in the east and mid-west of the continent, but they may also have had earlier beginnings than their most dramatic and best reported cases suggest—

[6] 'The Kickapoo Prophet's Speech, dated St Louis, February 10th, 1827' in the Indian Office documents, cited by J. Mooney, op. cit., p. 696. This section leans on Mooney's account, op. cit., pp. 692-6.

[7] From the Annual Reports of the Commission of Indian Affairs to Secretary of the Interior, cited in J. Mooney, op. cit., p. 706.

[8] There are early but sparse accounts of resistance to Christianity from the west: a peasant woman who went into a trance in the early nineteenth century exhorted Indians to continue to sacrifice to Chupa, an idol worshipped in the area who had appeared to her and who had said that Indians would die if they were baptized. The account is in a report to the Gobernador de la N. California, March 1 1805, reported in Robert F. Heizer, 'A Californian Messianic Movement of 1801 among the Chumash', American Anthropologist, 43, 1 (January–March 1941), pp. 128–9. The word 'messianic' appears to be very loosely used. Leslie Spier, The Prophet Dance of the Northwest and its Derivatives: The Source of the Ghost Dance (George Banta, Menasha, Wisc., 1935), chapter II, reports a woman who preached the doctrine of the end of the world (and probably preached a golden age and revival of the dead) among the Athapascans about 1812.

the 1870 *Ghost Dance*, and movements begun by Smohalla and Wovoka. Among many North American tribes there appears to have been 'an old belief in the impending destruction and renewal of the world, when the dead would return, in conjunction with which there was a dance based on supposed imitation of the dances of the dead, and a conviction that intense preoccupation with the dance would hasten the happy day'.[9] How old such a belief was, is, of course, a matter of conjecture, but periodically the idea was revived, and provided the occasion for renewed attempts to dance-in the new dispensation, particularly when men arose as prophets, claiming to have 'died' and returned to life.[10] The myth appears to have been known to all the tribes of the north-western interior from the Paviotso in the south (California) to the Sekani in the north (central British Columbia). Natural calamities portended the early end, and among the Modoc a dance occurred each year when the Aurora was sighted to prevent the sky from burning: in this case the dance was not associated with the return of the dead. Many variants of these ideas existed, however. Among some tribes, when periodic prophecy was renewed, normal activities would be suspended (sometimes for a whole summer) whilst the dancing was held. Earlier reports suggest the idea of the world getting old and belief in its early end predominated, whilst more modern accounts more often mention the coming of the Creator to destroy the whites.[11]

[9] L. Spier, op. cit., p. 5.

[10] L. Spier, op. cit., pp. 10–11. Spier's attempt to trace back the doctrines of the 1870 Ghost Dance to an earlier Prophet dance has some support from archaeological evidence. William Duncan Strong, in 'The Occurrence and Wide Implications of a "Ghost Dance Cult" on the Columbia River suggested by Carvings in Wood, Stone and Bronze', *American Anthropologist* 47, 2 (April–June 1945), pp. 244–61, considers that depopulation among the Indians of the Columbia River probably preceded white contact, and may have induced death and revival cults.

[11] L. Spier, op. cit., p. 8. According to Spier, on whom these paragraphs largely rely, stories of people who knew the land of the dead were told among the Bella Coola and Tlingit tribes, and visits by shamans to the dead to seek the lost souls of their ailing patients was a supposed curing method among the Haida, Bella Coola, Nootka, and Kwakiutl, in British Columbia, the Klalam, Twana-Skokomish, and Salish of south Puget Sound, and the Chinook. World renewal without the concept of cataclysm was also a well-known myth. How far the idea of dances and ceremonials for the assurance of plenty and freedom from disease for the ensuing year was necessarily associated with the idea that without these ceremonies the world would decline, I do not know. Philip Drucker in 'A Karuk World-Renewal Ceremony at Panaminik', *Varia Anthropologica*, University of California Publications in American Archaeology and Ethnology 35, 3 (University of California Press, Berkeley, California, 1936), pp. 23–8, relates that exoteric and esoteric ceremonials were performed for particular towns by 'priests'. A. L. Kroeber and E. W. Gifford in 'World Renewal: A Cult System of Native Northwest California', *Anthropological Records* 13, 1 (University of California Press, Berkeley and Los Angeles 1949), pp. 1–155, give detailed reports of these dances among the Yorok, Karok (Karuk), and Hupa, and specifically mention that the rites ward off cataclysm, in addition to militating against famine and disease. There were two spectacular dances. The dances had continued, in some cases, into the 1930s and 1940s.

Christian influences were diffused over large areas of the west at quite early dates, even before the penetration of the area by whites, and this, according to Spier, may have been facilitated by the pre-existing *Prophet Dance*—the cult associated with the recurrent prophecies of world-end and renewal.[12] Christianity had been diffused by a band of twenty-four Iroquois who had travelled across the country in 1816–25. They settled among the Flatheads in Montana, who, in 1831, sent to St Louis for a missionary before any had penetrated their territory. A semi-Christian religion, including prayers before meals, the use of crosses, the Lord's prayer, and a prohibition of hunting on Sundays, was disseminated to the Nez Percé, Chinook, and Cayuse in the 1830s, and became associated with a form of the Prophet Dance among the Nez Percé, and their neighbours the Salish and Sahaptin, according to the accounts of early travellers. Christian teachings may have been spread north to the Upper Columbia and Snake Rivers by Garry, a Spokan boy, who was educated by Sir George Simpson of the Hudson's Bay Company, and who rejoined his tribe in about 1830.[13]

The restorative prophecies of Smohalla

In this background of diversely diffused and conjoined aboriginal and faintly Christian elements, the *Smohalla* cult emerged in the 1850s or 60s, and by the 1870s it was the vital religion of probably 'all the Sahaptin tribes and linked Cayuse, and had found adherents among the Wishram, adjacent on the west, and the Spokan on the north'.[14] The

---

[12] Ibid., pp. 30–1.

[13] Ibid., pp. 30–8. Cora Du Bois, *The Feather Cult of the Middle Colombia* (George Banta, Menasha, Wisc., 1938), attributes the spread of Christianity much more to the influences coming from Fort Vancouver. In British Columbia, religious movements had arisen in response to very limited contact. Among the Babines, a prophet, Uzakle, had brought into being 'a wonderful religious movement among the natives of the extreme north-west, both Tsimpians and Dénés, a commotion which can rightfully be compared to the Messiah crazes of later days'. This appears to have occurred soon after the first encounter with Roman Catholic missionaries in the 1840s. Uzakle's preaching led to incredulity and derision on the part of a man named 'Kwes, a member of a band settled at Rocher Deboulé, but he was subsequently afflicted by cataleptic fits and thereafter set himself up as the founder of a new religion. The tenets of this faith were a mixture of Christian and native precepts, including atonement and repentance for sin; the sign of the cross; conferment of names (in imitation of Christening perhaps); and 'heathenish dances'. He acquired a remarkable reputation for prophecies. The movement appears to have been entirely pacific, and was probably not millennialist, but is an instance of very early assimilation of Christian influences. A. G. Morice, *The History of the Northern Interior of British Columbia*, 2nd Edn (William Briggs, Toronto 1904), pp. 234–6.

[14] Ibid., p. 21.

doctrine of the Smohalla cult was identical with that claimed for the Prophet Dance cult—the message of world destruction, the ageing 'Earth woman', and the resurrection of the dead—but its doctrinal peculiarity lay in its emphasis on the annihilation of the whites at the time of the end. Its dance-form was quite different, however, and its ritual was apparently derived from Christianity. It was, as with so many other new Indian religions, regarded by its followers as the product of new and unique inspiration, and was credited to a particular individual, the man from whom it got its name (a circumstance which reflects the importance of prophetism among hunting peoples, where new cults necessarily arise from inspiration, and have little chance of institutionalization apart from absorption into the tribal way of life as such).

Smohalla or Smowhala (the name means Dreamer, and is the name of both the man and the cult) was born about 1815–20, among the Wanapum Indians of eastern Washington (also called Sokulk, and of Sahaptin stock). He was essentially a traditionalist prophet, who acquired his visions when a young man, and wove his symbols with traditional elements of his people's way of life. The details of Smohalla's early life are only partly known, and subject to dispute. He attended Catholic missions in his youth, and he had a slight knowledge of forms of service, and of French. In early manhood he distinguished himself as a warrior.[15] He probably began preaching in the 1850s. He had sought a vision before he learned the Washat dance, and some accounts suggest that it was then that he learned his symbols, his calendar of six seasons, and his songs.[16] The symbols which, at some stage, Smohalla placed on his flags, were a star, the sun, and the moon, and, in the wood-carving that he made, the effigy of a bird, on which his messenger visited him in his period of spiritual isolation. He was known as a medicine man, and the spread of his teachings facilitated the confederation of tribes which joined in the Yakima War of 1855–6. His message may have been largely that of the Prophet Dance. Whether Smohalla had already claimed to have 'died' or was at this stage teaching the main substance of his later religion is open to dispute, although the latter seems likely. Mooney recounts that sometime after the Yakima War, Smohalla was involved in a fight with Moses, a chief of the 'up-river people' (known variously as Sinkiuse, Isle de Pierre, Columbias, or Kawachkin), and was beaten by Moses and left for dead. He is reputed then to have crawled to a boat, travelled far down-river,

[15] J. Mooney, op. cit., p. 717.
[16] Click Relander (Now Tow Look), *Drummers and Dreamers* (Caxton Press, Caldwell, Idaho, 1956), p. 70.

and been rescued by white men. It is said that he subsequently went to Mexico, Arizona, Utah, and Nevada, and there learned his famous calendar. On returning to his people, the story goes, he claimed to have been in the spirit world, and to have learned of the anger of the 'great chief above' at Indian apostasy. According to this account, he introduced a new ritual with elements of Catholic, and perhaps Mormon, practice after his return.[17] In the 1950s, however, the remnant of the Wanapum Indians knew no story concerning Smohalla fighting Moses, or of his going on a journey.[18]

Smohalla's religion was an expression of his strong resistance to the ceding of Indian lands to the whites and to the removal of Indians to the reservation. His people had not signed the treaty of 1855 with Governor Isaac I. Stevens of Washington Territory, by which many of the Yakima and Walla Walla tribes had accepted places on the reservations, and he appears to have been instrumental in keeping Indians off the reservations, or, in the case of some of the Umatilla, persuading them to leave. He was, of course, not alone in opposing the growing white pressure on the land, but it was he who was mainly responsible for the ideological justification of the resistance. His teaching, the dreamer faith *Washani* (worship, sometimes known as the Dreamer cult) was a mixture of various older and diffused elements. Essentially, it canvassed a return to the Indian way of life. It rejected the white man and his ways, and was believed to predict a cataclysm after which the ancestors would return to clear the land of white men and restore the former way of life. 'Their model of a man is an Indian. They aspire to be Indians and nothing else. . . .'[19] At Priest Rapids, where he settled with many of his followers, the cult was associated with the salmon, the abundance of which, at the appropriate season, was said to be produced by Smohalla's use of his bird emblem. The earth was the mother: agriculture, tilling the soil, or parcelling the land, were all rejected as a violation of the earth.

Smohalla complained that the white men took the land from the Indians. When he was told that Indians did not till the soil or make it useful, he replied that he understood that beyond the seas white men also kept land untilled, for deer, and that even when Indians did plant the soil, they were still not free from the white man's greed. He pointed to the fate of Chief Joseph and Nez Percé, as an example. He was urged to let his young men work. He replied, 'Men who work cannot

[17] J. Mooney, op. cit., pp. 717–8. L. Spier, op. cit., whilst not disputing the account of the fight, doubts whether Smohalla could have made such an extensive journey.

[18] C. Relander, op. cit., p. 180, although Smohalla's rivalry with Moses was well known, ibid., p. 65.

[19] From a Commissioner's Report, cited by J. Mooney, op. cit., p. 711.

dream, and wisdom comes to us in dreams'. Fishing was right, but the work of the white man hardened the soul and the body. Challenged because the Indians dug up roots, he said,

> We simply take the gifts that are freely offered. We no more harm the earth than would an infant's fingers harm its mother's breast. But the white man tears up large tracts of land, runs deep ditches, cuts down forests and changes the whole face of the earth. . . . Every honest man knows in his heart that this is wrong. But the white men are so greedy they do not consider these things.

Of the wisdom that came in dreams, Smohalla said, in a sentiment pre-echoing the Peyote cult, 'Each must learn for himself the highest wisdom. It cannot be taught in a few words.' One might also learn by singing and dancing with the Dreamer at night. The dreams and visions were informed by tribal lore, in which the prophet was himself deeply versed.[20] His doctrine had many continuities with the Prophet Dance, but his flag, with the red spot which represented his heart, and his calendar, were elements that he had himself added to these traditions.

The ritual of Smohalla's religion was, however, not merely tribal in its tradition. He learned a dance, the Washat dance, at the time of the death of his daughter, and claimed then to have died with her, and to have been sent back to his people to urge upon them the old ways. He brought back a song to be sung every seventh day, and the Wanapum dance, which would restore the country and the things belonging to it to the Indians.[21] He gave out feathers for the dance, with which men would rise up after death, and the dance itself, for which the seven oldest and wisest men were to drum, could be danced as a delirious frenzy. When it was over, feasting took place. But there were also circular dances, a berry dance in autumn, and a salmon dance when

[20] The quotations in this paragraph are from Smohalla's discourse with an American officer: E. L. Huggins, 'Smohalla, The Prophet of Priest Rapids', *Overland Monthly* (San Francisco) XVII, Second Series (January–June 1891), pp. 208–15.

[21] C. Relander, op. cit., pp. 82 ff. The story of Smohalla's death and return to life is typical of claims made on behalf of many religious leaders who arose among the tribes in the region of the Columbia River. The idea that Smohalla was 'just one prophet in a whole series of Washani dreamers', put forward by C. Du Bois, *The Feather Cult* . . ., op. cit., p. 5 (and again, p. 16) may be discounted. The several other prophets on whom Du Bois gathered information, and many of whom were said to have died and come to life again, all lacked certain characteristics of Smohalla's teaching. None propounded so coherent and unqualified a return to native practices, and none preached any sort of millennialism. All of them, including Jake Hunt, founder of the Feather Cult, accepted a much more conventional Christian eschatology, and expected to join the dead in heaven. Du Bois does not see the significance of these distinctions. The prophets who arose among the Umatilla and Yakima, whose teachings she recounts, preached a much more accommodative doctrine than Smohalla. In view of these distinct differences, it is curious that C. Relander, op. cit., p. 50, says, 'His Dreamer religion was practically synonymous with the Feather Cult. In regions where the two merged they quickly intermixed. . . .'

the salmon began to run in April, and these were all part of the pattern of indigenous religion. In Smohalla's services there were lamentations for the dead, and accounts of trance visions—variations of practices more widely known. There were also prayers in response to a bell, and genuflections; and the permanent buildings of the cult (the tule-mat long-houses) face east—all of which features are clearly attributable to Christian influences.[22]

The millennial element in Smohalla's teaching was apparently secret for some time, but it was also an essentially pacific millennialism. Although hostilities occurred between the forces of the government and tribes that had taken up the cult, his teachings appear to have had much less to do with the fighting than the very real sufferings of the Indians as white encroachment on their land continued.[23] The treaty of 1855 with the various tribes of the area was broken when gold was discovered, and white speculators moved into the area. Chief Joseph, with a band of the Nez Percé, who refused to be a party to the treaty of 1863, by which the invaders' claims were conceded, roamed the Wallowa valley. More whites entered the area, and, in 1876, the attempt was made to persuade Joseph to take his band into the Lapwai reservation. Toolhulhulsote, the principal Dreamer priest of Joseph's band, answered General O. O. Howard and the commissioners who met the group in terms of Smohalla's doctrine. The earth was the mother and should not be disturbed with hoe or plough; men should live by the spontaneous products of nature; the sovereignty of the earth was such that men could neither sell it nor give it away. The Indians were persuaded to go to the reservation, when they were attacked by a band of white robbers, and the Nez Percé retaliated with raids against neighbouring white settlements. So began Joseph's remarkable campaign in which, with great hardship and privation, he led his people over 1,000 miles until he was forced to surrender by Colonel Nelson Miles.[24] The promises made to Joseph at surrender were never kept, but his speech on that occasion illustrates the despair which, as had the Palouses before them,[25] this group of Nez Percé now experienced:

I am tired of fighting. Our chiefs are killed. Looking Glass is dead. Toolhulhulsote is dead. The old men are all dead. It is the young men who say yes or no. He who led the young men is dead. It is cold and we have no blankets. The little children are freezing to death. My people,

[22] L. Spier, op. cit., pp. 41–5.
[23] C. Relander, op. cit., p. 122, writes, 'Smowhala was a man of peace, who preached it, lived it and abided by it'.
[24] J. Mooney, op. cit., pp. 711–15.
[25] On the Palouses, and their struggle, see C. Relander, op. cit., pp. 87 ff.

some of them, have run away to the hills and have no blankets, no food. No one knows where they are—perhaps freezing to death. I want to have time to look for my children, and see how many of them I can find. Maybe I shall find them among the dead. Hear me, my chiefs. I am tired. My heart is sick and sad. From where the sun now stands, I will fight no more forever.[26]

Smohalla was wrongly blamed for the resistance of the Nez Percé, but he lived on quietly with his followers at Priest Rapids, and took no part in the campaigns. His religion was actively opposed by the Rev. James H. Wilbur, the Methodist minister at Yakima reservation, who for a time was also Indian agent, and who forbade stick and ball games, and traditional Indian gambling, and who, like the Rev. Myron Eells in Puget Sound, became an opponent of Indian nativism and indigenous religion (in marked contrast to the attitude of the Shakers to Tenskwatawa, and the Quakers in their encouragement of Handsome Lake).[27] General Miles sent Major J. W. MacMurray to discovery the grievances of the Indians in the 1880s, and he learned a great deal about Smohalla's faith from his stay at Priest Rapids, and of his opposition to the Indian homestead laws.[28] Smohalla died in 1895, after becoming blind towards the end of his life. He was succeeded by his son, Yoyouni, and subsequently by Puck Hyat Toot, his nephew, who, in the 1950s was the last leader of the faith, which was still maintained in its purity in the last mat-house, although the Wanapums had been moved from their ancestral fishing grounds by the government in 1942, after the government had built dams and bridges over the Columbia River. Only a tiny group of Wanapums remained, and the ritual objects of the Smohalla cult were to be buried when Puck Hyat Toot died, since then there would be no one to receive them from him.[29]

The Ghost Dance of 1870

The diffusion of the Smohalla religion, and the imitation of it by other prophets, many of whom made similar claims to have died, and who

[26] From the Annual Report of the Secretary of War, cited by J. Mooney, op. cit., p. 175. On the epic of the Nez Percé see Merrill D. Beal, '*I Will Fight No More Forever*' (University of Washington Press, Seattle 1963).

[27] On Wilbur, see C. Relander, op. cit., pp. 126, 196. On Myron Eells, and the (Indian) Shakers, see pp. 353–64. On the relation of the (American) Shakers and the Shawnee Prophet, see pp. 229–36. On the role of the Quakers in the religion of Handsome Lake, see pp. 387–97. The (American) Shakers and the Quakers were, of course, both introversionist European sects, and showed their sympathy for aboriginal religion, which relied on inspirationalism not dissimilar, in some respects, from their own.

[28] An account is given in J. Mooney, op. cit., pp. 716 ff.

[29] C. Relander, op. cit., pp. 225, 239.

returned with visions of heaven, or of the ancestors, is a matter of great complexity on which full information is lacking. Other prophets were reported among the Umatilla and the Skempah.[30] Local leaders of the cult became virtually prophets in their own right, propounding a broadly similar faith in the resurrection of ancestors who would descend to join the dance, and teaching their own songs. But the central ideas of the cults are the same, and sometimes many specific items are identifiable: thus Jake Hunt (Titcamnashat) claimed visionary and healing powers and distributed feathers to his followers, who gathered regularly at Warm Springs.[31] The names *Dreamers* and *Feather* cult were indiscriminately applied, and the specific influence of one prophet or another cannot be traced. The whole represents a cultural complex of somewhat varying teachings and rituals, some of which drew on older elements, which spread over a very wide area of Washington, Oregon, and California in the 1860s and 1870s.[32] In California, this diffuse tradition provided the background for the Ghost Dance of 1870, and may have been associated with the emergence of the *Shaker* religion of Puget Sound, although Smohalla is said to have disliked the Shaker religion, since it was christianized, and since it did not seek, as did the congeries of Dreamer cults, the Feather cult, and the Smohalla religion, to preserve Indian ways. The lines of communication of these cult movements, as they passed from tribe to tribe, is not our specific concern, but it must be remembered that what are seen as 'new movements' by agents or local settlers may indeed be merely diffused patterns from other tribes, or revivals of older beliefs by particular prophets and proselytizers, who find a favourable circumstance for an intensification of ideas and rites which, in similar form, have been well known in the past.

The tribes of California in and soon after 1870 learned and practised a purportedly new cult, which has become known as the Ghost Dance, since its leaders maintained that the dance would bring back the dead at the overturning of the world.[33] Its origins have long been traced back

[30] Ibid., pp. 150–4, for a number of cases.
[31] Ibid., pp. 156–61. See pp. 351–3.
[32] L. Spier, in 'The Ghost Dance of 1870 Among the Klamath of Oregon', *University of Washington Publications in Anthropology* 2, 2 (November 1927), pp. 39–55, says, 'It may well be asked if the two Ghost Dance movements, the Smohallah cult, the Shaker religion, and similar beginnings . . . do not really represent just so many phrasings of an old and recurring cult pattern in this general area' (p. 52). We are again faced with the difficulty of determining the distinguishing criteria of a movement, but it seems reasonable to regard the principal cults as distinct movements, although sharp changes sometimes occurred within one cult, and separate cults often embraced many cultural characteristics in common. Both revolutionist and thaumaturgical responses were in evidence.
[33] This Ghost Dance of 1870 is not to be confused with the Ghost Dance which began with the Paiute prophet, Wovoka (Jack Wilson) and spread to many of the Plains tribes in 1890. See pp. 292–306.

to the Paiutes, and it appears to have been either a development independent of the Smohalla cult, or to be a separate derivation from an earlier common source.[34] A much earlier shaman named Winawitu, who had preached rejuvenation by dancing, and amity with the whites, was vaguely remembered among the Shoshone, Bannock, Washo, and Paviotso, and after him Wodziwob (Waugh-zee-waugh-ber) had prophesied the return of the dead among the Paviotso at Walker Lake, western Nevada, in 1869. His message was that with the return of the dead there would be paradise on earth, life eternal, and no distinction between races. His associate Weneyuga (Frank Spencer) preached the same ideas to the Washo in 1870, and carried it to another group of the Paviotso, who lived in the eastern part of the Klamath reserve. There appeared to be no special ritual associated with these teachings (which varied somewhat in the mouths of different proselytizers), and the Paviotso used their round dance in association with them, but acquired new songs, learned by the shaman while in trance.[35] The impression of Cora Du Bois was that

> . . . the 1870 and 1890 Ghost Dances were not radical departures from Paviotso shamanistic concepts. . . . The behaviour patterns which became attached to these cults, outside of western Nevada, were not necessary correlates of an adventist doctrine among the Paviotso. Foreign tribes in accepting the prophecies, not only placed them in a new context, but also attached to them Paviotso traits, which were merely in solution among the originators. In the process of doctrinal borrowing they made these common Paviotso traits necessary concomitants of the cult. In fact, they may almost be said to have created the cult as a dynamic and specific movement.[36]

Initially, the teachings provoked in each tribe an epidemic of local dreaming and trances until new local leaders arose and imposed their own authority, often adding some local variant to cult practice. In some tribes, the return of the dead was the dominant and urgent theme at the outset, sometimes given direct personal application when individuals sought to liberate some recently dead relative. Among the Karok of the lower Klamath River, the initial idea was that the dead

[34] A. L. Kroeber, 'A Ghost Dance in California', *Journal of American Folklore* XVII (January–March 1904), pp. 32–5, believed that this cult, as he recounted it among the Yurok and Karok, had probably originated among the Paiutes. L. Spier in *The Prophet Dance* . . ., op. cit., p. 24, considers that the Paviotso (Paiute) got this dance not from Smohalla, but probably from either the Modoc, among whom a prophet dance had existed as early as 1840–50, though it was probably not associated with the return of the dead (ibid., pp. 10–11) or from the Oregon Ute.

[35] C. Du Bois, 'The 1870 Ghost Dance', *Anthropological Records* 3, 1 (University of California Press, Berkeley 1939), pp. 1–151 (p. 6). This and subsequent paragraphs rely considerably on this source.

[36] Ibid., p. 7.

were coming back to wreak vengeance on the whites, with the cultural hero of the tribe in the van of the returning dead. But at no point were there plans for overt aggression in association with the cult: the whites were simply to be exterminated by supernatural action when the advent occurred.[37]

Enthusiasm had often not played itself out when a second wave of interest in some variant form of movement was introduced. Thus it appears that one line of transmission of the early cult was from the Paviotso to the easternmost Achomawi, and from them to the northern Yana, Wintun, and Hill Patwin. Among the Wintun and Hill Patwin a variant which became known as the *Earth-Lodge* cult developed, which stressed the end of the world, from which the faithful were to be protected by subterranean shelters—earth lodges. Emphasis shifted from the earlier preoccupation with the return of the dead to earth to communication with the dead in dreams. But by the time this cult had reached the northern Californian tribes, where it was known as the *Warm House* cult, the idea of resurrection became reasserted. An elaboration of this cult, probably begun by a Patwin prophet, Lame Bill, who had also been prominent in the Earth-Lodge cult, then occurred among the Patwin and Wintun, and was known as the *Bole-Maru* movement, which gradually abandoned the idea of world catastrophe, and emphasized the supreme being and the after-life. Each local dreamer had his own revelations, and, arising among tribes, the ceremonial life of which had been especially rich, this movement had much greater elaboration of ceremonial than its predecessors, including a secularized form of the old Patwin Hesi dance, cloth costumes, a ball dance, and a flagpole. The Earth-Lodge cult, which had been most vigorously adopted by the Pomo, who built seven lodges, was superseded by the Bole-Maru movement, which spread widely, and which in the early 1930s was still in existence in Patwin and Pomo areas.[38]

Phases of these cult movements succeeded each other, and overlaid each other, like geological strata, one enthusiasm replacing the

---

[37] Ibid., pp. 15, 130. L. Spier, in 'The Ghost Dance of 1870 . . .', op. cit., p. 43, writes of the cult in northern California: 'Here, however, its effect was not inflammatory, for the California Indians were doubtless too well aware of their own impotence to attempt driving the invading whites from their land.' It is not necessary, however, to present a revolutionist response in terms of alternatives of positive action and expectations of supernatural action. The wishful myth of such a movement is not a consciously adopted stance arising from an awareness of impotence in pursuit of articulated goals. The very dream-like quality of the experience in the Ghost Dance, and in some other millennialist movements, indicates how completely the myth and the associated performance of ritual (usually dancing) is divorced from conceptions of direct plans for action. That it has sometimes been associated with military action, but has also often ignored readily available opportunities for it, confirms the idea of the autonomy of the religious response.

[38] This paragraph relies on C. Du Bois, op. cit., especially, pp. 1–3, 50, 131–3.

previous one, as the cults acquired new features in being transmitted and retransmitted from tribe to tribe. Thus the Achomawi received the original Ghost Dance from the Paviotso and transmitted it to the Yana, Wintun, and Hill Patwin, only to receive the Earth-Lodge cult at a later date from the Wintu. They then in turn transmitted it to the Klamath reservation, where a group of Paviotso lived from whom the earlier dissemination had begun. The Shasta received three waves of these enthusiasms, and the Klamath two, in 1870 or 1871, and in 1873; and subsequently are reputed also to have received the Smohalla cult, in 1875–85.[39]

Relative deprivation and sequences of response

Two sociological problems are worthy of consideration in relation to the 1870 Ghost Dance and its successors: the circumstances that were conducive to the receptivity of the cults; and the sequence of changing response that the different phases appear to represent. The first of these issues has received more attention from the anthropologists, who traced the diffusion of the cults, particularly among the Klamath, Modoc, and Paviotso, who shared the Klamath reservation. The central ideas of the Ghost Dance as the Klamath received it from Wenyuga[40]—a natural calamity, earthquake, flood, and drought, with dancing all night to bring back the dead, which was Wenyuga's teaching[41]— acquired an additional feature. 'The news told that Kemu'kumps, the Klamath cultural hero, was coming from the south, and the dead were on their way to the land of the living.'[42] They received a form of ceremonial which was of a type new to them, but since shamanism had been forbidden on the reservation, the cult offered opportunities for individuals who had never enjoyed it before to acquire prestige.[43] The movement acquired almost complete adherence from the Klamath, who numbered about 1,200 individuals.

The Ghost Dance was transmitted to the Modoc, some of whom lived in the more remote part of the reservation, by Doctor George. Under Captain Jack (Keintpoos), that group of the Modoc fought the whites in the following year, in the Modoc War, but this 'can only

[39] Ibid., p. 12. Du Bois has attempted to trace the paths of diffusion of the various movements from detailed interviewing.
[40] Ibid., p. 7.
[41] Ibid., p. 4 ff.
[42] L. Spier, op. cit., p. 45; C. Du Bois, op. cit., p. 130.
[43] L. Spier, op. cit., p. 44.

indirectly be attributed to the Ghost Dance'.[44] The second wave of diffusion, as the Earth-Lodge cult, came to the Klamath in 1873 through an Achomawi slave, Pitt River Charlie, and from them passed to the Modoc. Dancing was revived, until finally suppressed by the authorities in late 1873.[45] The precise characteristics of the two cults is subject to varying interpretations, but at least in the second wave fainting had become more distinctly associated with trance states, and individual trances, at home as well as in the lodges, had become usual.[46] The Klamath built three refuge houses, the Modoc only one. The Klamath dance lasted five nights, and entranced dancers were tended by the dreamers or prophets. Ghosts appeared to those in trances, instructing them in the dance and giving them new songs.

New cult millennialist movements among North American Indians were explained by Kroeber as responses to the impending destruction of the native way of life.[47] But the Klamath, according to Spier, 'had not as yet suffered seriously from the incursions of the whites' of whom there were few in the vicinity, although they were irritated by the soldiery, and lived on a reservation. 'Their situation was still aboriginal, and any disturbance of their life so slight as to be no more than a predisposing influence in favor of the messianic movement.'[48] The Modoc, however, had fought against the whites, had been forcibly removed to the reservation, and one group of Modoc came into conflict with the whites again during their period of participation in the cult. Nash suggests that 'Nativistic cults arise among deprived groups. They follow a shift in the value pattern, due to suppression and domination, and are movements to restore the original value pattern which they do by the construction of a fantasy situation.'[49] The Modoc were in a much more pronounced state of conflict with the whites than the Klamath, who had readily signed a treaty and settled down to the idea of the reservation. The white authorities had a more direct and positive influence on the Klamath, seeking to introduce a democratic

---

[44] C. Du Bois, op. cit., p. 130. L. Spier, op. cit., p. 45, is also of this opinion: 'The severe dislocation of their life undoubtedly would have made of the Modoc a most fertile field for the messianic idea. Yet there is no evidence that the cult was more than a predisposing influence of the war.'

[45] L. Spier, op. cit., p. 45–6.

[46] These characteristics are attributed with more certainty to the second stage than to the first by Philleo Nash, in 'The Place of Religious Revivalism in the Formation of the Inter-cultural Community on Klamath Reservation', pp. 377–442 in Fred Eggan et al. (Eds.), *Social Anthropology of North American Tribes* (University of Chicago Press, Chicago 1937), pp. 420, 430.

[47] A. L. Kroeber, *Handbook of Indians of California*, Smithsonian Institution Bureau of American Ethnography Bulletin 78 (Government Printing Office, Washington 1925) pp. 868–73.

[48] L. Spier, op. cit., pp. 44–5.

[49] P. Nash, op. cit., p. 377.

style of chieftainship, encouraging them to take up individual farming, and trying to suppress shamanism.[50] New productive techniques were introduced, and schooling and apprenticeship began in the 1860s. Nash considers that the policy among the Klamath conferred greater gains on chiefs and slaves than on commoners and shamans. The more remotely located Modoc had a more uniform experience of deprivation, and did not receive the various benefits which the Klamath experienced.

The theory of relative deprivation which is implicitly invoked both by Spier and Nash is not easily applied even when data is much more abundant than in this instance. The external and objective indices of deprivation stand in uncertain relationship to the sense of deprivation which individuals experience. The only evidence for such 'felt' deprivation, in this case, is the behaviour that follows the objective circumstances of change. The unknown is derived from the known, and is then invoked to explain the known. Spier sees cults as associated with occasions when chiefs acquired power as shamans lost it.[51] This may suggest why alien ceremonial forms were so readily acceptable to the Klamath, whose circumstances otherwise, on Spier's assessment, differed from those predicated as conducive to cult movements—the awareness of the destruction of native life. Yet the effects of disruption of native life, and the awareness of it, are also difficult to assess, and we know from other cases that new religious responses occur after very much less interference than the Klamath had experienced.[52] Spier is, of course, principally concerned to show the influence of cultural diffusion in the process of social change.

Nash regards differential deprivation as an explanation of the incidence of the cult and also of its changing pattern, but he finally considers that both acculturation and resistance to it were occasions for deprivation. When skills were introduced which did not produce the expected rewards, deprivation occurred just as fully as when such skills were not available or were resisted. The cults expressed in ritual

[50] Ibid., pp. 397–408.

[51] L. Spier, op. cit., p. 44. This was not necessarily a general circumstance among other tribes. It did not occur in southern and central California, for example, perhaps because there was no external pressure to reduce shamanism as there was on the Klamath reservation. See A. H. Gayton, 'The Ghost Dance of 1870 in South-Central California,' *University of California Publications in American Archaeology and Ethnology* 28, 3 (1930), pp. 57–82 (p. 81).

[52] See for example the evidence from Highland tribes in New Guinea: R. M. Berndt, 'Reaction to Contact in the Eastern Highlands in New Guinea', op. cit. The significance of even very limited indirect contact emerges in the case of the Coast Salish, even though Suttles professes agreement with Spier in asserting that the forms of the Prophet Dance preceded white contact and were not specifically a reaction to it. Suttles shows that the dance existed among the Coast Salish before very much white contact, although indirect contact had already caused new epidemic diseases, and the fur trade had had effects on social stratification: Wayne Suttles, 'The Plateau Prophet Dance Among the Coast Salish', *Southwestern Journal of Anthropology* 13, 4 (Winter 1957), pp. 352–96.

symbolism the attitudes of acceptance or rejection of white culture. Thus there was stronger anti-white feeling among the Modoc. Among the Klamath, those nearest to the agency were the people least likely to be involved. He provides evidence of a much longer persistence of cult activities than does Spier, and sees the change from Ghost Dance to Earth-Lodge cult to Dream cult (until 1878) as indicating a shift of interest in the self. The Earth-Lodge cult was propitious for those who had sought social recognition and never received it, since it provided more opportunity for individual trances and visions both at home and in the dances. Different people were involved, and the Dream Dance phase persisted for three years at the upper end of the reservation among the Modoc. The difference of shaman and non-shaman was initially reduced in the Dream Dance, until the shamans incorporated the Dream Dance into their own activities. Though it is not the burden of Nash's discourse, this may indicate a reassertion of power on the part of the shamans.

Spier's main contention in regard to the Ghost Dance of California and the subsequent cult movements, including the Smohalla cult, is that an aboriginal form of the Prophet Dance had been widely diffused over the western United States before extensive white contact had occurred, and that this dance and its myths may be regarded as auto-chthonous. Consequently, although the threat of the destruction of the native culture might, at this period, predispose men to accept a new cult, none the less many basic cultic elements were already known, and neither contact nor deprivation provided explanation of their incidence, much less of their mythical and ritual content.[53] Aberle, contending against this view, has suggested that cults may arise as a native response long before the cultural collapse of the tribal way of life is threatened. He puts forward two factors conducive to the acceptance of cult movements: experience of deprivation (in its various forms); and the need to absorb the impact of a new and more powerful culture. The Prophet Dance and the Ghost Dance were, he suggests, attempts to cope with problems created by the constantly changing contact with western culture: the cults might or might not be borrowed, and might or might not result from deprivation following contact, but 'classifica-tion as to historical origin does not provide us with a classification as to function'.[54] Spier and his associates have further contended that cults do not arise simply from deprivation, or from contact which gives rise

[53] This thesis is put forward both in L. Spier, op. cit., and more especially in L. Spier, The Prophet Dance . . ., op. cit.

[54] David F. Aberle, 'The Prophet Dance and Reactions to White Contact', Southwestern Journal of Anthropology 15, 1 (Spring 1959), pp. 74–83.

to deprivation, although they acknowledge that a variety of tensions, disenchantments, and deprivations moulded the later course of these cults.[55] They also posit that cults of rejuvenation might arise without deprivation: the desire to see ancestors and to solemnize the process of life-renewal may have existed without distress as a precipitating agent. They suggest that the 1890 *Ghost Dance* (and by implication the 1870 Ghost Dance) '. . . did not spring full panoplied from conditions of distress; an older form was turned to nativistic and revivalistic account when acculturation conditions became intolerable'.[56] The debate is reduced to a matter of points of emphasis.

The second issue arising from the 1870 Ghost Dance is the changing orientations within the successive waves of the cults which so rapidly succeeded one another. The emphasis on return of the dead, cataclysm, and the anti-white elements which arose in the early Ghost Dance and in the early diffusion of the Earth-Lodge cult, at least among some tribes, appear to have steadily given way to other activities and to a rather different response to the world. Among the Klamath, individual dreaming increased during the Earth-Lodge cult and the interest moved from group to individual symbolism, and this emphasis persisted in the Dream Dance which followed. Eventually the doctrine of the return of the dead disappeared. The dead were now encountered in dreams. There was a considerable amount of sickness, general anxiety, and an absence of doctrine.[57] Among the Modoc, the anti-white feeling fomented in the Modoc war later passed into symptoms that were met by pseudo-shamanistic treatment.[58] Curing became an added feature in some cases: this was so even among the Klamath, for whom curing the sick at a dance was at variance with previous practice. 'The sick were cured at these dances in the manner now characteristic of the pseudo-Christian Indian sect of Puget sound, the Shakers; the hands were rubbed down the body of the patient and clapped together to

[55] L. Spier, W. Suttles, and Melville J. Herskovits, 'Comment on Aberle's Thesis of Deprivation', *Southwestern Journal of Anthropology* 15, 1 (Spring 1959), pp. 84–8.

[56] Ibid., pp. 87–8. Spier and his associates are here suggesting more distress than Spier had conceded in the case of the Klamath. These authors make the surprising claim, incidentally, 'that in Africa the deprivations and disbarments inherent in the colonial situation have given rise to almost no nativistic movements looking towards the restoration of the past'. African conditions were certainly very different—the absence of such extensive white settlement even in the areas of their greatest incursion, and the fact that the conditions of livelihood were not so uniformly destroyed as they were for North American Indians, among other things. None the less, movements such as Massa in the Ivory Coast; the Nyabingi in Uganda and Ruanda; Dina ya Msambwa and other Kenyan movements; and aspects of the Yakañ cult and the Maji-maji rebellion—and there are other cases—suggest restorative nativism. Some of them may have involved more people than either of the two Ghost Dances, although they were not diffused over so wide a territory.

[57] P. Nash, op. cit., p. 430.

[58] Ibid., p. 431.

shake off the sickness.'[59] On the Siletz reservation, much further north in Oregon, curing by blowing and by touching with feathers became part of the cult.[60]

Disillusionment and discontent appear to have occurred after the dance had been held periodically for a season or two when, despite several nights of dancing, the dead had not reappeared, and this may have been responsible for the return to a preoccupation with curing. The Bole-Maru cult, which introduced elaborate ceremonials, institutionalized the curing element, in that the local leader of the cult was expected to be a healer. The cult stimulated new dreaming, and the principal dreamers became both the expositors of the doctrine and the active proselytizers.[61] Ethical and eschatological elements grew in importance, with emphasis on a flowery after-life (translated in the 1930s as 'heaven'). There were injunctions against drinking, stealing, and quarrelling. The Christian conception of a 'Father' grew in this cult.

The important shift of response from a generally revolutionist to a renewed thaumaturgical concern, and a re-shaping of shamanism, appears to be evident over the whole of the west-coast regions in which the Ghost Dance had its impact. The diversity of local accretions of practice to fit in with indigenous preconceptions hardly affected this process. The promise of the Ghost Dance was an early return of the dead and, generally, a restoration of a past way of life, perhaps attended with a catastrophe which would destroy the whites (although informants in later decades generally denied that this element had existed). The intensified interest in dreaming (which had been absent in the earlier versions of the cult as they had occurred in some areas[62]) and the search for new curative power, indicate both the need of the communities for their tested curative practitioners, the shamans, and the persistence of personal over collective and communal preoccupations when a programme of collective salvation failed.

The Ghost Dance of 1890

The more celebrated Ghost Dance, which spread over the tribes of the Plains in 1890, also had its origin among the Northern Paiute of Walker

[59] L. Spier, 'The Ghost Dance of 1870 . . .', op. cit., p. 50. On the Shakers, see pp. 353–64.
[60] C. Du Bois, op. cit., p. 28.
[61] Ibid., pp. 101, 132–3.
[62] Thus, among the tribes of central and southern California trances were not part of the experience of the Ghost Dance. Later versions of the cult did not apparently affect these tribes, the shamans of which tended to retain the monopoly of contact with the spirit world. A. H. Gayton, op. cit., pp. 79–81.

Lake Reservation in Nevada. The prophet was Wovoka (Jack Wilson), the son of Tabivo (Numataivo, which is translated as 'White man') 'who was undoubtedly Jack Wilson's father'.[63] Mooney confused him with Wodziwob, the inspirer of the 1870 Ghost Dance, but Tabivo was a shaman and not a prophet. Of Wovoka himself we have better information than for earlier Indian prophets. He was visited by Mooney while his teaching was still of great importance, and he was known to local whites who have left some records of his life. He was alive when the earlier ideas of a Ghost Dance had been diffused, and these were part of his own cultural inheritance. He was probably taught shamanistic arts by his father. Some reports deny that he took up shamanism until later life, when he certainly dispensed advice, feathers, and special paint, used in the Ghost Dance, long after the Ghost Dance itself had come to an end.[64] But for a few journeys, he lived his whole life in Mason Valley, where he was born.

The Paiutes were a relatively weak and peaceful tribe. Some years before Wovoka's birth they had been involved in a battle with a company of miners who sought to steal their squaws, and whose force, under Major William Ormsby, the Paiutes had successfully ambushed. The Paiutes had finally surrendered to the whites in 1862. Wovoka inherited the whole tradition of the Ghost Dance of 1870. He may also have learned something of Christian ideas of the resurrection from the Mormons, who, since they saw the Indians as remnants of the tribes described in the Book of Mormon, 'took an active interest in the religious ferment then existing among the neighbouring tribes and helped to give shape to the doctrine which crystallized some years later in the Ghost Dance'.[65] Because he had worked for a settler family, the Wilsons, and been half-adopted by the family (hence the name Jack Wilson), Wovoka had acquired some knowledge of Christian theology, and, according to one account, had often been taken into the house, and had heard David Wilson read the Bible to his family.[66]

[63] C. Du Bois, op. cit., pp. 3–4.

[64] Many Indians continued, both by visits and letters, to seek guidance from Wovoka for many years after the Ghost Dance had ended, and even in 1920 some continued to believe that he was, as he had claimed from the time of his revelation, 'endowed with power to predict and control meteorological phenomena'. Grace M. Dangberg (Ed.), 'Letters to Jack Wilson, the Paiute Prophet, Written between 1908–1911', Smithsonian Institution Bureau of American Ethnology Bulletin 164, Anthropological Papers No. 55 (Government Printing Office, Washington 1957), pp. 279–96 (p. 287).

[65] J. Mooney, The Ghost Dance and the Sioux Outbreak of 1890 (Phoenix Books, Chicago 1965: originally published as Part 2, Fourteenth Annual Report of the Bureau of Ethnology to the Secretary of the Smithsonian Institution, 1892–3: Government Printing Office, Washington 1896), p. 5. In this section, all page references to Mooney are from the Phoenix edition. Wovoka's daughter and son-in-law later became Mormons.

[66] Paul Bailey, Wovoka: The Indian Messiah (Westernlore Press, Los Angeles 1957), pp. 23–7.

Whether Wovoka had heard anything of the (Indian) Shakers is disputed: one report suggests that he spent two summers as a paid hand in California, and there, although not going to a Shaker church, he saw the trance states, and may have sought to emulate what he learned of the founder of the Shakers, John Slocum.[67]

Whatever the sources of inspiration, Wovoka's own experience and his message were clear. He had, apparently, occasionally called seances and sought to work miracles, perhaps by the legerdemain characteristic of the Indian shaman.[68] In the winter of 1888–9 Wovoka became ill, and while he was sick there occurred, in January 1889, an eclipse of the sun which caused great alarm among the Paiutes. On his recovery, Wovoka preached a message to his people. He claimed to have visited the spirit world during his illness and to have seen there a land of game, and all the people who had died in the past. God commissioned him to return to his people, and to tell them to live peaceably, to love one another, work, and not to lie or steal, and to put an end to all their old practices that savoured of war. If they obeyed, they would be reunited with the dead, and death and sickness and old age would be no more. God had given him a dance, to be performed for five days at periodic intervals, to hasten the occasion of the return of the dead.[69] He preached that men must not fight or harm each other, and he condemned the traditionally extravagant mourning customs (killing horses and gashing oneself) by saying, 'When your friends die, you must not cry'. God, he claimed, had given him power over the elements, and had established him as His deputy in the west (which in itself almost seems to suggest the imprint of Christian conceptions, and the need for their special application to the Indian).

The teaching and the associated dance were quickly disseminated after the first performance of the dance at Walker Lake in January 1889. Delegates came from other tribes, and carried the knowledge of the Ghost Dance across the Plains. New railways had made travel very much easier, and there was, in addition, a sense in which Indians now

[67] Ibid., pp. 40–54.

[68] J. Mooney, op. cit., p. 15. Some of his earlier tricks are described by P. Bailey, op. cit., pp. 63–71. In Bailey's account, Wovoka is credited with a long trance prior to the occasion of the eclipse, and of giving a promise at that time that the dead were alive and in paradise. His ethical teachings are credited to that occasion, and likewise his dance and his use of feathers to induce the trance state. According to Bailey, Wovoka was afflicted with scarlet fever at the time of the eclipse on 1 January 1889, when he again swooned. Thereafter the escape of the sun from the monster that the Paiutes thought was eating it was attributed to Wovoka's intercession with God. In this revelation, after his recovery, Wovoka is reputed to have said that the whites would be swept away, and that Indians would become young again, and game would return. He claimed invulnerability after this trance, and had five new songs for affecting the weather. P. Bailey, op. cit., pp. 76 ff.

[69] This account is the one given by J. Mooney, op. cit., p. 14.

recognized their common condition, and responded to the common designation applied to them by white men. A millennialist doctrine of a return of the ancestors and a restoration of the former way of life attracted the people of many tribes as a gospel of hope in a world of increasing despair. The names of the prominent apostles of the new teaching and the new dance are well known. The proselytizer of the southern tribes, the Southern Arapaho, Caddo, Wichita, and Kiowa was an Arapaho, Sitting Bull.[70] He was regarded, even by the government's investigator, as a sincere man whose teachings were likely to dispose the Indians to live in better accord with their white neighbours.[71] Sitting Bull called a dance in September 1890, near the Cheyenne and Arapaho agency, on the bank of the North Canadian River, Oklahoma. The dance was attended by some 3,00 Inodians, including Caddo, Wichita, Kiowa, and Apache, and this was the greatest occasion of the Ghost Dance in the south. Visions were acquired in this dance, and Sitting Bull hypnotized some of the dancers so that they might see the happy world. The visions were readily incorporated into the songs.

Exaggerated accounts of the Indian messiah circulated among whites, and reports of the dance even by sophisticated observers were not always accurate. The Ghost Dance was attributed to a Cheyenne who lived among the Arapaho in late 1890, and who added the content of his own visions to the central teachings of Wovoka. There were apparently varying stories of cataclysm—cyclones, earthquakes, landslides.[72] Others thought that Sitting Bull was the originator of the dance, and reported new fantasies among the Cheyenne about seven nights and days of rain which had (or would) drown all the white soldiers (except General Nelson Miles).[73] The effect of inter-tribal association of the Indians, which reservations had also very much promoted, were evident in the dissemination of the new dance. The members of one tribe used the songs and dances of another until they acquired visions for songs of their own, and prescriptions for variations in the procedures of the dance.[74] The search for authentic revelation was also considerable, and some tribes sent their delegates to Wovoka to learn the message at first hand. The northern branch of the Cheyenne

[70] Not to be confused with Sitting Bull, the great chief of the Sioux, referred to on pp. 302 ff.

[71] J. Mooney, op. cit., pp. 146–56.

[72] Alice C. Fletcher, 'The Indian Messiah', *Journal of American Folklore* IV, 12 (January–March 1891), pp. 57–60.

[73] George Bird Grinnell, 'Account of the Northern Cheyenne Concerning the Messiah Superstition', *Journal of American Folklore* IV, 12 (January–March 1891), pp. 61–9.

[74] This section relies on Donald N. Brown, 'The Ghost Dance Religion Among the Oklahoma, Cheyenne', *The Chronicles of Oklahoma* XXX, 4 (Winter 1952–3), pp. 408–16. See also, J. Mooney, op. cit., p. 156.

(living in Wyoming) sent Porcupine, who returned to the reservation in 1890.[75] From them the Cheyenne in Oklahoma heard of the message, and the Arapaho, allies of the Cheyenne, sent Black Coyote and Washee to the northern reservation to learn the dance. Subsequently, the Southern Cheyenne and the Arapaho sent their own delegation to Wovoka, and on this occasion his instructions were written down. Very soon the new dance had superseded all other dances among these tribes, and a 'crow dance' was evolved by Grant Left Hand.[76]

The Caddo were one of the tribes who were keenest in the Ghost Dance, perhaps because they had an enthusiastic apostle, Nishkuntu (John Wilson), who was half-Delaware, part Caddo, and part French. He was one of the first to go into a trance; 'from that time [he] became the high priest of the Caddo dance. Since then his trances have been frequent, both in and out of the Ghost Dance, and in addition to his leadership in this connection he assumes the occult powers and authority of a great medicine man, all the power claimed by him being freely conceded by his people.'[77] He claimed to know what heaven was like, and consulted the 'father' in a trance state, to discover remedies for the sick. Indeed, from his subsequent religious activity in the Peyote cult, John Wilson ('Moonhead') ranks with his namesake, Wovoka (Jack Wilson) as one of the great innovators in Indian religion.[78]

The Kiowa were also well-disposed to the dance. In 1881, one of their young medicine-men, Datekan, had made medicine to bring the buffalo back, and in 1887 Paingya, another medicine-man, prophesied that as the whites had destroyed the buffalo, so God would destroy the whites. He drew the whole tribe to his tent by promising to bring down fire from heaven to destroy the agency, the school, the white race, and all Indian unbelievers. He promised, too, that the white man's bullets would be harmless. The Kiowa welcomed the Ghost Dance when it came, and seven leaders were appointed by the Arapaho, Sitting Bull. One of their dreamers, Bianki (Asatitola, the Dreamer), a remarkable man who had invented his own system of ideographic writing, had visions of meeting the ancestors in all their full regalia, dancing the

[75] A song composed by Porcupine, among the Northern Cheyenne, ran:

Our Father has come . . .
The Earth has come . . .
It is rising, eye ye . . .
It is hunting, Ahe e ye . . .

each line being repeated: Donald N. Brown, op. cit.
[76] Ibid., loc. cit.
[77] J. Mooney, op. cit., p. 161.
[78] On John Wilson's role in the Peyote cult, see pp. 423 ff.

Ghost Dance. They sent a delegation, but the principal emissary, Äpiatan, who had lost a child over whom he grieved a great deal and who dreamed of communicating with her again, wrote home, after meeting Wovoka, that the messiah was a fraud. The Kiowas had ideas of Wovoka as a type of Christ, and this, Äpiatan had not found him to be. For a time the Kiowa abandoned hope, although they organized another great dance under Bianki and others, in September 1894.[79]

The remarkable character of the Ghost Dance of 1890 is the extent to which it was diffused among Indians of tribes which had not previously had very much, if any, association. Inevitably, it acquired local variants as it spread. The Shoshone believed that both races would live together; the Paiute themselves believed that a flood would come; the Kiowa and Arapaho believed that a new earth would slip over the existing one. There were increasing variants of dance procedure as new dreamers arose, especially after Sitting Bull's missionary activity in Oklahoma, and there was a tendency, for example on the part of Porcupine, the Cheyenne, and among the Kiowa, to regard the distant person of Wovoka as a sort of Christ figure. But more remarkable than the differences was the unifying effect, however brief, of a common faith for erstwhile hostile tribes. 'Only those who have known the deadly hatred that once animated Ute, Cheyenne and Pawnee, one toward another, and are able to contrast it with their present spirit of mutual brotherly love, can know what the Ghost-dance religion has accomplished in bringing the savage to civilization.'[80] Perhaps Mooney's judgement is extreme, but the effect was none the less remarkable.

Not all Indian tribes were affected, of course. The 1890 Ghost Dance made little progress westwards beyond the Rockies (although it was taken up by the Washo, Bannock Utes, and Gosiute) and it has been suggested that the profound shock of culture contact and destruction of the native way of life was felt most keenly on the Plains at this time. In some regions there were already established 'new' religions— such as the Shakers in Washington, the Smohalla religion further east, and the teaching of Känakûk and the Potawatomi Prophet among the Kickapoos, Potawatomi, Sauk, and Fox, who were not much influenced by the Ghost Dance.[81] Nor were the Comanches, who had made their outbreak in 1873, much affected: the only ones to take up the dance were the Swift Stingers band, the one group which had not

[79] The foregoing paragraph relies entirely on J. Mooney, op. cit., pp. 163–73.
[80] Ibid., p. 25.
[81] Ibid., pp. 48–9, 158–9, A. L. Kroeber, *Handbook of California Indians*, op. cit., pp. 868–9, propounded a theory of 'immunization' by the earlier experience of 1870, in relation to the Californian tribes whose cultures were now totally destroyed.

participated in the millennialism associated with the Sun Dance of eighteen years before.[82] 'The Osage gave but little heed to the story, perhaps from the fact that as they are one of the wealthiest tribes in the country, they feel no such urgent need of a redeemer as their less fortunate brethren.'[83] Mooney was, in effect, an early exponent of the deprivation thesis. The Navaho, close neighbours of the Paiute, knew of the movement, but were unaffected. It has been suggested that they, too, were not as yet a particularly deprived people, that their life 'was integrated round a stable cultural pattern'.[84] But it has also been urged that the Navaho have a distinct fear of the dead, and that their return would be a matter of foreboding rather than of rejoicing, since ghosts often work evil.[85]

The Ghost Dance and cultural revitalization

The Ghost Dance affected many tribes, but, despite the high degree of similarity of the received teaching, its consequences were remarkably variable. The Pawnee and the Sioux were both peoples experiencing social circumstances that rendered them highly susceptible to millennialist teachings. The Pawnees, who had numbered perhaps 9,000 people, had been one of the large groups between the Mississippi and the Rockies, and they had concluded treaties with the whites in 1818

[82] E. A. Hoebel, op. cit., p. 303. The Northern Ute, some of whom were present at Wovoka's second performance of the Ghost Dance, at Pyramid Lake, were very little affected by the Dance. At this time however, they did adopt the Sun Dance, which had not hitherto been part of their ritual. J. A. Jones, 'The Sun Dance of the Northern Ute', Smithsonian Institution: Bureau of American Ethnology, Bulletin 157, *Anthropological Papers* No. 47, 1955, pp. 203–63. That tribes which had long practised the Sun Dance, the Arapaho, Cheyenne, and Dakota (Sioux) should have seized upon a completely alien rite, such as the Ghost Dance, and particularly one coming from a poor and despised people, the Paiutes, whilst the Utes (near neighbours of the Paiutes) and the Comanches should have adopted the alien Sun Dance at times of cultural stress, leads Shimkin to observe that, 'In all cases, there appears to be a correlation between the prior close functional integration of a ceremony and its psychological rejection at a time of overwhelming crisis': D. B. Shimkin, 'The Wind River Shoshone Sun Dance', Smithsonian Institution: Bureau of American Ethnology, Bulletin 151, *Anthropological Papers* No. 41, pp. 397–484, 1953, p. 435. The 'power' of culturally familiar ceremonial was known, but since circumstances of distress prevailed, and had not been affected by the known methods of invoking supernatural power, new vehicles were, one may suppose, much more attractive than old ones.
[83] J. Mooney, op. cit., p. 159.
[84] This is the interpretation of Bernard Barber, in 'Acculturation and Messianic Movements', *American Sociological Review* 6 (October 1941), pp. 663–8.
[85] This aspect of Navaho religion is emphasized by W. W. Hill in 'The Navaho Indians and the Ghost Dance of 1890', *American Anthropologist* 46 (October–December 1944), pp. 523–7. It is also mentioned by A. F. C. Wallace, in his Introduction to J. Mooney, op. cit., p. x. Fear of the dead among the Northern Ute is also a factor advanced to explain their lack of interest in the Ghost Dance: J. A. Jones, op. cit., pp. 227, 239.

and 1825; in 1833 they signed away some of their lands for annuities, agricultural implements, schools, and other advantages of white civilization. They were afflicted by new diseases arising from their contact with the whites, and they suffered from the westward migration of eastern tribes enforced by the whites. Tribal warfare was changing, especially as the buffalo which they hunted became fewer, and their old enemy, the Dakota Sioux, were evolving new methods of assault against them. After some years of attempting to adjust to a farming economy on the Platte River in Nebraska, the entire tribe, now only 2,026 people, moved south away from the marauding Sioux to a new reservation south of the Arkansas River, in 1875. The government policy was to discourage all old Pawnee customs, and to promote individual ownership of land and the break-up of the traditional Pawnee villages.[86]

Between 1875 and 1892, the Pawnee diminished in numbers from 2,026 to 759. New diseases afflicted them in Oklahoma; their attempts at agriculture were subject to diverse problems that were beyond their capacity to solve; and their social and ceremonial life was disrupted. Without the opportunity for prowess in war and their former responsibility for the welfare of their people, who now depended increasingly on the government agents, chiefs lost influence. Their medicine lost its power in the new circumstances. Without the sacred meat of the buffalo, the rituals could not be performed. The spring revival of games had ceased, and the great witch-doctor performances of magic ceased after 1878. The medicine bundles were buried with the medicine men when their apprentices did not understand their use, and even where, as in families, the bundles were handed on, the lore was increasingly lost.[87] The old societies for hunting and war atrophied, now that the buffalo had gone. 'Ceremonies, becoming functionless, became extinct.'[88] The rich aesthetic pattern and the past excitements of Pawnee life were replaced by a dreary, monotone existence: they were, in 1892, at a cultural impasse.

Into this situation came the Ghost Dance, which had been learned by a Pawnee, Frank White, from the Arapaho, Sitting Bull, the principal proselytizer in Oklahoma. White had visions of the recently dead Pawnees (and at the rate of population decline that they were experiencing, the memories of the dead must have loomed large for all

[86] Alexander Lesser, *The Pawnee Ghost Dance Hand Game: A Study in Cultural Change* (Columbia University Press, New York 1933), pp. 1–38. This paragraph and those following rely on this source.
[87] A. Lesser, 'Cultural Significance of the Ghost Dance', *American Anthropologist* 35 (January–March 1933), pp. 108–15.
[88] A. Lesser, *The Pawnee Ghost Dance Hand Game . . .*, op. cit., p. 50.

Pawnees). He organized dances and urged the Pawnee to dance the new kingdom into being. Trances were experienced and visions occurred. 'These visions became sanctions not only for special developments of the Ghost Dance, and of the hand games, but also for important revivals of old aspects of Pawnee life, which before this had ceased to function.'[89] The white man's ways were to be abandoned, and a high wind would soon blow all white people away, together with all those who did not dance. The buffalo and the dead would return. After a brief period, Frank White's exclusive leadership was challenged, although the practice by which the receiver of a vision needed to get proper ritual instruction from one who knew (the role White had appropriated), was closer to the old Pawnee pattern. Now, visions instructed individuals directly, and seven leaders of the Crow sub-division hypnotized the participants in the dance. Individuals now began to sponsor feasts at which a dance would take place, thus acquiring proprietary rights to determine the actual pattern of ceremonial.

The Pawnee Ghost Dance developed as a revitalization movement of Pawnee culture.[90] The meaning of the medicine bundles was now re-learned through visions: the dead instructed the living. The old societies were re-organized, the old songs were taught, and the old games were played again. In effect, the Ghost Dance redirected men to the past, although what they now forged was, necessarily, a blending of old and new. 'The Ghost Dance proved not only a force for cultural revival, but with a return to the past as an inspirational source and guide, and vision sanctions as immediate drives, the doctrine was an impetus to cultural development.'[91] The old games were now restored and, more significant, ritualized. Ceremonial forms were learned in visions, and this was particularly so for the hand game (in which two teams compete for hidden counters). The paraphernalia and ritual of the game now came to resemble the lore involved in the old medicine bundles. Luck in the game was an indication that supernatural forces were working for the winner. Since, in the world at large, luck was with the white man, and this was something which the message of the Ghost Dance promised to end, so the game came to symbolize and to indicate the extent of one's contact with the influence of the spirit world. The concept of luck was broadened through the Ghost Dance into a sign of greater faith. Ghost Dance game bundles now became similar to the

[89] Ibid., p. 62.
[90] The term 'revitalization movement' was coined by A. F. C. Wallace: 'Revitalization Movements: Some Theoretical Considerations for their Comparative Study', *American Anthropologist* 58 (April 1956), pp. 264–81. It was not employed by Lesser, but the Pawnee Ghost Dance is an excellent case for Wallace's category.
[91] A. Lesser, op. cit., p. 117.

old medicine bundles, with sacred objects, rituals, drums, waiters, game leaders, and smoke offerings, some of which items were also evident in the simultaneously emerging Peyote cult.[92] Dancing, feasting, and speech-making were common, and in the period of the direct influence of the Ghost Dance so were trances, when the practices performed at the games were the same as those of the Ghost Dance itself.[93]

Thus the game from the past became a new ritual, now that war and hunting had ceased to be significant in Pawnee life. Women were permitted to participate, although they never had in the past, and this, too, may indicate the increasing importance of women in a society the economy of which was forcibly being transformed from hunting to agriculture. (A similar tendency became increasingly evident in the Peyote cult.) Although they had not formerly done so, chiefs participated in the games, presiding in place of the priests who had presided in the past. Play in itself was perhaps also vital to the recovery of a way of life for the Pawnees, since this had disappeared through the years of struggle in Nebraska, and in the first decade and a half in Oklahoma.

The effects of such revitalization do not, of course, long persist. It constitutes an adjustment, a reinvigoration in a situation of despair and decline, in which the past, its sanctified meaning, and ritual expression are dead.

> Carrying out most of the rituals was impossible; developing new ritual forms based on the visions and associated with the old life of planting, hunting and war, was also impossible. The old ritual ceremonies were not only occasions of sanctity to the Pawnee, but also affairs of dramatic beauty. The ritual movements, and gestures, and symmetry, and order of the performance, the complexity of associations and acts to be remembered and performed, constituted an intellectual and aesthetic experience for the participant and observer. All this was missed by the people. The ceremonial hand game became at once a mode for creative, intellectual effort. . . .[94]

But a revitalization of the culture does not change material conditions. The Pawnee were forced into individual ownership: whites came and settled among them. Their separate way of life was doomed as a long-term prospect, although the games, in a de-ritualized form, persisted for several decades, and provided social occasions for a people now scattered on individual allotments. The Pawnee Ghost Dance hand game was the transformation of 'a gambling game into a complex

---

[92] Ibid., p. 168. On the Peyote cult, see pp. 414–41.
[93] Ibid., p. 220.
[94] Ibid., pp. 328–9.

ritual'. But over time 'ritual tends to relapse once more into mere games'.[95]

The Ghost Dance and militant action

The effect of the Ghost Dance among the Pawnee was necessarily that of a pacific restorative teaching. The Pawnee had for a long time abandoned the war-path, and their rapid decline in numbers precluded a revival of military activity. The millennial hope was a dream of a supernatural cultural restoration, which encouraged something of an actual restoration. The self-fulfilling aspiration, which is a common characteristic of the effect of religious faith, induced the Pawnees to create something for themselves because they fervently wished and prayed for its supernatural creation. It would be too facile to suggest that the effect of the Ghost Dance among the Sioux was a diametrically opposite one: to do so would attribute too much to the influence of the teaching as such. The so-called 'Sioux Outbreak' of 1890, when about three hundred Sioux were killed at the 'Battle' at Wounded Knee Creek, reflects, as the competent authorities saw at the time, the whole unhappy history of the Sioux people in their final struggle with the whites. The Ghost Dance was, at best, no more than an incidental factor.[96]

The Sioux were a large nation, and the last to be subdued by the whites. They were gathered into several tribes, and in 1890 were settled on several reservations in Dakota. Only a few years before they had been free, and had inflicted a dramatic defeat on Custer's force at the Little Big Horn. Sitting Bull, the chief of the Hunkpapa Sioux, had for some years been in Canada evading the American army, and he had somewhat reluctantly returned, with a starving band, to accept life on the reservation at Standing Rock. Recollections of recent wars with the whites, and the raids on the Pawnees and others, were still fresh. Glory in war, so recently a major cultural goal, was no longer available. The Sioux had experienced a dramatic change in their way of life

[95] Ibid., p. 330. Murray Wax in 'Les Pawnees à la recherche du Paradis perdu', *Archives de Sociologie des Religions* 4 (July–December 1957), pp. 113–22, pursues a similar analysis, emphasizing that in this period of anxiety the search for 'power' had become a search for 'luck'.

[96] This was the opinion of Commissioner Morgan, who put the Ghost Dance as the eleventh of the items in the background of the rising; of Dr. T. V. McGillycuddy, the former agent of the Pine Ridge reservation; of General Nelson Miles, who in his statement of the causes of Indian dissatisfaction did not mention the Ghost Dance. The reports are given in J. Mooney, op. cit., pp. 74–80.

within a very short time. They had progressively lost their lands as white settlement had led the government to impose successive treaties on the Indians, reducing their territory and their freedom. These grievances and government failure to produce the promised rations, on which reservation Indians lived, now that the buffalo had gone, had led to despair and anger among the Sioux, whose young men hankered after the chance to win glory in war, as those only a few years their senior had done.

The Sioux learned about the new messiah in the west in 1889 and sent a delegation to visit Wovoka; subsequently they sent a second delegation. Wovoka's message to the Sioux was to live in peace with the white men, who would soon be buried under a new land which was to descend upon the old. Red men would rule the world, and the returning ancestors would be led by the Messiah who once came to live on earth with the white men, but who had been killed by them. The delegates believed, as Kicking Bear told the story, that Wovoka had shortened their journey when they were tired, and they claimed to have seen their own dead relatives.[97] Whether from Wovoka's own claim to invulnerability, or from an independent vision to Black Elk, the Sioux were told by Kicking Bear of a shirt through which no bullets would pass.[98] The dance spread over the various Sioux reservations: the Brulé Sioux danced vigorously at the Rosebud reservation, where Short Bull and Mash-the-Kettle produced 'wonders' to convince their tribesmen of the new power. Such was the reputation of the Sioux, particularly on account of their defeat of Custer, that wild rumours spread among the white population concerning their purpose in dancing the Ghost Dance. The name of Sitting Bull was one to terrify the settlers in Dakota, and he was readily confused by the press with the Arapaho of the same name, and was thought to be mobilizing the tribes for war.[99] Sitting Bull of the Hunkpapa Sioux remained at his own camp in the Standing Rock reservation, watching the dance that Kicking Bear had introduced to his followers, although he appears not to have participated in the Ghost Dance himself.[100]

The real trouble among the Sioux appears to have arisen from the precipitate action of a new and inexperienced agent at Pine Ridge

[97] David Humphreys Miller, *Ghost Dance* (Duell, Sloan and Pearce, New York 1959), p. 54. This account rests largely on Indian sources, and may somewhat overstate, in some particulars, the Indian case.

[98] D. H. Miller, op. cit., p. 80, attributes the shirt to Black Elk, from whom he got some of his information, and who was Miller's adopted father. See also John G. Neihardt, *Black Elk Speaks* (University of Nebraska Press, Lincoln, Neb., 1961; first published 1932).

[99] D. H. Miller, op. cit., pp. 107–8.

[100] J. Mooney, op. cit., p. 92, says that Sitting Bull said that they had to dance in order to live. D. H. Miller, op. cit., p. 112.

reservation—a recent political appointment of an unsuitable man, in the tradition of American agency appointments—who persistently called for troops, such was his alarm at the Ghost Dance, which he, like many whites, mistook for a war-dance. Troops came to the Sioux country. Short rations had made the Indians defiant, but an experienced agent like McGillycuddy, who had maintained the reservation without a soldier for seven years, recommended that the troops should be removed. The arrival of the army had alarmed the Sioux, who felt that this meant a white attack, and towards the end of 1890 a large party broke camp and fled to a stronghold in the Bad Lands. The agent at Standing Rock reservation, James McLaughlin, had a deep-seated dislike of Sitting Bull, and had advised that if he, Kicking Bear, and one or two other chiefs were removed, then the trouble would subside.[101] Fearing that the Army were intent upon sending in Buffalo Bill Cody, who knew Sitting Bull, he sent in Indian police to arrest the old chief. Six policemen were killed in the struggle which occurred when Sitting Bull's men resisted the Indian police, and so were Sitting Bull and his son, Crowfoot.[102]

A series of incidents followed, with depradations of white property by Indians, and cruel attacks on innocent Indians by white ruffians. Troop movements alarmed the Sioux, and some fled to the party which had gone into the Bad Lands. The tragedy at Wounded Knee was a military blunder against a small party of relatively defenceless and very hungry Indians under Big Foot, who on 29 December 1890 were moving towards the Pine Ridge agency. While the soldiers were attempting to disarm the Indians, a medicine-man, Yellow Bird, showed some resistance, and took exception to a soldier handling one of the women in too familiar a fashion. He rose and reminded the Sioux of their invulnerability in the ghost shirts which they were wearing. Just how the firing began is subject to dispute, but the Indians were mainly unarmed.[103] Although no one was expecting an engagement, the troops suddenly panicked and fired into the Indian camp, killing many of them at once, together with a number of their own comrades, who were

[101] James McLaughlin, *My Friend, the Indian* (Houghton Mifflin, Boston 1910), p. 180, wrote, 'Crafty, avaricious, mendacious and ambitious, Sitting Bull possessed all the faults of an Indian, and none of the noble attributes. . . .'

[102] J. Mooney, op. cit., p. 101. Sitting Bull had for a time been induced to take part in Buffalo Bill Cody's Wild West Show in the 1880s. D. H. Miller, op. cit., pp. 177–192, suggests that McLaughlin had given his policemen plenty of whisky, and that he profited from the looting of Sitting Bull's cabin. Miller also recounts that one of the Indian policemen obtained hospitality in Sitting Bull's lodge, in order to admit his comrades, and that the police, perhaps in fear, desecrated Sitting Bull's body after his death.

[103] See J. Mooney, op. cit., pp. 115–9; D. H. Miller, op. cit., pp. 224–30.

in the line of fire.[104] What followed was a pitiless massacre. The majority of the three hundred Indians who died appear to have been women and children, some of them shot down three miles from the camp site where the firing began.[105] There were bodies 'scattered along as they had been relentlessly hunted down and slaughtered while fleeing for their lives'.[106] The Indians believed that the soldiers were seeking revenge for Custer's defeat.

The large party that had fled to the Bad Lands had at this time agreed to come into the agency, but the firing at Wounded Knee Creek caused new panic, and further skirmishes occurred, in one of which the 7th Cavalry were led into an ambush and were rescued only by the Negro 9th Cavalry, who had earlier been brought in as a re-inforcement when hostilities had seemed likely. The Sioux, hungry and bewildered, were divided about the action they should take. Finally, on 16 January, General Nelson A. Miles, a man widely trusted by the Indians, who was now empowered by Congress to make various offers, effected a peace with the Indians through a number of the chiefs, such as Young-Man-Afraid-of-his-Horses, who had remained un-affected by the disturbances and who saw the hopelessness of war with the white men.

Despite the fighting, there *never was* a Sioux uprising. The outbreak was a response of panic and despair, not an act of aggression. The Ghost Dance had been a gospel of hope, and in the mouths of the more extreme leaders, such as Kicking Bear and Short Bull, it had en-couraged first defiance of, and then resistance to, the Americans. But it was not, in itself, the prompter of a military campaign, and the principal action that occurred was largely caused by the presence of troops and the behaviour of the troops themselves.[107]

The Ghost Dance passed quickly among the Sioux, associated as it was with a hope that had turned to bitterness. It scarcely survived among other tribes, though some revived it for a few years after the season of its greatest vigour in 1890. Wovoka was dejected by the military encounters of the Sioux, and he accused them of having distorted his teaching. The messages he gave to later delegates, for

[104] Charles A. Eastman (Ohiyesa), author of *From the Deep Woods to Civilization* (Little Brown, Boston 1916; first published 1902), a Sioux who had already been trained as a doctor, and who was working at the Pine Ridge agency at the time of the Battle of Wounded Knee, wrote, p. 109, 'At dusk the Seventh Cavalry returned, with their twenty-five dead, and I believe thirty-four wounded, most of them by their own comrades who had encircled the Indians, while few of the latter had guns.'

[105] Ibid., p. 109; J. Mooney, op. cit., p. 119 ff.

[106] C. A. Eastman, loc. cit.

[107] This paragraph relies on J. Mooney, op. cit., and D. H. Miller, op. cit.

example those from the Cheyenne and Arapaho, who visited him in
October 1892, discouraged them, although many continued to believe,
and Wovoka retained his prestige as a wonder-worker for many years
after the Ghost Dance itself was dead.[108]

Conclusion

The millennialism of the movements discussed in this chapter is
associated essentially with the restoration of the physical, social, and
cultural conditions of the past. It differs from the millennialism of
many Christian movements, which postulate the creation of a *new*
dispensation on earth, or in heaven, or both. A sense of history and
progress is involved in any such projection of present wishes into a
future blissful state, and North American Indians, like any other pre-
literate peoples, lacked the time-perspective involved in futuristic
millennialism. They had only a general, imprecise and largely mythical
conception of their past history.[109] But they were aware of their present
sufferings, and they identified them with the magical power of their
enemies. What they sought was a new way of life, new power, and new
techniques (whether associated with their traditional practices or as
new moral prohibitions, or new rituals, particularly ritual dances) that
would make that power manifest.

That the movements should have focused so strongly on the restoration of the past, indicates the very limited extent of acculturation of
many North American Indians, and their persisting sense of their
separate way of life. They had acquired elements of white culture,
particularly the horse and firearms, but these they had absorbed into
their own culture, and conferred aboriginal meanings upon them. In
other respects, they were conscious of the deleterious consequences of
association with the white men, and their millennialist movements
frequently included the idea of purging their way of life of these afflictions—alcohol; marital infidelity; disease; and high mortality. The
restored way of life to come after the cataclysm was to be free of these
things. Two distinctive prohibitive dispositions were common: one
against the use of artefacts of white culture (although this was not

---

[108] D. N. Brown, op. cit., p. 416; G. M. Dangberg, op. cit.
[109] Thus Smohalla indignantly rejected the idea that the white man had introduced the
horse to the Indians, and asserted to the contrary that in the past the Indians had had much
better horses than now. E. Huggins, op. cit.

always associated with millennialism).[110] The other enjoined moral precepts which suggested that when the Indians had freed themselves from 'sin', the new dispensation would be supernaturally brought into being. (Obviously, where the use of alcohol was involved, the two prohibitive tendencies converged.) The prohibition of the appurtenances of white culture occurred in the Smohalla cult, as it had been in the more militant millennialism of Tenskwatawa. The second disposition was particularly marked in the preaching of Känakûk. Each of these orientations might steadily acquire a more intrinsic (and less magical) significance, of course, implying that obedience to these injunctions would in itself forge a new way of life. This sometimes occurred as the hope of supernatural action receded. Where these dispositions, and particularly the second, were strongly enjoined, a revolutionist movement had greater likelihood of persisting beyond the first flush of disappointment, and of continuing in being as a more introversionist response to the world.[111]

All of these movements manifested a strong sense of collective calamity and a demand for collective redemption. It was by corporate action that they would be saved, and it was their way of life, above all other temporary or individual afflictions, for which redemptive action was desired. Frequently these movements demanded that everyone must take part in the rituals, and sometimes supernatural sanctions were said to operate against non-participants.[112] But the social bases of corporate response were disappearing. Tribes were involved in closer association with each other on the reservation, and the diffusion of new patterns of supernatural action, such as occurred in the Ghost Dances and in the borrowing of the Sun Dance by tribes which had not previously performed it, led to a diminished significance of tribal identity. Travel, white contact, the loss of tribal functions in warfare and hunting, and the declining significance of distinctly tribal religious practice, promoted the same consequences. Thus, *Indian*, as distinct from *tribal*, identity became of increasing significance, as the Ghost Dances themselves made manifest, but, simultaneously, purely individual troubles became a more important focus for religious responses. The individualism, which was part of the cultural pattern of many Indian

[110] Relatively few accounts of the destruction of property are given in the records of North American Indian religious movements (such as occurred, for example, so commonly in Melanesia). Property was not so significant an item in these cultures. One instance of destruction of property, though in response to non-millennialist restorative teachings, is reported of converts to the Feather cult, promoted by Jake Hunt among the Wishram, at Spearfish, Columbia River, although this appears also to be an isolated instance in this cult. C. Du Bois, *The Feather Cult . . .*, op. cit., p. 26.

[111] On North American introversionist movements, see pp. 387 ff.

[112] This was the case in the Ghost Dance of 1870 among Californian tribes.

tribes, was enhanced, but within a new context—that of the wider society (Indian society, and, increasingly American society). The tribe was no longer there, providing the social-structural and normative framework within which individualistic aspirations could work themselves out. New possibilities of voluntaristic action developed—not least in the religious sphere. The shamanism of the past, with its individual applications, provided the basis for the thaumaturgical religious movements of the future.[113]

[113] On North American thaumaturgical movements, see pp. 349 ff.

10

Commodity Millennialism

NOT all revolutionist religious movements are associated with warfare, rebellion, or guerilla terrorism. Such an association occurs only in certain circumstances when revolutionist religion becomes an agency for the mobilization of psychological resources for social and cultural defence. Since traditional magic has failed, new magic, prophecies, or charisma must be discovered if the 'magic' of the invader, so evident in his military capacity, is to be countered. The powerful emotions released in such a situation are readily drawn into a religious response to evil circumstances. Since less-developed peoples depend on local communal social organization, the emotions are subject to much less self-control and are more easily summoned for collective behaviour. Great emotional intensity is a characteristic of the new religions that arise among them, in which the processes of institutionalization, which routinize and formalize (and in western societies intellectualize) religious exercises, have not occurred. It is the spontaneity, emotional intensity, and the sense of power engendered in such movements that stimulates collective action.

Where indigenous society was constituted of many small and mutually hostile groups (as in New Guinea, Australia, New Zealand and, in large part, North America) such collective action could become warfare only where cultural contact extended slowly. Such a process occurred in North America: armed conflict continued over a long period, facilitated by the extensive terrain suited to nomadic hunters but, until specific technological advances had been made, not for white settlement; by the initially much lower disparity of strength between natives and invaders than was the case in later periods of conquest elsewhere; and by the intermittent wars between English and French rival colonists. Consequently, despite the relative smallness of most North American tribes, warfare was a feasible response, encouraging new associations among tribes. In miniature, a similar pattern emerged in New Zealand.

Because Melanesian peoples were in small localized units, warfare against the invader was rarely an effective possibility after the first encounter. Colonial administration was effective relatively quickly, and inter-tribal warfare was suppressed early. A revealing instance of the ease with which white dominance was attained, occurs in the settlement of the Purari delta, on the southern coast of British New Guinea. Sir William Macgregor, the first lieutenant governor, visited the area in 1894 with two other Europeans and twenty armed native constables.

> Traveling by a decrepit steam launch, they [reached] the large Koriki village group of Kairu'u. Here . . . the people were confidently hostile to the point of openly announcing that they would kill all members of the patrol before morning. Attack, however, did not come that night, but with reinforcements from other Koriki villages it was estimated that more then five hundred warriors had been gathered by the time Sir William's party was ready to depart on the next day. These disposed upstream and down on both banks of the fifty-yard-wide stream. In addition, war canoes were in the water for close-quarter attack. The entire force had been placed under the command of the most important Kairu'u chief, a man named Kauri, who had impressed Sir William as a leader of ability. As the launch headed upstream the bowmen on the banks fired a co-ordinated volley, and the war canoes moved in for attack. But the patrol, with incredibly good fortune, escaped casualty, and their return volley had great effect. Within minutes the Koriki battle lines had been dispersed and the launch pulled away to safety. In retrospect it seems probable that this experience had considerable psychological effect on the Koriki and paved the way for advancing administration influence. The Kairu'u people and their allies had gone to battle on their own terms, with a great advantage in numbers and initiative, and under experienced leadership. But they had been defeated in short order without inflicting injury on their enemy. A growing respect for administrative authority and personnel would appear to have begun here.[1]

This was perhaps reinforced in the area by 'what the Purari knew of the punishment the Goaribari received as a consequence of their massacre of the [James] Chalmers party [in 1901]. A punitive expedition of troops from Queensland moved against the Goaribari, killing many of them and destroying much property.'[2] The size of the Koriki force, five hundred men, was far greater than the normal war party in New Guinea, where fighting units were usually organized only at the village level.

Thus in New Guinea there was neither the time nor the space that facilitated the long-drawn-out, if sporadic and intermittent, military conflict between indigenes and invaders that occurred in North America, in the context of which early revolutionist religion developed. Nor were tribes large enough, as in South Africa, to engage in wars

[1] Robert F. Maher, *New Men of Papua* (University of Wisconsin Press, Madison 1961), p. 37.
[2] Ibid., p. 37 n.

and rebellions over a long period, in association with new religions of the revolutionist type. The technical superiority of the whites and the smallness of Melanesian tribes precluded even effective rebellion. Thus religious agencies could not be used, as they were in the Mau Mau movement in Kenya, to foster political ends. In that case, although the tribal culture had in some degree decayed, it had not been abandoned as an inferior thing: it could still be invoked to induce social unity, and it still stood as an effective symbol for another way of life at least for one large and powerful tribe.[3]

Revolutionist religion and cultural continuities

New religious movements in Melanesia are most remarkable not only for their profusion, but also for their localism and for the similarity, over a wide area and a considerable span of time, of their predominant concerns. The revolutionist religious responses in this area—and most cult movements have been revolutionist—have not normally been associated with military activity. Aggressive gestures certainly occurred in *some* movements, but it would be facile to regard every occasional murder of an unpopular trader or the imitation of military exercises as of real revolutionary intent. The fundamental response of new Melanesian cults has not been to reject white men, much less their culture.

Revolutionist religion is a demand for the transformation of the social situation: in the South Seas that demand has been expressed as a search for economic betterment and status opportunities. This expression of traditional Melanesian preoccupations gives the new movements their generic name, 'cargo cults'. Incipient nationalism; the expression of anti-white feelings; the search for the native past—have at times all been associated aspirations: but all have been subsidiary to the dominant concern for the realization of new opportunities to seek social status by traditional means—the proof of ability by the accumulation of wealth.

Cargo cults differ sharply from revolutionist movements such as the Ghost Dance obsession to restore the native past; or the Hau Hau movement in its struggle for the land; or the Ras Tafaris with their racist animus and their search for another ('old' and 'new') country. Like other revolutionists, cargo cultists seek access to power, and like other such cultists among colonial peoples, power at least the equivalent

[3] On Mau Mau, see pp. 364–8.

of that enjoyed by colonists, missionaries, soldiers, traders, or settlers. The demand for enhanced power is the key to whatever specific cultural content a revolutionist movement takes as its primary focus. Supernatural command of cargoes is the Melanesian cult equivalent of the demand of militarily active revolutionist movements for power to withstand bullets, or (as in nativistic movements) to control the environment as in the past, or (as in western revolutionist sects) to sit at the right hand of God.

Since trade goods occupied an important place in Melanesian cultures, being the means by which an individual established his status in many societies, the arrival of materially well-endowed Europeans, with many new and useful commodities, was by no means universally unwelcome to the natives. The demand for these goods was quickly developed, and natives were eager for power similar to that of Europeans to conjure up cargoes from beyond the seas. The assumption that these shiploads of commodities came from the ancestors was widespread, and in the search to emulate the European many aspects of white behaviour that implied either power or ritual significance were imitated.

Thus in many unassociated cult movements similar elements of white culture acquired sudden importance, as cultists practised to acquire the economic power of Europeans. Words of command were one obvious manifestation of power in white society, since in response to them men obeyed, sometimes engaging in complex, unified, and co-ordinated action. Pieces of paper with writing on them—letters—appeared intrinsically powerful, because in response to them action was summoned and decisions communicated. Paraphernalia such as aerials or telegraph poles appeared to have almost magical significance, and their use was simulated in some cults. Even the building of wharfs or airstrips, roads, and storehouses to receive the much wished-for cargo, entailed, in addition to rational planning, a much more significant element of magical thinking. The cults organized spectacular and collective action, which it was supposed would be automatically efficacious.[4] And although wharfs do not quite produce steamers nor airstrips planes, there is a sense in which the cults demonstrate the self-fulfilment of prophecy. Dramatic events do occur, and there *are* concrete products, even if they fall short of what the cultists expect. And in the hysteria that often accompanies these movements intense power is felt, and its cause easily objectified.[5]

[4] Jean Guiart, 'Conversion to Christianity in the South Pacific' in S. L. Thrupp, op. cit., pp. 122–38.
[5] On such hysteria, see above, the cult movements in the Eastern Highlands, pp. 216 ff., and below, in the Vailala Madness, pp. 317 ff.

Diffusion and diversity

Elements such as those referred to above are found in a large number of Melanesian movements. It is easy to describe the 'typical' cargo cult because so many specific items and patterns of behaviour are replicated or have their close equivalents in cult after cult. This circumstance raises two issues: the extent of diffusion of cult movements and the associated question of specific origins; and the extent to which differences do obtain among these movements.

The cargo cult is not one movement: there have been many more or less similar movements preoccupied with cargo. Well over a hundred different cults have been reported among peoples widely spread over this vast region. The broad similarity of cultural preoccupations goes some way to explain similarities spontaneously occurring. But diffusion and recrudescence have also occurred. Whether the Koreri myth was indigenous or not, there have been, as we have seen, many separate outbreaks of Koreri enthusiasm in the Schouten Islands.[6] We know too that important elements in the *Joe Gimlet* or *Sivioli* cult in Samoa were picked up from the *Mamaia* cult in Tahiti in the early nineteenth century.[7] The initiators of the later cults in the Madang area in the years just before and just after the war were acquainted with earlier movements.[8] It is unlikely that participants in the Jonfrum movement were unacquainted with movements that had earlier troubled other islands in the New Hebrides, and this movement in turn became a source of rumours elsewhere at later dates.

Whichever ideas and prophecies have been diffused, however, we have no reason to suppose that anything like the pattern of the Peyote religion occurred in respect of cargo cults.[9] The outbursts were themselves often ecstatic and of relatively brief duration, and some of the phenomena of hysteria were certainly local and spontaneous. Ideas may, of course, have travelled long distances and inspired local prophets, and in some circumstances even Christian teachings may have been enough to stimulate the emergence of a cult.[10]

There are also significant differences between the ideas and behaviour associated with various movements. Even within one specific region,

[6] See pp. 199–206.
[7] See J. D. Freeman, op. cit., pp. 185–200. On Mamaia, see W. E. Mühlmann, *Arioi und Mamaia: Eine Ethnologische religionssoziologische und historische Studie über Polynesische Kultbünde* (Franz Steiner Verlag, Wiesbaden 1955), pp. 194–243.
[8] See pp. 327 ff.
[9] See pp. 422 ff.
[10] For discussion of this possibility, see pp. 342, 442.

where later cultists know all about earlier cult expectations and rituals and may have participated in them, new variations occur. Oscillation between acceptance of white culture and emphatic nativism is found. Some movements are more pronouncedly anti-white than others. Some are quasi-Christian, and others demand complete dissociation of their followers from the missions.

Nor do cults all arise at similar stages of cultural contact. In the Eastern Highlands a cult precedes European contact; in Tanna the first cult movement develops decades after the settlement of missionaries and administration. Once arising, a sequence of cults in one area may differ from that occurring in another. The cults do not in themselves necessarily grow increasingly anti-white, nor are less unfriendly cults followed by cults that are more unfriendly and more symbolically militant.

However, some distinctions do occur. We have already considered Melanesian cults that are essentially preoccupied with new patterns of garden magic. Gestures imitative of European practices are incorporated in a cult like the Taro cult,[11] but it is in itself neither revolutionist nor yet a cargo cult in the normal sense of the term. Later we shall consider cults that reveal a much stronger appeal to rational procedures of social action than do the cargo cults now to be discussed. Some correlation of length and intensity of exposure to European culture and education must be presumed in the shift from cults with distinctly mystical ideas about the production of cargo to those movements in which mystical and religious ritual are subordinated to systematic, empirically-validated procedures of work and organization.

Frequently, the extent to which a movement is magical or rational reflects almost exclusively the experience and capacity of the leader. And here we see a significant variable which must in itself destroy any ready correlation between the stage of cultural contact experienced by a particular group or tribe and the degree of mysticism of the cults that outcrop among them. For cargo cultism is in considerable measure voluntaristic religious practice. Not every man need join a movement that is active in his village or among his people. A leader or a prophet usually mobilizes only a section of his society, and in one society there must inevitably be some people who are more, and some less, acculturated to western ideas, from among whom he wins his following according to the ideology that he himself puts forward. Of course, where men have so tenuous a grasp on the social reality in which they are involved as is the case in Melanesia, a powerful and dynamic figure such as a Yali may swing his following towards social construction or nativistic ritual in accordance with his own varying interpretations of what is to

[11] On the Taro cult, see pp. 74–5.

be done. Or, perhaps among less-advanced groups, the prophet may be a man of less than average emotional stability who becomes the catalyst bringing a new movement into being on the strength of visions: adolescents have not been infrequently cast in such roles, but the more significant Melanesian cults appear to have required the potential 'big man' as a fitting leader, whose high status commands respect and obedience.[12]

As is evident from the recrudescent Koreri movement, and from the cult in the Eastern Highlands, cargo cults may now arise at virtually any stage of cultural contact. Even tribes who have not seen westerners now meet them with cargo expectations on first encounter. The cargo idea is diffused certainly throughout New Guinea, and perhaps through most if not all of the islands of Melanesia. The existence of the cargo beliefs does not, of course, imply with any certainty that a cargo cult will develop:[13] it is merely a propitious pre-condition. But pre-existence of the belief facilitates the emergence of a cult among those whose experience of culture contact has been only slight. Given such a belief, a cult may be touched off by relatively ordinary events. Such was the case among the Semeira.

A spontaneous cargo cult

The Semeira, a group of the Kaowerabedj people of the Mamberamo River in New Guinea, had experienced relatively little cultural contact when the first cult movement was reported from this area in the late

[12] Te Ua, prophet of the Hau Hau movement, is an example of an emotionally unstable prophet. Adolescents as prophets are reported among the Xhosa in South Africa (see pp. 239–41). They were frequent among the Tukuna in Brazil, according to Curt Nimuendajú (Unkel), *The Tukuna*, op. cit., pp. 138–40, when movements inspired by adolescent prophets subsequently passed under the control of a shaman. The visions of a youth stimulated cult activity in Tangu: see Kenelm O. L. Burridge, *Mambu: A Melanesian Millennium* (Methuen, London 1960), p. 175. A cult was begun by a girl, Polelesi, in Garialand in 1947, according to Peter Lawrence, *Road Belong Cargo: A Study of the Cargo Movement in the Southern Madang District in New Guinea* (Manchester University Press, Manchester 1964), p. 162. Cyril S. Belshaw in 'Recent History of Mekeo Society', *Oceania* XXII, 1 (September 1951), pp. 1–23, speculates on the extent to which native political activity may canalize aggressive feelings engendered by guilt in the emergence of the prophetess, Filo, who had dreams and visions of cargo in the Mekeo region of the central division of Papua in 1941. Filo had married a kinsman of too close a degree of relationship before uttering her prophecies (which induced a great deal of hysteria). One is however also struck by cases of prophets of whom little is reported except that they are recently bereaved, which may also be sufficient to induce dramatic mental reactions.

[13] Raymond Firth in 'The Theory of "Cargo" Cults: A Note on Tikopia', *Man* LV, 102 (September 1955), pp. 130–2, notes that incipient cargo ideas existed on the Polynesian island of Tikopia, but that no cult had arisen: in explanation of this Firth attaches importance to the lack of a charismatic leader.

1950s.[14] A child had died, and its father and uncle sought to discover who had killed it by mixing its flesh with that of a fish. Instead of divining the 'murderer', they conjured up Djewmé, the goddess of the afterworld, and a group of *warria*, spirits of the dead. They ordered that the child's body should be interred before decomposition (which was not a tribal custom) and that a house should be built over it. That night Djēwmé and the spirits reappeared and promised to return for ever with a cargo of axes, tobacco, machetes, and outboard motors. Traditionally Djēwmé is thanked after the burial of a man's bones by a feast at which gifts of food are exchanged to resolve old enmities, and at which singing and dancing occur. Part of the traditional belief is that the spirits will return bringing food gifts from the spirit world.

When the visions associated with the child's death were seen the account of them spread rapidly, affecting other tribes, and a cult movement began. Excitement mounted at the prospect of cargo, and houses were built to receive it. Later there was an accretion of stories typical in cargo cults, that Europeans had hitherto kept all wealth to themselves although it had been intended that they should at least share it with natives. In this instance these stories appear to have arisen with one Banni, who took the cult to the Airmati tribes, and who was himself a much embittered native who demanded to know why Europeans kept 'factories' to themselves, and why the natives did not get 'factories'. Banni promised the natives that they would soon live in brick houses and persuaded them to burn down their own. Later, after more than one lapse and recrudescence of cult enthusiasm, a feast of several nights' duration for which many pigs were killed was held after the death of a bachelor. When the food ran out a period of relative famine followed, and the subsequent deaths caused a renewal of the cult, with Banni explaining that the Europeans had now stopped the cargo.

Such a cult displays various continuities with traditional feast-giving and the preoccupation with wealth, but that a movement erupts in which there is more intense expectation of a much larger quantity of wealth than ever before can be attributed only to increased acquaintance with the material goods of Europeans. The sense of relative deprivation of an intensely acquisitive people can only be enhanced by that ever-increasing flow of commodities in the possession of Europeans. The cult expresses the urgency induced by awareness of an ever-extending cultural gap in the material accoutrements of life, and the growing self-disparagement and sense of inferiority of the natives.

[14] Gottfried Oosterwal, 'A Cargo Cult in the Mamberamo Area', *Ethnology* II, 1 (January 1963), pp. 1–14.

Reports of cargo cults by no means always comment on the psychic state of the cultists, but Oosterwal reports that when singing the words of the cargo song, 'They [Djēwmé and the spirits] bring along the cargo for us', the 'people . . . become very highly excited; they shout and shriek them rather than sing them, and it seems as though their repetition alone were enough to bring the desired material wealth'.[15] The impression of such emotional intensity to will something into being exactly resembles that of, for example, would-be curers of disease in the Aladura churches of West Africa.[16] To comment on their psychic state is not to say that native cultists are deranged or insane, or even that they are intellectually inferior. It is simply to acknowledge that cult movements summon emotional expression that transcends rational control: they manifest the intensity of feeling involved as people seek to will things to happen. Although some early reports echo the commonplace settler judgement that 'the natives have gone berserk again', we can reject this facile prejudice without disregarding important data about psychic aspects of religious behaviour or leaping (all too often with intense passion) to the verdict that natives are just as rational as we are.[17]

Cargo and hysteria

A movement the profound emotional character of which is well documented is the *Vailala Madness*, an enthusiastic outburst that broke out in 1919 among the Western Elema of the Gulf Division, on the southern coast of Papua, more than a hundred miles west of Port Moresby. The cult was marked by the onset of giddiness, referred to as 'head-he-go-round', which sometimes affected whole villages simultaneously, particularly at the beginning of the cult's development. The cult leaders were the most affected, some of whom, when questioned, asserted, 'I no savvy. God he savvy.' Affected individuals would stand and sway, moving backwards and forwards, uttering gibberish as they did so. This phenomenon appeared to occur spontaneously in many instances, but it was also stimulated (and perhaps simulated) in others, and some natives lost considerable weight as a consequence of vigorous

[15] Ibid., p. 10.

[16] Author's own field observation; see p. 182.

[17] The strongest objection to the use of the term 'irrational' in respect of cult movement and cult behaviour comes from I. C. Jarvie, *The Revolution in Anthropology* (Routledge, London 1964), especially p. 92; *idem*, 'Theories of Cargo Cults', *Oceania* XXXIV, 1 (September 1963), pp. 1–31, especially pp. 27–30.

participation in the cult's activities. The automatic behaviour was associated with stories of visions of the ancestors and promises of their return with a cargo of tobacco, calico, knives, axes, and foodstuffs.[18]

The Western Elema had had an LMS missionary settled among them since the 1880s, and between that time and the time of the Vailala Madness there had been a considerable impact of western culture, and this despite the absence of anchorages on the coast. The missionaries had built a compound; used a water-pump and a steam press for making wooden planks; had a small boat, rickshaws, and cows. Slowly the Elema had accepted some aspects of Christianity, and its rituals were replacing pagan rites in some respects.[19] Some men had probably been involved in mining operations in the early years of the century when the area 'received a considerable amount of expatriate commercial attention'.[20] The Anglo-Persian Oil Company had also been active in the district and had employed many natives.[21] Plantation work had been introduced, and the administration had obliged the Elema to grow rice, which they did not wish to do. In 1918 taxation had been opposed. In 1919 there had been a rise in copra prices and a high demand for native labour. In 1918, Luluais, native officials, had been appointed, although they did not fit into the traditional social structure of New Guinea peoples.

The Madness appears to have begun when a native recently afflicted by the death of his father and brother went into a trance, had visions of deceased kinsmen and of the ancestors, and gave prophecies of the coming of a steamer with cargo for the natives. Many other ideas were added as the movement spread, constituting an emporium of native fantasies about the heaven which they were to inherit from the ancestors and things it would contain—usually the accoutrements of European culture. Strong elements of mission teaching were incorporated into the different versions of the cult, and many of those who became its adherents described themselves as 'Jesus Christ men'. God and Christ were seen in visions. For some, heaven was a place where they would wear long clothes—perhaps derived from the sight of the Roman Catholic missionaries on Yule Island.

Elements of Christian ethics were sometimes also expounded by the cultists. The ancestors exhorted men to be honest, not to commit

---

[18] The primary source for the Vailala Madness on which this section principally relies, is F. E. Williams, *The Vailala Madness and the Destruction of Native Ceremonies in the Gulf Division* (Papuan Anthropology Reports, 4, Port Moresby 1923).

[19] Glynn Cochrane, *Big Men and Cargo Cults* (Clarendon Press, Oxford 1970), p. 44, on which this paragraph chiefly relies.

[20] Ibid., p. 48.

[21] P. Worsley, op. cit., p. 79.

adultery, to keep the sabbath, to abandon traditional ornaments and nose and ear perforations, to tidy up the villages, to be clean in eating, and to wash. There was also imitation of plantation, or possibly police, discipline: the leaders regularly ordered the community to 'fall in'. The obviously powerful items of white culture, albeit almost magically conceived—the Bible and the letter—were both in evidence. Illiterate natives would pretend to read from the Bible, and pieces of paper with marks on them were carried about as 'letters'. The painted flagpoles which became a feature of the cult in each village were claimed by one trader to be imitations of the Persian Oil Company's wirelesses.[22]

In each village that was affected a cult 'temple' was built called a 'hot house', most probably because heat was associated with the power of 'big men' in the past. Men entering the temple were said to become 'hot'—inspired. A pole of between fifteen and thirty feet in length was kept in the temple, and from it messages were received from the dead— it was a medium of communication between the living and their ancestors. The pole was credited with a will of its own, and although it was carried by at least two men it was believed to be able to detect miscreants and to perform a general divinatory role. The pole was also credited with protective power against sickness in some instances. One of the most forceful injunctions of the cult was the maintenance of funerary feasts for the dead. Tables were laid with cloths and flowers in European style and natives, dressed in their best clothes, spent their time sitting at them. Relatives of the recently dead gave periodic feasts. The ancestors were also awaited with presents, gathered on to platforms by the 'big men' of the movement.[23]

The cult spread to other villages as local evangelizers took it from the points of its origin west into the Purari delta and eastwards to the Biara River.[24] At this point of origin, the cult died out within nine months, except for a few mild incidents.[25] For a time its leaders had acquired considerable authority, displacing those who had achieved their status as local leaders in more traditional ways. But although the cult itself was not, even on the most liberal estimates, of very long duration, it persisted long enough to cause the destruction in many places of the traditional ceremonies and rituals, and to achieve in a sudden outburst of frenzy the abandonment of many aspects of local

[22] Ibid., p. 85.
[23] G. Cochrane, op. cit., p. 53, and F. E. Williams, 'The Vailala Madness in Retrospect in E. E. Evans-Pritchard (Ed.), *Essays Presented to C. G. Seligman* (Kegan Paul, London 1934), pp. 369–79.
[24] P. Worsley, op. cit., p. 89.
[25] G. Cochrane, op. cit., p. 55, quoting the resident magistrate, G. H. Murray, gives the place of origin as Arihava. P. Worsley, op. cit., p. 85, says it began at Iori,

culture that missions had been condemning and upon which planters had poured contempt for many years.[26]

The Vailala Madness was a powerfully emotional expression of the expectation of, and the demand for, the transformation of native life. It both proclaimed and in part attained that transformation. Despite the preoccupation with the ancestors, the movement was in no sense nativisitic: the ancestors were merely the agents whose authority was invoked *to destroy the traditional* and to establish new rituals of greater power, and who would themselves bring the cargoes of commodities that, hitherto, only white men had enjoyed. There was no teaching of the restoration of the life of the past. The visions, ideals, and practices of the cult were an amalgam of traditional and European elements. What else could they be for men who saw two such sharply contrasted ways of life, who clung to the failing but still indispensable reassurance of the past whilst hazily perceiving and coveting the appurtenances of a new culture?

It is not easy to say to what extent the movement was anti-white. Reason for resentment against white men, and particularly against traders, planters, and other employers of labour, the natives certainly had. But there is no report that the cult had any promise of a 'reversal of roles' of black and white men in the dispensation to come. Black men were promised that they would get light skins in some variants of the enthusiasm, and the ancestors were traditionally regarded as white (white men were sometimes mistaken for dead ancestors[27]). Worsley, who sees cargo cults as pre-political movements of protest, emphasizes black-white relations and 'anti-white sentiments',[28] although he himself quotes Williams in referring to Kori, one of the principle disseminators of the Madness, as 'a rather singular personality, more than usually cunning, but nevertheless a very faithful and energetic friend of the Government'.[29] Retrospectively, it is not difficult to regard cargo cults as spontaneous outbursts of feeling against oppression waiting for a coherent and 'rational' political ideology. The 'class struggle' is

[26] On the apa-Hevehe ceremony, which the Elema discarded, see G. Cochrane, op. cit., pp. 17–32.

[27] P. Worsley, op. cit., p. 85. In common with other South Sea Islanders, the Elema are reputed to have regarded the first Europeans they saw as spirits of the dead: J. Chalmers, *Pioneering in New Guinea* (The Religious Tract Society, London 1887), pp. 42, 43.

[28] P. Worsley, op. cit., p. 90. See also p. 81. He takes the 'rudeness' of natives while in the entranced condition as further evidence (p. 88), although there is other evidence to show that natives were quickly 'brought to their senses'. He believes that the organization of the movement was 'tighter' than Williams suggests, although I do not interpret his evidence (that of Murray) as implying that. He also believes that Williams over-emphasized the psychological aspects and underestimated the 'political significance of the movement' (pp. 78–9).

[29] Ibid., p. 85.

exported to the colonies and race differences become the surrogates of relationships between classes.

But cargo cults embody a number of diverse and often contradictory elements.[30] Although it is true that in the colonial situation, where political activity is suppressed or closely controlled, religious activity may become the only possible means of collective expression, it is also true that natives conceive of their problems in religious terms. It is only at much later stages and with a much more sophisticated indigenous population that religion becomes a conscious agency of political feeling. To meet this fact by regarding the cargo cult, or a similar movement, as a collective manifestation in search of 'true consciousness' is to lose sight of the reality for the sake of the theoretical scheme into which it has to be fitted: in its own way it is to hold the native in as much contempt as does the benighted planter.

What the Vailala Madness manifested was the attempt to absorb new information, new concepts, and new artefacts, to wish into being a new order of affluence and, as Cochrane has illustrated, new opportunities for status.[31] The Europeans, with their obvious power, were the new 'big men' of Elema society, in many ways behaving in ways exactly comparable to those of the men who, by dint of industry, cleverness, and judicious marriages had, in the past, amassed wealth, special knowledge, and reputation. Like them, the Europeans accumulated crops, acquired trade goods (of even more impressive kinds), performed mysterious acts clearly directed to ancestors, gave orders and were obeyed, made decisions, healed diseases by superior magic, and fed their adherents in a patron-follower relation as did the big men of old.

By the end of the First World War, Elema social structure was severely disordered. The old overseas trading relations had collapsed with new patterns of work; shell-money, the traditional form of wealth for a variety of activities, was in short supply and reciprocal obligations were thus difficult to meet. Plantation life had disrupted the rhythms of the old society: there was no time for the old ceremonies, '. . . there was no longer any ritual framework within which the Elema could establish their identity'.[32] The Europeans treated the natives as men of no status, 'rubbish men'. What the Vailala Madness sought to effect was to provide a way whereby 'big men', those protectors of the

[30] Ibid., p. 90.
[31] The logic of cults for natives is well brought out by C. S. Belshaw, 'The Significance of Modern Cults in Melanesian Development', *Australian Outlook* 4, 2 (June 1950), pp. 116–25. G. Cochrane, op. cit., gives particular emphasis to native concern for status.
[32] Ibid., p. 49.

community of the past, could re-emerge among them. Had Europeans assumed the full responsibilities of the old 'big men', sharing, competing, involving themselves in native society, the cult might not have been necessary at all. The cult leaders were themselves would-be 'big men' of the new world which they envisaged, and their cult was a way of seeking status for themselves and a way of seeking to create a new form of social organization.

The Jonfrum movement: a recrudescent cult

Whilst certain features are common to many Melanesian movements— and in particular the need of natives to make sense of European behaviour, to explain European wealth, and to seek ways to reduce cultural disparities—other elements are not given the same emphasis in all movements (or in the available reports about them). The *Jonfrum* movement on the island of Tanna, New Hebrides, occurred after much longer experience of contact than the Vailala Madness; it was apparently much less characterized by extreme hysterical behaviour; it was, once begun, recrudescent. It is less readily analysed in terms of the displacement of local 'big men' and the attraction of the cult for those who aspired to this role, which may reflect the character of Tanna social structure at the time of the cult outbreaks, or may only reflect the fact that we know so much less about the prophets and the leaders of the movement.

Tanna was a fertile island with a population of about 5,700 in 1940 when, after two centuries of contact with whites its first reported cargo cult, the Jonfrum movement, broke out.[33] The Presbyterian mission settled on the island in 1848. There had been difficulty in establishing missions originally, until they gained success by curbing the traders and the recruiters of labour for the plantations in New Caledonia, Fiji, and the sugar-cane fields of Queensland.[34] The system, known as 'blackbirding' was little more than a thinly disguised slave-trade. French shippers had also recruited women from the island.[35] The missionaries brought law and order to Tanna, whose people were

[33] G. L. Barrow, 'The Story of Jonfrum', *Corona* (Journal of HM Colonial Service) III, 10 (October 1951), pp. 379–82, uses this title. Other writers refer to 'John Frum'. The usual explanation of the name is that 'Frum' alludes to the 'broom' with which whites would be swept off the island.
[34] J. Guiart, 'Culture Contact and the John Frum Movement on Tanna, New Hebrides', *Southwestern Journal of Anthropology* 12, 1 (Sping 1956), pp. 105–16.
[35] Loc. cit.

unpopular with other islanders for their avarice and their reputation as sorcerers and poisoners.[36]

The missions imposed their own morality on the Tanna islanders. Kava-drinking, prostitution, and warfare were brought to an end, and in 1914, some eight years after the establishment of the Anglo-French Condominium, the mission appropriated wide tracts of land 'in trust' for the natives. In practice, the land was rented to natives who agreed not to engage in 'heathen practices' on 'mission' land. The missions had also sought to stabilize land-holdings, which suited the most recent conquerors of land, who therefore became Christian, but alienated the conquered, who, under traditional customs, would have had the opportunity to fight to get their land back.[37]

Until 1912 the Presbyterian mission was the *de facto* government of Tanna, and in the 'Tanna law' period native courts operated, with Christian converts judging issues, often very severely.[38] In that year a government agent was appointed, but mission influence remained profound, and by 1920 nearly four natives were at least nominally Presbyterian to every one who was still heathen. In 1932 the Seventh-Day Adventists opened a mission at Port Resolution, and in the following year a Roman Catholic mission was begun, albeit with little success.[39]

The war brought a sudden change of circumstances to Tanna, which apart from subsistence agriculture had a cash crop, copra, and which, even in 1940, exported young male labour to other islands. Copra prices slumped and there was widespread idleness and shortage of money. During 1940 a 'little man with bleached hair' and 'a coat with shining buttons'[40] began preaching in the south-west of the island. His message was that Tanna would become a flat, fertile land following a cataclysm. Natives would get back their youth; there would be no more sickness; nor would there be need to work or to rear pigs, for Jonfrum would supply. The missions, government, agents, and police would all have to go; European money would have to be suppressed; natives from other islands would have to return to their homes, and ancient customs would be restored, in particular kava-drinking, dancing, and polygamy.[41]

Whether this teaching is to be taken as anti-white is disputable.[42]

[36] Patrick O'Reilly, 'Jonfrum is New Hebridean "Cargo Cult"', *Pacific Islands Monthly* XXI, 6 (January 1950), pp. 67–70, and XXI, 7 (February 1950), pp. 59–65.
[37] J. Guiart, op. cit.
[38] J. Guiart, 'Conversion to Christianity in the South Pacific', op. cit.
[39] J. Guiart, 'Culture contact . . .', op. cit.
[40] P. O'Reilly, op. cit.
[41] Ibid., on which this paragraph relies.
[42] P. Worsley, op. cit., p. 154, says that there was no anti-white preaching at the beginning of the cult.

Certainly J. M. Nicol, who had been resident Agent since 1916, did not take alarm until May 1941. In the meantime Jonfrum had urged natives to spend all their money, since it would be useless in the future and once it was used the traders would have to leave the island.[43] The villagers dispersed to their traditional lands, and deserted the mission— and by mid-May there was no one at Dr Armstrong's Presbyterian morning service. All but one of the native assessors deserted, reducing the whole of the District Agent's organization overnight.[44] The police, for whom Nicol now sent, arrived on 30 May and arrested a native, Manehevi, who refused to say where he got his gold-buttoned coat. He was illiterate but pretended to read from a book. He was exposed for a day, sentenced to three years' interment and five years' banishment from Tanna. Nine other natives received sentences of a year's imprisonment. The chiefs declared themselves to have finished with Manehevi and imposed a voluntary fine of £100 upon themselves as a token of good faith.

In September 1941, Resident Nicol intercepted a letter from a former police-boy, Joe Nalpin, who from prison in Port Vila, capital of the New Hebrides, had written to a west-coast chief about Jonfrum. Jonfrum was now called 'King of America', and Nalpin offered to send his son to bring him from America if a house were built to receive him.[45] Jonfrum was also identified with Karaperamun, god of the island's highest mountain, Mount Tukosmeru. In December, Nicol reported anti-British feelings in the island, and sent twenty natives to Port Vila as disturbers of the peace. At the end of 1941, three sons of Jonfrum were reported in eastern Tanna, and one of them gave messages through a young girl. Young boys and girls were dedicated to these new gods, and lived together in a common dwelling.[46] There was a new run on the stores for meat, rice, sugar, and knives. The unrest increased and the three reputed sons of Jonfrum were arrested for one year's detention at Vila. America's entry into the war precipitated new rumours—Americans were black and there would be new money.[47]

The Americans provided work for Tannese men at Vila, and most

---

[43] P. O'Reilly, op. cit., says there were two European traders, Wilkinson and Bannister. G. L. Barrow, op. cit., refers to four traders, three British, one French. P. Worsley, op. cit., p. 157, refers to a Chinese store, presumably on the island.

[44] J. Guiart, 'Culture contact . . .', op. cit.

[45] G. L. Barrow, op. cit., says that Nalpin referred to America before she was involved in the war, although knowledge of America on Tanna was slight. P. Worsley, op. cit., p. 156, cites a source suggesting that the 'Coming of the Americans' was an old theme, existing before the war.

[46] P. Worsley, op. cit., p. 157.

[47] P. O'Reilly, op. cit.

of them wanted to go. Nearly 1,000 indentured for labour, but despite American generosity and the abundance of war surplus, their high expectations, derived from the Jonfrum cult, were unfulfilled and by October 1943 many had returned home chastened.[48] The most serious outbreak of the cult occurred in that month under a new leader, Ne Loiag.[49] He proclaimed himself King of America and Tanna, and two hundred of his followers began the building of an airstrip in northern Tanna for the planes full of cargo which the Americans would soon send. Nicol sent for twenty reinforcements. He arrested Ne Loiag, whose followers now actively sought to free him. They also attacked other natives for not working on the airstrip. The situation was serious and Nicol, requesting one hundred men, cabled, 'Nearly whole island making common cause with Loiag supporters'. He brought an American major to demonstrate a tommy-gun and to tell the cultists that the Americans did not want an airstrip. But Loiag, as 'King of America', threatened to get his planes to come and bomb. He was eventually declared mentally unbalanced and sent to an asylum.

Although for some time no further dramatic outbreaks occurred, dancing and kava-drinking persisted. The social structure of Tanna, as the Presbyterian mission had sought to mould it, had collapsed at the very first impact of this recrudescent cult movement.[50] When Armstrong attempted to recommence his mission at Lenakel in 1943, only fifty children from a population of 2,500 people attended. By 1951, there was still 'little return' to the missions.[51] Meanwhile there had been a further period of Jonfrumist activity in April 1947, when Bannister's store was raided and the coloured labels were torn off many of the goods at the order of one Iokaeye. The new manifestation of the movement expressed Jonfrum's dislike of colours 'John Frum like black now white'.[52] Iokaeye and fourteen others, all of whom had been involved in the outbreak of October 1943, were arrested and imprisoned. After this some effort was made to organize native co-operatives, probably influenced by the co-operative cult movements on the island of Malekula, but in 1952 there was a reintroduction of garden magic, and visions of warships coming from the land of the dead with the ancestors were seen—a collective expectation that persisted for a month and a

[48] G. L. Barrow, op. cit.
[49] Spelling of this name varies: Barrow gives Ne Loiag; O'Reilly, Loiag; and Worsley, Neloaig and Nelawihang.
[50] J. Guiart, 'The John Frum Movement in Tanna', Oceania XXII (March 1952), pp. 165–77.
[51] G. L. Barrow, op. cit.
[52] P. Worsley, op. cit., p. 159.

half in part of the island.[53] New rumours circulated, coinciding, as
Worsley points out, with a dramatic fall in copra prices.[54]

The Jonfrumists appear to have been principally mission people.
O'Reilly comments that 'it has not been real heathens nor the most
fervent Presbyterians who have been the most involved but those who
have come into contact with the mission ways without having altogether
abandoned heathenism'. In this Guiart concurs.[55] But Worsley says at
least of the early period, that 'Dominican services were equally
neglected', and of the period following 1943, that 'Pagans, too, provided
recruits' to the cult.[56] Whatever may have been the case on Tanna,
in other cases cargo enthusiasm was no respecter of religious divisions.

Persisting themes and spasmodic cults

Just what significance should be attached to the difference between
what is described as the recrudescence of a particular cult and what is
called the development within one area of a succession of cults (some
of which may also be partially contemporaneous rivals)? In fact
whether the Koreri movements or the successive Jonfrum outbursts are
to be regarded as one recrudescent cult or as a series of successive movements, depends on the criteria of identity that we employ. Koreri and
Jonfrum tend to be seen as one cult because of the continuity of relatively
stable elements of specific myth which each of them manifests. In Biak,
the Koreri cult invokes the Manseren legend, which is long-established,
and even appears as 'traditional' mythology: in Tanna, Jonfrum, apart
from some tenuous identification with a traditional island deity,
appeared in 1940 as something new. But in both cases each new
manifestation of enthusiasm brought accretions to the basic mythology.

Yet between outbreaks there is no persisting organization in either
case (if the over-sophisticated term 'organization' is ever really appropriate to cults of this kind). Leadership is not continuous, although
there may be—and on Tanna we know that there were—some individuals who were involved in successive pullulations of cult activity.
But this is also the case with movements in one area that we regard as

[53] J. Guiart, 'Culture contact . . .', op. cit.
[54] P. Worsley, op. cit., p. 160. One ought not, perhaps, to make too much of such co-
incidences: there is no general correlation of cult-outbursts and price changes, and economic
determinism can easily be overstated. See L. P. Mair, 'The Pursuit of the Millennium in
Melanesia', British Journal of Sociology IX, 2 (June 1958), pp. 178–9.
[55] P. O'Reilly, op. cit.; J. Guiart, 'The John Frum Movement . . .', op. cit.
[56] P. Worsley, op. cit.

relatively distinct cults. The cults occurring in the Madang district, to be discussed below, illustrate the point. Well-identified individuals are found who are involved in, or who are well acquainted with, a particular cult, and who then become prominent in another.

Although these cults in the Madang area lack the persistence of stable, central mythological systems, there are continuities: the differences might even be regarded as variants—albeit significant ideological variants—in a persisting thematic framework. This district, at least in the early stages of cult development, was perhaps too fragmented socially and culturally for any mythology to sustain a widespread and persistently recrudescent movement. Perhaps, too, the experience of local peoples was for some time too differentiated in respect of the extent of cultural contact—for instance in the measure of christianization—for one body of myth to carry sustained conviction. The process of social change, in the two decades chiefly in question, was also dramatic, affecting different groups rather differently, both in respect of the measure of their past acculturation and for adventitious reasons. Yet what did exist was a common psychological climate. The disparities of wealth, status, and power between themselves and white men was evident: there was a need for interpretation of this disparity, and a need for prescribed action to make these things available to natives.

It is in this sense, then, that although actual cargo cults may be seen as transient, amorphous and poorly-organized forms of sectarianism, they are in themselves merely more emphatic and crystallized developments of long sustained, if oscillatory, responses to acquaintance with European (and in some cases earlier Indonesian) culture. Thus it is that some of the best authorities distinguish between persisting belief and spasmodic cults. Peter Lawrence, from his intimate knowledge of cultism in the southern Madang district of the north coast of New Guinea, distinguished 'cargo beliefs', which he believes have existed virtually in continuous sequence from the earliest European contact, from 'cargo movements'.[57] Burridge's concept of the 'myth-dream' which awaits to be activated by some charismatic figure, who can articulate it and who offers himself as a model for the 'new men' of the indigenous society, is essentially similar in this respect.[58] Sierksma sees particular leaders whose personal neurosis provides expression for what amounts to a 'collective neurosis'.[59]

[57] P. Lawrence, *Road Belong Cargo* . . ., op. cit.
[58] K. O. L. Burridge, op. cit.
[59] Fokke Sierksma, *Een nieuwe hemel en een nieuwe aarde* (Mouton. The Hague 1961).

Cultural continuities and discontinuities

Cultural contact alone demands some response from native peoples, and initially such response must be made in terms of indigenous religion. Europeans are incorporated into the indigenous world-view as new manifestations of the supernatural, as ancestor spirits or deities with whom must be instituted some reciprocal relationships, similar to those by which both native religious life and inter-group trading relationships are conducted.

This broad ideological response makes apparent the continuities of traditional culture that persist in cargo movements. The cargo cult, no less than the myth-dream or the cargo belief that precedes it, depends on well-established categories of thought—the lacunae of which, and the opaqueness of which, as judged in relation to western categories of thought, do much to explain cargo enthusiasm. The cults themselves have sometimes been described as essentially conservative;[60] sometimes as revolutionary.[61] Both judgements can be defended: movements differ one from another, and they also change over time (and not always, or only, from a conservative to a revolutionary position). Moreover, a single movement may, even at a given moment of time, maintain a conservative perspective, seeking to absorb Europeans and aspects of European culture within a traditional framework of values and assumptions, and may, simultaneously, envisage the realization of its goals as the material, millennial transformation of native life.

The cargo cult is thus manifestly not merely a defensive response to protect native society and culture from invaders. It is not specifically a religious aid for military activity (although at times it may embrace something approaching that). It is not explicitly 'nativistic' in orientation, and often it accelerates the already existing process of abandonment of past practices. It is by no means an unequivocal religious assertion of political aims. Certainly, it may at times reveal facets of all of these orientations, but none of them adequately summarizes the complexity of these movements. The succession of enthusiasms of the Madang district of New Guinea makes this apparent.

[60] P. Lawrence, op. cit., pp. 224–31.

[61] P. Worsley, op. cit., p. 226, discusses the revolutionary potential of such movements; T. Bodrogi, 'Colonization and Religious Movements in Melanesia', *Acta Ethnographica Academiae Scientiorum Hungaricae* II, 1–4 (1951), pp. 259–90, refers (p. 282) to the 'revolutionary discontent' of cargo cultists, seeking 'the right way towards a solution'. Both of these writers tend to see millennial movements as pre-political expressions of a type of class struggle.

Madang is a town on the north-eastern coast of what was formerly German New Guinea. The peoples in the area of dense bush around Madang lived in small villages, engaging in primary subsistence agriculture and hunting. Although linguistically fragmented and with some variations in traditional religious conceptions, the cultural level and world-view of these peoples was basically homogeneous. The degree of economic specialization was low, and production was for need and exchange at fixed values without conceptions of gain or profit.[62] These peoples had no distinct concept of the supernatural: deities and spirits were part of the everyday world, the former having created the world and given men their way of life, and the latter being available to assist in the manipulation of the environment. The relationships with these beings were regarded as reciprocal, and were as materialistic, anthropocentric, and pragmatic as human relationships. Ritual was a technology by which to manipulate the physical world, and 'big men' were those who had acquired more than average success in economic activities through their ritual knowledge.[63]

Both Lawrence and Burridge believe that a 'cargo belief' prevailed among Madang peoples—and by extension among perhaps most Melanesian peoples—from the very beginnings of European culture contact. The first Europeans were identified with deities, attempts were made at appropriate reciprocal relationships; gifts were exchanged, and the expectation excited that more of the valuable artefacts of European culture would be acquired in due course and in response to the appropriate ritualistic gestures.[64] Specific cargo cults, however, arose only when the expectations aroused by contact had been disappointed. In the Madang area the appropriation of land for plantations followed the annexation of the north-eastern mainland by the German New Guinea Company. Labour recruiting, dispossession, the eventual interference with native customs and in particular the suppression of warfare, the introduction of missions, and of a head-tax all occurred in this area between 1884 and 1914.

In the early years of this century the coastal peoples are said to have come to realize that Europeans were human beings after all, and there are reports of myths that explained the very different cultural attain-

---

[62] P. Lawrence, op. cit., p. 10; K. O. L. Burridge, op. cit., pp. 31, 60, says that the simple possession of cash and goods is pointless for Melanesians, unless it is linked to community, moral, political, and economic values: hence a theft, except perhaps for a sorcerer, would be of no advantage.

[63] I have retained the phrase used by G. Cochrane, op. cit., K. O. L. Burridge, op. cit., refers to 'managers'. P. Lawrence, op. cit., occasionally uses the term 'big men', but the concept is not a significant item in his analysis.

[64] P. Lawrence, op. cit., pp. 63–5.

ments of natives and the invaders. There were many variants of such myths as they were accommodated to local religious traditions, but typically they related a similar story. Two creator gods who were brothers had quarrelled: one chose a native vessel and sailed away. The other built a ship of European type, filled it with cargo and with native artefacts, and then offered a choice between these—between a rifle and a bow and arrow, or a canoe and a dinghy—to natives in each village. All chose native artefacts. This deity then went on to another country and gave to the whites the artefacts of advanced culture.[65] The common elements of this particular myth are found elsewhere in New Guinea: in the more northerly parts of the Madang area, a very similar myth attributed brotherly origins to white men and black; black men sinned, albeit by chance, but white men have an obligation to share their good luck with their less fortunate brothers.[66]

Such myths, even when associated, as they were perhaps in abortive risings that occurred in the Madang area, do not constitute more than necessarily religious allegories that account for the contemporary state of things. They do not, as yet, amount to a new response to the world, but do give moral grounds for condemning those who take advantage of cultural differences. Even a later myth which accommodated more fully European self-explanations, and which was a guide to action intended to induce the cargo to come, scarcely amounted to a cult. This theory accepted Christian concepts, identifying Ham, son of Noah, as the progenitor of the black race, for whose sins God had banished him to New Guinea. Missionaries, as the descendants of Ham's brothers, had come to New Guinea to bring Ham's descendants a better way of life, symbolized by cargo.[67]

Transference of allegiance from one deity to another when the first had failed to produce material blessings occurred in traditional religion. Christianity was now to be tried out, to see if it would bring cargo for natives as it did for white men. Old customs were given up. There were widespread conversions, and the claims made for

[65] Ibid., pp. 70–2.

[66] K. O. L. Burridge, op. cit., pp. 164–74. Burridge places more emphasis on the idea of some early sin and subsequent 'guilt' on the part of *kanakas*, which cost them their cargo inheritance, than does Lawrence, who regards the concept of sin as quite alien to the southern Madang peoples, and who writes, op. cit., p. 247, 'Even in cargo doctrine there was no hint that the natives' present economic inferiority was due to the sinfulness of their forbears [*sic*].'

[67] P. Lawrence, op. cit., pp. 75 ff. Although Lawrence does not discuss the possibility, the idea of the sinful Ham as the progenitor of the 'inferior' black people has a considerable history in the fundamentalist tradition of western Christianity, and has been not infrequently invoked to explain and justify the different achievements and competences of white and coloured peoples as part of God's plan. It was used particularly to justify negro slavery in the United States, as a racially differential extension of a theory of original sin.

Christianity by missionaries fed cargo ideas partly because Melanesians lacked any sense of historical time with which to interpret missionary promises and their own prospects. Christian phrases carried hidden implications concerning cargo, and although native mission helps knew this and fostered these ideas, the missionaries themselves did not, and this contributed to many mutual misunderstandings. In the 1930s it is estimated that many more than 50 per cent of 'the natives of Madang and the Rai Coast . . . subscribed to quasi-Christian cargo doctrines'.[68]

Eventually this belief in cargo from Christian worship gave place to frustration, and the typical Melanesian idea that the missionaries were cheating by not revealing the vital parts of their religion by which they themselves acquired the cargoes that came to them from overseas.[69] Mission education was often academic and its use was not clear to Melanesians. Alternatively, Europeans were now thought to be diverting cargoes that were destined for natives by changing the labels. An indigenous deity (Manup) was identified with Christ in the *Letub* cult, occurring in part of the Madang district in the late 1930s. He was said to be crucified and held captive by 'the Jews'. The effect of the new myth with its appropriate ritual was, much more than the preceding cargo beliefs, towards transformation of the native way of life. The ritual was designed to free Jesus (Manup) so that he might return to New Guinea with cargo, first to the ancestors and then to the people. Pagan ceremonies were revived and a syncretistic cult evolved. Hymns and prayers were still offered, but sacrifices were also made to the spirits of the dead. Tables were put up and covered with clean cloths, decorated with flowers in bottles, and heaped with gifts. In these respects, and in the 'general shaking and uncontrolled antics of some of the dancers', who were thought to be in communication with the dead,[70] the Letub movement resembles the quite independent Vailala Madness of the south coast of Papua.

Simultaneously with the Letub cult, another movement was in progress north-west of Madang at Tangu, where Mambu, a former mission helper, began to preach that a new order was coming. The ancestors were making cargo for *kanakas* (natives) but white men were switching the labels and taking the goods for themselves. *Kanakas* were thus entitled to take their property by force if need be. Soon the ancestors would come with cargo for all; work in the gardens would

---

[68] Ibid., p. 81.
[69] This idea was, of course, common to many (but by no means to all) cargo-cult movements.
[70] Ibid., p. 95.

cease, and all existing property would be destroyed. Taxes should not be paid to whites, but to him, the Black King. Children should be withheld from mission schools, since mission natives would be consumed in the holocaust when the ancestors returned. Mambu prayed at the graves of the dead, and baptized the genitals of his followers, whom he told to abandon their laplaps and to wear European clothes. Thus he taught that a new material culture, modelled on the European, was to come *from* the ancestors. He was believed to work miracles and to produce not cargo, but money, and in some respects money was the key to cargo.[71] In 1938 he had a large following: whole villages gave up work and held themselves aloof from Europeans.[72]

Mambu and the prophets of the Letub cult, and of other similar movements in the area, at this time were only marginally innovators. More especially they were activators of a persisting preoccupation among the natives. Only in the changing attributions and identifications of particular native and Christian mythical beings, and in the detail of prescribed activites, do these cults significantly differ from the congeries of beliefs about cargo that preceded them. The idea that life, or at least the material culture, will be transformed now finds expression in specific activities. The cargo itself stimulates ideas of a millennium, a blissful future in which those things to which men attach most importance will be vouchsafed. Melanesians, like all millennialists, were unclear about the further implications of their millennial dream— about changes in social structure, the bases of authority, the quality of human relations in the world to come. They would live in some measure as Europeans lived, enjoying all those things that Europeans possessed: from the deities or the ancestors there would be unlimited supply.

In some variants of the Madang cargo cults of the late 1930s and early 1940s, typical Christian injunctions were incorporated as *sine qua non* for the arrival of the cargo. Men were not to steal, fight, commit adultery, and were to live soberly, and in peace. Sorcery in particular had been a cause of offence to the cargo deity, promoting as it had, feuds and even warfare. Obedience to the ten commandments was enjoined in a cult led by a former native policeman, Tagarab. Europeans were said to have persuaded natives to pray to the wrong God, but now they would be punished, and the natives themselves would become white. This cult was a rival to the Letub cult and each was adopted in various localities according to the way in which its theory of divinity fitted in with local religious traditions. Each re-

[71] K. O. L. Burridge, op. cit., pp. 132–3, 180–92.
[72] Helga Uplegger and W. E. Mühlmann, 'Die Cargo-Kulte in Neuguinea und Insel-Melanesian' in W. E. Mühlmann, *Chiliasmus und Nativismus*, op. cit., pp. 165–89.

garded the other as false and as a cause of the delay in the coming of cargo.[73] Their exclusivism, albeit based as yet on distinctly tribal variations, itself indicates the growing significance of voluntarism in religious belief and practice.

The most dramatic development of cargo cultism in the Madang district occurred after the Second World War, drawing into one new enthusiasm natives from a wider area than previously: many of the followers of the Letub cult, of Tagarab, and of Mambu were recruited to the new movement when it emerged in the late 1940s. In the most thoroughly documented study of a cargo cult, Lawrence traces the complexity of the origins of the cult and of the career of the Melanesian around whom it centred, Yali, a Rai Coast native born in Ngaing about 1912.[74]

Yali was an illiterate man who worked so long with Europeans that he came to prefer pidgin English to his native tongue, although 'he had no knowledge of English itself'.[75] He had served in the police just before the war, and then with Australian forces to whom, in contrast with many natives, he remained completely loyal. During and just after the war he was in Australia on occasions. This and his daring escape from a Japanese ambush after being landed behind enemy lines, gave him a reputation with both the Australians and the *kanakas* of being a most exceptional man. He had been a sergeant of police, and while in Australia heard many wartime promises about the future of New Guinea after the war: he himself made one propaganda broadcast for the Australians along these lines. For Yali this was a promise that New Guinea would become like Australia.

After the war, the Australian administration employed Yali to give talks urging the natives to co-operate with the administration, and promising them that if they worked they would enjoy a better standard of life. He was explicitly told not to become involved in cargo cult activities, but to the Melanesians Yali was already an unrivalled leader (especially since many who had been leaders in local society had been imprisoned or disgraced for collaboration with the Japanese during the war). He was virtually a messiah, who had seen 'cargo' being produced, and who himself believed that the Australians meant to bring and distribute commodities to Melanesians.

What Yali sought to do initially was to persuade natives to re-organize their lives. They were to live in larger settlements (which the

[73] P. Lawrence, op. cit., pp. 98–105.
[74] Ibid., pp. 116 ff., upon whose detailed analysis this account relies.
[75] Ibid., p. 127. H. Uplegger and W. E. Mühlmann, op. cit., also describe Yali as illiterate, and Lawrence explicitly contradicts Worsley, op. cit., p. 218, who said that Yali could read and write English.

administration had long sought to encourage), and to keep open the roads; they were to live in every way like Europeans, by digging and using latrines, washing daily, laundering their clothes. Sorcery was to be outlawed and feuds were to end. Women were encouraged to have more children, and infanticide and abortion were to be discontinued. Children were to attend mission schools, and good relationships with Europeans were to be maintained. Yali was obeyed, not only in the southern Madang district, but as far away as Bogia and Tangu, many miles up the coast in the area of the old Mambu cult.[76] But obedience was given because Yali's instructions fitted into a familiar pattern: this was now the authentic ritual that would bring the cargo. In some instance army camps were the model for the new villages: in others the new rules were obeyed collectively to the sound of a whistle.

Yali appointed 'boss boys' in villages, and quickly they became relatively autonomous; certainly they were not under regular or direct control by him. Some of them were imbued with cargo ideas, and throughout 1947 there were sundry local prophecies of cargo, with a variety of ritual prescriptions. In one case extensive sexual promiscuity (perhaps a reaction to the mission injunction against polygyny which for a time Yali was induced to support, and perhaps due to garbled accounts of brothels in Australia) became vital to inducing cargo to come. In another a flood was predicted and villagers left their homes to join the young prophetess, Polelesi, at a place of safety where cargo would also be received. In a third, led by one Kaum, who had been active before the Japanese invasions, a tidal wave to destroy Europeans was predicted.

In 1947 Yali, together with nine other natives, was summoned to Port Moresby to be informed of administrative schemes for New Guinea. Rumours among the natives suggested that he was going for cargo, or for military equipment for war against the Europeans, or that he would return as a District Officer, and at Sangpat the locals built a house for him laid out like the administration station at Saidor. The course was a disappointment to Yali. All that he saw was generally familiar to him, but what he learned incidentally from a native who was a trainee-teacher was that Europeans did not all believe in the Christian story of creation: many believed in evolution—that man, as it was crudely put, was descended from *monki* (monkey).

This idea explained why Europeans kept useless pets and lavished care upon them; it explained why Europeans kept animals carefully in cages (as Yali had seen at Brisbane Zoo); it explained the emphasis on

---

[76] K. O. L. Burridge, op. cit., p. 197; and p. 137, where he says, 'For Tangu, Yali seemed to be beyond and above any other kind of man they had met'.

animal husbandry, which he saw at an agricultural station: Europeans *really* believed in totems. All this was explicable in terms of traditional Ngaing religion. It also revealed that missionaries had been deceivers (Yali had never been a Christian) since they had stopped the natives from worshipping their own gods. He had earlier been in some trouble with the administration for speaking against polygyny (at the instigation of Roman Catholic priests) since this had caused a great deal of hardship and some suicides when men had abandoned their polygynous wives. Now he learned, on enquiry, that natives were to remain free with respect to their religion, and in particular that traditional ceremonies could be organized.

To Yali, all of this meant that he had a licence to encourage natives to revive pagan religion, and that it was from their own gods that benefit would come—not European cargo, but improvement in crops, game and herds. He was now convinced that Europeans would not reveal the secret of their religious rituals—the secret by which cargo was produced—any more than a traditional tribesman of New Guinea would reveal the secret of his religion, the rituals that gave him success. In any case, it was wrong traditionally to use rituals to which one had no right by descent or purchase. Yali abandoned the idea of European cargo, but was bitterly disillusioned about Europeans and about the promises that he felt had been given to him in Australia during the war.

On his return Yali rejected the various local cargo cultists who sought to put him at the head of their movements, principally because of 'his fear of being accused of stealing other people's religious secrets' and not through rational disbelief.[77] He began his attack on missions and reinstituted traditional ceremonies. When, however, a new prophet, Gurek of Hapurpi, came preaching that the old Rai Coast deities were the real cargo deities, and told Yali that the Roman Catholic missionaries had collected and taken 'to Rome' the masks of these old gods (in fact for a museum), Yali was convinced of the duplicity of the missions, and came to believe that by a return to paganism cargo would in fact be realized. The table ritual of older cults—of clean clothes and flowers in bottles—was resuscitated, and traditional ritual for crops, hunting, and pig-husbandry began again. All the old deities could now share in the cult, and the old rivalries of cults derived from differing tribal gods were swept away.

For a time Yali, who had been made a Foreman Overseer in the Department of Native Affairs, a paid post, retained both the good will of the administration and the commanding respect of the native

[77] P. Lawrence, op. cit., p. 184.

population over a wide area. He became for all offences except the most serious the virtual judicial authority of the area, and he used the meetings of headmen, which he called in his official capacity, to promulgate cargo-cult teachings. But the prolongation of the newly revived traditional ceremonies, the difficulties of planters in getting native labour, and the new contempt for the missions, eventually led the administration first to curtail and then to investigate Yali's activities. The extent of trouble was not really great, and Lawrence says that the complaints were

> mainly European uneasiness and resentment at the decay of pre-war colonial social order. The natives were showing their teeth. Settlers could no longer count on automatic obedience to their slightest commands, and the missions were forced to compete with other ideologies.[78]

Eventually charges of illegally depriving natives of their liberty (although Yali's 'sentences' were not served in a jail) and of inciting one of his unofficial 'policemen' to commit rape (a charge which Yali denied) led to Yali's arrest and imprisonment for six and a half years.

Cargo cults, perhaps even less than new religions among other pre-literate peoples, are never well-defined movements. They are transient outbursts, drawing men in for a period, waxing and waning, giving place to similar but rival movements, and proceeding on confused and sometimes contradictory notions and expectations. To the mass of followers the doctrinal niceties propounded by prophets are of less importance than instructions for appropriate ritual, and often the sheer excitement of the idea of inducing cargo produces spontaneous hysteria and convulsions which, in turn, permit many individuals to receive dreams, spirit messages, and inspiration of their own.

Even the cults that persist rely more on what might still be called 'collective representations' in the Durkheimian sense than on any well-articulated and formally conceived principles of organization. Even when wharfs are built or airstrips constructed, or new villages settled and military drill performed, it would be an error to credit these activities to planned decisions, or to attribute to those sponsoring them a capacity for creating organized structures. Like other ecstatic millennial movements, cargo cults do not present evidence of evolving organizational skills. Even Yali's movement depended for its chain of command on his bureaucratic authority as a paid official, and, latterly, on the loyalty of 'boss boys', who were often kinsmen, affines, or men with whom he had traditional trading and exchange obligations.[79] It

[78] Ibid., p. 216.
[79] Ibid., p. 263.

is only as the millennialist element recedes that rational organization grows.[80]

Of course, the cults arise on various assumptions of what is 'common sense' to those involved. Given the materialistic values and animistic assumptions of Melanesian societies, the intimate dependence for success in war, agriculture, and trade on ritual practices, and the impact of aliens materially so much more successful, emulation, competition, and phantasy-action for wish-fulfilment are all understandable developments. The cultists seek to devise a procedure along the lines of previously successful procedures, or to build upon presumed similarities of activity and purpose between themselves and Europeans, which will now bring about the transformation that they desire. From the external point of view they do not behave rationally, but certainly, given the limited knowledge that they possess, their behaviour has a certain limited situational logic.[81]

But the Melanesian native is a man in transition from one system of logic to another. The intimations of his own culture become decreasingly compelling. Already by the First World War, the artefacts of traditional culture were being displaced among coastal tribes in the Madang area. Old rituals were less convincing because new methods of production were being learned and new implements were being used which did not depend on the old ritual assumptions. Thus from the early demand for reciprocal trade relations with the invader who would provide superior material implements, the demands for cargo gradually expanded. Eventually it is what is conceived as 'the whole way of life' of the European which is sought, and not just steel axes, knives, calico, and corrugated iron. The whole way of life itself is of course very imperfectly perceived from the fragment of European society that is visible to natives; it does not provide a basis for them to grasp the complex nexus of productive procedures in advanced civilization, and they lack the historical sense of time by which to understand their development.

The demand for the way of life of Europeans is, when religiously conceived, thorough-going millennialism, a manifestation of the revolutionist response. But such a demand is inevitably equivocal because so imperfectly grasped. The vision of European life is coloured by native assumptions, and often it is to be attained by procedures that are nativistic attempts to re-awaken the native past. Yali, who for a moment saw that each people had its own deities and must expect its

[80] See pp. 476 ff.
[81] On the distinction between these two types of rationality see Steven Lukes, 'Some Problems about Rationality', pp. 194–213 in B. R. Wilson (Ed.), *Rationality* (Blackwell, Oxford, and Harper, New York 1970).

own specific benefits from them, and even abandoned the demand for cargo, succumbed at the instigation of Gurek to using his nativistic revival for the ultimate goal of inducing the gods to send a European cargo—and Yali was an exceptional native, if not yet (by western standards) a rational man. Ecstatic millennialism must be irrational, of course: the causal explanation of what is predicted makes leaps beyond the bounds of legitimate inference, and presents prospects which defy all previous experience (when objectively viewed and with full knowledge). The fantasies of fairy stories persist in western society, and now de-mythologized, religious representations of man's past and future are tolerated: these are the repositories of millennial dreams in the western world.

Cargo cults and Christianity

Precisely because the custodians of western millennial myths were among the first and have been the most consistent and persistent of the diffusers of western culture in Melanesia, so a question arises concerning their role in the development of native millennialism. Christian missions may have stimulated cargo-cult development in several ways, not all of which are directly attributable to the specific ideological content of Christianity itself. In varying degrees Christianity (i) had a disruptive effect on indigenous culture; and (ii) introduced specifically new ideologies to native peoples.

From their establishment missions sought to disrupt existing religious systems, and doing so they frequently tore the fabric of indigenous social organization. Obviously they were not the sole diffusers of white culture, and traders, planters, and labour recruiters also played significant parts in this process. But the missionaries set about the matter more explicitly; they set themselves up as the natives' friends and made the disorganization of at least certain elements of indigenous life their goal; and they stayed. Their influence in these respects was greater in Polynesia, where they arrived earlier than in Melanesia, often a long time before governmental administrators were appointed.[82]

[82] Polynesians sometimes accepted Christianity very rapidly (for example on Onoi Lau, Tabuai, and Manua), but their acceptance may have been *more specifically* of the material culture of white men. Thus in Hawaii, Kamehameha I quickly used the white men's guns to establish his ascendancy over other chiefs: in 1820 Kamehameha II fought a battle with those who opposed his abandonment of traditions. All this occurred *before* the arrival of missionaries on Hawaii. See F. Sierksma, op. cit., p. 22, and David Malo, *Hawaiian Antiquities* (translated by N. B. Emerson) (Hawaiian Gazette Co., Honolulu 1903).

In Tahiti, for instance, the missions fought a prolonged battle with Tahitan culture, from their first contact with the island at the end of the eighteenth century, when LMS missionaries had sided with a local chief, Pomare (mistaking him for the king of the island, and eventually helping him to usurp that office). Christian interference with polygyny, idolatry, and with many details of native life, including tattooing and the wearing of flowers in the hair, amounted to a puritan dictatorship which eventually produced anti-Christian cult reactions.[83] In Tonga, where missionaries arrived in 1822, and settled in 1826, the effect they had was similar. They forbade dancing, foot-races, and boat-races; they demanded pre-marital chastity and fidelity after marriage, ideals which 'clashed bitterly with traditional Polynesian attitudes to sex'.[84] The implications of the Wesleyan brand of Christianity that they imposed were particularly disliked by chiefs, who were unprotected by the conventions which prevailed in Europe,

> Their teaching that all men were equal in the sight of God . . . their belief that everyone was a sinner by nature and that in order to get to heaven everyone, irrespective of rank, had to submit to certain moral discipline, and their preaching that no one, chief or otherwise, had any right to appropriate to himself any property belonging to another, were foreign to Tongans, and were particularly unpopular with the chiefs.[85]

Melanesian social systems, lacking the clearly articulated and elaborate system of social stratification that prevailed in Polynesian islands, did not suffer to the same extent from Christian egalitarianism (an egalitarianism that was imposed *upon* natives, rather than shared *with* them). But the missionaries with their cultural artefacts disrupted their traditional system of social mobility in which 'big men' emerged

---

[83] For a detailed account of the impact of Christianity on Tahiti, and the development of an indigenous counter-movement, see W. E. Mühlmann, *Arioi und Mamaia . . .*' op. cit. A shorter account of Christian impact (but not of cult reactions) is given in Peter Henry Buck (Te Rangi Hiroa) *Anthropology and Religion* (Yale University Press, New Haven 1939). For a general history of missionary influence in Polynesia, see Aarne A. Koskinen, *Missionary Influence as a Political Factor in the Pacific Islands* (Suomalaisen Tiedeakatemian Tolmituksia Anneles Academiae Scientiarum Fennicae, Sarja Ser.B., Nide-Tom 78, 1, Helsinki 1953). Koskinen discusses Hawaii, Tonga, and Fiji as well as Tahiti. George H. Lane-Fox Pitt-Rivers, *The Clash of Cultures and the Contact of Races* (Routledge, London 1927), discusses the consequences of missionary prohibitions, particularly of nudity, polygyny, and amusements. He instances the harm done by the forcible dismissal of polygynous wives, and reports cases of girls kidnapped by missionaries to prevent polygynous unions. Some admission of the unfortunate consequences of interference with native customs, particularly of sabbatarianism and of the prohibition of kava-drinking and tobacco, is made by the Christian writer John Wear Burton in *Modern Missions in the South Pacific* (Livingstone Press, London 1949).

[84] Sione Lātūkefu, 'The Opposition to the Influence of Wesleyan Methodist Missionaries in Tonga', *Historical Studies: Australia and New Zealand* 12, 46 (April 1966), pp. 248–64.

[85] Ibid., p. 259.

by dint of work, organizing ability, and marital alliances, often attributed to ritual ability and to power as a sorcerer.[86]

The interference with pig-rearing, with initiation rites, polygyny, kava-drinking, and dancing (since dancing was sometimes associated with lasciviousness), were all more immediately oppressive in many instances.[87] On the island of Tanna in the New Hebrides, missionaries had effective control of the island for a considerable time, and their policy of holding coastal land in trust for (Christian) natives caused considerable uprooting of families who moved down to live near the mission.[88] There is evidence, too, that mission Christians not infrequently enjoyed the power acquired by their adherence to the white man's religion and became the most exacting taskmasters of less-willing fellow-Melanesians: in effect they used Christianity as a way of climbing into positions of authority.[89]

At later dates, as they became increasingly aware of the integration of pagan religion with other aspects of indigenous life, missionaries adopted more circumspect tactics in dealing with local customs.[90] The Roman Catholics were, as has been traditional for them, anxious to interfere with local religion only in so far as was necessary to establish the superiority of the church.[91] They preferred to neutralize shrines by sprinkling holy water rather than to destroy them. None the less, many aspects of traditional life were antithetical to mission ideas, and particularly polygyny, against which the Roman Catholics were no less severe than the Protestants. Abrupt demands that mission Christians put away their polygynous wives frequently led not only to individual misery and suicides, but also to the dissolution of the networks of native relationships within local and descent groups.[92] Perhaps most important of all, after two decades of mission and other contact, many native institutions were in decay. The power of indigenous religion may not have ended, but for the lacunae of a partially disintegrated society,

[86] A man might gain in reputation by acknowledging an accusation of being a sorcerer in some societies, as in Tangu, according to K. O. L. Burridge, op. cit., p. 65; G. Cochrane, op. cit., p. 9, says of the Elema that 'big men' were necessarily sorcerers. Those who controlled ritual secrets among Madang societies were the men in leadership roles, according to P. Lawrence, 'Lutheran Mission Influence on Madang Societies', Oceania XXVII, 2 (September 1956), pp. 73–89.

[87] This point is stressed by J. Guiart, 'Report on the Native Situation in the North of Ambryn (New Hebrides)', South Pacific 5, 12 (March 1952), pp. 256–67. (The former Presbyterian missionary subsequently sought some modification of Guiart's comments; W. F. Paton, 'The Native Situation in the North of Ambryn', South Pacific 6, 5 [August 1952].)

[88] J. Guiart, 'The John Frum Movement . . .', op. cit.

[89] P. Lawrence, 'Lutheran Missions . . .', op. cit.

[90] Ibid.

[91] P. Lawrence, Road Belong Cargo . . ., op cit., p. 57.

[92] Ibid., pp. 152, 161.

Christianity, one of the agencies of disruption, offered some new solutions—some of them easily misinterpreted into cargo terms.

Apart from its influence in disturbing existing cultures, Christianity may have contributed in a number of ways to the development of cargo cults. Because Melanesians associated ritual activities with economic success, Christianity was already cast in the role of being the fundamental source of the white man's cargo. Once Melanesians had experienced the superior economic and military power of whites, and once they had taken in the idea that the white men were strenuously offering them their religion (and not, as was the Melanesian practice, keeping their rituals strictly secret) then they believed that fervent attention to the rituals and taboos of the new religion would produce cargo.[93] It was this reaction which produced dramatic waves of conversion in various areas. By this reasoning, when cargo did not arrive, natives came to believe that the missionaries had really withheld the secret—torn out a page of the Bible, deceived them about the really significant rituals (such as floral table decorations or telegraphic communication).[94] A reversion to nativism then sometimes occurred.

Misunderstanding native assumptions and values, missionaries often declared that the white man's success was indeed attributable to his faith in God, and offered Christianity as the basis of salvation for man and society. They did not make a very fine distinction between spiritual and material concerns, and they were, perhaps, even inclined to claim at least an idealized form of material culture for Christian influence. In pidgin English their precise meanings could rarely be expressed. When natives saw that many white men were far from practising Christianity and yet were prosperous, they came to doubt that Christianity was indeed the real ritual basis for material well-being.

Finally, it must be remembered that many missionaries were fundamentalists, men who believed in the literal second coming, the destruc-

---

[93] P. Lawrence, 'The Madang District Cargo Cult', *South Pacific* 8, 1 (January–February 1955), pp. 6–13, describes this process for the Jam people of Madang in the 1930s. See also P. Lawrence, *Road Belong Cargo . . .*, op. cit., pp. 73–85, 259.

[94] In addition to the importance of floral table decorations reported above in the Vailala Madness (1919), the Letub cult (1937), and in Yali's movement (1948), K. O. L. Burridge, *New Heaven New Earth* (Blackwell, Oxford 1969), p. 60, reports of Manam Island (off the north-eastern coast of New Guinea) in 1952, that '. . . an administrative officer . . . knowing that flowers in vases were almost sure indications in the area of imminent cargo activity, set himself the task of looking for just these signs. Realizing, however, that the officer was looking for flowers in vases, Manam Islanders not only determined to hide them from him, but became more convinced than they had been that there must be some exceptional magical potency in arranging flowers in vases. This might well be the very secret of European dominion and superior capacities for which they were looking.'

tion of the world, resurrection of the dead (ancestors) and the establishment of a period of bliss under the reign of Christ.[95] Their own time-sense in these respects was often hazy, but must have fed the immediate expectations of the natives, who conceived of creation as occurring only three or four generations in the past, and for whom the millennial future was imminent. That second-adventist preaching occurred among many orthodox missionaries is clear. Guiart, writing of the New Hebrides, saw that they

> laid great stress on the Apocalypse. Over and over again I have seen Presbyterian and Seventh Day Adventist teachers walking about the hills in Espiritu Santo and Malekula to show the heathen sets of brightly coloured pictures of the life of Jesus. The last picture of the set, by contrast in tones of black and red, always depicted the Day of Judgement according to the Book of Revelation of St. John.[96]

In Polynesia, the often spontaneous adoption of Christianity by natives amounted to a revival of the authentic Christianity of early times, since 'Christianity was originally millennial'.[97]

In certain instances particular cults were touched off by adventist preaching. A well-known case is that of the Kukuaik movement on Kadar Island in 1941, which began immediately after a sermon about the second coming.[98] (Both Tagarab and Yali, who were later to be involved in cargo cultism in the Madang area, were acquainted with this cult, when, as native policemen, they were members of the party sent to arrest its leaders, and Tagarab was deeply impressed by what he heard.[99]) But even in an instance of this type, the particular sermon is perhaps no more than the light that ignites fuel already accumulated from other sources. Undoubtedly the cults mobilize aspirations drawn from indigenous culture, as Oosterwal has argued.[100] We may accept

[95] This point is made by A. A. Koskinen, op. cit., pp. 102 ff, who says of the teaching of early Polynesian missionaries that adventism was very common. Of the Mamaia movement in early nineteenth-century Tahiti, J. D. Freeman, op. cit., p. 190, writes that it 'had pronounced chiliastic beliefs acquired from the Protestant missionaries of the islands. It was declared and believed that "the end of all things was nigh at hand", and that when the millennium came, the faithful would enter heaven immediately.' In the Articles of Faith that they compiled while aboard the ship *Duff*, the missionaries affirmed that they looked to the second coming of Christ.

[96] J. Guiart, 'Conversion to Christianity in the South Pacific', op. cit., p. 127.

[97] Ibid., p. 137.

[98] Ibid., p. 123.

[99] P. Lawrence, op. cit., pp. 99, 122.

[100] G. Oosterwal, 'Cargo Cults and the Seventh Day Adventists', *The Ministry* XXXV, 10 (October 1962), pp. 10–13. Oosterwal is himself a Seventh-Day Adventist. K. O. L. Burridge in *Mambu . . .*, op. cit., p. 234, has commented that 'Adventist teaching is not uncomplementary to cargo expectations'.

that movements 'arise almost spontaneously when a pagan tribe gets its first contact with Christianity and accepts it only in part'.[101] Even without the influence of Christianity, new movements of incipient cargo-ism have occurred.[102] None the less, Christian adventism and millennialism correspond too closely to some aspects of native cults to be dismissed as irrelevant to their emergence. Natives do not initially have a clear apprehension of their own social structure, and the cargo cults as such could not provide conceptions of a transformed world order from indigenous sources.[103] From a growing sense of self-identity as a community, *kanakas* came to envisage, in however rudimentary a way, an alternative social system. In part this complex of ideas was fed by Christian prohibitions and exhortations to certain standards of conduct, and perhaps by Christian millennial ideas.

The sequence of cults

The process of cultural diffusion is inevitably uneven. The beginnings of contact between Europeans and Melanesians were random and occurred at very different times in different places. Subsequently, the pace at which more intensive contact occurred and the type (missions, blackbirders, planters, prospectors, administrators, or troops) also varied. Cults appear to have arisen at many stages of contact: many may have gone unreported. In some places not conspicuously different from others, and having been exposed to similar circumstances of culture contact, there appear to have been no cult movements at all.[104] But we lack well-documented cases of matched samples in which to trace the influence of one diverging variable.

We cannot strictly, therefore, regard cults as occurring in 'half-way cultures',[105] but all the cultures concerned have undergone or are undergoing some degree of actual or anticipatory disruption. This

[101] Georg Höltker, 'How "Cargo-Cult" is born', *Pacific Islands Monthly* XVII, 4 (November) 1946), pp. 4, 16. Another Christian defence of missionaries is provided by R. Inselmann, ' "Cargo Cult" Not Caused by Missions', *Pacific Islands Monthly* XVI, 11 (June 1946), pp. 44. Inselman attributes disruption of native life to blackbirders and whites other than missionaries.

[102] See pp. 216 ff.

[103] P. Lawrence, *Road Belong Cargo* . . ., op. cit., p. 28, writes 'Nobody in any of these societies . . . clearly understood its total social structure. Rather individuals conducted their affairs from a purely egocentric standpoint: in terms of person to person relationships. . . .'

[104] J. Guiart, ' "Cargo Cults" and Political Evolution in Melanesia', *Mankind* 4, 6 (May 1951), pp. 227–30, says that there have been no cults in New Caledonia, but there, agitation has taken the forms of equity-claims and strikes.

[105] The phrase is that of C. S. Belshaw, op. cit. It is specifically subject to criticism by J. Guiart, op. cit., p. 227.

circumstance may be regarded as productive of bewilderment and confusion, and this *both* for men who had thus far only heard tales about white men *and* for men like Yali who had seen a great deal of European life. Yet all of these movements are attempts by men rooted in indigenous culture to comprehend white civilization, to explain it and, in considerable part, to acquire it. Whilst European forms of wealth do not entirely displace native forms, or their traditional uses, European artefacts are seen as superior to many native products, and new activities demand these superior instruments.[106]

Cargo becomes the symbol for the transformation of the social order which is now expected, however inarticulate or contradictory are the ideas that are entertained about that transformation. The cults are, as Stanner has suggested, religious because the natives see themselves as so powerless that they need a redemptive act from an other-wordly source to resolve the problem of cultural inferiority that they suffer.[107] They are the attempt to induce an *Ausgleich* between the now seriously enlarged gap between cultural ideals, as expressed in myth, and the reality of enhanced deprivation in the face of superior European culture. The cargo cults may, therefore, be seen as a projective theodicy. Unlike the theodicies of literate religions, which transfer adjustment to another sphere, the cults anticipate the outworking of remedial measures in this world and in the near future, even though these remedies are all-embracingly transformative beyond the bounds of imagination or articulation. The focus is on cargo because this is the specific pre-occupation of Melanesian cultures, and the increase of wealth is the practical concern of so many indigenous ritual practices. This, then, is the specific cultural form of the revolutionist reponses to the question 'What shall we do to be saved?', with salvation depicted in persisting indigenous terms.

The revolutionist response is, however, a less likely indigenous response than a purely thaumaturgical orientation: it is itself a transmutation of perspective, caused, we may say, by the disruption of culture contact. The stuff out of which it is produced is thaumaturgical, and the evidence of purely magical elements in cargo cults is conspicuous. Magic on such a scale induces fear and hysteria, which is

---

[106] W. E. H. Stanner, 'On the Interpretation of Cargo Cults', *Oceania* XXIX, 1 (September 1958), pp. 1–25, complained that '. . . anthropologists study almost everything about cargo cults except cargo'. He asked 'Is cargo a substitute for traditional wealth, a complement to it, or an addition to it?' In part the point has been met by G. Cochrane, op. cit., p. 6, who found that even in 1967 European commodities had not replaced traditional forms of wealth in transactions between natives in the Solomon Islands.

[107] W. E. H. Stanner, op. cit., and *idem*, *The South Seas in Transition* (Australasian Publishing Co., Sydney 1953), p. 68, where the redemptive element is also emphasized.

reported of many movements. A particularly suggestive indication of the basically thaumaturgical orientation is provided in Kamma's analysis of the Koreri movements on Biak.[108]

Kamma regards the Manseren myth as not only a creation legend, but as a theodicy explaining the gap between the ideal—the world of a past golden age—and the actual. We are told that 'at first the movements were directed against sickness and death'.[109] These are typical concerns of thaumaturgical practice. 'The position of the forerunner (*Konoor*) was often a natural extension of the function of the medicine-man or shaman, who in his struggle against sickness and death was the obvious choice for it', although shaman were not prophetic innovators in their normal roles.[110] The xenophobic element in the movements was not original; it occurred only because of the negative reactions of the missions and the administration to the movement. Thus, as in some instances in Africa, the revolutionist orientation is in part induced by the restrictive administrative attitude towards thaumaturgical movements.

As between cults in different regions, the process of cultural contact was so piecemeal and so haphazard that no simple conformity to chronological sequence can be expected. Widely divergent orientations often co-existed. Thus at the very time that the latter-day cargoism of Yali's movement was still evident at Tangu in northern New Guinea, on Manam Island (a few miles off the coast) a movement of very different type was flourishing. Manam had experienced white culture a generation earlier than Tangu, and most people had been baptized by the end of the Second World War. In 1952, all the ingredients of a cargo movement seemed to exist on Manam, but although they knew about Yali, the islanders had not taken up the cult that had been disseminated on the mainland.[111] Instead, under Irakau, villages were being systematically organized for production along commercial lines. There were those who 'tried to push him [Irakau] into the role of prophet',[112] and some villagers when they said their prayers away from the mission 'added to the names of the Trinity "*Irakau na Yali*, Amen".'[113] But Irakau remained simply a businessman. On Manam it was possible, at least for some, to transcend the reversion to magical thinking and cargo cultism which still produced prophets and characterized movements on the less-Europeanized mainland.

[108] F. C. Kamma, *De Messiannse Koreri-bewegingen . . .*, op. cit.
[109] J. Pouwer, 'Cargo Cults', *Oceania* XXVIII, 3 (March 1958), pp. 247–52. Pouwer summarizes and follows Kamma's analysis.
[110] Ibid.
[111] K. O. L. Burridge, *Mambu . . .*, op. cit., pp. 138–40.
[112] K. O. L. Burridge, *New Heaven New Earth*, op. cit., p. 59.
[113] K. O. L. Burridge, *Mambu . . .*, op. cit., p. 234.

Cargo cults reveal thaumaturgical, revolutionist and quasi-rational orientations—and this broadly in accordance with the degree of exposure to western ideas. The Taro cult indicates an early thaumaturgical concern.[114] The Vailala Madness, the Mambu cult, and the Jonfrum movement are revolutionist movements, albeit with thaumaturgical aspects. The Paliau movement and Marching Rule reveal oscillating and equivocal rationalism with strong revolutionist elements.[115] There is a shift, too, in the extent of emotional self-control in these movements, from the involuntary hysteria among the natives of the East Central Highlands,[116] to the more manipulated, perhaps simulated and certainly stimulated, shaking of the Vailala Madness and the Letub cults, and further to the attempts at elimination of all such motor reactions in the Paliau movement. In the early cults, hysteria and lack of emotional control is itself ascribed to the power of mystical forces. Powerful subjective feelings necessarily predicate powerful external entities, and become an evidence of the spiritual forces that are at work. Growing control of feelings is associated with the increased application of reason to the production of cargo (even though some of the early inferences—i.e. the floral table decorations—are mistaken). Steadily, local reasoning about how to produce goods comes to conform increasingly to European experience.

The 'modernization' of goals (from improved taro crops to the demand for western equipment); the increased levels of emotional control and the regulation of fear and impulse-ridden behaviour; and the gradual simulation of co-ordinated activity in systematic and persistent patterns of work, may, without disparagement of native abilities, be regarded as increasing rationality.[117]

Two other processes are associated with these changes in the orientation and emotional tone of Melanesian movements, both of which indicate, if not any specific increase in rationality at least a change in the sense of self-identity which facilitates social action on a larger scale and towards more clearly formulated ends. The first is the increasing tendency for Melanesians to acquire the habit of thinking of themselves as such instead of as men of a local group or a tribe. This is evident in the Koreri movements, in the increasing association of different groups

[114] See pp. 74–5.
[115] See pp. 468–74, 476–83.
[116] See pp. 216 ff.
[117] I do not ignore the strictures on this subject of, *inter alia*, I. C. Jarvie, 'Theories of Cargo Cults . . .', op. cit., and *idem, Revolution in Anthropology*, op. cit. Cargo cults are native attempts at explanation of a situation which, given what the natives know, are not necessarily irrational according to the logic of their situation. I write, however, as a western observer, using western standards, and making western judgements: my use of the term 'rational' is not intended to imply a particular quality of intellect.

in the later cults of the Madang district, and among many other cults. The achievement is not, of course, attributable simply to the revolutionist orientation of cargo movements. Europeans had proscribed warfare, imposed central administrative areas, and fostered the tendency to describe natives as *kanakas* over against Europeans.[118] None the less, the process is one with its equivalents in other parts of the third world. As Lawrence has emphasized, however, the emergence of an embryonic nationalism is not necessarily correlated with the sense of pan-native identity, nor has it led to a specific sense of civic responsiblity.[119] It may indeed be the case that neither incipient nationalism nor conscious political identity is capable of producing a sense of civic responsibility.

The second development is for more recent cults to manifest a more explicitly political orientation. This might be seen as a further manifestation of the process of secularization evident in the shift from thaumaturgical to revolutionist, and thence to rational economic concerns. It would be easy to exaggerate the unilinearity of the process.[120] The bias of western observers is to see in religious preoccupations hidden political intents; and of many western administrators, to so deal with religious movements that a political or even a military animus is engendered. The recognition of cults as political movements has of course been considerably stimulated because they are often the only manifestations of indigenous expression at a time when the modern West is anxious to encourage political self-determination in colonial territories: up to a point the political element in movements was first induced accidently by repression, and then encouraged because of the absence of any other significant expression of political interest.[121]

---

[118] P. Lawrence, op. cit., p. 231, writes, 'Already possessing a basically common culture and now having in Pidgin English a *lingua franca* capable of expressing it, they began to feel that they belonged to a society far wider than that of their forbears [sic]: the common native society of the whole area.' Lawrence considers (p. 257) that the growth of this sense of solidarity was a by-product, not a master-plan.

[119] Ibid., pp. 257–8.

[120] Ibid., pp. 265–6, where Lawrence seeks to qualify the opinion of P. Worsley, op. cit., by showing that his interpretation of Yali's movement ignored the extent to which people still believed in cargo ideas. Cargo beliefs had become a virtual part of the local culture. On this general subject see also the discussion in Judy Inglis, 'Cargo Cults: The Problem of Explanation', *Oceania* XXVII, 4 (June 1957), pp. 249–63.

[121] G. Cochrane, op. cit., p. 124, writes, 'The Legislative Council debates which reflect the views of elected Solomon Island leaders, show that the people are basically satisfied with their present system of government. They have no real desire for independence, nor even a desire to assume a greater degree of responsibility for their affairs. But in the prevailing climate of world opinion and in view of the 1960 UN Declaration on the abolition of colonialism, the British Government has no wish to stay in the islands any longer than is strictly necessary.' And on p. 125, 'Local government council meetings show the operation of the traditional "big man" relationship with ordinary men. There is little discussion, all the motions of the President are inevitably carried unanimously.'

11

From Magic to the Millennium—and back

It is only at certain historical moments and in a particular concatenation of circumstances that revolutionist movements emerge. Such movements mobilize men by creating a new and induced awareness of the commonality of their conditions, and the need for supernatural action at a societal or cosmic level to produce effective change. This awareness is not a sophisticated consciousness of social circumstances. It does not imply accurate perception of the structure of the social order, nor a clear conception of its operation. It is, rather, a widely diffused apprehension that things are wrong, and the wish that they should be better. The ideology that welds so many men together and stimulates them to action has little or no analytical content, and produces little empirical evidence. Rather it presents a dream, a vision, a wish, and projects it as a prospect for the real world. It is a fantasy that fires the imagination and conforms to widely felt longings, which now acquire a focus and perhaps even a stimulus for action.

Since the millennial dream draws so little support from empirical reality, and since fantasy does not remain fresh, revolutionist responses are not easily sustained at even levels of commitment over long periods. Men have individual problems which are only incidentally and occasionally shared with others, and the solutions for which lie, or appear to lie, in personal relationships with others, or with the powers of the cosmos, rather than in the circumstances of the collectivity, or the relations of the society with other societies. The demand for thaumaturgy, as we have seen, is endemic, and especially so in societies in which medical and religious practice are closely identified, and in which a wide range of worldly activities require the reassurance of supernatural goodwill. The revolutionist response is a consequence of a stimulated awareness that the difficulties that men experience are common difficulties, having their origin within the social system, or in the unbalance between the community and its natural environment, or in the disordered relations of the community and those men who come from another society and another culture.

The salvation of the community, and perhaps of the wider society, has usually been expressed in traditional ceremonial, in rain-making, war-dances, or renewal rites. But this communal search for salvation has been a traditionalized and ritualized matter, of which individuals have not been consciously aware. The ceremonials have expressed a necessary relationship of the community to the powers that protect it, or that it must placate in self-defence. The revolutionist response is equally communal (and among less-developed peoples it is initially tribal or racial, rather than individually voluntaristic), but it is also an expression of a new consciousness of the need for communal salvation. It is a cognition, however strangely evaluated, of the collective circumstance, and it is cognition with a degree of acuteness that traditional communal ritual never required. Suddenly men are brought to acknowledgement that the cause of their discontents lies in the structural and processual circumstances of their society, or in new influences affecting their traditional social order. The revolutionist response to the world is the demand that these circumstances be altered, and altered at once.

The revolutionist response readily subsides again when hope of divine intervention fails. Men resume their effort to work out their own salvation, and forget the salvation of their community, their society, or their race. The stable demand for thaumaturgical and therapeutic services steadily erodes the fading hope of a time and place free from all such needs, and free from the oppression of other men. For a time, millennialism may draw some strength from thaumaturgical pre-occupations, particularly in the promise of a future time when illness and old age will not occur. But men cannot live by such promises: the needs for healing and reassurance are immediate. Thus, it is a commonplace that the millennialist and revolutionist response gives place again to thaumaturgy. But sometimes, the thaumaturgy is itself of a new type, is itself infused with the effects of the catalytic experience of the revolutionist movement.

Some of the patterns of millennialism may persist, even if the specific content of the millennial hope wanes. The former distribution of power, the limitations of access to the supernatural, exemplified in the practice of shamans, may be broken by the revolutionist movement. The new dream of a changed set of social circumstances has been communicated through new agents, and has been received and personalized by others. The trance states, the shaking, the onset of power in the face of events too dramatic to be contemplated without perturbation, by-pass the conventional channels of communication concerning the supernatural. Unless old shamans can appropriate new roles in dissemination of the new cult, the cult will present a threat to their power. New roles are established temporarily, even if they are not so readily institutionalized.

New styles of association occur, affecting the relations of the sexes, age-groups, and tribes. When such transformation has been wrought, the community is unlikely to revert entirely to the patterns that previously prevailed. Traditional roles may now need new validation, and even though the millennial visions fade and are discredited, the means of acquiring power through more dramatic visions may persist. The exclusive monopoly of the shaman is broken. New patterns of thaumaturgy are likely to follow in the wake of a revolutionist movement, as the wider promise of the millennium is whittled down to more personal prospects of healing, and the other immediate concerns of everyday life. Even if the notion of a millennium persists, the emphasis shifts from it, but the changed pattern of roles associated with it may now affect the evolution of thaumaturgical practice.

The *Feather* cult of the Middle Columbia River, which arose among those tribes in which the religion of Smohalla, the prophecies of a variety of other dreamers, and the curative practices of the north-west coast *Shakers* were disseminated, was one such reassertion of thaumaturgical concerns. The prophecies of Smohalla were distinctly revolutionist, even though the movement was itself also somewhat withdrawn from wider associations with the world, and emphasized the continuities of the native way of life. Its real hope was the coming restoration of the Indian past. But among the many prophets who arose among the tribes on the Columbia River this was a unique message, although it was one that was echoed in the Ghost Dance of 1870, which spread south and west into California, and again in the Ghost Dance of 1890, which spread mainly east across the Plains.

The minor prophets of the Columbia River region appear to have been largely disseminators of relatively conventional christianized eschatology. Thus Luls, one of the Umatilla prophets, during a period in which he 'died', had visions of the people in the clouds. If Indians would but keep their hearts clean, they too would go to the beautiful places inhabited by their dead relatives. Dancing, drumming, and emphatic sabbatarianism marked his preaching.[1] More emphatically nativistic ideas were preached to the Cayuse by Hununwe, an old woman, who also 'died', and who received a vision of the dead. She emphasized the need to wear buckskin rather than the clothes of the white man, but her message, and that of her husband, Nukshai, who succeeded her after her (real) death and after his own experience of 'dying', was a set of ethical prescriptions for going to heaven, rather than either a millennial message or a fully introversionist ideal.

[1] An account of Luls, and of other prophets among the Umatilla and neighbouring tribes, is given in Cora Du Bois, *The Feather Cult of the Middle Columbia* (Banta, Menasha, Wisc., 1938).

Shramaia of the Skin Indians used a bell and a bird raised on a pole, and had a flag, in the same fashion as Smohalla. His message was quietistic: 'Whatever the white man planned for us could not be changed', and the white men were coming to build a church, a court-house, and a jail.[2] He acknowledged four ways of salvation, the American, the Catholic, the Methodist, and the Indian, and his teaching was essentially accommodative.

The Feather cult itself may be traced back, indirectly, to Lishwailait, a Klikitat Indian, who appears to have been very much affected by his mother's death at some time about 1850, and who had visions of her in the conditions of the after-life, where people did not age. She gave him messages about the creation of the earth and its fullness, and directed him not to mourn for her. He appears to have had the power of discern-ing spirits, but he was not a curer. His teaching resembled the Washani faith, which was common among the Indian tribes of the area, and incorporated Christian ideas. The founder of the Feather cult (also called the *bum-bum* or *pom-pom* religion, from its use of the drum), Jake Hunt, was a Klikitat who appears to have drawn some inspiration from Lishwailait. He became inspired after the death of his third wife (to whom he was devoted) and her child, between 1898 and 1904, and after some contact with the Shakers, who had by this time disseminated their cult to the Yakima reservation, and who had been engaged in therapeutic practice for Jake Hunt's family. At this time Jake Hunt, perhaps imitating some of his relatives, had a vision of Lishwailait dressed in buckskins, with a drum and eagle feathers.[3]

Jake Hunt's household was at this time in a state of tension and hysteria. The double bereavement had left them vulnerable to any supernaturalist interpretations, and the sustained activity of the Shakers disposed them to strong religiosity, even though the Shakers rejected local visions. In this context, a variety of events occurred which began to shape the new Feather cult. Whether Jake Hunt experienced 'death' and return to life is not clear, although it was the common legitimation for new revelations. Certainly he had visions of the ancestors, singing Washani songs. He was given a command to convert people, and, expelling the Shakers from his family, he pro-claimed himself by a new name, Titcamnashat, the Earth Thunderer. He acquired the ability to read men's thoughts, to anticipate visitors, to detect any whisky that was brought into his encampment, and to locate lost objects (a capability often claimed by the Shakers). Accord-ing to his half-brother, who was a shaman, he had had spirit familiars

[2] Ibid., p. 14.
[3] This account rests entirely on C. Du Bois, op. cit.

when he was a young man, and he now claimed to get his messages from an eagle (hence the name Thunderer, from Thunderbird). Although he did not use shamanistic practices in healing, the continuities with traditional shaman practice are significant.

Jake Hunt set out to proselytize in response to the command he had received in a vision, and became known as a healer. He converted people at the Yakima reservation, but failed in a curing challenge among the Walla Walla and Nez Percé. At Warm Springs he converted some Paviotso (Paiute) who carried the new faith to the Klamath reservation on the borders of California and Oregon, where other Paviotso lived. At Spearfish, on the Columbia River, he built a long-house, and performed cures, and there is a report of some of his converts destroying their European furniture and re-installing Indian artefacts. This touch of emphatic nativism, also symbolized in his dress and regalia, does not conceal the central importance of his healing and thaumaturgical practice.

The initiation of a new convert required that the leader should obtain a vision and transfer it to the initiate, causing him to spin around (hence the name sometimes used for the movement of the *Spinners*). From feathers, the neophyte saw all his past sins, which he then had to confess, with vomiting as part of the purification process. The successful initiate was given eagle feathers for himself. Any of the members might organize a meeting, at which each participant, often holding a feather in the hand, would spin in his place while songs were sung. In many ways the faith was similar to the Washani faith common to the area, but curing was one of its distinctive differences—and this may have been borrowed from the Shakers. They, however, regarded the therapeutic practice of the Feather cult as little better than the shamanism which they themselves so strongly disavowed.

When a cure was sought a group of cultists would normally respond to the call, as among the Shakers, although one might be sufficient. 'The curers pray for power. The drums convey to them the nature and seriousness of the illness.'[4] The patient would lie in the centre of the floor with his feet to the east, and usually the leader, three assistants, and drummers and bell-ringers would begin the process of therapy. The patient would be brushed with eagle feathers to remove the malady, and the leader might be led to the afflicted part of the body to grip the evil to pull it off. Jake Hunt himself had a special reputation for his ability to cure alcoholics. 'Even the Shakers, with their marked hostility to the Feather cult admit his success in this respect.'[5]

4 Ibid., p. 34.
5 Ibid., p. 37.

The Feather cult was not millennialist, but accepted the conventional eschatology of going to heaven after death. The nativist element, represented in the buckskin clothes of Jake Hunt, did not persist, though long hair and moccasins were considered to be desirable for men. It shared many moral precepts with the Washani faith but was more severe concerning alcohol, although less austere than the Shakers in this and other moral prescriptions. The cult appears to have been a revitalization of the Washani faith, which was itself composed of traditional and some Christian ideas, but to it Jake Hunt had added practice and curing of a semi-shamanistic type.

New patterns of thaumaturgical practice

The Feather cult was an amalgamation of the therapeutic practices of the Shakers; of the already christianized Washani religion, with its traditional festivities for the salmon and the berries; and the prophetic revelatory styles, by that time well established among the tribes on the Columbia River. The Shaker Church was the most important of the thaumaturgical movements to arise among the North American Indians. Their tradition was a mixture of the accepted styles of prophetism; an amended and revitalized thaumaturgy, enjoying many continuities with earlier shamanistic practice; and procedures, forms, and organization derived from the Christian denominations. Its early emphasis on millennialism, which may have been derived from echoes of the 1870 Ghost Dance, or, as seems more likely, may have been inspired by Christian millennial ideas, and the gradual recession of this teaching into complete obscurity, make of this movement a primary example of the mutation of the revolutionist response into the thaumaturgical preoccupation.

The Shaker Church had its origins in 1881 in the visions of John Slocum, of the Squaxin band of the Skokomish tribe, who lived in south Puget Sound in the state of Washington.[6] Slocum was a logger of about forty at this time, an illiterate man who had lived a careless life, with a fondness for pony-racing and whisky. He was married and had fathered thirteen children, most of whom had died in infancy.[7] The Indians of the area had long before ceded their land to the whites, and become wards of the government. They were plagued by recurrent

[6] Homer G. Barnett, *Indian Shakers: A Messianic Cult of the Pacific Northwest* (Southern Illinois University Press, Carbondale 1957), pp. 6, 41. The account in the following paragraphs leans heavily on this source.
[7] Ibid., p. 6.

fears of being further dispossessed of the land, and, in 1874, the nearby Puyallup reservation was, against Indian wishes, sold off in individual allotments, perhaps because the number of whites in the area had increased.[8] Native customs had long been frowned upon by the local agents, and after 1871—such was the fear of the whites that all Indian ceremonials were war-dances—all native dances were prohibited.[9] The pattern of Indian life had been further affected by many decades of contact, by the introduction and availability of whisky, the effect of white disease, and the various other importations of the white man, against which the native had few cultural or physical defences.

The exact circumstances of John Slocum's 'death' and resuscitation with a vision of heaven subsequently became subject to various accumulations of myth. That some message from God would be given to the Indians was predicted by Big Bill, a local Indian of religious disposition, some time before John Slocum 'died', and a group who were at odds with the Congregationalist missionary Myron Eells, and the agent, his brother Edwin, were already holding their own services at Big Bill's house, and claiming to be Catholics. Thus a group of anti-mission religionists was already in being and ready to accept a new message.[10] Slocum had 'died', preparations were made for his funeral, when, in the presence of his wife and others, he returned to life, with a message of his experience. An angel had confronted him with the wickedness of his life, 'and he was instructed to return to earth to bear witness of his transformation and to lead other sinners into the Christian way of life'.[11] For this purpose he was given the chance to return to the world to preach his message for a period, and was instructed to build a church before the next Sabbath day. Slocum's preaching initially inspired many of the local Indians. One of his followers later declared, 'We never heard such a thing as man dying and bring word that there was a God'.[12] After some months the excitement and interest waned as the novelty of

[8] Marian W. Smith, 'Shamanism in the Shaker Religion of Northwest America', *Man* LIV, article 181 (August 1954), pp. 119–22.

[9] June McCormick Collins, 'The Indian Shaker Church', *Southwestern Journal of Anthropology* 6, 4 (Winter 1950), pp. 399–411.

[10] H. G. Barnett, op. cit., pp. 48–9, 344–6. Barnett also gives the various versions of Slocum's death, pp. 11–44.

[11] H. G. Barnett, op. cit., p. 6. John Slocum told James Wickersham, the local lawyer who helped the Shakers to organize a church, that the angel of his vision had told him to look down at his body, lying dead below, and, he continued, ' "I did, and saw it lying down. When I saw it, it was pretty poor. . . ." When I came alive, I tell my friends "Good thing in heaven. God is kind to us. If you all try hard and help me we will be better men on earth." ' cited by J. Mooney, *The Ghost Dance and the Sioux Outbreak of 1890*, 1896 Edn, op. cit., Part II p. 752.

[12] These were the words of Mud Bay Louis (Louis Yowaluch), cited in H. G. Barnett, op. cit., p. 49.

Slocum's vision and the impact of his message began to wear off, and he himself slipped back into his former ways.

Slocum again fell ill, and this crisis had a much more enduring effect on the new movement which, thereafter, was to spread far beyond Puget Sound. Slocum's illness very much affected his wife, Mary, who experienced a hysterical seizure, 'praying, sobbing and trembling uncontrollably as she approached Slocum's body'.[13] As her convulsion subsided, Slocum recovered somewhat, and this was attributed to the seizure. Thus, the idea of shaking as a therapeutic procedure was established in the waning religion that John Slocum had founded. Shaking was something that many could experience. It was a manifestation of power, and it became more important than either the early ethical prescriptions or the millennial message in promoting the diffusion of the new movement beyond its immediate locality of origin.

Thereafter, the Shaker Church underwent many vicissitudes. A number of divergent elements were evident in its early years. Visions were acquired by different individuals, and various new elements were added, in particular hand-shaking; crossing oneself; the use of candles and an altar—all part of the Catholic tradition which the local group of anti-mission Indians had claimed as their own. Rumours associated with Shaker proselytizing declared that those outside the new movement would suffer great misfortune, and some propounded an idea found elsewhere among Indian religious cults, that those who did not join would be turned into animals. In particular, ideas of the early end of the world were disseminated. There were stories of people being turned into angels, dying and coming to life again, whilst shaking, and the therapeutic practice of brushing off the evil that was supposed to come to the surface of the body both persisted.

The millennial element was conspicuous, and one active proselytizer, Big John, received a vision that he was Christ Incarnate, and that his wife was the Virgin Mary. With a considerable following, he rode on horseback through the streets of Olympia, with arms outstretched, like the crucified Christ. Although he was imprisoned, new millennial ideas arose, and 4 July was prophesied to be the day of Christ's return; this date was later repeatedly reset, and many were repeatedly frightened as the predicted time drew near.[14]

The millennial hope faded in the course of a few years, and the persecution that the church experienced from the agent and his missionary brother led to a period of quiescence on the part of the Shakers, with the normal provision of the religious services of the missionary. Curing

[13] H. G. Barnett, op. cit., p. 7.
[14] Ibid., pp. 55, 56, 92; J. Mooney, op. cit., p. 749.

meetings continued, however, and became the abiding concern of the cultists. When, in 1891, the opportunity arose for the church to emerge into the open again, it was evident that Shaker practices had not lapsed. Even so, without the assistance of a white lawyer, James Wickersham, it is doubtful whether the movement would have acquired the permanence and the prestige that it attained in this period. By the Dawes act of 1887, Indians who resided apart from their tribe and adopted the habits of civilized life became American citizens, and when Washington became a state in 1889, the citizen Indians became citizens of the state. Subsequently, in 1891, the United States District Court ruled that citizens of the state could not be placed under the jurisdiction of an Indian agent, and Wickersham tested the new law in a case involving the sale of alcohol to an Indian. It now became possible for the Shakers to organize and to establish themselves as a church, free of the general supervision of Indian agents. With Wickersham's assistance the leading Shakers constituted themselves as a religious body, and in June 1892 the Church was organized on a regular basis in Mud Bay, at the house of Mud Bay Louis (Yowaluch).[15]

The new faith was diffused fairly rapidly over a wide area of the west coast. It spread to the eastern parts of Washington state, where it contended with the Washani religion, the Smohalla cult, and finally with the Feather cult.[16] It spread south through Oregon and into California, and north to Vancouver Island.[17] Many churches were built, although many later fell into decay when meetings were more commonly held in houses, and as former enthusiasts allowed their interest to flag. In some areas, the Shakers drew out all the people from Catholic missions, although elsewhere, particularly in Canada, Catholic Indians were not drawn in.[18] Enthusiasm, and especially the power acquired by shaking hands, which often immediately caused the newcomer to begin to shake, were features of its early spread. Groups travelled to sick people at Yakima, Klamath, Warm Springs and other distant reservations, and in the course of time their success facilitated the acceptance of the new religion, despite the embargo which the Shakers put on whisky, tobacco, and sometimes on gambling, dancing, and other pastimes. In the 1930s, twenty-five Shaker churches were reported as in use; others had fallen into decay.[19]

[15] H. G. Barnett, op. cit., pp. 57–8; J. Mooney, op. cit., p. 758.
[16] See pp. 280–3, 350 ff.
[17] M. W. Smith, op. cit., p. 119.
[18] H. G. Barnett, op. cit., pp. 65–6.
[19] Ibid., pp. 58–85. Of the number of Shakers, Barnett (p. 84) says that it is impossible to estimate, but 'it is certain that a rather large number of Indians in the northwestern states have at one time or another been significantly affected by the Shaker cult'.

The fact that the Shakers have kept no records, and have readily accommodated somewhat diverse ideas of the faith and its practice, indicates that, despite the accommodation of the religion to the formal organizational style of a western church, it remained essentially a typical native cult movement.[20] It shared with other Indian movements the willingness to allow any individual to sponsor meetings, to undertake curing, to become actively involved in proselytizing. Neither doctrinal rigour nor constitutional authority existed to impede the freedom that particular persons might claim in their interpretation of, participation in, and dissemination of the faith. Ministers were not paid officials, nor was it necessary that a minister be present at a church service. They were neither divinely appointed nor the possessors of special esoteric knowledge. Barnett says, 'the definitions of leadership embodied in the Shaker constitution have proved to be irrelevant to needs of the organization'.[21]

The sanctions of the church have always been weak, and whilst the occasion for formal schism scarcely existed, the opportunities for divergence in faith and practice, and for rivalry, were uninhibited. Many offices remained unfilled for long periods. The office of bishop did not provide adequate leadership for the movement, and the incumbents became the objects of contention, particularly in the late 1920s and 1930s, when controversy arose about the extent to which the Shakers were Christian or should use the Bible. Peter Heck the Bishop and the older party opposed the use of the Bible in services. All the power that was needed, and all the legitimation for it, were in the shake itself. The ensuing conflict eventually led to the emergence of rival bishops, each claiming jurisdiction over the Church, one embracing and the other eschewing the use of the Bible in services.[22]

Syncretism and shamanism among the Shakers

With far less desire than, for example, West Africans for the adoption of the forms of organization prevailing in the dominant culture, the

[20] Ibid., p. 110. The Church in Washington acquired two documents, regarded by them as Articles of Incorporation and Rules and By-Laws, in 1910, in order to organize themselves under the laws of the State. On the Rules and By-Laws, Barnett (p. 112) comments that it is a 'confusion of ritualistic, dogmatic and ethical elements'. According to Erna Gunther, 'The Shaker Religion of the Northwest', pp. 37–76 in Marian W. Smith (Ed.), *Indians of the Urban Northwest*, Columbia Contributions to Anthropology No. 36 (Columbia University Press, New York 1949), Shakers elsewhere had acquired such legal forms at a rather earlier date.
[21] Ibid., p. 129.
[22] Ibid., pp. 114–24 for an account of this conflict. See also E. Gunther, op. cit., p. 67 ff.

Indian Shakers embraced a limited and imperfect constitutional model of the denomination to meet a particular situation. They needed it to assert their legality as a religion in the face of persistent persecution. But they had no experience of the operation of a formal constitution, and no particular disposition to use constitutional procedures. The history of the divisions and rivalries among the Shakers illustrates the importance of individual personality, the inadequacy of their constitutional forms, and their limited capacity to employ them, or to evolve forms of association more appropriate to their needs. The physical distance between churches, and the general sparseness of Indian population, have clearly made the denominational pattern (itself so suited to urban environments and higher population density, where its implicit voluntary character was more self-evident and more meaningful) much harder to sustain than, for example, in West African thaumaturgical movements. Although the teachings and worship of the Church had from the very beginning a strong Christian imprint, and this has tended to grow—giving rise to the campaign of the unsuccessful minority who sought to establish the use of the Bible, and who claimed explicit Christian status for the visions of John Slocum—none the less, the forms of denominational organization have never received regular acknowledgement.

The Shaker religion is regarded as having gone furthest of all North American Indian prophet cults in the direction of adopting Christian forms.[23] Services were held in a single room with simple furnishings, with benches along the wall, so that the centre might be used for dancing and curing ceremonies. In common with other cults in the north-west, a bell announced the service half an hour before it began, usually on Sunday morning. Some of the members wore robes—white dresses and shirts were once the form—but this was always considered to be an individual matter. Although the shaking was more frenzied in services in the early days than later, it persisted as a regular, seemingly uncontrolled, but in fact almost stereotyped activity. The shaking occurred to particular songs with sustained repetition of syllables that had no sense (there were also other more conventional songs). Many songs were said to have come to individuals in visions, and some resembled evangelical songs. The concepts of original sin, atonement, and redemption were very little emphasized. 'They all pray aloud, individually and spontaneously.'[24]

    [23] E. Gunther, op. cit., p. 60; H. G. Barnett, op. cit., p. 285, says that Slocum's own teachings were derived almost wholly from Christian sources. This account of Shaker worship relies on these two sources.
    [24] H. G. Barnett, op. cit., p. 239; also p. 153.

The similarity of many of the characteristics of worship procedures—the repeated choruses leading to dancing (or shaking); the simultaneous individual prayer—with those of thaumaturgical movements elsewhere, for example those in West Africa, is striking. Nor do these elements spring directly from the Christian mission inheritance which is common to the new religions of both these areas. They appear to be spontaneous developments of similar patterns of worship. Sin is not seen as being against God, but rather as a cause of personal distress. Confession is a catharsis, less for spiritual regeneration than for immediate relief. There is no general expectation of confession, although some have set themselves up as confessors. Authorities disagree about the extent to which the Christian conception of reward in the life after death is emphasized in Shakerism. John Slocum had a vision of heaven, but 'this was apparently not vivid enough to bring the imagination of his followers to focus upon it'.[25] The real concern of the Shakers is not the conventional eschatological concern of Christendom, but rather the thaumaturgical preoccupation, which is itself so characteristic of indigenous religion.

> All Shakers are anxious about their souls, but their interest is in keeping them in their bodies rather than in providing for them after death. Their thinking does not run to speculation about the after-life. Heaven when it is thought of, is vaguely imagined as a good place somewhere up above without positive attributes or inducements.[26]

The acquisition and use of power are the vital concerns of the faith, as they were of the old cultural complex. From it come prestige, health, and even prosperity (though Shakers nominally condemn healing for payment as shamanistic).

The primary concerns of the Shakers in the use of power are with healing and inspiration. It is a wonder-working faith, and virtually an accommodation in Christian mould and with official approval of the continuance of the shamanistic functions (and some of the shamanistic forms) of the past. Its early Christian millennialism was quickly superseded, but Slocum himself preached a distinctly millennial message, and some of his early successors were even more profoundly stirred by messianic aspirations.

> The end of the mundane order of things was imminent; the millennium was to be heralded by the second appearance of Jesus Christ and would be marked by the final judgment of all souls, the destruction of the

[25] Ibid., p. 156. E. Gunther, op. cit., p. 51, maintains that sermons emphasized rewards in heaven.
[26] H. G. Barnett, loc. cit.

wicked, the reunion of the saved, and the eternal rule of right, truth and justice.[27]

This may be regarded as the expression of a revolutionist response, even though, as Barnett points out, the cult never expressed any anti-white orientation, nor did it proclaim the restoration of the Indian way of life.[28] The absence of these items may be attributed to the Christian origin of its millennialism. This was certainly not autochthonous millennialism, and it quickly mutated into a re-formulation of indigenous thaumaturgical concerns. For, despite the absence of a restorative orientation, there was a 'pronounced feeling among most Shakers that their religion belongs to the Indian'.[29] As with most millennial expectations, the call for faith in the advent had little power beyond the early disappointment of hope postponed. Slocum himself lost his sense of urgency; his wife introduced the preoccupation with healing. Thus, a movement that had its first impetus as a revolutionist response to a situation of considerable despair, in which all traditional cere-monial was prohibited, sustained itself by re-legitimizing, under the cover of law, the Indian's abiding expectation of religious salvation—salvation in the present world and in the body, rather than by the early overturn of the world, or in post-mortem states of bliss.

Healing was the primary element in the Shaker movement. It might be undertaken in the church, or in a home, very much in the manner of a sacramental ceremony, with an elaborate ritual in which bells, candles, chanting, parading, and stamping were important. The Shakers sometimes healed by 'brushing' the patient's body. They might also 'rub' the body, and when inspiration occurred grasp the afflicted part to extract the evil from it. Finally, there was a more dramatic technique of pushing, pulling, and pummelling the patient, and this was sometimes a group effort. At times the healer was over-come by the strength of the sickness as he grasped it in his fists, and grappled with it. The curing ceremony was more exciting and spiritually liberating than the normal Sunday worship service, and a congested pattern of disorder might occur on the church floor, as healers, patients, and bell-ringers moved about, trying to 'get up the shake' and occasion-ally speaking in tongues. Shakers might seek personal healing by brushing motions, rubbing their limbs, and 'brushing' themselves with candlelight. The sessions might continue from the early evening into the small hours, and thus stand in sharp contrast to the Sunday

[27] Ibid., p. 286.
[28] Ibid., pp. 141–2.
[29] Ibid., p. 141.

morning worship services, which after the early days became more closely regulated, and ended more punctually at noon.[30]

The indigenous religious practice of the north-west coast involved the reliance of the individual on the spirit which he encountered in isolation. The spirit gave him a power, and this was true for shamans and for others. These powers had to be validated by pragmatic demonstration in the acquisition of skills. A man might become ill by displeasing his spirit, but he might also suffer from the activities of shamans, against whom he needed protective spirits. The inspirational element in Shakerism showed continuity with these ideas. Individual shaking was the manifestation of his encounter with a spirit-power. The spirit was not now met in isolation, but in the community. Songs were acquired from the spirit in a similar way, and although the guardian spirit has now become the 'spirit of God', the function of the spirit, and man's relationship to it, have marked similarities.[31]

The traditional shamans cured by 'visiting the land of the dead' to recapture their patients' souls that had been stolen by the dead.[32] It was not said that they 'died' in undertaking this visit, but the similarity to the experience of Slocum himself is notable, and the frequency of this legitimation of prophecy in other parts of Washington, if not among the Puget Sound tribes themselves, is well established.[33] Shamans cured by pitting their own power against that of the intrusive power to which the sickness was attributed. To destroy the intrusive power was to destroy its owner, who might be killed by the operation of the shaman. Other shamanistic ideas, that sin might be brushed off, blown off, or sucked out, were prevalent on the north-west coast.[34]

Many of these elements were inherited by the Shakers, even though Slocum himself turned against shamanism at his conversion. There is some evidence that the early Shaker cures were also thought to involve killing.[35] Shakers were frequently pitted against shamans or other healers in their early performances. They had concepts of being able to shake off the evil or sometimes to shake loose the soul if it had 'got stuck' somewhere. Even where sickness was seen more specifically as a consequence of sin, some parallel exists between ridding the person of

[30] This paragraph relies on the detailed account of Shaker healing by Dale Valory, 'The Focus of Shaker Healing', *Kroeber Anthropological Society Papers* (Berkeley, California), Vol. 35 (Fall 1966), pp. 67–112.

[31] This paragraph relies on J. M. Collins, op. cit.

[32] M. W. Smith, op. cit., p. 120.

[33] See, for example, the accounts above of the Feather cult and the religion of Smohalla: pp. 283–3, 350 ff.

[34] These characteristics are discussed in T. T. Waterman, 'The Shake Religion of Puget Sound', *Annual Report of the Board of Regents of the Smithsonian Institute, 1922* (Government Printing Office, Washington 1924), pp. 499–507.

[35] M. W. Smith, op. cit., pp. 120–1.

sin and extracting an intrusive object. Indeed, in some places the early Shakers revived the idea of 'Indian devils', and non-Shakers were sometimes vilified, for example among the Yoruk, as nocturnal agents of death.[36] 'The first Shakers were obsessed by shamanistic threats.'[37] The conflict persisted between the two, as between two alternative patterns of thaumaturgical practice, sometimes coming into open competition. Just as witches in Africa were said sometimes to visit the aladura churches, so the shamans sometimes appeared at Shaker services, ready for a trial of strength. Again, just as is often claimed by African members of aladura churches, the ability to recognize witches in disguise was claimed by some Shakers. Shakerism had, indeed, partly emerged in the vacuum created by the prohibition of so many shamanistic rites, but the shamans were still practising. The Shakers did not imitate all forms of shamanistic practice: they avoided, for example, the fire tricks and the piercing and cutting of the body that constituted part of the more professional shamanistic repertoire. But the 'power sing' of the shaman had its equivalent in the Shaker Church.[38] The Shakers acquired reputations for finding lost objects, much in the fashion of shamans, but 'the preponderance of revelations have for their purpose the discernment of disease, the exposure of shamans and the persecution of witches'.[39]

The ethical precepts of Shakerism were in many respects those of mission Christianity, although sanctions have rarely been effective in reforming or expelling the wayward. There has been a general prohibition against smoking and drinking, and particular individuals have practised a more austere code, eschewing horse-racing and gambling. But personal ethics have not always been of a high standard; animosity among the officers of the church has been frequent, and the agencies of control have been weak. The evidence from the lives of individual Shakers suggests that marital inconstancy has been as prevalent as among other Indians. As with other thaumaturgical religions, ethical concerns have not been the major preoccupation of the church. The condemnation of shamanism and of other movements —for example the Feather cult—and the elimination of sin and disease by confession and cures, in order 'to feel good again', have been much more predominant concerns.[40]

[36] H. G. Barnett, op. cit., p. 138.
[37] Ibid., p. 167.
[38] M. W. Smith, op. cit., p. 121.
[39] H. G. Barnett, op. cit., p. 199.
[40] H. G. Barnett, op. cit., p. 142, credits the Feather cult (the pom pom religion) with a strict reactionary response to white acculturation. This appears to be an over-statement from the available evidence: the cult appears to have been conservative rather than reactionary, although this might be an appropriate description of the religion of Smohalla. See pp. 350 ff.

The Christian impetus, from which Shakerism sprang, acquired periodic reinforcement with the conversion to the faith of Indians who had experienced mission training and Christian conversion. Subsequently, the increasing experience of Pentecostalism may have had its influence on the movement. The older Shakers believed in conversion by the acquisition of power, demonstrated by shaking. Those who came later, and particularly the 'progressives', emphasized the importance of accepting the Scriptures and Christian injunctions in order to attain salvation.[41] The absence of a restorative emphasis in the faith, and the willingness of many to accept the influence of Christianity, illustrate the extent to which the movement differed from the attempts of other earlier, and even contemporaneous, Indian movements to preserve the separate Indian way of life in a mould of the past. The Shaker movement did not seek assimilation to the dominant culture, but it did attempt some type of accommodation of the native to a way of life which, whilst separate from that of white men, borrowed acceptable forms from the dominant culture, in order to sustain a pattern of activities, and a style of reassurance, uniquely needed by many among the indigenes.

The cultural disorganization which had overtaken the coastal tribes of the north-west—in the changing regulation of land; the smallpox epidemics; the prohibition of traditional ceremonials; and the increasing involvement in wage labour—appears to have been associated with an increase in the fear of the practitioners of evil magic. The 'surge of witch hunts that marked the emergence of Shakerism' indicates this.[42] Slocum himself appears to have been involved in family disagreements in which he suspected that evil magic was being employed against him.[43] His own revelation proposed a means of breaking the power of the shamans, or providing new curative practices, and of restoring some ceremonial order to native life. It was not a re-affirmation of the past, nor even a perpetuation of the traditions, such as they were, of the present. Rather it was a new thaumaturgy, a new power, with which to challenge and defeat the old. In some measure it met the requirements of the white man concerning religion, and adopted reassuring aspects of Christianity, but it remained an Indian way, and used Indian forms.

Later, when shamans had become few or non-existent, it could be said that 'for many individuals the emotion experience of shaking is a

[41] Ibid., pp. 146–8.
[42] Ibid., p. 352. That there was a rise of witchcraft in the period in which Shakerism arose is the opinion of Elizabeth Colson, in an unpublished manuscript cited by Dale Valory, op. cit., p. 102.
[43] Ibid., pp. 351–2.

healing instrument. It *is* a medicine, the fulfilment of a prophecy for the afflicted and oppressed, an unmeasured gift for the faithful'.[44] Shakerism was an essentially thaumaturgical movement. The epithet 'messianic', used of the movement by Barnett, is a misnomer if it suggests particular faith in a messiah. Slocum was, on his own account, only a prophet. The adventist phase of the movement soon gave place to other preoccupations in which no messiah was promised, while the prophet himself was eclipsed in importance, even in his own lifetime, by the emergence of more vigorous leaders, for although his name has lived on in the movement, little is known about his later days.

Millennialism and thaumaturgy: sequences and alternations

The rapid supersession of early millennialism by persistent thaumaturgical interests among the Shakers recalls the similar processes that occurred among the aladura churches in Nigeria, even though millennialism was a less-persistent and less-recurrent concern in West Africa.[45] The Shaker case also parallels the relation of these two responses in many western Christian movements, without displaying, however, that degree of institutionalization which, in advanced societies, relegates both of these concerns to subsidiary positions. In all the denominations and many sects in western societies both millennialism and thaumaturgy are recessive in both doctrine and practice to the dominant conversionist orientation, with its more conventional eschatology and its pastoral and counselling functions. In other instances from less-developed societies, the supersession of revolutionist outbursts by new thaumaturgical orientations tends to occur in what are recognized as distinctly new movements, and it is not always evident that the same clientele is involved in each case. They occur as two responses that impress themselves on observers as being relatively discrete, and their exact relation to each other is often far from clear. But sometimes, at least, well-known people are involved in the earlier and later stages of a movement (or in the two different movements, if they are seen as such) and the implication is that the religious world-view of some people, at least, has undergone a process of mutation. Perhaps simultaneously, such shifts are also associated with the attraction of new types of adherent, and perhaps the loss of others. There is rarely evidence, in the conditions of less-advanced countries, even in the gross terms of

[44] Ibid., p. 353.
[45] On the aladura churches, see pp. 160 ff.

changing age and sex composition of a movement's following (always assuming that a 'following' can be readily defined) of such selective dispositions. We can merely assume, when a movement under the same leadership shows a changing orientation to the world, that there may occur both a process of mutation in the world-view of a continuing clientele, and the selective withdrawal of some and recruitment of others.

Part of what is promised for the millennium is the elimination of the threats, illnesses, and tensions of everyday life. It is always a transformative experience, not only in its eradication of political and social oppression, as this has been collectively experienced, but also in the prospect of permanent relief from physical ailments, personal problems, and fears and tensions in social relationships. It includes, specifically, the cessation of illness, the ageing process, and death, and the disappearance of the evil and the evil-doers (witches), real or imagined, that exist in everyday life. The millennium itself is to be brought into being by stimulating supernatural action, often by praying, dreaming, or dancing (which, in ascending order, may reveal degrees of emotional abandonment and intensity relevant to differing stages of cultural development) and the completion of certain material preparations (barn-building, wharf-building, or crop-burning). Whilst each of these aspects is often evident, the distinction between the millennialist or revolutionist orientation and the thaumaturgical is more than merely a matter of (relative and culturally bounded) universalism on the one hand, and particularism and demands for purely personal benefits on the other. Revolutionist responses envisage a total social transformation, which, whilst it is envisaged to include new principles of physical constitution and causation, is very much more concerned with the transformation of the power structure, and the inter-ethnic and inter-cultural relationships prevailing in the society. The two orientations—the revolutionist and thaumaturgical solutions—may occur with alternating emphasis, and may simultaneously attract different social strata into the activities of one movement.

This circumstance may facilitate the simultaneous, or alternating, expression of the two responses in particular movements, or congeries of movements, reflecting either the divergent aspirations of the body of adherents, the styles of different leaders, or the changes in the external situation to which the movements respond. Periods of acute tension, associated with economic, political, and military events in the wider world, which have repercussions on the lives of less-developed peoples, may stimulate excitements and expectation conducive to revolutionist religion. Examples of such events are the recruitment by colonial authorites of soldiers, or by plantation-owners and mining companies of labour; the sudden collapse of overseas markets; or the impact of war in which the colonists are elsewhere engaged. In periods when such influences are not in evidence, we may expect movements to settle down to a more routinized concern with the persistent thaumaturgical demands of their clientele.

But revolutionist responses are not merely rejoinders to external circumstances. They may also be summoned by much more local conditions, and the combination of unsettling influences from the wider world and the impact of local stimuli and local decisions may be necessary elements in the emergence of a revolutionist movement. One such factor is the response of colonial authorities to new movements that are basically thaumaturgical in orientation. Such movements may, particularly if they give rise to activities which disturb established routines, be interpreted as political manifestations. Religious behaviour, particularly when it is ecstatic, spasmodic, and extensive, and when it leads to the disruption of normal (particularly work) activities, is readily misunderstood. This was so not only in the case of the Ghost Dance, which had millennialist significance—although of only a pacific kind—but also in that of the more regular ceremonials among North American Indians. Because work was disrupted by his sabbatarianism, William Wadé Harris was deported from the Ivory Coast, although his mission was not even remotely millenarian. The Lumpa Church in Zambia, which had probably passed the zenith of its influence, and which, while watched, had not been considered as a threat by the colonial authorities, was quickly accused of being 'anti-political' by the enthusiasts of the first Zambian government and by UNIP members, and was brought into direct military action against government troops.[46] Such appears also to have been the government response to the earliest manifestations of the entirely thaumaturgical practice of Simon Kimbangu, the similar spark to touch off a whole sequence of revolutionist movements in the Congo.

The alternation of revolutionist and thaumaturgical orientations that were subsequently manifested by the congeries of new religious movements that arose in the wake of Kimbangu, and sometimes in his name, among people of the areas where his initial thaumaturgical mission had had influence, illustrates the difficulty with which such responses acquire institutionalized form. It also reveals the complex pressures in the Congolese situation and the bewilderment of the

[46] On the Ghost Dance, see pp. 292–306; on William Wadé Harris see pp. 174–5; on the Lumpa Church, see pp. 94–100.

natives, who appear to have been susceptible, at least intermittently, to almost any new style of religious practice or prophecy. Many such styles were provided—by local prophets, as well as by missionaries of the various movements who moved into the Congo in a struggle for the souls of the Congolese, in spiritual repetition of the political struggle for Africa half a century before. Within the new religious movements arising in the Congo, however, no clear mutations of one response to another were conspicuous after the initial redirection of primitive thaumaturgy into more revolutionist channels, at least in the colonial period. Kimbangu's own movement moved from thaumaturgy to revolutionism; that of Matswa from almost conscious political intentions became distinctly mystical; the Kakists evolved in various phases and sequences at different times and places.

Thaumaturgy and the reaction of the administration

Simon Kimbangu was a Congolese from the Bas-Congo, whose influence came to be particularly significant in the area bounded by the river Congo to the north, by the Matadi-Léopoldville railway to the south, the Kwilu on the west, and the Inkisi on the east; and in the southern part of the (then) French Moyen Congo.[47] Kimbangu came into prominence in 1921, after he received his 'call' to preach and heal. He had been a catechist of the English Baptist mission who had failed his examinations, and who appears to have been dissatisfied with his inability to rise further in the mission.[48] His 'call' came after he had left his home village, Nkamba, near Thysville, and gone to Léopoldville to seek work. After many revelations, he returned to his village to begin his mission. He was, apparently, devoted to his Bible, and one commentator has said of the teaching that he propounded, 'If he incorporated . . . primitive beliefs in his doctrine it was not from policy, but because they formed a part of his own cultural heritage. In the domain of ritual he was strongly influenced by tradi-

---

[47] This is the area given by J. Van Wing in 'Le Kibanguisme vu par un témoin', *Zaïre* (Revue Congolaise) XII, 6 (1958), pp. 563–618. Van Wing was a Redemptorist missionary in the area for many years. (He employs the French corruption of the name, Kibangu.)

[48] This is the interpretation of Georges Balandier, *Sociologie actuelle de l'Afrique Noire* (Presses universitaires, Paris 1955), p. 427. The matter of his examination failure is not mentioned by other authorities, but is regarded as having a determining influence in his career by this author: G. Balandier, 'Messianismes et Nationalismes en Afrique Noire', *Cahiers Internationaux de Sociologie* xiv, 1953, pp. 41–65.

tional pre-Christian concepts, but doctrinally he upheld the pure tenets of Christianity.'[49] This may be an overstatement of the extent of his orthodoxy, although he specifically enjoined the faith of Jesus, and there appears to have been nothing in his teaching to which at least the Protestant missions would have taken exception.[50] The *minkisi*, medicines, idols, and fetiches, were everywhere destroyed at his instigation. His work was followed by a widespread demand for Bibles, and up to this point, Kimbangu appears comparable to William Wadé Harris, who had preached in the Ivory Coast and western Gold Coast some seven years before.

The healings for which he quickly acquired a reputation, even though there were many unsuccessful cures, brought large numbers of Africans on pilgrimage to visit Kimbangu at his house in Nkamba, and there he built an enclosure, in which services were held. The hospitals were deserted as news of the new healer spread, and he began to send out his assistants to lay hands on people; others began similar practices in imitation.[51] After a period in which people filled the Protestant missions in general sympathy with the new movement, there followed a period in which both followers and catechists left both Protestant and Catholic missions to become his disciples. At Nkamba people became possessed of spirits, and Kimbangu professed to discern whether the possession was good; to those individuals he gave a Bible, and they became prophets; if evil spirits were involved, Kimbangu cast them out.

One of the most dramatic effects of *Kimbanguism* was the wholesale destruction of *minkisi*, fetiches, throughout wide areas where the influence of the new prophet was felt. This was not a new phenomenon in this part of the Congo, which had experienced the impact of Christianity as long as four-and-a-quarter centuries before, when Diogo Cão had visited the Congo, built a church, exchanged gifts, and persuaded the natives to burn their idols, in 1482 and in the years

---

[49] Harold W. Fehderau, 'Kimbanguism: Prophetic Christianity in the Congo', *Practical Anthropology* 9 (July–August 1962), pp. 157–78 (p. 159). According to P. H. J. Lerrigo, 'The Prophet Movement in the Congo', *International Review of Missions* 11 (1922), pp. 270–7, imitators of Kimbangu quickly arose, some of whom showed distinctly nativistic tendencies, and some of whom were decidedly anti-white, promising that God would drive out the white people and that therefore it was useless to plant gardens.

[50] The judgements of Protestant and Catholic missionaries on Kimbangu are often sharply in contrast, and the severity of the Catholic missionary judgement is reflected at times in Balandier's work, where he has followed Van Wing's early commentaries.

[51] This account of the rise and development of Kimbanguism relies particularly on the thorough and detailed study by Efraim Andersson, *Messianic Popular Movements in the Lower Congo*, Studia Ethnographica Upsaliensia XIV (Almqvist & Wiksells, Uppsala, 1958), pp. 52 ff.

following.[52] New movements begin by an assault upon the old gods and medicine, and it is possible that the burning of fetiches had occurred on several occasions as new religious conceptions were received in particular areas. The *Kyoka* movement in north Angola, in 1872, had had a similar effect, and Harris had achieved exactly the same result in the Ivory Coast.[53]

Just what role Kimbangu appropriated for himself at this juncture is not entirely clear. It seems likely that all that he did was done in the name of the Christian orthodoxy in which he had been trained. Balandier says that he regarded himself as a prophet, and has no hesitation in calling him a 'messiah', although this appears to be an appelation that his followers conferred upon him only later.[54] Initially he had not favoured natives' leaving the missions, and he had declared that he did not wish to establish a church of his own. His preaching was originally neither anti-mission nor anti-white, but events conspired to push him into the role of the native Christ, and he may himself have dramatized his performance, as he recognized the appeal to the Congolese of a black messiah, and as his fame spread.

The pilgrimages made to his village were quickly a source of concern to the administration. Special trains had to be put on to carry the numbers of passengers eager to reach the Thysville area and hear Kimbangu. The abandonment of the missions alarmed the missionaries, particularly the Catholic missionaries, who found that Catholic rosaries, scapularies, and images were being discarded along with the fetiches of the older pagan religions.[55] When the natives abandoned

[52] Ibid., pp. 29 ff. The lower Congo had borne the brunt of white contact, including severe dislocation of local life before the Matadi–Leopoldville railway was built in 1898. But long before this, prophet movements had arisen. The most famous is the sect of Antonians, so-called because one Dona Beatrice had claimed to be possessed by the spirit of St Antony, and subsequently claimed that Christ was born in San Salvador. The sect had come to play an important part as a political opposition to the King, Pedro IV, and the clergy who supported him, before Beatrice was burned as a heretic in 1706. The forces gathered under her associate, Chibenga, were defeated in 1709. See Erika Sulzmann, 'Die Bewegung der Antonier im alten Reiche Kongo', pp. 81–5 in W. E. Mühlmann, *Chiliasmus und Nativismus,* op. cit.: short accounts are to be found in René Lemarchand, *Political Awakening in the Belgian Congo* (University of California Press, Berkeley and Los Angeles 1964), pp. 168–9; and in Jean Comhaire, 'Sociétés secrètes et Mouvements prophétiques au Congo Belge', *Africa* XXV, 1 (January 1955), pp. 54–68.

[53] On Harris see W. J. Platt, *An African Prophet,* op. cit.

[54] G. Balandier, *Sociologie actuelle . . .,* op. cit., p. 428. Of Kimbangu's background (he was probably born in 1889), J. Van Wing, op. cit., p. 566, writes, 'Son père était un nganga (féticheur) renommé dans la région, qui, comme ses congénères, se livrait à des tremblements et des convulsions, quand il proférait les incantations rituelles que réclame la mise en action d'un nkisi (fétiche). Simon doit avoir été souvent témoin de ces manifestations impressionnantes qui sont sensées signifier que le sujet a été saisi par un esprit. Il a été élevé par une tante très devouée. Il ne semble donc pas avoir connu sa mère.'

[55] This according to Jules Chomé, *La Passion de Simon Kimbangu,* 2nd Edn (Les Amis de 'Présence Africaine', Bruxelles 1959), p. 16.

the corvée imposed for the Matadi–Léopoldville railway, the situation appeared increasingly serious to the authorities. Morel, the administrative officer at Thysville, sought to have a talk with Kimbangu, who was not, however, particularly co-operative. The movement was now infiltrated by more pronounced anti-white elements, who caused incidents which gave the authorities more concern about its development. In June 1921 Simon Kimbangu was arrested, but he escaped. His home village was now attacked by the authorities, and Kimbangu became celebrated in a new way. The ideas of an adventist movement with a distinctly revolutionist orientation now became more prominent. Kimbangu came to be seen as a champion of the Africans, and as the ruler of Africa. His followers were arrested, and eventually Kimbangu, following closely the fashion of Christ, returned to his own village and permitted himself to be arrested.[56]

Even at this stage, after no more than a few months of activity, the movement, largely by the intervention of the authorities, had been transformed from a rather ecstatic manifestation of thaumaturgical power, panoplied in Christian form, into a revolutionist movement. With the arrest of Kimbangu a martyr was created, a symbol of identification, and although he did not conceive of himself as a liberator of the Congolese from the colonial authorities, he was readily cast in that role. The oppression of the movement was itself perhaps more significant in promoting this mutation than the general background problems being experienced by the Congo at that time—the unrest following the war, the fall in prices for the goods which the country exported, and the loss of income and employment by the natives. The authorities politicized a religious movement, which had arisen for the distribution of therapeutic benefits. Now it was pushed into a position where resistance was inevitable, even though passive, and in consequence of which an antagonistic ideology became imperative. The relatively innocuous thaumaturgy, had it been left alone, or been handled by the sympathetic Swedish Protestant missionaries, might have dwindled away, or been re-canalized into a more orthodox

[56] E. Andersson, op. cit., pp. 63–6, provides a full account of these episodes. These earlier anti-white incidents are referred to in Charles André Gilis, *Kimbangu: Fondateur d'Église* (La Libraire Encyclopédique, Bruxelles 1960), p. 40. Some commentators have ascribed a much more self-conscious political role to Kimbangu, but this is almost certainly mistaken— the common mistake of political commentators, who are sometimes disposed to see as most important the political consequences of religious movements, and then to ascribe political intentions to those whose religious activities become significant in the political process. Virginia Thompson and Richard Adloff in *The Emerging States of French Equatorial Africa* (Stanford University Press, Stanford, California, 1960), say of Kimbangu that he 'used religion as a screen from behind which he attacked white rule' (p. 481). They repeat this emphasis on p. 310. This is certainly a misinterpretation.

stream of Christianity. But the tolerance displayed by the Protestant missions itself became a matter of concern to the authorities and the Catholics, and they were accused of engaging in a conspiracy to encourage Kimbangu. Some Catholic missionaries sought to get the Protestants expelled.[57]

The trial of Kimbangu appears to have been a travesty of justice, and was conducted in a hostile atmosphere, according to Protestant commentators. Catholic commentators called for sterner measures against the new movement, and have since maintained that Kimbangu's trial was conducted according to the rules of law.[58] This suggestion is refuted, apparently properly so, by the equally partisan account of Chomé, who wrote,

> De ce procès où l'on fit rétroagir la compétence du tribunal spécial, où tout se fit avec une hâte fébrile, où les accusés furent dépourvus de toute défence, où le principal accusé comparut et demeura devant son Juge, chargé de chaînes, où le même accusé, entre deux audiences, fut douché et frappé de douze coups de chicotte sur l'ordre du juge, ce procès, le Révérend Père Van Wing, S.J. nous dit, en 1958, qu'il se déroula 'selon toutes les règles du droit'.[59]

The trial took place in a military court, although military law had been imposed only after the events had occurred on which the accusations against Kimbangu rested. Kimbangu was sentenced to death, but this sentence was subsequently commuted to life-imprisonment. He lived out the rest of his life in prison in Elizabethville, where he died in 1950.

The arrest and imprisonment of Kimbangu set the seal on the mutation into a revolutionist movement of an originally thaumaturgical revival which undoubtedly had many affinities with former witch-finding movements. No outbreak of military activity occurred, but periodic rumours of Kimbangu's return created situations essentially similar to those arising in millennialist and adventist movements. To

[57] J. Chomé, op. cit., p. 24. Chomé provides evidence that the Catholics used excommunication against those associated with Kimbangu, and persuaded the government to undertake military reconnaissance in the affected villages. J. Van Wing, op. cit., pp. 564, 571, 580 ff., says that the American Baptists at Nsona-Mbata welcomed Kimbanguism as the spirit of God; that Kimbangu used the terminology of Protestantism, but in fact was acting as a witch-doctor, with baptism employed as a purification from witches. He emphasizes that the Catholic missions were not affected, but had this been so, it is difficult to see why the Catholic missions should have been so concerned about a movement occurring within Protestantism.

[58] J. Van Wing, loc. cit.

[59] J. Chomé, op. cit., pp. 64–5. Chomé gives the text of the judgement, pp. 66–72. E. Andersson, op. cit., p. 67, in an account less partisan than that of Chomé, also considers that the trial took place in a very hostile atmosphere.

many of the Bakongo, Kimbangu had proved his invincibility, since the death sentence had not been carried out. The movement now went underground, and took on many local variants. Anti-white feeling was intensified, and some cultists left the areas of white settlement, withdrew from white schools, and practised new rituals of commemoration of Kimbangu, in expectation of his return, and also that of the ancestors, for whose coming the roads were kept in good repair.

In 1923, thousands of natives demonstrated in Thysville for the release of Kimbangu, and similar incidents occurred elsewhere. The attitude of the authorities oscillated between cautious observation and repression, and the attitudes of the missionaries, differing from area to area, affected the extent to which the movement was associated with, or separated from, their influence. In some instances, in the early 1920s, sympathetic missionaries made of the new wave of religiosity something akin to a religious revival. The administration imposed a licensing system on all catechists of the Catholic and Protestant missions, but new local prophets arose, until they, too, were eventually arrested. The movement also affected the French Congo. In the Boko area, where the movement stood closer to orthodox Protestantism, the authorities prompted by the Catholic missions, accused the Protestants of employing unsuitable evangelists, and eventually forced the dismissal of 77 catechists in one district. The expulsion of the natural native leadership from the missions forced the new religious impetus out of the orbit of Protestant control, and into a more nativistic orientation and more secret forms of organization.[60] Repressive measures quietened both regions in the late 1920s, but Kimbanguism was not dead.

The dominant ideas that were increasingly disseminated in the 1930s were explicitly revolutionist. A war would occur in which the whites, and those natives who collaborated with them, would be destroyed, since they had betrayed the call of Jesus. The ancestors and heroes would arise, and this within a few months. Adherents were to avoid all mission Christians, Catholic and Protestant, and also to hold themselves aloof from pagans. A variety of taboos were promulgated in association with this teaching. Such was the message of Yoane Mvubi. Others had a more explicit nationalist and political message, in which Kimbangu was hailed as a political liberator. In seven years or so the movement had changed from one 'in which spiritual revival was the central feature even if elements of nationalism were by no means

⁶⁰ E. Andersson, op. cit., pp. 68–95.

lacking . . . into a movement almost entirely hostile to foreigners and with obviously national and even revolutionary aims.'[61]

These millennialist ideas were, however, associated with outbursts of much more emphatic thaumaturgical religion and ecstatic manifestations. Throughout the whole region of the Lower Congo, *Ngunzism*— the outcropping of local prophets with messages ranging from xenophobic millennialism to animistic cults, including ancestor worship— became epidemic. Forest meetings now became the occasion not only for the abandonment of mission regulation, but for the general relaxation of all patterns of social control at the behest of the prophets and the spirits. One such meeting, of which there is a report, was highly ecstatic, with jerks, confessions, speaking in tongues, lecherous dancing (which was traditional), healings, and attempts to resuscitate the dead. Hymns, sung prayers, shaking, and fire-ordeals to prove sinlessness, occurred in a highly orgiastic context.[62]

Successors to Kimbangu

Detribalization was proceeding steadily in the Belgian Congo in the 1930s, and this was a process accelerated by the war. The failure of the Belgians to develop educational and political institutions, or to provide leadership opportunities for natives, has been associated with the process of industrial and economic growth which they had fostered.[63]

[61] Ibid., p. 100. The terms in which Yoane Mvubi expressed his message have something of the resonance of Jehovah's Witnesses. There is no evidence that he had been influenced by them, however, either from their American headquarters, or from the African offshoot, Kitawala. Kitawala had first penetrated the Belgian Congo in Katanga, far away on the Northern Rhodesian border, when Mwane Lesa had introduced his witch-finding baptism and general Witness teachings in 1925. (See pp. 83–4.) It had made further inroads in the late 1920s, and spread rapidly in the 1930s in Elisabethville, Albertville, Jadotville, and elsewhere in the south-east. It was dissolved in Katanga in 1937 by provincial edict, after pronounced demands for the equality of black and white. In 1942, under Bushiri (Mulumozi wa Yesu—representative of Jesus) the Kitawalans planned a rising at Nyamasa and Muhulu, and an attack against Europeans at Costermansville. A rising occurred at Jembe, where fifty-eight rebels were killed. In 1944, Kitawalans were blamed for an insurrection among the Makumu in Orientale and Kivu. It was not until 1948 that Kitawala appeared sufficiently menacing in Leopoldville, at the other end of the country, to warrant an edict enforcing dissolution. R. Lemarchand, op. cit., p. 172; Crawford Young, *Politics in the Congo* (Princeton University Press, Princeton, N.J., 1965), pp. 287–8.

[62] Ibid., pp. 103–4; Karl Aldén, 'The Prophet Movement in Congo', *International Review of Missions* XXV (1936), pp. 347–53.

[63] Belgian policy had been to leave educational matters to the missions. In 1954, discontent with the very restricted curriculum of the education provided by the Catholic missions was expressed in the Coulon Report, which led to the first, albeit modest, endeavour in lay education in the Belgian Congo. The static political policy of the Belgian government also came under attack in the same period. See R. Lemarchand, op. cit., pp. 146 ff.; 153–4. The economic policy in the Belgian Congo was, however, much more dynamic than that in the

In these circumstances, the new native leaders necessarily took on either anti-white attitudes, or offered distribution of benefits (physical healing and psychic security) for which demand far exceeded the supply provided through mission and administrative channels, and which were still sought in native rather than European styles. The charisma of Kimbangu was now claimed by large numbers of prophets with divergent teachings, and the situation was one in which recurrent charismatic leadership was related to a persistent charismatic demand.

Charismatic leadership is most readily claimed in the religious sphere, or, as long as political activity is not bureaucratized or routinized, in politics. But the religious sphere was the only one in which really significant native leadership could be sustained. The prophet was not more acceptable to the authorities than the would-be politician, of course, since they readily identified religious movements with political unrest, but the prophet had advantages in this situation which a would-be native politician could not enjoy. His promises were non-empirical, and he could always claim the benefit of the strategic ambiguities of supernatural promises and prophecies, whereas the criteria of failure and success in political enterprises were capable of much more definitive judgement. It is understandable, in these circumstances, that political and religious leadership among the indigenes were sometimes difficult to distinguish, and particularly so where the religious orientation was millennialist. The extent to which religious agencies were consciously employed either as a front for political ends, or as a means of more easily mobilizing a clientele, is not easily decided. It is certainly possible that even a sophisticated leader, like the *evolué* Matswa André, more than half-believed the religious ideas that became associated with his mission.

Unlike Kimbangu, who began as a Christian thaumaturge, and who became the symbol (never actually the leader) of semi-political and certainly revolutionist movements, Matswa began his activities as a much more political figure, who was eventually deified by a religious movement. He was born in 1899, and went to school in Brazzaville in the (then) French Congo. He served in the First World War and subsequently in the French campaigns in the Rif in 1924–5, and spent some years in Paris, where he associated with left-wing groups and pan-

French Congo, and this was a specific cause of grievance to André Matswa in the late 1920s, about which he complained to the French government when founding the *Amicale*: V. Thompson and R. Adloff, op. cit., p. 480. Africans were being more systematically transformed into skilled workers in the Belgian Congo than anywhere else in Africa in the post-war period, although trade unions were not allowed: Basil Davidson, 'The Congo and Angola', *West Africa*, Nos. 1939, 1940, 1942, 1943 (April 24; May 1; 15; 22, 1954).

Africanists. There he successfully founded, under his assumed name of A. Grenard, *L'association amicale de Originaires de l'Afrique Équatorial Français* (Amicale Balali), intended to help Africans in Paris, and succeeded in obtaining a subsidy for this *utilité publique* from the French government. With two associates, he obtained permission to make collections in the French Congo. He recruited a following in Bangui and Libreville, and especially among the Bakongo. His activity quickly became interpreted as pan-African, and he encouraged passive resistance to the administration. The movement soon acquired affinities with Kimbanguism.[64]

When the authorities prosecuted Matswa, they found that the chiefs, who had contributed funds to his cause, had widely divergent ideas about what the money was for; some thought that it was for funeral ceremonies; others that it was for a bank; others believed it would give them social equality with Europeans. But, whatever they thought, and despite proof of financial irregularities, they regarded Matswa as a leader, and his imprisonment for three years and banishment for ten conferred martyrdom upon him, and stimulated demonstrations and passive resistance. Matswa became something of a legend: he escaped from the Tchad in the mid 1930s but was again arrested in 1940, and even his death whilst still in detention in 1942 did nothing to arrest the growth of the movement which took his name. The movement he founded became known as the *Lusambulu lua Bougie* or *Lusambulu lua Bois Sacré*, from the candles used in the rites that were practised, and the wood used in making protective amulets. Shrines arose, and the movement acquired strength, particularly in the towns. Whether this religious activity occurred simply in response to Matswa André's death, or had received impetus from him whilst he was at liberty, is not clear. It was later exploited by the Abbé Fulbert Youlou, who became President of the French Congo after independence, and who, for a time, was thought to be the reincarnation of Matswa—who was now the Jesus of the mixed pagan and Christian cults in which his name was revered.[65]

The progress of Kimbanguism proper was given a fillip in the mid 1930s by the arrival in the Belgian Congo of the missionaries of the

---

[64] E. Andersson, op. cit., pp. 117 ff.; G. Balandier, *Sociologie actuelle . . .*, op. cit., pp. 398–9. V. Thompson and R. Adloff, op. cit., p. 480.

[65] E. Andersson, op. cit., pp. 120–5; Matswaists persisted in voting for their dead leader until Youlou's appearance. Later when Youlou became President of the (former French) Congo Republic, the Matswaists refused to pay taxes and to assist the census, just as they had done before independence. Two outbursts of rioting occurred in 1959, and the Youlou government deported 500 Matswaists. The Matswaists retaliated, and thirty-five were killed in a further encounter with government forces. V. Thompson and R. Adloff, op. cit., pp. 484, 492; *The Times*, 29 July 1959.

Salvation Army. The success of the Salvationists was enormous.[66] They appeared as something quite new to the natives, emphasizing joy, hand-shaking, easy confession, and salvation. They were not identified with the old missions, and had no part in the agreements which existed among the other Protestants at work in the Congo. The uniform and the manifestation of military discipline contributed to the attraction, and it appears that even the letter 'S' on their collar lapels was interpreted by the natives as a sign for Simon (Kimbangu). Shaking hands with a Salvationist officer became a purifying experience, and people travelled ten days or more to see the Army, shake hands with the officers, and touch the flag. Those who died *en route* for the Salvationist mission stations were regarded as wizards, who had been affected by the superior power of the new evangelists, who were regarded as anti-witchcraft thaumaturges. So great was the press of people seeking the Salvationists' ministrations that the border between the French and Belgian Congo was closed.[67] Ideas of the resurrection were disseminated, and a new adventist expectation arose. After some time, the Salvationists recognized that the conversions they had made were of people whose religious conceptions diverged radically from their own. Some who had been expelled from missions welcomed the Salvationists as a new agency through which to acquire prestige without the rigours of mission supervision. Eventually the Salvationists learned to scrutinize their converts more closely, expelled many of them, and dissociated themselves from the nativist Salvationist movement which now broke away on its own.

One of those caught up in the Salvationist enthusiasm was a mission-educated native, Simon Mpadi, who had been expelled for adultery. After being in the movement for some time, he offered to organize Salvationists in some 150 villages, the care of which the Salvationists themselves had decided was beyond their resources. His loose association with the Salvationists enabled him to establish a uniformed following, known as the *Kakists*. The Salvation Army later expelled him for desertion, and since natives were not permitted to organize new religions in the Belgian Congo he was arrested. Mpadi made a number of escapes from prison, and became involved in a popularized form of Salvationism and in new expressions of Ngunzism. In 1944, he was deported to Elizabethville, but the Kakist movement continued. It had a highly hierarchic organization, in which Mpadi had established himself as chief of the apostles of Simon Kimbangu. The uniforms, insignia, and hierarchic ranks were evidently influenced by both

[66] J. Van Wing, op. cit., pp. 594–5, E. Andersson, op. cit., pp. 126 ff.
[67] This account rests principally on E. Andersson, op. cit., pp. 130–7.

Catholicism and Salvationism, with remnants of primitive tradition. The church used especially the numbers three and twelve as sacred numbers for its organization—giving Kimbangu twelve titles or 'personalities', such as the Prophet, the Sacred, the Saviour, the Leader, the Flag, the Ladder to heaven, etc.[68]

The cult abandoned images, including the cross, and imposed a variety of taboos appropriate to the people of Israel. Confession and prayer were emphasized and redemption for sins: these were Christian elements. But the ancestor cult continued to flourish, and communication with the ancestors, trance states, religious ecstasy, and curing were part of the movement's practice. These thaumaturgical concerns did not exclude strong anti-mission and anti-white orientations. The uniform gave the idea of an ultimately military effort, and in the war years the expectation of the return of the black saviour was associated with the idea of the victory of the Germans, which would effect the liberation of the Congolese.

While Mpadi was detained other Kakist leaders emerged, and there were eventually a number of movements under different leadership with varying emphases, sharing certain common features such as the uniform. After 1944, Kufinu Philippe (also known as Mavonda Ntangu), who claimed visions and inspiration from Kimbangu, came to the fore. Mavonda Ntangu's movement grew, especially at the frontier of the French and Belgian Congo, recruiting former Salvationists in the more southerly areas of its influence and former Catholics in the north. The names of Kimbangu and Matswa were revered, but although the movement had this revolutionist inheritance, it appears to have been primarily a reassertion of new thaumaturgical powers. One rank of leaders devoted themselves to 'smelling out' good times for meetings— which were usually held in the forest—detecting sins, and prescribing appropriate penalties. Sick persons were allotted to particular officials, and while healing (by means of 'brushing' the patients) was taking place, the rest of the congregation sang as loudly as they could. Shaking and the use of sacred water were part of the cult rituals; dreams were recited and interpreted; water from the sacred groves was mixed with earth from the graves, and this was even thought of as a type of 'corpse-juice' of very special potency. Mavonda Ntangu himself claimed all the typical powers of the thaumaturge, including the ability to make mystical flights. Yet the inheritance of some Christian ideas also persisted: the headquarters was known as Ngetsemane; there was confession of sins; prayers were in the names of God and the Holy Spirit.[69]

[68] G. Balandier, 'Messianisme . . .', op. cit.
[69] E. Andersson, op. cit., pp. 151–75.

Ntangu called his movement 'The Salvation Army', and was an active proselytizer. The practices of the Kakists in other areas probably differed considerably, and the blending of Catholic, Salvationist, and traditional rites and beliefs was subject to considerable variation. What was apparent, however, in these recrudescent manifestations of Ngunzism, was the thaumaturgical bed-rock on which millennialism has occasionally found sufficient soil to blossom forth as a distinctive creed. Andersson considers that the messianic features have steadily increased, but it appears to have been an uneven growth, with a sustained concern with healing, ancestor worship, and miracles. Reverence for Kimbangu persisted, but leaders like Mpadi, Matswa, and Ntangu were also periodically taken into the hierarchy of messianic beings. The upsurgence of the Munkukusa movement in 1951 indicates that protection from witchcraft persisted as a preoccupation of the masses.[70] Even Kimbangu, the messiah himself, on the model of earlier messiahs, rested his claim to eminence on his healing practice. Such a claim was in the native tradition—to it was now added a specifically Christian, particularly biblical, legitimation.

> That Kimbangu had been strongly influenced by the nkisi cult and its banganga is proved by his method of faith-healing. He did, certainly, pray, and practise the laying on of hands in accordance with the Biblical model, but he shook also. At a later stage, the ecstatic element was intensified: he shook, rolled his eyes, and jumped high in the air, just like a banganga. He had religious songs sung in wild ecstasy, for this gave him healing power. And the movement was taken still further back on the traditional paths by Kimbangu's disciples.[71]

Such has been the diversity of the movements in the Congo, however, and such the fluidity of the designations, that it cannot with certainty be said that particular movements, except as purely local manifestations, have demonstrated an even course of mutation from one dominant religious response to the other. Thus *Mvungism* appears to have arisen among the Bayaka in the 1950s with a strong anti-fetichist orientation, reminiscent of that of Kimbangu himself, but adapted to the usages of that tribe. Association with those who were not baptized was refused, and strong expectations of the *Parousia*[72] were encouraged. The movement, founded in Mayama by Nanga, used the symbolism of Kimbangu, Matswa, and Mpadi, and employed apocalyptic threats to enforce unity. It solemnly celebrated the anniversary of the death of Matswa, emphasized the black saviour, and reinterpreted Christian feasts to fit

[70] On the Munkukusa movement, see pp. 89–91.
[71] E. Andersson, op. cit., p. 222.
[72] J. Van Wing, op. cit., pp. 603 ff.

into the requirements of ancestor worship.[73] Simon Mpadi returned from prison in 1960, to direct once again his Mission de Noirs en Afrique, most of whose members were among the Bakongo, especially among the Bantandu and Belemfu. The movement emphasized healing, and sustained a happy atmosphere among its largely rural members. Simon Mpadi claimed to be heir to the title of king of the Congo. Dressed in red, with crown and sceptre, to the accompaniment of drums and cymbals, Mpadi held court, and 're-created' a legendary past.[74]

Political independence of the two Congolese republics introduced a period of new uncertainties, once the exaggerated initial expectations of what independence would mean had been disappointed. The religious movements of the inter-war and post-war years were heavily implicated in the disturbances. After the Second World War, the movements had shown an increasing ability to unite the peoples of different tribes: the Bakongo among the Kakists were prepared to espouse a doctrine of loving one's neighbour, 'even one's enemies, even the Bayaka and the Bangala'.[75] The messianic movements began to appear as reactions against the continuous process of group disintegration that had been occurring.[76] The old pattern of Ngunzism had scarcely facilitated such a process, since these movements had frequently been short-lived and highly local. The invocation in Mayama of the symbolism of Mpadi, Matswa, and Kimbangu was one attempt to bring together the various dispersed groups of religionists who claimed ultimate descent from Kimbanguism.[77] Two movements arose in the 1960s with the aim of reuniting the native churches, the *Catholic Democratic Union*, which had government support, and the *Good Shepherd*, in which a number of groups were also involved.[78] In general, the religious affiliations of the Congolese remained as complex as their

[73] G. Balandier, *Sociologie actuelle* . . ., op. cit., pp. 466–70.

[74] G. Bernard and P. Caprasse, 'Religious Movements in the Congo: A Research Hypothesis', *Cahiers Économiques et Sociaux* (Lovanium, Congo) III, 1 (March 1965), pp. 49–60.

[75] G. Balandier, 'Messianism and Nationalism in Black Africa' (translation of the article of the same title in *Cahiers Internationaux de Sociologie*, op. cit.), pp. 443–60 in Pierre L. van den Bergh, *Africa: Social Problems of Change and Conflict* (Chandler, San Francisco 1965), p. 454. The Bangala are not in fact a tribe, although for a long time such a tribe was thought to exist, and the name was applied to various tribal groups who were not Bakongo. See C. Young, op. cit., pp. 242–5.

[76] G. Balandier, 'Messianism . . .', op. cit., p. 457. This is also the interpretation of Benôit Verhagen and Laurent Monnier, 'Problèmes concrets et concepts de Science Politique en Afrique: Application au Bas-Congo', *Cahiers Économiques et Sociaux* I, 4 (June 1963), pp. 79–91. These writers perhaps ante-date the extent to which Kimbanguism polarized the nationalist sentiments of the Bakongo, in suggesting that this occurred in 1921, unless this result is specifically regarded as subsequent to Kimbangu's arrest and trial. That it facilitated this process is, of course, indisputable.

[77] G. Balandier, *Sociologie actuelle* . . ., op. cit., pp. 466–70.

[78] Guy Bernard, 'The Nature of a Sociological Research: Religious Sects in the west of the Congo', *Cahiers Économiques et Sociaux* (Lovanium, Congo) II, 3 (November 1964), pp. 261–9.

disturbed political affiliations in this period, and some independent sect leaders were considerably involved in the political scramble which marked the early 1960s.

One newly designated movement was *Kintwadism*, which restored the concepts of Bantu theodicy, particularly those of the Bakongo. The God of the Bakongo was manifested in a force, the Mpeve, acting in each individual, which, however, might be assimilated to the Holy Spirit, as a source of inspiration. Mpeve provoked trances, and gave messages. He was held to have guided Simon Kimbangu, and to have fought the *bandoki* (witches). Prophets arose in this movement, employing the curative water from the sacred rivers. Locations were given biblical names. Bernard saw Kintwadism arising from 'the progressive exhaustion of traditional society since the fifteenth century, and by self-doubts . . . concerning the surviving culture'. It appeared as an endeavour to establish something distinctive in Congolese cultural traditions. In the post-colonial period it lost its messianic character except in certain of its missions. Charles Kisolokele, the son of Simon Kimbangu (and a man who might have been the President of the Kongo Central, and who occupied posts in the central government in early days of independence) declared that Kintwadism was not just for the Bakongo but for all Congolese. The movement only slowly sloughed off its old messianism, however. In 1960 the graves of the ancestors were made tidy, ready for the regaining of the paradise lost. In many respects the movement, for which no doctrinal definition was available, was simultaneously engaged in the attempt at the reconstruction of society, and the destruction of the old tribalism. Through its parades, and the discipline of the guards who maintained order at its ceremonies, the movement appeared to be effectively establishing something of the groundwork of a new morality.[79]

In the French Congo the Matswaists, who had strongly supported the Abbé Youlou as President, were soon dissatisfied by the experience of independence and became quickly involved in disturbances against the new government. The movement may have been used by the politicians, much as Léon Mba, who became President of the Gabon, had used the Bwiti cult among the Fang as an agency for his success.[80] The pattern, indeed, appears to be that where native political develop-

[79] This section relies entirely on Guy Bernard, op. cit. It is not possible to say to what extent Bernard identifies Kintwadism with the more formal expression of Kimbanguism as manifested in L'Église de Jesus-Christ sur la terre par le prophète Simon Kimbangu (EJCSK). He appears to regard it as a separate phenomenon, as an association which sought to draw together those who regarded Kimbangu as their spiritual forebear. The EJCSK is discussed in Chapter 14.

[80] On Léon Mba's rise to power in the Gabon, and his use of the Bwiti Cult among the southern Fang, see V. Thompson and R. Adloff, op. cit., pp. 313–4; 349.

ment was restricted in colonial territories, and where direct administrative rule prevailed (in contrast to indirect rule through chiefs and traditional agencies), some sect leaders were men who otherwise might have been politically active. Such was Matswa André himself, and Emmanuel Bamba, a latter-day Kimbanguist who became heavily involved in politics, and who was finally shot as an enemy of the government formed by a rival faction. Even those with no direct connection with the indigenous religious movements were aware of their importance and the legitimation they could acquire for their leadership from such sources. Thus Joseph Kasa-Vubu, first President of the (former Belgian) Congo was depicted in photographs circulating in Léopoldville at the time of independence as receiving his powers from Jesus Christ at the behest of Simon Kimbangu.[81] Alternatively, once independence was granted, sect leaders were in a good position to use their mass support to take advantage of the new political opportunities.

The millennial response in the congeries of movements arising from Kimbanguism appears to have arisen most dramatically in periods of external crisis for Congolese society. A colony under direct administrative control, with little political but considerable industrial development, was one in which the external economic and political events communicated themselves more directly than in many parts of Africa, where indirect rule and the maintenance of the economic, social, and political agencies of the past, cushioned the effect of external affairs much more. The economic depression following the First World War and the depression at the beginning of the 1930s were both associated with revolutionist outbreaks in the Congo, even though the first of these responses was in part induced by the oppressive measures of the administration. The later development of revolutionist religion occurred in the Second World War and the troubled years which followed. The continuing interest in thaumaturgy, the obduracy of government policy, and the sense of threat felt by the Roman Catholic missions, all contributed to keep the new movements in being. They fulfilled functions similar to the numerous voluntary and cultural

[81] Paul Raymaekers, 'L'Église de Jesus-Christ sur la terre par le prophète Simon Kimbangu: Contribution à l'étude des mouvements messianiques dans le Bas-Kongo', *Zaïre* (Revue Congolaise) XIII, 7 (1959), pp. 675–756 (p. 682). Kasa-Vubu had been president of the *Association pour le maintien d'unité et l'expansion de la langue Kikongo* (ABAKO) which was an early semi-political organization devoted to cultural nationalism among the Bakongo. God and the ancestors were cited as powerful helpers of ABAKO, and the movement tried to push the grievances of sectarian movements into political channels, whilst not becoming identified with them. Its leaders clearly welcomed the opportunity to invoke Kimbangu as a precursor, particularly once ABAKO became a major political force at the time of independence. R. Lemarchand, op. cit., pp. 173–4; R. Lemarchand, 'The Bases of Nationalism among the Bakongo', *Africa* XXXI, 4 (October 1961), pp. 344–54.

associations which arose in the Congo after the Second World War, in providing new bases for social integration in parts of the country that had experienced profound economic and cultural change. When natives were given political opportunities in the mid 1950s, both associations and religious movements became political spring-boards, and although the millennial strain in the Kimbanguist cults did not immediately disappear, thaumaturgy, cultural nativism, and institutional religious organization became apparent in the evolution of the tradition.

Conclusion

In societies which lack specialist therapists, and in which spiritual purification is associated with physical healing, new religious movements, even if they are initiated by millennial dreams, are likely to acquire thaumaturgical functions. Thaumaturgy is, indeed, more immediately impressive than unredeemed promises of world transformation by supernatural action. (Christianity itself may have owed as much to the stories of miracles as to the expectations of the new kingdom, particularly over the long run.) The millennial idea is stronger when it can be identified with a known personage, a messiah who will one day return and inaugurate a new dispensation. But the credit he initially enjoys rests on his reputation as a thaumaturge and a martyr. Even where, as with Matswa André, political activity leads to martyrdom, it is in the thaumaturgical cult that the leader is canonized and memorialized, not as a practical and rational leader—for in those terms he failed: his following understood him as a saviour but had little comprehension of the significance of his pragmatic political endeavour.

The case of Matswa André, like that of the millennialism of John Slocum, reveals the ease with which revolutionism, whether activist or entirely pacific, subsides into more immediate, personal, and individual concerns. The promise of the end of the dispensation, or of a new social order, being for a time unfulfilled, commands less enthusiasm than the prospect of relief from sickness, witches, and evil. Whilst revolutionism is liable to lose its pristine vigour relatively quickly and to lapse into thaumaturgical preoccupations, movements with a profound thaumaturgical orientation, such as Kimbanguism, may, in the face of repression, become the seed-bed for more radical religious aspirations. The history of the Belgian Congo had been punctuated by war, insurrection, and mutiny, and a sensitive administration transformed a christianized witch-purging cult (and it undoubtedly appeared more effective in the elimination of witchcraft, where self-fulfilling prophecy established its infallibility, than in curing physical ailments) into a recrudescent messianic and millennial movement. But even oppressive opposition did not sustain the millennialist orientation of the Kimbanguists in an unalloyed form. Thaumaturgical preoccupations persisted and recurred. The persecution of the early (millennialist) Shakers was, of course, much milder, but they were fewer, and the power of the white man was self-evident. The millennium also failed, and but for its secondary development of thaumaturgical powers the movement might, indeed, have disappeared.

The transfer of government from the hands of the white colonists to the Congolese leaders, some of whom were well disposed towards, and well regarded by, the sects, did not bring to an end confused sectarian responses to the world. The Matswaists resisted the regulation of the man they had regarded as an heir to Matswa, Fulbert Youlou, and Simon Mpadi returned to his preoccupation with his inheritance from Simon Kimbangu of the kingship of the Congo. Such movements acquire new functions once the immediacy of the millennial prospect recedes. They become opposition groups, without regard to the relational meaning of opposition and the definition of what it is they oppose. They have found a solidarity in circumstances of oppression and difficulty, and the basis of their integration—whether it be as a reinvigorated tribalism, or as a new association of the detribalized—requires such conditions of duress. Identification with the group may, in its significance for the individual members, transcend the assessment of external situations, and the appropriate orientation towards them. This is the strength of the religious commitment, and 'irrational' as it might be labelled by those committed to theories of the inevitability of social change, it is itself an objective datum in a given situation. The ends which such groups have sought, the mixture of physical relief and supernatural hope, are not attainable in the political sphere, nor by the mere provision of secular medical services. The changes in governments, educational programmes, and medical facilities, do not automatically dissolve the desire for power and for relief from an oppressive world. The thaumaturgical demand persists: and intermittently, perhaps shorn, as in some cases it might be, of nationalistic, xenophobic, and racist elements, the millennial dream recurs.

12

Intimations of Introversionist Responses

THE mutation of revolutionist aspirations into thaumaturgical pre-occupations may, in many respects, be regarded as the reassertion of traditional religious concerns. The demand for therapy, for a dispensation from the normal laws of physical causation, is ubiquitous among mankind. Among less-developed peoples thaumaturgical demand is the primary and persisting religious orientation. Revolutionism, dramatic as it often is, is infrequent, episodic, and ephemeral. Revolutionist religion does not, in lapsing, always revert to thaumaturgical preoccupations, however. Millennialism has sometimes acted as a catalyst for a permanent restructuring of values as it has been superseded by another religious response—the introversionist. In western Christendom, and also in the context of Russian Orthodoxy, the introversionist response has characterized the most persistent sectarian movements. It represents a relatively stable institutionalization of sectarianism. It might, at times, be regarded as an over-institutionalization, a rigidification, not only of religious practices, beliefs, and procedures, but also of the entire pattern of life of a new community. What is rigidified is not, in fact, the actual pattern of the past, although it may be represented as such (or as a perfected pattern of social order). It is always a reconstruction, but in acquiring special sanctity, such a reconstructed way of life may be perpetuated, and even fossilized, as a total social system.

What was sanctified and fossilized, in such cases, was the way of life of a particular stratum of the population—whether they were peasants, like the Amish, or small businessmen, tradesmen, minor professionals, and clerks, like the Exclusive Brethren.[1] Sometimes, of course, an essentially new pattern of life was evolved out of older elements and once established, sanctified and given permanency.[2] In the case of less-

[1] On the Amish, see J. A. Hostetler, op. cit.; on the Exclusive Brethren, see B. R. Wilson, 'The Exclusive Brethren: A Case Study in the Evolution of a Sectarian Ideology' in B. R. Wilson (Ed.), *Patterns of Sectarianism* (Heinemann, London 1967), pp. 287–342.

[2] This was virtually the case with the Rappites and the Amana Society (the Society of the Truly Inspired). On the Rappites, see K. G. Arndt, op. cit.; on the Amana Society, see Bertha M. H. Schambaugh, *Amana That Was and Amana That Is* (The State Historical Society of Iowa, Iowa City 1932).

developed peoples, what such an introversionist movement perpetuated was necessarily the tribal, or the native, way of life, and the cases to be examined all illustrate the attempt to create and retain a social system and a form of religious practice different from those of the dominant culture, and representing the continuance of the native past.

The subsidence of revolutionist responses into thaumaturgy is, in part, a rejection of the catalytic impulse of the millennial aspiration, a reassertion of the primacy of personal, local, and immediate tensions and problems, and an abandonment of the demand for a more collective, corporate, communal, and perhaps societal and supra-societal, salvation. Whereas older thaumaturgical practice often functioned for the community as well as for individuals, with the breakdown of tribal life, the community functions of religion can be fulfilled less readily, and the resumed preoccupation with thaumaturgy tends to be much more individual. In contrast, the introversionist response implicitly assumes a corporate salvation, whether the individual is assumed to be eligible for salvation by his voluntary participation in the new rites and beliefs, or whether it is vaguely extended to all those who share tribal or ethnic identity; whether, that is to say, the society of the elect is forged anew, or is merely a re-clustering and re-gathering of a previously existing tribal (or supra-tribal) society. Christianity, from its very beginnings, was a religion of voluntary choice, in a society where the mixture of faiths and peoples made choice increasingly appropriate in religion: it provides an ancient model for the creation of new voluntaristic communities. But the specific Christian influences to which less-developed peoples have been exposed have rarely been introversionist, and have more usually been conversionist, as we have already seen in the cases from South and West Africa.[3] In one case considered below, however, Christian introversionism reinforced local dispositions. But, such are the differences in the assumptions concerning participation, and so little developed in pre-literate society is the concept of voluntary membership, that even in this instance communal allegiance, rather than exclusivist individual choice, is the more evident phenomenon.

We have already said that new religious movements among less-developed peoples are not sects in the sense in which the term is used in western society. They lack the organizational characteristics normally associated with sectarian movements, and they usually lack the exclusivity and the voluntarism implicit in the Christian tradition. Whether those new movements among less-advanced peoples that most closely approximate to introversionist sects arise from preceding

[3] See Chapter 6.

revolutionist movements, or whether they come forth more autonomously as new religious expressions, the organizational definiteness of
Christian sects is normally lacking. The revolutionist precursors themselves typically manifest only rudimentary styles of organization. They
are transitory, often ecstatic, movements which frequently undergo
swift changes in tone, activity, leadership, and direction. They offer
few stable patterns of structure and procedure for subsequent movements to incorporate. Where more introversionist responses are
autonomously manifested, they tend to borrow the organizational
patterns of kinship and tribal structure, sometimes modified to accommodate inter-tribal association.

The extent to which a new religious movement of a more or less
introversionist type is itself a mutation of a revolutionist movement is
not easily decided. Since the organizational elements are so rudimentary,
their persistence is not to be looked for as a guide to the continuity of
movements through a sequence of responses. Because of this organizational vaugeness, the movement as a unit *per se* is less easily defined as
one continuing entity. The type of continuity found in western European
movements, in which there is an on-going organization, a stabilized
set of procedures, and at least a nucleus of core personnel (and often,
also of clientele), is rare. Such organization, procedures, and membership, once recognized, undergo amendment in observable and continuous ways until a new response is evident: the mutation of sect
response is discerned with much less difficulty.

In simpler societies all that can be seen is often little more than a
sequence of religious responses among the new movements that arise
successively. In the context of a more advanced and heterogeneous
society, such a sequence would be insufficient evidence on which to rest
a hypothesis of differential responses to cultural contact and circumstances of cultural change.[4] But in a simple society, the relative homogeneity (despite the new pluralism of co-existent invader and aboriginal
systems, and differential acculturation) and the relative smallness,
make such direct proofs of continuity less important. If two differing
responses arise in sequence, we may, even without evidence of the
direct involvement of the same persons, relate these to different stages
of the acculturation process, and to the changing relationships between
invaders and indigenes. But, in some instances, the argument is
strengthened by the actual continuity of personnel and procedures from

---

[4] In a complex and heterogeneous society such a procedure would be to commit the
equivalent of what has been called the 'ecological fallacy'—the attribution of traits true of
only a small part of a population to the whole population. In a simpler society, and particularly among the tribes of North America and New Zealand, many of which were quite small,
such a risk scarcely exists.

one movement to another of a different type. Alternatively, changes of response occur within what is clearly one on-going movement.

Some new movements, which, allowing for the wide cultural divergencies, may be said to approximate in many respects the introversionist sects of Christendom, have arisen relatively late in the process of culture contact. To consideration of these we shall shortly turn. Yet not all movements with introversionist orientations have emerged merely as secondary responses following the disappointment of the hopes of revolutionist movements. Introversionism sometimes appears, both in western and less-developed societies, as an autonomous and primary response to the prevailing situation, and not merely as a reaction to the failed prophecies of millennial movements, although it is often that. It may be withdrawal from the wider society of a group of people who share a similar sense of disenchantment with the world. Introversionist responses frequently follow revolutionism because a revolutionist movement acts as a catalytic phenomenon. It voices urgent demands and more vivid dreams. It crystallizes more acute discontents which more swiftly bring to birth a movement demanding action (or, more appropriately, expecting supernatural action) which is to be sudden and soon. The introversionist response has no such urgency, and no such immediate prospect. Its participants withdraw from the world in resignation, but such withdrawal is effectively possible only if those who participate can create a viable basis for a new withdrawn community (whether such withdrawal is vicinally or only socially effected). Among less-developed peoples the autonomous introversionist movement would appear to rely on the quietistic prophet. His message is largely ethical, but it is also ethnically circumscribed; it is compelling whilst yet making no promises for more than the maintenance of a separate way of life now and ultimate good in some future dispensation, which might be heavenly or terrestrial—but, if terrestrial, then remote.

The Gai'wiio' religion of the Iroquois

Perhaps the first of the introversionist faiths to arise among the North American Indians, the religion of Handsome Lake (Ganio'dai'io), was less a transformation of a revolutionist response than an aid in the accommodation of the Iroquois Indian peoples to life as a dominated minority. It was in part a perpetuation of the way of life of the Indian past, but, no less impressively, it was also an abandonment of the past. Most significantly of all, it facilitated the adjustment of Indian life to

radically transformed circumstances. The new faith was assisted by
the presence of the Quakers among the Iroquois, and it was perhaps
their influence, their endorsement of the inspiration of Handsome Lake,
and their willingness to nurture the accommodation of aboriginal life
to a selected range of traits learned from the white culture, which really
established the new religion as an identifiable and distinctive
phenomenon.

Gai'wiio', the Good Word, as the new religion was known, was a set
of precepts, legitimated by visions, for the selection and rejection of
elements from the Indian past, and their accommodation to a similar
selection of traits from European culture. Some such adjustment of the
two cultures at a normative level, with exhortations against the un-
assimilable elements in each, was already canvassed before the visions
of Handsome Lake had occurred, but it was only through those
visions and the authority that they claimed that the normative prescriptions already noised abroad in Iroquois society acquired the
legitimacy of a prescribed way of life. It was, perhaps, only through the
instrumentality of the Quakers that the visions were recorded as
revelations and became the basis of a religious movement.

The Iroquois tribes had experienced a very long process of association with the white settlers by the time of the revolutionary war. The
typical experience of the Indian: loss of land; European diseases; the
curse of alcohol; the impact of missionaries; and the history of misunderstandings, double-dealing, and fraud—was, by this time, part o
their common past experience. To it was added defeat in war and, in
the Revolution, alliance with the British, the losing side. The circumstances of the frontier, for white and Indian alike, produced lonely,
uprooted people, with low standards of living and a fragile, uncertain,
social structure. Aggressiveness and alcoholism reflected the emotional
instability of the frontier way of life.[5] The period after the Revolution
was one of increased uncertainty for the Iroquois, and the need for
new adjustment was acutely felt. Not all of the Iroquois accepted the
American victory—Joseph Brant and the Mohawks continued to be
allies of the British in Canada—but Gaiänt'wakǎ, Cornplanter, one
of the leading Seneca, did his best, by visiting American leaders and
negotiating in Washington, to bring about a reconciliation between
the revolutionaries and the Seneca, who had sought to remain British
subjects. There he became well known, and was regarded by Quakers
and Moravians whom he met as being as good as converted to Chris-

---

[5] These factors are emphasized by Anthony F. C. Wallace, 'Handsome Lake and the
Great Revival in the West', *American Quarterly* IV, 2 (Summer 1952), pp. 149–65.

tianity.[6] The Quakers were interested in the Iroquois, and worked among them, and in 1798 five Quakers stayed among the four hundred Seneca at Burnt House, Cornplanter's village. Some of them were at hand when Handsome Lake recounted his visions.

The Quakers, of whom three, Henry Simmons, Jr, Joel Swayne, and Halliday Jackson, stayed in Cornplanter's house over the winter of 1798 and into the summer of 1799, were not seeking land for themselves nor even to convert the Indians. They came essentially to teach them how to cultivate the soil and to spin, and they were convinced that if they succeeded in this, then the Indians would come to adopt moral and social values which the Quakers believed were necessary to the implementation of that technology. 'By guiding the Seneca into an economic system which stressed private property and profit, they confidently expected their ultimate acceptance of an ethical and moral, and eventually religious code which emphasized the voice of conscience, sobriety, cleanliness, industry and marital stability; in a word the Protestant type of religion.'[7] In ten years they had indeed transformed the Seneca way of life, and through the instrumentality of Handsome Lake, Cornplanter's half-brother, who lived in the same house, an Iroquois religion had been propounded and was spreading.

Although the Quakers did not seek to proselytize among the Senecas, they found that the Indians were interested in the white man's religion, and asked them a good deal about it. They were prepared to agree with the Quakers about the deleterious influence of whisky and the white man's dances, and Cornplanter and the chiefs forbade any more whisky to be sold among them.[8] Quaker goodwill was apparent to the Indians, and Handsome Lake evolved a strong admiration for them.[9] Their preoccupation with moral improvement reinforced the aspirations of many Iroquois to resist the attraction of the more debilitating artefacts of civilization. The Iroquois had, of course, had long exposure to aspects of Christian belief. 'Under the constant pressure of representatives of various European religious sects since the time of the Jesuits, the "pagan" Iroquois naturally have absorbed, willy nilly, a

[6] Merle H. Deardorff, 'The Religion of Handsome Lake: Its Origin and Development', pp. 77–107 in William N. Fenton (Ed.), *Symposium on Local Diversity in Iroquois Culture* (Smithsonian Institution, Bureau of American Ethnology, No. 149, 1951), p. 84.
[7] A. F. C. Wallace, op. cit., p. 159, on whom this paragraph relies. He comments on the Quaker attitude to the Indians, 'One would almost think that they had read Max Weber's *Protestant Ethic and the Spirit of Capitalism*', but the Quaker message is interestingly at variance with Weber's assumptions about the relationship of Protestantism and capitalism. The Quakers were here rather economic determinists, expecting religious impulses to follow from a particular mode of production!
[8] M. H. Deardorff, op. cit., p. 88.
[9] A. F. C. Wallace, op. cit., p. 158.

certain amount of our ethics and biblical teachings.'[10] But Indian ideas also persisted.[11] Henry Simmons saw a witch killed with knives during his stay, and revelation through dreams was well known in the community, even if the content of the dreams was increasingly christianized. One young man dreamed of punishments in the after-life, and in particular of a punishment for drinking, which consisted of being made to drink molten-pewter—a vision similar to that which was later revealed to Handsome Lake.[12] Visiting the other world in dreams and returning with a message of repentance and reform was also an established form of prophecy among the Iroquois at this time. Thus not only was Handsome Lake's experience of a vision an already institutionalized phenomenon among the Seneca, but many of his injunctions for reform 'had actually been instituted in his own community before June 15, 1799, the date of his first visions'.[13]

Yet prophetism was perhaps the essential way of legitimizing cultural reformation. Simple decision by political leaders was not sufficient to supersede long-established patterns, or to coerce those who had adopted new habits of a deleterious kind. Authority was never easily sustained in Indian tribes, and there were limits to the legislation for which a council could win acceptance. Even though the reforms had been canvassed, and were already in some measure instituted, religious justification and religious sanctions for their infringement were probably indispensable if they were to be properly accepted and maintained. In societies with relatively small social units, each of which has a high degree of autonomy, extensive authority is scarcely known. Only the prophet, asserting the supernatural sources of his power, can really claim authority over wider social groups. His prophecy is largely a re-affirmation of existing values, and a re-telling of stories already known, and has to be so to acquire credibility, but it is the supernatural claim of prophecy which is the means of conferring validity on its content.

Handsome Lake was born in 1735, in the Seneca village of Conawagas. His family had moved after the Seneca lost their lands. He served in the revolutionary war as a soldier with the British, but his life was characterized by dissoluteness and drunkenness, and for four years he had suffered from a wasting disease. In June 1799, Handsome Lake 'died', and on two subsequent occasions he received visions, which were

[10] Alanson Skinner, a review of *The Code of Handsome Lake* by Arthur C. Parker (cited below), *American Anthropologist* 17, 1 (January–March 1915), pp. 180–4 (p. 181).

[11] For an account of aspects of Iroquois traditional religious beliefs, see William M. Beauchamp, 'Civil, Religious and Mourning Councils and Ceremonies of Adoption of the New York Indians', New York State Museum (New York State Education Department) *Bulletin* 113, Archaeology, 13 (1906), pp. 341–451.

[12] M. H. Deardorff, op. cit., p. 89.

[13] Ibid., loc. cit.

written down by the Quakers who were with the Seneca. His teachings have come down in different versions: those copied by the Quakers, Henry Simmons and Halliday Jackson, and those standardized and written down by the Gai'wiio⁵ priests, as well as a somewhat divergent oral tradition.[14] When, in February 1800, the Indians gathered at Cornplanter's village for religious ceremonies, he took the opportunity of the occasion to urge people to abandon strong drink, and the visions of Handsome Lake were propounded. Halliday Jackson was asked to give his opinion of them and, after reflection, he 'told them that they would do well to observe the sayings' of Handsome Lake.[15]

Handsome Lake's vision was of four messengers who came to call him to repentance, and who promised to give him a message in which they would uncover all evil, and which he should then proclaim. The ethical prescriptions of the Gai'wiio⁵ teachings were a set of injunctions for Iroquois life. Whisky and rum were to be abandoned. Witchcraft was condemned, since witches made diseases. They were to confess publicly or privately. Charms were forbidden, and so was abortion. The married were to live together, and rear their children well. Young people were to be told when to marry, and mothers-in-law were to cease interfering with their married children. Small children were not to be unjustly punished. The young were to help the aged. Handsome Lake proscribed evil-speaking of the parentage of children. He exhorted hospitality; charity; the abandonment of gossip, vanity, boasting, and pride. Animals were to be well treated. He opposed theft, borrowing, and failure to pay for commodities. Men were to help each other, and repent of their sins.[16]

A considerable part of the Code of Handsome Lake is concerned

[14] The versions obtained by the Quakers at the time were recorded by Halliday Jackson, who heard the third vision in Handsome Lake's account to the council in 1800: the two earlier visions were recorded by Henry Simmons, Jr, who wrote them down from Handsome Lake, or from an interpreter. See A. F. C. Wallace, 'Halliday Jackson's Journal to the Seneca Indians', *Pennsylvania History* XIX, 2 (April 1952), pp. 117–47, and XIX, 3 (July 1952), pp. 325–49. Wallace sees this document as bearing 'the same relation to the Handsome Lake religion as would a newly discovered eye-witness account of the Sermon on the Mount to Christianity' (p. 120). The version standardized by Gai'wiio⁵ priests was committed to writing but was lost by Chief Cornplanter (a descendant of the Cornplanter referred to above) and had to be rewritten. This version is printed in A. C. Parker, *The Code of Handsome Lake*, New York State Museum, Museum Bulletin 163, Education Department Bulletin 530 (University of State of New York, Albany, N.Y., 1 November 1912). Parker considered this to be a definitive text, but it has since been recognized that divergent traditions exist: some recitals of the code take four or five days, rather than the three which Parker thought was the rule. Each longhouse where the religion is maintained has some autonomy, but inter-longhouse discussions take place at Tonawanda, where the sacred belts of the faith are kept, according to M. H. Deardorff, op. cit., p. 100 n.

[15] A. F. C. Wallace, 'Halliday Jackson's Journal . . .', op. cit., p. 333.

[16] This paragraph and those following rely principally on the Code, as presented in A. C. Parker, op. cit.

with the continuance of past practices and the acceptance of some of the white man's ways. Simmons was told by Handsome Lake that 'the Indians liked some of the white people's ways very well, and some Indian ways very well. It would take some time to lead the Indians out of their set ways.'[17] This sounds almost like a conscious attempt to arrive at an accommodative solution for a people suspended between the prescriptions of two cultural complexes. Of the thirty-three dances which the Seneca had, Handsome Lake condemned many, particularly totem dances, since they might harm other people. The revelation he had was that four amusements were appropriate: the Great Feather dance, the Harvest dance, the Sacred Song dance, and the Peach Stone game. He exhorted his followers to go to the festivals, and to stay throughout. There should be thanksgiving and, since the wild animals had gone, it was appropriate to keep cattle and pigs for feast food. It was wicked to turn good food into evil drink (fermented drinks). He permitted the Burning of the White Dog ceremony.[18] His vision reflected the prevalent fear of witches among the Iroquois: the Great Spirit decreed that they should be killed. He rejected the anniversary mourning customs, which he said added to the sorrows of the dead; he prescribed ten days of mourning, and a feast at which the souls of the dead would participate.

The accommodative elements in Handsome Lake's teaching are evident in what was revealed to him of the ancestors: that they

> have never reached the true lands of our Creator, nor did they enter the house of the tormentor, Ganos'ge. It is said that in some matters they did the will of the Creator, and in others they did not. They did both good and bad, and none was either good or bad. They are therefore in a place separate and unknown to us, we think, enjoying themselves.[19]

This represents a distinct divergence from the essentially restorative message of movements like the Smohalla cult and the Ghost Dance, in which the ways of the ancestors were extolled, and true happiness was to be had only in living according to their practice. The visions of the ancestors in those movements was of people enjoying themselves, but doing so in the rectitude of a confirmed way of life from which white elements had been eliminated. The accommodative aspects of Gai'wiio⁶ are pronounced. They are evident, too, in the claims made for the

[17] M. II. Deardorff, op. cit., p. 92.

[18] In the Oneida community, where Roman Catholicism was strong, the followers of Handsome Lake, to make Gai'wiio⁶ teaching more acceptable, denied that he had permitted the Burning of the White Dog ceremony, although it is known that he had in fact enjoined it on his followers. M. H. Deardorff, op. cit., p. 102.

[19] A. C. Parker, op. cit., p. 56, Section 66 of the Code.

Gai'wiio' teaching as such. Handsome Lake prophesied that all would follow him. The messengers had said that they thought the world would continue for three generations long (or three hundred years). 'Then will the Gai'wiio' be fulfilled.'[20] Those who refused the good word would suffer hardships.

The prophet himself was given curing power, and there were prescriptions for the use of tobacco as a medicine. He was also given prophetic power. But neither of these features is nearly so striking as, on the one hand, the ethical prescriptions, and on the other, the accounts of the actual visions. Nor is the cataclysmic and millennialist element in the Code of sufficient significance to consider the movement as in any sense revolutionist. Handsome Lake predicted the time of the end, when the earth would fail to bring forth its sustaining foods, when there would be a plague, and many men would claim to have spoken to the Creator, and there would be many wonders. All the powers of nature would be suspended, and the earth would be destroyed by fire. Those who had been generous on earth would enjoy blessings thereafter. But this cataclysm was set forth in time for three generations (or for 300 years—A.D. 2100) and thus more resembled the formal millennial teaching of the orthodox Christian denominations than that of adventist sects. It reflected, perhaps, the teachings of Christianity as he had heard them, blended with the Iroquois conceptions of the path of the soul after death. The sections of the Code in which the cataclysm is discussed echo something of the tone of the books of Ecclesiastes and Revelation.

From aboriginal teachings, Handsome Lake emphasized the earth journey of the soul. In his vision he went on a journey to the afterworld which recapitulates Iroquois conceptions, and which reads a little like *Pilgrim's Progress*. There he saw what happened to the greedy; the prison which is the law of the whites; the church, which was difficult for Indians; and the house of George Washington (who had dealt generously with the Iroquois after their opposition to the revolution), the only white man with a house near to the Creator, which appears almost as a symbolic accommodation of the Iroquois to the now established American state. The neighbouring section of the Code warns the Iroquois to remain neutral in the new war between the Americans and the British (the war of 1812, in which Tecumseh was active on the British side, and for recruitment to whose cause the Iroquois had been canvassed).

The fourth messenger who escorted Handsome Lake in his visionary

[20] Ibid., p. 44, Section 39 of the Code.

after-life journey showed him the scars on his hands and feet, and revealed himself as a man killed by the white people, who had now shut the doors of heaven so that they might no longer see him till the earth had passed away. This Christ-figure had said that none of his people now believed in him, although Handsome Lake declared that half of the Iroquois believed in him. The idea of a saviour killed by his own people is one which the Indians seized on in the teaching of the missionaries: the same idea was to recur in the Ghost Dance, with the implication of the greater worthiness of the Indians to receive a saviour. Other Christian features occurred in the visions, including a devil with a cloven hoof, horns, and a tail. In the after-life there would be no chance for the wicked to repent. There were two roads, that for those who, when warned on earth, had repented, and another for the wicked. The wicked were being punished, and among them were the drinkers, the witches and the wife-beaters, those using secret powers to attract men, adulterers, quarrellers, fiddlers, and gamblers. There he also saw Red Jacket, an Indian chief who had opposed Handsome Lake, being punished in the after-life for selling reservation land—an adaptation of Christian sanctions to a peculiarly Indian evil. In heaven there was a narrow way for the righteous, leading to pleasant lands where there was abundance and where dead relatives would meet. After his own death, which he predicted, Handsome Lake promised to stretch forth his hands for those who would follow his teaching.

The significance of the Code of Handsome Lake was the strong ethical content it provided for the Iroquois, in establishing both the principles and the sanctions for an Indian way of life. Elements of old Iroquois beliefs were set into a pattern of simulated Christian teaching. Its aim was reform rather than restoration: certainly it revitalized the culture of the Iroquois. It has impressed commentators by the emphasis on conscience and by its almost puritanical moral dogma.[21] 'Whatever may be the merits of the prophet's teachings, they created a revolution in Iroquois religious life.'[22] The Code reflects Handsome Lake's own preoccupations—the fear of witchcraft, which was rampant; his need to overcome his craving for alcohol; his dejection over the disloyalty of a son; his sorrow at the loss of a favourite niece; his guilt over his dissolute life; and his wish to be cared for, as a man who, although he had inherited a noble title, had never exerted any influence until this time.[23] But it also reflects the preoccupations of the Iroquois themselves

[21] A. F. C. Wallace, 'Handsome Lake . . .', op. cit., p. 154.
[22] A. C. Parker, op. cit., p. 11.
[23] A. F. C. Wallace, 'Handsome Lake . . .', op. cit., describes these circumstances (p. 152).

—the growing concern about alcohol;[24] their insecurity of tenure of the land; their decaying religious system and the loss of meaning of their ceremonial life.

The prophet's teaching presented in a fairly coherent form much that was known to many Indians, whether diffused from Christian culture or as a common response to it. Its accordance with the injunctions of the Quakers and its endorsement by them (and they were, of course, people particularly well disposed to inspirationalist procedures) no doubt further facilitated its acceptance. The approval of Cornplanter (though he was more of a progressive than Handsome Lake), who was, if not of a noble house like Handsome Lake himself, a very influential man among the Seneca, was important to its acceptance. (Cornplanter may, indeed, have been eager to mould the new teaching to his own conception of his how people should develop, for he appears to have tried to get Handsome Lake to prophesy 'prematurely'.[25]) The teachings gained a particular impetus from the commendation which they received from President Thomas Jefferson, given over the hand of the Hon. Henry Dearborn, Secretary of War:

> Brothers—The President is pleased with seeing you all in good health after so long a journey, and he rejoices in his heart that one of your own people has been employed to make you sober, good and happy; and that he is so well disposed to give you good advice, and to set before you so good examples. Brothers—If all the red people follow the advice of your friend and teacher, the Handsome Lake, and in future will be sober, honest, industrious and good, there can be no doubt but the Great Spirit will take care of you and make you happy.[26]

A copy of the commendation was held by all the chiefs of the six nations, and was taken virtually as a licence to profess and teach the new faith. The teachings of the prophet spread, and it became the practice for them to be recited at all annual midwinter festivals of the various Iroquois reservations in New York and Ontario.

The close similarity of many features of Handsome Lake's visions and those of Tenskwatawa, the Shawnee Prophet, who was his exact contemporary as a prophet during the later years of Handsome Lake's activity, is remarkable. Handsome Lake's first visions and teaching occurred before Tecumseh had disseminated the Shawnee Prophet's message, and others after Tenskwatawa had lost support

---

[24] The first temperance petition recorded in the United States was from the women of the Six Nations (the Iroquois tribes) to Joseph Brant, the Mohawk chief, in 1802, according to Mabel Powers, 'The Legacy of Handsome Lake', *Christian Century* LXXXIV, 2 (9 January 1957), pp. 47–8.

[25] This is indicated in Section 52 of the Code in the version given by A. C. Parker, op. cit., p. 50 (see also footnote 1, page 50).

[26] The message is given in A. C. Parker, op. cit., p. 10.

following the action of Tippecanoe. It is not possible to say in which direction the lines of influence flowed: they may have gone in both directions.[27] The marked similarities, however, should not conceal the differences. Tenskwatawa preached a much more emphatically restorative gospel, with xenophobic elements.[28] The militaristic character is lacking in Handsome Lake's teaching, and the millennial promise is remote and more christianized in comparison. Despite the fact that the prophecy of Handsome Lake was 'uttered by a scion of one of America's most martial tribes, the Code of Handsome Lake is conceived in a spirit of peace'.[29]

The Code urges men to return to Indian virtues. The incorporated Christian elements are indianized. It does not envisage a union with Christianity so much as the absorption of those elements of the Christian faith that are appropriate to the Iroquois circumstance. Although many Christian Iroquois have remained sympathetic to Gai'wiio', at the council of the tribes in 1820 at Tonawanda, the various groups made their choice between the Christian faith and the religion of Handsome Lake. The new faith appropriated the Christian saviour, but did so by making him virtually exclusively an Indian saviour, and indeed a Gai'wiio' saviour. Handsome Lake was opposed to schools; and although his Code permitted farming, he did not approve of producing for the market. His strong native disposition is evident in the strength of his condemnation of witches. But neither witches nor healing, both of which were mentioned in the Code, nor the millennial idea (it can scarcely be characterized as a millennial hope) are central features. The Code is an attempt to restore the dignity of Iroquois life, not through the old military virtues, once so highly prized, but in the acceptance of a separate way of life, and the quiet fulfilment of religious obligations. The ecstatic performances of the past were to be abandoned. The rituals were to commemorate the peaceable concerns of the Iroquois (Handsome Lake added a Strawberry Feast), and the ethical system was to be enjoined by four agents (angels) of the community. The introverted character of this new system of values is evident in the moving annual ceremonies at which the visions are recited. The Iroquois had bowed to the inevitable, and

[27] M. H. Deardorff, op. cit., p. 96, cites reports of the extent to which the fame of Handsome Lake had spread. Shawnee delegates visited him in 1807. A. Skinner, op. cit. (p. 183), says 'It seems improbable that Handsome Lake was not influenced by the Shawnee Prophet. The latter was already in the field when Handsome Lake commenced his work [this seems to be untrue] and as it is known that Seneca youths had broken away from the tribe to join the followers of Tecumseh, it would be strange if some of the Shawnee doctrine had not reached the ears of Handsome Lake.'

[28] On the teachings of Tenskwatawa see pp. 231–2 and especially footnotes 33 and 37.

[29] A. Skinner, op. cit., p. 183.

had sought to recapture something of the unity and integrity of their former way of life. Their values, however, no longer expressed assertive militancy, but rather past tribal glory recollected in tranquillity, and future individual bliss contemplated in pious application of a new ethical code.

Despite the forebodings which commentators at the beginning of this century had about the Gai'wiio' religion, which then appeared to be in a state of decline, the movement has persisted, and in the 1950s the faith was still practised by about 7,000 of the 15,000 Iroquois in New York State and Ontario.[30] Ten longhouses were known at that time, and those at the St Regis and Caughnawaga settlements had been established since the end of the First World War.[31] The Gai'wiio' members from Onondaga and the Canadian Oneida, who were of long standing in the faith, spent time in training people as local preachers. Local traditions have varied, and different preachers have brought their own emphasis, but, typical of an introversionist sect, the Gai'wiio' faith has shown itself to be enduring, localized, and accommodative of local inspiration within the broad context of its scriptural inheritance. It has remained Iroquois, and has, indeed, become the religious expression of Iroquois identity.

The successors of the Hau Hau movement

The Gai'wiio' religion came to the Iroquois at a period of cultural crisis and insecurity about the future of the people and their occupancy of the land. Guided by a European introversionist sect, they found their own pattern of native introversion, in which, with a very limited accommodation to white culture, they sought to forge precepts for a new normative pattern for Iroquois life. They had not experienced a recent millennial disappointment, although they had seen the overthrow of their allies and protectors, the powerful soldiery, by the settlers, from whom they had less reason to expect good treatment. The *Ringatu* faith, in its establishment among the Maoris, has much in common with the Gai'wiio' religion, and the impress of circumstances, allowing for all the specific historical and cultural differences, may reasonably be compared with that experienced by the Iroquois.

In the case of the Maoris, a recent revolutionist faith had prompted

[30] W. M. Beauchamp, op. cit., p. 415, regarded the faith as fast dying out in 1906; A. C. Parker, op. cit., p. 6, said that the teaching was waning in 1912. A. F. C. Wallace, 'Handsome Lake . . .', op. cit., p. 149, gave this estimate in 1952.
[31] M. H. Deardorff, op. cit., p. 77.

them to military action. They had suffered disappointment in war
and in their literal acceptance of biblical and prophetic utterances
about the outcome of their military and political endeavour.[32] The
revolutionist response and revolutionary action, which in this instance
had been conjoined, had failed. Nativistic millennialism was no longer
a credible prospect for the Maori. Many of them were ready now for
some new religious accommodation to the situation. They had long ago
abandoned aboriginal religion for Christianity, but orthodox Christianity
now strongly identified with those who had burned their homes and
pillaged their lands. Some new supernatural interpretation of the
world was now needed. Maori separateness had already acquired
expression in the King movement. But that movement was less concerned with a distinctive Maori way of life than with a system of Maori
authority to replace a government no longer trusted by the tribes.
Neither the King movement nor Hau Hau were explicitly nativistic,
even though the latter resorted to aboriginal ideas for some of its
content and practice. Each was heavily infused by the conceptions of
white religion. The King's followers remained Christians, and although
Hau Hau 'threw away the scriptures' it retained many biblical concepts
and personages in its teaching.[33] It was to be expected that new
developments of Maori faith should also be influenced by Christianity.
The new religious response, however, was not to come from a disillusioned follower of the Hau Hau movement, but from a government
supporter who found himself, by accident, indicted with the rebels.

At an important engagement in the war against the Hau Hau, the
government forces besieged and captured an important fortified
village, Waerenga-a-hika, where they took three hundred prisoners.
The battle destroyed the Pai-marire, or Hau Hau religion, in the area
of Poverty Bay on the east coast of North Island.[34] Te Kooti Rikirangi
had not fought with the rebels, but because he was locally accused of
theft, a local chief had pushed him on to the boat on which the prisoners
from the village were being taken to the Chatham Islands for deporta-
tion. In the island prison, Te Kooti, who had been educated in a mission
station, became the leader of a new religion, declaiming the Scriptures

[32] For the Hau Hau movement, see pp. 248–52. S. Barton Babbage, *Hau-hauism* . . ., op.
cit., p. 72, writes 'Although Christianity was accordingly rejected, it is not strange that
religious enthusiasm was invoked in the political struggle. Its [Hau-hauism's] end left the
Maori in a curiously unsettled state; his faith in Pakeha justice and truth undermined, his
belief in Christianity shaken, his land still in danger, and his confidence in himself weakened.'

[33] Robin W. Winks, 'The Doctrine of Hau Hauism', *Journal of the Polynesian Society* 62, 3
(September 1953), p. 227.

[34] The account here, and in the following paragraphs, rests principally on William
Greenwood, 'The Upraised Hand, or the Spiritual Significance of the Rise of the Ringatu
Faith', *The Journal of the Polynesian Society* 51, 1 (March 1942), pp. i–vi and 1–81.

and holding services. Of the old Hau Hau faith, he retained one element, the upraised hand, Ringatu, but he transformed its meaning from that of an act warding off bullets to a gesture of homage to God. His teaching emphasized solace in the circumstance of captivity, and the Old Testament, and especially the Psalms, had a special appeal for him.

On 4 July 1868 Te Kooti planned and executed a dramatic escape from prison, and from the Chatham Islands. With 163 men, 64 women, and 71 children, he captured the provisions schooner which came to the Islands, and forced the white crew to set sail for New Zealand. On the way, he quelled a mutiny led by Te Warihi, whom he denounced as a Jonah who was causing a storm which was raging. According to the story, when Te Warihi had been thrown overboard the storm subsided. Te Kooti successfully evaded capture by the whites, and for a time he became a nuisance to the government, planning raids against both settlers and Maoris loyal to the government. He applied the vengeance pattern of the Maoris against the officers and chief who had him deported.[35] Over time, thirty-three Europeans and thirty-seven 'friendly' Maoris were killed in the skirmishes with Te Kooti's men, but 120 of Te Kooti's followers were killed at Ngatapa-pa early in 1869. He escaped to the King country in 1873, and there he established himself near the present township of Te Kuiti and preached his religion. He was finally pardoned in 1883, and lived until 1893.

In some respects the Ringatu faith began by working out, or tidying up, the remnants left over from the earlier government struggle against Hau Hauism, but the Ringatu faith itself was not Hau Hauism.[36] Little has been written on it, and it has itself no written matter for its liturgy or its preaching, which is all memorized, as were the teachings of the old *Whare Wananga*, and Maori genealogies.[37] In many respects, such as the order of precedence which was followed, the Ringatu faith followed old Maori custom, but its teaching was essentially biblical, and the leader of a service had to know by heart the Psalms, hymns, and *panuis* (medleys of biblical verses, traditional in the Ringatu faith). The Bible was heavily *tapu*, and Ringatu followers had extensive knowledge of it. Ancient songs and chants were included in the services, and in this mixture of Maori traditions and Christian beliefs there was a literal application of Old Testament stories to the Maoris as a people in bondage.

[35] A. T. Ngata and I. L. G. Sutherland, 'Religious Influences', pp. 336–73 in I. L. G. Sutherland (Ed.), *The Maori People Today* . . ., op. cit., p. 355.
[36] W. Greenwood, op. cit., p. 33.
[37] A. T. Ngata and I. L. G. Sutherland, op. cit., p. 357.

The Ringatu maintained the twelfth of the month as a holy day, because 12 was a common biblical number. On such occasions people came from long distances, often staying for two nights in the church (there were no special buildings, and they often used tribal meeting-places that were open to all). Meetings had a strong communal character, reinforced by the use of ancient songs. The *panuis* composed by Te Kooti himself were well known and were repeated by the *tohunga*, or religious specialist, from memory: were a speaker to make a mistake it was instantly recognized and regarded as very unfortunate. The *tohunga*, although a specialist, wore no special vestment, and the communal character of the Church has not been compromised by the emergence of a priesthood. Several services were held during the course of one night, and between services discussion, usually of a religious topic, would take place. The communal character of the gatherings was most evident in the appointment of stewards, or policemen, *pirihimanas*, whose functions were to ensure the maintenance of order and good conduct in the meetings and to make arrangements for cooking and sleeping.[38]

The *tohungas* were elected by the local congregation, which might dismiss them if they became careless. They received no remuneration, but they acquired a legal status in order to perform the simple marriage ceremonies and burial rites practised in the Church. The *ture* was the *tohunga* who looked after one parish, and he had to be well versed in the law of the Church. The *takuta* was a *tohunga* who conducted faith-healing services, and there might be several such within one parish. Above the local level, a district leader presided, and here the Ringatu Church has met with difficulty in evolving an appropriate model. 'Bishop' was the ecclesiastical title familiar to them, and such leaders were thought of as bishops for some time. Subsequently, the inappropriateness of the title was recognized, and the style was changed to the more secular designation of 'president'. At a later date, they reverted to an early usage of Te Kooti, and called such a leader a *poutikanga*, mainstay. The Church was badly fragmented for many years, and in the 1930s a *poutikanga* for the unity of the Ringatu Church was appointed; biennial conferences were organized, with a constitution of a European type.[39] The slowness of the emergence of a denominational structure illustrates the *gemeinschaftlich* character of Ringatu, and is reminiscent of the slow denominational development of the Congregationalists, Baptists, and Unitarians in Britain and elsewhere. Some degree of local autonomy has persisted, and some branches have

[38] W. Greenwood, op. cit., pp. 53–4, 39–40.
[39] Ibid., pp. 50–1.

maintained rather different special festivities of their own. Organizational rationalization and unification were accompanied by doctrinal rationalization: 'After his election in 1937, Paora Teramea, present *poutikanga* . . . succeeded in injecting much more consistent doctrine, which, while fundamentally Maori, is Christian as well.'[40]

The Ringatu Church manifests a qualified introversionism. Like other such movements among less-developed people, its concerns are distinctively ethnic. The remnant that withdraws does so as an ethnic group, preserving a distinctive (though not an aboriginal) way of life. Its concept of salvation is less that of the elected saints of God, and more that of a cultural community—a salvation appropriate for *this* people, in *this* world. Such a movement becomes a vehicle for the preservation of particular facets of the native way of life. The way of life it sustains is always an accommodation to the dominant culture, a compromise between life-patterns drawn from both the aboriginal past and the culture of the invader, but its cultural meaning to the faithful is of a separate native way. Like introversionist movements in western Christendom, the Ringatu Church undertook no proselytizing. It represented a withdrawn remnant, for whom a separate faith reinforced ethnicity in the assertion of distinct identity. Thus there was no special ceremonial when a man 'joined' the Ringatu Church—it was treated as if he were claiming a birthright.

The model of the introversionist sect of western society does not wholly apply to Ringatu. Some elements represent continuity of past traditions, rather than distinctive introversionist features: one is the practice of faith-healing. Although there is no direct evidence, some have regarded faith healing as the feature which attracts the Maoris to the Ringatu faith. It is both a survival from pre-*pakeha* times, and has, of course, the explicit legitimation of scripture, but it is especially appropriate to the *mate Maori* afflictions that are regarded as peculiar to the Maori.[41] Such indigenous afflictions, said to occur only among the natives, are clearly a manifestation of the psychological responses of less-developed peoples to the dominant culture of the invader. (Essentially similar afflictions are reported of some North American Indians as a type of troubled soul. The ailment is especially exacerbated in bereavement and other circumstances of more acute sadness.[42]) This type of healing may, indeed, be closely akin to the reassurance provided

---

[40] R. W. Winks, op. cit., pp. 235–6.
[41] A. T. Ngata and I. L. G. Sutherland, op. cit., p. 360.
[42] Sickness which was a type of sadness of melancholia was sometimes the subject of curing among North American Indians: see C. Du Bois, *The Feather Cult* . . .' op. cit., p. 34. Grievous bereavement had been the recent experience of several North American Indians who became prophets: Handsome Lake, Smohalla, and Jake Hunt were prominent examples.

by the religious group in the form of the security of the new context and the re-creation of community life in the face of the overwhelming superiority of the dominant culture which cannot be imitated, and the dominant society which cannot be joined. Faith-healing may, however, also be seen as a continuity of traditional thaumaturgy. If the white culture is to be abandoned, it is understandable that this limited therapeutic practice must, as of old, continue in the framework of religious institutions. Faith-healing as such is acceptable because Christianity enjoins healing in this way; thus it replaces earlier aboriginal therapeutic practice.

Ringatu faith arose first among former members of the Hau Hau movement, and it remained strongest on the east coast and around the Bay of Plenty, the area in which Hau Hau had thrived. Its membership in the 1930s was drawn from the tribes at Opotiki, those in the Urewera country (who were among the few who had not been evangelized by Christian missionaries), the majority of those about Whakatane, and a few outlying groups. These are principally the Tuhoe people. During the first half of this century there have been between 4,000 and 6,000 adherents. The faith is a mixture of nativism and introversion, and relies on the ethnic and tribal elements of the past. Ringatu is a legitimation, in the new biblical terms, of separate native community life, which is, however, a very considerable modification of the traditional way of life.

In contemporaneous movements among other tribes, a more emphatic nativistic and anti-white orientation is to be discerned. One such movement grew up around Te Whiti among the Taranaki tribes, who felt that they had suffered particular injustice in the wars over their disputed lands.[43] He led a pacific movement of resistance to government services, particularly in education and health, and celebrated the eighteenth of the month to commemorate the day on which the first shot had been fired at Waitara in 1860. His followers had no distinct practice of worship, although they chanted the ancient songs, adapted to themes of oppression and injustice, and accompanied them with traditional dances. They turned from the Wesleyan mission, but 'did not revert to their old gods, and nothing in their ritual or observances suggested the idea of a religious sect or church'.[44] The *Ratana* movement, founded by Wiremu Ratana, who arose as a faith-healer who could deliver men from black magic, combined the characteristics of thaumaturgy with the worship of God, and to the

[43] A. T. Ngata and I. L. G. Sutherland, op. cit., pp. 361–2.
[44] Ibid., p. 362.

Trinity was added a hierarchy of angels, complemented by a corresponding network of religious functionaries. Ratana built a township of Wanganui, and appears to have attracted the de-tribalized as well as those who had not found sufficient opportunity for assertion in their own tribal groups. The movement held aloof from the government's development schemes. It grew rapidly, particularly in the days of Ratana's own miracle-working, and was still considerable in the 1960s.[45]

These movements are characterized by the belated rejection by considerable numbers of Maoris of white culture and the orthodox forms of the white religion, following the long period of relatively eager acceptance of the ways of the invader and the abandonment of many aboriginal practices and beliefs. Apart from indigenous prophets and movements, of whom there are several others in addition to those mentioned above, the Mormons, who made their first impact in the 1880s, succeeded in winning considerable allegiance among the Maoris, and this, too, represented a tacit rejection of British culture and religion, and included both a millennialist and an introversionist element of response.[46] The resort of the Maoris, after their failure in arms and the disappointment of their revolutionist hopes, was to retreat into the native culture by building religious barriers to reinforce the barriers of ethnicity. The response of withdrawing from the world was facilitated by the fact that the world had been taken over by the *pakeha*: and thus their religious reaction repeated only some of the aspects of withdrawal of the typical introversionist responses of western Christendom. Yet, in some ways, culturally transplanted minorities, such as the Amish, the Hutterians, and some groups of Doukhobors, represent in American and Canadian societies—albeit with the preservation of the sense of a different historical moment as well as of a different cultural tradition—groups comparable to the introversionist Maori movements.

---

[45] A. T. Ngata 'Tribal Organization', in I. L. G. Sutherland (Ed.), *The Maori People Today* .. ., op. cit., p. 182; A. T. Ngata and I. L. G. Sutherland, op. cit., pp. 364–6. In 1955, the Ratana Church had 154 persons registered as officiating ministers under the New Zealand Marriage Act (at the same time the Ringatu Church had 46, and the Church of Te Kooti Rikirangi, a schismatic group, had 6): *New Zealand, Official Year Book*, 1956, p. 80. In the 1961 Census, the Ratana Faith claimed 21,954 adherents (some 13.14 per cent of all Maoris) and the Ringatu Church had 5,275 (3.16 per cent). J. J. Mol, 'Integration versus Segregation in New Zealand Churches', *British Journal of Sociology* XVI, 2 (June 1965), pp. 140–9.

[46] In 1926 the Mormons were reported as having 3,416 members among the Maoris (compared with 11,567 Ratana members and 4,540 Ringatu at that date) according to Felix M. Keesing, *The Changing Maori*, Memoirs of the Board of Maori Ethnological Research, Vol. 4 (Avery, New Plymouth, N.Z., 1928), p.143. In 1961, they had 12,179 members, representing 7.3 per cent of Maoris. At this date, the three movements accounted for almost 24 per cent of Maoris. Ratana and Ringatu each had some non-Maoris, and the Mormons had 5,709 non-Maoris in New Zealand, according to J. J. Mol., op. cit.

An autonomous introversionist response

That introversionist movements among under-developed peoples show less continuity with previous revolutionist responses than do some of the introversionist sects of Christendom, may be attributed to the lower level of conscious organization prevailing among such peoples. For them, ethnic identity replaces the more deliberate voluntarism found within Christian countries. Most movements along less-developed peoples are fluid at the edges. Ethnicity is itself almost a claim of eligibility to participate, and formal membership is a virtually un-known concept. Thus, especially in their early stages, new movements tend to belong to everyone, or potentially so. Consequently direct continuities between revolutionist and subsequent movements cannot be so readily shown. The general succession of responses is not always conspicuous either. The slow acculturation of the Iroquois appears to have induced an introversionist ethic without a preceding revolutionist phase. The abrupt breakdown of harmonious relations with the Maoris produced a sequence of responses. The dramatic change in the circum-stances of Plains cultures precipitated their acceptance of the revolu-tionist Ghost Dance, and subsequently of more introverted responses. With the Algonquins, long and steady acculturation was again associ-ated with a more quietistic response, once the military phase of relations (and, in the case of the Delaware Prophet and Tenskwatawa, its attendant millennialism) had passed. Long after their last military struggle with the whites, an introversionist response occurred among some Algonquin tribes in the *Powwow* cult. Just as in advanced countries some introversionist sects appear to have arisen without a particularly marked millennialist phase, so among less-developed peoples, persisting movements like the Powwow, displaying a qualified introversionism, have come into being as independent movements, without a preliminary experience of disappointed millennialism.

The Powwow cult (also variously called *Dream Dance* or *Drum Dance*) was probably diffused from the Sioux to the Chippewa, Potawatomi, Kickapoo, Fox, Sauk, Winnebago, and Menomini.[47] It is misleading to regard it, as one investigator has done, 'as one form of the messiah cult'.[48] The cult has no messianic aspect and not even a particular

[47] J. S. Slotkin, *Menomini Powwow* (Milwaukee Public Museum Publication in Anthro-pology, 4, Milwaukee, Wisc., 1957).

[48] S. A. Barrett, 'The Dream Dance of the Chippewa and Menominee Indians of Northern Wisconsin', *Bulletin of the Public Museum of Milwaukee* I, iv, (November 1911), pp. 251–369 (p. 256). Barrett offers no evidence for this view. Elsewhere his account makes plain the conventional eschatology of the movement: 'The most important part of the faith is the hope of the devotees for reward in the ordinary spirit world in return for good deeds and upright living in the present world' (p. 298).

conception of a millennium. Just as the Comanche, Ute, and Shoshone adopted the Sun Dance, so the Powwow cult is an example of the borrowing of an alien cultural form to meet needs and to express concern for which the older traditional rituals appear to be inadequate.[49] The dance and the teachings of the Powwow cult, however, while essentially Indian, were an approximation to an introversionist response—emphasizing withdrawal from the white man's world rather than the expectation of its supernatural transformation.

The woodland Chippewa and Menomini in Wisconsin had long been exposed to acculturating influences, and when the dance first came to them, with a strong ethical message and with the traditional legitimation of a vision, it appeared both as a native religious expression, and yet, simultaneously, as a new and more effective method of adjusting to a new set of circumstances for which old and decaying ceremonial was not adequate. The older ceremonials, particularly the medicine dance, were relatively infrequently performed. The cult of the medicine dance was esoteric, and to learn its lore was costly in time and effort. The Dream Dance, Drum Dance, or Powwow, was at once a more public ritual, which a man could learn about at less cost and with less effort. Although the principal rituals were practised seasonally, it also provided other procedures for regular, and eventually usually weekly performance. The conditions of insecurity and the manifestation of the powerful (and weekly performed) rites of the white churches probably influenced the development of Powwow.

The introduction of the Drum Dance was the work of a Sioux girl who, in 1876, whilst fleeing from the white soldiers who had killed all the other members of her band, concealed herself for about twenty hours in a lake. Eventually the spirits offered her help, and told her that she must teach a new dance to all the Indian tribes. The girl apparently went from tribe to tribe teaching the dance, enjoining Indians to put away the small drums they had used and to use larger ones, and to discontinue their war and pipe dances in favour of the new dance. Only the new large drum would be sufficient to keep away bad spirits.[50] The dance appears to have spread to the Chippewa in the late 1870s, and from them to the Menomini. To the original story there was an accretion of various myths—of the girl acquiring invisibility and so

---

[49] On the Sun Dance of the Comanches see p. 275. On the Utes, see pp. 298 n., 413 n.

[50] This account is from B. G. Armstrong and T. P. Wentworth, *Early Life Among Indians* (Bowron, Ashland, Wisc., 1892), ch. 10, cited by J. S. Slotkin, op. cit., Appendix I, p. 155. The Sioux girl was travelling around at this time, and the evidence from this source suggests that the dance and ritual was known to the Algonquin tribes in the late 'seventies, a decade before S. A. Barrett, op. cit., had supposed. The account in the following paragraphs relies principally on J. S. Slotkin.

escaping the soldiers, for example—but the more important aspects are the organization of the cult, the rituals and the ethical injunctions.

The central rituals of the Powwow consisted of both weekly and seasonal performances. The drum, which was invested with power from the spirits, was the central object of the cult. It was itself sacred, and was a symbol of the supernatural, much as the cross or the altar in Christianity. It was also a symbol of the world. In the rituals the beat of the drum, undertaken in unison by the principal officers of the cult, was all-pervasive. To this beat the dances were performed. The officers of the organization symbolized different spirit beings. One, usually the drum-owner, impersonated the Great Spirit; others the thunderbirds who were protective agents for the tribe; yet four more represented the spirits of the four cardinal points of the compass.

At one time the drum was given to a group, but, and this seems to be typical of the reversion to individual proprietorship evident in North American Indian cults, the drum eventually came to be possessed by one individual, the drum chief. Where the principles of formal organ-ization are little known, and where any such organization is an alien importation, the tendency is for either kinship structure or individual proprietorship to be reasserted and to become the basis for collective endeavour. The drum chief was responsible for selecting the other members of the organization, all of whom had important ritual functions—drumming, singing, dancing, offering sacrifices, attending to the dancing ground, and looking after the pipes which form so important a part of the sacrificial system. Women participated as helpers to the singers, and one, the drum woman, represented the Sioux woman to whom the cult had been first revealed.

The purpose of the rituals was to strengthen the ties between the members and the spirits. The normal weekly rite consisted of songs, most of which were sung four times. It is possible that the first songs which were sung were intended to discharge bad spirits, with later ones that expressed the joy of living, although this does not appear to have been formally established.[51] Special handshake songs are included. The songs among the Menomini were largely Chippewa or Potawatomi. The dancers danced as each song was sung, although over the years the dancing became less ecstatic and more of a formality. There were prayers and the drum chief usually preached, both on the ethical injunctions of the faith and on the original myth of the acquisition of the cult. The pipes were smoked by the officials as an offering to the spirits: they symbolized a pipe of peace among mankind. Like the drums, the pipes were embellished with symbolic designs. The seasonal rites

[52] J. S. Slotkin, op. cit., p. 14.

secured the help of the spirits for the forthcoming season. Gatherings on these occasions used to last several days, until the influence of the white man's working week made such prolonged religious festivities difficult to organize. Food was also consecrated (invested with spirit power) and became part of the sacrificial offering in these rites, which also included private songs for the support of the male officials, each of whom danced while his song was being sung. The elaborate belts, decorated with feathers, were used by the men who represented the thunderbirds, and who danced to protect the weaker members of the community: others also danced with the belts, to acquire special protection. Special rites were undertaken to bring individuals who were in mourning back into the community of their fellows, and in the early days of the dance there were customs acquired from the Plains cultures, particularly the divorce songs, in which divorces were solemnized, and warrior songs—although these were somewhat inconsistent with the brotherly ethic of the Powpow. (These particular features did not survive among the Menomini.) An important feature of the seasonal rituals was the presentation of gifts to people from other tribes who were present. This epitomized the central ethical ideals of the Powwow.

The ethical injunctions recounted as the instructions of the Great Spirit (or the spirits) to the Sioux woman emphasized a few simple propositions, which are remarkable when the warlike virtues of the Indian past are recalled. The dance was given for all Indians, and the drum was a manifestation of the Great Spirit's will to help his people, the Indian people. Indians were not to fight each other or cheat each other.[52] They were not to be angry, nor to be jealous. They were to help each other in every way. The ethic was taught by exhortation and by formal didactic orations in the Powwow. The cult had no specific eschatology but inherited the general pantheon of Indian spirit beings, both good and evil, and accepted the need to make offerings to the good, and to placate the evil (although this last item became increasingly vestigial). The spirits themselves, as represented in the drum, were the fountain-head of help for all Indians in all their enterprises, including such common tasks as deer-hunting and berry-picking.

The central characteristics of the Powwow were its nativist emphasis and its pan-Indianism. Yet between the two there is some degree of inconsistency. Since each tribe has a distinctive inheritance, a restorative or conservative faith could not easily be other than tribal. But by the late nineteenth century, tribes that had experienced so long a period

[52] S. A. Barrett, op. cit., p. 284, 'This creed is all-embracing and demands for the stranger the same consideration as is accorded the tribesman and blood relative'.

of acculturation and acquaintance with white dominance as the Algonquin tribes had come increasingly to accept the dichotomy of Indian and white, and the white man's easy assumption that all tribesmen were simply Indians. The Powwow itself emphasized Indianness, and consequently its conservatism was the conservatism of the lowest common denominator rather than that of particular tribal traditions. Like other nativistic movements, what is sought to preserve was far from being traditional or aboriginal, although it was represented as such. The Dream Dance ritual and the ethic of the Powwow were themselves markedly deviant from older Indian values, even though they embraced many elements derived from the past. Some versions of the myth of the establishment of the Powwow emphasized the dichotomy very sharply, asserting that this was a religion given specifically to Indian peoples, something suited to them and not to white men.[53] Adherents by no means always regard it as proper for white men even to know about their religion.[54] Whilst any Indian might join the Powwow, those who were Roman Catholics were not admitted to membership. That was the white man's way.[55]

The Powwow and its dances superseded the older dances of the tribes in which it gained adherents. The war dance and the buffalo dance, for reasons which their very names suggest, were rarely performed by the early 1950s. The medicine dance still lingered on among the older people, but the situation appeared to have changed con-

[53] One of Slotkin's informants recounted the vision of a relative concerning the way he should go after he had been associating with the Catholics. In the vision he was looking for a trail, and his accounts proceed: 'And when I come to a place there where them roads fork, I didn't know what to do. So I follow one of them trails. And I come to a place. Oh, I see lot of Indians . . . they're all Catholics. . . . And I looked around there, and I seen that stairway . . . all decorated with flowers . . . going towards Heaven. But it must be about six foot; that's where that stairway was hanging. And them Indians, you know, they want to go to Heaven. They couldn't make it. Some of them they reach the stairway, and they're trying to start . . . [to] go to Heaven . . . I seen somebody coming down the steps there; he had that long stick; he pushed them Indians off. He says "You don't belong here; you ain't supposed to come here. You, Indian, why don't you follow that [other] trail? That's where you belong." That looks like a white man taking charge of that stairway. . . . He tell them, "You can't go over there. You got a place to go; you follow that trail down there; that's where you belong. You don't belong here." That's what that boss [Great Spirit] told me to tell you. . . .' The 'boss' went on to tell the visionary that only white people got through the (Catholic) stairway, and that the Indians had the medicine dance and the drum dance, which was their way. The Great Spirit sent the man back to earth to live, and told him to practise his own, Indian, religion; only then would he get into heaven. J. S. Slotkin, op. cit., pp. 24–5.

[54] S. A. Barrett, op. cit., says (p. 369) 'The whole ceremony is strictly non-esoteric, and any person, regardless of race or creed is welcome to participate in it'. J. S. Slotkin, op. cit., p. 9, found the Powwow people 'suspicious of white men and their ways'; although his informants asked him to record their religion, particularly to help them convey the meaning of this waning cult to the younger generation, none the less they felt that they were not to talk about it (p. 10), and Slotkin encountered some opposition (p. 124).

[55] Ibid., p. 14.

siderably since the first decade of the century, when this aboriginal ritual still existed in some measure of purity. Even at that time, the Powwow had replaced many older ceremonies among the Chippewa and Menomini.[56] It offered a simpler, more regular and more reassuring access to the spirits and their protective power than the older rituals, and, in being so readily available to all, it manifested the breakdown of the hierarchy in tribal structure as well as the distinctions between tribes. Like other new cults, it provided roles for women. It created new segmentary roles, which was appropriate to the breakdown of tribal life, and which reflected the gradual effect on Indian culture of the impingement of white society. It adapted the 'power' concept of Indian religion to the new concerns of a changing social situation. And yet, with all these functions of accommodation, the Powwow was also capable of representing itself as distinctively Indian, proper to the Indian way of life.

In its early days, the Powwow cult was also known as the Dream Dance, and this presumably related to the vision experience of the Sioux girl, since there was no evidence of trance inducement or vision quests in the Powwow dances. Slotkin reported, 'I could not find anything unique about the present role of dreams in the Pow-wow'.[57] Dream messages were often claimed among the Menomini '. . . so it is not surprising that a few years ago Keme·wam's daughter had a dream ordering that her father's drum organization be revivified after it had been allowed to become inactive'.[58] Visions in which people were instructed by the Great Spirit to join the movement, or which legitimated it as the appropriate Indian way, were reported both in this period and in the first decade of the century.[59] But the cult did not concentrate on the inducement of visions in the way ascribed by some commentators to Peyote.[60]

It would be surprising were any new religious movement among a pre-literate people entirely devoid of thaumaturgical aspects, since the

[56] Ibid., p. 13; S. A. Barrett, op. cit., pp. 255, 256.
[57] J. S. Slotkin, op. cit., p. 81.
[58] Loc. cit.
[59] S. A. Barrett, op. cit., found that the Chippewa and Menomini maintained a book in which they had recorded a number of confirmatory visions given to a local girl. She had been visited by angels, who told her that the markings on a scroll which they carried, 'indicate the duration of the earth under present conditions and further that if the people would only believe in the messages sent to them by the Great Spirit and mend their unrighteous ways three lines more could be added to those already on the scroll and that much more grace given before the end of the world' (p. 329). See also footnote 53 on p. 408.
[60] The Powwow cult was a different experience from Peyote, being much more emotionally expressive and collective in character. J. S. Slotkin, op. cit., p. 14 n., who knew both cults well, wrote 'The Powwow is . . . quite different from the individualistic and comtemplative Peyotism. I found it impossible to study the two simultaneously; the rapid shift in world view and mood necessary, was too great for successful identification [of the investigator with the participants, presumably].'

acquisition of power is such an intense preoccupation, and an agency for curative practice is an abiding need. The medicine dance was still practised in the earlier days of the Powwow, and as long as this more elaborate ritual with its extensive range of therapeutic procedures flourished, the Powwow, which was in no sense a direct rival, and members of which normally accepted the traditional medicine dance, appears not to have acquired curative functions. At some stage, at least among the Menomini, an accretion of therapeutic practice occurred, and some of the functions of the medicine dance were acquired by the Powwow. Over time the Powwow healing rite fell into desuetude, and in the 1950s this supplicatory procedure for curing had not been in use for a number of years.[61] The Powwow itself was by this time in decline.

Conclusion

Unlike the revolutionist movements, which in such societies are essentially restorative, these introversionist religions do not promise to *restore the past*, but simply to *preserve the faithful* in a native and separate way of life. Tacitly they endorse the surrender of those cultural traits that have had to be abandoned: the Powwow did not sustain the virtues of the warrior, any more than did the code of Handsome Lake. These movements seek to establish a completely new structure of values, whilst yet insisting that these values are native values, inappropriate to, and not derived from, the white culture. There was, thus, a new consciousness of native identity, and of the differences in knowledge, reasoning, and emotional balance between the white man's mind and culture and those of the indigene in his culture. And this was so even where, as in the Ringatu Church, a considerable inheritance from the Christian faith had been acquired: there were applications of that faith—particularly of the Old Testament stories— that were held to be more appropriate to the native. The absorption of Christian elements had become, not the imitation of the religion of the white man, but its appropriation. The strong implication was that the white man had in fact rejected this faith, had crucified his saviour, had played the part only of the elder son in the vineyard, while the native was the more worthy younger son who, at first rejecting, had finally responded to the wishes of the master. The native way of life was in itself, as it now existed, and as it was sanctified in the new introverted faith, the manifestation of readiness to do the will of the master. The

[61] Ibid., pp. 13–14, 149.

white man, with his greed, his theft of land, his destruction of the game, and with his tremendous power, had clearly profited from his religious knowledge, but he had perverted it. The natives had learned from the white man of the power of evil, and of new virtues and values which the white man himself did not sustain. They had lost the cultural, diplomatic, and military struggle. Their power had failed. Thereafter, communal power as such ceased to be their central religious pre-occupation.

The wishes, dreams, and ideals of these new movements are not for a return to the past pre-contact days: increasingly those times cannot be imagined. They are for the preservation and separation of the native way of life. Thrust into common situations of oppression and disadvantage, the tribal particularism of the past is abandoned, just as its structure and its military preoccupations have had to be abandoned. War chiefs disappear, and in their place arise new styles of leaders—leaders who can promise supernatural compensations for a new social circumstance, who can reassure and protect by spiritual conviction rather than by military prowess.

The new religions emphasize a new community. They are rarely capable of embracing the totality of the communities of the past, since a new voluntarism has become possible with the diminution of the need for protection from military dangers. They frequently assert an ethic for the whole community, even though the rites and beliefs are not maintained by all. The boundaries of the old community are, however, no longer so significant socially, and since they are not religiously sanctified, the new community quickly ignores tribal limitations, and comes to do so explicitly in some cases. Ethnicity replaced tribal, linguistic, or cultural unity, as increased mobility occurred between tribes, and as the reservation system and the wars brought an increase in peaceful inter-tribal intercourse. A new conception of a religious in-group emerges: its boundaries within the ethnic group are sometimes vague, particularly at the beginning, but the ethnic group defines the limits of its application. Increasingly, over time, voluntary adhesion comes to define the membership. The ethnic group becomes the constituency from which some elect to participate in their faith. Those within the faith create their own internal hierarchy, which necessarily reflects the degree of acquaintance with ritual and belief. The faith for all natives steadily becomes the faith of some natives, and comes to stand over against other voluntaristic expressions of native solidarity (as the Powwow people disapproved of the Peyotists; or the Ringatu believers came to believe that Te Kooti's prophecies were a warning against Ratana). Only a minority of the native community is drawn to the new faith that seeks to preserve the native way of life, and over time they find themselves in opposition both to other introversionist faiths, and to indigenes who either cling to the past and seek to restore it, or who seek to become acculturated to the dominant white culture.

What, then, the introversionist religions offer, is an accommodation to the present. They are sometimes seen as conservatives (just as the millennialists might be seen as reactionaries who seek to restore what has gone) but they seek to conserve only a range of elements of the received tradition, and often embrace entirely new revelations and new forms within which to accomplish the preservation of this separate way of life. Their innovations are, however, essentially supernaturalist, and not political or economic, and thus they stand in sharp contrast to those natives, usually called 'progressives', who seek to participate in the dominant white culture by accepting its values and its rationality, or who rebel against it in essentially similar (but ethnic or racist) terms.

The community that the introversionists preserve is in fact a new community, a community which increasingly has voluntary choice as its basis, even though it continues to speak for 'the native way'. Their apartness, not only from the white culture, but also from fellow natives who stand outside their faith, becomes more manifest. Voluntary allegiances replace tribal distinctions as the basis of new divisions, socializing men to divergent conceptions of the world, and focusing on different preoccupations. They distribute new roles, and find functions even for the women who once had so much less a part in religious activities. Religion becomes the primary badge of identification, establishing distinctions within the ethnic group, and it is appropriate that all should be able to wear such a badge. Whatever the style of the introversionist movements, whether they are intellectual and orderly like the Ringatu Church and Gai'wiio', or expressive and somewhat ecstatic like the Powwow, or reflective and withdrawn like the Peyote cult, they become the potential expression of new and distinctive communities. Such communities do not always emerge from introversionist movements, although there are some evidences of separatism along religious lines. The religious orientation is not always strong enough to establish clear boundaries based on voluntary commitment to replace the ascriptively-based social boundaries of the past. In everyday life devotees do not effectively withdraw from their fellow tribesmen or their ethnic group. Material circumstances do not always admit such withdrawal—although, and the case is marked especially in the Peyote cult, distinctive religious allegiance may at times create frictions even if it is not strong enough, or lacks the opportunity, to

establish real divisions.⁶² In other cases the semi-introversionist movement becomes a tolerated expression of the separate way of life. Among
minority peoples even to express such distinctiveness may demand too
much effort in face of hopelessness, demoralization, and the pressures
of acculturation.

⁶² The divisive effects of introversionist religious movements have been reported in a
number of cases, particularly of Peyotism, the best documented and most widely diffused
introversionist sect among a less-developed people. J. A. Jones, 'The Sun Dance of the
Northern Ute', Smithsonian Institution: Bureau of American Ethnology, Bulletin 157,
Anthropological Papers No. 47 (1955), pp. 203–63, wrote (p. 232), 'Today, on the Unitah and
Ouray Reservation, peyote is taken by most of the fullblood Ute in weekly ceremonies. It has
become a year-round integrating factor for those who identify themselves with Indian
culture, and according to administrative officials is the biggest stumbling block to a real
integration of the whole people that exists today.' It causes factionalism because the ruling
clique, who are mainly halfbloods, do not generally become Peyotists. Among the Pueblo
Indians at Taos, New Mexico, Peyote was originally seen as an innovative cult, opposed by
conservatives. It produced schisms and factions in the pueblo, particularly because it represented inter-tribalism, which, in a society with relatively unimpaired social organization, was
resented. Later the Peyotists moved into leading positions in the pueblo, although they were
only a minority (50–70 cultists in a community of over 900 people). William N. Fenton,
'Factionalism at Taos Pueblo, New Mexico', Smithsonian Institution: Bureau of American
Ethnology, Bulletin 164, *Anthropological Papers* No. 56 (1957), pp. 297–344.

13

The Peyote Cult—An Introversionist Movement?

INTROVERSIONIST religions respond to the world by withdrawing from it. The world is alien and irredeemable. The sectarians can do nothing for it, worldly men will do nothing and God has already fore-ordained history. All that good men can do is to gain salvation by leaving the world and cleaving to God. The faith takes man out of the world into a private realm, a protective community, insulated from the tensions of life in the wider society. In western Christendom this response has been made effective by severe ethical injunctions against association with the world, by strong avoidance regulations, sometimes reinforced by vicinal segregation and withdrawal into closed communities. Lacking the strength of rigorous socialization and the internalization of puritanical moral rules, such as has been the inheritance of many Christian groups, and usually without the opportunity to remove themselves to a new social context, new religious communities among less-developed peoples use the distinctiveness of their rites as an insulation from the world. Drugs are not infrequently one means of withdrawal, and their use as stimulants, sedatives, or hallucinogens is found in various religious movements (the Ras Tafarian use of marijuana, and the Bwiti use of ibiota, are examples). In the *Peyote* cult, the principal object of ritual, and virtually of devotion, is the small cactus button (*Lophophora williamsii* Lamaire) from the consumption of which the movement takes its name.

The exact properties of peyote, a succulent turnip-like cactus from which the tops are used, and which grows in southern Texas and northern Mexico, have been disputed.[1] The drug is not addictive, but

[1] Peyote was originally thought to be a narcotic drug and an intoxicant, with harmful properties: Robert E. L. Newberne and Charles H. Burke, *Peyote: An abridged compilation from the files of the Bureau of Indian Affairs* (Haskell Institute, Lawrence, Kansas, 1925). These opinions have subsequently been modified. In mature plants there are nine alkaloids and both strychnine-like and morphine-like properties which are somewhat antagonistic in action, according to Omer C. Stewart, 'Washo-Paiute Peyotism. A Study in Acculturation', *University of California Publications in American Archaeology and Ethnology* 40, 3 (1944), pp. vi and 63–142 (p. 63). For an account of recent research on the pharmacological aspects of peyote, and on its medical and psychiatric aspects, see Weston La Barre, 'Twenty Years of Peyote Studies', *Current Anthropology* 1, 1 (January 1960), pp. 45–60. For a discussion see Caroll G. Barber, 'Peyote and the Definition of a Narcotic', *American Anthropologist* 61 (1959), pp. 641–5, and the correspondence that followed, ibid., 62 (August 1960), pp. 684–9.

even the extent to which it stimulates visions is a matter of disagreement, although many who partake of it certainly obtain visions, and not always of a reassuring kind.[2] It can cause nausea and headaches, and the vomiting associated with it is often regarded as a form of purification—an interpretation found in other North American Indian movements. Exhilaration, greater mental capacity, and a sense of well-being are commonly attributed to it.[3] It was used in some tribes before the development of an actual Peyote cult, but its dissemination through the Plains to many quite remote Indian societies has been essentially as a religious movement, in which the attributes of the cactus buttons themselves are perhaps less important than the cultural meaning which their ritual use has acquired.

Religious activity centring on the peyote button was observed among the Indians by the Spanish invaders of Mexico from the sixteenth century, when it was perhaps a relatively minor cult.[4] The Apache probably used it for cultic purposes in the 1770s, but the spread of Peyotism among North American Indians did not occur until the last quarter of the nineteenth century.[5] The exact course of its diffusion, the conditions which prompted it, and the extent to which even in its early days it was christianized, are subjects on which investigators have disagreed.[6] The ritual use of peyote, although without the important elements of Plains culture which subsequently came to distinguish the cult, may have spread from the Carrizo to the Lipan Apache in the Galveston–Houston area of Texas in the early nineteenth century.[7] Some important elements of later cult practice—the acquisition of

[2] Ruth Shonle, 'Peyote, Giver of Visions', *American Anthropologist* 27, 1 (January–March 1925), pp. 53–75, emphasized the continuities of Peyote practice with the vision-quest of the Plains cultures. She cites the case of John Rave, the Winnebago Peyotist innovator (see below), as an instance of a man who, at first, acquired fearful visions from peyote.

[3] These are the general attributes referred to by Vincenzo Petrullo, *The Diabolical Root, A Study of Peyotism, the new Indian Religion among the Delawares* (University of Pennsylvania Press, Philadelphia 1934), pp. 6–7.

[4] O. C. Stewart, op. cit., pp. 63, 64; V. Petrullo, op. cit., p. 15.

[5] O. C. Stewart, op. cit., p. 64.

[6] The differences are between M. E. Opler, W. La Barre (who largely agree about the early history of Peyote), J. S. Slotkin, and O. C. Stewart. Opler and La Barre give *the cult* a longer history than does Slotkin, who thinks that the Peyote religion was invented in the second half of the nineteenth century in the Gulf, South-west, or Southern Plains: J. S. Slotkin, *The Peyote Religion* (Free Press, Glencoe, Illinois, 1956), p. 32. O. C. Stewart, op. cit., has emphasized the therapeutic aspects of Peyotism as against the sociological theories of acculturation. He has also argued, in *Ute Peyotism: A Study of a Cultural Complex*, University of Colorado Studies: Series in Anthropology, No. 1 (University of Colorado Press, Boulder, Colorado, 1948), that the Christian elements of Peyotism were not late accretions to the cult, but were primary and integral to it. This view is rejected by W. La Barre, op. cit.

[7] This view, and the evidence for it, is offered in Morris E. Opler, 'The Use of Peyote by the Carrizo and Lipan Apache Tribes', *American Anthropologist* 40, 2 (April–June 1938), pp. 271–85.

visions, the passing of the drum and rattle among the participants as they sang, and the ceremonial breakfast—were in evidence then. But the use of the mound for an altar, and of the whistle and the feathers, and the appearance of the morning woman with water, were not yet part of the cult as the Lipan Apache knew it.

A generally similar ceremony to that which came into being among Plains Indians apparently occurred among the Mescalero Apache, who performed it from about 1870 until about 1910, although it was 'maintained entirely within the traditional bounds of Apache ceremonalism'.[8] This practice was without Christian elements, and appeared rather as 'an intensification of aboriginal religious values and concepts at many points'.[9] Peyote was used as an agency conferring power, and in this respect it was typical of Indian supernatural concerns. Power came in dreams, and was associated with a revealed ceremony, and with songs that came from the same supernatural source, and peyote was used in the same way. But among the Mescalero, who were 'a tribe of shamans', Peyotism never became a cult or a society with regular members and officers: the ceremony still belonged to the shaman, and even though it was also a co-operative effort, particularly in its use as a curative agency, it was also a demonstration of power. In this context, Peyotism became a new shamanistic practice. Among the Lipan, masked dancers were not admitted to Peyote meetings, perhaps reflecting the rivalry between practitioners of the new magic and of the old. Since the intrusion of the whites had gradually prevented Mescalero assertion of prowess against other tribes in war, rivalries among shamans may have been accentuated in the first period of reservation life, and Peyote, as the new way of power, became an important shamanistic weapon.

The search for power was particularly acute in a tribe with so emphatic a shamanistic tradition as the Mescalero, but this search for inspiration, protection, and salvation was part of a widely diffused cultural response among North American Indian tribes. It was an orientation to which, as it was diffused and as it evolved, the Peyote cult was admirably suited, since it accommodated both the individual search for a vision, and the need for Indians to draw together, to combine their power, and to express their solidarity in the face of the dominant and powerful intrusion of the white men. It was a new reassertion of the Indian way, but it was also an adaptation of it to

[8] M. E. Opler, 'The Influence of Aboriginal Pattern and White Contact in a Recently Introduced Ceremony, The Mescalero Peyote Rite', *Journal of American Folklore* 49 (January 1936), pp. 143–66 (p. 144).
[9] Loc. cit. This paragraph relies entirely on Opler.

new conditions. The old visions—of prowess in the war, or in the hunt, or protective medicines, or success in the competitive search for prestige—were increasingly rendered meaningless in the 1880s by the imposed peace of the white men and the disappearance of the buffalo and other game. What new dreams might Indians seek? What was now the way of salvation? When the objective circumstances which gave fantasies their necessary plausibility had been destroyed, the pleasure of old dreams was also destroyed. Perhaps all men need to dream, and feel the need particularly when their life circumstances have been profoundly disrupted. Plains Indian cultures had institutionalized dreaming, but the culturally prescribed content of dreams was now not only irrelevant but positively traumatic. Circumstances scarcely provided new cultural content for dreaming now that the active attempts to dance into being the Indian past had failed. And the individual was scarcely capable of finding an occasion for establishing the importance of dreams. Peyote sustained the significance of dreams, and provided occasions for them, even if their content was less readily described than the spiritual reassurance that they provided. Whereas visions had once transmitted the received values of the culture with specific injunctions for acting them out in everyday life, now the reassuring effect of being in the context of spiritual power had to suffice, whether visions as such were precise or vague.

For a time, dreams of the past and of its restoration were enough. The most vigorous dreamers, the creative dreamers or their imitators, could communicate such a vision to a tribe or to several tribes, and stimulate new patterns of acting out the ceremonial of the dream to bring the past back into being. Such dreams, especially where conditions were rapidly changing, led to ecstatic and urgent action. Where groups could insulate themselves and could perpetuate the past in some measure, they tended, as with Smohalla, to quietistic millennialism. The more ecstatic exercises failed for the majority of Indians, who could not enjoy the freedom of remote regions as did Smohalla and the Wanapums, and then the attempt to preserve 'the Indian way' replaced failed dreams of the restoration of the past. Conditions were now more collectively experienced, and although the dreams were still individual they were no longer lone quests for visions: visions now affirmed the need of shared experience and shared response. Dreaming both symbolized withdrawal from the world of white men, and was its realization. Peyote was the agency through which such introversion could be manifested.

The beginnings of the cult: ritual, myth, and ethic

The adoption of peyote by various tribes occurred over several decades from the 1870s onwards. It was not an entirely new thing for Indians to employ a drug-bearing plant as a focus of ritual. They were acquainted, of course, with numerous herbal remedies as the focus of a good deal of shamanistic practice. Among Plains Indians there were mescal-bean societies, which thrived before the introduction of peyote, although they were not of great antiquity. The bean (*Sophora secundiflora*) was not in itself an object of worship, but the medicine societies which had grown up about its use, had their own dances, medicine bundles, and paraphernalia.[10] It seems unlikely that the rituals employed were themselves influential in the development of the Peyote cult, but peyote, like the mescal bean before it, 'was fitted into the prevailing ceremonial patterns of Plains culture'.[11] But at least, the idea was established of making a new power, derived from a plant, into an object of ceremonial attention.

The exact evolution of the central characteristics of the Peyote cult cannot now be traced, although numerous innovations have been recorded, and the cult leaders responsible for them are known. The cult acquired new characteristics as it spread, and some ritual items fell into desuetude as the cult was disseminated from one tribe to another. Time, too, played its part; certain features (for example the permission for women to be present) occurred with increasing frequency among those tribes that received the cult at later dates.

Peyote was known both in Mexico and among some Plains peoples as a therapeutic agent and as a power useful, for example, as a protector in war long before the cult itself evolved. It was kept in the war bundles of some tribes—the Comanches and the Shawnees.[12] It was used individually to obtain revelations, and perhaps to induce a trance state before a dance.[13] The pattern of activities which became the ritual of the Peyote cult appears to have evolved, perhaps in the 1870s. The Kiowa and Comanches were two of the first tribes among whom the cult was observed, and among the latter it is thought to have begun

[10] W. La Barre, *The Peyote Cult* (The Shoe String Press, Hamden, Conn., 1964), p. 7, considers that the use of the mescal bean facilitated the introduction of the Peyote cult at a later date. This point is somewhat disputed by Rudolf C. Troike, in 'The Origins of Plains Mescalism', *American Anthropologist* 64, 5:1 (1962), pp. 946–63, on which this paragraph largely relies.

[11] Ibid., p. 961.

[12] W. La Barre, op. cit., p. 26.

[13] J. S. Slotkin, op. cit., p. 32.

about 1875.[14] The Kiowa experienced two late millennialist outbursts in the 1880s, one under Buffalo-Bull-Coming-Out in 1881–2, and another, in 1887–8, under Baigya. These movements were essentially similar to many others, with a dance and ceremony, the promise of the return of the buffalo, and the threat of resistance to whites. A whirlwind would come to destroy white men and all their works, and a group known as the *Sons of the Sun* arose to promulgate these teachings. This group was strongly opposed to Peyotism, which they regarded as being at enmity with the ten medicine bundles of the tribe. After the failure of the millennial hope, Lone Bear and some others among the Sons of the Sun themselves turned to the Peyote cult and became staunch peyote-users.[15] The conservatives thus accepted the new religion when their own medicine had proved to be inadequate: the millennial response was replaced by the introversionist religion, and the millennialists themselves assumed a new response to the world.

The Kiowa and the Comanches became early adepts of the new faith, and Quanah Parker, the great Comanche chief, who finally led his people into the reservation after long resistance, himself turned to Peyotism after it had cured him of an illness.[16] From Oklahoma, where these tribes were settled in this period, Peyotism was steadily diffused to other tribes of the Plains. The Comanches, too, had had their recent experience of millennialism under the prophet Ishatai ('Coyote Droppings'). 'Until their collapse and the failure of their venture with Coyote Droppings there was no functional reason for them to rely on a drug as the means to supernatural power, although they had access to it, and, indeed, had used it in a limited way for some time.'[17] Peyotism symbolized withdrawal and the search for a different type of life from that which had so manifestly failed in the struggle with the white man.

The essential characteristics of the Peyote rite may be broadly described without regard to the more or less minor variations in practice among various tribes.[18] The basic ritual of the all-night meeting took place in a tipi around a crescent-shaped earthen mound (a moon) and a ceremonially built fire. A special drum, gourd rattle, and carved staff were passed around as the ritual for singing. The occasion for a meeting was usually to procure a healing, to allay troubles, to ensure

[14] This is the date given by Ernest Wallace and E. Adamson Hoebel, *The Comanches* (University of Oklahoma Press, Norman 1952), p. 332. The date of 1890 given by R. Shonle, op. cit., is now generally recognized as too late.

[15] W. La Barre, op. cit., p. 112.

[16] Loc. cit.

[17] E. Wallace and E. A. Hoebel, op. cit., p. 332.

[18] There are many detailed accounts of Peyote cult meetings, with specific regard to differences of paraphernalia, ritual, and symbolism. I have drawn this account principally from W. La Barre, op. cit., pp. 43–52; and V. Petrullo, op. cit., pp. 48 ff.

welfare, or to show hospitality and goodwill to friends. Special meetings might celebrate the first four birthdays of a child, and in more recent times public holidays have also been occasions for the practice of the cult. Meetings were sponsored, and the sponsor, who usually had a particular purpose in organizing the meeting, paid for it and supplied the peyote. He chose the road-chief, or leader, who would supply the paraphernalia to be used. Other officers were the fire chief, who tended the fire and lit the pipes, the drummer, and (possibly) the cedar chief. Ceremonial dress used to be usual, and some older participants used to paint their faces. Meetings were once confined to old men and warriors, but in later years some tribes allowed women to be present, though not usually to participate. The meeting largely consisted of singing, prayer, and the consumption of peyote. Set songs were often used for opening and closing the meeting, which continued through the night (in many cases in a tipi). Silent prayer, which might be directed to the earth-creator or to a more christianized conception of God, and smoking were followed by an intense blessing ceremony. All participants were expected to eat (usually four) peyote buttons, and they might subsequently consume more during the night.

As soon as peyote had been consumed, the principal ritual of passing of the staff and drum from person to person, in strict order and often with elaborate and precise procedures, would commence. Each person would sing four songs as the staff came to him, with a friend who would drum for him. At midnight cedar wood would be put on the fire for a blessing to be obtained from its smoke, accompanied by a midnight song. Water was brought at this time and a number of ritual acts were performed, before the meeting resumed its pattern of singing until dawn, when water was again brought, this time by a woman. The leader then sang four morning songs and sometimes followed this with instruction, particularly for any younger persons who were present. Afterwards the company would close the meeting and partake of a morning meal which the women had prepared. General social intercourse might be followed by another meal at noon.

Both a myth and an ethic are associated with the Peyote ritual. The myth, which varies somewhat from tribe to tribe, everywhere embraces broadly similar elements. As known among the Kiowa, one of the earliest tribes to have the Peyote cult, the myth described how an Indian girl, who had gone to the hills to bewail the absence and presumed death of her brothers, lost her way and, worn out with grief, lay down to sleep. In her dreams the peyote spirit visited her and promised that her brothers should be found, and that where her head rested she would find that which would restore them to her. The spirit gave further instructions and vanished. Next day, she dug up the peyote which she found where her head had rested, and returned to her camp with the plant and the story of her vision. Under her direction the sacred tipi was set up with its crescent mound. Songs were sung, prayers said, and peyote was eaten, and in their visions the old men saw where the lost warriors were wandering. The warriors were recovered from the enemy country, and since then 'peyote is eaten by the Indians with song and prayer that they may see visions and know inspiration, and the young girl who first gave it is venerated as the Peyote woman'.[19] The spirit of peyote was sometimes identified with Christ.[20] Thereafter, for believers peyote became something uniquely given to Indians for sustenance, healing, and spiritual inspiration. It became the symbol of the Indian approach to the divine, and the provider of the visions so important in traditional Indian religion.

The ethic of the Peyote cult shared much with that of other introversionist movements, which frequently arise from inspirationalism. Since inspiration is not available to everyone, the good life can ultimately be known only to those whose hearts or minds have been charged with the divine power. This strong pietistic current found a parallel in the Peyote cult. Only from eating peyote could wisdom be acquired. It could not be described or revealed, because it surpassed the power of words to communicate. Peyote was the teacher, just as for Smohalla dreams had been the teacher.[21] The holy 'in-group' following the Peyote Road was essentially a group enjoying a mystic bond. Outsiders could not penetrate its mysteries or understand its meaning. But there are other ethical implications which hold in bounds any possible antinomianism which might arise—as it so often does in

[19] This account follows James Mooney, 'The Kiowa Peyote Rite', *Der Urquell*, N.S., 1 (1897), pp. 329-33. Cited in J. S. Slotkin, op. cit., pp. 22-3. This myth may be compared with that of the origin of the Powwow religion, see pp. 405-6.

[20] This appears to be particularly often the case with tribes who were late in receiving the cult, or who had been subject to considerable acculturation and Christian missioning before the adoption of Peyote—for example the Menomini, among whom Christ was sometimes portrayed as the bringer of peyote, according to J. S. Slotkin 'Menomini Peyotism: A Study of Individual Variation in a Primary Group with a Homogeneous Culture', *Transactions of the American Philosophical Society*, N.S., 42, Part 4 (December 1952), pp. 565-600 (p. 573). John Wilson, the leading innovator among the Delaware Indians, taught that the cup of water that was used in the cult symbolized the blood of Christ. Christian elements were sometimes present in other relatively early versions of the cult. Victor Griffin, a Quapaw, who amended the styles of altar employed, and who embraced specific Christian elements, rejected peyote as a medicine and proclaimed it to be the first step in the seven paces taken by Jesus to reach the Father: V. Petrullo, op. cit., pp. 97 ff., 109.

[21] This need to participate in order to understand was frequently asserted: see, for example, J. S. Slotkin, 'Menomini Peyotism . . .', op. cit., p. 571, who refers specifically to the doctrine and rites; and V. Petrullo, to whom his Delaware informants stressed that peyote itself was the teaching—Indians should not be asked about it, peyote should be asked (op. cit., pp. v, 89).

pietistic religion. Peyote was said by some to be 'tricky' to use. It was, after all, a source of power, and a man must lead a straight life or peyote would shame him. It was not easy to eat, and there was sometimes a suggestion that to get wisdom men must be prepared to suffer. The meetings thus had some connotation of the ordeal and the proof of worthiness. It could bring bad consequences for the guilty.[22]

Peyote itself was held to teach men an ethical system, the Peyote Road. Brotherly love, care of the family, self-reliance, and the avoidance of alcohol (this last being almost a universal injunction of all new religious movements among North American Indians). The Road would lead to bliss in the next life as well as to material well-being, health, long life, and tranquillity in this one.[23] In some contexts, at least, Peyote exhorted love, hope and charity, ambition and honesty, as things necessary for a man to lead a happy life. The visions were held to reward and punish past actions, and to reveal to the faithful all the knowledge that they needed in life.[24] Among the Southern Utes and the Gosiutes, where large proportions of the people were involved in the cult, it exercised functions of social control, and even provided a degree of political cohesion, although this appears to have been an incidental function rather than a prescription deriving from cult ethics.[25]

Diffusion and innovation

The diffusion of the Peyote cult took place after many tribes had been moved to reservations, and had begun a new way of life, living in peaceful association with other Indians, and in dependence upon, and subjection to, the white man. It reflected these changed circumstances, and its diffusion was facilitated by, and was an adjustment to, the new inter-tribal character of Indian life. The Kiowa, Comanche, and Wichita reservation was the centre from which the cult spread over the Plains, facilitated by inter-tribal visiting, the division of one tribe between reservations (which was common), and the contacts

[22] W. La Barre, op. cit., pp. 94–7.
[23] These are the features mentioned by J. S. Slotkin, *The Peyote Religion*, op. cit., pp. 70–1. They are given in much the same form for Peyotism among the Navaho, David F. Aberle, *The Peyote Religion Among the Navaho* (Aldine, Chicago 1966), p. 13.
[24] These characteristics are given for Peyotism among the Washo and Paiutes by O. C. Stewart, 'Washo-Paiute Peyotism . . .', op. cit., p. 65.
[25] Marvin K. Opler, 'The Character and History of the Southern Ute Peyote Rite', *American Anthropologist* 42 (July–September 1940), pp. 463–78; and Carling Malouf, 'Gosiute Peyotism', *American Anthropologist* 44, 1 (January–March 1942), pp. 93–103.

being formed in the new Indian boarding-schools, which together created a complex pattern of contemporaneous and successive lines of communication about Peyote. Some prestige attached to tribes who had the cult earlier, and visiting in order to learn the ritual and teaching of prominent exponents led to the common circumstance of Peyote meetings being celebrated by groups comprising men of more than one tribe. The cult, which is known to have been practised in sixteen tribes before the end of the nineteenth century and which was found in sixty-one by 1955, became a vehicle for the expression of the new sense of identity as 'Indian'.[26]

A number of active missionaries of Peyotism are well known. Some of them were also innovators, who added their distinctive teachings to the cult, and acquired followings of their own within the broad and tolerant boundaries of Peyotism. One of these was John Wilson, the half-Delaware, part-French, and part-Caddo, who among the Delaware became for a time in 1890 a prominent enthusiast of the Ghost Dance, and who was one of the first to go into the trance during the Caddo Ghost Dance. John Wilson was obviously a religious innovator who had been a healer and who had also known the older mescalin rites.[27] He claimed, on learning of peyote, to have sought visions and to have been guided by the peyote spirit itself to establish a new variant of the ritual as it had come from the Kiowa and Comanche. He took the name Moonhead, from the 'Big Moon' form of earth-mound altar which, in the 1890s, he introduced among the Delawares, and which he set in opposition to the 'little moon' tradition, which was defended by Elk Hair, a conservative figure who had been a champion of the old Delaware religious practices, which were increasingly difficult to perform in the impoverished conditions of the reservation.[28] John Wilson 'claimed that he alone, or such men as he appointed, had the power to build the Moonhead or Big Moon shrine, and that these leaders in turn had the power to confer the right of building Moons upon others'.[29] He had been influenced by Roman Catholics at an earlier time, and he introduced (or emphasized) Christian elements in the cult, and claimed association with Christ in the visions that he had, but he taught the Indians to look for Christ through Peyote and not in the Bible, which was for whites.

Like many Indian religious innovators, John Wilson took a fee for introducing others to his spirit-given secrets, and for passing on the

[26] This paragraph, and the one following, rely principally on W. La Barre, op. cit.; V. Petrullo, op. cit.; J. S. Slotkin, *The Peyote Religion*, op. cit.

[27] W. La Barre, op. cit., pp. 151–61.

[28] V. Petrullo, op. cit., pp. 32–46.

[29] Ibid., p. 44.

power to build the altars of his vision. He acquired considerable fame among various other tribes, and spread his version of the cult to the Caddo, Wichita, Osage, and Quapaw, and received gifts from them for his ritual performances. The pattern of ceremonial that he promoted appears also to have influenced Peyotism among the Kickapoo, Omaha, and Potawatomi. He was the living embodiment of an almost professional prophet who ranged through a variety of available religious ideologies and practices, becoming prominent in each. He had espoused the Ghost Dance, but subsequently adopted (or returned to?) Peyotism, in each case anticipating, and perhaps also stimulating, the widespread adoption of these patterns of religious response.[30]

The new cult spread rapidly, acquiring minor accretions and accommodating itself to the divergent experience and degree of acculturation of different groups. The Winnebago, half of whom had been removed from their ancestral territory in Wisconsin to Nebraska, acquired Peyote relatively early. The man who introduced it, John Rave, had been a wanderer, who met the peyote-eaters in 1893-4 in Oklahoma. Rave had been a drinker, had 'married many times', and had been abroad with a circus, when he was introduced to the Peyote religion.[31] He had sought a vision in childhood, after the traditional pattern, but had never received one, and thus he had never become a member of the most important society of the medicine rite. His later experience, and the unhappiness of his people in Nebraska, produced a man curiously torn between two cultures. Initially, he was passive about traditional practices, but, as an illiterate, he could not very strongly identify with the white culture. Peyote came to him at a time of crisis and healed him of a disease, which appears to have been a typical psychological malaise—a strong sense of alienation with suicidal and homicidal tendencies. His early visions under the influence of peyote reflected the anguish of his mind: he saw snakes, and experienced aggression and fear of death before he received a vision of God. Rave then became a firm adherent and proselytizer of the cult. He appears 'to have come to the conclusion that the whole Winnebago heritage was an obstacle in their rehabilitation, and must therefore be abandoned'.[32] Peyotism was a new source of inspiration.

[30] W. La Barre, op. cit., p. 153, says 'Gradually . . . Wilson turned from the Ghost Dance to peyote'. William W. Newcomb, Jr, 'The Peyote Cult of the Delaware Indians', *The Texas Journal of Science* XVIII, 2 (June 1956), pp. 202–11, says that John Wilson became a Peyotist about 1880—ten years before the Ghost Dance. This is not necessarily incompatible with La Barre's statement: Wilson might have become a *prominent* Peyotist only after the Ghost Dance, even if he knew the rite before.

[31] This and the following paragraph are drawn from Paul Radin, 'Religious Experiences of an American Indian', *Eranos-Jahrbuch* XVIII (Sonderband), Zürich (1950), pp. 249–90.

[32] Ibid., p. 283.

Through peyote, Rave became known as a healer. His ethical prescriptions were similar to those of the traditional culture—the condemnation of evil, gambling, conceit, selfishness. To them was added avoidance of alcohol, and—this was a rejection of the spiritual agencies of the past—tobacco. Originally, he did not 'think of God, either the Christian God or the old Winnebago earthmaker, as the source of his life and dispensation, or as responsible for his recognition of the holy'.[33] It came simply from peyote itself. His success was considerable, and in seventeen years he had converted half the Winnebago people to Peyote. Another innovator had, in the meantime, come to change the character of Winnebago Peyotism, and this in the direction of Christianity. Albert Hensley introduced the Bible: the New Testament was used and the Trinity was referred to, and a form of baptism was accepted (John Rave would dip his hand into an infusion of peyote and rub it on the forehead of the new member 'in the name of God, the Son and the Holy Ghost, which is called God's holiness').[34] Hensley taught that peyote opened the Bible to the Indian, and Rave, although passive about these ideas, added them to the Peyote cult. Subsequently, Hensley quarrelled with Rave, after Rave, who was the leading Peyotist among the Winnebago, permitted a man of bad character to occupy one of the leading ritual positions. Rave took a position similar to that of the early Catholic church in asserting that 'the efficacy of the peyote, and of any position connected with its cult, was in no way connected with the character of the performer, and that it was inherent in the peyote and the peyote ritual'.[35]

The spread of Peyotism continued through a variety of agencies: sometimes there were men who sought to make money and gain prestige from the introduction of a new rite; sometimes kinship, friendship, and marriage were the agencies of diffusion.[36] By 1960, it was said to be 'the

[33] Ibid., p. 286.
[34] P. Radin, 'A Sketch of the Peyote Cult of the Winnebago: A Study in Borrowing', *Journal of Religious Psychology* 7, 1 (January 1914), pp. 1–22 (p. 5).
[35] Ibid., p. 11.
[36] W. La Barre, op. cit., mentions John Wilson and the Quapaw, Victor Griffin, as such, pp. 64–5; Ben Lancaster, among the Washo and Northern Paiutes, was another: W. La Barre, 'Twenty Years of Peyote Studies', op. cit., p. 53. An instance of the importance of kinship ties is revealed in P. Radin, 'The Autobiography of a Winnebago Indian', *University of California Publications in American Archaeology and Ethnology* 16, 7 (15 April 1920), pp. 381–473. (This work was published later, with supplementary materials, as *Crashing Thunder* [New York 1926].) The Indian concerned, S.B., went to a Peyote meeting and experienced a black-out. Although he was not entirely convinced, he sought to please his sister and brother-in-law, who were ardent enthusiasts of the christianized form of Winnebago Peyotism. They showed him a passage in the Bible which said that it was a shame for a man to wear his hair long (in traditional Indian fashion). He described his reaction: 'I looked at the passage. I was not a man learned in books, but I wanted to give the impression that I knew how to read, so I told them to cut my hair. . . . After my hair was cut I took out a lot of medicine that I

major religious cult of most Indians of the United States between the Rocky Mountains and the Mississippi . . . and additionally in parts of southern Canada, the Great Basin and east-central California'.[37] Within two years of its introduction among the Washo-Paiute, around Lake Tahoe in California and Nevada, in the late 1930s, it had spread to fourteen communities.[38] It had been introduced to the Northern Ute by the Oglala Sioux, Samuel Lone Bear (also known as Roan Bear, Loganberry, Pete Phelps, and Cactus Pete) between 1908 and 1916, and to the Southern Ute between 1914 and 1916. The Towaoc Utes were the principal contact for Navaho who picked up knowledge of peyote from working as herdsmen among the Utes, or from going to school with them, and, perhaps most especially, from the Navaho habit of using Ute shamans to deal with witchcraft illnesses. The Navaho probably became most extensively acquainted with it during the period when the government ran camps to provide employment for them and the Utes in the period from 1933 to 1942.[39] 'In 1951 Navaho Peyotists numbered between 12,000 and 14,000 in a population of about 70,000 Navaho. The cult has membership as high as three fourths of the population of some northern communities . . . but is known only by reputation in some communities in the northwestern reservation.'[40]

Peyotism as an introversionist mutation

The Peyote cult did not spread so rapidly among Indians as the 1890 Ghost Dance, but its message, being essentially quietistic, had less drama and less urgency than the Ghost Dance. There were fewer sanctions against non-believers in an introversionist religion, since less was lost by abstention. At the same time, Peyotism was more willingly

---

happened to have in my pockets. These were courting medicines. There were many small bundles of them. All these, together with my hair, I gave to my brother-in-law. Then I cried and my brother-in-law also cried. Then he thanked me. He told me that I had understood, and that I had done well' (pp. 438–9). He was still not convinced and had acted, on his own admission, only to please his brother-in-law, but subsequently he acquired visions at Peyote meetings, and then was converted. The instance illustrates both the importance of kinship in disseminating the cult and also the emotional significance of the surrender of the old and acceptance of the new.

[37] W. La Barre, 'Twenty Years . . .', op. cit., p. 45.
[38] O. C. Stewart, 'Washo-Paiute Peyotism . . .', op. cit., p. 77.
[39] D. F. Aberle and O. C. Stewart, *Navaho and Ute Peyotism: A Chronological and Distributional Study*, University of Colorado Studies: Series in Anthropology, No. 6 (University of Colorado Press, Boulder, Colorado, 1957), pp. 5, 25, 33 ff.
[40] Ibid., p. 25. More than 35 per cent of the Navaho were Peyotists by 1964, according to D. F. Aberle, *The Peyote Religion . . .*, op. cit., p. 125.

diffused than introversionist religions in the Christian tradition, since its eligible constituency was the entire Indian people: its introversion was not only of self-selected converts, but potentially of the entire ethnic group. If it spread less rapidly than the Ghost Dance, once it did so it showed far greater persistence. In some tribes Peyotism eventually declined, but in others it has retained its hold, and increased its numbers. It is noticeable that its principal areas of early diffusion were the Plains, and some of its converts, Frank White, the Pawnee, and John Wilson being the most conspicuous, were men who had been leaders in the Ghost Dance.

Although the spread of Peyotism has continued to the present time, the beginnings of its dissemination were in the period of the Ghost Dance itself. Mooney believed that it spread rapidly after the Ghost Dance lost its impetus,[41] and others, though uncertain about the extent to which the new cult was a substitute for the old, acknowledge that it 'diffused rapidly around the turn of the century'.[42] La Barre wrote, 'In the Plains, peyotism largely followed the Ghost Dance frustrations of anti-White sentiment and preached conciliation instead. . . '.[43] The Ghost Dance provided the occasion for many inter-tribal contacts, eliminating in its urgency differences and divisions that might normally have prevented swift cultural diffusion from one tribe to another. In some respects it opened the way for Peyote, which, however, being less urgent, encountered considerably more conservative resistance in many cases. The Ghost Dance was the catalyst, and Peyote was a recognition of the weakness of the Indian in changing circumstances, from which he could do no more than withdraw. Thus

> . . . as with the Shawnee and others, Pawnee peyotism was early involved in the Ghost Dance excitement. The leader claimed from peyote the same sort of revelations acquired in the Ghost Dance, and taught that while under the influence of peyote one could learn the rituals belonging to the bundles and the societies. One usual Pawnee feature was the use of the special Ghost Dance form of painted tipi for peyote meetings. . . .[44]

Just as the Ghost Dance led to the revival of the old games among the Pawnee, so it also facilitated the emergence of the new cult, with Frank White, once the dominant *owner* of the Ghost Dance among the Pawnee, as the principal adept of Peyote. The idea that peyote might restore the lost knowledge of the medicine bundles in itself illustrates the concern with revitalization of the past, although the new cult was,

[41] James Mooney, statement to US Congress House, Committee on Indian Affairs, 1918, pp. 67–74, cited in J. S. Slotkin, *The Peyote Religion*, op. cit., p. 35.
[42] Ibid.
[43] W. La Barre, *The Peyote Cult*, op. cit., p. 43 n.
[44] Ibid., pp. 118–9.

by contrast with the hand games, distinctly introversionist, and Lesser somewhat disparagingly characterizes it as 'a religion of sleep and forgetfulness, an inactive and slothful attempt to avoid the issues of life'.[45]

The Ghost Dance was one distinctive response to a rapidly changing socio-cultural situation—the response of despair converted by fantasy into ecstatic hope. Peyotism, it has been suggested, represented an alternative accommodation.[46] Whatever culture contact they had previously experienced, the circumstances of the Plains Indians had been radically altered by the 1890s. Apart from the effects of disease and alcohol, Indian peoples were now subject peoples. The last fighting on the Plains had occurred in the 1870s, and since then the white man had been sovereign. The last bison herd disappeared in the south in the late 1870s, and the northern herds were extinct by 1883; to military defeat was now added economic dependence for most of the tribes. The loss of land, the attempts to enforce agriculture, the pledges and broken treaties, the breakdown of social structure into smaller units under the allotment policy, the increased imposition of schooling, and the impact of the various missions, left disorganized societies, lacking in internal social control, unable to sustain traditional values, and incapable of accepting those of the invaders. All that held meaning for the Indian had been swept away, and the ceremonies which had sacralized those meanings, consolidated tribal life, and sanctified men's purposes, had become irrelevant to the new circumstances. Into the social, cultural, and religious vacuum came the new cults, fictively aggressive, in the case of the Ghost Dance, when actual aggression could no longer be employed, and passively withdrawn, in the instance of Peyotism.

The older religious system was now too difficult to celebrate: Peyotism was seen to be easier. It had simpler rituals, cost less, and was detached from the important military and hunting values of the ceremonials of the past.[47] But by no means everyone was prepared to abandon the old religion. Just as some had resisted the Ghost Dance, which was less easily withstood, there were many who saw Peyotism as an assault on the Indian way of life. At first this was true even among the Comanches,[48] and it occurred elsewhere. Among the Pawnee, Sky

[45] Alexander Lesser, *The Pawnee Ghost Dance Hand Game* (Columbia University Press, New York 1933), p. 329. See also pp. 117–8.

[46] Bernard Barber, 'A Socio-Cultural Interpretation of the Peyote Cult', *American Anthropologist* 43 (1941), pp. 673–5, expounds this thesis.

[47] V. Petrullo, op. cit., p. 76, was told by one of his informants, 'The old Delaware religion is too heavy for us who are becoming few and weak. It is too difficult; Peyote is easy in comparison.'

[48] See p. 419.

Chief, head of the doctors' dance, and Good Buffalo, leader of the buffalo dance ceremonialists, were both opposed to it, although at a later time they both came to use peyote.[49] Peyote represented a considerable abandonment of the past, and the more emphatically Christian it became—and this appears to have been the trend in some instances—the more clearly was it set over against the earlier traditions. The medicine-men usually opposed it, unless it appeared to be a new vehicle for their practice, as apparently it did among the Kiowa-Apache.[50] Iowa Peyotism, which was vigorous in 1914, had 'driven out of existence almost all the other societies and ancient customs of the tribe', and among the Winnebago, where the Christian character of the cult was marked, participation excluded activity in other societies, and led to abandonment of aboriginal practices and the destruction of their paraphernalia.[51]

Peyotism, then, began as something of an innovative cult which tended to compete with, and sometimes destroy, older religious ceremonials which were becoming functionless and difficult to perform.[52] In the course of time, however, Peyotism itself came to be regarded as a conserving agency, preserving distinctly Indian values. In consequence, it was challenged by those who sought a more total adaptation of Indian life to the standards prevailing in white society. Thus, the Towaoc community of Utes, which was more primitive than its neighbours, accepted Peyotism as a type of revivalism of ancient Ute conceptions, while at Ignacio, where Peyotism had existed longer, it was not accepted by the whole community.[53] Among the Menomini, the Peyotists were, by the mid-twenteith century, among the transitionally acculturated group between the more conservative practitioners of the Medicine Lodge and Dream Dance groups on the one hand, and the most acculturated members of the society on the other. The Peyotists in Spindler's sample were people raised by conservative parents, but the cult itself represented a 'unique integration of native-oriented power, curing, vision concepts and behaviours, and Western-oriented

[49] W. La Barre, op. cit., pp. 117–8.

[50] Charles S. Brant, 'Peyotism Among the Kiowa-Apache and Neighboring Tribes', *Southwestern Journal of Anthropology* 6, 2 (Summer 1950), pp. 212–22.

[51] W. La Barre, op. cit., pp. 115–6.

[52] S.B., the Winnebago, whose conversion Radin recounted, learned that all that he had done in the past was evil. 'It is false, this giving of [pagan] feasts . . . the Medicine Dance, and all the Indian customs.' P. Radin, 'The Autobiography . . .', op. cit., p. 449. Peyote did not, however, even after years of practice, completely replace traditional religion in all tribes. Even among the Delaware, who had been early in accepting Peyote, the old religion continued; by no means all Delaware were even nominal Peyotists, and in the Second World War the Delaware Big House ceremonials were briefly revived. W. W. Newcomb, Jr, op. cit., p. 210.

[53] M. K. Opler, 'The Character and History of the Southern Ute Peyote Rite', op. cit.

elements of Christian ideology'.[54] The individual doubted the old way of life, yet felt more Indian than white.

Among the Unitah Utes, there was opposition to the introduction of Peyotism, when it first arrived in 1914, among both the conservative elements and the more educated.[55] Among the Navaho, who were much less acculturated than, for example, the Menomini, opposition was largely traditional in the 1940s: opponents also dominated the tribal council, and these were among the most politically conscious men in the Navaho nation. The most acculturated were probably outside Peyote in the 1960s, but the cult was then seen as 'a mode of expressing rejection of the traditional system still relatively strong among the Navaho and of the American system, a mode of coping with feelings of helplessness, and a way of engendering a total reorientation which assists in adjusting to wage work and cash cropping'.[56] Among the Potawatomi, where the high degree of christianization of Peyote perhaps facilitated its widespread acceptance, nominal allegiance was considerable in the 1960s, but young married adults were not part of the cult.[57]

Peyotism appears, then, to have been both an agency in which some, much simplified and adjusted, expression of Indian native identity was maintained, and, simultaneously, to have been a cultural innovation. It was easier than all the old ceremonies for which neither the objective environmental conditions nor the social structural base remained. It was still the expression of something distinctively Indian, which its mythology emphasized, and a ritual that accommodated some elements of the religious preoccupations of that past. Understandably, it appeared first as the solvent of the Indian way of life, and subsequently as the preservative for it.

The continuities with the past are particularly evident in the role of visions in Peyotism—about the significance of which there has been considerable divergence of opinion. The individual's search for a vision was an integral part of the culture of the tribes of the Plains, and the easy adoption of Peyote among them was early seen as something facilitated by its 'vision-giving power'.[58] Elsewhere, the vision was part

[54] George Dearborn Spindler, 'Personality and Peyotism in Menomini Indian Acculturation', *Psychiatry* 15 (1952), pp. 151–9 (p. 153). Where practitioners of more conservative cults persist, Peyotists even in the 1960s were disdained as people who rejected the old ways—for example by members of the Drum religion among the Potawatomi. Robert L. Bee, 'Potawatomi Peyotism: The Influence of Traditional Patterns', *Southwestern Journal of Anthropology* 22, 6 (Summer 1966), pp. 194–205.

[55] O. C. Stewart, *Ute Peyotism . . .*, op. cit., p. 16.

[56] D. F. Aberle, op. cit., p. 309.

[57] R. L. Bee, op. cit.

[58] R. Shenle, op. cit., p. 58. Shonle expounds the thesis that the spread of the cult was very much influenced by its role as a continuance of the concern about visions in Plains cultures.

of a puberty rite, but among Plains tribes the vision at puberty was the first of many occasions on which the individual would seek and obtain visions. Mourning, guidance for revenge, initiation into some societies, the organization of a war party, were all occasions calling for visions. Thus Peyote represented the preservation of a religious tradition, even if specific and directive visions had so much less significance in the new conditions: conspicuously the Plains Peyote cult did not take over the rituals of the Mexican Tarahumare, from whence Shonle believes the cult may have come, but moulded it to local requirements.

Visions had been of considerable importance among some other tribes. They featured prominently in the conversion of John Rave and other Winnebago.[59] Revelation in the collective situation replaced the search for individual visions among the Menomini, even if most visions were brief and fleeting impressions, with elaborate and detailed visions coming relatively rarely (and then perhaps having more specific religious significance).[60] Visions were important to the Delaware. Even though some of Petrullo's informants declared that 'Peyote should not be eaten for the visions', they said so perhaps as a polemical point in favour of the conservative traditions of Elk Hair against the rite as introduced by John Wilson, against whom it was said '. . . it is customary for the followers of Wilson to ask one another after the meeting what they saw or experienced. Some of them do not even wait until the meeting is over but they whisper and discuss the various experiences, the objects, the visions they claim to see all night long, during the meeting.'[61] Instruction was said to come in visions, and certainly many cult innovations were legitimated, as was perhaps traditionally necessary, by visions. The hankering for visions and for proofs of spiritual power persisted long after visions lost their recognizable social function, outside the religious and therapeutic context.

It is possible that the cult has in fact attracted adherents for different reasons, according to the past preoccupations of the tribe; the role accorded to the cult by those who have introduced it; its relation to shamans and their therapeutic activities; and the particular age-groups which have first espoused it. La Barre is of the general opinion that although doctoring was the commonest reason given for calling a Peyote meeting, 'the vision-producing psychological effect is probably the major reason'.[62] Among the Great Basin tribes, Stewart believed

---

[59] According to the accounts of P. Radin, 'Religious Experiences . . .', op. cit., and 'The Autobiography . . .', op. cit.

[60] J. S. Slotkin, 'Menomini Peyotism . . .', op. cit., p. 569; G. D. Spindler, op. cit., p. 152.

[61] V. Petrullo, op. cit., p. 66. They were also of importance among the Comanches; see E. Wallace and E. A. Hoebel, op. cit., p. 332.

[62] W. La Barre, op. cit., p. 58.

that curing was the major function of the Peyote cult, and that visions were of much less significance.[63] The dispute may really turn on the specificity of visions, and be resolved in the terms proposed above. It would be surprising were any religion arising among a less-developed people not to claim general therapeutic and thaumaturgical functions. What is true of the Washo and Northern Paiute in this respect may also be more generally true.

> All Washo-Paiute are conscious of their position as an under-privileged minority, and appear to feel the need for stability and self-aggrandisement. Some desire physical improvement, others spiritual; all desire something. Peyotism has provided both physical and spiritual solace for the few who have believed and remained active. It is merely one of many possible means of attaining inner security.[64]

The difficulty in sustaining the necessary ritual of past religious activity, and the inapplicability of the 'received' traditions of what one might experience in a vision, left a vacuum in Indian life. There had to be new occasions for solemnized gatherings, and a reinterpretation of the Indian way to salvation, the more particularly in the conditions of intense despair and anomie. The inward-looking Peyote cult, which combined both the individual experience of the past with the social solidarity of the wise (those who permitted Peyote to instruct them), necessarily took on many aspects of traditional culture. Where traditional medicine was under attack, or lacking prestige because of past failures, Peyotism provided shamans with new opportunities to win a clientele. 'No doctrine of the cult commands members to go forth and convert other tribes.'[65] But such proselytizing was considerable, and the agents were often men who made, and perhaps sought, wealth by setting up in the new medicine, and by offering the new solace through a legitimated ritual. If, as seems likely, a principal affliction among Indians was an essentially cultural malaise, Peyotism, as an introverted religion of withdrawal, as a consolidation of the culture according to new precepts, was well equipped to provide therapy. Visions and healings, both frequent in thaumaturgical religion, were merely continuities in the context of a new religious response, a response which did not fit men to take their part in the world—there was no world to which they really belonged—but one which preserved for them an enclave of their own and a promise (and in the visions a manifestation, perhaps) of the salvation of their people.

[63] O. C. Stewart, 'Washo-Paiute Peyotism . . .', op. cit., p. 86 n.
[64] Ibid., p. 98.
[65] Ibid., p. 96.

Peyotism, Christianity, and organization

No less disputed than the matter of visions and healing has been the extent to which the Peyote cult was an adaptation, in particularly Indian guise, of Christianity. The controversy has been bedevilled by the conscious simulation of Christian styles of organization as deliberate procedures of defence for a cult which, because of its use of a drug, and perhaps because of the effect of all-night meetings, met with hostility and, sometimes, persecution from the Government's Indian agents and others. Conscious adoption of church organization may have accompanied the unconscious adoption, equally as a defence-mechanism, of Christian terminology and concepts. The mythical figures of Peyotism's origins became identified with biblical figures, just as African deities in Brazilian *candomblés* acquired scriptural counterparts.[66] There may, however, also have been conscious and sincere efforts to accept the Christian message, and to interpret it through the beliefs and rites of Peyote.

The early Arapaho ceremony had no discernible Christian elements, although these appeared by 1912.[67] The Winnebago acquired these from Hensley, and they were accepted by John Rave.[68] Among the Oto, Jonathan Koshiway, who had been an evangelist with the Mormons, introduced Christian elements into the cult.[69] As early as the 1880s, John Wilson had legitimated his ritual by claiming to have seen Christ and to be his forerunner: his followers tended to identify him with Christ himself.[70] Stewart believes that Peyotism may have acquired its Christian characteristics in the eighteenth century, and that it was disseminated as a relatively stable constellation of traits among the tribes of North America, but this view appears to be outbalanced by what is known of the innovative capacities of many of Peyote's proponents. Stewart emphasizes their role in disseminating, but not in amending, the cult.[71] Certainly, Peyote, as presented to recent observers, shows considerable evidence of Christian influence,

[66] J. S. Slotkin, op. cit., p. 579, notes that among the Menomini the Great Spirit is understood as God; the Son (sometimes Jesus) is regarded as a cultural hero who gave the white version of Christianity to white men, and Peyote to the Indians; the Good Spirit is the Holy Ghost; angels are fused with the traditional Indian spirits of the four cardinal points. Since sin, redemption, incarnation, crucifixion, and judgement are not mentioned this sounds like superficial syncretism rather than something 'essentially Christian', as Slotkin elsewhere claims.

[67] R. Shonle, op. cit.

[68] See p. 425.

[69] W. La Barre, op. cit., p. 167.

[70] V. Petrullo, op. cit., p. 46.

[71] O. C. Stewart, *Ute Peyotism . . .*, op. cit., p. 19 ff.

particularly in the confession of sins and the ethical code promulgated among the cult leaders. In the twentieth century, Peyotism has been put forward as the Indian form of Christianity. The Bible, the Trinity, and confessions have been incorporated, and in some cases crucifixes and rosaries have been in even longer use.[72] But elsewhere, for example among the Gosiute, the Bible is not used in meetings, but only in the ideological defence of Peyotism.[73] The long process of acculturation itself makes the accretion of Christian elements to Indian religion thoroughly expectable. The power of the white man made his faith impressive, even if that faith seemed curiously divisive, and of relatively little influence in the everyday world of the whites. It was readily assimilated in other North American Indian traditions, and by other minority peoples. It would be remarkable if new religions among peoples undergoing major social and cultural upheaval were not to assimilate concepts, terms, and mythical personages from a dominant tradition so much more inventive, elaborate, and viable than their own.

Yet the extent to which Peyotism also provided a new scene for rival practices in the shamanistic tradition should not be overlooked. Almost every tribe evolved rival patterns of Peyote practice, however minor were the details of procedure, and however tolerant were the adherents in attending the meetings of one rite or another. The variations were the possessions of the particular road chiefs, who owned their rites in the traditional fashion of a man who had received a vision of how to communicate with the supernatural. Christianity sometimes became an issue in the struggle, as between Elk Hair and John Wilson among the Delaware, and the other groups whom they influenced with their Little Moon (original Kiowa) rite and Big Moon (Wilson) rite. Among the Southern Ute, Peyotism fitted the pattern of traditional shamanistic curing practices, and the Peyote chief at Towaoc, himself a shaman, resisted, throughout the early years of this century, the Christian influences of the rite introduced by Sam Roan Bear. In the much more acculturated Ute community at Ignacio, Peyotism was more accommodative of Christianity, and was opposed by shamans.[74] Other divisions also occurred among the Ute, between those who accepted the 'old Ute way' of Sam Roan Bear, and those adopting the 'Tipi way', disseminated from Oklahoma.[75]

[72] J. S. Slotkin, *The Peyote Religion*, op. cit., pp. 45–7.

[73] C. Malouf, op. cit., p. 101.

[74] M. K. Opler, op. cit., and *idem*, 'Fact and Fancy in Ute Peyotism', *American Anthropologist* 44, 1 (January–March 1942), pp. 151–9.

[75] O. C. Stewart, op. cit., p. 5. The dispute between M. K. Opler and Stewart centres essentially on the extent to which Peyotism among the Ute (and more widely) may be seen as a continuity of past traditions, or as the acceptance of an entirely new cult, which Stewart believes to have been diffused as a cultural whole, Christian elements included.

Although the cult was considerably christianized among the Potawatomi, the old tradition of shamanistic 'combat' with threats and
counter-threats, which could not find very easy accommodation in
actual Peyote meetings, was continued in the rivalries between two
groups of cultists. One group objected to the policy of the *Native North
American Church of God*, which legitimated peyote but which, to the
objectors, was too much an expression of conformity to white values.[76]
Even among the Menomini, among whom there were only three dozen
active Peyotists in the late 1940s, there were two distinct rites, the Cross
Fireplace and the Half Moon, of which the former represented a much
more Christian style of ritual, and the latter a more traditional Indian
pattern, although Slotkin refers to Peyotism in general as an essentially
Christian faith, adapted to traditional Indian beliefs and practices.[77]
In these cases there is manifested the factionalism of Indian society and
the struggle for power between individuals, which the adoption of a
Christian type of organization, a 'chuch', has been insufficient to dispel.

Peyotism has changed over the course of the eighty years in which it
has been thriving among North American Indians. Some styles of
ritual have proved very acceptable while other practices have lapsed.
In general Peyotism has manifested the increasing acculturation of
Indians to the white culture, even though Peyotism itself has come to be
regarded by some acculturated Indians as a conservative force.
Christian concepts have been absorbed, in ideology and ritual (as well
as in the deliberate organization of Peyotism on the Christian denominational model). Among the Delaware, differences at two meetings
with a twenty-year interval between them have been noted. At the
earlier meeting there was a crucifix on the altar, at the later one none;
whereas only the road chief had smoked at the earlier meeting, at the
later meeting everyone smoked corn-husk Bull Durham cigarettes; at
the early meeting women had been given only peyote tea, but twenty
years later they were given green or dried peyote, and men drank tea;
whereas women did not sing at the first meeting, at the meeting in the
1950s women sang with permission of the road chief; in the 1930s the
occasion ended when the participants filed out and washed, but two
decades later the meeting closed with the Lord's Prayer.[78] Some

---

[76] R. L. Bee, op. cit., p. 177.

[77] J. S. Slotkin, 'Menomini Peyotism . . .', op. cit., pp. 574-5.

[78] These comparisons between Petrullo's report of Delaware Peyotism, and his own
experience, are provided by W. W. Newcomb, Jr, op. cit. Shamanistic curing, by the use of a
feather which had been in smoke and by a sucking procedure, were also undertaken at this
later meeting, which had not occurred in the meeting twenty years before. It is quite possible,
however, that shamanistic curing of this kind might well have been permitted at the earlier
date, also. Unfortunately, despite the abundance of reports on Peyotism, even detailed field
studies have relied on relatively few attendances at Peyote meetings. Newcomb's report here

differences may have been adventitious, since the absence of a definite priesthood and the legitimation by visions of particular rites introduced by prominent individuals facilitate many minor variations in cult performance. One noticeable trend, however, is the increased participation of women in Peyote meetings.[79]

The evolution of Peyotism from a new religious practice into a well-established religious organization indicates both the increasing acculturation of Indians and the rationalization and routinization of religious responses. The model of how to stabilize, defend, and present to the world a set of religious practices was borrowed from the white culture. Religion among Indians was no longer an expression of the anxieties felt, and reassurances sought, in the prosecution of an integrated round of life-activities: it had become something more separate, voluntaristic, and compartmentalized, and the emergence of formal organization was both a recognition and an enhancement of that process. Although not so directly influenced in their teachings as was Handsome Lake by the Quakers, nor so attractive to any white sect as was Tenskwatawa to the Shakers, nor yet so directly and so centrally prompted by a friend of the kind that Judge Wickersham was to the Puget Sound Shakers, none the less, the Peyotists saw that the adoption of denominational organization was an important safeguard for a faith that was not, as aboriginal Indian religion had been, deeply rooted in daily-life activities.

The persecution of the Peyotists began long before the cult was well known or widely spread. Officials had made regulations against it without governmental authorization at the Kiowa, Comanche, and Wichita agency in Oklahoma in 1888. In this period almost every expression of Indian native culture was subjected to official scrutiny, and much of it to prohibition. The session laws of Oklahoma prohibited the practice in 1899, and arrests of Peyotists took place in 1907. The

---

cited was of a single meeting. Stewart, who wrote with great assurance, and polemicized about Ute Peyotism, did so after attending only three meetings. Even Aberle, in his splendidly thorough account of Peyotism among the Navaho, mentions attendance at no more than eleven meetings. The fewness of such attendances stands in sharp contrast to the practice of sociologists who have participated in sect meetings in western society. (In addition the sociologists have not had to work through interpreters, and have had much less to learn about the cultural background.) The limited participation of anthropologists studying Peyotism perhaps explains the presence of sharp controversies in the field, as generalizations have been propounded on the strength of relatively slender empirical enquiry.

[79] Considering the importance of Peyote in providing roles for men, especially after the loss of warrior and hunting activities, and the traditional restriction of religious practice to males, the slowness of this development is not surprising. As Indians have settled to a more regular work order, the importance of Peyote in providing an arena for male activity has perhaps declined.

law was repealed in 1908, after Quanah Parker, the Comanche chief, had testified against it. Subsequent attempts at its re-enactment in 1909, and later, failed. Under these threats of persecution, Indians were induced to consider ways of defending their new source of spiritual power. A very early association of 'mescal-bean eaters' (Peyote was often confused with the mescal bean) arose in the first decade of the century, and, in 1909, this was constituted as a 'union church', but the first incorporation of a Peyote denomination was sponsored by Jonathan Koshiway.[80] Koshiway sought to negotiate with Protestants for their recognition of the Peyote cult.[81] When this failed, he and other Otos incorporated the *First Born Church of Christ*, at Redrock, Oklahoma, in 1914. The Church was confined to one tribe, it remained small, and its articles did not make clear that the use of peyote was essential.[82]

The Native American Church was incorporated in Oklahoma in 1918, perhaps on the earlier initiative of James Mooney.[83] The Church was inter-tribal, although it was limited to Oklahoma, and its members included Southern Cheyenne, Oto, Ponca, Comanche, Kiowa, and Kiowa-Apache. Subsequently, groups in other states obtained their own charters in similar terms, and in 1944, when a national charter was needed, the Church became a national organization, which (in 1955) established itself under the name of the *Native American Church of North America*, to which groups in various states could affiliate. Some did so, while others remained independent. The evolution of this organization was associated with the spasmodic persecution which the Peyotists encountered in various places, and its defence was to claim that Peyotism was a branch of Christianity. It claimed the same God; belief in the Trinity; the ten commandments; and the use of the Bible. Peyote was used as a sacrament—suited to those who, like the Indian, are 'weak', as suggested in Romans 14, 1–3. Although the Church lacked an officially promulgated doctrine, since Peyotism was individualistic, many biblical citations were employed to defend the use of peyote. The Indians represented the faith as a way of humility.[84]

The charter of the Church is explicit about its purposes, emphasizing the importance of the Christian religion, morality, sobriety, industry

---

[80] The 'mescal-bean eaters' are referred to as a loose inter-tribal association which had spread to New Mexico from Oklahoma and Nebraska by 1906, by C. Burton Dustin in *Peyotism and New Mexico* (C. Burton Dustin, Albuquerque *c.* 1960).

[81] W. La Barre, op. cit., p. 167.

[82] The history of these persecutions is drawn from O. C. Stewart, 'The Native American Church (Peyote Cult) and the Law', *The Denver Westerner's Monthly Roundup* XVII, 1 (January 1961), pp. 5–18.

[83] J. S. Slotkin, *The Peyote Religion*, op. cit., pp. 58 ff.

[84] Ibid., pp. 62 ff.

charity, right-living, self-respect, and brotherly union, and most particularly, in Article II, it declares:

> The purpose for which this corporation is formed is to foster and promote the religious belief of the several tribes of Indians in the State of Oklahoma, in the Christian religion with the practice of the Peyote sacrament as commonly understood and used among the adherents of this religion. . . .

Various states legislated against the use of peyote, after the First World War, but there were difficulties in applying the law since it was not entirely clear whether the laws covered Indian reservations. The law which prohibited the use of peyote in Utah was repealed in 1935, and this marked the change from the period of restrictive legislation in many states to a more liberal attitude with the later repeal of restrictive laws in Iowa, Texas, and New Mexico. The Native American Church was responsible for fighting cases brought under the various state laws, and their efforts were attended with some success.[85] Among the Navaho, the tribal council, which had very considerable power, was bitterly opposed to the use of peyote, and prohibited its use in 1940. The liberal attitude of John Collier, the U.S. Commissioner for Indian Affairs in the late 1930s and 40s, led to a struggle between his tolerant attitude towards peyote and the opposition of the Navaho tribal councillors. The complexities of tribal, state, and federal policies, led to sporadic persecution, legislation, and appeal, throughout the 1950s and 1960s, in Nevada, Arizona, and Utah.[86]

Persecution was undoubtedly the factor that prompted the organization of the Native American Church, and which caused it to emphasize its acceptance of the Christian tradition. Peyote is a contemplative religious movement, in which men emphasize their spiritual inadequacy, and search for spiritual reassurance, and physical and spiritual well-being. They meet at night, with relatively few persons gathering together, for activities which have little public significance and no public communication to make. These elements conform to those of the

[85] This paragraph rests on O. C. Stewart, op. cit.

[86] A thorough account of the highly complex legal processes among the Navaho, the role of the Native American Church and the American Civil Liberties Union, will be found in D. F. Aberle, op. cit., pp. 109 ff. The legal dispute led to pronounced disagreement between Dr Clarence Salsbury, Commissioner for Public Health in Arizona, who opposed the Peyote cult, and made widely published statements against it, and anthropologists who defended the cultists. Five anthropologists, W. La Barre, D. P. McAllester, J. S. Slotkin, O. C. Stewart, and Sol Tax, published a statement in *Science* CIV (1951), pp. 582–3, in which they protested at the attacks. In *Science* CV (1952), pp. 503–4, John Collier, the Commissioner for Indian Affairs, issued a statement of his concurrence with the anthropologists, and deplored the laws that prohibited the activities of the Native American Church. Both statements are extensively cited in Vittorio Lanternari, *The Religions of the Oppressed*, translated by Lisa Sergio (MacGibbon and Kee, London 1963), pp. 64–6.

introversionist sect—and introversionist sects do not normally evolve organizational structures to promote their concerns. They do so, perhaps, only when facing persecution. It is by retreat into a sanctified ethnicity, rather than by the assertion of distinctive *doctrines* of with-drawal that the introversionism of Peyote is manifested. Since they have no need of articulated doctrine, there would not—but for persecu-tion—have been need for a formal organization structure, and in actuality it is of little importance in the practice of the faith, except in defending the rights of Peyotists. The public face of the Native American Church makes of the Peyote cult a more conspicuous entity than would spontaneously arise from an introversionist response to the world. Because ethnicity rather than doctrine is the ultimate base for the group, this duality may occur without the sense of explicit contradiction.

If persecution has led to greater emphasis being given to Christian elements, then it may be argued that these Christian teachings do not have the 'essential' quality which Stewart and Slotkin have attributed to them. Both were staunch defenders of Peyotism, appearing at trials, and signing manifestos on behalf of Peyotists: perhaps this disposed them to support the principal ideological defence-mechanism of the movement. Perhaps La Barre goes too far in saying that 'such Christian elements as were added had a largely propagandist function'[87] if by this is implied too conscious and calculated an appeal to Christianity as a 'front'. But at the same time, even in highly tolerant societies, religious practices have often been defensible only by exegesis in the dominant religious tradition, and this was an obvious course for Peyotism. But even without persecution, in the normal course of increased acculturation of Indians, some assimilation of Christian elements seems probable.

The organization of the Native American Church made explicit what was already a marked characteristic of the Peyote cult—the inter-tribalism of the movement. Although temporary inter-tribal involvements had occurred earlier in millennial movements, association in more persistent patterns of ritual practice and, subsequently, in the responsibility for an organization, was a new phenomenon. Reservation life; the suppression of warfare; the common dependence on the white man's rations; and subjection to his regulation, were all as important as the increasing literacy among Indians, and the use of postal and rail services, and eventually motor transport, in facilitating the new sustained inter-tribalism. Peyotism was, if not yet an alternative to tribalism as a basis of association, none the less a movement with a growing self-consciousness. Although some pluralism was found, for

[87] W. La Barre, op. cit., p. 43 n.

example among the Potawatomi in the 1960s, indicators of a tendency towards group apartness, and even endogamy, had appeared long before in other tribes.[88] Peyotists, both among the Navaho and the Taos Pueblo, established group relationships of mutual assistance along lines that transcended kinship.[89] In each case the fierceness of controversy about peyote reduced the possibility of pluralism and enhanced the in-group identification of the cultists, who created new group solidarities. If the more active Peyotists identified themselves as a group within a tribe, the associations across tribal lines were just as conspicuous, and were so at earlier dates.[90] At many of the meetings for which reports are available, men of different tribal groups were present.

The fact of distinct ethnicity has remained too strong as a source of identity in Indian life for Peyotism to have created a completely distinctive in-group, except in cases where considerable persecution and animosity have forced men to take sides—as in some Navaho communities. But Peyotism has been one of the vehicles promoting the sense of Indian—as distinct from tribal—identity, so that the cult became 'an Indian defence against the consequences of white domination'.[91] The decline of tribal ceremonies, and the absence of an occasion on which tribesmen as such might gather for some collective expression of unity, particularly where they had become dispersed, indicates the difficulty of the maintenance of purely tribal religious practice. The decline of Indian languages, and the borrowing of dancing and rituals from other tribes—the Sun Dance, the Powwow, or Peyotism—indicate how much the Indian was coming to see himself as such, rather than as the member of a particular tribe.

[88] On the Potawatomi, see R. L. Bee, op. cit. An instance of tendencies towards endogamous attitudes among Peyotists is provided in the response of the girl whom S.B., the Winnebago, sought for a wife, who said that she 'wanted a man who ate peyote and who paid attention to the ceremony'. P. Radin, 'The Autobiography . . .', op. cit., p. 446. This might, as Radin suggests, have been no more than the sentiments a Winnebago girl would traditionally express concerning traditional religious practice: however, that the sentiment should become attached to an inter-tribal cult is not without importance.

[89] D. F. Aberle, op. cit., pp. 16, 219–20. William N. Fenton, 'Factionalism at Taos Pueblo, New Mexico', Smithsonian Institution: Bureau of American Ethnology, Bulletin 164, Anthropological Papers No. 56 (1957), pp. 297–344, discusses the way in which adhesion to the Peyote cult broke up families at Taos, pp. 327–8.

[90] Thus, at the Delaware meeting reported by W. W. Newcomb, Jr, op. cit., there were present Winnebagos, Sioux, and Shawnees, and the Delawares often attended meetings among the Osages and Quapaws. This degree of inter-tribal association, whilst impressive, is certainly not, as is said by V. Petrullo in 'Peyotism as an Emergent Indian Culture', Indians at Work Vol. 7, No. 8 [cover gives Vol. 8, in error] (April 1940), pp. 51–60, the first step 'to arouse and develop an awareness' in the Indian 'that his affinities extend beyond tribal bounds'. Pontiac and Tecumseh certainly, and Hiawatha probably, are claimants to that accolade, even though Peyotism has been the most effective and sustained step in that direction.

[91] J. S. Slotkin, op. cit., p. 7.

Peyotism as introversionism? The case of the Navaho

The Peyote cult acquired its initial impetus as a widespread Indian religious response after the failure of the Ghost Dance. As Slotkin has said, '. . . the peyote cult's present importance is probably due to diffusion from the tribes of the Kiowa, Comanche and Wichita Agency, after the failure of the Ghost Dance of 1889–91'.[92] The sequence in which a revolutionist response is succeeded by introversionism is a pattern well known among sects in advanced countries. In this case there are two distinct movements, with different points of origin, and the sequence is rather of the popularity of each in turn, than of specific changes of orientation within one on-going movement. Additionally, Peyotism became an accommodation for many other needs felt by disorganized tribesmen. Thus, although the dominant and expectable response of the Peyotists is introversionist, none the less there is no set, automatic sequence of responses. There are new beginnings. It is not the disillusionment of the members of an on-going organization, but the emergence of a completely new pattern of activity, which steadily replaces the ecstatic millennial dream. Again, Peyotism continued to spread long after the echoes of the Ghost Dance had fallen silent. For some, it was not a secondary introversionist response, but a primary response of men whose social circumstances induced in them introspection and sensitivity.[93] For some, the needs for compensation were first experienced in conditions in which millennialism had never been widely attractive, even though occasional outbursts had been known. Such was the case with the Navaho.

The Navaho had remained unaffected by the two Ghost Dances disseminated from the Paiutes in 1870 and 1890.[94] They were the largest of the Indian tribes, occupying wide areas of Nevada and Arizona and parts of some neighbouring states, and they were among the last Indians to experience widespread contact with white Americans. They had been resistant to Christianity, accepting Spanish Catholicism in the areas where the missions penetrated, largely for material gain, but remaining traditionalist in their basic religious orientations.[95] Their lack of susceptibility to the Ghost Dance has been attributed to

[92] J. S. Slotkin, 'Peyotism, 1521–1891', *American Anthropologist* 57, 2 (April 1955), pp, 202–30 (p. 212).
[93] J. S. Slotkin, *The Peyote Religion*, op. cit., p. 76.
[94] See p. 298.
[95] William H. Hodge, 'Navaho Pentecostalism', *Anthropological Quarterly* 37, 3 (July 1964), pp. 73–93.

two circumstances: (i) to the absence of material deprivation among the
Navaho in the periods when the California tribes were undergoing the
profound shock of contact (prior to 1870) and when the Plains tribes
were first encountering life on reservations; and (ii) to their fear of
ghosts. 'The idea of resurrection, that a man, having died, may live
again and appear to his survivors . . . is positively abhorrent to Navaho
psychology.' Contact with the dead was the worst thing that could
happen to a man. 'Fear of the dead, the "ghost", amounts to a tribal
phobia; it is the most universal of all reactions' among the Navaho.[96]

Although the promise of the returning ancestors through the Ghost
Dance made no appeal to the Navaho, they were not entirely free from
rumours of doom. These stories lacked a restorative quality, however,
and were seen as threats to the Navaho themselves, rather than as
selective agencies that would destroy the whites. A Navaho visionary
called Mexican John had dreamed of a flood which would wipe out
the tribe: 'the flood never appeared . . . and somehow, or other,
Mexican John "was killed" '.[97] This is the brief account of one such
panic. Another occurred in 1922. 'At Todanestya, the Wetherills . . .
in the summer of 1922 heard the bells of moving flocks one day, and
saw the People [i.e. the Navaho] fleeing as they had fled at the coming
of the soldier in 1908. With flocks and herds, they rode past the trading
post.' When Asthon Sosi (the Slim Woman, as the Navaho called
Louise Wetherill) asked where they were going, she was told that they
were going to the Black Mountain to escape the flood that was coming.
An old man had been struck by lightning and left for dead, and after
many days he had come back to life, and told what he had seen and
heard. 'He told of a great flood, which would destroy all their flocks
and cornfields.' The flood was to come from the great water in the
east. Cornfields were left without care and ruined. Apparently the
prophet had heard from a missionary of Noah's Ark and the great
flood that God had sent to visit a sinful people. Since the missionary
declared the Navaho to be also very sinful, and that God would punish
them, the idea had arisen in this old man's mind of the flood coming
to the Navaho.[98]

---

[96] Gladys A. Reichard, 'The Navaho and Christianity', *American Anthropologist* 51, 1
(January–March 1949), pp. 66–71 (p. 67). Clyde Kluckhohn and Dorothea Leighton, *The
Navaho*, Rev. Edn (Doubleday Anchor, New York 1962) report that the Navahos have no
belief in a glorious after-life; that death and everything connected with it are horrible to the
Navahos; and that this abhorrence of death, and the morbid avoidance of the dead, 'rests
upon the fear of ghosts' (p. 184).

[97] Bernard Haile, 'A Note on the Navaho Visionary', *American Anthropologist* 42, 2 (April–
June 1940), p. 359.

[98] Francis Gillmor and Louisa Wade Wetherill, *Traders to the Navahos: the Story of the
Wetherills of Kayenta* (Houghton Mifflin, Boston 1934), pp. 234–5, 54.

Such incidental outbursts of panic share only a few of the elements found in millennialism: they do not constitute a revolutionist response to the world. Peyotism among the Navaho was not a successor to a millennial movement. It was communicated to them from neighbouring tribes, particularly the Ute, and it met particular needs of sections of the Navaho at the time. When Peyotism first made its appearance among them in the 1930s, the Navaho were the least-acculturated Indian people. They had suffered less interference with their traditional way of life than most tribes; they had not fought against the Americans; and they had not been forcibly moved from ancient lands to new reservations. Although they had not entirely escaped distressing involvements with the government and with white men, in general they had been protected by their agents from incursions by whites; they had not been severely pressed to stay within the bounds of the reservation; and they had succeeded at different times in getting additional land.[99]

The particular distress that the Navaho suffered had been principally associated with the programme of stock reduction in the 1930s. The area on which the Navaho maintained their flocks was considerably over-grazed, and the government imposed limitations on stock-holdings in the 1930s. The process caused both hardship and resentment among the Navaho, who had no conception of the cumulative effects of over-grazing, but believed that nature balanced these things. There were minor outbursts of violence, but by 1945 the Navaho flocks had been reduced to what the range could carry. Thereafter increase of stock began again, but this period was one in which drought, war, population increase, and severe blizzards in the late 1940s, caused the Navaho great hardships.[100]

The Navaho acquired Peyotism from the Ute at Tawaoc, and the movement took root in the early 1930s, just at the time of the beginning of their troubles with stock reduction, when the balance of Navaho life, and the religious conceptualization of it, had been disrupted. Not only were the Navahos faced with poverty, but increased dependence on wage-work outside the community threatened old patterns of reciprocity, so important in the past.[101] Local clan organizations could no longer maintain social control, and although traditional religion continued, fewer young men were coming forward as apprentices to learn the old shamanistic arts as 'singers'. Peyotism grew steadily, and although it came in christianized form, it was well fitted to assimilate local traditions, and to fulfil functions important to the Navaho.

[99] This paragraph relies, as do those which follow, on D. F. Aberle's detailed study, *The Peyote Religion* . . ., op. cit., pp. 23–45; 344–6.
[100] Ibid., pp. 52 ff.
[101] Ibid., p. 202.

The central figures of Peyote myth were identified with biblical personages: Jesus was mentioned in prayers; the sign of the cross was used; some even saw peyote as the blood of Christ.[102] Peyote itself was the teacher, and the less-acculturated northern groups emphasized its mystical and magical attributes, the revelations, visions, mystical insights, and its power to bring good fortune. Among the more-acculturated southern Navaho Peyotists, contemplation, introspection, and the moral message of Peyotism were more emphasized than visions and magic.[103] Curing was everywhere a central concern of the Peyotists, some three-quarters of whom were drawn into the cult to procure healings, often after the traditional 'sings' of the Navaho shamans had failed.[104] But once people belonged to the faith, their interests tended to become differentiated. The Peyote road chief was, in some respects, rather like the traditional 'singer' in Navaho ceremonies. Often he legitimated his acquisition of knowledge by a ceremony in a similar way, and some 'singers' became road chiefs.[105]

The strong opposition to Peyotism came from various sources: the traditionalists were one. Traditional 'singers' in particular claimed that it was an alien, borrowed religion, not a medicine given to the Navaho. A Peyote meeting, however, was cheaper than a traditional 'sing', and in the opposition of the shamans undoubtedly lay a fear of competition from a growing and successful cult. The sense of tribal identity remained strong: the Navaho, even in the 1960s, did not feel themselves to be just 'Indian'—they were still Navaho. The missions, and some of the more acculturated and 'progressive' Navaho, who wanted to identify with American society, also opposed the movement, '. . . peyotism is caught in a pincer movement in which extreme traditionalists and extreme modernists with Christian orientations, form the two arms'.[106]

Despite opposition, which took the form of legislation in the tribal council, raids on meetings, and arrests, Peyotism grew, fulfilling important functions in the life of many Navahos. It offered an explanation which released men from the need to placate the supernatural so that order might continue among men, nature, and the supernatural powers. It became the solvent of traditional practices that were out of joint with the times, such as mother-in-law avoidances. In asserting that the Indian was weak, it helped the Navaho to accept a new relationship with his fellow men and the deity without self-assertiveness

[102] Ibid., pp. 153, 148, 13, 176.
[103] Ibid., pp. 189–90.
[104] Ibid., p. 185.
[105] Ibid., pp. 197–9.
[106] Ibid., p. 223.

or techniques to compel the spirits to grant favours. By promulgating an ethic, Peyotism helped to internalize normative standards at a time when traditional sanctions and agencies of social control had broken down. It provided substitute kinship bonds when such bonds were under strain, and when traditional reciprocity was hard to maintain, but which men feared to abandon.[107] Its visionary quality provided reassurance and an enhanced sense of personal worth, whilst its curing functions were necessary if it was to replace the older religious practice and gain widespread voluntary allegiance among a less-developed people.

Aberle's investigation of Peyotism among the Navaho convinced him, both from the time of the appearance of the movement, and from the examination of those who had joined and those who had not, that 'membership of the cult was associated with the amount of livestock lost in the process of reduction, and with pre-reduction holdings'. This finding he interpreted in terms of relative deprivation: the Peyotists were likely to be those who had experienced the larger discrepancies between legitimate expectations and the actual situation.[108] Acculturation he came to regard as a factor inhibitory to the spread of Peyotism, but the causes of acceptance or rejection depended less on the degree of an individual's acculturation than on the situation in which he found himself, in the effects of external relations on the reservation community rather than in the effects on individuals of education and missions.[109] Peyotists were much more likely to experience bad dreams than non-Peyotists, and this, and the high pre-reduction livestock holdings, were the two best predictors of those who would be Peyotists.[110] What was also of great significance in determining the level of the cult in Navaho communities was its availability, which was assessed by mileage from the principal centre of dissemination.[111]

Relative deprivation is regarded by Aberle as the circumstance from which revolutionist movements (transformative movements, in Aberle's terminology) arise. Among the Navaho only very transient and localized

[107] Ibid., pp. 202–4.

[108] Ibid., p. 252

[109] Ibid., pp. 278–310.

[110] Ibid., p. 270. Allen T. Dittman and Harvey C. Moore, 'Disturbances in Dreams as Related to Peyotism among the Navaho', *American Anthropologist* 59, 4 (August 1957), pp. 642–9. It seems important to ask, however, whether the experience of Peyotism itself might not—whether for physiological or psychological reasons—induce bad dreams. Those who frequently enter into dream situations under the influence of a drug may very much affect the normal dream functions of their psychosomatic systems.

[111] This theory is also expounded in D. F. Aberle and O. C. Stewart, *Navaho and Ute Peyotism*, op. cit., pp. 104–5.

transformative responses came into evidence: the Navaho remained empirical in their approach to their problems, and realized that they enjoyed better circumstances in relation to the government than did their Ute and Apache neighbours. But he believes that at the time of livestock reduction, the Navaho might have been ready to manifest a revolutionist response. 'If livestock reduction had not been accompanied by a variety of ameliorative efforts that increasingly involved Navahos in Government-directed work-programmes, it seems possible that the reduction might have led to a magical transformative movement'[112]— that is to say, to a movement which might have taken up and disseminated some of the restorative visions that occurred to one or two 'prophets' in this period, and some of which had strong anti-white connotations. Government programmes, in moderating the effects of reduction, and the availability of the Peyote cult, led those Navaho who felt most acutely deprived to seek salvation in this movement, rather than to espouse a new millennial dream.

It seems equally possible that the gradualism of the impact of government upon the Navaho, both over the many decades since they had been brought under supervision at Fort Sumner in the 1860s, and in the effect of stock-reduction, was a factor inhibiting revolutionist response. The Ghost Dance on the Plains followed the dramatic and relatively sudden collapse of the life-circumstances of many Plains tribes. But by the 1930s, when the Navaho began to adopt the Peyote cult, they had experienced a long process of steady adjustment. Not least important in that process was the increasingly evident fact that the white culture was a dominant culture of immense power. The revolutionist responses of the past had often been associated with military action—indications that, with a little spiritual power, Indians believed that they could still triumph. The Navaho had never engaged in war with the Americans, and this particular type of millennialism did not meet their conception of their relations with the government. Even a more entirely super-naturalist millennialism may, in the face of increasingly abundant evidence of the white man's power, have seemed implausible. The Navaho traditional way of life was not, in the 1930s, so far affected that the restorative aspect of millennialism had great cogency. Peyotism offered itself, even though an alien importation, as a preservative of the Indian way. That it preserved in an entirely passive way, by encouraging introspection rather than by action or ecstasy, fitted the tempo of the encroachments on the Navaho way of life and the Navaho economy.

[112] D. F. Aberle, *The Peyote Religion*, op. cit., pp. 350–1.

Conclusion

The Peyote cult among the Navaho, no less than elsewhere, is basically a response of withdrawal from involvement. Its functions of curing, communal organization, the creation of a new internalized ethic, the rejection of alcohol, and the maintenance of an Indian way, all fit into the matrix of the rejection of the wider world. Aberle, who does not distinguish between conversionist and introversionist sects (calling all of them 'redemptive'), writes, 'peyotism is a mode of expressing rejection of the traditional system and of the American system, a mode of coping with feelings of helplessness, and a way of engendering a total re-orientation which assists in adjusting to wage-work and cash cropping.'[113] It is the internalization of new norms which performs the adjustive aspect of the Peyote movement, the acquisition of a sense of the meaning of existence instead of living from day-to-day, and of standards of hard work, family care, planning for the future, peaceability, and personal discipline (over alcohol and adultery).[114] A conversionist sect might induce its votaries to accept these ethical requirements, but such sects emphasize very much more the changed heart of the man who has entered into a relation with God, and this change is more of an emotional condition than a new ethical perspective; it is expressed emotionally, even ecstatically. The cultivation of piety and withdrawal from the world even whilst remaining within it, is more of an intro- versionist orientation. The Peyote meeting is just such an enclave, separated from the white society, somewhat persecuted by it, and separated from Indians who do not adopt these special sanctifying practices, who do not withdraw as a 'gathered remnant'. The emergence of somewhat exclusive communities of Peyotists, strongly in evidence among some tribes, including the Navaho, is a further substantiation of the introversionist character of Peyote.

Redemption, regarded as such, was not simply what Peyotists sought, since that was available to the Navaho from the missionaries who had long been active among them. Most of these missionaries had a distinctly conversionist orientation,[115] and offered a religious system

[113] Ibid., p. 309. In the V-way, a variant pattern of Peyotism, practised among some Navaho (after a local vision concerning the proper procedures of the ritual), confession is more strongly emphasized, and the adherents believe in 'total purity, and in the banishing of all sin and hate from their hearts', ibid., p. 165.

[114] Ibid., pp. 155, 181, 351.

[115] G. A. Reichard, op. cit., wrote, 'there are Protestants who do not believe in eternal damnation—I have not met any of these among the missionaries to the Navaho, theology being mainly of the fire-and-brimstone type'. On the number of missionaries among the Navaho who were aggressively fundamentalist, and the fewness of practising converts among the Navaho, see C. Kluckhohn and D. Leighton, op. cit., pp. 132–3.

much more obviously accommodative to the dominant norms of American society, in the idealized form in which they are presented by educative and religious agencies. But the Navaho have shown great resistance to christianization. The Navaho traditionally saw the gods as existing for man's benefit: he need not abase himself, as conversionist Christianity, with its strong preoccupation with sin, demanded. Yet, in the Peyote cult, the Navaho presented himself as weak and humble, needing instruction. He did so, however, in the context of an Indian movement, withdrawn from the ideas and practice of white society. The Peyote cult might inculcate the moral ideas of white society, but it did not do so in general adjustment to it, as would a conversionist faith, but rather in separation from it. The internalization of the new values was a guarantee not of conscious accommodation, but rather of the integrity of sustained independence.

Like other new North American Indian religions, Peyotism shows a distinctively different organizational form from the denominations of western Christendom, even though it has consciously imitated them. The imitation, like that of the Shaker Church some years before, was largely for defence from persecution and the attainment of rights. The structure had little relationship to Peyote practice, and at the grass-roots level, there has often been a vagueness among Peyote adherents about the activities and purposes of the Native American Church. Meetings on private initiative for named purposes (even though these purposes were perhaps only part of the movement's significance) and the persistence of private proprietorship of access to supernatural power show marked continuities with other indigenous practice. The bureaucratic structure of conversionist denominations, so well adopted by African thaumaturgical movements, was not approximated by North American Indians.

Lack of rigorous organization prevented divergence of ritual practice and belief from becoming the occasion of schisms, although different traditions often became the focus for rivalry. In general, however, Peyotists have been tolerant of the variant practices of rival road chiefs. The struggle of the shamans found new and more innocuous form within the central traditions of the new cult. The absence of an effective, well-articulated system of organization beyond the level of the almost *ad hoc* character of authority in the local meeting (in which the prestige of a particular road chief, rather than the hierarchization of offices, is what matters) reflects a characteristic found elsewhere in introversionist movements. The tendency to withdraw into new communities (rather than to create new organizations) and to rely on local social structure, is found in introversionist movements among European peasant strata.

It stands in sharp contrast to more vigorous voluntarism, which is the basic principle of organization among conversionist movements and a consequence of their distinctive response to the world. Other aspects of communal orientation are also conspicuous. Just as the Shaker spirit was met in the community rather than individually as of old, so the Peyote vision is communicated among a group rather than as an isolated experience of the individual. Traditional demand is now supported more distinctively in a group situation, the only situation in which the encounter with the supernatural—no longer the basic for the individual's life-course—can now be legitimated. The individual acquires his songs from the group circumstance, and it is back to the group that they are given.

14

The Rational Mutation of Religious Responses

DEVIANT religious responses to the world, as manifested in social movements, display distinct capacities for mutation. Not only the movements themselves, but also the particular processes of change that they undergo are powerfully influenced by the relation between, on the one hand, the culture and social conditions of the indigenes, and on the other, those of the advanced peoples who have dominated them. Cultural response to conquest itself varies. The North American Indians and the Maoris resisted—belatedly in the Maori case—the impress of white culture. Substantially dispossessed of their lands by the invaders, they rejected assimilation to the way of life and the values of the people who engulfed them. As their own social organization was destroyed, and as any possibility of assimilation to the dominant system disappeared, new patterns of response emerged. Ethnicity became the basis and bulwark of the new religious orientation and the new pattern of community life which sometimes arose with the new movement. Once tribal life was in decay, *ethnic* allegiance gained steadily over *tribal* allegiance: but from within the ethnic group a new voluntaristic principle came into operation as the basis for the new religiously-inspired communities. This re-girding of cultural loins was the assertion of a persisting, if much modified, way of native life.

New movements necessarily legitimated themselves by claiming to belong to the native past, and offered a separate path of native salvation. Necessarily, they retained much of the old thaumaturgical practice of the past, albeit in modified form. Thus the Shakers of the north-west coast and the Ratana movement perpetuated styles of thaumaturgical practice which, although by no means aboriginal, were none the less sufficiently separate and distinct even from white religio-therapeutic practice, and perpetuated sufficient elements from the indigenous cultural inheritance, to pass themselves off as such. At the same time, these movements avoided outright rejection of the primary religious concepts of the dominant culture, whilst asserting that the dominant religion *per se* was inappropriate to native needs. The Ringatu movement, the Menomini Powwow, and the Peyote cult similarly asserted

450

their nativistic quality. Their mythological legitimation emphasized revelation specifically for natives, and in so doing they abandoned all the tribal particularism of past native life, accepted a lowest common denominator of native cultures, and synthesized a style of religious practice that was innovative in its absorption of old and imported patterns. None the less, these movements remained emphatically different from anything in the dominant culture. They perpetuated a pattern of segregation, and a self-conscious ethnic particularism. Threats to the group reinforced these responses, and they functioned like introversionist sects in the dominant culture, preserving an inner and special piety, which in this case was also the remnant of ethnic and cultural traditions, or at least a representation of them even if traditions were no longer really known.

This response is in marked contrast to the extensive assimilation of western forms and styles by West Africans. The introversionist orientation has had less appeal there, since tribalism still represents the past, and has become an issue for the opposition of the young to the old. Traditional religious dispositions persist in the entirely new and legitimated contexts of the spiritual churches. Thaumaturgy adapts and finds new styles; old practitioners assimilate their procedures to those of the missions and of western society; and new ones—men who have been brought up with both traditional concepts and those of mission organizations—arise. The rational organizational form houses the thaumaturgical content. Introversion is alien: indeed, extroversion becomes almost a requirement for the whole culture, as well as for new movements, as a way of demonstrating parity of approach with the imported religions. Political independence has given a curious rationale to religious distinctiveness: the African mind, African religion, African spirituality have acquired respectability and autonomy, and particularly so in the search for a cultural ideology, such as *negritude*. The determination to recover the past, to prove its compatibility with, and perhaps its superiority to, the imported culture of the west, is not confined to the fantasy of the Black Muslims: it exists in some measure in West Africa, too.[1]

The impress of the modern world is such, however, that the pressure for rationalization, seen so clearly in the denominationalism of the West African thaumaturgical movements, is not confined to mere

---

[1] Thus in Ghana, during the régime of Kwame Nkrumah, when the search for an ideological underpinning for his political ambitions stimulated acceptance of the philosophies of *negritude*, pan-Africanism, and Russian-style communism, 'research' into 'African religion' was officially promoted—for instance at the shrine of Akonade in Larteh. Both the herbalistic and divinatory aspects of the system were studied, with a view to legitimating the religions of the African past.

organizational forms. Steadily it begins to affect religious ideas them-selves. A process of secularization occurs, as the sanctity of the past, of the culture, the way of life, the people, is lost. As instrumental relationships and the institutions of modern society which embody them—the work order; the rational-legal system of law and economy; political institutions and the bureaucracy (at times extending into military organizations); the educational system and scientific procedures —supersede the communal and affective bases of traditional societies, so religious movements also undergo rationalization. As structural and cultural differentiation occurs, the affective spheres of life and the agencies of social support and reassurance cease to be co-terminous with whole—now increasingly cosmopolitan—local communities, and become more specifically confined to the sub-communities of those of like culture or to self-selected communities of those sharing common life-orientations. Regulation of the individual passes from the com-munity at large to more formal agencies of social control, more external and remote systems of regulation. The provision of solace becomes professionalized to an increasing extent, and the psychic gratification supplied by the thaumaturge is transformed into faith in science and medicine, administered by peoples who in themselves become decreas-ingly mysterious, mere administrators of impersonal knowledge decreasingly worthy of the blind faith which was once thought to make men whole.

The new religious movements among less-developed peoples display tendencies to increasingly routinized and rational responses. This means, necessarily, that religion loses something of its magical orienta-tion, and accepts increasingly the logic of economic, political, bureau-cratic, and educational institutions copied from the western world. We have noted this phenomenon in the forms of organization that West African spiritual churches have copied, not only from the missions, but from the mission-sponsoring denominations of western countries.

Rationalization also occurs not simply in organizational structure, but also in the actual mutations of religious responses of less-developed peoples. It would be too much to assert that from religious heterodoxy emerges secular orthodoxy in one sphere or another, but the process is sometimes almost an analogue of the function of the Protestant ethic in promoting consequences of a rational kind (and this not only in the economic sphere, to which most attention has been paid, but also in the evolution of political, and particularly democratic institutions).[2]

[2] The reference here is to the new emphasis on rudimentary procedures for the maintenance of order, the conduct of meetings, and decision-making found within some of these new religious movements, and not to the political institutions of the state-societies in which they arise.

The particular direction in which religious responses have come to manifest a greater degree of rationality has been a consequence of a diverse set of influences, some of which have been more influential in one circumstance than another. The particular imprint of the mission in a given area may have done much to promote, or retard, specific developments. The traditional preoccupations of the traditional culture have also heavily conditioned this development. Religious responses have also been affected by the opportunities that have existed for other social movements to evolve, with which the new religions may have co-operated, or from which they may have needed to make distinct their own sphere of interest. Most important of all, perhaps, has been the relative strengths of indigenous and invading populations, and the consequent effect on the native social system. The number of variables in each situation would require an extensive and detailed analysis of each given case. All that can be offered here are very tentative intimations of the relative strength of some of these items as they are revealed by broad comparisons.

New religious responses among less-developed peoples have had a prospect of development that few of the sects arising in advanced nations have had. The new movements have a future. They are themselves dynamic responses to changing circumstances, and because they are sometimes the most manifest expression of native independence, native aspirations, and native concerns, they may become a key to the prospects of new nations. The many similarities in such movements have been the basis for the standard typology that has been used in this discussion, but there are also emphatic differences—the pre-occupation with witchcraft in Africa; the almost obsessive concern with trade goods in Melanesia; the secularism of revolutionist responses in Central and East Africa; and the very limited manifestation of any sort of millennialism in West Africa. These divergences become even more striking when one sees that in the Congo the revolutionism of the Kimbanguist movement, although giving rise to many different organizations that underwent different processes of mutation, did produce a movement that aspired to be a national church; whilst in Kenya religious responses were associated with educational independence; and in New Guinea with the emergence of new patterns of producer co-operatives.

Among *minority* indigenous peoples—the North American Indians and the Maoris—we see new religious movements disavowing overt processes of rationalization. There is not, except in self-defence, the will to promote a church structure—which in itself would arise only in a much more unified society than either of these native peoples represent—nor yet does religion become an agency for the re-organization of other social institutions along rational lines. The new movements, in becoming introversionist, reinforce piety, and concentrate on the re-organization of the community as such. The balance of the dominant and minority cultures appears here to be the crucial determinant of the mutation of religious response: religion becomes the agency in which is preserved the distinctive culture and the distinctive community of the group. Immigrants before they are assimilated manifest the same pattern, sometimes clinging in their religion to the language and customs of their past, sanctifying even the secular aspects of their own older tradition. But for a muted development of pan-Indianism, evident in the Peyote cult, the Powwow, and perhaps more incidentally in the Shaker movement, there has been very little rational mutation of religious movements among these peoples.

The institutionalization of a millennial movement

The direction of the mutation occurring among the millennialist movements in the (former Belgian) Congo has been affected by the sudden acquisition of political independence. Millennialism is always an at least partially transcendentalized conception of political relationships. What is sought in such movements is power—power for the believers themselves, or for the constituency (tribal, racial, or stratificational) from which they come. It represents a collective salvation. As long as the political control of the natives of the Congo remained in the hands of the whites, millennialism, once uttered, recurred, both in the Kitawala movement and in the congeries of movements that arose in the wake of the thaumaturgical teaching of Simon Kimbangu, and which claimed him as their predecessor. The prospect was never hopeless, as it became in South Africa, where religious independence —with implications for political independence—has, in the 'Ethiopian' churches, only muted expression. When Congolese independence came, millennialism in the xenophobic style in which it had recrudesced under Matswa, Mpadi, Ntangu, and other prophets, was, in some degree, anachronistic—although by no means abandoned by all of the persisting sectarian movements. But Kimbangu himself—so much identified as the opponent of white rule (and with so little justification) —ceased to be a returning messiah, a cultural hero, arriving with the ancestors, as he had often been depicted in the past. He became (however inappropriately, considering his own doctrines) the Winstanley, the Babeuf, the Tolstoy, or the Garvey of the liberation that followed.[3]

A religious clientele is not, however, converted into a political association even by the dramatic declaration of national independence (which some certainly thought would be the beginning of the millennium). Even this 'millennium' had been slow to come, and in the meantime some branches of Kimbanguism had acquired functions other than those of stimulating millennial hopes. When the Kimbanguists proper dared to appeal for recognition in the increasingly liberal atmosphere of the Belgian Congo in the mid 1950s, they did so as a movement modelled on the respectable denominations of western Christendom, and one prepared to take its place as the national church of the country. Over the years, and particularly following the Second World War, there had been a remarkable proliferation of voluntary associations, many of them tribal and kinship associations, but all of them with more prospect of acquiring political functions than had the religious movements, which had disavowed all political motives.[4] As these new vehicles for cultural expression arose, so they, rather than the erstwhile messianic movements, inherited the political future. The sects were not altogether superseded, however: the politicians looked to them for supernatural legitimation. The prospect for the Kimbanguist movement was more distinctively in the religious field than it had been for some time.

A variety of movements claimed to be the successors to Kimbangu, but the most impressive of them was the organization that took the name *L'Église de Jesus-Christ sur la terre par le prophète Simon Kimbangu* (EJCSK). Its relation to the Kintwadi ('association') movement is not easily discerned, and there was probably considerable overlap, but the EJCSK emerged as a relatively rationally-organized religion once the new policy of tolerance was instituted in the mid 1950s. It had ceased to announce the end of the world, and it eschewed the mythical restorative ideals of Simon Mpadi, whose newly revived movement became preoccupied with the somewhat legendary accounts of his inheritance of the mantle of Kimbangu, and the days of oppression.[5] The new Church, with its headquarters at Nkamba, where Kimbangu had lived, and where his widow and three sons were then living,

[3] Thus President Kasa-Vubu and others were present to pay respects when Kimbangu's bones were transported from Elisabethville to Matadi-Mayo in April 1960. R. Lemarchand, *Political Awakening in the Belgian Congo*, op. cit., p. 173. According to J. Van Wing, who visited Kimbangu in prison in 1947, at this time Kimbangu himself was thoroughly disillusioned, and wanted to be baptized into the Catholic Church: J. Van Wing, 'Le Kibanguisme . . .', op. cit., p. 580.

[4] R. Lemarchand, op. cit., p. 167–8.

[5] G. Bernard and P. Caprasse, 'Religious Movements in the Congo . . .', op. cit., pp. 49–60.

became the centre for various Kimbanguist movements, and the EJCSK allowed other groups to be associated with it, without taking full responsibility for them.[6]

The EJCSK had a doctrine and liturgy that were largely Protestant, with emphasis on baptism by immersion, public confession, and free interpretation of the Bible, and its leaders regarded it as a development of Protestantism. They attempted to eliminate the more ecstatic practices inherited from the past, particularly shaking, nocturnal dancing, and polygamy, although the mixture of its constituency— from sophisticated *evolués* to illiterates for whom the name of Kimbangu still had a messianic ring and who sought ecstatic experience and healing from their religion—was a circumstance imposing some diversity upon, and flexibility within, the EJCSK. The Church published its programme of activities, and its catechisms (one of which made no mention of Kimbangu, although the others—in French, Kikongo, and Lingala— did ŝo). The Church insisted upon its respect for authority, although it remained somewhat opposed to missions, which it regarded as alien, in contrast to its own claim to be Congolese Christianity. It published its own rules (including the ten commandments) which demanded that its members should not smoke; engage in quarrels; calumnate their neighbours; retain fetiches. It concluded its statement on these matters, '*à suivre*', which perhaps indicated the extent to which the movement encouraged flexibility and the prospect of its own evolution.[7]

The Church disavowed a political role, although the distinction between religion and politics was not, as Raymaekers emphasizes, always easily understood by Africans.[8] Since it expressed a willingness to be regarded as a state religion, and since, after independence, it gained the same standing for its ministers as that accorded to Roman Catholic priests and Protestant ministers, the Church authorities were clearly aware of their dependence on political relationships.[9] It was led by many young men who had obtained important positions in the state, and 'it is not surprising to discern a willingness to become 'a State religion in protest against the imported character of the other religions'.[10] Its impressive organization imitated the structure of advanced denominations and voluntary associations, with legal representatives, and a central and regional hierarchy, as well as publications on the Church's teaching and constitution. Its rigour in

[6] P. Raymaekers, 'L'Église de Jesus-Christ sur la terre par le prophète Simon Kimbangu . . .', op. cit., on which this section relies to a considerable extent.
[7] Ibid., p. 695.
[8] Ibid., p. 703.
[9] G. Bernard and P. Caprasse, op. cit., p. 58.
[10] Loc. cit.

practice may, of course, have been much less than all of these developments tended to suggest.[11]

The EJCSK had not, apparently, sloughed off, and perhaps had not
entirely sought to slough off, the thaumaturgical inheritance of its past.
The demand for effective agencies against witchcraft and the provision
of therapeutic relief continued in the Congo after independence as
before. The *Dieudonné* movement manifested, in Kikwit (Kwilu), east
of the Bas-Congo, in the mid 1950s, the continuing preoccupation with
the destruction of fetiches and sorcery accusations.[12] In the same
province, Kwilu, the *Mpeve* sect, also known as BenaSimon (people of
Simon) an offshoot of Kimbanguism, although basically concerned
with essentially thaumaturgical attempts to invoke the spirits, came
into conflict with the authorities, in 1962, after resisting various
measures of the new Congolese independent provincial government of
Kwilu, and had to be suppressed, as the Dieudonné sect had been by
the Belgian authorities a few years earlier. Thaumaturgy and civil
disobedience were obviously closely associated, particularly in a period
of inflation, in which ordinary western medicaments, such as aspirins,
had become very expensive, and in which tribal healers were again
thriving.[13] The Kintwadist movement, with which the EJCSK was
connected, had the same preoccupations, and used holy water and
encouraged prophetic visions.[14] The EJCSK itself charged the Catholic
and Protestant missionaries with opposing supernatural revelation,
which, the Kimbanguists implied, was a way of denying the worth of
Congolese Christianity.[15]

Yet, with all this, the attempt was made to draw on distinctive
Congolese traditions to create a church which might take on functions
similar to those of the religious institutions of more advanced nations.
Religious unification and centralization were a rationalizing step
towards the creation of supra-tribal identity, and although Kimbanguism has belonged most peculiarly to the extreme west of the
Congo, the Bas-Congo, with later dissemination in Kwilu, it had
acquired more prestige than any other movement in the struggle for
distinctly Congolese native independence. It had fed political movements, but had not abandoned the central religiosity of its own past.
The process of secularization does not occur so quickly.

[11] P. Raymaekers, op. cit., p. 722.
[12] J. Van Wing, op. cit., p. 611 ff.
[13] Renée C. Fox, Willy de Craemer, and Jean-Marie Ribeaucourt, ' "The Second
Independence": A Case Study of the Kwilu Rebellion in the Congo', *Comparative Studies in
Society and History* VIII, 1 (October 1965), pp. 78–109 (pp. 90–2).
[14] G. Bernard, 'The Nature of a Sociological Research . . .', op. cit.
[15] P. Raymaekers, op. cit., p. 704.

This was evident from the persistence of thaumaturgical movements, and from the recrudescence, in the unsettled years of independence, of new millennial and thaumaturgical responses, when the prospects of independence—the secularized millennial hope—proved disappointing. Although the EJCSK was not itself involved, in Kwilu the earlier waves of Kimbanguist and other sectarianism fed the semi-communist rebellion of the Mulelists in the struggle for what was called 'La Deuxième Indépendence'. The failure of the native government to fulfil the extravagant promises of the new political parties, such as the Parti Solidaire Africain in Kwilu, led to deep disillusionment.[16] When Pierre Mulele, a close associate of Antoine Gizenga, Vice-President of the Congo under Patrice Lumumba, organized the villagers of Kwilu, after internecine feuding had deprived these men of office, he did so according to a crude utopian Marxism, assisted by the typical assertions of millennialist activists. Mulele was regarded as being invulnerable to bullets, and obedience to his injunctions (most of which were practical, but which included such typically nativist injunctions as abstinence from all things European) would, it was believed, confer invulnerability on the rebels in the cadres that he trained. Only obedience to him would ensure fertility, and preserve children from illness. He was cast as the thaumaturge who was omnipresent and omniscient. The rebels needed a magical ideology and a millennial prospect to spur their efforts: political programmes were in themselves not enough.[17] Their aims, however, were those of political revolution, and even though thaumaturgical elements were involved, their goal was practical and realizable. They were not thorough-going millenarians.

The unsettled conditions of the Congo facilitated the recrudescence of millennial dreams, as material circumstances became less secure than they had ever been before. Yet despite this political regression, the achievement of the EJCSK is still a testimony to the possibility of rational mutations of primitive religious responses. It is comparable to the acceptance of rational organization by the spiritual churches in West Africa, but the revolutionism in its tradition gave it far greater access to political associations than had been available to the sects of Ghana and Nigeria. In circumstances such as those of the Congo, where political outlets existed, the millennial strain might have died away entirely, had the indigenes shown themselves capable of establishing stable government and progressive policies, giving at least some

[16] R. C. Fox, et al., op. cit., p. 91, provide illustration of these disillusionments. This paragraph rests on this source.
[17] Ibid., pp. 98–101. In other areas, rebels were rendered 'invulnerable' by sorcerers who treated them with special magic.

satisfaction to the exaggerated expectations of the populace. The frustrations of the acute political and social anarchy of the Congo in the early 1960s kept millennialism alive—in the service of internecine struggles within tribes, classes, and parties. The introversionist mutation, so typical of millennial sects arising among native *minorities* and among depressed strata in advanced societies, was never a likelihood in so disturbed a situation as the Congo, where dreams of supernatural power suddenly seemed almost realizable by political action. The over-stimulation of expectation, and the deprivation and frustration that followed were quite unlike the resignation into which the intro-versionist sect lapses, satisfied as it has to be with an enclave and a way apart. For the Congolese sectarian, the millennial prospect could be identified with the political prospects of the whole people. The illusion of the millennium was enlarged and, for some time at least, provided a self-sustaining mechanism of alternating dreams and disappointments, as entirely supernatural visions were harnessed to purely political and military action.

Pan-Indianism: the religious contribution

New religions among North American Indians contributed very much less consciously to the process of rationalization than new movements occurring in some other cultures. Pan-Indianism began with the defensive alliances of related tribes, such as the enduring league of the Iroquois, and the Creek confederation in the seventeenth century and, later, the briefer associations of tribes in the military campaigns of Pontiac and Tecumseh, both of whom used religious cement to re-inforce Indian solidarity in the face of an ethnically defined enemy. But even here, the Indians were almost pawns in the struggle, siding with the French, English, or Americans in battles which, whatever the outcome, were part of a long war that they must lose. With the emergence of the prophetic movements, and particularly the two Ghost Dances, awareness of Indian identity increased, as tribes with very different cultural traditions were drawn into a new pattern of ritual which itself hastened the decay of their own old ceremonials. In this period a set of beliefs, or a dance style, or songs in one tribal language not understood by other tribes, were transmitted from tribe to tribe: and there was also the more local borrowing of ceremonies by one tribe from another, such as occurred with the Sun Dance among the Comanches and Utes. There was also the diffusion of myths, and the acknowledgement that ritual forms and myths that purported to be history were not unique tribal possessions, but had been learned from other peoples. So it was with the story of the Powwow (Dream Dance) and with Peyote.

Peyotism has sometimes been regarded as constituting a form of nativistic nationalism for Indian peoples, a defence against white domination.[18] It arose at the time of decay of tribal culture, when traditional ceremonies and religious life were losing their meaning. Peyotism represented the detachment of religion from the active lives of its adherents. As the old and regular routines of life were replaced by uncertainty and aimlessness, so religion ceased to legitimate practical activities and was necessarily quietistic. Whilst Peyotists were taught to integrate religious ethics with everyday experience, in a manner common among introversionist sects, their procedures and practices were less clearly, or at least less directly, connected to biological rhythms and work routines. It was less elaborate, less egocentric, and less tribocentric than the traditional systems. Earlier, so much of Indian religion had been related to the life activities of individuals, their search for guidance, reassurance, justification, and salvation. Now religious activity became an end in itself, with a certain ethical appendage. Peyote was almost a prolonged inducement of reverie for the past, theoretically the tribal past, but increasingly simply the past of the Indian. Its dissemination from the Kiowa, Comanche, and Wichita reservation in Oklahoma, where it may have taken its general shape as a cult movement, throughout and beyond the Plains, was undoubtedly an important factor in the diffusion of the new sense of common Indian identity, which men in similarly oppressed circumstances, and faced with a common oppressor, were coming to recognize.

But if Peyote may be described as pan-Indian, it is less easy to attribute to it more than a contributory role in the development of a common sense of Indian identity. It arose in circumstances in which there were much more impressive evidences of commonality of identity among tribesmen: the reservations; the new boarding schools; the allotment system which promoted the disintegration of tribal unity; the increased geographic mobility; the heightened possibilities of inter-tribal marriage. Peyote becomes almost one of these circumstances itself, even if its particular contribution was to provide expression, ideological defence, and ritual forms for new Indian culture. Other agencies were more important than this introversionist and quietistic religion, which, although it was steadily diffused and carried from one tribe to another by active proselytizers, was never conversionist in

[18] J. S. Slotkin, *The Peyote Religion*, op. cit., p. 7.

orientation. Recruitment was haphazard, at the whim very often of individuals who sought prestige or wealth from the new rituals, rather than because of religious injunctions to promote salvation.

The other agencies were not rapidly developed, and they were mainly political in form. The five tribes of the Cherokee, Seminole, Chickasaw, Creek, and Choctaw attempted, at the time of the admission of Oklahoma to statehood, in 1907, to join forces to establish an Indian state. It was a temporary, but an early, non-military alliance of Indian peoples for a conscious political end. The First World War, which evoked a spontaneous demonstration of Indian patriotism, even though Indians were not subject to military service, brought into being veterans' clubs among Indians, which, paradoxically, may have enhanced the sense of common Indian identity. Improvement associations and defence leagues had existed, sometimes ephemerally, since the late nineteenth century, and the new Indian legislation of the American government, in the 1930s, produced widespread responses from the various tribes. In 1944, an all-Indian organization was founded at Denver, and in 1961, the National Indian Youth Council, which became an even more vigorous defender of Indian rights, leading to Indian candidatures for public office in the elections of 1964. These agencies were slow to evolve, and, faced with the dominance of white America, they have not been particularly effective in practice. The struggle of the National Indian Youth Council on behalf of the fishing and game rights of the more than forty tribes in Washington state has been hailed as the first time that many tribes had joined together to solve a common political problem.[19]

In comparison with the activities of the Indians of Alaska and British Columbia, these were slow developments. The Alaska Native Brotherhood, which was founded as early as 1912 among the Tlingit and Alaskan Haida, sought both to reduce aboriginal practices, particularly the potlatch, as well as to fight for Indian rights in matters of voting, reservation policy, and racial discrimination.[20] In British Columbia, a land committee, formed among the Niska in 1890, had led to petitions and to the organization of the Allied Tribes of British Columbia in 1915.[21] The Indians of the far north-west coastal regions had, of course, been longer exposed to processes of acculturation than had the Indians

[19] Shirley Hill Witt, 'Nationalistic Trends Among American Indians', *Midcontinent American Studies Journal* 6, 2 (Fall 1965), pp. 51–74 (p. 65). This paragraph leans on this source.
[20] Philip Drucker, *The Native Brotherhoods: Modern Intertribal Organizations on the Northwest Coast*, Smithsonian Institutions: Bureau of American Ethnology (Government Printing Office, Washington 1958), pp. 42 ff.
[21] Ibid., p. 95.

of the Plains and mountain region of the United States, but their pan-Indian progress was, even so, more impressive and quite secular.

Even in the realm of cultural pan-Indianism, the Peyote cult did not in itself play so prominent a role, although it came before the evolution of secularized forms of pan-Indian expression. When these occurred, however, in the Indian Powwows and the inter-tribal clubs, they became much more conscious vehicles of Indian culture, and existed to express Indian identity in an avowed way that has never been part of the purpose of the Peyote cult. The dissemination of English as the *lingua franca* of Indians has perhaps been more important than the Peyote cult in forging conspicuous links. The dissemination of Plains culture, and the assimilation of quite innovative styles of costume and dance, has had the explicit purpose of fostering Indian identity. The Powwows, which centre round these performances, largely for the purpose of displaying Indian culture to both Indians and whites, are consciously sponsored by tribal councils of various groups, and have led to a circumstance in which a Pawnee might sing Ponca songs without knowing that they are not those of his own tribe. In some small tribes, such as the Quapaw and Kansa, pan-Indian culture has become the only culture which the tribe has.[22] Members of many tribal groups were involved in this new self-conscious national culture, although it has sometimes also been opposed by traditionalists within these same tribes, and, paradoxically, this opposition has even led to inter-tribal contacts of quite remote tribes seeking to preserve their traditional way of *tribal* life in the face of pan-Indianism—such was the case among the Hopi, Seminole, and Iroquois.[23] Local nationalism prevailed among the Navaho.

The Peyote cult had become, by the mid 1960s, 'the main present-day religion of more than fifty tribes from California to Michigan'.[24] Its association with cultural pan-Indianism is limited, although Peyote meetings have sometimes been organized for participants in the intervals of the activities at the Powwows, at least in the Great Lakes region.[25] At the same time, Peyote did give rise to disputes within tribes, and was seen by some, even at this date, as being a corruption

[22] James H. Howard, 'Pan-Indian Culture of Oklahoma', *Scientific Monthly* 81, 5 (November 1955), pp. 215–20. Even in New England, the Powwow circuit has become a prominent event: Ernst Schuskey, 'Pan-Indianism in the Eastern United States', *Anthropology Tomorrow* VI, 1 (December 1957), pp. 116–23.

[23] Robert K. Thomas, 'Pan-Indianism', *Midcontinent American Studies Journal* 6, 2 (Fall 1965), pp. 75–83 (pp. 79–80).

[24] S. H. Witt, op. cit., p. 68.

[25] Gertrude Protosch Kurath, 'Pan-Indianism in Great Lakes Tribal Festivals', *Journal of American Folklore* 70 (April–June 1957), pp. 179–82.

of Indian traditions, and particularly of tribal traditions. Although the cult is the principal religious expression of Indian ethnicity, it has not played a very active role in promoting this new sense of identity, outside the confines of the cultists themselves. It is, indeed, a sanctification of ethnicity, and the ethnic way of salvation, but it is not the public manifestation of Indian ideology. It is a retreat into the ethnic enclave, rather than the promotion of Indian nationalism. That it brings tribesmen into new connections is clear, but Peyotism is not a religious justification of national destiny. It is not a national church in the way in which European societies had national churches, nor even in the way in which the Kimbanguists have appropriated this role in the Congo. Its formal organization has not been a proclamation for the Indian people, but a defence for the Peyote religion itself. It remains an introversionist, not a nationalistic, response.

Religious responses and civic purposes

Deviant religious responses tend to express the alienation of men from civic involvement. Among minority peoples the opportunity for civic involvement is limited, and once the millennial phase has passed there is a clear tendency not only to participate, but deliberately to withdraw into the confines of a communally organized system. The wider society, the only society in which civic concerns are appropriate, is rejected. In western Christendom, it is in the developed sectarianism of groups that have appropriated to themselves the role of the social conscience, that civic concerns arise among sectarians, as for example among the Quakers. Even then, the participation in civic matters is restricted, entered into only on the sect's own terms. In less-developed societies, particularly in those where the indigenous population has remained a majority, religious protest has often been a response to political, economic, and social arrangements and to the cultural dominance of the invader. Eventually, whether the invader has remained and stabilized his rule, as in South Africa, or has granted partial autonomy or total independence to his former wards, as in Melanesia and in some parts of Africa, the protest of deviant religiosity has tended to become attenuated. Even though the concern of such movements might be—most typically—the provision of healing agencies which claim superiority to those of the dominant culture, the organization that provides such services may acquire other functions.

The welfare provisions of some African sects, and the acquisition of a sect territory on the model of a tribal homeland, have been noted above. These may be more the provision of benefits for believers than the distribution of welfare to the community at large, but they take the form of a manifestation of new civic concern. The development of medical and welfare facilities for a wider public by the Kardecists and even by the Umbandists in Brazil is an indication of the mobilization of religious sentiments of goodwill which transcend the confines of the movements themselves. These, of course, are sects without boundaries, and it is easier for such groups to come into the service of the wider community than for sects with a closely defined membership.[26] The model of the mission has undoubtedly stimulated welfare orientations of this kind, and even spiritualistic churches, in West Africa as well as in Brazil, have sponsored public institutions—schools, hospitals, rest homes are the most usual undertakings—perhaps partly in imitation of mission practice. As with the missions, the motivation has often been a mixture of goodwill, the urge to proselytize, the manifestation of accomplishment, and the opportunity for the self-enhancement of the movement and its personnel. Such efforts also fulfil the function of redirecting the energies of a clientele when the actual benefits from religion itself have palled, or when the excitement of religious activity appears insufficient to sustain commitment. Clearly, this pattern can develop only where some considerable articulation of a movement's authority-structure has occurred, and where men are not simply indulging in a set of rites, but are bound to an organization.

The relationship of religious allegiance and voluntary associations for secular purposes was of vital importance in the promotion of civic concern in nineteenth- and early twentieth-century Europe and America, and particularly so in Protestant movements, in which self-help, the absence of powerful hierarchies, and the principles of grass-roots democracy were most fully developed. Within the limitations of

---

[26] Clearly the sectarian response which I label Reformist and which, since the late nineteenth century, the Quakers have espoused, makes social works into a religious activity *per se*. The *raison d'être* of the movement becomes philanthropy. Since the late nineteenth century social concern for outsiders has become an increasingly important subsidiary orientation for a number of movements, most conspicuously the Salvation Army. In other cases particular issues of concern for outsiders have developed from specific aspects of a movement's teaching. Thus the doctrinal emphasis on Old Testament dietetic prescriptions have given impetus to general concern for medical welfare, including anti-smoking clinics and medical missionary work, among the Seventh Day Adventists. Perhaps from their distrust of orthodox medical use of pharmacological therapy, the Scientologists have entered the field of rehabilitation of drug-users. Since the Second World War the Christadelphians have developed charitable concerns for outsiders which far transcend their early preoccupation with providing assistance for Jews: in some respects this movement illustrates some shift from an introversionist position to responses closer to 'reformist'. On this last point, see B. R. Wilson, *Religious Sects* (Weidenfeld, London; McGraw-Hill, New York 1971).

the political situation, such voluntary bodies have grown in association with religious movements (sometimes ultimately shaking themselves free from religious concerns, much as has occurred with hospitals, schools, colleges, benefit societies, youth associations, and similar institutions in western societies).

In South Africa, the impetus which new religious responses and independent groups have given to political causes has, perforce, been somewhat muted, but one development has been the emergence of the powerful *manyanos*, the women's movements. That these are *women's* movements indicates one of the contributions to civic involvement which is not uncommon in protesting religions—the increase of opportunities for women to participate in religious affairs is often the beginning of their increased opportunity for involvement in social affairs generally. The *manyanos* in the African movements were an imitation of the form of women's organizations established by the more orthodox churches. They spread to many of the independent churches, whether thaumaturgical ('Zionist') movements or 'Ethiopian' movements. The women conducted their own meetings and evolved their own uniforms, and the movements began to undertake social, judicial, and religious functions for their members.[27]

The *manyanos* represented both new civic concerns, providing women with recreation, training in conducting public affairs, and informal education, and a search for more authentic religious experience. Although they are usually independent of the ministers of the churches to which they belong, the *manyanos* are religious organizations, with a general atmosphere of 'weeping and sighing', and they provide a general catharsis for their members.[28] Increasingly, however, the young women seek to reduce the emotional expression of these organizations, and seek more formality in the proceedings, and less of the carry-over into the new christianized forms of traditional preoccupations with divining and herbalism.[29] If the *manyanos*, perhaps particularly those of the African independent churches, have not acquired all the characteristics of the women's voluntary associations of western society, this in itself indicates simply that secularization is a slow process and that the redirection from emotionally oriented concern with spiritual and physical well-being to concern with social and civic affairs takes time. The fact of the independent organization of women is itself a very considerable evidence of the process of rationalization.

[27] The paragraph relies on Mia Brandel-Syrier, *Black Women in Search of God* (Lutterworth Press, London 1962).
[28] Ibid., p. 34.
[29] Ibid., p. 210.

Millennial magic and economic enterprise

The principal focus of the millennialist movements in Melanesia has been uniformly economic. The millennial dream, whilst often including the return of the ancestors, has typically concentrated on the prospect of the sudden availability of various objects of European manufacture. Elements of 'cargo' ideas have sometimes occurred in Africa in millennial movements, but their importance in Melanesian movements has been far greater. The millennial movements themselves have frequently been more than mere attempts to dance into being an age in which cargo commodities would become abundant—practical steps to receive the cargo, by building wharfs, airstrips, or by engaging in disciplined drill, have usually accompanied the purely ritualistic activity. At times these efforts have been destructive of existing property, and at times they have been self-contradictory, in placing an embargo on the very types of commodities—European commodities—that the millennial age was to provide in such abundance. But this, perhaps, has been an incidental manifestation of strong anti-white feeling associated with the desire to acquire the goods which the white men have.

It is for anthropologists and comparative ethnologists to account for the cultural factors which cause Melanesians to be so preoccupied with the economic benefits of civilization. In the relatively small tribes and even smaller relatively autonomous village units of Melanesian society, productive capacity and trading ability were powerful determinants of prestige, rivalling chieftainship. The opportunity for economic achievement existed in Melanesian society, and no doubt this strong emphasis on the artefacts of material well-being made the European appear so immensely successful in the eyes of the indigenes. The eagerness to accept European products fitted neither a pattern of restorative millennialism nor one of perpetuative introversionism. Native Melanesian culture, although drastically affected by the activities of European mining companies and planters, was also relatively readily abandoned in the face of cultural contact, compared to the persistence of native ways of life in other less-developed societies. Several factors may account for this, particularly the greater disparity between the indigenes and the invaders from the very early days of contact. Invasion on any scale occurred at a date when European technology was very much more advanced than it had been in the first two-and-a-half centuries of steady cultural contact with North American Indian peoples. Native resistance to the invaders was never on the scale of warfare, such as occurred in Africa or even among American Indians, and conquest was easily achieved. The basis for tribal alliances did not exist among so many mutually antagonistic groups, locked in local raiding, head-hunting, and cannibalism. The Melanesians were economically oriented, but like the Indians of the Canadian and Alaskan north-west, their search for gain had no outlet except in the elaborate and prestige-conferring ceremonials and feasts which punctuated the life of gardening, fishing, and trading.

From the earliest contact, the emphasis of the colonists was on the salvation of the native. Education, medical care, and the reduction of aggression were all early aspects of the colonial endeavour: there was never a pretence of simply living as neighbours to native societies as there had been in South Africa and America. Nor was there extensive expropriation of land. The European came, in greater measure than could ever have appeared to be the case in large parts of Africa and America, to teach and guide the native. Some economic exploitation certainly occurred, but not to the extent that it took place in societies suitable for extensive European settlement. Consequently, quite apart from the divisiveness and hence the relative powerlessness of Melanesian society, the struggle for political autonomy was not brought into such marked relief. Melanesians sought material wealth in their traditional cultures. They were under the impression that the primary concern of the missionaries and government agencies was to benefit the native. The sight of western wealth, particularly during the Second World War, but in some limited measure before this, made Melanesians dream of possessions like those of the Europeans.

The issue in respect of which Melanesian movements manifested increased degrees of rationality was the endeavour to increase wealth: the methods were an imitation of European behaviour and artefacts.[30] If religious techniques were the first to be employed, this was an obvious procedure for savages. And it was one that was reinforced by the missionaries, who taught that from God, the white man's God, all good things came, and who readily attributed civilization and European wealth to the power of religion. It was largely their recognition of the remoteness of religious activity from productive activity among Europeans, that induced Melanesians to imitate other European procedures in the hope of making religion work, and it was their impatience with the results of Christian belief that induced them to take supplementary, or alternative, measures. To a people for whom religion was pragmatic and who expected ancestor spirits to protect and provide, or to suffer dismissal, the association of the two sets of techniques, spiritual and practical, was self-evidently necessary.

[30] See Chapter 10.

Marching Rule and the Malekula Co-operative

The *Marching Rule* movement of the Solomon Islands has been regarded by some writers on Melanesia as at once the expression of acute political consciousness and the result of growing awareness of economic deprivation—in short, of the emergence of a relatively sophisticated appraisal of social conditions and a capacity for rational action to attain well-articulated goals.[31] At most, this characterization may have held for some of the leaders of the movement: the mass of the rank-and-file following appear to have entertained quite different conceptions.

The Solomon Islands, an archipelago 900 miles long, of six large and many small islands, had experienced some labour recruiting and some missionary activity before the British Protectorate was declared in 1893. White men had been periodically killed, and the Navy had even shelled villages by way of reprisal. Land had been appropriated mainly for copra plantations, for which native labour had been recruited, but it was not until the 1930s that all areas of the archipelago had been brought under control. In 1937 there were forty-two Europeans, 417 natives, and five Chinese in the administrative service.[32] But the punitive expeditions that had followed the occasional murder of European officials had established the reputation of the District Officers as very formidable war-leaders, far more powerful than native 'big men'.

Many of the former functions of the 'big man'—as judge, tax-gatherer, and feast-giver, as well as warrior chief—were now fulfilled by the District Officer. He acquired the role of 'big man'—although this was traditionally an achieved (not an ascribed) status. Simultaneously, mission influence, particularly that of the South Seas Evangelical Mission, had worked to prevent natives from rising in social status, by the prohibition of bride-price and feast-giving. On the plantations, managers were aggressive and tough, behaving like traditional enemies: rather than work for them, natives preferred

---

[31] This is expressed most explicitly by P. Worsley, op. cit., p. 182, where he writes of Marching Rule. 'It would be a mistake to pay too much attention to the millenarian aspect of this movement to the exclusion of the more important political, social and economic demands which are the ordinary stuff of world politics. The demands for minimum wages, for improved educational and social services, for independence and self-rule, for national self-expression etc. are the important features of Marching Rule, not the lingering myths of the Cargo.' These points are rebutted in considerable detail by G. Cochrane, *Big Men and Cargo Cults* (Clarendon Press, Oxford 1970).

[32] G. Cochrane, op. cit., on whom the following paragraphs principally rely.

European service.[33] Together, these influences worked towards the derogation of native status: 'big men' were now necessarily Europeans; natives, their opportunities for achievement and social mobility circumscribed, became conscious of themselves as 'rubbish men'.[34] Cochrane sees the Solomon Islanders' loss of eligibility to attain high status as the background circumstance of discontent out of which the Marching Rule movement arose.[35]

The name 'Marching Rule' has been said to be derived from *ma-asinga*, meaning 'brother' in a dialect of the Are-Are language,[36] but it seems more probable that it originates in a hymn that natives had learned in the South Seas Evangelical Mission.[37] The movement probably began in the Labour Corps of Solomon Islanders formed to help Allied troops on Guadalcanal in 1943. By 1945 it had spread to Malaita, Ulawa, and San Cristoval, and in 1947 to Florida and Ysabel.[38] The outbreak of the movement coincided with the impact of military activity on Guadalcanal, but whatever significance may be attributed to such dramatic cultural contact in stimulating the cult, it spread to other islands where military action between the Allies and the Japanese did not take place. Stories, rumours, and expectations that henceforth things would be different were, given energetic leadership, sufficient to stimulate the diffusion of the movement once it had begun.

The presence of large numbers of American troops may have encouraged ideas about the prospects of a new social order, even though, Cochrane tells us, 'only 12 per cent had come into close contact with the Americans through service in the Defence Corps or Labour Corps'.[39] In behaving so differently from government officials, missionaries, and traders, they undoubtedly created an impression that influenced far more Solomon Islanders than those whom they actually encountered.

---

[33] Ibid., p. 80.

[34] Ibid., p. 83.

[35] Ibid., pp. 89–90: ' "Marching Rule" was an attempt to give validity and impact to indigenous notions regarding the nature of status and power in [the] new society where the Melanesians found themselves without power or status.'

[36] This derivation is given by R. R. A. Wouters, 'La "Marching Rule" ', *Sociaal Kompas* VI 2, (1958–9), pp. 45–55. The same derivation is offered by Worsley, op. cit., p. 173 n. The name Masian Rule was also known, according to William Burrows, 'The Background to Marching Rule', *Pacific Islands Monthly* XX, 11 (June 1950), pp. 37–8. C. S. Belshaw, 'The Significance of Modern Cults in Melanesian Development', *Australian Outlook* 4, 2 (June 1950), reports a 'Chair and Rule' movement from Santa Ysabel, stimulated by a missionary who urged the natives to agitate for a seat on the nominated Advisory Council.

[37] G. Cochrane, op. cit., p. 95, says that the hymn, *We're marching along together* . . ., 'was sung on the way to work in the mission gardens . . .'.

[38] C. H. Allan, ' "Marching Rule": A Nativistic Cult of the British Solomon Islands', *South Pacific* 5, 5 (July 1951), pp. 79–85 (reprinted from *Corona*, March 1951).

[39] G. Cochrane, op. cit., p. 95.

They were less readily accounted for by traditional cultural concepts,[40] and in the cargo myth of Marching Rule, Americans, who were to be the bringers of cargo, were always contrasted with the British. The equality of white and negro American soldiers, and the presence of Fijian troops may also have stimulated ideas for change.[41]

The Marching Rule movement spread during the period of economic disruption following the war. From Cochrane's careful study it does appear, however, that the desire to regain a sense of cultural integrity and status, and the need to overcome the feeling of inferiority, of being only 'rubbish', together constituted the background of the movement's appeal, even though the movement expressed itself in political as well as economic terms. The economic programme of the movement included both a powerful myth of a coming cargo, to be brought by the Americans and to be stored in huts built by the members of the movement and distributed to faithful adherents, and a more rational attempt to re-organize native economic activities, particularly by the institution of communal farms.

The ambivalence of this economic programme was paralleled by confusion in the prevailing attitude towards the government.[42] Such

[40] Loc. cit. The Americans were not thought of as 'big men' of the traditional type: they were too kind and generous. 'Americans gave away their possessions "like children": they were thought to be foolish, since they did not ask for anything in return. Solomon Islanders acted as scouts for the Americans in the jungle and they knew that they were better soldiers than the Americans. This military service, in which the leaders of the "Marching Rule" movement were prominent, had placed the Americans in the position of having an obligation which it was thought that they would repay. The obligation was to be repaid by bringing "cargo" ' (pp. 95–6). The different attitudes to natives of Americans and colonists were paralleled in earlier contacts between natives and white men of nationalities other than that of the colonial authorities; Hans Fischer in 'Cargo-Kulte und die "Amerikaner" ', Sociologus 14, 1 (1964), pp. 17–30, points to the example of the early 'German Wislin' movement. None the less, the numbers, the equipment, and the generosity of the Americans are all on a scale unprecedented by earlier culture contact, and the frequency of the invocation of Americans as the bringers of cargo is not found of other nationals in earlier movements. All over Melanesia, cargo cultists have continued to pin their faith on the arrival or return of the Americans, from the Jonfrum movement in the New Hebrides to a succession of movements in New Britain and New Ireland. In Rabaul, New Britain, a 'helicopter cult' occurred in 1961, when natives waited in the mountains to be taken to the United States in helicopters from an American ship, believed to be just over the horizon. Earlier cultists had expected a submarine to convey them to America. On Watom Island, leaders of another cult distributed eggs 'which they believed would hatch into a squad of armed United States soldiers' (Sunday Telegraph, 12 February 1961). In 1964, a cult known as 'the President Johnson cult' arose in New Hanover, off New Ireland, during the first general election in Papua–New Guinea (February 1964), and led to violence in the following September. 'Led by two natives named Bos Mailik and Oliver, members of the cult want President Johnson to come to the island to rule over them. They refuse to pay taxes and say they will use money instead to "buy" President Johnson' (The Times, 26 September 1964).

[41] This point, widely made in connection with Melanesian millennial movements, is emphasized by P. Worsley, op. cit., p. 172.

[42] G. Cochrane, op. cit., p. 85, following Allan, says that the movement preached non-co-operation with government, but P. Worsley, op. cit., p. 175, implies that at least at the outset there was a desire for co-operation with the administration.

contradictions and oscillations are entirely to be expected among a people at a low level of cultural development experiencing dramatic cultural contact, even though some of the movement's leaders were relatively sophisticated.[43] Nori, Timothy George, Aleki, and Vouza were all men who had experienced close contact with Europeans, and in the establishment by the two first-mentioned of nine administrative districts on Malaita, each with its own subordinate hierarchy of chiefs, there was a clear indication of some political *savoir faire*.[44] Yet even here, the line between articulate conceptions of rational organization and the influence of purely imitative magic is difficult to draw. When natives see words of command apparently creating their own effects on human behaviour; when they observe that written 'orders' are obeyed; when they perceive the importance attached to rules of procedure in meetings—it is none the less not always clear whether they attribute strictly magical power to these intrinsic items (the powerful word, the written formula, the ritual that constrains the external world) or whether they begin to see some of the principles of rational organization.

Imitation is apparent in the organization of district, sub-district, village, 'line' chiefs (for each clan within a village), and farmer chiefs. People were marshalled for work on communal farms; guards patrolled the settlements and maintained discipline. Eventually 'customs chiefs' were established to deal with those who offended against traditional customs approved by the movement, who failed to pay taxes, who broke the movement's rules, or who refused to accept Marching Rule authority and teaching. Offenders were sometimes imprisoned in the movement's jails. A code of customs was established, dealing with a wide range of subjects, including the treatment of single women, suitors, wives, sexual intercourse, land-ownership, control of pigs, and swearing, among other things. Young men were enjoined not to work on the plantations unless for very high wages. New settlements were established and scattered tribes were drawn together—a process long and unsuccessfully advocated by the British administration (and a development found in other less apparently 'rational' cult movements in New Guinea). The model for these villages appeared to be a mixture

[43] P. Worsley, op. cit., p. 174, says that most of the leaders 'were drawn from the ranks of hereditary political, religious and military leaders or from amongst mission teachers'. G. Cochrane, op. cit., p. 70, maintains that in Solomon Islands' societies there were no hereditary authority ranks or statuses; he adds, p. 85, that six of the nine district leaders appointed in Malaita were mission teachers.

[44] The role of Vouza, referred to by P. Worsley, op. cit., is somewhat obscure in the published sources. He became one of the four Malaita islanders elected to the Advisory Council (ibid., p. 182). For his earlier career, see Hector McQuarrie, *Vouza and the Solomon Islands* (Gollancz, London 1945).

of government and mission advocacy and the pattern seen in American military camps.[45]

Wartime earnings and American generosity provided the natives with wealth taxable by the movement, and among its promises were the establishment of schools, the provision of social welfare, and development programmes. Simultaneously there was also the myth of coming cargo: the Americans would return with tobacco, candy, tinned goods, knives, fish lines, axes, and calico. To observe the coming of the cargo, watch-towers were erected, and to house the goods many storehouses were built. It is perhaps impossible to assess the balance between millennial dreams and magical thinking on the one hand, and the degree of awareness of rational planning and procedures for the attainment of future goals on the other. What can be said is that Marching Rule manifested a degree of economic and political rationality not found in the characteristic cargo cult. Cochrane is, however, no doubt correct to emphasize the significance of cultural continuities—the Marching Rule leaders were like the 'big men' of old, exacting tribute, promising the periodic distribution of welfare, and manifesting *mana*. Marching Rule, which showed strong nativistic inclinations in consciously seeking to preserve traditional customs, was a new means by which to assert cultural integrity.[46]

Marching Rule was at once a millennial movement, a vehicle of economic and political discontent, and in some respects a terrorist organization. It had picked up the ideas of native councils and courts, which had been begun before the war; it had organized economic boycott, to a point where in 1947–8 labour had become very scarce in Malaita;[47] and it had organized widespread refusal to pay taxes. Oscillating between nativistic and futuristic perspectives, it was at times avowedly anti-administration. 'Sometimes it is a desire for independence and return to the days of before the white man came: sometimes it embodies a firm belief in the return of the Americans, whom the natives consider would make far better rulers than the British. But in every case there is a desire to be rid of the present administration.'[48] The leaders were not beyond manipulating their following with ruses devised to encourage the belief that the cargo was soon to arrive.[49] Trickery alternated with coercion: the Marching Rule courts were a method of imposing policy on natives; non-adherents

[45] This paragraph relies on C. H. Allan, op. cit.
[46] G. Cochrane, op. cit., pp. 89–90.
[47] *Pacific Islands Monthly* XXI, 1 (August 1950), news-item, p. 41.
[48] Rt. Rev. S. G. Caulton, Bishop of Melanesia, 'The Marching Rule Delusion', *Pacific Islands Monthly* XXI, 1 (August 1950), p. 77.
[49] Ibid.

were penalized and sometimes expelled into the bush; some died through being made to work long hours in the communal gardens; the discipline imposed by the leaders was more severe than that of traditional 'big men' or British administrators.[50]

After the movement had sought to establish its authority in some areas, the British administration arrested the movement's leaders in 1947, and subsequently demolished the palisades that had been erected around the settlements. Hostility and periodic demonstrations persisted. The missions, particularly the South Seas Evangelical Mission, whose missionaries had been away during the war and who refused natives the use of mission stations for political activities, suffered severely.[51] In 1952 a new High Commissioner established a council for Malaita, and the Marching Rule men were finally satisfied, even though the amount of political power they gained was very slight indeed. Nor had they gained economically. But, as Cochrane emphasizes, they now had their own 'big men' once again, as council members —evidence that Melanesians were no longer all regarded as 'rubbish men', since some of them were treated as the equals of Europeans.

> Wages were not increased, the 'cargo' did not come and yet the leaders made peace. . . . The early council members' only concern was with the status of the President. Salana Gaa's, the 'Marching Rule' leader, was the first President of the Council. They voted him a salary of $4,000 a year which the D.C. turned down. At the same time, they thought that employees of the council in the sub-districts should work for 10s a month. But there was a measure of the difference between 'big men' and ordinary men.[52]

Quite apart from their function, councils and assemblies have an intrinsic significance as status-distributing agencies. The more sophisticated individuals among under-developed peoples not infrequently become preoccupied with constitutions, charters, and procedural devices, partly for their instrumental, but also for their symbolic significance. This particular element of Marching Rule practice was revived more than a decade after the movement's demise. Three men from South Mala made use of the Bible to legitimate the objects of Marching Rule by creating a constitution for an indigenous Anglican church which was to be self-supporting. The ideas in the charter were taken from the Marching Rule movement, but the object was to re-establish the mission and to draw back members lost in the late 1940s when Marching Rule was at its height. The purpose of the new organi-

[50] P. Worsley, op. cit., pp. 177, 181; G. Cochrane, op. cit., p. 92.
[51] R. P. A. Wouters, op. cit., p. 50, 'La "Marching Rule" a été la ruine de la S.S.E.M. qui avait travaillé pendant cinquante ans aux îles Salomon du Sud'.
[52] G. Cochrane, op. cit., p. 94.

zation was to promote economic and material advancement, this time within the community of the church. As in Marching Rule, team-work was to be the basis for the cultivation of gardens, and voluntary subscriptions were levied to support the new pattern of indigenously-controlled church activity.[53]

In societies in which local entrepreneurship is hampered by lack of individual capital, by traditional obligations of reciprocity between leaders and supporters which impede capital accumulation by individuals and restrict personal innovation and initiative, new economic opportunities can be realized only through quasi-political re-organization or community co-operatives. The development of a consciously new form of social organization can occur most easily when the existing social structure has been disrupted—by war, as in the case of the Solomons and the initiatives in the Purari Delta and the Admiralty Islands, to be considered below, or by the creation of new settlements, as in the case of Malekula. The arbitrary event (sometimes intensified by the charismatic leader) opens the way for a new pattern of rational organization.

The *Malekula Co-operative* movement was more explicitly prompted by economic concerns than was Marching Rule. In the New Hebrides, a number of refugees had been settled in north Malekula. In 1939, this surplus population established a co-operative movement with the idea of profits going to the community. The island had been affected by the Jonfrum disturbances on Tanna, and the co-operatives expected to be able to produce sufficient for themselves without dealing with the distrusted European traders.[54] But the idea of a co-operative was associated with the ideas of a coming cargo: the prospect of quick and manifold returns for effort led to intense excitement. Although the movement encountered difficulties, the effort of planting was continued until 1941.[55] The government of the Condominium became concerned about the movement, particularly after the island had been unsettled by the wartime experience of the unwonted generosity of the American troops. As a co-operative effort natives cleared roads for the lorries that were expected to arrive with goods from America. The white population was coerced into association with the new movement, and government intervention induced the leaders to purge it of its cargo-cult aspects. Although the planters, who feared the shortage of labour, and mis-

---

[53] An account of this development is given in Nicolas Peterson, 'The Church Council of South Mala: A Legitimized Form of Masinga Rule', *Oceania* XXXVI, 3 (March 1966), pp. 214–30.

[54] P. Worsley, op. cit., p. 161.

[55] J. Guiart, 'The Co-operative Called "The Malekula Native Company". A Borderline Type of Cargo Cult', *South Pacific* 6, 6 (September 1952), pp. 429–32.

sionaries, who disliked the fact that recruitment to the movement cut across the lines of mission allegiance, remained opposed, the movement settled down as a regular producer co-operative, with some degree of government supervision.

Each of these movements manifests the same convergence of religious means and economic and political goals, with the increased resort to more rational procedures to achieve the immediate and pragmatic ends that are sought. Leadership is not so sophisticated that one can appropriately speak of the manipulation of the masses by leaders who simply voice religious ideas that they themselves do not share, yet often the leaders appear to have perceived some of the appropriate steps towards the realistic attainment of their goals. That deliberative courses of action should lead to exaggerated expectations and fantasy projections is not surprising. If God helped those who helped themselves, as the Christian missionaries taught, for instance in the parable of the talents, this expectation was also part of traditional belief, and, perhaps most important, it also fitted the very strong emotional orientations of those who now began work to attain greater wealth. Work was hard, and only intense desire could have induced strenuous labour: it did so through the mediating agency of profound conviction.

That the intensity of desire was independent of particular belief systems is evident in the development of determined efforts to transform the culture, and to enjoy economic advancement, which have occurred in Melanesia without the intermediation of a cargo-cult movement. The sense of cultural inferiority and the imitation of European styles sometimes came about without manifestations of anguish about the past or religious promises about the future. The experience of some men with the Australian forces or in civilian employment was sometimes enough to stimulate economic endeavour. Such a man was Tommy Kabu, who sought, in this same early post-war period, to create a new economy for the Purari Delta tribes of the western coastal region of Papua.[56] The development of Port Moresby had brought the old trading relations with the Motu peoples who came on long visits in their big canoes to an end: Kabu wanted to build a new trading system with gardens in the Delta and markets in Port Moresby.[57] His plan was to create a producer co-operative, and so transform not only the economy but the whole ceremonial system that was so closely interrelated with the Papuan search for social honour.

[56] This paragraph relies largely on R. F. Maher, *New Men of Papua*, op. cit., especially pp. 55–78.

[57] Report of the Department of Education, New Guinea, 'Community Development in the Purari Delta', *South Pacific* 5, 10 (December 1951), pp. 208–14. (The report calls Kabu, Tomu Kabu.)

His efforts resulted in the re-siting of villages on higher ground, and the attempt to grow, transport, and market taro through the formation of a *kompani*. That the absence of European book-keeping, inadequate knowledge of techniques, difficulties of co-ordination, and lack of articulation between family holdings and *kompani* work, together brought the scheme to failure does not detract from the importance of a co-operative effort by tribes that had previously been mutually hostile, and the collection of enough money to buy a boat. Even in this movement, which lacked all the overtones of the cargo cult, Tommy Kabu's prestige was such that, during the period of greatest enthusiasm, he was believed to be married to a daughter of the King of England. He was almost a living cultural hero, even though his plans were entirely rationalistic. As a man with a knowledge of business and the system of shares, he was a prestigious model for his Papuan associates. He was identified with a millennium to come, yet his enterprise remained free from millennial outbursts. There were exaggerated expectations, but of the results of work, not of prayer or dancing; of human efforts, not of the benevolence of the ancestors. Such endeavour was not undertaken entirely without reference to the supernatural and 'certain groups were found equipped with wooden rifles and posted to guard villages and gardens for the purpose of excluding "evil spirits" '. None the less the rational character of the enterprise is scarcely impugned by this defensive measure.[58]

The Paliau movement: cult beliefs and rational action

The rational mutation of religious orientations does not occur automatically. There is no regular set of stages through which a living movement necessarily passes: at most there is a rough sequence, although different phases sometimes co-exist or alternate uncertainly. Men whose dominant orientations are rational may, in the tenuous grasp they have of organizational procedures and of the sequence of cause and effect in the world in which saving, co-operating, capitalizing, and credit systems operate, half-believe that what is achieved is magical. Religious men may promote behaviour that, in the longer or shorter run, is conducive to the discipline and stability that systematic economic activity requires. There is no automatic mutation of a movement that has a religious conception of ends to one that embraces pragmatic ends. At most there is a changing balance of dispositions,

[58] Ibid., p. 211.

which may either involve changes of leadership or personnel, or, more slowly, reflect the effects of a changed process of socialization.

The complexity of these responses, and the steady but uneven shift of dispositions, is most clearly manifested in the Paliau movement in the Admiralty Islands, of which our knowledge is owed to Theodore Schwarz and Margaret Mead, who were working on the largest island, Manus, during the period in which the movement underwent a (second) cargo-cult phase, and to the studies that Margaret Mead had conducted some twenty years earlier.[59] The Admiralty Islands had a population of 15,000 consisting of three groups—Manus, who lived on Great Admiralty (Manus Island) and who were fishers and traders; Usiai, who lived in the interior of Manus Island and who were gardeners; and Matankor, who lived on the smaller islands and who were fishers and gardeners. These groups cannot properly be called tribes, since there was no common language or culture, but each group was gathered in a number of villages which, before government was established by the Germans in 1912, had engaged in periodic warfare among themselves.

The natives were steadily influenced by European civilization. Some became migrant workers; others worked on local plantations; in the 1930s the Manus adopted Roman Catholicism—pidgin English became increasingly known, war between villages ceased, and European currency was introduced. All of these developments affected traditional economic and social organization, and young men became more difficult to recruit into village life. The war intensified the process of cultural contact, with the Japanese and then with the Americans. One million American troops passed through the Admiralties: and the diversity of races among them, their general friendliness to natives, and the abundance and scale of their equipment made a great impression.[60] But, overall, the islanders 'suffered little physical deprivation' from the European control of their culture. 'Most villages lost little land' by pre-war colonization;[61] the Japanese made little impression; the incursion of the Americans, however, undoubtedly created a new awareness of the inferiority of native life, and provoked a keen desire for higher living standards and more material goods.

The war brought many young men from different parts of Melanesia

---

[59] This section relies principally on Theodore Schwarz, 'The Paliau Movement in the Admiralty Islands, 1946–1954', *Anthropological Papers of the American Museum of Natural History* (New York) 49, Part 2 (1962), pp. 207–422. For a narrative account see, Margaret Mead, *New Lives for Old* (Gollancz, London 1956).

[60] According to H. Uplegger and W. E. Mühlmann, 'Die Cargo-Kulte in Neuguinea und Insel-Melanesian', op. cit.

[61] T. Schwarz, op. cit., p. 224.

together, and their association may be regarded as another important background circumstance in the dissemination of cult movements and ideas of social change. Once the war was over, several of the younger men in the various Manus villages sought to re-structure their traditional way of life. Their special concern was the wasteful ceremonial expenditures which they believed were a cause of their failure to experience economic gain: in particular they attacked bride-wealth, the repayment of which kept young men in bondage to their kinsfolk for years after marriage.[62] Some of the leaders, for example Lungat on the island of Nriol, claimed that their ideas had come to them in dreams.[63] This may be regarded both as an attempt to provide supernatural legitimation for innovation and as a reflection of the emotional intensity with which a new state of affairs was envisaged and wished for. Such plans were always difficult to realize, however, both because of the opposition of older men, and in this case perhaps more acutely because there was only a hazy conception of how alternative social arrangements might be instituted and operated. The period after the war was marked not only by discontent and uncertainty, but also by gambling fever.[64]

Even before the war, some natives had tried to modify native life: most conspicuous among them was Paliau. He had observed that the large feasts on which a man's prestige depended caused the dissipation of wealth and left natives too poor to pay their taxes. He induced the *luluai*, government-appointed headman, of his village to accept a sum of his own savings as the beginning of a borrowing fund for impecunious taxpayers. He had served for several years as a policeman, and in the war he was a sergeant in charge of 280 police at Rabaul. Subsequently he served the Japanese as a policeman, for which he was treated with suspicion by the Australians when they returned. During the war he had had several dreams, and claimed to have met and talked with Jesus. He had uttered prophecies, but he later said that some accounts of his visions had become exaggerated. He returned to Baluan in the Admiralties in 1946 and gave his first message, a story of creation and the mission of Jesus to the natives. The Australian government and the Germans and Japanese before them had prevented the true message of Jesus being delivered. God had given to America this message for black men. The Americans had come to teach the natives, but had been prevented by the Australians. God had not forgotten New Guinea, and

---

[62] A discussion of this pattern of relationships in traditional Manus society is to be found in M. Mead, *Growing Up in New Guinea* (Morrow, New York 1930).

[63] T. Schwarz, op. cit., p. 235.

[64] This response is known elsewhere in circumstances of anomie. The Pawnees turned luck into a major focus of proof of supernatural power after the decay of their traditional culture.

if Australia did not now help them, another country would come to do so. Paliau's story was written down in note-books by those natives who could write, as *The Long Story of God*.[65]

Paliau taught that the missions had lied to the natives: each man was both God and man. Confession was unnecessary, but men should shake hands to make up their quarrels. Although Paliau did not demand that his followers should abandon the missions, his reinterpretation of Christianity, and his idea that missionaries got paid for the number of converts they made (why otherwise would they leave home?) were serious challenges. He saw the importance of attempting to define just what was needed to reorganize native life, and a great deal of his teaching was concerned with the need to straighten out *thinkthink*—thought. He rejected, in particular, the atomistic character of the old society: the Manus, Matankor (he was Matankor himself), and Usiai were to work together, and to institute a *newfela fashion*, that is, a new way of life. The old ceremonies were to be set aside; bride-price was to be fixed and paid in cash; villages were to co-operate; men were not to go away to work for Europeans, but rather to stay at home and work. A *pesman* (face-man?) was appointed to organize each village, and the principal concern was to prevent dissipation of the wealth which had been acquired from the discarded surplus of the Americans. A fund was to be established, along the lines on which work-boys had often pooled their money, and decisions were to be made in village meetings.

Although it had religious overtones, Paliau's movement was not simply a new set of beliefs. Schwarz considers that 'he was not simply a cult leader proclaiming the imminence of the millennium when the desired state of equivalence with the white man would be attained through supernatural means'.[66] But a cargo cult did develop from the dissemination of these ideas. Paliau had invoked special revelation to justify his plans: rational procedures were associated with supernatural direction. For those who followed him, with high expectations of what would quickly be achieved, the manipulation of the world by magic was the obvious way to give expression to their emotional orientation. An ecstatic cult movement erupted because the first steps proposed by Paliau 'seemed scarcely related to their ultimate goals and could be conceived only by some mystic linkage that made them ritual keys to immediate supernatural fulfillment'.[67]

Individuals arose in different places whose excitement at the prospects of the new movement led to dreams of the coming of a cargo, to be

[65] T. Schwarz, op. cit., pp. 238–58.
[66] Ibid., p. 265.
[67] Ibid., p. 266.

brought by Jesus and the ancestors. Old goods were to be destroyed—canoes, the church, everything that spoke of the past: even the money which had been collected in the movement was thrown away at Mouk, a village on Baluan. Other cargo cults had been known in the area, and the ideas associated with them were familiar. Visions occurred, lights were seen, and planes, cars, and other supernatural manifestations presaged the early return of the ancestors. *Thinkthink* became the intense effort to reach out for God, and convulsions and shaking became widespread. In some villages there was marching and American flags were hoisted. Paliau himself was affected by these manifestations, and although he did not confirm them, neither did he disavow these prophecies uttered by others. The cult spread rapidly from island to island, and Paliau's ideas of people of different villages loving one another were caught up in the new movement. The hats and books of the *luluais* were burned in some villages.[68]

The progress of the cult, which lasted only a short time, manifested both the intensity and anxiety of the natives. It came as a catalytic experience, with both intense yearnings for the past, as manifested in the ancestor cult, and eagerness for the future, however uncertain it might be.[69] The *guria*, shaking, which lasted for four days in some places, was almost a self-evident cultural swan-song. The burning of the hats and books, the insignia of office of the *luluais*, was symbolic of the native desire to attain autonomy. The marching and the American flags were manifestations of the difficulty with which the natives had absorbed the meaning of recent events. The destruction of existing possessions, in such curious contrast with the expected return of the ancestors, expressed the hope of making all things new. Older men, who had opposed the *newfela fashion*, were caught up in the cult, and the young ones were equally affected by the epidemic of shaking and intensity of expectation.

When the cult subsided, it did so not because the ideas had been wrong, but because, as natives saw it, for some reason they had not quite managed to get the cargo, although it had been very near. Millennial ideas were not abandoned, nor were rational procedures simply espoused in their stead. The millennium had been narrowly missed, but this time, in contrast with so many cargo cults, there was a return to the programme of work activity and new organization that had come into being before the cult movement began. The thirty-three villages that had been affected by the cult were now bound in the movement, and looked to Paliau for guidance.[70]

[68] Ibid., pp. 266–82.
[69] On the ancestor cult on Manus, see M. Mead, *New Lives for Old*, op. cit.
[70] T. Schwarz, op. cit., p. 283.

The government intervened, arrested some of those who had burned their badges of office, and detained Paliau and gave him a course of instruction in which the policy of the government was explained. The movement persisted. New villages were settled, some of them very much larger in size than had ever existed before. Emphasis on moral regeneration, with the avoidance of anger and evil thinking, became stressed as the more literate leaders resumed control after the visions of the cargo had faded. When Paliau returned, in about 1950, he found that the movement was losing momentum. Meetings were held but the process of decision-making and its relation to practical activities were little understood. Young men had returned to work for Europeans, or were conspicuously idle.

In this period of stagnation a second phase of the cargo-cult idea arose, and appeared as a type of mystical revitalization of the movement itself. The focus of the new cult was very much on the ancestors, whose messages sought to strengthen morality, and to insist on tidy cemeteries with decent interment of the bones of the dead. The dreamers who received the messages of the new cult promised each village a teacher, who would give the true teaching of Jesus; they emphasized the nearness of the time of the Last Day, which was set for Easter Day, 1954, when the world would be levelled out into a park-like condition. Drilling, uniforms, proper procedure at meetings, with one thing decided at a time (a point Paliau had persistently made) were part of the instructions of the ancestors. The ghosts detected the use of love-charms (although these practices had supposedly been abandoned when the Paliau movement had begun), and in various ways the cult sought to reinvigorate the ethical prescriptions of the movement. Many aspects of the cult, particularly the wailing of the ghosts who returned with messages, were similar to the ideas prevailing in the old religion; but there were also ideas drawn from the Seventh-Day Adventists, whose mission teachings were well known; and there were the ideas of the Paliau movement itself.[71]

The new cult phase occurred at a time when the south coast of Manus Island expected to get a council from the Australian administration, and Schwarz considers that the cult may have been an attempt to hasten the day of the end before the council was inaugurated. The council implied the 'hard work road', whereas the cult sought a supernatural short-cut to the millennium. It was led, largely, by the

[71] Schwarz considers that there was no direct influence by the Seventh-Day Adventists, who had missionaries in the area, although he says that emphasis on Revelation and Judgement Day 'make the cult and the Seventh Day Adventists seem almost indistinguishable in belief' (ibid., p. 317).

more illiterate men, who could not play so active a part in the movement proper, and it was adopted by those villages and hamlets with the
lowest prestige.[72] It was, in a sense, a rival bid for leadership, and a
compensatory device for groups who were otherwise likely to be dis-
advantaged by the stabilization of a new order of society under the
council. But the cultists also claimed that they were restoring aspects of
the *newfela fashion* that had fallen into decay, and in some of the
villages the cult introduced an austere pattern of life, with the prohibition of gambling, whistling, singing, and ukelele-playing.

The second cult was much more divisive of the movement than the
first had been. The cult leaders and their opponents, one of whom said,
'Nothing simply materializes. Everything comes from hard work',[73] all
claimed Paliau as their leader, and sought vindication from him. Paliau
finally condemned the cult as something that would destroy the
movement, though he also condemned the fact that so much of his
early teaching had fallen into desuetude. The children were undis-
ciplined; chairs and tables were not being used; meetings were badly
conducted; and gambling had been resumed. He forbade further talk
of ghosts or cargoes, and sought to establish amity among his following
so that the movement might work in co-operation with the new
council that was to be established on the south coast in 1954. Once
established, the council was seen as government recognition of the
movement, and it sought to expand its influence to villages which had
not been previously associated with the movement, or which were not
nominally under the council's control.

The rationality of Paliau's movement did not stem directly from the
cargo-cult responses, but stood rather in considerable contrast with
them. Yet, the cults were almost necessary consequences of the new
incentives and expectations that were arising in Melanesian society.
They were the short-cut to the realization of the new ends that men
sought. They were also a manifestation of the will to terminate the
existing dispensation, even if, initially, they were themselves often
couched in the language and custom of the past, and expressed both
restorative ideals and the desire for all the artefacts of western civilization. In Paliau's teaching there was a general secularity which,
although he too was affected by the cult ideas, generally led away
from magical expectations, and emphasized the acquisition of discipline
and skills as the way to reach a social order. That these procedures
should have been mistaken for magical instrumental means to bring
the millennium into being is not itself surprising, considering the very

[72] Ibid., pp. 333, 383-4.
[73] Ibid., p. 322.

limited knowledge of western civilization that was available to the natives from the type of cultural contact that they had experienced. The dramatic manifestations of the cult, the *guria*, trances, visions, and tongues, reflected the anxiety at the adoption of new techniques, and the excitement at the prospect of success. For people with a limited sense of time, the possibilities of transformation were incalculable. The high aspirations embraced by the movement—the assumption of white culture—were an assertion of present deprivation, and faith in its amelioration. The difficulty and gradualness of the intervening steps was what was not realized. The mood of the movement was urgent, and although the procedures were rational, the conjoining of end and means was very imperfectly understood.

15

Conclusions

Concepts and categories

THE conceptual framework adopted in this study of new religious movements among less-developed peoples was borrowed from a typological scheme developed in respect of the sects of advanced society, which was intended to exhaust the logic of religious deviance.[1] The use of such a framework should make apparent the divergences of response within movements, and provide some type of measuring rod against which to trace changes in a movement's orientation over time. Obviously, to discuss movements in terms of orientations is not to specify their cultural content, to indicate, for example, the extent to which a revolutionist response is nativistic and restorative, or futuristic or imitative. These are important cultural variables, and the analysis has sought to indicate the type of social circumstances in which the content of a movement's concern is broadly restorative or broadly imitative. In plotting the mutation of responses some indication of the broad shifts of consciousness have also been suggested.

The dominant orientations in the new movements arising among less-developed peoples are thaumaturgical and revolutionist, responses for which I have used the terms *magical* and *millennial* as rough approximations. But thaumaturgy is a more encompassing term than magic, and the revolutionist response embraces more than millennialism. The term *millennial* is a misnomer if the strictly Christian implications of the word are borne in mind, whilst in common usage *magic* does not always include belief in the power of witch-finders as well as of witches. In these pages it is belief in empirically unjustified practices and procedures which affect personal well-being.

Such practices and procedures are predominantly personal in application—rarely extending beyond individuals to families or communities. The revolutionist response in contrast is always social— tribal or ethnic—and rarely localized to the merely communal. Analytically, magical and millennial solutions—the thaumaturgical response and the revolutionist response—are polar opposites both in

[1] See Chapter 1.

484

the diagnosis of, and in the prescription for, whatever men find to be wrong with their social experience. Yet we have seen that in tribal societies, and perhaps in some societies somewhat more advanced than that, the two conceptions are capable of successively, and even simultaneously, dominating the minds of men. In certain, perhaps rare, instances in small tribal societies the elimination of witchcraft almost *is* a prospect of the millennium—such are the limitations of any wider conception of social structure in a world of such confined horizons. The analyst is reminded of the limitations of his conceptual apparatus in embracing the complexity of the world, even if he remains committed to the belief that only by comparison, and hence of widely applicable concepts for comparison, is explanation likely to be advanced.

A number of widely employed terms for new religious movements have been eschewed in this essay. *Messianism* is one. The messianic element is usually only one in the general complex of millennialism, and by no means an indispensable element at that. The term is unfortunately frequently used of movements in which there is no specific promise of a messiah. Worse, messianism is often confused with prophetism. The role of the prophet and the charismatic leader calls for fuller investigation than the blanket term *messianism* invites.

Culturally specific designations, *Ethiopian* or *Zionist*, are clearly valueless for cross-cultural analysis. The term *cargo cults* indicates the specific focus of movements arising in one cultural area, but our analysis has led us to draw some tentative distinctions between so-called cargo cults with a predominantly thaumaturgical orientation both from those that manifest a distinctly revolutionist response, and from yet others in which both of these orientations are steadily subordinated to apprehension of the rational measures instituted to bring about an improvement of social experience. All these three terms stand close to empirical data, initially in the self-conceptions of the votaries themselves. Their danger is that they are subsequently applied to movements which have only a few characteristics in common, or which share only the cultural context, with those for which the categories originated.

The terms *nativistic* and *syncretic* are the summary description of movements by an external observer. The former term is defined as 'any conscious, organized attempt on the part of a society's members to revive or perpetuate selected aspects of its culture'.[2] Despite Linton's refinement of this concept and his attempt to relate it to psychological attitudes of conquered peoples in different relationships with their

[2] Ralph Linton, 'Nativistic Movements', *American Anthropologist* 45 (April–June 1934), pp. 230–40 (p. 230). See the discussion, with which I concur, of K. O. L. Burridge, *New Heaven New Earth*, op. cit., pp. 102–3.

conquerors,[3] nativism *per se* is too widely found in new movements for it to be the basis of a very fruitful comparative analysis.[4] There is always a nativistic element in new movements which arise in cultural contact situations, even when the main concern is a desire to acquire the technically superior goods of the invader, since until a movement ceases to be religious—supernaturalist in its primary reference—it will inevitably be tied to cultural assumptions about the means to attain its goals. All movements, however impressed by the invasive culture, begin with existing preconceptions: whatever may be desired from outside, as ethnocentric movements, their votaries are entirely unaware of what they would necessarily lose of their native way of life in attaining the millennium. (The point applies not only to tribal peoples, of course: the same appears to be true of Christian adventists, and even of those with firmly delineated conceptions of a heavenly hereafter.)

Movements as different as that of Smohalla, the Jonfrum movement, and Peyotism are clearly not equally nativistic, but all are emphatically pro-native. All seek in some measure to preserve some elements of what they understand to be native culture, although all of them—again in differing degrees—have acquired goals, means, artefacts, techniques, or styles from other cultures, including the intrusive culture of the dominant invaders from whom they are seeking to protect themselves. As Aberle has pointed out, Peyotism is paradoxically more nativistic for the second generation of Peyotists than for the first: the one-time innovators appear as later-time conservatives.[5]

The designation *syncretic* takes us no further. Since all the movements we have examined have—almost certainly—arisen only after cultural contact with invaders or fore-knowledge of them, they all incorporate mythical elements drawn from exogenous as well as endogenous sources. The Tupi-Guaraní migrations *may* have been prompted by indigenous ideas of finding a world without evil, but such ideas *may* incorporate mythical elements diffused from Christianity. The Eastern Highlands

[3] Ibid.

[4] I agree with Munro S. Edmondson, 'Nativism, Syncretism and Anthropological Science', *Middle American Research Institute Publication 19* (Tulane University, New Orleans 1960), pp. 181–204, who writes (p. 184), 'nativism is the self-conscious, overt manifestation of ethnocentrism in one of its most sharply defined and exclusive or divisive aspects. A clearly structured and explicit ethnocentrism in any dimension of cultural organization is thus definable as nativism, for a people can only identify itself with its present or past experience . . . the future time aspect of [millennialism] is more apparent than real, and although it is obvious that any matter involving identification must include expectations of the future . . . Zion, Salvation, the messiah or the "cargo" ship are extrapolated from a real past and present rather than from a "real", or nationally projected, future. . . . Nativism and ethnocentrism are conservative forces, . . . always standing in opposition to cultural innovations: one cannot rest his identity on the uncertainties of the future.'

[5] D. F. Aberle, *The Peyote Religion Among the Navaho*, op. cit., p. 339.

tribes of New Guinea knew of the artefacts of western culture and had developed (or learned) a myth about these commodities, even if their behaviour reflected an unlearned, uncontrolled, basic physiological response to the dangerous unknown. Such a movement is, however, clearly less-consciously attempting to preserve or restore a traditional way of life than the Ghost Dance of 1890, most of whose participants had certainly absorbed more of the elements of white culture than had the Eastern Highlanders. By the time that Wovoka uttered his prophecies there was a well-established native tradition of millennialism— but a tradition that had been influenced by many years of the dissemination of Christian ideas. Paradoxically, the Eastern Highlands cult was much less nativistic than the Ghost Dance, but was also much less syncretic. Syncretism, then, also seems to be an inadequate primary point of reference for such movements: it has its most obvious application to the independent Christian or semi-Christian churches in Africa that have separated from the missions but which sustain a significant element of mission Christianity.[6]

Widening Linton's concept of nativism, A. F. C. Wallace has coined the term 'revitalization movement', which he defines as 'a deliberate, organized, conscious effort by members of a society to construct a more satisfying culture'.[7] Those concerned must see their culture as a system, and the process involves both the attempt to change individual cognitive orientations and social reality. He offers Gai'wiio, the Wesleyan revival, Sudanese Mahdi-ism, the T'ai-p'ing rebellion, the Ghost Dance, and Christianity itself as examples. Nativistic movements and cargo cults he regards as sub-classes, and millennial and messianic movements as special types: while most denominations and sects are also to be called revitalization movements. All organized religion may be regarded as relics of old revitalization movements—devitalized revitalization movements, it seems!

Concepts of such general application tend both to reiterate very broad truths, but also to overlook significant differences between movements which comparative analysis and terms of less ambitious generality and abstractness might elucidate. All movements arise to attain some goal; all enjoin men to use their energies and resources in particular ways, to forswear certain activities and anathematize others. Such prescriptions and taboos are important elements of a culture, and many movements—albeit often only those that are more settled—go further, in prescribing the model of relationships to prevail between

---

[6] On such movements, see D. B. Barrett, op. cit.

[7] A. F. C. Wallace, 'Revitalization Movements: Some Theoretical Considerations for their Comparative Study', op. cit., p. 264.

men. But not all new religious movements seek to institute a new culture. Many of them seek only to provide immediate release from stress— and stress is a factor not less important for Wallace than for Smelser.[8] Thaumaturgical movements, from itinerant witch-finding cults in Africa to the settled *candomblé* shrines in Brazil, fall outside the framework of Wallace's analysis: yet such movements have been abundant in human history, and represent an important human concern: even in movements with broad transformative ends, the thaumaturgical sometimes becomes an important alternative focus of attention.

Wallace's analysis of revitalization movements follows such a movement through its life-cycle, from the originating point of the 'steady state' of the culture in which individual stress arises as the first point of departure for a revitalization movement, to a final 'new steady state'. But many of the movements which his concept covers are millennial movements, which, in the nature of the ideology that they espouse, never attain a 'new steady state'—unless they relinquish their specific conception of cultural renewal. Conversionist movements—the Wesleyan revival would be classed as such—do of course fit into Wallace's scheme rather better: but their explicit aim is *not* cultural revitalization, it is the change of heart and mind of men who have claimed salvation by faith. The transformation of the culture, particularly of its institutional structure, is at most a latent function of conversionist religion, not 'a deliberate effort to construct a more satisfying culture'. It could be argued that such a consequence is almost always only a latent content of a specifically religious movement (since millennialist movements cannot succeed, and conversionist movements have aims that differ fundamentally from that of the creation of a culture), whilst neither thaumaturgical nor manipulationist movements take the culture as point of reference.

Reformist movements could attain such revitalization very gradually, but they might easily cease to be religious movements in the process—a development which, be it conceded, Wallace envisages. Utopian movements do have such a goal, but as an empirical fact manifest little success either in its attainment, or indeed in sustaining support for their activities. It is only in the introversionist movement that cultural revitalization appears to be consciously sought and actually attained, and then often at a cost of withdrawal from the wider world. Even to the Peyote cult, which organizes a predominantly introversionist response, Wallace's analysis is not easily applied. The Peyotists are not members of 'a society' but of many, and the new culture that they espouse is less created by them than received by them. Only rarely do

[8] N. J. Smelser, *Theory of Collective Behaviour* (Routledge, London 1962).

they constitute a majority within a community, thus rather than revitalizing a society, they appear more likely to create separate enclaves within many societies. Nor does Peyotism fit into an analysis of a society passing from one 'steady state' through the activities of a revitalization movement to another 'steady state'. In so many instances Peyotism was a successor to at least one other movement, and sometimes to several. Wallace is perhaps especially impressed by the case of the Gai'wiio' religion, in respect of which his thesis has perhaps greatest plausibility.

The terms 'acculturative' and 'accommodative' usually refer more to the latent functions of the movements, as observers see them, than to the conscious aims of their leaders. Thus the conscious attempt to revitalize a culture by Handsome Lake, which Linton might describe as 'nativistic' and which Wallace described as 'revitalization', Voget describes as 'reformative-nativist', and this he appears to see as 'acculturative'.[9] There is no necessary contradiction, of course, only a shift of emphasis. New movements which introduce Christian elements, as in many places the Peyote cult has done; or western constitutional forms, as West African independent churches have done; or which, even if sometimes for the wrong reasons, imitate the procedures of western practice, as in many Melanesian movements—may all be regarded as having a generally acculturative effect. But the term can be applied to millennialist movements only by more tortuous functionalist argument. It also appears to have more relevance in contexts where dominant white culture is more or less permanently established over subordinate native peoples, as in North America, than to newly independent societies, even though a process of europeanization is occurring widely throughout the world.

Nor have I found any special cogency in the concept of accommodative movements, if that term is applied to movements which help indigenes to adjust to their circumstance of subordination in particular societies. Such movements, in contrast to millennialism, may be said to be those which teach natives that they can assimilate certain white and indigenous traditions, and establish a 'native way', different from but not opposed to the 'white man's way'. Gai'wiio' and Peyotism are conspicuous examples, and so too are the separated churches in Africa that permit polygyny within a context of otherwise more or less orthodox Christianity.[10] The concept applies primarily to established

[9] Fred. W. Voget, 'Acculturation at Caughnawaga: A note on the Native modified group', *American Anthropologist* 53 (April–June 1951), pp. 220–32; *idem*, 'The American Indian in Transition: Reformation and Accommodation', *American Anthropologist* 58 (April 1956), pp. 249–63.

[10] E. Andersson, *Churches at the Grassroots* (Lutterworth, London 1968), p. 45.

and settled movements: ephemeral cults are rarely strictly accommodative, even though they often express vigorously the religious
felt-needs of the indigenous population, as in the various thaumaturgical cults pullulating in various African countries.

The conscious thrust of new religious movements is always contra-
culturative in respect of the imported religion of the missions. But
the missions are not themselves an absolute standard of orthodoxy,
representing as they now do many diverse perspectives within the
general Christian (and sometimes also the Muslim) tradition. The
governments of many recently tribal states are not identified with
mission Christianity of any particular persuasion, and are committed
either to neutrality in religious matters or to pluralism. Such movements that have persisted from colonial times to times of independence
are sometimes claimed as precursors of nationalism, pre-political
expressions of anti-colonialism, the true inheritors of native cultural
tradition, or the repositories of indigenous values. Such claims by no
means always withstand close scrutiny, but the important point is that
with the change of the wider social situation, new religious movements
necessarily seek new self-conceptions. Terms such as 'acculturative'
and 'accommodative'—largely the creation of American anthropologists looking at movements among North American Indians—do
not convey very much when one looks at movements that arose in
contexts with quite different relationships between colonial and
indigenous cultures. The model for acculturation is less easily defined,
and indeed the whole concept of social system, and the functionalist
analysis associated with it, appear to have little relevance to tribal
groups that have been welded into new, artificial, and often still brittle
state-societies.

If a concept such as 'acculturative' appears to reflect a particular
social situation and a particular stage in the relations of super-
ordinate and subordinate peoples, some typologies for new religious
movements appear to be too ethnocentric and culture-bound. The
specifically Christian character of many widely employed concepts
was discussed in the opening sections of this work: other classificatory
schemes have been evolved in respect of particular areas, and lack
ready applicability to other contexts. Fernandez distinguishes expressive
movements from instrumental movements.[11] Expressive movements
appear to have much in common with movements with thaumaturgical
concerns. *Instrumental* is a less convincing category to employ of religious
movements, but Fernandez appears to apply it principally to move-

[11] J. W. Fernandez, 'African Religious Movements: Types and Dynamics', *Journal of
Modern African Studies* 2, 4 (December 1964), pp. 531–49.

ments that adopt church-type structures and which are often schisms from mission churches. Using these dichotomous variables together with the dichotomy of acculturated and traditional orientations, he produces a fourfold table of separatist, messianic, reformative, and nativist movements. The categories are explicitly related to African movements, and Fernandez does not suggest that they have wider application: but even in Africa how do we use such a classification for the powerful independent churches which appear to employ western organizational forms to satisfy traditional expressive functions, such as the aladura churches?[12]

Perhaps the closest scheme to the one employed in this study is that of David Aberle, who distinguishes movements that seek change at a supra-individual level from those seeking change at the individual level.[13] Among those seeking supra-individual change he distinguishes those seeking total change (transformative movements) and those seeking partial change (reformative movements); among movements that seek only individual change he distinguishes again those which seek total change (redemptive movements) and those seeking only partial change (alternative movements). This scheme is intended to embrace all social movements and not only the religious, however, and Aberle's examples of reformative movements (child-labour laws; women's suffrage) clearly do not arise from any supernaturalist world-view. Similarly his alternative movements are typified by those that canvass changes in personal practices and standards (for example, the dissemination of birth-control propaganda). Whilst the category of sectarian response that I label *reformist* corresponds to Aberle's reformative movements, there appear to be no independent religious movements that fit the 'alternative' category. Sects are usually value-oriented movements, seeking total change at cosmic, social, or individual level. The category of transformative movements is close to the category of revolutionist movements: the community, the society, or the wider culture is the point at which supernatural action will be effective. The category of redemptive movements incorporates movements that organize at least two types of response—the conversionist and the thaumaturgical, which I have found it important to distinguish one from the other. The introversionist response seems to me to differ both from the demand for the change of society and from that for the change of the individual, demanding something of both.

There are no definitive typologies. The foregoing is offered simply to justify the need for categories different from those already established in

---

[12] See Chapters 5 and 6.
[13] D. F. Aberle, op. cit., pp. 315 ff.

the literature for the type of comparative exercise undertaken in this essay, and to indicate the relation between different attempts to bring conceptual order into a bewilderingly complex field of human behaviour.

From magic to the millennium

Whatever may be its theological content, for the sociologist salvation has meaning only as an experience in this world. Men may seek salvation from evil conceived in many forms—from anxiety; illness; inferiority feelings; grief; fear of death; concern for the social order. What they seek may be healing; the elimination of evil agents; a sense of access to power; the enhancement of status; increase of prosperity; the promise of life hereafter, or reincarnation, or resurrection from the grave, or attention from posterity; the transformation of the social order (including the restoration of a real or imagined past social order). The common core of all these specific forms of salvation is the demand for reassurance. Of the various theodicies that organize appropriate promises and command the appropriate activities to cope with these specific apprehensions of evil, two responses are widely found among the less-developed peoples—the thaumaturgical and the revolutionist (at later stages of cultural contact introversionist response may also occur).

Thaumaturgy is the primal manifestation of religion in tribal societies. The revolutionist response is occasional, episodic, unenduring. Among some peoples—in West Africa for instance, or among the Navaho—whilst not entirely unknown, millennialism has been of rare and only localized incidence. Even where it has occurred more commonly, the revolutionist response is transitory. Of all the forms of religious response to the world, it alone is incapable, *in its own terms*, of attaining any measure of success. Thaumaturgy apart, all other religious orientations, in promising objective change, make that promise dependent on changes in subjective orientation, and can then subsequently point to changed subjective attitudes as a measure of success. The thaumaturge, it is true, also claims to be able to affect external circumstances and makes few direct demands of his client, but thaumaturgy does affect mental attitudes, reassures men, confirms their diagnoses (in witch-finding), utilizes trickery and self-confirming devices (in ordeals), and normally escapes objective test. Only millennialism stakes all on a prophesied external event to occur cataclysmically, suddenly, and soon, and proceeding from the action of an external agency.

Thaumaturgical belief is not only the pristine religious orientation, it is also more persistent than millennialism. The many little failures of magic are less disturbing to believers than the one big periodic failure of the millennium, and are more easily explained away.[14] Given the localism implicit in tribal societies, the lack of consciousness of social structure, the persistence of a world-view expressed in a personal idiom, it is understandable that magic should be the acceptable means for the solution of problems. Incipient millennialism itself is often heavily infiltrated with magical ideas. The demand for new commodities in the cargo cults is often more of a demand for magical benefits for the community than a demand for millennial transformation, at least in the earlier cults. Thaumaturgy is the bed-rock of such cults, even if from this base a revolutionist orientation develops. Not even the use of the language of military command, together with drilling, marching, and the use of mock rifles, is indisputable evidence of the wish to transform the social order *in toto*. They are the symbols of potent magic for those who do not understand the social structural implications of order, hierarchy, role-relationships, and all else that lies behind the short sharp military words that summon co-ordinated responses. Marching natives in Melanesia with imitation rifles need not be planning, perhaps not even envisaging, revolution.

To say this is not to deny that there are real causes of the discontent that has led to native risings, nor to underestimate the purposes of tribes that have taken up arms against white invaders. It is rather to recognize the inter-penetration of elements; and to make apparent the dramatic rarity of fully-fledged millennialism. Europeans have frequently mistaken, or misrepresented, the causes of native unrest. Both magic and millennialism have sometimes been blamed for disturbances the real cause of which (very often the expropriation of land) Europeans may not have wanted to concede.[15] They have chosen to blame witchdoctors for inciting rebellion[16] when all that they have done is to provide warriors with protective magic, much as bishops might bless Christian soldiers. To native peoples witch-doctors are men who do good: since they have always met with the condemnation of Europeans might it not be that Europeans were themselves powerful witches?[17] Such are the accusations and counter-accusations of magic (albeit with

[14] Of course, millennialists adjust their claims when prophecy fails—re-set dates; argue (as long as some magical elements persist in their culture) that proper procedures were not followed; or assert—as Jehovah's Witnesses have done—that the prophesied advent has in some sense occurred and that the present is only an interim before all becomes manifest.

[15] The opposite case also occurs, of course, in which socially disruptive but purely religious activity is treated as politically inspired—see the case of Kimbanguism above, pp. 368–73.

[16] See, for example, G. M. Theal, op. cit., III, pp. 91–2.

[17] Europeans faced this general accusation when Xhosa cattle were dying of lung disease in 1854–5; ibid., p. 198.

some differences of meaning) that occur in colonial warfare. In certain circumstances the thaumaturge might also claim a prophetic role,[18] promising not only protection but also supernatural intervention in battle and the creation of a new social order. When this occurred millennialism—a stronger and more convincing ideology of revolution —could be indicted as *the* cause of a particular native uprising. Its real significance in such cases was normally, however, less as a cause of rebellion than as an agency establishing unity among different tribal groups.

The expression of fully-fledged millennialism, with a prophet and a promise of the establishment (or the re-establishment) of the good life following a cataclysm in which all enemies and all evil would be destroyed, appears to have evolved only slowly following the contact of invading and indigenous peoples. Pre-existent indigenous myths of world destruction do not always experience the accretion of those other millennial elements which together constitute a thoroughly revolutionist response.[19] This response demands that men should have acquired a future sense and a future tense: in doing so they obtain a new dimension of social consciousness and create new forms of social organization. Whereas new magic may gain many adherents, whether it appears to succeed or to fail, it leaves the system of social relationships little changed. Millennialism always promises social transformation, and although always erronecus, it none the less creates a new conscious expectation of social change. Sometimes it prompts men to begin to make the millennium. The new age does not come, but the effort of work, organization, and the futuristic (or restorative) ethic has important consequences. A new framework of order is established. Even in restorative millennialism a new basis of social identity is created: in futuristic millennialism, the tendency is towards the establishment of a more rational order, as men themselves begin to take on the powers once ascribed to the gods, and to construct their own social institutions —not perfectly but with growing self-consciousness.

The revolutionist response has arisen in four distinct sets of circumstances. It has arisen in close association with war when it occurs as a transmutation of the traditional promise of the tribal magician into the more universal prophecy of protection and assistance for a new collectivity of peoples (as with the Delaware Prophet, Tenskwatawa, and Te Ua). It has occurred when notions of magical assistance in

[18] Many prophets were also witch-finders and curers—Tenskwatawa, the Shawnee Prophet, Handsome Lake, and Mwana Lesa are prominent examples.
[19] Here I differ from M. I. Pereira de Queiroz, *O Messianismo* . . ., op. cit., pp. 14–15, in attributing less importance to pre-existing myth than she does.

acquiring harvests and trade goods have been extended to become a transformative vision of changed status and material wealth for whole communities. It has arisen when white men have applied unduly politicized concepts to new thaumaturgical movements, and so have made of the widespread demand for more potent magic the demand for a counter-culture to that of the colonial administrators, as in the case of Kimbanguism. Finally, even in the millennium dreamed of in deep cultural despair, the Ghost Dance, the sense of Indian identity as against tribal identity gains new cogency in a myth of collective salvation.

In all of these cases a new conception of the social organization of the collectivity occurs: a glimmering sense of a different future is acquired. The idea of social change is grasped. The deities who hitherto have sanctioned custom, now—suddenly—become the initiators of change (even if that change is restoration). When men acquire a notion of the ancestors or the spirits initiating change they have experienced a radical transformation of consciousness. This transformation is perhaps rooted more in millennialism—despite its inherent incapacity to fulfil the promised changes it proclaims—than in any other single historical phenomenon. Although millennialism is an ideology of change, the real change which it inaugurates is a latent function rather than the realization of its promise. That other shifts of consciousness must come about before conscious and planned social change can occur is clear, and the burden for action is then laid on human effort rather than divine ordinance.

Rationalization and the introversionist alternative

Over the course of time, both thaumaturgy and recrudescent revolutionist responses undergo rationalization. Sometimes such development occurs within a movement: more typically, given the lack of persistence generally found in new enterprises among less-developed peoples, it is evident in the changing character of successive movements, or in the differences between movements arising at earlier and later stages of cultural contact. The specific form of increasing rationalization differs from context to context with the given preoccupations of local culture; with the opportunities for learning from Europeans; with the availability of models of rational organization. There is growth in scale of eligible clientele—of catchment area—as new movements overstep tribal boundaries, especially when their common condition gives force to the invaders' conception of tribal peoples as merely 'natives'. The given agglomerations of society—the family, the kin group, the settled community are transcended, and the traditional institutions of reciprocity, from trading relations to marital arrangements, are suspended for new, more voluntaristic, units of allegiance and new procedures.

The shift has all the appearance of a sudden break from status to contract: but of course, the 'contract' often becomes the new basis for status. Social organization is rationalized and existing communal structure is set aside, but often only to be re-instituted on new premises: kinship ties are replaced by shared religious commitment. Fictive kinship, surrogate tribalism, and selective communitarianism are bases of allegiance perhaps as compelling as the indigenous phenomena for which they substitute and which in some measure they replace. The impulse promoting this enlarged social organization is, however, immediately compromised by the absence of alternative models from those of kinship and local community—the forms which from childhood have for all indigenes appeared to be the permanent group-constellations of human kind.

The reassertion of folk values and folk structures which qualify the rational impulse for new bases of social integration is particularly conspicuous when a revolutionist response is superseded by introversionism, which implies a return to reliance on the gathered community—the only location in which men feel that they can experience salvation. It is found in some degree among the North American Indians in the Peyote cult, and among the Maori.[20] It is those who are —from circumstance or from choice—little affected by westernization who are most likely to adopt this reassertion of community organization. The new religions arising among them are claimed as the continuance of indigenous traditions, but in fact they are innovations which preserve not the actuality so much as the spirit of separate, authentic, cultural integrity. The spirit depends more perhaps on the sense of gathered community than on the specific rituals which give these communities

[20] Apart from the Ringatu movement considered above, Te Whiti O Rongomai built a model village for his Maori followers in the essentially introversionist movement that is known by his name. The Ratana movement began in 1918 as a form of Maori Christianity, condemning nativism and desecrating the t'apu (sacred) places. It had the approval of the Methodists (and for a time of the Anglicans). The hostility between tribes was overcome and the movement began as a Christian Maori revival movement. It established itself as an independent Church in 1925, and in 1927 a temple was built, when the leader Tahupotiki Wiremu Ratana was said to have 'closed the Bible'. The temple was to some not just a house of prayer, but a Whare t'apu, filled with secret, spiritual power. At Ratana Pa, the movement had its own separate community, and although less locally confined than Ringatu and the Te Whiti movement, it often embraced whole communities. For a full account, see J. McLeod Henderson, Ratana: The Origins and the Glory of the Movement (Polynesian Society Memoir 36, Wellington, N.Z., 1963).

their *raison d'être*. Rationalization—widely evident in various movements —is expressed through the specific cultural intimations of particular regions (commodity preoccupations in Melanesia; the control of thaumaturgy in Africa), which are developed to the exclusion of, or at least to the neglect of, other issues. Where deprived and defeated indigenous minorities persist, their rejection of assimilation to the intrusive white culture is also their resistance to the full impress of rationalization. Their semi-introversionist movements, as a reassertion of community, represent a radical alternative to rationalized social re-organization.

New religious movements are significant as embodiments of new initiatives among less-developed peoples. They are important not simply as charismatic impulses, to which Weber attributed so much weight in the process of social change, nor simply as the moments of social effervescence which caught the imagination of Durkheim, but because any re-appraisal of the social situation among people whose world-view always embodies strong reference to the supernatural, must be expressed as a new religious impulse. It is within *religious* phenomena that secularization must first appear. It is within the religious perspective that new and more rational procedures will be adumbrated; it is within a framework of religious wish-dreams that a new world will be envisaged. That world may remain entirely and forever unattainable, but if, as in so many Melanesian movements, it is a world embracing the artefacts of white civilization, then an approximation to it will be attained only by a more effective appreciation of the relationship between efficient means and more clearly formulated ends, by rational reorganization of social groups and the employment of empirically validated techniques and procedures. For the un- reasoned vision to be realized, even in some small measure, demands the sustained exercise of reason. The charisma of a Paliau or a Tommy Kabu irrevocably leads towards the establishment of a social order that tends more and more to the exclusion of the arbitrary and the wilful that characterizes the charismatic.

Conscious organization, often in imitation of Europeans—at first badly and then, with education, pretentiously (as in the case of the Church of the Lord, Ghana See)—marks the full force of rationaliza- tion. In the Church of the Lord and in the Paliau movement the need for order, discipline, and control are self-consciously expressed. The wilful poetry of religion is tamed. New constitutions and new structures now regulate behaviour. For a time these instruments facilitate religious association—perhaps for a long time. Eventually they threaten it; the spirit they embody stands out against the search for magical cures for personal ills and against millennial dreams of social salvation. The instrumentalism of the new movements militates against both, just as it provides alternative structures for those embodied in the family, kin-group, and local community.

Comparative method and some problems of explanation

In setting out the distinctions between different movements and the distinctions between the types of circumstance in which they have arisen, some very broad indicators of causal elements are necessarily implied. Beyond this in a broad comparative study it is perhaps not possible to go. Each movement can be finally explained only in relation to very specific conditions, in which such elements as the nature of indigenous mythology, the primary focus of indigenous cultural goals, the cumulative character of cultural contact, the speed and content of cultural diffusion, the specific teachings of missions, and the nature of contacts between indigenes and invaders would all need to be specified. One would need to know something about the social positions of those espousing a new teaching and of those ignoring it; the personality of leaders and something of their personal history; the sequence of events immediately before the development of a distinct new movement. Some of these data are sometimes available in the detailed accounts of particular movements, but the more specific the material the more difficult becomes the exercise of comparison. Comparison is useful as long as broad categories are employed. The problem of broad categories—such as *anomie, charisma, relative deprivation, nativism,* and *culture-shock*—is their tendency to become catch-all phrases, glib formulae by which the uninformed, looking for summary solutions to intellectual problems, parade a spurious sophistication. This debasement of the conceptual coinage adds to the problems of comparative sociology by reducing the rigour and the exact specification of abstract propositions.

None the less, we can point to very broadly similar circumstances in which disrupted economic conditions, confusions of authority-structure, the effects of cultural contact, the breakdown of stable norms and expectations, and the existence of relatively deprived groups may be identified. What cannot be derived from these general conditions are the items mentioned in the foregoing paragraph, which stand closer to the explanation of a particular set of social consequences. For similarity of general circumstances does not necessarily lead to the development of new social movements. There are cases of societies in which economic exploitation, relative deprivation, cultural shock, and anomie are identifiable but in which no millennial movements have occurred and from which we have no reports of new cults of popular thaumaturgy.

Nor is it sufficient to point to the absence in such instances of charismatic leaders. Whilst a leader may often be prominent in the emergence of movements, we also find men who make bids for leadership but who are socially unacceptable—who are regarded as lunatics, deviants, or agitators. *Charisma* as a term expresses less a quality of person than of relationship; it contains the acceptability of a leader by a following, the endorsement of his personality, and the social endowment of power. There are those who seek endorsement and endowment who are denied them. And there are instances, to propose a new concept, of charismatic demand, of situations in which men mobilize as a following and look for a leader. Where traditional authority-structures fail, the social demand for a new leadership—as in the Bas-Congo after the arrest of Kimbangu—may create a context in which prophetism is socially awaited. So may the occasion produce the man, or even, as in the Congo, a succession of such men. To say this is not, of course, to deny that the obverse case may exist, in which men of exceptional ability attain charisma—where supply is enough to stimulate demand.

Charisma is a sociological, and not a psychological, concept. But precisely for this reason—because it expresses a social relationship and is a mode of legitimizing leadership, it does not serve us well as a causal category. Society, or at least a section of it, endows a leader. On his part, he must have some grounds on which a claim to exceptional competence can rest: on theirs, there must already be an ethos propitious to the mobilization of sentiments. But *charisma* expresses the balance of claim and acceptance—it is not a dynamic, causally explanatory, concept; it relates to an established state of affairs, when the leader is already accepted, not to the power of one man to cause events to move in a particular direction.

Such general propositions as that which declares that new movements are attempts to 'make sense' of a disordered world tell us something significant about these phenomena. But this one (possible) function of a new movement may be neither exhaustive nor pre-eminent: it certainly offers us nothing approaching causal explanation. Indeed it does little more than offer us an old functionalism without the connotations of irrationality which the concept of latent functions has usually carried. The new vision of the world which a movement disseminates is, too, not simply an intellectual reorientation: it is shot through with highly emotional preoccupations. The new comprehension of the prevailing situation embraces emotions, evaluations, and wishes, as well as what pass for facts. New religious movements—least of all millennial movements—are not prompted by intellectual demand to see things 'as they are' or by the desire to understand objective truth in a detached way. What is sought are guidelines for behaviour that will attain specific soteriological goals. Given the strong demand for salvation, one may, of course, refer to cult action as a response to 'the logic of situation' as participants perceive it, and self-evidently participants will seek to present their action as rational, their reasoning as logical. But 'the logic of that situation' incorporates conceptions of salvation which —and as detached observers of more extended knowledge and with all the benefit of hindsight we may say this—are simply not warranted and not attainable.

However ingenious may be the interpretation of causal forces that magical and millennial movements canvass, they never constitute impressive demonstrations of intellectual reconstruction. Emotional orientations are too dominant, and evaluations too inseparably incorporated in factual observations, for that. Certainly, once we have full information about local knowledge (and local ignorance), historical events, cultural preconceptions, and other data of this kind, the new magical or millennial teachings do become understandable. But neither the contemporary self-hatred of many western intellectuals (and their corresponding romantic sympathy for third-world cultures), nor the prevailing doubt about the 'ultimate validity' of our conceptual categories should persuade us to deceive ourselves: magic does not work; the millennium will not come.

New movements represent demands for salvation, and if those demands include new ways of 'making sense' of things, then it is the search for salvation that prompts it. We need not ignore the fact that men (no less in simpler societies than elsewhere) are capable of compartmentalizing experience, of seeking salvation according to certain intimations which do not—even according to their own standards— really finally 'make sense'. The ideology which is offered is usually ephemeral, incapable of withstanding rigorous examination or careful definition, or even complete articulation. Furthermore, it is certainly very rare that all men in a given situation accept the new attempt to 'make sense': in the case of most movements there are many men who reject as unconvincing what some of our commentators describe as 'the logic of the situation'. Shall we say that those who do not become votaries of new movements, all of which eventually fail, are the men who in their situation are irrational?

One is not obliged, in having made this point, to regard new movements as manifestations of mania, as merely the outworking of neurotic dispositions. The causes of new movements are laid in the unprecedented disruption of social circumstances. For sociologists this is the starting point of analysis. Obviously movements may themselves contribute to disruption, may, as they become recrudescent, contribute to situations in which the return to stable norms and expectations becomes difficult. It may also be the case that many personal psychopathologies may be mobilized in such movements, just as revolutions mobilize men at odds with their societies for many reasons other than abstract passion for social justice. Leaders may indeed exercise abnormal psychic dispositions, and catch the momentary frailty of other men exposed to circumstances of exceptional stress. Men faced with intense new anxieties may be the victims of emotions which in less stressful circumstances would be disciplined or sublimated. New movements may, if they persist, come to institutionalize new safeguards on men's emotions, in the form of new mores, norms, values, and sanctions, new bases upon which men can safely conduct their relations with each other. But in the early stages, in the ecstasy of millennialism, in the first new hopes for new miracles and new therapy, it is the breakdown and abandonment of previous assumptions and codes of discipline, of earlier norms and goals, rather than the institutionalization of new ones, which is more impressive. The new movements appear less as a consequence of mania, than as the response to conditions in which men feel the need to act out their emotions in new forms.

It is the dramatic cult movements that have called forth general explanations—the derogatory, perhaps condemnatory, 'explanations' in terms of mania; and the defensive attempts to relate millenarianism to the logic of the situation. New thaumaturgical cults have been accorded less general, and less ideological, explanations. Yet new thaumaturgy is more widespread, more widely endemic, more frequent in early stages of cultural contact, more likely to be overlooked, than new millennialism. It is less conspicuous, less dramatic, less socially disrupting. Religious movements may be characterized typologically by their broad orientations, and we have found it useful in this study to offer such characterization. But in the real world we know that the interpenetration of these orientations frequently occurs, and particularly in less-developed societies. The breakthrough in social consciousness that the millennial vision represents is continually compromised by the subsidiary search for new magic. No explanation of new movements that confines itself to ideal-typical millennialism alone is likely to be adequate except at a level of considerable theoretical remoteness from the real world.

The formulation of a general theory incorporating causal explanation of cult movements appears to go far beyond the possibilities of ordering the complex body of available data. At best we can have models of the type propounded by Smelser; we can have general specification of social conditions and stages of consciousness, in the manner followed in these pages; we can resort to broad (often ill-defined) sociological concepts as, in a somewhat unrigorous fashion, Lanternari has done; or we can abandon comparative general theories in favour of detailed analysis of particular movements, of which we have several excellent examples, particularly those of Aberle, Andersson, Burridge, Cochrane, and Lawrence.[21]

This last choice is less than sociologists would wish, committed as is the subject to abstract generalization, and the search for encompassing theoretical formulations. Yet it should be plain that sociology cannot progress without thorough, detailed, individual studies, even though it is more general relationships and comparative procedures to which the discipline is committed. The tasks of the historian or the ethnographer and that of the sociologist should be mutually informative: without the bricks of detailed monographs, sociological theories will be worthless, but in undertaking more general comparative analysis sociology may help the historian and ethnographer to make better bricks.[22]

Epilogue

Man's dreams of magical or millennial solutions for personal and social problems do not entirely disappear even in advanced societies in which productive operations and social relationships are predominantly organized according to empirical and rational principles, but both magic and millennialism become marginal and attenuated. Modern men expect their blessings mainly from the welfare state, scientific medicine, the development of technology, the availability of education, the operation of impersonal legal institutions, and disinterested agencies for the maintenance of social order. Yet within the world-view of those who count themselves Christians, thaumaturgical elements of the old style may persist. There is sustained demand for additional benefits of an essentially psychic kind—reassurance, solace, conferment of worth, a place in which to attain a measure of public esteem in a context in which to be known 'as a person' and not merely as a role-performer. Dealing with the individual as a total person, religious movements

[21] D. F. Aberle, op. cit.; E. Andersson, *Messianic Popular Movements* . . ., op. cit.; K. O. L. Burridge, *Mambu* . . ., op. cit.; G. Cochrane, *Big Men and Cargo Cults*, op. cit.; P. Lawrence, *Road Belong Cargo* . . ., op. cit.

[22] For a discussion, see B. R. Wilson, 'Sociological Methods in the Study of History', *Transactions of The Royal Historical Society* 5th Series, Vol. 21 (1971), pp. 101–18.

persist: in a role-articulated and increasingly rationalized social system, this is their feeble magic, extolled in the rhetoric of legendary miracles and special personal salvation.

At the fringes of Christian orthodoxy, somewhat more dramatic manifestations of this ancient thaumaturgical appeal are given prominence—in healings, and in the self-confirming miracles of glossalalia, the 'interpretation of tongues' (by power of the Holy Spirit), and discernment of spirits in Pentecostal groups. But even here the miraculous is only faintly claimed: the gift of prophecy ceases to be full thaumaturgical prophecy—foretelling is interpreted as the much more routinized activity of forth-telling. In seeking to work wonders that pass beyond the restrictive scope of even the literally interpreted license of the gospels, Spiritualism too keeps magic and the spirit of primitive thaumaturgy alive in the margins of advanced society.[23]

The very dilute thaumaturgy of Christian orthodoxy has long been culturally accommodated (even if Christianity itself becomes more of a cultural abnormality). The old form of Christian millennialism, cither by the 'spiritual' reinterpretation of the literal biblical promises of the advent or by the doctrine of the post-millennial advent, has been pushed even further to the margins. In the major denominations, it is found only among small minorities; it flourishes more vigorously among minority sects such as Jehovah's Witnesses, and perhaps, in highly secularized form, in the spasmodic socio-political enthusiasms that capture the minds principally of the young.

The old magic, then, persists only in the interstices of the institutionalized processes of advanced society, and the old millennialism only at its peripheries. The thaumaturge and the prophet have also become distinctly marginal men. Esoteric knowledge which defies empirico-rational analysis, and the capacity to predict cataclysmic change that conforms to no known set of testable propositions, can command the complete attention of very few in contemporary advanced society. There is a diminution of trust in strictly *personal* qualities (as distinct from impersonal, technical expertise). Modern men do not look for a man—or a god—to 'come and save us': they look to impersonal, consciously evolved agencies and organization, and to scientific procedures of enquiry and prescription.

Yet these two primary orientations to the world are not extinct even in advanced society. They emerge in new, more individuated forms. Men remain eager to find solutions for the tensions that living must always generate: when scientific procedures, elaborate social organiza-

[23] See Bernice Martin, 'The Spiritualist Meeting' in David Martin and Michael Hill (Eds), *Sociological Yearbook of Religion* 3 (SCM Press, London 1970), pp. 146–61.

tion, and deliberative planning fail to assuage existing tensions (and perhaps create new ones) men sometimes resort to magical and millennial wish-dreams. In day-dreams, fantasy, and dreams men accept magical solutions to personal and perhaps to social problems. Modern societies institutionalize such fantasies in newspaper strip-cartoons of supermen, or in the synthetic characters of film and television, of which James Bond is the most visible contemporary representative. Such provision falls short of collective behaviour: the audiences are passive; fantasy is synthetic and prefabricated; its production is a rational, planned profit-seeking operation; the engagement of individuals is segmentary and its duration in time is calculated and costed; the images are distributive rather than collective.

There is a somewhat more collective form in which the new-style magical and millennial orientations are reincarnated in advanced society, and that is in the new manipulationist sects of the modern world, which, by means that claim to be scientific, metaphysical, and religious, offer men the prospect of greater success in the world by the enlargement of their natural faculties and intelligence, of greater command over themselves and their personal environment. These new religions tend to imitate the impersonality, the obsession with science and technology, that characterize modern society, and to demand from their clientele only calculated investment for calculated return, only segmentary and partial commitment.[24]

These phenomena, however rationalized and compartmentalized they become, however accommodated to a time-ordered social system, indicate man's ambivalent hankering for magical and millennial solutions. This aspect of human yearning is no less a part of men's attempt to organize his world, however peripheral its social expression has become, than his instrumental striving and conformity to the demands of the increasingly consciously-organized system. The search for the unprogrammed in the increasingly programmed society is a commentary on the further limits of planning and rational organization: it is a commentary on the persistence of demand for fantasy, for colour, and in its more trivial respects, for ceremony, pageantry, and the sentiments engendered by traditional performances, in an impersonal, calculating, instrumental, and progressive society. The demand for fantasy—for freedom, as it is often expressed—is a type of persisting irrationality in a rational world, reminding us of the fragility of our very complex social order, of the delicacy of the socialization process on which it rests, and of the untamed, perhaps untameable, element of man's spirit.

[24] On this, see B. R. Wilson, *Religious Sects*, op. cit., pp. 141–66.

Bibliography

ABERLE, DAVID F. 'The Prophet Dance and Reactions to White Contact', *Southwestern Journal of Anthropology* 15, 1 (Spring 1959), pp. 74–83.
The Peyote Religion Among the Navaho (Aldine, Chicago 1966).
ABERLE, DAVID F. and STEWART, OMER C. *Navaho and Ute Peyotism: A Chronological and Distributional Study*, University of Colorado Studies: Series in Anthropology, No. 6 (University of Colorado Press, Boulder, Colorado, 1957).
ADEJOBI, E. O. ADELEKE. *The Bible Speaks on the Church of the Lord*, 2nd Edn (Free Town, Sierra Leone, January 1950).
Mount Tabborrar's Anniversary (The Royal Press, Tka, probably 1962).
Holy Matrimonial Guide (no place of publication, n.d.).
ALDÉN, KARL. 'The Prophet Movement in Congo', *International Review of Missions* XXV (1936), pp. 347–53.
ALLAN, C. H. 'Marching Rule: A Nativistic Cult of the British Solomon Islands', *South Pacific* 5, 5 (July 1951), pp. 79–85.
ALONSO, ISADORO. *La Iglesia en America Latina: Estructuras ecclesiásticas* (Feres, Freiburg, Switzerland, and Bogotá, Colombia, 1964).
AMES, MICHAEL M. 'Magical Animism and Buddhism: A Structural Analysis of the Sinhalese Religious System', *Journal of Asian Studies* XXIII (June 1964), pp. 21–52.
'Reactions to Stress: A Comparative Study of Nativism', *Davidson Journal of Anthropology* 3, 1 (Summer 1957), pp. 17–30.
ANDERSSON, EFRAIM. *Churches at the Grassroots* (Lutterworth, London 1968).
Messianic Popular Movements in the Lower Congo, Studia Ethnographica Upsaliensia XIV (Almqvist and Wiksells, 1958).
ANGULO, JAIME DE and FREELAND, J. S. 'A New Religious Movement in North-Central California, *American Anthropologist* 31, 2 (April–June 1929), pp. 265–70.
ANSON, PETER F. *Bishops at Large* (Faber, London 1964).
ARMSTRONG, B. G. and WENTWORTH, T. P. *Early Life Among Indians* (Bowron, Ashland, Wisc., 1892).
ARNDT, KARL J. R. *Georg Rapp's Harmony Society 1785–1847* (University of Pennsylvania Press, Philadelphia 1965).
ASSIMENG, J. M. *A Sociological Analysis of the Impact and Consequences of some Christian Sects in Selected African Countries*, Unpub. D.Phil. thesis, University of Oxford, 1968.
BABBAGE, S. BARTON. *Hauhauism: An Episode in the Maori Wars 1863–6* (A. H. & A. W. Reed, Wellington and Dunedin 1937).

BABBIE, EARL R. 'The Third Civilization: An Examination of Sokagakkai', *Review of Religious Research* 7 (Winter 1966), pp. 101–21.

BAËTA, C. G. *Prophetism in Ghana* (SCM Press, London 1962).

BAILEY, PAUL. *Wovoka: The Indian Messiah* (Westernlore Press, Los Angeles 1957).

BALANDIER, GEORGES. 'Messianismes et Nationalismes en Afrique Noire', *Cahiers Internationaux de Sociologie* XIV, 1953, pp. 41–65.
Sociologie actuelle de l'Afrique noire (Presses universitaires, Paris 1955).

BANTON, MICHAEL. 'An Independent African Church in Sierra Leone', *Hibbert Journal* LV (October 1956), pp. 57–63.

BARBER, BERNARD. 'A Socio-Cultural Interpretation of the Peyote Cult', *American Anthropologist* 43 (1941), pp. 673–5.
'Acculturation and Messianic Movements', *American Sociological Review* 6 (October 1941), pp. 663–8.

BARBER, CAROLL G. 'Peyote and the Definition of a Narcotic', *American Anthropologist* 61 (1959), pp. 641–5.

BARNETT, HOMER G. *Indian Shakers: A Messianic Cult of the Pacific Northwest* (Southern Illinois University Press, Carbondale 1957).

BARRETT, DAVID B. *Schism and Renewal In Africa* (Oxford University Press, Nairobi 1968).

BARRETT, S. A. 'The Dream Dance of the Chippewa and Menominee Indians of Northern Wisconsin', *Bulletin of the Public Museum of Milwaukee* I, iv (November 1911), pp. 25–369.

BARRETT, STANLEY R. *God's Kingdom on Stilts: A Comparative Study of Rapid Economic Development.* Unpubl. Ph.D. thesis, University of Sussex, 1971.

BARROW, G. L. 'The Story of Jonfrum', *Corona* (Journal of H.M. Colonial Service) III, 10 (October 1951), pp. 379–82.

BASTIDE, ROGER. 'Religion and the Church in Brazil' in T. L. Smith and A. Marchant (Eds.), *Brazil: Portrait of Half a Continent* (Dryden Press, New York 1951).
Le Candomblé de Bahia (Rite Nagô) (Mouton, Paris 1958).
Les religions africaines au Brésil (Presses universitaires de France, Paris 1960).

BATTIS, EMRYS. *Saints and Sectaries* (University of North Carolina Press, Chapel Hill, N.C., 1962).

BAXTER, P. T. W. 'The Kiga', in A. I. Richards (Ed.), *East African Chiefs* (Praeger, New York 1959).

BEAL, MERRILL D. *'I Will Fight No More Forever'* (University of Washington Press, Seattle 1963).

BEATTIE, JOHN 'Group Aspects of the Nyoro Spirit Mediumship Cult', *Rhodes-Livingstone Journal*: Human Problems in British Central Africa, XXX (December 1961), pp. 11–38.

BEAUCHAMP, WILLIAM M. 'Civil, Religious and Mourning Councils and Ceremonies of Adoption of the New York Indians', New York State Museum (New York State Education Department), *Bulletin* 113, Archaeology, 13 (1906), pp. 341–451.

BEAVER, R. PIERCE. 'Expansion of American Foreign Missionary Activities since 1945', *Missionary Research Library Occasional Bulletin* V, 7 (4 June 1954).

BECKER, HOWARD. *Systematic Sociology on the Basis of the Beziehungslehre und Gebildelehre of Leopold von Wiese* (Wiley, New York 1932).

BEE, ROBERT L. 'Potawatomi Peyotism: The Influence of Traditional Patterns', *Southwestern Journal of Anthropology* 22, 6 (Summer 1966), pp. 194–205.

BEIDELMAN, T. O. 'Witchcraft in Ukaguru', in J. Middleton and E. H. Winter (Eds.), *Witchcraft and Sorcery in East Africa* (Praeger, New York 1963).

BELL, R. M. 'The Maji-Maji Rebellion in the Liwale District', *Tanganyika Notes and Records* 28 (January 1950), pp. 38–57.

BELSHAW, CYRIL S. 'The Significance of Modern Cults in Melanesian Development', *Australian Outlook* 4, 2 (June 1950), pp. 116–25.

'Recent History of Mekeo Society', *Oceania* XXII, 1 (September 1951), pp. 1–23.

BENNETT, JOHN W. *Hutterian Brethren* (Stanford University Press, Stanford 1967).

BERGER, PETER L. 'The Sociological Study of Sectarianism', *Social Research* 21 (Winter 1954), pp. 467–85.

The Sacred Canopy (Doubleday, New York 1967).

BERNARD, GUY. 'The Nature of a Sociological Research: Religious Sects in the west of the Congo', *Cahiers Économiques et Sociaux* (Lovanium, Congo) II, 3 (November 1964), pp. 261–9.

BERNARD, GUY and CAPRASSE, P. 'Religious Movements in the Congo: A Research Hypothesis', *Cahiers Économiques et Sociaux* (Lovanium, Congo) III, 1 (March 1965), pp. 49–60.

BERNDT, RONALD M. 'A Cargo Movement in the Eastern Central Highlands of New Guinea', *Oceania* XXIII (September and December 1952), pp. 40–65, 137–58.

'Reaction to Contact in the Eastern Highlands of New Guinea', *Oceania* XXIV (March and June 1954), pp. 190–228; 255–74.

An Adjustment Movement in Arnhem Land, Northern Territory of Australia (Mouton, Paris and The Hague 1962).

BESSELL, M. J. 'Nyabingi', *Uganda Journal* VI, 2 (October 1938), pp. 73–86.

BLAIR, EMMA H. (Ed.). *The Indian Tribes of the Upper Missouri Valley and Region of the Great Lakes* (Arthur H. Clark Co., Cleveland, Ohio, 1912).

BODROGI, T. 'Colonization and Religious Movements in Melanesia', *Acta Academiae Scientiorum Hungaricae* II, 1–4 (1951), pp. 259–90.

BOHANNAN, PAUL. 'Extra-Processual Events in Tiv Political Institutions', *American Anthropologist* 60, 1 (February 1958), pp. 1–12.

BORHEK, J. T. 'Role Orientations and Organizational Stability', *Human Organization* 24, 4 (Winter 1965), pp. 332–8.

BRACKMAN, RICHARD W. 'Der Umbanda-Kult in Brasilien', *Stadenjahrbuch* 7/8 (1959–60), pp. 157–73.

BRANDEL-SYRIER, MIA. *Black Woman in Search of God* (Lutterworth Press, London 1962).

BRANT, CHARLES S. 'Peyotism Among the Kiowa-Apache and Neighboring Tribes', *Southwestern Journal of Anthropology* 6, 2 (Summer 1950), pp. 212–22.

BREWSTER, A. B. *The Hill Tribes of Fiji* (Lippincott, London 1922).

BROKENSHA, DAVID. *Social Change at Larteh, Ghana* (Clarendon Press, Oxford 1966).

BROWN, DONALD N. 'The Ghost Dance Religion Among the Oklahoma Cheyenne', *The Chronicles of Oklahoma* XXX, 4 (Winter 1952–3), pp. 408–16.

BRUYN, J. V. DE. 'The Manseren Cult of Biak', *South Pacific* 5, 1 (March 1951), pp. 1–11.

BUCK, PETER H. (Te Rangi Hiroa) *Anthropology and Religion* (Yale University Press, New Haven, Conn., 1939).

BUELL, RAYMOND L. *The Native Problem in Africa* (Macmillan, New York 1928).

BURRIDGE, KENELM O. L. *Mambu: A Melanesian Millennium* (Methuen, London 1960).
New Heaven New Earth (Blackwell, Oxford 1969).

✓ BURROWS, WILLIAM. 'The Background to Marching Rule', *Pacific Islands Monthly* XX, 11 (June 1950), pp. 37–8.

BURTON, JOHN W. *Modern Missions in the South Pacific* (Livingstone Press, London 1949).

BUSIA, K. A. *Report on a Social Survey of Sekondi-Takoradi* (Crown Agents for the Colonies, London 1950).

BUTT, AUDREY J. 'The Birth of a Religion', *Journal of the Royal Anthropological Institute of Gt. Britain and Ireland* 90, Pt. I (January–June 1960), pp. 66–102.

CALLEY, M. J. C. *God's People: West Indian Pentecostal Sects in England* (Oxford University Press, London 1965).

CATO, A. C. 'A New Religious Cult in Fiji', *Oceania* XVIII (December 1947), pp. 146–56.

CAULTON, S. G. 'The Marching Rule Delusion', *Pacific Islands Monthly* XXI, 1 (August 1950), p. 77.

CHALMERS, J. *Pioneering in New Guinea* (The Religious Tract Society, London 1887).

⟶ CHAMBERLAIN, ALEXANDER F. 'New Religions Among the North American Indians . . .', *Journal of Religious Psychology* 6, 1 (January 1913), pp. 1–49.

CHINNERY, E. W. P. and HADDON, A. C. 'Five New Religious Cults in British New Guinea', *Hibbert Journal* XV (1917), pp. 448–63.

CHOMÉ, JULES. *La Passion de Simon Kimbangu*, 2nd Edn (Les Amis de Presence Africaine, Brussels 1959).

CHRISTENSEN, JAMES B. 'The Tigari Cult of West Africa', *Papers of the Michigan Academy of Science, Arts and Letters* XXXIX, Pt IV (1954), pp. 389–98.
'The Adaptive Functions of Fanti Priesthood', in W. R. Bascom and M. J. Herskovits (Eds.), *Continuity and Change in African Cultures* (University of Chicago Press, Chicago 1959).

CLARK, E. T. *The Small Sects in America*, Rev. Edn (Abingdon Press, New York and Nashville 1947).

CLOIN, TIAGO. 'Aspects socio-religieuses et sociographiques du Brésil', *Social Compass* V, 5–6 (1959), pp. 200–37.

COCHRANE, GLYNN. *Big Men and Cargo Cults* (Clarendon Press, Oxford 1970).

COMHAIRE, JEAN L. 'Religious Trends in African and Afro-American Urban Societies', *Anthropological Quarterly* XXVI (1953), pp. 95–108.
'Sociétés Secrètes et Mouvements Prophétiques au Congo Belge', *Africa* XXV (January 1955), pp. 54–8.

COLLINS, JUNE MCCORMICK. 'The Indian Shaker Church', *Southwestern Journal of Anthropology* 6, 4 (Winter 1950), pp. 399–411.

COLLINS, ROBERT O. *The Southern Sudan 1883–1898: A Struggle for Control* (Yale University Press, New Haven, Conn., 1962).

COOK, LLOYD A. 'Revolt in Africa', *Journal of Negro History* XVIII, 4 (October 1933), pp. 396–413.

COOK, SCOTT. 'The Prophets: A Revivalistic Folk Religious Movement in Puerto Rico', *Caribbean Studies* 4, 4 (January 1965), pp. 20–35.

CORFIELD, F. D. *Historical Survey of the Origins and Growth of Mau Mau* (HMSO [Colonial Office Cmnd. 1030], London 1960).

CORY, SIR GEORGE E. *The Rise of South Africa* Vol. I–IV (Longmans, London 1910–26; Vol. VI, Cape Times, Cape Town 1940).

CRONON, EDMUND D. *Black Moses: The Story of Marcus Garvey and the Universal Negro Improvement Association* (University of Wisconsin Press, Madison 1955).

CUNNISON, IAN. 'A Watchtower Assembly in Central Africa', *International Review of Missions* XL (1951), pp. 456–69.

DABBS, JACK A. 'A Messiah among the Chiriguanos', *Southwestern Journal of Anthropology* 9, 1 (Spring 1953), pp. 45–58.

DA CUNHA, EUCLIDES. *Rebellion in the Backlands (Os Sertões)*, trans. Samuel Putnam (Phoenix Books, University of Chicago Press, Chicago 1944).

DAMMANN, ERNST. 'Das Christusverstandnis in nachchristlichen Kirchen und Sekten Afrikas', in E. Benz (Ed.), *Messianische Kirchen, Sekten und Bewegungen im heutigen Afrika* (E. J. Brill, Leiden 1965).

DANGBERG, GRACE M. (Ed.). 'Letters to Jack Wilson, the Paiute Prophet, Written between 1908–1911', Smithsonian Institution: Bureau of American Ethnology, Bulletin 164, *Anthropological Papers* No. 55 (Government Printing Office, Washington 1957), pp. 279–96.

DAVIDSON, BASIL. 'The Congo and Angola', *West Africa* Nos. 1939, 1940, 1942, 1943 (April–May 1954).

DEAN, JOHN C. (Ed.). 'Journal of Thomas Dean: A Voyage to Indiana in 1817', *Indiana Historical Society Publications* VI, 2 (1918), pp. 273–345.

DEARDORFF, MERLE H. 'The Religion of Handsome Lake: Its Origin and Development', in W. N. Fenton (Ed.), *Symposium on Local Diversity in Iroquois Culture*, Smithsonian Institution, Bureau of American Ethnology No. 149 (1951), pp. 77–107.

DEBRUNNER, H. W. *Witchcraft in Ghana* (Presbyterian Book Depot, Kumasi 1959).

DITTMAN, ALLEN T. and MOORE, HARVEY C. 'Disturbances in Dreams as Related to Peyotism among the Navaho', *American Anthropologist* 59, 4 (August 1957), pp. 642–9.

DOUGALL, J. W. C. 'African Separatist Churches', *International Review of Missions* XXV (1956), pp. 257–66.

DOUGLAS, MARY. 'Techniques of Sorcery Control in Central Africa', in J. Middleton and E. H. Winter (Eds.), *Witchcraft and Sorcery in East Africa* (Praeger, New York 1963).

DRAKE, BENJAMIN. *Life of Tecumseh and of his Brother the Prophet, with a historical Sketch of the Shawanoe Indians* (Rulson, Cincinnati and Quaker City Publishing House, Philadelphia 1856).

DRIBERG, J. H. 'Yakãn', *Journal of the Royal Anthropological Institute of Gt. Britain and Ireland* LXI (July–December 1931), pp. 413–20.

DRUCKER, PHILIP. 'A Karuk World-Renewal Ceremony at Panaminik', *Varia Anthropologica*, University of California Publications in American Archaeology and Ethnology, 35, 3 (University of California Press, Berkeley, California 1936), pp. 23–8.

The Native Brotherhoods: Modern Intertribal Organizations on the Northwest Coast (Smithsonian Institution: Bureau of American Ethnology, Government Printing Office, Washington 1958).

DU BOIS, CORA. *The Feather Cult of the Middle Columbia* (George Banta, Menasha, Wisc., 1938).

'The 1870 Ghost Dance', *Anthropological Records* 3, 1 (University of California Press, Berkeley 1939).

DU PLESSIS, J. *A History of Christian Missions in South Africa* (Longmans, London 1911).

DURKHEIM, ÉMILE. *Elementary Forms of the Religious Life* (The Free Press, Glencoe, Illinois 1957).

DUSTIN, C. BURTON. *Peyotism and New Mexico* (C. Burton Dustin, Albuquerque *c.* 1960).

EASTMAN, CHARLES A. (Ohiyesa). *From the Deep Woods to Civilization* (Little Brown, Boston 1916: first pub. 1902).

EBERHARDT, JACQUELINE. 'Messianisme en Afrique du Sud', *Archives de Sociologie des Religions* 4 (June–December 1957), pp. 31–56.

ECKERT, GEORG. 'Prophetentum und Freiheitsbewegungen in Caucatal', *Zeitschrift für Ethnologie* 75–6 (1950), pp. 115–25.

ECKVALL, ROBERT B. *Religious Observances in Tibet: Patterns and Functions* (University of Chicago Press, Chicago 1964).

EDEL, MAY MANDELBAUM. *The Chiga of Western Uganda* (Oxford University Press, New York 1957).

EDMONDSON, MUNRO S. 'Nativism, Syncretism and Anthropological Science', *Middle American Research Institute Publication 19* (Tulane University, New Orleans 1960), pp. 181–204.

EISTER, A. W. 'Towards a Radical Critique of Church-Sect Typologizing', *Journal for the Scientific Study of Religion* VI, 1 (Spring 1967), pp. 85–90.

ELLIOTT, ALAN J. A. *Chinese Spirit-Medium Cults in Singapore*, London School of Economics, Monographs in Social Anthropology, No. 14 (London 1955).

EVANS-PRITCHARD, E. E. 'Witchcraft', *Africa* VIII, 4 (October 1935), pp. 417–22.

Witchcraft, Oracles and Magic Among the Azande (Clarendon Press, Oxford 1937).

'Foreword' in J. Middleton and E. H. Winter (Eds.), *Witchcraft and Sorcery in East Africa* (Praeger, New York 1963).

FEHDERAU, HAROLD W. 'Kimbanguism: Prophetic Christianity in the Congo', *Practical Anthropology* 9 (July–August 1962), pp. 157–78.

FENTON, WILLIAM N. 'Factionalism at Taos Pueblo, New Mexico', Smithsonian Institution, Bureau of American Ethnology, Bulletin 164, *Anthropological Papers* No. 56 (1957), pp. 297–344.

FERNANDEZ, JAMES W. 'Christian Acculturation and Fang Witchcraft', *Cahiers d'Études Africaines* Vol. II, 2 (1961), pp. 244–55.

'The Idea and Symbol of the Saviour in a Gabon Syncretistic Cult', *International Review of Missions* LIII (July 1964), pp. 281–9.

'African Religious Movements—Types and Dynamics', *Journal of Modern African Studies* 2, 4 (December 1964), pp. 531–49.

'Politics and Prophecy: African Religious Movements', *Practical Anthropology* 12, 2 (March–April 1965), pp. 71–5.

FERREIRA DE CAMARGO, CANDIDO P. *Kardecismo e Umbanda: Uma interpretação sociológica* (Livraria Pioneira Editôra, São Paulo 1961).

FERREIRA DE CAMARGO, CANDIDO P. and LABBANS, J. 'Aspects socio-culturels du spiritisme au Brésil', *Social Compass* VII, 5–6 (1960), pp. 407–30.

FIELD, M. J. *Religion and Medicine of the Gã People* (Oxford University Press, London 1937).

Search for Security (Faber, London 1960).

FIRTH, RAYMOND. 'The Theory of "Cargo" Cults: A Note on Tikopia', *Man* LV, 102 (September 1955), pp. 130–2.

'Ritual and Drama in Malay Spirit Mediumship', *Comparative Studies in Society and History* IX, 2 (January 1967), pp. 190–207.

FISCHER, HANS. 'Cargo-Kulte und die "Amerikaner"', *Sociologus* 14, 1 (1964), pp. 17–30.

FISHER, HUMPHREY J. Ahmadiyyah: *A Study in Contemporary Islam on the West African Coast* (Oxford University Press, London 1963).

'Muslim and Christian Separatism in Africa', in *Religion in Africa*, Proceedings of a Seminar held in the Centre of African Studies, University of Edinburgh, 10–12 April 1964, pp. 9–23.

FLETCHER, ALICE C. 'The Indian Messiah', *Journal of American Folklore* IV, 12 (January–March 1891), pp. 57–60.

FOX, RENÉE C., CRAEMER, WILLY DE, and RIBEAUCOURT, JEAN MARIE. ' "The Second Independence": A Case Study of the Kwilu Rebellion in the Congo', *Comparative Studies in Society and History* VIII, 1 (October 1965), pp. 78–109.

FREEDMAN, MAURICE. 'Religion and Society in South Eastern China', *Man* LVII (April 1957), pp. 56–7.

FREEDMAN, MAURICE and TOPLEY, MARJORIE. 'Religious and Social

Realignment among the Chinese in Singapore', *Journal of Asian Studies* XXI, 1 (November 1961), pp. 3–23.

FREEMAN, J. D. 'The Joe Gimlet or Siovili Cult: An Episode in the Religious History of Early Samoa', in J. D. Freeman and W. E. Geddes (Eds.), *Anthropology in the South Seas* (Thomas Avery, New Plymouth, N.Z., 1959).

FRETZ, JOSEPH W. *Pilgrims in Paraguay* (The Herald Press, Scottsdale, Pennsylvania, 1953).

FUCHS, STEPHEN. *Rebellious Prophets: A Study of Messianic Movements in Indian Religions* (Asia Publishing House, London 1965).

GANN, L. H. *A History of Northern Rhodesia* (Chatto and Windus, London 1964).

GAYTON, A. H. 'The Ghost Dance of 1870 in South-Central California', *University of California Publications in American Archaeology and Ethnology* 28, 3 (1930), pp. 57–82.

GERTH, H. H. 'A Mid-western Sectarian Community', *Social Research* XI, 3 (September 1944), pp. 354–62.

GILIS, CHARLES A. *Kimbangu: Fondateur d'Église* (La Libraire Encyclopédique, Brussels 1960).

GILLMOR, FRANCIS and WETHERILL, LOUISA W. *Traders to the Navahos: the Story of the Wetherills of Kayenta* (Houghton Mifflin, Boston 1934).

GILSENAN, M. D. 'The Decline of Sufi Orders in Modern Egypt', *Muslim World* LVII (1967), pp. 11–18.

GLOCK, CHARLES Y., RINGER, BENJAMIN B., and BABBIE, EARL R. *To Comfort and to Challenge* (University of California Press, Berkeley and Los Angeles 1967).

GLUCKMAN, MAX. *Custom and Conflict in Africa* (Oxford University Press, London 1955).

GOMBRICH, RICHARD F. *Precept and Practice* (Clarendon Press, Oxford 1971).

GOODWIN, GRENVILLE and KAUT, CHARLES. 'A Native Religious Movement Among the White Mountain and Cibecue Apache', *Southwestern Journal of Anthropology* 10 (Winter 1954), pp. 385–404.

GOODY, JACK. 'Anomie in Ashanti', *Africa* XXVII (1957), pp. 356–62.

GORER, GEOFFREY. *Death, Grief and Mourning* (Cresset Press, London 1965).

GORST, JOHN E. *The Maori King: or, Our Quarrel with the Natives of New Zealand* (Macmillan, London 1864).

GÖTZEN, GUSTAV, GRAF VON. *Deutsch Ostafrika im Aufstand* (Reimer, Berlin 1909).

GREENWOOD, WILLIAM. 'The Upraised Hand, or the Spiritual Significance of the Rise of the Ringatu Faith', *The Journal of the Polynesian Society* 51, 1 (March 1942), pp. i–vi; 1–81.

GRESCHAT, HANS-JÜRGEN. ' "Witchcraft" und kirchlicher Separatismus in Zentral-Afrika', in E. Benz (Ed.), *Messianische Kirchen, Sekten und Bewegungen im heutigen Afrika* (E. J. Brill, Leiden 1965).

GRINNELL, GEORGE B. 'Account of the Northern Cheyenne Concerning the Messiah Superstition', *Journal of American Folklore* IV, 12 (January–March 1891), pp. 61–9.

GROVES, C. P. *The Planting of Christianity in Africa*, Vol. II (Lutterworth Press, London 1954).

GUIART, JEAN. ' "Cargo Cults" and Political Evolution in Melanesia', *Mankind* 4, 6 (May 1951), pp. 227–30.

'Report on the Native Situation in the North of Ambryn (New Hebrides)', *South Pacific* 5, 12 (March 1952), pp. 256–67.

'The John Frum Movement in Tanna', *Oceania* XXII (March 1952), pp. 165–77.

'The Co-operative Called "The Malekula Native Company". A Borderline Type of Cargo Cult', *South Pacific* 6, 6 (September 1952), pp. 429–32.

'Culture Contact and the John Frum Movement on Tanna, New Hebrides', *Southwestern Journal of Anthropology* 12, 1 (Spring 1956), pp. 105–16.

'Conversion to Christianity in the South Pacific', in S. L. Thrupp (Ed.), *Millennial Dreams in Action* (Mouton, The Hague 1962).

GUNTHER, ERNA. 'The Shaker Religion of the Northwest', in M. W. Smith (Ed.), *Indians of the Urban Northwest* (Columbia University Press [Columbia Contributions to Anthropology No. 36], New York 1949).

GWASSA, G. C. K. and ILIFFE, JOHN (Eds.), *Records of the Maji Maji Rising* Pt I, Historical Association of Tanzania Paper No. 4 (East African Publishing House, Nairobi 1968).

HAILE, BERNARD. 'A Note on the Navaho Visionary', *American Anthropologist* 42, 2 (April–June 1940), p. 359.

HARLAN, ROLVIX. *John Alexander Dowie and the Christian Catholic Apostolic Church in Zion*, a Dissertation submitted to the Faculty of the Graduate Divinity School, University of Chicago, 1906.

HARRISON, PAUL M. *Power and Authority in the Free Church Tradition* (Princeton University Press, Princeton 1959).

HARTMAN, FRED. *Occupation and Colonization of German East Africa*, Unpub. M.A. thesis, University of California, 1934.

HARTWEG, F. E. 'Das Lied von Manseren Mangundi (Biak Sprache)', *Zeitschrift für Eingeborenen-Sprachen* XXIII, 1 (October 1932), pp. 46–58.

HAWLEY, FLORENCE. 'The Keresan Holy Rollers: An Adaptation to American Individualism', *Social Forces* 26 (March 1948), pp. 272–80.

HAWTHORN, HARRY B. (Ed.). *The Doukhobors of British Columbia* (University of British Columbia Press, Vancouver 1955).

HEIZER, ROBERT F. 'A Californian Messianic Movement of 1801 among the Chumash', *American Anthropologist* 43, 1 (January–March 1941), pp. 128–9.

HELD, G. J. *The Papuas of Waropen* (Martinus Nijhoff, The Hague 1957).

HENDERSON, J. MCLEOD. *Ratana: The Origins and the Glory of the Movement* (Polynesian Society Memoir 36, Wellington, N.Z., 1963).

HENDERSON, W. O. 'German East Africa 1884–1918', in V. Harlow and E. M. Chilver (Eds.), *History of East Africa* (Clarendon Press, Oxford 1965).

HENRY, THOMAS R. *Wilderness Messiah: The Story of Hiawatha and the Iroquois* (William Sloan Associates, New York 1955).

HERSKOVITS, MELVILLE J. 'African Gods and Catholic Saints in New World Negro Belief', *American Anthropologist* 39:4 (1937), pp. 635–43.

HEWARD, CHRISTINE. 'The Rise of Alice Lenshina', *New Society* 98 (13 August 1964), pp. 6–8.

HILL, W. W. 'The Navaho Indians and the Ghost Dance of 1890', *American Anthropologist* 46 (October–December 1944), pp. 523–7.

HIMMELHEBER, HANS. 'Massa-fetisch der Rechtschaffenheit', *Tribus* (Zeitschrift für Ethnologie und ihre Nachbarwissenschaften) Stuttgart, 4/5 (1954/5), pp. 56–62.

HOBSBAWM, E. J. *Primitive Rebels* (Manchester University Press, Manchester 1959).

HODGE, WILLIAM H. 'Navaho Pentecostalism', *Anthropological Quarterly* 37, 3 (July 1964), pp. 73–93.

HODGKIN, THOMAS. *Nationalism in Colonial Africa* (Muller, London 1956).

HOEBEL, E. ADAMSON. 'The Comanche Sun Dance and Messianic Outbreak of 1873', *American Anthropologist* 43, 2, Pt 1 (1941), pp. 301–3.

HOFFMAN, CARL VON. *Jungle Gods* (Henry Holt, New York 1929).

HOGBIN, H. IAN. 'Native Christianity in a New Guinea Village', *Oceania* XVIII (September 1947), pp. 1–35.

'Pagan Religion in a New Guinea Village', *Oceania* XVIII (December 1947), pp. 120–46.

HOLAS, B. 'Bref Aperçu sur les principaux cultes syncrétiques de la Basse Côte d'Ivoire', *Africa* XXIV (1954), pp. 55–60.

Le Separatisme religieux en Afrique noire (Presses universitaires, Paris 1965).

HOLLENWEGER, WALTER J. *Enthusiastisches Christentum* (Zwingli Verlag, Zürich 1969).

HOLT, P. M. *A Modern History of the Sudan* (Weidenfeld and Nicolson, London 1961).

The Mahdist State in the Sudan, 2nd Edn (Clarendon Press, Oxford 1970).

HÖLTKER, GEORG. 'How "Cargo-Cult" is born', *Pacific Islands Monthly* XVII, 4 (November 1946), pp. 4, 16.

HOOKER, J. R. 'Witnesses and Watchtower in the Rhodesias and Nyasaland', *Journal of African History* VI, 1 (1965), pp. 91–106.

HORNEY, KAREN. *Neurotic Personality of Our Time* (Norton, New York 1937).

HOROWITZ, MICHAEL M. 'The Worship of South Indian Deities in Martinique', *Ethnology* II, 3 (July 1963), pp. 339–46.

HOROWITZ, MICHAEL M. and KLASS, M. 'The Martiniquan East Indian Cult of Maldevidan', *Social and Economic Studies* (Jamaica), 10, 1 (March 1961), pp. 93–100.

HORTON, ROBIN. 'African Traditional Thought and Western Science', *Africa* XXXVII, 1 and 2 (January and April 1967), pp. 50–71; 155–87.

HOSTETLER, J. A. *Amish Society* (Johns Hopkins Press, Baltimore 1963).

HOWARD, JAMES H. 'Pan-Indian Culture of Oklahoma', *Scientific Monthly* 81, 5 (November 1955), pp. 215–20.

HUGGINS, E. L. 'Smohalla, The Prophet of Priest Rapids', *Overland Monthly* (San Francisco) XVII, Second Series (January–June 1891), pp. 208–15.

HULSTAERT, G. 'La Sorcellerie chez les Mongo', in M. Fortes and G. Dieterlen (Eds.), *African Systems of Thought* (Third International African Seminar, Salisbury, December 1960) (Oxford University Press, London 1965).

HUNTINGFORD, G. W. B. 'Nangi Witchcraft', in J. Middleton and E. H. Winter (Eds.), *Witchcraft and Sorcery in East Africa* (Praeger, New York 1963).

INGLIS, JUDY. 'Cargo Cults: The Problem of Explanation', *Oceania* XXVII, 4 (June 1957), pp. 249–63.

INSELMANN, R. ' "Cargo Cult" Not Caused by Missions', *Pacific Islands Monthly* XVI, 11 (June 1946), p. 44.

ISICHEI, ELIZABETH. *Victorian Quakers* (Oxford University Press, London 1970).

JAHODA, GUSTAV. 'Money Doubling in the Gold Coast', *British Journal of Delinquency* VIII, 4 (April 1958), pp. 266–76.

JAMES, EDWARD (Ed.). *A Narrative of the Captivity and Adventures of John Tanner, during thirty years Residence among the Indians in the Interior of North America* (Ross and Haines, Minneapolis 1956).

JARVIE, I. C. 'Theories of Cargo Cults', *Oceania* XXXIV, 1 (September 1963), pp. 1–31.
The Revolution in Anthropology (Routledge, London 1964).

JONES, J. A. 'The Sun Dance of the Northern Ute', Smithsonian Institution: Bureau of American Ethnology, Bulletin 157, *Anthropological Papers* No. 47 (1955), pp. 203–63.

KAMMA, F. C. 'Messianic Movements in Western New Guinea', *International Review of Missions* XLI (1952), pp. 148–60.
De Messiannse Koreri-bewegingen in het Biaks-Noemfoorse cultuurgebied (J. N. Voorhoeve, The Hague 1954).

KARIUKI, JOSIAH M. *'Mau Mau' Detainee* (Oxford University Press, London 1963).

KEESING, FELIX M. *The Changing Maori*, Memoirs of the Board of Maori Ethnological Research, Vol. 4 (Avery, New Plymouth, N.Z., 1928).

KENYATTA, JOMO. *Facing Mount Kenya* (Secker and Warburg, London 1938).

KING, WINSTON L. *A Thousand Lives Away: Buddhism in Contemporary Burma* (Cassirer, Oxford 1964).

KITZINGER, SHEILA. 'The Rastafarian Brethren of Jamaica', *Comparative Studies in Society and History* IX, 1 (October 1966), pp. 33–9.
'Protest and Mysticism: The Rastafari Cult of Jamaica', *Journal for the Scientific Study of Religion* VIII, 2 (Fall 1969), pp. 240–62.

KLAUSNER, JOSEPH. *The Messianic Idea in Israel: From its Beginning to the Completion of the Mishnah* (Macmillan, New York 1955).

KLIEWER, FRITZ. 'Die Mennoniten in Brasilien', *Stadenjahrbuch* (São Paulo) 5 (1957), pp. 233–46.

KLOPPENBURG, BOAVENTURA. 'Der Brasilianische Spiritismus als Religiöse Gefahr', *Social Compass* V, 5–6 (1959), pp. 237–55.

KLUCKHOHN, CLYDE. *Navaho Witchcraft*, Papers of the Peabody Museum of American Archaeology and Ethnology, Harvard University, XXII (The Museum, Cambridge, Mass., 1944).

KLUCKHOHN, CLYDE and LEIGHTON, DOROTHEA. *The Navaho*, Rev. Edn (Doubleday Anchor, New York 1962).

KNOOB, W. J. 'Ethnologische Aspekts der religiösen Bewegungen in südlichen Afrika', in W. E. Mühlmann, *Chiliasmus und Nativismus* (Reimer, Berlin 1961).

KNOX, RONALD. *Enthusiasm* (Oxford University Press, Oxford 1950).

KÖBBEN, J. F. 'Prophetic Movements as an Expression of Social Protest', *International Archives of Ethnography* XLIX, Pt 1 (1960), pp. 117–64.

KOSKINEN, AARNE A. *Missionary Influence as a Political Factor in the Pacific Islands*, Suomalaisen Tiedeakatemian Toimituksia Anneles Academiae Scientiarum Fennicae, Sarja Ser. B., Nide-Tom 78, 1 (Helsinki 1953).

KRIGE, J. D. 'The Social Functions of Witchcraft', *Theoria* (Pietermaritzburg) 1 (1947), pp. 8–21.

KROEBER, A. L. 'A Ghost Dance in California', *Journal of American Folklore* XVII (January–March 1904), pp. 32–5.
    Handbook of Indians of California, Smithsonian Institution: Bureau of American Ethnography, Bulletin 78 (Government Printing Office, Washington 1925), pp. 868–73.

KROEBER, A. L. and GIFFORD, E. W. 'World Renewal: A Cult System of Native Northwest California', *Anthropological Records* 13, 1 (University of California Press, Berkeley and Los Angeles 1949), pp. 1–155.

KROEF, JUSTIN M. VAN DER. 'The Messiah in Indonesia and Melanesia', *Scientific Monthly* LXXXV, 3 (September 1952), pp. 161–5.
    'Patterns of Cultural Change in Three Primitive Societies', *Social Research* 24, 4 (Winter 1957), pp. 427–56.

KROPF, A. *Das Volk der Xosa-Kaffern in östlichen Südafrika* (Berliner evangelischen Missions-gesellschaft, Berlin 1889).

KURATH, GERTRUDE P. 'Pan-Indianism in Great Lakes Tribal Festivals', *Journal of American Folklore* 70 (April–June 1957), pp. 179–82.

LA BARRE, WESTON. 'Twenty Years of Peyote Studies', *Current Anthropology* I, 1 (January 1960), pp. 45–60.
    The Peyote Cult (The Shoe String Press, Hamden, Conn., 1964).

LA FONTAINE, JEAN. 'Witchcraft in Bugisu' in J. Middleton and E. H. Winter (Eds.), *Witchcraft and Sorcery in East Africa* (Praeger, New York 1963).

LALIVE D'EPINAY, C. A *Haven of the Masses* (Lutterworth Press, London 1970).

LANTERNARI, VITTORIO. *The Religions of the Oppressed; A Study of Modern Messianic Cults*, trans. Lisa Sergio (Alfred Knopf, New York; MacGibbon and Kee, London 1963).

LĀTŪKEFU, SIONE. 'The Opposition to the Influence of Wesleyan Methodist Missionaries in Tonga', *Historical Studies: Australia and New Zealand* 12, 46 (April 1966), pp. 248–64.

LAWRENCE, PETER. 'The Madang District Cargo Cult', *South Pacific* 8, 1 (January–February 1955), pp. 6–13.

'Lutheran Mission Influence on Madang Societies', *Oceania* XXVII, 2 (September 1956), pp 73–89.

Road Belong Cargo: A Study of the Cargo Movement in the Southern Madang District in New Guinea (Manchester University Press, Manchester 1964).

LEACOCK, SETH. 'Fun-Loving Deities in an Afro-Brazilian Cult', *Anthropological Quarterly* 37, 3 (July 1964), pp. 94–109.

LEAKEY, L. S. B. *Mau Mau and the Kikuyu* (Methuen, London 1952).

Defeating Mau Mau (Methuen, London 1954).

LEHMANN, F. RUDOLF. 'Weltuntergang und Welterneuerung in Glauben schriftloser Völker', *Zeitschrift für Ethnologie* Vol. 71, Heft 1–3 (1939), pp. 103–15.

LEMARCHAND, RENÉ. 'The Bases of Nationalism among the Bakongo', *Africa* XXXI, 4 (October 1961), pp. 344–54.

Political Awakening in the Belgian Congo (University of California Press, Berkeley and Los Angeles 1964).

LERRIGO, P. H. J. 'The Prophet Movement in the Congo', *International Review of Missions* II (1922), pp. 270–7.

LESSER, ALEXANDER. 'Cultural Significance of the Ghost Dance', *American Anthropologist* 35 (January–March 1933), pp. 108–15.

The Pawnee Ghost Dance Hand Game: A Study in Cultural Change (Columbia University Press, New York 1933).

LEVINE, ROBERT A. 'Witchcraft and Sorcery in a Gusii Community', in J. Middleton and E. H. Winter (Eds.), *Witchcraft and Sorcery in East Africa* (Praeger, New York 1963).

LINDIG, WOLFGANG H. 'Wanderungen der Tupi-Guaraní und Eschatologie der Apapocúva-Guaraní', in W. H. Mühlmann, *Chiliasmus und Nativismus* (Reimer, Berlin 1961).

LINDIG, WOLFGANG H. and DAUER, ALFONS M. 'Prophetismus und Geistertanz Bewegung bei nordamerikanischen Eingeborenen', in W. E. Mühlmann, *Chiliasmus und Nativismus* (Reimer, Berlin 1961).

LINTON, RALPH. 'Nativistic Movements', *American Anthropologist* 45 (April–June 1943), pp. 230–40.

LOEWEN, JACOB A., BUCKWALTER, ALBERT, and KRATZ, JAMES. 'Shamanism, Illness and Power in Toba Church Life', *Practical Anthropology* 12, 6 (November–December 1965), pp. 250–80.

LOMMEL, ANDREAS. 'Modern Cultural Influences on the Aborigines', *Oceania* XXI, 1 (September 1950), pp. 14–24.

LOUIS, WILLIAM R. *Ruanda–Urundi 1884–1919* (Clarendon Press, Oxford 1963).

LUKES, STEVEN. 'Some Problems about Rationality', in B. R. Wilson (Ed.), *Rationality* (Blackwell, Oxford and Harper, New York 1970).

MCCLELLAND, E. M. 'The Experiment in Communal Living at Aiyetoro', *Comparative Studies in Society and History* XI, 1 (October 1966), pp. 14–28.

MACINTYRE, ALASDAIR. 'Is Understanding Religion Compatible with Believing?' and 'The Idea of a Social Science', in B. R. Wilson (Ed.), *Rationality* (Blackwell, Oxford and Harper, New York 1970).

MCLAUGHLIN, JAMES. *My Friend the Indian* (Houghton Mifflin, Boston 1910).

MACLEAN, JOHN PATTERSON. 'Shaker Mission to the Shawnee Indians', *Ohio Archaeological and Historical Quarterly* XI (1902), pp. 215–29.

MACLEOD, WILLIAM CHRISTIE. *The American Indian Frontier* (Knopf, New York 1928).

MCQUARRIE, HECTOR. *Vouza and the Solomon Islands* (Gollancz, London 1945).

MAHER, ROBERT F. *New Men of Papua* (University of Wisconsin Press, Madison 1961).

MAIR, LUCY P. 'The Pursuit of the Millennium in Melanesia', *British Journal of Sociology* IX, 2 (June 1958), pp. 175–82.

'Witchcraft in the Study of Religion', *Cahiers d'Études Africaines* 15, Vol. IV, 3 (1964), pp. 335–48.

MALO, DAVID. *Hawaiian Antiquities*, trans. N. B. Emerson (Hawaiian Gazette Co., Honolulu 1903).

MALOUF, CARLING. 'Gosiute Peyotism', *American Anthropologist* 44, 1 (January–March 1942), pp. 93–103.

MARTIN, BERNICE. 'The Spiritualist Meeting', in David Martin and Michael Hill (Eds.), *Sociological Yearbook of Religion* 3 (SCM Press, London 1970), pp. 146–61.

MARTIN, DAVID A. 'The Denomination', *British Journal of Sociology* XIII, 1 (March 1962), pp. 1–14.

Pacifism (Routledge, London 1965).

MARTIN, MARIE-LOUISE. *Kirche ohne Weisse: Simon Kimbangu und seine Millionenkirche im Kongo* (Friedrich Reinhardt Verlag, Basel 1971).

MARTY, MARTIN E. 'Sects and Cults', *Annals of the American Academy of Political and Social Science* 332 (November 1960), pp. 125–34.

MARWICK, MAX G. 'African Witchcraft and Anxiety Load', *Theoria* (Pietermaritzburg) 2 (1948), pp. 115–29.

'Another Modern Anti-Witchcraft Movement in East Central Africa', *Africa* XX, 2 (1950), pp. 100–12.

'The Continuance of Witchcraft Beliefs', in P. Smith (Ed.) *Africa in Transition* (Max Reinhardt, London 1958).

'Some Problems in the Sociology of Sorcery and Witchcraft', in M. Fortes and G. Dieterlen (Eds.), *African Systems of Thought*, Third International African Seminar, Salisbury, December 1960 (Oxford University Press, London 1965).

Sorcery in its Social Setting: A Study of the Northern Rhodesian Ceŵa (Manchester University Press, Manchester 1965).

MAYER, PHILIP. *Townsmen or Tribesmen: Conservatism and the Process of Urbanization in a South African City* (Oxford University Press, Cape Town 1961).

MEAD, MARGARET. *Growing Up in New Guinea* (Morrow, New York 1930).

New Lives for Old: Cultural Transformation—Manus, 1928–1953 (Gollancz, London 1956).

MELLAND, FRANK, and YOUNG, CULLEN. *African Dilemma* (United Society for Christian Literature, London 1937).

MERTON, ROBERT K. *Social Theory and Social Structure* (Free Press, Glencoe, Ill. 1957).

MESSENGER, JOHN C. JR. 'Religious Acculturation among the Anang Ibibo', in William R. Bascom and Melville J. Herskovits, *Continuity and Change in African Culture* (University of Chicago Press, Chicago 1959).

'Reinterpretations of Christian and Indigenous Belief in a Nigerian Nativist Church', *American Anthropologist* 62, 2 (April 1960), pp. 268–78.

MÉTRAUX, ALFRED. 'Migrations historiques des Tupi-Guaraní', *Journal de la Société des Américanistes* (Paris) N.S. XIX (1927), pp. 1–45.

'Les hommes-deux chez les Chiriguano et dans l'Amérique du Sud', *Revista del Instituto de Ethnologia de la Universidad nacional de Tucumán* II, 1 (1931), pp. 61–91.

'Messiahs of South America', *The Interamerican Quarterly* III, 2 (April 1941), pp. 53–60.

'A Quechua Messiah in Eastern Peru', *American Anthropologist* 44, 4 (October–December 1942), pp. 721–5.

'The Guaraní', in J. H. Steward (Ed.), *Handbook of South American Indians* Smithsonian Institution, Washington D.C., Bureau of American Ethnography, Bulletin 143, Vol. III (1948), pp. 69–94.

'The Tupinamba', in J. H. Steward (Ed.), *Handbook of South American Indians* Smithsonian Institution, Washington, Bureau of American Ethnography, Bulletin 143, Vol. III (1948), pp. 95–133.

MIDDLETON, JOHN. 'The Lugbara', in A. I. Richards (Ed.), *East African Chiefs* (Praeger, New York 1959).

MIDDLETON, JOHN and WINTER, E. H. (Eds.), *Witchcraft and Sorcery in East Africa* (Praeger, New York 1963).

MILLER, DAVID HUMPHREYS. *Ghost Dance* (Duell, Sloan and Pearce, New York 1959).

MILLER, HAROLD. 'Maori and Pakeha, 1814–1865', in I. L. G. Sutherland (Ed.), *The Maori People To-day: A General Survey* (Oxford University Press, Oxford 1940).

MILLER, J. GRAHAM. 'The Naked Cult on Central West Santo', *Journal of Polynesian Society* 57, 4 (December 1948), pp. 330–41.

MITCHELL, ROBERT C. 'Christian Healing', in V. E. W. Hayward (Ed.), *African Independent Church Movements*, International Missionary Council Research Pamphlets No. 11 (Edinburgh House Press, London 1962).

'The Babalola Revival: A Non-Arrested Prophet Movement' (mimeographed).

MOL, J. J. 'Integration versus Segragation in New Zealand Churches', *British Journal of Sociology* XVI, 2 (June 1965), pp. 140–9

MOONEY, JAMES. *The Ghost Dance Religion and the Sioux Outbreak of 1890*, Fourteenth Annual Report of the Bureau of Ethnology to the Secretary of the Smithsonian Institution (Government Printing Office, Washington 1896).

'The Kiowa Peyote Rite', *Der Urquell* N.S., 1 (1897), pp. 329–33.

'Prophets', in F. W. Hodge, *Handbook of American Indians* Vol. II, Smithsonian Institution, Washington, Bureau of Ethnology, Bulletin 30 (1910).

The Ghose Dance Religion and the Sioux Outbreak of 1890, edited by A. F. C. Wallace (Phoenix Books, Chicago 1965).

MOORE, JOSEPH G. 'Religious Syncretism in Jamaica', *Practical Anthropology* 12, 2 (March–April 1965), pp. 63–70.

MORICE, A. G. *The History of the Northern Interior of British Columbia*, 2nd Edn. (William Briggs, Toronto 1904).

MORTON-WILLIAMS, P. 'The Atinga Cult among the South-Western Yoruba: A Sociological analysis of a Witch-finding Movement', *Bulletin de l'Institut français d'Afrique noire* T. XVIII, ser. B. Nr. 3–4 (1956), pp. 315–34.

MQOTSI, L. and MKELE, N. 'A Separatist Church: Ibandla Lika Krestu', *African Studies* 5, 2 (June 1946), pp. 106–25.

MÜHLMANN, WILHELM E. *Arioi und Mamaia: Eine ethnologische religionssoziologische und historische Studie über Polynesische Kultbünde* (Franz Steiner Verlag, Wiesbaden 1955).
  'Die Mau Mau Bewegung in Kenya', *Politische Vierteljahrschrift* 2, 1 (March 1961), pp. 56–87.

MÜLLER, ERNST W. 'Die Koreri-Bewegung auf den Schouten-Inseln (West Neuguinea)', in W. E. Mühlmann, *Chiliasmus und Nativismus* (Reimer, Berlin 1961).

NASH, PHILLEO. 'The Place of Religious Revivalism in the Formation of the Intercultural Community on Klamath Reservation', in F. Eggan *et al.* (Eds.), *Social Anthropology of North American Tribes* (University of Chicago Press, Chicago 1937).

NEIHARDT, JOHN G. *Black Elk Speaks* (University of Nebraska Press, Lincoln, Neb., 1961; first pub. 1932).

NELSON, GEOFFREY K. *Spiritualism and Society* (Routledge, London 1969).

NEWBERNE, ROBERT E. L. and BURKE, CHARLES H. *Peyote: An abridged compilation from the files of the Bureau of Indian Affairs* (Haskell Institute, Lawrence, Kan., 1925).

NEWCOMB, JR, WILLIAM W. 'The Peyote Cult of the Delaware Indians', *The Texas Journal of Science* VIII, 2 (June 1956), pp. 202–11.

NGATA, A. T. and SUTHERLAND, I. L. G. 'Religious Influences', in I. L. G. Sutherland (Ed.), *The Maori People Today: A General Survey* (Oxford University Press, Oxford 1940).

NIDA, EUGENE A. 'The Indigenous Churches in Latin America', *Practical Anthropology* 8, 3 (May–June 1961), pp. 97–110.

NIEBUHR, H. RICHARD. *Social Sources of Denominationalism* (Holt, New York 1929).

NIMUENDAJÚ UNKEL, CURT. 'Die Sagen von Erschaffung und Vernichtung der Welt als Grundlagen der Religion der Apapocúva-Guaraní', *Zeitschrift für Ethnologie* 46, 1 (1914), pp. 284–403.
  The Tukuna (University of California Publications in American Archaeology and Ethnology 45, Berkeley and Los Angeles 1952).

NORRIS, KATRIN. *Jamaica: The Search for an Identity* (Oxford University Press, London 1965).

NOTTINGHAM, J. C. 'Sorcery Among the Akamba in Kenya', *Journal of African Administration* XI, 1 (January 1959), pp. 2–14.

NUNEZ, JR, THERON A. 'Creek Nativism and the Creek War of 1813–

1814', *Ethnohistory* 5: 1, 2, and 3 (Winter 1958; Spring 1958; Summer 1958), pp. 1–47; 131–75; 292–301.

'NYANGWESO' (pseud.). 'The Cult of Mumbo in Central and South Kavirondo', *Journal of East Africa and Uganda Natural History Society* 38/39 (May–August 1930), pp. 13–17.

OBEREM, UDO. 'Die Aufstandsbewegung der Pende bei den Quijo, Ost-Ekuadors im Jahre 1578' in W. E. Mühlmann, *Chiliasmus und Nativismus* (Reimer, Berlin 1961).

OBERG, KALVERO. 'Afro-Brazilian Religious Cults', *Sociología* (São Paulo) XXI, 2 (May 1959), pp. 134–41.

ODUWOLE, SAMUEL OMOLAJA. '*Ell Tieggah Vicottieorrius*', *The Holy Cross* [*in the Church of the Lord*] (no place of publication, n.d.: probably 1962).

OGOT, BETHWELL A. 'British Administration in the Central Nyanza District of Kenya, 1900–1906', *Journal of African History* IV, 2 (1963), pp. 249–73.

OOSTERWAL, GOTTFRIED. 'Cargo Cults and the Seventh Day Adventists', *The Ministry* XXXV, 10 (October 1962), pp. 10–13.

'A Cargo Cult in the Mamberamo Area', *Ethnology* II, 1 (January 1963), pp. 1–14.

OPLER, MARVIN K. 'The Character and History of the Southern Ute Peyote Rite', *American Anthropologist* 42 (July–September 1940), pp. 463–78.

'Fact and Fancy in Ute Peyotism', *American Anthropologist* 44, 1 (January–March 1942), pp. 151–9.

OPLER, MORRIS E. 'The Influence of Aboriginal Pattern and White Contact in a Recently Introduced Ceremony, The Mescalero Peyote Rite', *Journal of American Folklore* 49 (January 1936), pp. 143–66.

'The Use of Peyote by the Carrizo and Lipan Apache Tribes', *American Anthropologist* 40, 2 (April–June 1938), pp. 271–85.

ORDE BROWNE, G. S. J. 'Witchcraft and British Colonial Law', *Africa* VIII, 4 (October 1935), pp. 481–7.

O'REILLY, PATRICK. 'Jonfrum is New Hebridean "Cargo Cult" ', *Pacific Islands Monthly* XXI, 6 (January 1950), pp. 67–70; and 7 (February 1950), pp. 59–65.

OSITELU, J. O. *Catechism of the Church of the Lord (Aladura) throughout the World and the Holy Litany* (Ogere 1948).

The Book of Prayer with uses and powers of Psalms and Precious Treasures Hidden Therein (The Church of the Lord, Ogere Headquarters, Shagamu n.d.).

OSITELU, J. O. et al. *Order of the Official Robes for the Ministers and Members of the Church of the Lord (Aladura)* (no place of publication [Ogere?] n.d. [1948]).

OSKISON, JOHN M. *Tecumseh and His Times* (Putnam, New York 1938).

OESTERREICH, T. E. *Possession: Demoniacal and Other*, trans. D. Ibberson (University Books, New York 1966).

PARETO, VILFREDO. *The Mind and Society*, trans. A. Livingston and A. Bongiorno (Cape, London 1935).

PARKER, ARTHUR C. *The Code of Handsome Lake*, New York State Museum, Museum Bulletin 163, Education Department Bulletin 530 (University of State of New York, Albany, N.Y. (November 1912).

PARKMAN, FRANCIS. *The Conspiracy of Pontiac and the Indian War after the Conquest of Canada* (Little Brown, Boston 1917).

√ PARRINDER, E. G. *Religion in an African City* (Oxford University Press, London 1953).

'Islam and West African Indigenous Religion', *Numen* VI, 2 (December 1959), pp. 130–41.

√ 'The Religious Situation in West Africa', *African Affairs* 59 (January 1960), pp. 38–42.

PARSONS, ANNE. 'The Pentecostal Immigrants', *Journal for the Scientific Study of Religion* 4, 2 (1965), pp. 183–97.

√ PARSONS, ROBERT T. *The Churches and Ghana Society, 1918–1955* (E. J. Brill, Leiden 1963).

PATON, W. F. 'The Native Situation in the North of Ambryn', *South Pacific* 6, 5 (August 1952), pp. 392–6.

PATTERSON, ORLANDO. 'Ras Tafari: The Cult of Outcastes', *New Society* No. 111 (12 November 1964), pp. 15–17.

PAULME, DENISE. 'Une religion syncrétique en Côte d'Ivoire: le culte déima', *Cahiers d'Études Africaines* 9, Vol. II (1962), pp. 5–90.

PAUW, B. A. *Religion in a Tswana Chiefdom* (Oxford University Press, London 1960).

'African Christians and their Ancestors', in V. E. W. Hayward (Ed.), *African Independent Church Movements*, International Missionary Council Research Pamphlets No. 11 (Edinburgh House Press, London 1962).

'Patterns of Christianization among the Tswana and Xhosa-speaking Peoples', in M. Fortes and G. Dieterlen (Eds.), *African Systems of Thought* (Oxford University Press, London 1965).

PAUWELS, MARCEL. 'Le Culte de Nyabingi (Ruanda)', *Anthropos* XLVI, 3–4 (1951), pp. 337–57.

PECKHAM, HOWARD H. *Pontiac and the Indian Uprising* (Princeton University Press, Princeton, N.J. 1947).

PEEL, J. D. Y. *A Sociological Study of Two Independent Churches among the Yoruba*, Unpub. Ph.D. thesis, University of London (1965).

'Syncretism and Religious Change', *Comparative Studies in Society and History* X, 2 (January 1968), pp. 121–41.

Aladura (Oxford University Press, London 1969).

PEREIRA DE QUEIROZ, MARIA I. 'Messiasbewegungen in Brasilien', *Stadenjahrbuch* 4 (1956), pp. 133–44.

'Die Fanatiker des "Contestado" ', *Stadenjahrbuch* 5 (1957), pp. 203–15.

O Messianismo no Brasil e no Mundo (University of São Paulo, São Paulo 1965).

PETERS, VICTOR. *All things Common: The Hutterian Way of Life* (University of Minnesota Press, Minneapolis 1965).

PETERSON, NICOLAS. 'The Church Council of South Mala: A Legitimized Form of Masinga Rule', *Oceania* XXXVI, 3 (March 1966), pp. 214–30.

PETRI, HELMUT. 'Das Weltende im Glauben australischer Eingeborener', in A. E. Jensen (Ed.), *Mythe, Mensche und Umwelt* (Bamburg 1950).

PETRULLO, VINCENZO. *The Diabolical Root. A Study of Peyotism, the new Indian Religion among the Delawares* (University of Pennsylvania Press, Philadelphia 1934).
'Peyotism as an Emergent Indian Culture', *Indians at Work* 7, 8 (April 1940), pp. 51–60.

PHILIPPS, J. E. T. 'The Nabingi: An Anti-European Secret Society in Africa, in British Ruanda, Ndorwa, and the Congo (Kivu)', *Congo: Revue générale de la Colonie belge* I, 1 (January 1928), pp. 310–21.

PITT-RIVERS, GEORGE H. LANE-FOX. *The Clash of Cultures and the Contact of Races* (Routledge, London 1927).

PLATT, W. J. *An African Prophet* (SCM Press, London 1934).

PLOTNICOV, LEONARD. ' "Nativism" in Contemporary Nigeria', *Anthropological Quarterly* 37, 3 (July 1964), pp. 121–37.

POBLETE, R. and O'DEA, T. 'Anomie and the "Quest for Community": the Formation of Sects among Puerto Ricans of New York', *American Catholic Sociological Review* XXI, 1 (1960), pp. 18–36.

POS, HUGO. 'The Revolt of "Manseren" ', *American Anthropologist* 52 (1950), pp. 561–4.

POUWER, J. 'Cargo Cults', *Oceania* XXVIII, 3 (March 1958), pp. 247–52.

POWERS, MABEL. 'The Legacy of Handsome Lake', *Christian Century* LXXXIV, 2 (January 1957), pp. 47–8.

PRICE, A. GRENFELL. *White Settlers and Native Peoples* (Cambridge University Press, Cambridge 1949).

PRICE, FRANK W. 'The Younger Churches—Some Facts and Observations', *Missionary Research Library Occasional Bulletin* VII, 7 (15 July 1957).

QUAIFE, MILO M. (Ed.). *The Siege of Detroit* (Lakeside Press, Chicago 1958).

QUICK, GRIFFITH. 'Some Aspects of the African Watch Tower Movement in Northern Rhodesia', *International Review of Missions* XXIX (1940), pp. 216–26.

RADIN, PAUL. 'A Sketch of the Peyote Cult of the Winnebago: A Study in Borrowing', *Journal of Religious Psychology* 7, 1 (January 1914), pp. 1–22.
'The Autobiography of a Winnebago Indian', *University of California Publications in American Archaeology and Ethnology* 16, 7 (April 1920), pp. 381–473.
'Religious Experiences of an American Indian', *Eranos-Jahrbuch* XVIII (Sonderband), Zürich (1950), pp. 249–60.

RAMOS, ARTHUR. 'The Negro in Brazil', in T. L. Smith and A. Marchant (Eds.), *Brazil: Portrait of Half a Continent* (Dryden Press, New York 1951).

RANGER, TERENCE O. 'The Role of Ndebele and Shona religious authorities in the Rebellions of 1896 and 1897', in E. Stokes and R. Brown (Eds.), *The Zambesian Past: Studies in Central African History* (Manchester University Press, Manchester 1966).
'Witchcraft Eradication Movements in Central and Southern Tanzania and their Connections with the Maji Maji Rising', Seminar Paper

(mimeographed), 30 November 1966, University College, Dar-es-Salaam.

RAUM, O. F. 'Von Stammespropheten zu Sektenführern', in E. Benz (Ed.), *Messianische Kirchen, Sekten und Bewegungen im heutigen Afrika* (E. J. Brill, Leiden 1965).

RAWCLIFFE, D. H. *The Struggle for Kenya* (Gollancz, London 1954).

RAYMAEKERS, PAUL. 'L'Église de Jesus-Christ sur la terre par le prophète Simon Kimbangu: Contribution à l'étude des mouvements messianiques dans le Bas-Kongo', *Zaïre* (Revue Congolaise) XIII, 7 (1959), pp. 675–756.

READ, K. E. 'Effects of the Pacific War on the Markham Valley, New Guinea', *Oceania* XVIII, 2 (December 1947), pp. 95–116.

'Missionary Activity and Social Change in the Central Highlands of Papua and New Guinea', *South Pacific* 5, 11 (January–February 1952), pp. 229–39.

READ, W. R. *New Patterns of Church Growth in Brazil* (Eerdmans, Grand Rapids 1965).

REICHARD, GLADYS A. 'The Navaho and Christianity', *American Anthropologist* 51, 1 (January–March 1949), pp. 66–71.

RELANDER, CLICK (Now Tow Look). *Drummers and Dreamers* (Caxton Press, Caldwell, Idaho 1956).

REYBURN, WILLIAM D. and REYBURN, MARIE F. 'Toba Caciqueship and the Gospel', *International Review of Missions* ILV (1956), pp. 194–203.

REYNOLDS, BARRIE. *Magic, Divination and Witchcraft among the Barotse of Northern Rhodesia* (Chatto and Windus, London 1963).

RIBEIRO, RENÉ. 'Problemática Pessoal e Interpretação divinatória nos cultos afro-brasileiros do Recife', *Revista do Museu Paulista* X (1956/8), pp. 225–42.

'Brazilian Messianic Movements', in S. L. Thrupp (Ed.), *Millennial Dreams in Action* (Mouton, The Hague 1962).

RICHARDS, AUDREY I. 'A Modern Movement of Witchfinders', *Africa* VIII, 4 (October 1935), pp. 448–61.

RILEY, CARROLL L. and HOBGOOD, JOHN. 'A recent nativistic movement among the South Tepehuan Indians', *Southwestern Journal of Anthropology* 15, 4 (Summer 1959), pp. 355–60.

ROGERS, P. G. *The Fifth Monarchy Men* (Oxford University Press, London 1966).

ROSBERG, CARL G. and NOTTINGHAM, JOHN. *The Myth of 'Mau-Mau': Nationalism in Kenya* (Praeger, New York 1966).

ROSENFELD, ANATOL H. 'Macumba', *Stadenjahrbuch* III (1955), pp. 125–40.

ROTBERG, ROBERT I. 'The Lenshina Movement of Northern Rhodesia', *Rhodes-Livingstone Journal*: Human Problems in British Central Africa XXIX (June 1961), pp. 63–78.

'Missionaries as Chiefs and Entrepreneurs: Northern Rhodesia 1882–1924', *Boston University Papers in African History* I (1964), pp. 195–215.

The Rise of Nationalism in Central Africa (Harvard University Press, Cambridge, Mass., 1965).

ROUTLEDGE, W. S. and ROUTLEDGE, K. *People: With a Pre-historical The Akikuyu of British East Africa* (Arnold, London 1910).

ROUX, EDWARD. *Time Longer Than Rope* (Gollancz, London 1945); 2nd Edn (University of Wisconsin Press, Madison 1964).

SALER, BENSON. 'Religious Conversion and Self-Aggrandisement: A Guatemalan Case', *Practical Anthropology* 12, 3 (May–June 1965), pp. 107–14.

SAYERS, GERALD F. *The Handbook of Tanganyika* (Macmillan, London 1930).

SCHADEN, EGON. 'Der Paradiesmythos in Leben der Guaraní-Indianer', *Stadenjahrbuch* III (1955), pp. 151–62.

SCHAMBAUGH, BERTHA M. H. *Amana That Was and Amana That Is* (The State Historical Society of Iowa, Iowa City 1932).

SCHAPERA, I. 'Christianity and the Tswana', *Journal of the Royal Anthropological Institute of Gt. Britain and Ireland* 88, Pt I (January–June 1958), pp. 1–9.

SCHLOSSER, KATESA. *Propheten in Afrika* (Albert Limbach Verlag, Braunschweig 1949).
'Die Prophetismus in niederen Kulturen', *Zeitschrift für Ethnologie* 75–76 (1950–1), pp. 60–72.
Eingeborenenkirchen in Süd- und Südwest-Afrika (Walter G. Mühlau, Kiel 1958).
'Profanen Ursachen des Anschlusses an Separatistenkirchen in Süd- und Südwest-Afrika', in E. Benz (Ed.), *Messianische Kirchen, Sekten und Bewegungen im heutigen Afrika* (E. J. Brill, Leiden 1965).

SCHOOLCRAFT, HENRY R. *Information Respecting the History, Conditions and Prospects of the Indian Tribes of the United States*, Vol. VI (Lippincott, Philadelphia 1860).

SCHUSKEY, ERNST. 'Pan-Indianism in the Eastern United States', *Anthropology Tomorrow* VI, 1 (December 1957), pp. 116–23.

SCHWARTZ, GARY. *Sect Ideologies and Social Status* (Chicago University Press, Chicago 1970).

SCHWARZ, THEODORE. 'The Paliau Movement in the Admiralty Islands, 1946–1954', *Anthropological Papers of the American Museum of Natural History* (New York) 49, Pt 2 (1962).

SCOTCH, NORMAN A. 'Magic, Sorcery and Football among the Urban Zulu: A case of reinterpretation under acculturation', *Journal of Conflict Resolution* V, 1 (March 1961), pp. 70–4.

SHEPHERD, ROBERT H. A. 'The Separatist Churches of South Africa', *International Review of Missions* XXVI (1937), pp. 453–63.

SHEPPERSON, GEORGE A. 'Ethiopianism and African Nationalism', *Phylon* XIV, 1 (1953), pp. 9–19.
'The Politics of African Separatist Movements in British Central Africa, 1892–1916', *Africa* XXIV (July 1954), pp. 233–46.
'External Factors in the Development of African Nationalism with Particular Reference to British Central Africa', *Phylon* XXII, 3 (Fall 1961), pp. 207–25.

'Nyasaland and the Millennium', in S. L. Thrupp (Ed.), *Millennial Dreams in Action* (Mouton, The Hague 1962).

'Pan-Africanism and "Pan-Africanism": Some Historical Notes', *Phylon* XXIII, 4 (Winter 1962), pp. 346–58.

'Church and Sect in Central Africa', *Rhodes-Livingstone Journal*: Human Problems in Central Africa 33 (June 1963), pp. 82–94.

SHEPPERSON, GEORGE A. and PRICE, THOMAS. *An Independent African: John Chilembwe* (Edinburgh University Press, Edinburgh 1958).

SHIMKIN, D. B. 'The Wind River Shoshone Sun Dance', Smithsonian Institution: Bureau of American Ethnology, Bulletin 151, *Anthropological Papers* No. 41 (1953), pp. 397–484.

SHONLE, RUTH. 'Peyote, Giver of Visions', *American Anthropologist* 27, 1 (January–March 1925), pp. 53–75.

SIERKSMA, FOKKE. *Een nieuwe hemel en een nieuwe aarde* (Mouton, The Hague 1961).

SIMPSON, GEORGE E. 'Political Cultism in West Kingston, Jamaica', *Social and Economic Studies* 4, 2 (1955), pp. 133–49.

'Jamaican Revivalist Cults', *Social and Economic Studies* 5, 4 (1956), pp. 321–442.

'The Ras Tafari Movement in Jamaica in its Millennial Aspect', in S. L. Thrupp (Ed.), *Millennial Dreams in Action* (Mouton, The Hague 1962).

'The Shango Cult in Nigeria and Trinidad', *American Anthropologist* 64, 6 (December 1962), pp. 1204–19.

'The Acculturative Process in Trinidadian Shango', *Anthropological Quarterly* 37, 1 (January 1964), pp. 16–27.

SINCLAIR, KEITH. *The Origins of the Maori Wars* (New Zealand University Press, Wellington, N.Z., 1957).

SLOTKIN, J. S. 'Menomini Peyotism: A Study of Individual Variation in a Primary Group with a Homogeneous Culture', *Transactions of the American Philosophical Society*, N. S., 42, Pt 4 (December 1952), pp. 565–700.

'Peyotism, 1521–1891', *American Anthropologist* 57, 2 (April 1955), pp. 202–30.

The Peyote Religion (Free Press, Glencoe, Ill. 1956).

Menomini Powwow (Milwaukee Public Museum Publication in Anthropology 4, Milwaukee 1957).

SMELSER, NEIL J. *Theory of Collective Behaviour* (Routledge, London 1962).

SMITH, MARIAN W. 'Shamanism in the Shaker Religion of Northwest America', *Man* LIV, article 181 (August 1954), pp. 119–22.

SMITH, MICHAEL G. *Dark Puritan* (Dept. of Extra-Mural Studies, University of the West Indies, Kingston, Jamaica, 1963).

SMITH, MICHAEL G., AUGIER, ROY and NETTLEFORD, REX. *The Ras Tafari Movement in Kingston, Jamaica* (University College of the West Indies, Institute of Social and Economic Research, Mona, Jamaica, 1960).

'The Ras Tafari Movement in Kingston, Jamaica, *Caribbean Quarterly* 13, 3 (September 1967).

SMITH, THOMAS L. *Brazil: People and Institutions* Rev. Edn (Louisiana State University Press, Baton Rouge 1963).

SMITH, THOMAS L. and MARCHANT, ALEXANDER (Eds.). *Brazil: Portrait of half a Continent* (Dryden Press, New York 1951).

SOLT, LEO F. 'The Fifth Monarchy Men: Politics and the Millennium', *Church History* XXX, 3 (September 1961), pp. 314–24.

SPICER, EDWARD H. *Cycles of Conquest: The Impact of Spain, Mexico and the United States on the Indians of the Southwest, 1533–1960* (University of Arizona Press, Tucson 1962).

SPIER, LESLIE. 'The Ghost Dance of 1870 Among the Klamath of Oregon', *University of Washington Publications in Anthropology* 2, 2 (November 1927), pp. 39–56.

The Prophet Dance of the Northwest and Its Derivatives: The Source of the Ghost Dance (George Banta, Menasha, Wisc. 1935).

SPIER, LESLIE, SUTTLES, W. and HERSKOVITS, M. J. 'Comment on Aberle's Thesis of Deprivation', *Southwestern Journal of Anthropology* 15, 1 (Spring 1959), pp. 84–8.

SPINDLER, GEORGE D. 'Personality and Peyotism in Menomini Indian Acculturation', *Psychiatry* 15 (1952), pp. 151–9.

STANNER, W. E. H. *The South Seas in Transition* (Australasian Publishing Co., Sydney 1953).

'On the Interpretation of Cargo Cults', *Oceania* XXIX, 1 (September 1958), pp. 1–25.

STARK, WERNER. *The Sociology of Religion*, Vols. I–IV (Routledge, London 1966–1969).

STEWART, OMER C. 'Washo-Paiute Peyotism. A Study in Acculturation', *University of California Publications in American Archaeology and Ethnology* 40, 3 (1944), pp. vi and 63–142.

Ute Peyotism: A Study of a Cultural Complex, University of Colorado Studies: Series in Anthropology, No. 1 (University of Colorado Press, Boulder 1948).

'The Native American Church (Peyote Cult) and the Law', *The Denver Westerner's Monthly Roundup* XVII, 1 (January 1961), pp. 5–18.

STOEVESANDT, G. 'The Sect of the Second Adam on the Gold Coast', *Africa* VIII (1934), pp. 479–82.

STRONG, WILLIAM D. 'The Occurrence and Wide Implications of a "Ghost Dance Cult" on the Columbia River suggested by Carvings in Wood, Stone and Bronze', *American Anthropologist* 47, 2 (April–June 1945), pp. 244–61.

STUART, J. *A History of the Zulu Rebellion, 1906* (Macmillan, London 1913).

SULZMANN, ERIKA. 'Die Bewegung der Antonier im alten Reiche Kongo', in W. E. Mühlmann, *Chiliasmus und Nativismus* (Reimer, Berlin 1961).

SUMNER, MARGARET L. 'Mexican-American Minority Churches, U.S.A.', *Practical Anthropology* 10, 3 (May–June 1963), pp. 115–21.

SUNDKLER, BENGT G. M. *Bantu Prophets in South Africa* (Lutterworth Press, London 1948); and Rev. Edn (Oxford University Press, London 1961).

'The Concept of Christianity in the African Independent Churches', *Africa* 20, 4 (1961), pp. 203–13.

'Chief and Prophet in Zululand and Swaziland', in M. Fortes and G. Dieterlen (Eds.), *African Systems of Thought* (Oxford University Press, London 1965).

SUTHERLAND, I. L. G. *The Maori Situation* (Tombs, Wellington, N.Z. 1935).

SUTHERLAND, HON. WILLIAM. 'The "Tuka" Religion', *Transactions of the Fijian Society* (Suva, 1910), pp. 51–7.

SUTTLES, WAYNE. 'The Plateau Prophet Dance Among the Coast Salish', *Southwestern Journal of Anthropology* 13, 4 (Winter 1957), pp. 352–96.

SYMMONS-SYMONOLEWICTZ, KONSTANTIN. 'Nationalist Movements: An Attempt at a Comparative Typology', *Comparative Studies in Society and History* 7, 2 (January 1965), pp. 221–30.

TAIT, DAVID. 'A Sorcery Hunt in Dagomba', *Africa* XXXIII, 2 (April 1963), pp. 136–46.

TAYLOR, JOHN V. and LEHMANN, DOROTHEA A. *Christians of the Copperbelt* (SCM Press, London 1961).

TERRY-THOMAS, A. C. *The African Orthodox Church* (1956: no publisher or place of publication given).

THEAL, GEORGE MCCALL. *History of South Africa*, 4th Edn (Allen and Unwin, London 1915).

THOMAS, KEITH. *Religion and the Decline of Magic* (Weidenfeld and Nicolson, London 1971).

THOMAS, ROBERT K. 'Pan-Indianism', *Midcontinent American Studies Journal* 6, 2 (Fall 1965), pp. 75–83.

THOMPSON, BASIL. *The Fijians: A Study of the Decay of Custom* (Heinemann, London 1905).

THOMPSON, VIRGINIA and ADLOFF, RICHARD. *The Emerging States of French Equatorial Africa* (Stanford University Press, Stanford, California 1960).

THWAITE, DANIEL. *The Seething African Pot* (Constable, London 1936).

TOPLEY, MARJORIE. 'Some Occasional Rites performed by the Singapore Cantonese', *Journal of the Malayan Branch of the Royal Asiatic Society* XXIV, 3 (October 1951), pp. 120–44.

'The Emergence and Social Function of Chinese Religious Associations in Singapore', *Comparative Studies in Society and History* III, 3 (April 1961), pp. 289–314.

TREGEAR, EDWARD. *The Maori Race* (Willis, Wanganui, N.Z., 1904).

TROELTSCH, ERNST. *The Social Teaching of the Christian Churches*, trans. O. Wyon (Macmillan, New York 1931).

TROIKE, RUDOLF C. 'The Origins of Plains Mescalism', *American Anthropologist* 64, 5:1 (1962), pp. 946–63.

TURNBULL, COLIN M. 'Tribalism and Social Evolution in Africa', in J. Charlesworth (Ed.), *Africa in Motion: Annals of the American Academy of Political and Social Science* (July 1964), pp. 22–32.

TURNER, HAROLD W. 'The Litany of an Independent West African Church', *Sierra Leone Bulletin of Religion* I, 2 (December 1959), pp. 48–55.

'The Catechism of an Independent West African Church', *Sierra Leone Bulletin of Religion* II, 2 (December 1960), pp. 45–57.

'The Church of the Lord: The Expansion of a Nigerian Independent

Church in Sierra Leone and Ghana', *Journal of African History* 3 (1962), pp. 91–110.

'African Prophet Movements', *Hibbert Journal* 61, 242 (April 1963), pp. 112–16.

'Pagan Features in West African Independent Churches', *Practical Anthropology* 12, 4 (July–August 1965), pp. 145–51.

'Prophets and Politics', *Bulletin of the Society for African Church History* II, 1 (1965), pp. 97–118.

'A Methodology for Modern African Religious Movements', *Comparative Studies in Society and History* VIII (1965–6), pp. 281–94.

'A Typology for African Religious Movements', *Journal of Religion in Africa* I, 1 (1967), pp. 1–30.

African Independent Church, 2 Vols. (Clarendon Press, Oxford 1967).

TURNER, V. W. 'Ndembu Divination: Its Symbolism and Techniques', *Rhodes-Livingstone Papers* No. 31 (Manchester University Press, Manchester 1961).

UNDERHILL, RUTH M. 'Religion among the American Indians', *Annals of the American Academy of Political and Social Science* 311 (May 1957), 127–36.

UPLEGGER, HELGA and MÜHLMANN, W. E. 'Die Cargo-Kulte in Neuguinea und Insel-Melanesian', in W. E. Mühlmann, *Chiliasmus und Nativismus* (Reimer, Berlin 1961).

USHER-WILSON, L. C. 'Dina Ya Msambwa', *Uganda Journal* 16, 2 (September 1952), pp. 125–9.

VALORY, DALE. 'The Focus of Shaker Healing', *Kroeber Anthropological Society Papers* (Berkeley, California) Vol. 35 (Fall 1966), pp. 67–112.

VAN WING, J. 'Le Kibanguisme vu par un témoin', *Zaïre* (Revue Congolaise) XII, 6 (1958), pp. 563–618.

VERHAGEN, BENÔIT and MONNIER, LAURENT. 'Problèmes concrets et concepts de Science Politique en Afrique: Application au Bas-Congo', *Cahiers Économiques et Sociaux* I, 4 (June 1963), pp. 79–91.

VILAKAZI, ABSOLOM. *Zulu Transformations: A Study of the Dynamics of Social Change* (University of Natal Press, Pietermaritzburg 1962).

VILALDACH, ANTONIO DE VECIANA. *La Secta del Bwiti en la Guinea Española* (Consejo Superior de Investigaciónes Científicas [Instituto de Estudias Africanos], Madrid 1958).

VOGET, FRED W. 'Acculturation at Caughnawaga. A note on the Native-modified Group', *American Anthropologist* 53 (April–June 1951), pp. 230–2.

'The American Indian in Transition, Reformation and Accommodation', *American Anthropologist* 58 (April 1956), pp. 249–63.

WALLACE, ANTHONY F. C. 'Halliday Jackson's Journal to the Seneca Indians', *Pennsylvania History* XIX, 2 (April 1952), and XIX, 3 (July 1952), pp. 117–47; 325–49.

'Handsome Lake and the Great Revival in the West', *American Quarterly* IV, 2 (Summer 1952), pp. 149–65.

'Revitalization Movements: Some Theoretical Considerations for their Comparative Study', *American Anthropologist* 58 (April 1956), pp. 264–81.

'New Religions Among the Delaware Indians, 1600–1900', *Southwestern Journal of Anthropology* 12, 1 (Spring 1956), pp. 1–22.

WALLACE, ERNEST and HOEBEL, E. ADAMSON. *The Comanches* (University of Oklahoma Press, Norman, Oklahoma 1952).

WALLIS, WILSON D. *Messiahs: Their Role in Civilization* (American Council of Public Affairs, Washington 1943).

WARD, BARBARA E. 'Some Observations of Religious Cults in Ashanti', *Africa* XXVI (1956), pp. 47–60.

WATERMAN, T. T. 'The Shake Religion of Puget Sound', *Annual Report of the Board of Regents of the Smithsonian Institute*, 1922 (Government Printing Office, Washington 1924), pp. 499–507.

WATSON, WILLIAM. *Tribal Cohesion in a Money Economy* (Manchester University Press, Manchester 1958).

WAX, MURRAY. 'Les Pawnees á la recherche du Paradis perdu', *Archives de Sociologie des Religions* 4 (July–December 1957), pp. 113–22.

WEBER, MAX. *The Sociology of Religion*, trans. Ephraim Fischoff (Methuen, London 1965).

WEBSTER, JAMES B. *The African Churches among the Yoruba 1888–1922* (Clarendon Press, Oxford 1964).

WELBOURN, F. B. *East African Rebels* (SCM Press, London 1961).

WERBLOWSKY, R. J. ZWI. 'A New Heaven and a New Earth: Considering Primitive Messianisms', *History of Religions* 5, 1 (Summer 1965), pp. 164–72.

WESTERMANN, DIEDRICH. *Africa and Christianity* (Oxford University Press, Oxford 1937).

WHITE, C. M. N. 'Elements in Luvale Beliefs and Rituals', *Rhodes-Livingstone Papers* No. 32 (Manchester University Press, Manchester 1961).

WILLEMS, EMILIO. 'Cultural Change and the Rise of Protestantism in Brazil and Chile', *Kölner Zeitschrift*, Sonderheft 7 (1963), pp. 184–210.
'Religious Mass Movements and Social Change in Brazil', in E. N. Baklanoff (Ed.), *New Perspectives of Brazil* (Vanderbilt University Press, Nashville 1966).
Followers of the New Faith (Vanderbilt University Press, Nashville 1968).

WILLIAMS, F. E. *The Vailala Madness and the Destruction of Native Ceremonies in the Gulf Division*, Papuan Anthropology Reports 4 (Port Moresby 1923).
Orokaiva Magic (Oxford University Press, London 1928).
'The Vailala Madness in Retrospect', in E. E. Evans-Pritchard (Ed.), *Essays Presented to C. G. Seligman* (Kegan Paul, London 1934).

WILSON, BRYAN R. 'An Analysis of Sect Development', *American Sociological Review* 24, 1 (February 1959), pp. 3–15.
Sects and Society (Heinemann, London, and University of California Press, Berkeley 1961).
Religion in Secular Society (Watts, London 1966).
'Establishment, Sectarianism and Partisanship', *Sociological Review* 15, 2 (July 1967), pp. 213–20.
(Ed.), *Patterns of Sectarianism* (Heinemann, London 1967).
'A Typology of Sects', in *Types, Dimensions et Mesure de la Religiosité*, Actes de la Xe Conférence Internationale de Sociologie Religieuse (Rome 1969), pp. 29–56.

Religious Sects (Weidenfeld and Nicolson, London and McGraw-Hill, New York 1971).

'Sociological Methods in the Study of History', *Transactions of The Royal Historical Society* 5th Ser., Vol. 21 (1971), pp. 101–18.

WILSON, JOHN. 'British-Israelism: The Ideological Restraints on Sect Organization', in B. R. Wilson (Ed.), *Patterns of Sectarianism* (Heinemann, London 1967).

WILSON, MONICA. *Communal Rituals of the Nyakusa* (Oxford University Press, London 1959).

WINCH, PETER. 'Understanding a Primitive Society', in B. R. Wilson (Ed.), *Rationality* (Blackwell, Oxford and Harper, New York 1970).

WINKS, ROBIN W. 'The Doctrine of Hau-Hauism', *Journal of the Polynesian Society* 62, 3 (September 1953), pp. 199–236.

WISHLADE, R. L. *Sectarianism in Southern Nyasaland* (Oxford University Press, London 1965).

WITT, SHIRLEY HILL. 'Nationalistic Trends Among American Indians', *Midcontinent American Studies Journal* 6, 2 (Fall 1965), pp. 51–74.

WOBO, M. SAM. *A Brief Resumé of the Life-Course of Dr. J. O. Ositelu, Psy.D.* (Ogere Headquarters, The Church of the Lord, Shagamu 1955).

WOODCOCK, GEORGE and AVAKUMOVIC, IVAN. *The Doukhobors* (Faber, London 1968).

WORSLEY, PETER. *The Trumpet Shall Sound: A Study of 'Cargo' Cults in Melanesia* (MacGibbon and Kee, London 1957; 2nd Rev. Edn 1968).

WOUTERS, R. P. A. 'La "Marching Rule" ', *Sociaal Kompas* VI, 2 (1958–9), pp. 44–55.

YANG, C. K. *Religion in Chinese Society* (University of California Press, Berkeley and Los Angeles 1961).

YINGER, J. MILTON. *Religion in the Struggle for Power* (Duke University Press, Durham, N.C. 1946).

Religion, Society and the Individual (Macmillan, New York 1957).

YOUNG, CRAWFORD. *Politics in the Congo* (Princeton University Press, Princeton, N.J. 1965).

Anonymous Works

'A Visit to the Apostles and the Town of Aiyetoro', *Nigeria* 36 (1951), pp. 387–442.

'Aiyetoro', *Nigeria Magazine* 55 (1957), pp. 356–86.

'Cherubim and Seraphim', *Nigeria* 53 (1957), pp. 119–34.

National Opinion Poll Survey on Religion, January 1971.

Report of the Department of Education, New Guinea, 'Community Development in the Purari Delta', *South Pacific* 5, 10 (December 1951), pp. 208–14.

The Constitution of the Church of the Lord (Aladura) Ghana (comprising Definitions, Laws and Regulations) (mimeographed, n.d.).

The Fundamental Beliefs of the Church of the Lord (Aladura) Throughout the Whole World, Founded in Nigeria, 1930 (no place of publication, n.d.).

Towards a Quaker View of Sex (Friends Home Service Committee, London 1963).

Index of Authors

Index of Subjects

Index of Principal Movements, Tribes, and Persons

73 74 75 9 8 7 6 5 4 3 2 1